A History of Modern Aesthetics
Volume 2: The Nineteenth Century

A History of Modern Aesthetics narrates the history of philosophical aesthetics from the beginning of the eighteenth century through the twentieth century. Aesthetics began with Aristotle's defense of the cognitive value of tragedy in response to Plato's famous attack on the arts in *The Republic*, and cognitivist accounts of aesthetic experience have been central to the field ever since. But in the eighteenth century, two new ideas were introduced: that aesthetic experience is important because of emotional impact – precisely what Plato criticized – and because it is a pleasurable free play of many or all of our mental powers. The three volumes tell how these ideas have been synthesized or separated by both the best-known and lesser-known aestheticians of modern times, focusing on Britain, France, and Germany in the eighteenth century (Volume 1); Germany and Britain in the nineteenth (Volume 2); and Germany, Britain, and the United States in the twentieth (Volume 3).

Paul Guyer is the Jonathan Nelson Professor of Humanities and Philosophy at Brown University. He is author of nine books and editor of six collections on the philosophy of Immanuel Kant, including four focusing on Kant's aesthetics. He has been the recipient of numerous fellowships and prizes, including a John Simon Guggenheim Memorial Fellowship and an Alexander von Humboldt Foundation Research Prize. *A History of Modern Aesthetics* was facilitated by a Laurance Rockefeller Fellowship at the Princeton University Center for Human Values. Professor Guyer is a Fellow of the American Academy of Arts and Sciences and has been president of both the Eastern Division of the American Philosophical Association and the American Society for Aesthetics.

A History of Modern Aesthetics

Volume 2: The Nineteenth Century

PAUL GUYER
Brown University

CAMBRIDGE
UNIVERSITY PRESS

CAMBRIDGE
UNIVERSITY PRESS

University Printing House, Cambridge CB2 8BS, United Kingdom

One Liberty Plaza, 20th Floor, New York, NY 10006, USA

477 Williamstown Road, Port Melbourne, VIC 3207, Australia

314-321, 3rd Floor, Plot 3, Splendor Forum, Jasola District Centre, New Delhi - 110025, India

79 Anson Road, #06-04/06, Singapore 079906

Cambridge University Press is part of the University of Cambridge.

It furthers the University's mission by disseminating knowledge in the pursuit of education, learning and research at the highest international levels of excellence.

www.cambridge.org
Information on this title: www.cambridge.org/9781108733823

© Paul Guyer 2014

This publication is in copyright. Subject to statutory exception and to the provisions of relevant collective licensing agreements, no reproduction of any part may take place without the written permission of Cambridge University Press.

First published 2014
Reprinted 2016
First paperback edition 2018

A catalogue record for this publication is available from the British Library

Library of Congress Cataloging in Publication data
Guyer, Paul, 1948–
A history of modern aesthetics / Paul Guyer.
volumes cm
Includes bibliographical references and index.
ISBN 978-1-107-03803-5 (hardback)
1. Aesthetics, Modern – History. I. Title.
BH151.G89 2014
111'.850903–dc23   2013050046

ISBN 978-1-107-03803-5 Volume 1 Hardback
ISBN 978-1-107-03804-2 Volume 2 Hardback
ISBN 978-1-107-03805-9 Volume 3 Hardback
ISBN 978-1-107-64322-2 Three-Volume Hardback Set
ISBN 978-1-108-73382-3 Paperback

Cambridge University Press has no responsibility for the persistence or accuracy of URLs for external or third-party internet websites referred to in this publication, and does not guarantee that any content on such websites is, or will remain, accurate or appropriate.

Contents

Acknowledgments		*page* vii
Introduction		1

PART ONE GERMAN AESTHETICS IN THE FIRST HALF OF THE NINETEENTH CENTURY

1	Early Romanticism and Idealism: Schlegel and Schelling	11
	1. Back to Kant	11
	2. Hölderlin, Schlegel, and Romanticism	18
	3. Schelling	38
2	High Romanticism in the Shadow of Schelling	57
	1. Jean Paul	58
	2. Coleridge, Wordsworth, Shelley	63
	3. Mill	84
	4. Emerson	91
3	The High Tide of Idealism: Schopenhauer, Hegel, and Schleiermacher	106
	1. Schopenhauer	106
	2. Hegel	119
	3. Schleiermacher	144
4	In the Wake of Hegel	153
	1. Solger	154
	2. Vischer	159
	3. Rosenkranz	172
	4. Lotze	179

PART TWO (MOSTLY) BRITISH AESTHETICS IN THE SECOND HALF OF THE NINETEENTH CENTURY — 187

5 Ruskin — 191
  1. *Ruskin, Turner, and Truth* — 191
  2. *Truth as Sincerity* — 215
  3. *Conclusion, with an Excursus on Arnold* — 225

6 Aestheticism: The Aestheticist Movement — 229
  1. *Moralism and "Art for Art's Sake": From Cousin to Baudelaire* — 230
  2. *"This hard, gem-like flame": Pater* — 244
  3. *Wilde* — 257

7 Bosanquet and Tolstoy — 270
  1. *Bosanquet* — 270
  2. *Tolstoy* — 290

PART THREE GERMAN AESTHETICS IN THE SECOND HALF OF THE NINETEENTH CENTURY

8 In the Shadow of Schopenhauer — 299
  1. *Nietzsche: Introduction* — 300
  2. *Nietzsche: "The Dionysiac World View"* — 304
  3. *Nietzsche: The Birth of Tragedy* — 306
  4. *Nietzsche after The Birth of Tragedy* — 315
  5. *Von Hartmann* — 320

9 Neo-Kantian Aesthetics — 325
  1. *Fechner* — 327
  2. *Cohen* — 330
  3. *Cohn* — 346
  4. *Münsterberg* — 353
  5. *Dilthey* — 363

10 Psychological Aesthetics: Play and Empathy — 378
  1. *Spencer's Revival of the Concept of Play* — 380
  2. *The Aesthetics of Empathy: Robert Vischer, Lipps, and Volkelt* — 389
  3. *Groos: The Play of Animal and Man* — 409
  4. *Psychological Aesthetics in the United States: Puffer* — 418
  5. *Psychological Aesthetics in Britain: Lee* — 426

Bibliography — 439
Index — 457

Acknowledgments

Quotations from Friedrich Schlegel, *On the Study of Greek Poetry*, edited by Stuart Barnett, reprinted by permission from the State University of New York Press © 2001, State University of New York. All rights reserved.

Quotations from Wihelm Dilthey, *Selected Works Volume V: Poetry and Experience*, edited by Rudolf A. Makkreel and Frithjof Rodi, reprinted by permission from Princeton University Press © 1985. All rights reserved.

Introduction

Periodization is always one of the great challenges for historiography. Deciding how to define the nineteenth century in the history of aesthetics is no exception. For some purposes, such as political and diplomatic history, a "long nineteenth century," running from 1789 to 1914, that is, from the French Revolution to the outbreak of World War I, might make sense, although if the Revolution is considered well within the eighteenth century and the Napoleonic era considered a continuation of that era, then the nineteenth century might only run from 1815 to 1914, which is in any case exactly one hundred years. In aesthetics, there are many if not more possibilities, due to different developments in different national traditions or even within single national traditions. Thus, in the case of Britain, the eighteenth-century flourishing of the field was largely completed with Thomas Reid's *Essays on the Intellectual Powers of Man* of 1785 and Archibald Alison's *Essays on the Nature and Principles of Taste* of 1790, but it made sense to include Dugald Stewart in the eighteenth century, even though some of his relevant work was published only as late as 1810, because of his proximity to the intellectual world of those authors. In Germany, the situation is even more complicated. It would be perfectly natural to think of Kant's *Critique of the Power of Judgment* of 1790 as the culmination of the developments that began in Germany with Wolff and of the developments that began in Britain with Hutcheson and Hume, as well as conceiving of it as a conclusive rejection of a tradition that began in France with Du Bos, and then to think of everything coming after Kant as part of a new epoch. Thus, in German aesthetics, the nineteenth century might begin after 1790. But we have already treated several prominent authors whose main works in aesthetics were published later in the 1790s, or even the first decade of the 1800s, namely Schiller, Goethe, von Humboldt, and even Herbart, in the last chapter of the previous book, because of their intellectual proximity to Kant; and Herder's *Kalligone*, published in 1800, which some might regard as the last year of the eighteenth century and others as the first year of the nineteenth century, certainly had to be treated there because it is so explicitly a critique of Kant. However, a new school of philosophy, still conceiving of itself in relation to Kant but breaking more radically with his thought, namely the era of German Idealism, while it would become the dominant school of thought in Germany in the first half of the calendar's nineteenth century, and reverberate in Anglo-American thought for much of the second half of the century, began as early as 1794, with Johann Gottlieb Fichte's first *Wissenschaftslehre* ("Theory of Science"), before Schiller had even published his main essays in aesthetics; and Fichte's precocious colleague Friedrich Wilhelm Joseph Schelling was also well-embarked on his publishing career before the end of the 1790s. In addition, the broader German artistic and intellectual movement known as Romanticism, although that is generally considered a nineteenth-century movement, was also well under way before the end of the decade, and that movement had reverberations within academic philosophy. So, in the end, perhaps we can only say that in German aesthetics the eighteenth century continued into the 1790s and the nineteenth century began in the same decade, depending upon what figures and movements we are considering. And that is how I have proceeded and will continue to proceed, with some of the figures I have already discussed as part of the eighteenth century, such as Schiller, Goethe, and Herbart, nevertheless having remained active in the 1790s or well beyond, while others who are now to be discussed, such as the two Friedrichs, Hölderlin and Schlegel, representing the Romantics, and Schelling, the first representative of German Idealism, having at least begun their careers in the 1790s as well.

As we will see, the question where to begin the nineteenth century in the history of aesthetics is largely a question about where to begin it in Germany, since while in the eighteenth century there was great activity in the field in Britain and France as well as in Germany, although German aesthetics in that period was more affected by British and French developments than the other way around, in the first part of the nineteenth century Germany was definitely the center of new developments in aesthetics while the subject largely disappeared from the British or indeed the Anglo-American academy. Moreover, such extra-academic authors in Britain and America who did make significant contributions to the field, such as Samuel Taylor Coleridge, Ralph Waldo Emerson, and even

John Stuart Mill, to some considerable extent worked in the penumbra of the German philosophers, particularly Schelling. We will return to a truly independent British tradition in aesthetics only when we turn to the work of John Ruskin beginning in the 1840s, a figure who might seem to be more of an art (and social) critic than a philosophical aesthetician, but who was both so strongly influenced by the previous British tradition in aesthetics and had such an impact on the subsequent development of more philosophical aesthetics in Britain that he cannot be left out of our story. German aesthetics rather than its own eighteenth-century tradition was largely dominant in France in the first part of the nineteenth century too, as we will see when we comment on the work of Victor Cousin (although France will play a smaller role in the remainder of this work than it did in the eighteenth century).

When we try to find an end for the nineteenth century, developments in Britain and America will become as important as developments in Germany, and we will find that in all three national traditions we will again have to allow the end of the nineteenth century to overlap with the beginning of the twentieth century. In Germany, we can use 1914 as the dividing line between the centuries, because the two movements that still were dominant up until that date, namely Neo-Kantianism and the "empathy" schools, had their origins as early as the 1870s, and radically different movements, such as the aesthetics of Heidegger and his followers, did not begin until after the Great War – although Heidegger's unique form of realism began as a critique of Neo-Kantianism, thus the dividing line of 1914 may be sharp but is hardly an impermeable barrier. So our discussions of the aesthetics of Neo-Kantianism and empathy will continue past 1900, and indeed our discussion of the empathy school will include consideration of several American and British texts, deeply influenced by the German leaders of the school, published between 1905 and as late as 1913. In Britain and America, however, things are more complicated. The leading aesthetician in Britain at the turn of the century was Bernard Bosanquet and the leading aesthetician in America at that time was George Santayana; their first books in aesthetics respectively, Bosanquet's *History of Æsthetic* and Santayana's *Sense of Beauty*, were published just four years apart, in 1892 and 1896, and both authors could easily be treated as nineteenth-century figures. But even though Bosanquet published another important work in aesthetics as late as 1915, Santayana remained productive throughout the first half of the twentieth century, and thus, while I will treat Bosanquet's work as the culmination of nineteenth-century aesthetics in Britain, I will treat

Santayana as founding twentieth-century aesthetics in America. This means that Clive Bell's widely discussed *Art* of 1914, although it could easily be treated as a late document of the nineteenth-century "art for art's sake" movement, will be treated as part of twentieth-century British aesthetics, and that makes sense too, because Bell's work was so closely associated with the literary and artistic circle known as "Bloomsbury," focused around the two Stephens sisters, Virginia Wolff and Vanessa Bell (Clive's wife), and that is very much a movement of the twentieth century.

Another decision that has to be made here is where, both chronologically and nationally, to discuss the Italian Benedetto Croce. Italian aesthetics as such has not been and will not be part of the story told here, although a case could certainly be made that our discussion of eighteenth-century aesthetics should have made room for Giambattista Vico; but Croce was such an influential figure in British aesthetics into the 1930s and even beyond that British aesthetics in that period cannot be understood without him, and therefore his work will be discussed as part of the history of British aesthetics. And likewise, while the publication date of his first main work in aesthetics in 1902 and even his second main contribution in 1913 might allow for his inclusion in the nineteenth century, his impact on twentieth-century British aesthetics clearly calls for his inclusion there. So, in this work the history of nineteenth-century British aesthetics will conclude with Bernard Bosanquet, and, strange as it might seem, the history of twentieth-century British aesthetics will begin with Benedetto Croce.

So much for the chronology of this and the next volume. Now for a few words on the substance of the history of nineteenth-century aesthetics to be presented in this volume. As we saw in Volume 1, Kant's philosophy of fine art synthesized his version of the theory that the intrinsically pleasurable free play of our mental powers is the essence of aesthetic experience that was developed in mid-eighteenth-century Scotland and Germany with a version of the theory that aesthetic experience is a distinctive form of the apprehension of truth that had been the core of aesthetic theory since the time of Aristotle. Kant brought these two strands of aesthetic theory together in his conception of "aesthetic ideas" as the source of "spirit" in fine art and of genius as the uniquely artistic capacity for the creation and communication of aesthetic ideas, for, by means of this concept, he postulated that in both the production and the reception of fine art the imagination freely plays with and around the intellectual content furnished by ideas of reason. A natural response to Kant's twofold synthesis would have been to add to it the third main line of thought in eighteenth-century aesthetics, the emphasis on the emotional impact of art by such figures as Du Bos and Kames that Kant had held at arm's length, indeed explicitly rejected, and that a few in the 1790s, such as Heydenreich and Herder, had attempted to preserve. But that is not what happened. Instead, even Kant's twofold synthesis was quickly sundered by the next generation, and Kant's combination of the aesthetics of play with the aesthetics of truth as well as the aesthetics of emotional impact were rejected in favor of a purely cognitivist aesthetics. This is particularly evident in the three great aesthetic theories to take the stage after Kant, those of Schelling, Schopenhauer, and Hegel. While each preserved some of the outward trappings of Kant's aesthetics, they each transformed Kant's conception of aesthetic ideas as a form of free play with truth back into a more traditional conception of an apprehension of truth that is certainly different from other forms of cognition but does not really involve an element of free play. Schelling and Schopenhauer in particular both rejected Kant's idea that aesthetic experience is intrinsically pleasurable because it is a free play of our mental powers, replacing that theory with the view that for the most part aesthetic experience is pleasurable only because it releases us from the pain of some otherwise inescapable contradiction in the human condition. To borrow terms used by Edmund Burke a half-century earlier, they replace Kant's conception of aesthetic response as a "positive pleasure" with a conception of it as "the removal of pain" or "delight" as a merely "negative" or "relative" form of pleasure.[1] In particular, even though Schopenhauer recognizes that there is some pleasure in aesthetic response that goes beyond mere relief at the removal of pain, he explicitly identifies the pleasure of aesthetic experience with relief from all other emotions, thus clearly rejecting that the arousal of emotions in any form is an essential or characteristic aim of art. Thus both he and Schelling nevertheless maintain that all of the pleasure in aesthetic experience comes through cognition alone rather than from a free play of our cognitive powers. In the case of Hegel, while his thesis that artistic beauty is the sensible appearance of what he calls "the Idea" can be taken as his version of Kant's own theory of aesthetic ideas as the spirit of fine art, both the theories that aesthetic experience is a form of play and the theory that art aims at the arousal of emotions – which Hegel associates with Mendelssohn – are explicitly

---

[1] Edmund Burke, *A Philosophical Enquiry into the Origin of Our Ideas of the Sublime and Beautiful* (1757), Part One, sections III–V.

rejected. All three thus transmute Kant's aesthetics back into a version of cognitivism.

Before we turn to Schelling, we will begin this part with a brief discussion of the aesthetics of German Romanticism, to be represented here primarily by the work of Friedrich Schlegel although with a briefer comment on the work of Friedrich Hölderlin as well. From a philosophical point of view, the aesthetics of Romanticism might be regarded as a new version of the Neo-Platonism of Shaftesbury of a century earlier, thus presenting a potential for seeing art as offering the possibility of a three-way synthesis of our responses to the true, the good, and the beautiful; but Romanticism was a short-lived movement, at least in philosophy, shoved off the stage by Idealism precisely because its theory of art was not exclusively cognitivist; this is explicit in Hegel. And, pausing to look at a broader range of cultural figures in Germany, Britain, and America before we turn from Schelling to Schopenhauer, we will see that it was the philosophy of Schelling and not of Schlegel that was the dominant influence; thus, Jean Paul, Coleridge, and Emerson were all strongly influenced by Schelling. Meanwhile, within more professional philosophy, it was Hegel who dominated the scene in the decade before his death in 1831 and for several decades afterward, in spite of some resistance even in Berlin, such as from the theologian Friedrich Schleiermacher, who defended something closer to Kant's earlier theory of play. But Schleiermacher's lectures on aesthetics, which began shortly after Hegel joined him at the university in Berlin, did not have the same influence as Hegel's.

Hegel's influence would remain strong in Germany at least until about 1860, when Neo-Kantianism began, as much as a form of resistance to Hegelianism as a genuine revival of Kantianism. Thus leading aestheticians of the 1830s, 1840s, and 1850s, such as Christian Hermann Weisse, Friedrich Theodor Vischer, Karl Rosenkranz, and Rudolf Lotze, all worked within recognizably Hegelian frameworks, although we will see that some of these thinkers, especially Vischer, began to make room for the Kantian idea of free play and for the recognition of the emotional impact of art as well within the confines of their Hegelian framework. Friedrich Theodor Vischer's son Robert Vischer would emphasize the idea of "empathy," the reading of our own emotions back into inanimate objects, as one way of making room for an emotional response to art, and that would generate a whole school of German empathy theorists that had influence in Britain and the United States as well, lasting beyond 1900. At the same time, the Neo-Kantians, in both their Marburg and Southwestern schools, would make room for the emotional impact of art within a framework that is not particularly Kantian at all, by seeing art as a vehicle for the cognition of our own emotions. This approach will still be visible in Britain half a century later, in the aesthetics of R.G. Collingwood, although he was more overtly influenced by Benedetto Croce's idiosyncratic mixture of Kantianism and Hegelianism. That, however, will be addressed in Volume 3.

Meanwhile, Schopenhauer, although he had published his main work on aesthetics – the third book of *The World as Will and Representation* – the same year that Hegel merely began lecturing on the subject at Berlin (and when Schleiermacher gave his less influential lectures as well) was eclipsed by the fame of Hegel, and his star began to rise only later, especially during the years of pessimism that followed the failed liberal revolutions of 1848 across Europe. But once Schopenhauer's star did rise, he had enormous influence, on the practice of the arts, especially literature and music, but also within philosophy, if not exactly academic philosophy, through Nietzsche and the now less known Eduard von Hartmann (Nietzsche was an academic for a decade, but a classical philologist, not a philosopher). In the case of Nietzsche in particular, we will see that while his first book and his only book devoted exclusively to aesthetics, *The Birth of Tragedy*, was very much influenced by Schopenhauer, in some passages in later work he began to revive the Kantian idea of free play. We shall also see that the famous "art for art's sake" movement, identified more with literary figures such as Charles Baudelaire, Walter Pater, and Oscar Wilde than with professional philosophers, and certainly not overtly influenced by Schopenhauer, can nevertheless be associated with the Schopenhauerian idea of art as an instrument for detachment from concerns of ordinary life. That attitude in turn can be seen as carrying over into some twentieth-century movements, such as the Bloomsbury aesthetics of Clive Bell and Roger Fry, although again that will be a matter for Volume 3. At the same time, these British movements, both the later stages of the art for art's sake movement or aestheticism, as it is also called, as well as the Bloomsbury aesthetics of the early twentieth century – can also be seen as rejecting the underlying cognitivism of the main home-grown form of aesthetics in mid-nineteenth-century Britain, namely the aesthetics of John Ruskin, so Ruskin will also be considered in the present volume. I shall conclude this part by looking at two other *fin-de-siècle* theorists, namely Bernard Bosanquet and Leo Tolstoy, who, though very different in almost every way, nevertheless shared a reductive rather than expansive approach to aesthetic theory.

Bosanquet, part of the British Hegelianism that flourished in the late nineteenth century while Neo-Kantianism was replacing Hegelianism in German itself, maintained a basically cognitivist approach to aesthetic experience. Tolstoy, on the contrary, promulgated an aesthetics of emotional arousal, but one of such narrow scope – for him, the sole function of art is the communication of religiously beneficial emotions – that he set back the cause of recognizing the emotional impact of art as much as the Idealism of Schelling, Schopenhauer, and Hegel had done at the beginning of the century. Collingwood's argument that only the clarification of emotions and not the arousal of emotions can be a legitimate aim of art, to be considered in Volume 3, can be understood as a rejection of Tolstoy's view, even forty years later.

Around the same time as Nietzsche was taking some steps toward reviving the theory of play, the Berlin philosopher Wilhelm Dilthey, a much less orthodox Neo-Kantian than either his Marburg or Southwest contemporaries, developed a "poetics" that came as close as anything in the nineteenth century did to reestablishing a threefold synthesis of the aesthetics of truth, feeling, and play that had been hinted at by a few of Kant's immediate predecessors or successors but that had been rejected by Kant himself. However, Dilthey's version of a threefold synthesis would remain an isolated example of aesthetic nonreductivism in the nineteenth century.

These are some of the figures and themes to be considered in the present volume. Let us now turn to them.

PART ONE

GERMAN AESTHETICS IN THE FIRST HALF OF THE NINETEENTH CENTURY

1

Early Romanticism and Idealism

Schlegel and Schelling

1. BACK TO KANT

Let us begin with a brief review of the central themes of Kant's aesthetics that will be relevant to what follows. Kant began from the challenge posed by mid-eighteenth-century aesthetic theory, for example by Hume's essay "Of the Standard of Taste," by Gerard's *Essay on Taste*, and many other works ultimately going back to Du Bos, to explain how a judgment of taste, paradigmatically a judgment that a particular object is beautiful, can be made only on the basis of a feeling of pleasure in response to an object, independent of any determinate concept of or rule for that object, and yet be valid for all qualified observers of the object responding to it under appropriate conditions. Kant did not present this challenge merely as one raised by previous philosophers, but as one raised by common sense and practice. He began by accepting from Shaftesbury and Hutcheson that a judgment of taste must be disinterested, independent of any personal physiological, prudential, or moral interest in the existence of the object. But disinterestedness seems to be merely a necessary condition for universal validity: one's pleasure in an object might be independent of any identifiable interest, yet still be utterly accidental or idiosyncratic. To find a sufficient condition for the universal validity of the judgment of taste, Kant sought its ground in a mental state that is disinterested and free from regulation by determinate concepts but nevertheless can be reasonably expected from all normal human beings who themselves approach the object without an antecedent interest in or preconception of what the object ought to be. This state Kant claimed to find in the free play of the imagination and understanding in response to an object, an "apprehension of forms" in which "the imagination ... is unintentionally brought into accord with the understanding ... and a feeling of pleasure is thereby aroused,"[1] a "state of mind" in which the "powers of representation that are sent into play by [a] representation are hereby in a free play, since no determinate concept restricts them to a particular rule of cognition,"[2] which is also a state of the "animation of both faculties (the imagination and the understanding) to an activity that is indeterminate but yet, through the stimulus of the given representation, in unison."[3] Such a state of mind is pleasurable because it seems to us like the satisfaction of our general goal in cognition – finding unity in our manifolds of representation – in a way that is contingent and surprising precisely because it is not dictated by any concept of rule that applies to the object.[4] But it is also a response to the object that we can impute to others as what they too would experience under ideal or optimal conditions, because it involves nothing but cognitive powers which themselves must be imputed to others and assumed to work in the same way in them as they do in ourselves. This inference is what Kant called the "deduction of judgments of taste."[5]

Kant insisted that the universal validity claimed by judgments of taste does not merely rest on "psychological observations"[6] but must be grounded on an "*a priori* principle,"[7] although he made no explicit argument that we can know *a priori* that the free play of our cognitive powers will produce a feeling of pleasure or animation. In addition, his assumption that we can know *a priori* that the cognitive powers of others must work like our own even when not determined by particular concepts is, to put it politely, underargued. In the "Dialectic of the Aesthetic Power of Judgment" Kant restated the challenge of justifying the judgment of taste's claim to universal validity in the form of an "antinomy" between the "thesis" that "The judgment of taste is not based on concepts, for otherwise it would be possible to dispute about it (decide by means of proofs)" and the "antithesis" that the "judgment of taste is based on concepts, for otherwise ... it would not even be possible to argue about it (to lay claim to the necessary assent of others to this judgment)."[8] However, instead of then reiterating his previous solution to this dilemma, that the

---

[1] Kant, *Critique of the Power of Judgment*, hereafter *CPJ*, Introduction, §7, 5:190.
[2] Kant, *CPJ*, §9, 5:217.
[3] Kant, *CPJ*, §9, 5:219.
[4] Kant, *CPJ*, Introduction, section VI, 5:187–8.
[5] Kant, *CPJ*, §§ 21, 38.
[6] Kant, *CPJ*, §21, 5:239.
[7] Kant, *CPJ*, §36, 5:288.
[8] Kant, *CPJ*, §56, 5:338–9.

judgment of taste is based on a free and therefore indeterminate play of cognitive powers that can be assumed to work the same way in everybody under ideal conditions, Kant, whether in spite of or because of the inadequacy of his previous proof that these powers do work the same way in everyone, next argued that "all contradiction vanishes if I say that [determining ground of] the judgment of taste ... may lie in the concept of that which can be regarded as the supersensible substratum of humanity,"[9] the noumenal basis of our phenomenal, psychological powers that must be the same in all human beings. This assertion relocates the explanation of the non-derivability of particular intersubjectively valid judgments of taste from determinate concepts of their objects from the psychological theory of the free play of the faculties to a metaphysical theory of a common but noumenal and therefore inaccessible ground of the phenomenal psychologies of all human beings. It's unclear how Kant might have thought he could assert that the noumenal ground of all human psychologies must be the same when he ordinarily maintains that our concept of our noumenal selves can be made determinate only through the *moral* law.[10] Nevertheless, this introduction of the metaphysical conception of a noumenal basis for taste would be decisive for the aesthetic theories of Schelling, Schopenhauer, and Hegel, for they return not merely to a cognitivist theory of aesthetics but to a particular form of it that can be called a "metaphysical" or "speculative" version of cognitivist aesthetics.[11]

This leap into metaphysics to complete the deduction of judgments of taste played no role in Kant's own account of fine art or of the significance of either natural or artistic beauty, however, which turns on moral rather than metaphysical ideas. Kant presented his theory of fine art in the form of a theory of genius as the source of fine art. Kant begins his account of genius by using his idea of the free play of the cognitive faculties, not that of the supersensible ground that he would introduce in the subsequent resolution of the antinomy of aesthetic judgment. Leading up to his account of genius, Kant defines art in general as the human

---

[9] Kant, *CPJ*, §57, 5:340.
[10] See Kant, *Critique of Practical Reason*, 5:49, in Immanuel Kant, *Practical Philosophy*, ed. trans. Mary J. Gregor (Cambridge: Cambridge University Press, 1996), p. 179.
[11] See Jean-Marie Schaeffer, *Art in the Modern Age: Philosophy of Art from Kant to Heidegger*, trans. Steven Rendall (Princeton: Princeton University Press, 2000), Part Two, "The Speculative Theory of Art," and Joachim Ritter, *Vorlesungen zur Philosophischen Ästhetik*, ed. Ulrich von Bülow and Mark Schweda, *Marbacher Schriften, Neue Folge 6* (Göttingen: Wallstein Verlag, 2010), pp. 153–76 (lectures originally given in 1962).

power to produce a work through freedom rather than mere instinct and through skill rather than science, and then distinguishes "liberal" art from mere handicraft as an intrinsically agreeable rather than merely remunerative occupation.[12] But "liberal" or "aesthetic art" in general can produce a feeling of pleasure in its audience as well, in either of two ways – namely, through mere sensation, in which case it is "agreeable" art, or as "a kind of representation that is purposive in itself and, though without an end, nevertheless promotes the cultivation of the mental powers for sociable communication," in which case it is "beautiful" art.[13] Kant may initially seem to suggest that in order to appreciate beautiful art as such one may have to suppress one's knowledge that it is the product of intentional human production: as he famously says, "the purposiveness of its form must still seem to be as free from all constraint by arbitrary rules as if it were a mere product of nature."[14] But as he continues, he makes it clear that beautiful art produces a free play of our cognitive powers precisely because its form engages and unifies our imagination in a way that goes beyond whatever determinate concepts – concepts of its goal, its medium and genre, and its content – that we do know apply to it. This is the lesson of Kant's conception of genius as the source of art and of aesthetic ideas as what the artistic genius produces.

Beautiful art must be produced by genius because "The concept of beautiful art ... does not allow the judgment concerning the beauty of its product to be derived from any sort of rule that has a **concept** for its determining ground," and genius is precisely the "talent (natural gift)" for "producing that for which no determinate rule can be given, not a predisposition of skill for that which can be learned in accordance with some rule."[15] Beautiful art, Kant also says, must contain "spirit," so genius must be responsible for the spirit in art. He then explicates spirit in terms of the concept of aesthetic ideas. Spirit, according to Kant, is the "animating principle in the mind" in the production and experience of beautiful art, and that "by which this principle animates the soul ... is that which purposively sets the mental powers into motion, i.e., into a play that is self-sustaining and even strengthens the powers to that end."[16] What sets the mental powers into such a play, Kant continues, is an aesthetic idea, "that representation of the imagination that occasions much

[12] Kant, *CPJ*, §43, 5:303–4.
[13] Kant, *CPJ*, §44, 5:305–6.
[14] Kant, *CPJ*, §45, 5:306.
[15] Kant, *CPJ*, §46, 5:307.
[16] Kant, *CPJ*, §49, 5:313.

thinking though without it being possible for any determinate thought, i.e., **concept**, to be adequate to it, which, consequently, no language fully attains or can make intelligible." What Kant means by this is that a work of art on the one hand has intellectual content – Kant assumes without argument that fine art is paradigmatically representational or mimetic – but specifically *rational* content, a content of ideas that cannot be reduced to determinate concepts of the understanding, and on the other hand conveys this content through a wealth of materials of the imagination – intuitions – that cannot be derived from that content by any concept or rule but nevertheless illustrate it and convey it to us in a satisfyingly harmonious and therefore pleasurable way. Thus he says,

> One can call such representations of the imagination **ideas**: on the one hand because they at least strive toward something lying beyond the bounds of experience, and thus seek to approximate a presentation of concepts of reason (of intellectual ideas) ...; on the other hand, and indeed principally, because no concept can be fully adequate to them, as inner intuitions. The poet ventures to make sensible rational ideas of invisible beings, the kingdom of the blessed, the kingdom of hell, eternity, creations, etc.[17]

A successful work of fine or beautiful art sets the form and the content of a work of art and the mental powers for the intuition of that form and the intellection of that content into a free and harmonious play:

> Now if we add to a concept a representation of the imagination that belongs to its presentation, but which by itself stimulates so much thinking that it can never be grasped in a determinate concept, hence which aesthetically enlarges the concept itself in an unbounded way, then in this case the imagination is creative, and sets the faculty of intellectual ideas (reason) into motion, that is, at the instigation of a representation it gives more to think about than can be grasped and made distinct in it. (*CPJ*, §49, 315)

Genius is thus the ability to present rational ideas through particular artistic media and genres in imaginative ways that cannot be fully determined by any rules for the latter, and fine art is the presentation of such ideas. But such ideas are moral ideas, not overtly metaphysical ideas, and Kant's theory of genius is not overtly a theory of art as a form of metaphysical cognition, as it will become for the successors we are about to consider. "Not overtly," I say: to be sure, in the full development of Kant's moral philosophy, he does argue that our ideas of moral rationality and obligation *presuppose* metaphysical conceptions of our own freedom and

---

[17] Kant, *CPJ*, §49, 5:314.

immortality and of the existence of God, and thus those who react to Kant by developing a metaphysical theory of art might be regarded as synthesizing Kant's aesthetics with his own moral philosophy. But as we saw in our discussion of Kant in the previous volume, this was not the way he connected aesthetics and morality, and he allowed at most that the experience of beauty, not especially that of art, can *suggest* our own moral freedom to us, by way of analogy, not that it gives us any *knowledge* of that freedom.

Kant stresses that genius consists not just in the capacity to create such ideas for oneself but also in the ability to find ways to communicate them to others: "genius really consists in the happy relation, which no science can teach and no diligence learn, of finding ideas for a given concept on the one hand and on the other hitting upon the **expression** for these, through which the subjective disposition of the mind that is thereby produced" in the artist "can be communicated to others," namely the audience for art.[18] This in turn means that the genius must have the special gift not only of enjoying the free play of his own mental powers but also of stimulating the free play of these powers in others, so that they may not simply apprehend the object he has produced but, paradoxical as it may sound, enjoy a free play similar to his own and thus be stimulated but not dominated by his artistic success. The work of a genius must be "exemplary" originality[19] that stimulates the free play of the mental powers of its audience in general and of successive artists in particular. This point was not stressed by the immediate successors of Kant, but as we will see later, it would be stressed by that nineteenth-century thinker who most fully captured the spirit of Kant's aesthetics and then extended it to complete a threefold synthesis of approaches to aesthetic experience, namely Wilhelm Dilthey.

In his theory of aesthetic ideas and genius, then, Kant synthesized the old approach to aesthetic experience and one of the new approaches: beautiful art (and Kant subsequently extended this to beautiful nature)[20] makes sensible or palpable the most profound ideas of (*practical*) reason, which cannot be fully grasped through ordinary concepts of the understanding, but our pleasure in art does not come from our cognition of these ideas as such but from the free play between these ideas and the form and matter of the works by which they are conveyed, thus

---

[18] Kant, *CPJ*, §49, 5:317.
[19] Kant, *CPJ*, §46, 5:308.
[20] Kant, *CPJ*, §51, 5:320.

from the free play of our imagination with these ideas rather than from mere cognition of them. In aesthetic experience our cognitive powers are engaged with cognitions, but not for the sake of or to the end of cognition. As already suggested, Kant maintained this delicate position in the final piece of his aesthetic theory – that "the beautiful is the symbol of the morally good, and also that only in this respect (that of a relation that is natural to everyone, and that is also expected of everyone else as a duty) does it please with a claim to the assent of everyone else." Here Kant argued that the beautiful may and indeed ought to be taken as a symbol of the morally good because of a number of analogies between our experience of the beautiful and our moral experience, above all the analogy between "the **freedom** of the imagination ... in the judging of the beautiful" and "the freedom of the will ... as the agreement of the latter with itself in accordance with universal laws of reason" in "moral judgment."[21] But Kant did not say that our experience of the freedom of the imagination in the experience of beauty gives us actual knowledge of the freedom of our will. That, he had argued in the *Critique of Practical Reason*, can come only from our immediate awareness of our obligation under the moral law, the "fact of reason."[22] Aesthetic experience can at most give us a *feeling* of our freedom rather than *cognition* of it, although apparently it is sufficiently important that we have even a mere feeling of our freedom that we can demand the attention of others to the beautiful objects that give this feeling to us and their assent to our judgments of taste about them.

Schelling, Schopenhauer, and Hegel draw on many of these ideas. But they also turn Kant's idea of the free play of our cognitive powers back into the more traditional idea that aesthetic experience is actual cognition, and treat such cognition primarily as a source of the negative pleasure of relief from pain rather than as a source of positive pleasure presupposing no antecedent pain. Doing the latter, they go even further in excluding the emotions from our proper responses to beauty, in the case of Schopenhauer the beauty of nature as well as art, and in the case of Schelling and Hegel primarily the beauty of art.

We are now about to see how they do that. But first we will pause to look at the aesthetic theory of German Romanticism, which prepares the way for the cognitivist turn of German philosophical aesthetics after Kant.

---

[21] Kant, *CPJ*, §59, 5:353–4.
[22] *Critique of Practical Reason*, 5:30, 47–9.

2. HÖLDERLIN, SCHLEGEL, AND ROMANTICISM

It is customary to point to the epoch, or better the brief moment of "early German Romanticism" as the first stage of the movement of aesthetic theory beyond Kant and the "classicism" of such at least partial Kantians as Friedrich Schiller and Wilhelm von Humboldt.[23] Friedrich Hölderlin was present briefly in the still "classical" Jena of 1795, just before it was transformed into the seat of early German Romanticism the next year. The phrase "early German Romanticism" has come to refer to the philosophical, critical, and literary activity of a number of people working in close contact with one another, first in Jena and then in Berlin between 1796 and 1801. Goethe and Schiller had brought Johann Gottlieb Fichte to the university at Jena in 1794, and he attracted first students like Hölderlin and Schelling, and then the literary figures included in early German Romanticism, who took philosophy and literature in a very different direction from that of their original patrons. Leading figures in the group included the literary historian and philologist August Wilhelm Schlegel (1767–1845), the essayist and poet Friedrich von Hardenberg, who would call himself "Novalis" (1772–1801), the novelists and storywriters Ludwig Tieck (1773–1853) and Wilhelm Heinrich Wackenroder (1772–1798), the theologian Friedrich Daniel Ernst Schleiermacher

---

[23] For a general survey of "early Romanticism," see Ernst Behler, *Frühromantik* (Berlin: Walter de Gruyter, 1992). For philosophical treatments, see Walter Benjamin, *Der Begriff der Kunstkritik in der deutschen Romantik* (Bern: Francke, 1920; Frankfurt am Main: Suhrkamp Verlag, 1973), and Manfred Frank, *Einführung in die frühromantische Ästhetik* (Frankfurt am Main: Suhrkamp Verlag, 1989), with special emphasis on Schelling, as well as *Unendliche Annäherung: Die Anfänge der philosophischen Frühromantik* (Frankfurt am Main: Suhrkamp Verlag, 1997); the final twelve lectures of this book, focusing on Schlegel, have been translated as Frank, *The Philosophical Foundations of Early German Romanticism*, trans. Elizabeth Millán-Zaibert (Albany: State University of New York Press, 2004). See also Frederick C. Beiser, *The Romantic Imperative: The Concept of Early German Romanticism* (Cambridge, Mass.: Harvard University Press, 2003). Two classical surveys of German Romanticism are Rudolf Haym, *Die Romantische Schule: Ein Beitrag zur Geschichte des deutschen Geistes* (Berlin: R. Gaertner, 1870), and Ricarda Huch, *Die Romantik: Ausbreitung, Blüte, und Verfall* (Leipzig: H. Haessel, 1908). A recent survey, including discussion of its influence in later nineteenth- and twentieth-century Germany, is Rüdiger Safranski, *Romantik: Eine deutsche Affäre* (Munich: Carl Hanser Verlag, 2007). Briefer treatments of Schlegel's aesthetics include Andrew Bowie, *From Romanticism to Critical Theory: The Philosophy of German Literary Theory* (London: Routledge, 1997), ch. 2, and Schaeffer, *Art of the Modern Age*, ch. 2. A collection of papers is Walter Jaeschke and Helmut Holzhey, editors, *Früher Idealismus und Frühromantik: Der Streit um die Grundlagen der Ästhetik (1795–1805)* (Hamburg: Felix Meiner Verlag, 1990), with a companion volume of texts, or *Quellenband*, under the same title, edited by Walter Jaeschke, also (Hamburg: Felix Meiner Verlag, 1995).

(1768–1834), and the philosopher Friedrich Wilhelm Josef Schelling (1775–1854). We will return to the last two, whose most important contributions to aesthetics came after the moment of early German Romanticism. As our representative of the aesthetic theorizing of early German Romanticism, we will focus on several works of the leading theorist of this group, Friedrich Schlegel (1772–1829), the younger brother of August Wilhelm, but will first say a few words about Hölderlin.

Hölderlin

Hölderlin (1770–1843), who in the twentieth century came to be regarded as perhaps the greatest and most philosophical of all German poets, published some of his poems as well as the epistolary novel *Hyperion* and a translation of the *Oedipus* cycle of Sophocles during the decade and a half of activity preceding his mental breakdown in 1806, from which he never recovered; in spite of a brief attempt to become a teacher of philosophy at Jena, however, he published no work in philosophy at all while he was alive. Recent scholarship has shown, however, that he played a central role in the transition from Fichte's version of Kantianism to the absolute idealism of his university roommates Schelling and Hegel,[24] and he also left behind several essays on aesthetics that presaged and may also have influenced the full-blown systems of aesthetics developed by his friends. This work thus merits a brief look before we turn to the more representative Romanticism of Schlegel.

Hölderlin was born in a small town in Württemburg. His father died when he was two, and a week before Friedrich turned nine his beloved stepfather also died. He was destined by his mother for the ministry, and received a thorough education, culminating in the two-year course in philosophy at the university at Tübingen followed by the three-year course in theology in the university seminary, the so-called *Tübinger Stift*. There he roomed with his fellow Württemburger Hegel, exactly the same age, and they were subsequently joined by the precocious Schelling, five years their junior but the first to achieve worldly success when he became a professor at Jena in 1798, at only twenty-three. Hölderlin, who was already publishing poetry, himself went to Jena to study philosophy with Fichte in 1794, but gave up his hope of himself becoming a professor after only six months, and instead embarked on a career as a tutor, first to a son of Schiller's friend Charlotte von Kalb and then to a son of the

[24] See especially Dieter Henrich, *The Course of Remembrance and Other Essays on Hölderlin*, ed. Eckart Förster (Stanford: Stanford University Press, 1997).

banker Jacob Gontard and his wife Susette, with whom Hölderlin unhappily fell in love. He held a number of other such posts, each briefly, until his collapse in 1806, after which he was cared for during the remainder of his life by a Tübingen craftsman and his family (presumably at the expense of his own family).

Hölderlin's place in the general history of philosophy depends upon a brief paper called "Judgment and Being," discovered only in 1961 but apparently written in the spring of 1795 while Hölderlin was still in Jena, thus after his time with Schelling and Hegel at Tübingen but before his various subsequent conversations with them, as well as on a subsequent, only slightly longer piece called the "Earliest Systematic Program for German Idealism," which is in Hegel's hand but was at least once thought to represent joint work by Hegel with Schelling and Hölderlin.[25] Since this piece is now thought to be Hegel's work alone, I will comment only on "Judgment and Being" before turning to Hölderlin's posthumous papers directly on aesthetics. The key idea of "Judgment and Being" is that judgment (*urtheilen*) is a "primordial division" (*ur-teilen*) of an antecedent unity, thus that the process of knowledge is not the *constitution of unity* out of sheer diversity by a self (which must indeed constitute its own unity in the process) but rather the *reconstitution of an original unity* that precedes its various parts, including the conscious self, and that even if the conscious human self or the collectivity thereof can never fully complete the process of reconstituting this original unity for itself, nevertheless it is there all along, preceding the effort to reconstitute it, and this is in some way known to the self through an "intellectual intuition," a state of mind that in some way already unifies the two things – namely concept and intuition – that it is always the task of the conscious mind to combine. In Hölderlin's words,

> *Judgment* is in the highest and strictest sense the original separation of the object and subject already most intimately united in the intellectual intuition, that separation by means of which object and subject first become possible, the primordial division [*Ur-Teilung*]. In the concept of the division

[25] See H.S. Harris, *Hegel's Development: Toward the Sunlight 1770–1801* (Oxford: Clarendon Press, 1972), p. 249. The inclusion of this piece in Friedrich Hölderlin, *Werke – Briefe – Dokumente*, edited by Pierre Bertaux (Munich: Winkler, 1963), the first popular edition of Hölderlin's work to publish the newly discovered fragment *Urteil und Sein*, represents the older view that Hölderlin had a hand in the *Älteste Systementwurf* as well. My translations of Hölderlin in the present section have been made from this edition. English translations of the texts to be discussed can also be found in Friedrich Hölderlin, *Essays and Letters on Theory*, translated and edited by Thomas Pfau (Albany: State University of New York Press, 1988).

there already lies the mutual relation of the object and subject to one another, and the necessary presupposition of a whole, of which object and subject are the parts.[26]

Hölderlin's affirmative use of the phrase "intellectual intuition" makes the anti-Kantian animus of this position clear: for Kant, theoretical philosophy can concern itself only with the manifold of intuition that is given to the mind in order to be connected into the parallel wholes of the unity of apperception and the unity of the world of objects in accordance with the mind's own forms of intuition and thought (the categories), and any unity that the world or for that matter the mind itself may already have in itself is a matter beyond theoretical purview; but for Hölderlin, it is important that the mind already have some form of access to the primordial unity of being before it undertakes its task of reconstituting that unity in its own system or systems of representations; the mind recognizes that it is not creating unity out of nothing but is in some sense rediscovering a unity that already exists and that indeed in some way it already knows to exist. This is the crucial move from Kant's "transcendental idealism" to the "objective" or "absolute idealism" of the next generation, then to be worked out in great detail, in their own ways, by Schelling and Hegel.[27] A century later, Hölderlin's idea that being must underlie judgment (although not the specific text "Judgment and Being") would have a great impact on Martin Heidegger as well.[28]

The key idea of the aesthetics of absolute idealism is then that aesthetic experience is one if not the paradigmatic form of this "intellectual intuition" of the primordial unity of being, and art is one if not the paradigmatic form for the expression of the mind's recognition or reconstitution of this unity. As we will see, in the early work of Schelling, aesthetic experience and the creation of art are the paradigmatic form for the recognition and reconstitution of the unity of being, in later Schelling one of the necessary forms for this, while in Hegel they are

---

[26] Hölderlin, *Werke – Briefe – Dokumente*, p. 490.
[27] On "Judgment and Being," see Henrich, "Hölderlin on Judgment and Being: A Study in the History of the Origins of Idealism," in *The Course of Remembrance*, pp. 71–89, and Henrich, *Between Kant and Hegel: Lectures on German Idealism*, edited by David S. Pacini (Cambridge, Mass.: Harvard University Press, 2003), pp. 279–95. See also Eckart Förster, *The Twenty-Five Years of Philosophy*, trans. Brady Bowman (Cambridge, Mass.: Harvard University Press, 2012), pp. 278–9.
[28] Heidegger's interpretation of Hölderlin will be discussed in the treatment of Heidegger in Volume 3, Part One.

only a preliminary form for this. The gist of the idea of intellectual intuition is that somehow the sensory presentation of reality and the conceptual comprehension of it are already unified and do not need to be as it were forcibly brought together, and the gist of idealist aesthetics is that aesthetic experience is like this, that art expresses this fact about aesthetic experience, and that the full weight of the metaphysical importance of intellectual intuition can be borne by the aesthetic and artistic case. In an essay on "The Procedure of the Poetic Spirit," which is the longest of the surviving pieces on aesthetics (from around 1799, or the year before Schelling would offer his first philosophy of art), Hölderlin states the first point by saying that the possibility of poetry depends on "the receptivity of the material to ideal content and to ideal form,"[29] suggesting a kind of preestablished harmony between the reality that a poem is about with its poetic expression as well as a harmony within the poem as expression of this reality between its form and its content, or its perceptual and conceptual aspects. The aesthetic experience that goes into the creation of a poem as well as that triggered by it, that is, the experience of both artist and audience, thus intimate the unity of being as well as the preestablished harmony between being and the human experience of it ("judgment," in the terms of Hölderlin's earlier note). Hölderlin stresses the unity of intuition and intellect in the work of art and the experience of it in the further remark that the "ground of the poem, its significance [*Bedeutung*], should form [*bilden*] the transition between the expression, what is presented, the sensory material, what is actually expressed in the poem, and the spirit, the ideal treatment."[30] Several pages later, he adds that the harmonies inherent in the poem – between the outer world and the aesthetic experience, between the sensory and the intellectual within the aesthetic experience – are both primordial yet also progressively reconstituted, in this regard thus like all knowledge on his account:

> I say: it is necessary that the poetic spirit in its unity and harmonious progress also give itself an infinite standpoint in its work, a unity where in harmonious progress and alternation everything goes both forwards and backwards, and through its *thoroughly characteristic relation* to this unity it wins not only objective coherence, for the audience, but also felt and palpable [*gefühlten und fühlbaren*] coherence and identity in the alternation of opposites, and it is its final task in this harmonious alternation to keep a thread, a recollection, so that the spirit is never left in individual moments and again

[29] Hölderlin, *Werke – Briefe – Dokumente*, p. 508.
[30] Hölderlin, *Werke – Briefe – Dokumente*, p. 509.

in individual moments, but moves continuously from one moment to the next, and remains present in the different moods,

so that it, the aesthetic spirit and its experience, is then "the unifying point ... of the opposites ... so that in it the harmoniously opposed are neither opposed as separates nor united as opposed but are felt as in *one*."[31] It is not easy to put a precise sense on Hölderlin's torrents of words, but the general idea seems clear that the poem, thus the aesthetic experience that leads to and/or to which it leads, does not merely put together what is originally separate, but rather progressively, infinitely, and thus in some sense never completely but in some sense always, discovers the unity in what only appears to be separate but is already primordially unified. Finally, Hölderlin suggests that aesthetic experience not only has this quality but represents it to us, thus functions as a form of metaphysical insight: the vocation or destiny (*Bestimmung*) of poetry is to be "cognition [*Erkenntnis*] of the harmoniously opposed ... in its unity and individuality."[32] In the end, then, Hölderlin regards the spirit of poetry, and presumably the spirit of art more generally, as a form of metaphysical insight, and thus stands squarely in the cognitivist tradition in aesthetics. There has been no mention of play nor of emotion in his account of poetry; even when he spoke of what is *gefühlt und fühlbar*, felt and palpable, he was talking about the sensory aspect of intellectual intuition, thus of metaphysical insight, not about the experience of any ordinary human emotion. This is not to say that Hölderlin's own poetry is not deeply expressive of emotion; it is a claim about Hölderlin's theory, not his poetry. (Though I think few would allege to find any element of play or playfulness in Hölderlin's earnest poetry.)

The metaphysical cognitivism of Hölderlin's rudimentary aesthetics was to be worked out in great detail by his friends Schelling and Hegel, although whether with knowledge of his texts or on the basis of conversations with him or only on the basis of a common way of thinking we cannot say. So for details of such a view we should turn to them. But first we will consider the Romantic aesthetics of Friedrich Schlegel, far better known in their own time than the unpublished thoughts of Hölderlin, communicated at best to his two friends who enjoyed worldly success while he languished alone in his tower room in Tübingen.

[31] Hölderlin, *Werke – Briefe – Dokumente*, p. 515.
[32] Hölderlin, *Werke – Briefe – Dokumente*, p. 520.

Schlegel

Here we will focus on Friedrich Schlegel, who arrived in Jena the year after Hölderlin left and presumably knew nothing of his predecessor's philosophical thought.

Friedrich and August Wilhelm were sons, Friedrich the seventh and youngest child, of the minister Johann Adolf Schlegel and nephews of Johann Elias Schlegel, both literary figures of a previous generation (Johann Adolf Schlegel had been the translator of Batteux into German and Johann Elias a well-known playwright). August Wilhelm was allowed to pursue his philological interests directly, and matriculated as a student of the classics at the university at Göttingen in 1786. Their parents were concerned about the financial future of their youngest son, however, and apprenticed him to a banker in Leipzig at the age of fifteen, then allowed him to follow his brother to Göttingen in 1790, but only to study law. The next year, August Wilhelm left Göttingen to become a tutor to a family in Amsterdam, and Friedrich returned to Leipzig to continue his study of law, where he met von Hardenberg, who was studying to be a mining engineer. Friedrich quickly gave up law for the study of Greek and Roman literature. In 1794, he moved to Dresden, where he was able to live with an older, married sister, and continue his study of ancient literature as well as study the extensive collection of plaster casts of ancient sculpture that had been assembled for the Saxon royal family by the painter Anton Raphael Mengs. In 1795, August Wilhelm was invited to Jena by Schiller to work on his journal *Die Horen*. Von Hardenberg also went there to listen to Fichte, and the next year Friedrich Schlegel arrived to join his older brother. This was the beginning of the brief moment of early German Romanticism, which flourished in Jena for the next several years. By 1798, however, August Wilhelm had fallen out with Schiller, and Friedrich moved to Berlin in order to continue his literary career there: for the next two years in Berlin, he would edit the three volumes of the journal *Athenäum*, which presented the views of the early Romantics to the German literary public. In 1799, the leading philosopher of Jena, Johann Gottlieb Fichte, was forced out of his position in the aftermath of the "Atheism controversy," and in 1803 Schelling, who had also been teaching there since 1798, departed as well, at least in part because of the scandal over his affair and marriage with Caroline, previously the wife of August Wilhelm Schlegel. Following Fichte's departure, Friedrich Schlegel returned to Jena to matriculate in philosophy and offered courses, but attendance at his first lectures on transcendental philosophy (posthumously published in 1935) dwindled before the course was complete, and he and his wife, the former Dorothea Veit, originally Brendel Mendelssohn, a daughter of Moses, moved back to Berlin, then in 1801 on to Dresden and then Paris. Also in 1801, Ludwig Tieck arrived in Jena but Novalis died. Those events marked the end of the Romantic circle in Jena and the end of the moment of early German Romanticism. Schlegel would make his living as a private lecturer in Cologne for several more years (1804–8), but in 1808 he ultimately converted to Catholicism, became a political conservative, and went to work for the Austrian administration of Prince von Metternich in Vienna from 1809 to 1818, for which service he was awarded a "von" in 1815. In his last years, Schlegel lectured in Vienna. Friedrich Schlegel wrote and edited journals prolifically throughout his life. In addition to the works in aesthetics from 1794 to 1804, some of which will be discussed in what follows, he published a work on *The Language and Philosophy of the Indians* in 1808 – his brother edited the first Western editions of the *Upanishads* – which may well have been a source for Schopenhauer's fascination with Indian philosophy. In his final lectures in Vienna, he was outlining a "system of Christian philosophy," three volumes of which – *Philosophy of Life, Philosophy of History*, and *Philosophy of Language or of the Word* – were published before or shortly after his death. As we will see, Schlegel's turn from a secular to a Christian philosophy appeared in his works in aesthetics no later than 1804.

Before he arrived in Jena, the strongest philosophical influence on Friedrich Schlegel was Kant. The influence of Kant's aesthetics is evident in an early piece on "The Limits of the Beautiful" (1794). This work looks both backward and forward. In Schlegel's opening statement of his aims, he uses a Neo-Platonic formulation, reminiscent of Shaftesbury almost a century earlier: he will attempt, he says, "to exhibit the elements of beauty as they exist, not in the [*sic*] art only but also in nature and in love, and to prove that the proper combination of these three elements – the richness of nature, the purity of love, and the symmetry of art – will infallibly produce true, genuine, and majestic beauty. The idea of beauty, thus understood, cannot be regarded as distinct, either from truth, or from the abundance of living realities; it must not be severed from love ... nor from the sentiment of goodness." At least at the outset of his career, Schlegel thus recognized the possibility of a threefold synthesis of approaches to beauty. But what was of more immediate concern to him is not theory but present practice: he says that the beautiful is "everywhere defective, incomplete, and partial, presented to us in disjointed fragments, both in artistic representation and in reality."[33] In this context, the latter remark seems to imply that contemporary art itself is not living up to its potential, and needs to be reformed. It is often thought that the core idea of early German Romanticism is that since reality itself can never admit of a unified and complete comprehension, our representation of it is necessarily fragmentary, and the inexorably fragmentary representation of reality in art is precisely what makes art the paradigmatic vehicle for the representation of reality. If this were indeed the central thought of early German Romanticism, then it would seem that the Neo-Platonic ideal of the unity of beauty, truth, and goodness should disappear from Schlegel's subsequent work, supposed to be the paradigm of this movement. In fact, as we will see, although there are hints of an acceptance of the ineluctably fragmentary nature of art and beauty in Schlegel's central contributions of the later 1790s, the Neo-Platonic ideal that philosophy, moral sensibility, and the sense of beauty each offer distinct but co-extensive representations of reality as a unified and systematic whole, which in turn might ultimately be unified in art – an idea which, as we have seen, had not died with Shaftesbury, but had continued to live in Germany in the work of Karl Philipp Moritz and would animate Herder's critique of Kant's aesthetics as late as 1800 – would remain central to Schlegel's work.

The fact that Neo-Platonism would be the source for the critique of Kant six years after Schlegel wrote the essay we are now discussing would seem to raise a doubt about my opening suggestion that this early essay was written under Kant's influence. But this suggestion should not be rejected, for two reasons. First, as we have seen, in spite of his initial rigorous separation of aesthetic response from all conceptual content, Kant had ultimately insisted that all fine art does have intellectual, indeed moral content, and even added that because of the structure of aesthetic experience itself all beauty, natural as well as artistic, is a symbol of the morally good; in other words, Kant by no means completely rejected the Neo-Platonic identification of the beautiful, the true, and the good, although he did transpose it from a metaphysical into a symbolic key and certainly underplayed any emotional aspect of the aesthetic response to the representation of the good. And second, in the present work Schlegel grounded his Neo-Platonism in a Kantian conception of the free activity

---

[33] Friedrich Schlegel, "On the Limits of the Beautiful," in *The Aesthetic and Miscellaneous Works of Frederick von Schlegel*, trans. E.J. Millington (London: Bohn, 1849), p. 413.

of the mind as the core of aesthetic experience and the basis for its further cognitive and moral significance. He begins the central passage of the essay with a thought that sounds like it comes from Schiller's *Letters on Aesthetic Education*, although that work would be published only a year later:

> The soul needs a certain amount of intellectual enjoyment to give it strength adequate for the daily struggle in which it is involved. The energies of the mind are as completely shattered and destroyed by constant restraint, as they are relaxed and enfeebled by perpetual enjoyments. To make pleasure the sole object of life is to defeat our own intention; for man exists but in accordance with the decrees of nature, and her laws stand in constant opposition to his own desires. Life is a stern struggle between conflicting powers.

Then, in a move parallel to Schiller's, Schlegel turns to a Kantian account of aesthetic experience as offering us a kind of pleasure that can resolve or at least ameliorate our constant struggle with the constraints of human existence without sapping our moral resolve, that can indeed strengthen our moral capacity without sacrificing what is unique to itself:

> Pleasure, indeed, has a higher zest when spontaneous and self-created; and it rises in value in proportion to its affinity with that perfection of beauty in which moral excellence is allied to external charms. It must be a free spontaneous burst of feeling: *not* the result of certain means applied for the attainment of any particular object; for pleasure thus pursued becomes occupation rather than enjoyment.

Here Schlegel adopts Kant's conception that the purposiveness of the beautiful must be disinterested and subjective, that beauty cannot be equated with ordinary usefulness; indeed, he exclaims that "We call it desecration and pollution to employ holy things in ordinary uses." Then he continues:

> But is not the beautiful also holy? Man can by representation inform the understanding; by beauty he can improve the manners; works of art may supply material for contemplation; but the mind will gain little or nothing thereby. As all energy demands for its development a free unrestrained power of action, so the sense of beauty and its creative faculty are kindled in the soul only by the free enjoyment and habitual contemplation of its creations. This inward perception of the soul for the beautiful is far different from the superficial artistic taste which refuses to acknowledge a susceptibility to comprehend represented and ideal forms as a creative and

generative faculty for art. For beauty reigns supreme, not only in imitative works, but also in nature, in mankind, and in love.[34]

Here Schlegel's idea is that the essence of beauty is not imitation, but free exercise – or free play – of our mental powers, and that the benefits of the experience of beauty for the rest of our lives – nature, mankind, and love – follow from the fact that aesthetic experience is a form of freedom. This was of course the central idea of Kant's aesthetics and, as noted, the idea that Schiller was developing at the same time as Schlegel.[35]

In Schlegel's next significant work on aesthetics, however, the essay "On the Study of Greek Poetry" written in 1795 as the introduction to a never completed history of ancient poetry, and published on its own in 1797, Schlegel's thought adds a new twist. The central idea of the 1794 essay might be stated by saying that aiming for beauty in art at least under ideal circumstances also yields both truth and goodness, but what Schlegel argues the next year is that art aims for truth, although under ideal conditions that will also yield beauty. In particular, he argues, no doubt under the continuing influence of Winckelmann, that the artists of ancient Greece had naturally aimed for truthfulness to nature in their work, but because of the harmonious circumstances of their life and their holistic conception of nature had produced works that also had great beauty – "The bold nudity in the life and art of the Greeks and Romans is not animalistic crudity but, rather, uninhibited naturalness, liberal humanity, and republican candor"[36] – while modern artists, because of the less harmonious conditions of modern life and their more fragmentary conceptions of reality, aim to capture the truth of particular objects rather than any sort of universal truth, and thereby do not produce harmonious beauty but only the "interesting" or even the ugly. In this essay, which is still only a way station to the early Romanticism of

---

[34] Schlegel, "On the Limits of the Beautiful," pp. 416–17.
[35] Ruth Sonderegger presents an interpretation of Schlegel centered on the concept of play in *Für eine Ästhetik des Spiels: Hermeneutik, Dekonstruktion und der Eigensinn der Kunst* (Frankfurt am Main: Suhrkamp Verlag, 2000), especially Part II. She bases her interpretation primarily on Schlegel's 1798 review of Goethe's *Wilhelm Meisters Lehrjahre* (see pp. 131–41), though her conception of play seems to equate it with the construction of unity out of the fragmentary and contradictory, so play is simply the "formal *connection* of diverse elements" in contrast to "hermeneutical" interpretation, which is understood as the discovery of previously existing meaning (see pp. 137, 140). Schlegel's review can be found in Friedrich Schlegel, *"Athenäums"-Fragmente und andere Schriften*, ed. Andreas Huyssen (Stuttgart: Philipp Reclam jun.: 1978), pp. 143–64.
[36] Friedrich Schlegel, *On the Study of Greek Poetry*, trans. Stuart Bennett (Albany: State University of New York Press, 2001), p. 73.

the immediately following years, this is not considered to be a virtue of modern art, but a defect that Schlegel hopes may be overcome by a revolution in art.

Schlegel's claim about the Greeks is that at the height of their art they strove for objectivity, not beauty, but that since beauty and objectivity are virtually identical, they could not but produce genuine beauty. He arrives at his conception of beauty as objectivity by transforming Kant's conception of the universal subjective validity of aesthetic *judgment* into a conception of the objectivity of the beautiful *object*; in this way his essay is thus a first step toward the recreation of a theory of aesthetic experience as a form of cognition within the framework of Kant's own language that we will also find in Schelling, Schopenhauer, and Hegel. In principle, Schlegel maintains, it has always been known that objectivity is the essence of beauty, and moderns as well as ancients have striven for objectivity in art:

> Throughout the most varied forms and orientations, in all degrees of vitality, the same *need for a complete satisfaction,* a consistent striving for *an absolute maximum of art* expresses itself in all modern poetry. What theory promised, what one hoped to find in each idol – what was this but a *ne plus ultra* of the *aesthetic?* The more often the longing for a complete satisfaction that would be grounded in human nature was disappointed by the individual and the mutable, the more ardent and restless it became. Only the universally valid, enduring, and necessary – the *objective* – can fill this great gap; only the beautiful can still this ardent yearning. *Beauty* ... is the universally valid object of an uninterested pleasure, which, independent of the constraint of needs and laws, is at the same time independent, free, and necessary, entirely purposeless and yet unconditionally purposeful.[37]

The Kantian heritage of Schlegel's conception of beauty is unmistakable – it is purposiveness without a determinate purpose, independent and free yet at the same time necessary – but it is transformed from a universally valid experience into a "universally valid object," and with this transformation the goal of the artist is transformed from that of free exercise of the imagination to truthfulness to an object beyond his own work, and the goal of the audience transformed from the free exercise of its own imagination to appreciation of the artist's truthfulness. The Greeks, Schlegel then argues, were able to produce unparalleled beauty because they could be truthful to an objective, harmonious nature. There is no question in his mind that Greek art at its greatest moment achieved a perfection of beauty unparalleled before or since:

[37] Schlegel, *On the Study of Greek Poetry*, p. 35.

Greek poetry truly attained this *ultimate limit of the natural culturation* [*Bildung*] of art and taste, this *utmost pinnacle of free beauty*. Culturation has attained a state of *perfection* if the inner striving force has fully unfolded itself, if the intention has been completely achieved, and no expectation remains unfulfilled in the uniform completeness of the whole. This state is termed a *golden age* when an entire complex of concurrently existing elements obtains. The pleasure that the works of the golden age of Greek art affords ... is *complete and self-sufficient*. For this level of accomplishment, I know of no more appropriate name than *ultimate beauty*. Not simply a beauty about which nothing more beautiful could be thought but, rather, the complete example of the unattainable idea that essentially becomes here utterly apparent: *the prototype of art and taste*.[38]

And,

> Only where all elements of art and taste evolve, form, and complete themselves in equal proportion is the greatest beauty possible – that is, in *natural* culturation. In artificial culturation this *symmetry* is irrecoverably lost by the arbitrary division and mixture undertaken by the regulative understanding.... the greatest beauty is that which has become an *organically formed whole*, and which would be torn asunder by the smallest division, destroyed by the slightest excess.[39]

With his characterization of beauty as an "organically formed whole," Schlegel takes a step that Kant did not take – the characterization of the object of aesthetic judgment in terms of the object of teleological judgment – and that would be influential in aesthetics into the twentieth century. (We will see it, for example, in the early twentieth-century British philosopher G.E. Moore, not usually thought of as a Romantic!) But his argument about the Greeks is that they could produce such beauty because they lived a harmonious and natural life and merely aimed in their art to be truthful in their representation of this life. This argument emerges in his characterization of the greatest of all Greek artists, Sophocles, who "developed what Aeschylus invented," who "in perfection and serenity ... is the equal of Homer and Pindar, and [who] surpasses all his predecessors and successors in grace." In Sophocles, "Everything evolves *necessarily* out of a unity and even the smallest part belongs unconditionally to the *great law of the whole*," thus achieving "uniform completeness" and organicity. Sophocles achieves this precisely by not consciously seeking beautiful effects, but by naturally responding to the harmonies of life itself:

---

[38] Schlegel, *On the Study of Greek Poetry*, p. 55.
[39] Schlegel, *On the Study of Greek Poetry*, p. 58.

> The moderation with which he renounces even the most beautiful outgrowth and with which he would have resisted even the most alluring temptation to do damage to the equilibrium of the whole is ... a proof of his richness. For his law-governedness is *free*, his accuracy is *graceful*, and the *richest abundance* organizes itself of its own accord to a perfect yet pleasing harmony. The unity of his dramas was not mechanically forced; rather, it *emerged organically*. Even the smallest side-branch enjoys its own life and appears simply to relegate itself freely to its place in the ordered context of the entire formation [*Bildung*].... The whole as well as the various parts are precisely differentiated and pleasingly grouped in the richest and simplest conglomerations. And struggle and calm, act and contemplation, humanity and fate obligingly alternate and freely unite throughout the action ... Here there is not the slightest reminder of labor, art, and necessity. We are no longer aware of the medium; the shell vanishes, and we immediately enjoy pure beauty.... These formations appear not to have been made or to have become, but, rather, to have been eternally present, or to have originated out of themselves, as the goddess of love arose effortlessly and at once perfect out of the ocean.[40]

Sophocles could create ultimate beauty precisely because he did not strive for particular beautiful effects, but naturally responded to a harmonious nature. Aiming only for truthfulness, in such conditions he inevitably produced beauty.

The modern artist, however, no doubt because of the different circumstances of modern life, aims in his work for the truthful representation of idiosyncratic particulars, and thereby produces something interesting or even ugly, but not something beautiful. Schlegel makes this point often. "Nothing can better explain and confirm the artificiality of modern aesthetic development [*Bildung*] than the great *predominance of the individual, the characteristic, and the philosophical*, throughout the entire mass of modern poetry."[41] "The general orientation of poetry – indeed, the whole aesthetic development of modernity – toward the interesting can be explained by this lack of universality, this rule of the mannered, characteristic, and individual."[42] The focus on particulars inevitably disrupts uniform completeness or organic unity:

> In the particulars the representation can be truly splendid; yet, on the whole, it will still negate itself through *inner contradictions* ... The *ideality* of art is contravened when the artist defies his instrument, and when he foists representation – which should only be a means – into the place of

---

[40] Schlegel, *On the Study of Greek Poetry*, pp. 60–1.
[41] Schlegel, *On the Study of Greek Poetry*, pp. 30–1.
[42] Schlegel, *On the Study of Greek Poetry*, p. 35.

the absolute goal, and strives only for *virtuousity* ... The *objectivity* of art is contravened when, in the course of a universally valid representation, peculiarity gets involved, or quietly sneaks in, or flagrantly outrages. It is contravened by *subjectivity*.[43]

The modern artist consciously aims at truth, but truth of the wrong kind, truth about particulars rather than truths about the organic whole of the universe, and is therefore incapable of producing beauty; he produces subjectivity, not objectivity, but beauty lies in objectivity, truthfulness to the organic whole of nature.

One might think, then, that the answer to the problem for modern art is to return to the style of the Greeks; this is, after all, what Winckelmann had advocated, and what much eighteenth- and even early nineteenth-century art, so-called Neo-Classicism, attempted to do in many artistic media, including all forms of poetry and drama, painting, sculpture, and architecture, even music in its subjects if not its forms (think of the operas of Handel and Gluck).[44] But simply copying the accidental idiosyncrasies of Greek art, which in their original context did not detract from its underlying organic unity, will not solve the problem of once again achieving objective beauty, although this is all that many modern artists seem able to do:

> If it had only discovered the secret of the Greeks, the individuality of modern poetry would be at liberty to be objective within the individual. Instead, it wants to elevate its conventional idiosyncrasies to the status of a general law of humanity. Not satisfied being the slave of so many aesthetic, moral, political, and religious prejudices, it also wants to clap its Greek sister in similar chains.[45]

Only if modern art can recapture the inward spirit rather than the outward forms of Greek art can it achieve objective beauty:

> One should not imitate just *any one*, or a particular, *favorite poet*, or the *local form or the individual organ*: for *an individual "as such" can never be a universal norm*. The modern poet who wants to strive for genuine, beautiful art should appropriate for himself the ethical abundance, the unfettered law-governedness, the liberal humanity, the beautiful proportions, the delicate equilibrium, the splendid appositeness that is more or less scattered over the entire mass. He should also approximate the perfect style of the golden

---

[43] Schlegel, *On the Study of Greek Poetry*, p. 70.
[44] For a work with an emphasis on the visual arts, see Hugh Honour, *Neo-Classicism* (Harmondsworth: Penguin Books, 1968).
[45] Schlegel, *On the Study of Greek Poetry*, p. 73.

age, the genuineness and purity of the Greek poetic forms, the objectivity of the representation – in short, the *spirit of the whole: pure Greekness*.[46]

Easy to say, hard to do: Schlegel does not spell out how the artist working within the circumstances of modern life can recapture the attitude toward art that came naturally to the Greeks in their very different relation to culture and nature. And, as we saw earlier, at the very same time that Schlegel was advocating a return to "pure Greekness," Schiller was arguing that there was no returning from our "sentimental" poetry to the "naïve" poetry of the Greeks.

Whether there ever existed the idyllic relation between culture and nature that Schlegel and for that matter Schiller attribute to the Greeks is another matter; his account of the Greeks seems more like fantasy than fact – at the very least, it seems like a one-sided account of Greek life and art, as Nietzsche would later argue by means of his famous contrast between the "Apollonian" and "Dionysian" and his thesis that the epitome of Greek art in the tragedy of Aeschylus and Sophocles combines these two elements, an argument that could have been directed against this work of Schlegel's although Nietzsche does not mention it. One might be tempted to think that a recognition of the irretrievability of the organic wholeness of Greek art, if not the possibility that such organic wholeness never existed in the first place, would have driven Schlegel to what is often presented as the paradigmatic thought of early German Romanticism, the idea that art is always essentially fragmentary rather than whole because reality itself is always essentially fragmentary rather than whole.[47] This idea would still be undergirded by the supposition that the aim of art is to strive for truthfulness toward reality rather than to create beautiful forms independently of what reality may have to offer, but now a different conception of reality itself would dictate a different conception of beauty. In fact, however, although Schlegel suggests this new idea at a few points in the famous fragments published in the *Athäneum* between 1798 and 1800 – in which he and his collaborators,

---

[46] Schlegel, *On the Study of Greek Poetry*, pp. 83–4.
[47] See especially Frank, *Philosophical Foundations of Early German Romanticism*, ch. 12, pp. 201–19. The translator, Elizabeth Millán-Zaibert, distances herself from Frank's emphasis on the fragmentary and takes an approach to Schlegel's central work that is closer to the one to be suggested here when she says in her own work that "The interest Schlegel has in art is epistemological; ultimately he endorses the value of aesthetic reflection as a way of reconciling the finite with the infinite"; see her *Friedrich Schlegel and the Emergence of Romantic Philosophy* (Albany: State University of New York Press, 2007), p. 165.

chiefly his brother August Wilhelm but also Friedrich Schleiermacher, certainly adopted the fragment as a literary form – the majority of his characterizations of "romantic poetry" in this work continue to suggest that ultimate beauty lies in the artistic intimation of the organic unity of reality itself. If there is any substantive difference between Schegel's stance in the essay on Greek poetry of 1795 and the fragments of 1798–1800, it is chiefly in his greater confidence that modern poetry can actually achieve such beauty.

A fragment in which Schlegel suggests the fragmentary character of reality and therefore the not only inevitably but also appropriately fragmentary character of its representation in art is perhaps this one: "A. You say that fragments are the real form of universal philosophy. But what can such fragments do and be for the greatest and most serious concerns of humanity, for the perfection of knowledge? B. Nothing but a Lessingean salt against spiritual sloth ... or even the *fermenta cognitionis* for a critical philosophy ..."[48] What could be better than salt against spiritual sloth and the leaven for knowledge, or a higher vocation for art than to provide it? But in fact, the majority of the fragments in the *Athäneum* identify the "romantic poetry" that they praise with "universal poetry," a form of poetry that precisely by overriding the traditional divisions among genres – as Schlegel himself attempted to do in his 1799 novella of fragments *Lucinde*[49] – manages to express the entirety of reality in all its diversity yet interconnectedness. In his definition of romantic poetry in the famous §116, Schlegel writes:

> Romantic poetry is a progressive, universal poetry. Its aim isn't merely to reunite all the separate species of poetry and put poetry in touch with philosophy and rhetoric. It tries to and should mix and fuse poetry and prose, inspiration and criticism, the poetry of art and the poetry of nature; and make poetry lively and sociable, and life and society poetical; poeticize wit and fill and saturate the forms of art with every kind of good, solid matter for instruction, and animate them with pulsations of humor. It embraces everything that is purely poetic, from the greatest systems of art, containing within themselves still further systems, to the sigh, the kiss that the poetizing child breathes forth in artless song. It can so lose itself in what it describes that one might believe it exists only to characterize poetical individuals of all sorts; and yet there is still no form so fit for expressing the entire spirit

---

[48] Friedrich Schlegel, *Philosophical Fragments*, trans. Peter Firchow (Minneapolis: University of Minnesota Press, 1991), §259, pp. 54–5.

[49] Friedrich Schlegel, *Lucinde: Ein Roman*, ed. Karl Konrad Polheim, rev. ed. (Stuttgart: Philipp Reclam jun., 1999); *Friedrich Schlegel's Lucinde and the Fragments*, trans. with an introduction by Peter Firchow (Minneapolis: University of Minnesota Press, 1971).

of an author ... It alone can become, like the epic, a mirror of the whole circumambient world, an image of the age. And it can also – more than any other form – hover at the midpoint between the portrayed and the portrayer, free of all real and ideal self-interest, on the wings of poetic reflection, and can raise that reflection again and again to a higher power, can multiply it in an endless succession of mirrors.[50]

Schlegel's suggestion that romantic poetry can raise its reflection of reality to ever higher powers may be influenced by the concept of "potencies" that Friedrich Schelling was developing in his philosophy of nature in 1797–98, immediately preceding or at the time that Schlegel was writing this. But another fragment that follows shortly suggests that what really underlies his conception of the cognitive significance of romantic poetry is nothing less than Leibniz's monadology, a philosophical image that retained a tight grip on the German imagination long after Kant's critique of it, even in the period of the 1790s when the influence of Spinoza was at its zenith. Thus in §121 Schlegel writes:

> An idea is a concept perfected to the point of irony, an absolute synthesis of absolute antitheses, the continual self-creating interchange of two conflicting thoughts.... But one shouldn't call this mysticism, since this beautiful old word is so very useful and indispensable for absolute philosophy, from whose perspective the spirit regards everything as a mystery and a wonder, while from other points of view it would appear theoretically and practically normal.... But to transport oneself arbitrarily now into this, now into that sphere, as if into another world, not merely with one's reason and imagination, but with one's whole soul; to freely relinquish first one and then another part of one's being, and confine oneself entirely to a third; to seek and find now in this, now in that individual the be-all and the end-all of existence, and intentionally forget everyone else: of this only a mind is capable that contains within itself simultaneously a plurality of minds and a whole system of persons, and in whose inner being the universe which, as they say, should germinate in every monad, has grown to fullness and maturity.[51]

The "they" who say this are, of course, Leibniz and his followers. This fragment may initially suggest that the universe is inexorably contradictory, that individuals are insuperably different from one another, and may therefore seem to imply that art must be fragmentary because if its role is to represent reality then it can only represent something fragmentary and so represent it fragmentarily. But the passage concludes by suggesting that every individual in fact represents the entire universe,

---

[50] Schlegel, *Fragments*, §116, pp. 31–2.
[51] Schlegel, *Fragments*, §121, p. 33.

although from a particular point of view, the key idea of Leibniz's monadology,[52] and Schlegel's implication seems in the end to be that "universal poetry" is universal precisely because through the representation of something highly individual it can nevertheless represent the entire universe.

Sometimes in the *Athäneum* fragments Schlegel suggests this point by assimilating poetry to philosophy. Here, for example, he borrows Kantian rather than Leibnizian terminology to make what is at least a closely related point:

> There is a kind of poetry whose essence lies in the relation between ideal and real, and which therefore, by analogy to philosophical jargon, should be called transcendental poetry. It begins as satire in the absolute difference of ideal and real, hovers in between as elegy, and ends as idyll with the absolute unity of the two. But just as we shouldn't think much of an uncritical transcendental philosophy that doesn't represent the producer along with the product and contain at the same time within the system of transcendental thoughts a description of transcendental thinking: so too this sort of poetry should unite the transcendental raw materials and preliminaries of a theory of poetic creativity – often met with in modern poets – with the artistic reflection and beautiful self-mirroring that is present in Pindar, in the lyric fragments of the Greeks, in the classical elegy, and, among the moderns, in Goethe.[53]

By transcendental philosophy Schlegel seems to understand a philosophy that unifies the subjective and the objective by recognizing the forms of the objective world to be the forms of thought itself, which gives thought the power (some might think Pyrrhic power) to discover the nature of the outward from within; by transcendental poetry he seems to mean the same as what he meant earlier by universal poetry, poetry that in mixing all the genres that were previously kept apart manages to transcend its own subjectivity or the particularity of any individual and to grasp the entirety of the universe through a reflection in or by one individual of the standpoints of all others. In one of a second set of fragments, the "Ideas," Schlegel suggests that poetry

---

[52] See Leibniz, *Discourse on Metaphysics* (1686), §14; *Principles of Nature and Grace, Based on Reason*, §3; and *Monadology* (1714), §§56–9. The first work was not published until the beginning of the twentieth century, and could not have been known to Schlegel; but the other two were (posthumously) published as early as 1720, and were widely known throughout the eighteenth century, indeed, being far shorter than Leibniz's only book, the *Theodicy* of 1710, formed the basis for the popular conception of Leibniz's philosophy.

[53] Schlegel, *Fragments*, §238, pp. 50–1.

supersedes philosophy, but only because it seems better suited than philosophy to play the role of a Leibnizian monad, finding universality in particularity:

> Where philosophy stops, poetry has to begin. An ordinary point of view, a way of thinking, natural only in opposition to art and culture, a mere existing: all these are wrong; that is, there should be no kingdom of barbarity beyond the boundaries of culture. Every thinking art of an organization should not feel its limits without at the same time feeling its unity in relation to the whole. For example, one ought to contrast philosophy not simply with unphilosophy, but with poetry.[54]

Whether both philosophy and poetry or only romantic poetry can reflect or represent the whole universe through the standpoint of an individual is less important to Schlegel's aesthetic thought than his supposition that at least poetry can do this. The key claim of Schlegel's central period as an aesthetic thinker is thus not that poetry can only be fragmentary because it represents a fragmentary world, but rather that through its combination of what would on their own be only fragmentary methods or genres truly universal poetry can represent the world in its entirety – and presumably derives its beauty from that. The beauty of poetry lies precisely in that it offers more profound knowledge than philosophy itself. This is an idea, as we will see, to which the young Schelling would be sympathetic, although the continued assumption that art aims at cognition but the rejection of the claim that art offers deeper knowledge than philosophy will subsequently be the basis of Hegel's critique of Romanticism in the form of his thesis of the "end of art."

After his short-lived fiasco as a philosophy professor at Jena, Schlegel traveled to Paris and Brussels and then settled in Cologne. In these cities his attention turned from poetry to painting, and he wrote a series of reports on what he saw that were published as "Letters on Christian Art." There is a change in tone in these letters from his fragments of 1798 to 1800: not a change from a fragmentary to a holistic conception of the truth that can be grasped by art, for as we have seen he by no means committed himself to the fragmentary conception of aesthetic cognition, but rather a change from a secular to a religious interpretation of the truth about the world as a whole that is grasped and conveyed by the best art. This passage from the end of the letters conveys the new religious tone of Schlegel's aesthetics and prepares the way for his conversion to Catholicism in 1808:

---

[54] Schlegel, *Fragments*, "Ideas" §48, p. 98.

> In what, then, does this exalted beauty consist? ... The true object of the art should be, instead of resting in externals, to lead the mind upwards into a more exalted region and a spiritual world. While false-mannered artists, content with the empty glitter of a pleasing imitation, soar no higher, nor ever seek to reach that lofty sphere, in which genuine beauty is portrayed according to certain defined ideas of natural characteristics ... The light of hope dawned not on heathen intelligence; impassioned grief and tragic beauty bounded their purest aspirations. Yet this blessed light of hope, borne on the wings of trusting faith and sinless love, though on earth it breaks forth only in dim anticipations of a glorious hereafter, – this glorious hope, radiant with immortality, invests every picture of the Christian era with a bright harmony of expression, and fixes our attention by its clear comprehension of heavenly things, and an elevated spiritual beauty which we justly term Christian.[55]

Here the Neo-Platonist identification of beauty with both truth and love of Schlegel's 1794 essay has been replaced with the Christian association of "an elevated spiritual beauty" with faith, and beauty reveals not the coherent universe of the Leibnizian monadology but the "heavenly things" of religion. The change from his "early Romanticism" to his later attitude is a change from secular "transcendental" philosophy to Christian religiosity, and prepares the way for the marked presence of Christianity in the art of the later period of Romanticism, at least in Germany.

We will return later to the aesthetic conceptions of several other Romantic thinkers, Samuel Taylor Coleridge of England and Ralph Waldo Emerson of Massachusetts. It might be natural to discuss them in connection with Schlegel, who no doubt influenced them in various regards, but they did not follow him in his turn to an explicitly Christian religiosity. It will therefore be more natural to discuss them in the shadow of the aestheticians of absolute idealism, above all Schelling, to whom we therefore now turn.

3. SCHELLING

We begin our consideration of the aesthetics of German Idealism proper with the aesthetics of Friedrich Wilhelm Josef Schelling (1775–1854). Born near Stuttgart and educated along with Georg Wilhelm Friedrich Hegel and the poet Friedrich Hölderlin at the Tübingen Stift (seminary), where they were all close friends, Schelling was brought

---

[55] Schlegel, *Miscellaneous and Aesthetic Works*, pp. 145–6.

to Jena as a professor by Goethe in 1798, all of twenty-three years old, where he succeeded Fichte, and remained there until 1803, when he left for a position in Würzburg, accompanied by his wife Caroline, formerly the wife of August Wilhelm Schlegel. He had previously brought Hegel to Jena and they worked closely until Schelling's departure, although Hegel was not to succeed Schelling the way Schelling had succeeded Fichte. Schelling moved to Munich in 1806, where he held a position at the Royal Academy of Art, and lived there until 1820 and again from 1827 until 1841 (in the interval he was in Erlangen). Finally, in 1841, now elderly instead of precocious, he was invited to Berlin to occupy the chair first held by his predecessor Fichte (1801–14) and then by his protégé Hegel (1818–31). In this late period of his career, Schelling worked on a vast philosophy of mythology that has its roots in his early work in aesthetics, but which will not be considered here. Schelling's views in aesthetics first emerged in his *System of Transcendental Idealism*, published in 1800 when others of the Romantic group such as Friedrich Schlegel were already leaving Jena. In 1802–3 and 1803–4, Schelling gave a series of lectures on the philosophy of art, first in Jena and then in Würzburg, which was not published until his son's edition of the father's complete works in the middle of the nineteenth century,[56] but was well known before they were published. The young Schelling had enormous influence, not only on Hegel, who was present in Jena when the lectures were first delivered, but also on Schopenhauer, whose notebooks show his close study of Schelling's published works in spite of his invective against the trio of Fichte, Schelling, and Hegel. As we will see in the next chapter, Schelling also had great influence on many thinkers outside of German academic philosophy.

It is difficult to write about the philosophy of Schelling briefly: he was a prolific and protean philosopher, whose views often underwent such rapid metamorphosis that only a geneticist could discern the constancies in their underlying DNA.[57] Nor can his aesthetic theory (or theories) be

---

[56] Friedrich Wilhelm Joseph von Schelling, *Sämtliche Werke*, ed. K.F.A. Schelling, 14 vols. (Stuttgart: Cotta, 1856–61); the text of *Philosophie der Kunst* from that edition is reproduced in F.W.J. Schelling, *Ausgewählte Schriften*, ed. Manfred Frank, vol. 2: 1801–1803 (Frankfurt am Main: Suhrkamp Verlag, 1985).

[57] There is no detailed survey of Schelling's whole philosophical career in English. Surveys in other languages include Kuno Fischer, *Geschichte der neueren Philosophie*, vol. VII, third edition (Heidelberg: C. Winter, 1902) and Xavier Tilliette, *Schelling: Une Philosophie en Devenir*, 2 vols. (Paris: Vrin, 1970). Introductions to Schelling include Alan White, *Schelling: An Introduction to the System of Freedom* (New Haven: Yale University Press, 1983); Werner Marx, *The Philosophy of F.W.J. Schelling: History, System, and Freedom*, trans. Thomas

easily isolated from his larger projects: as he asserted in his 1800 *System of Transcendental Idealism*, the work that made his fame at age twenty-five and may still be his mostly widely read work although it by no means represents his final position on aesthetics or anything else,

> Art is at once the only true and eternal organon and document of philosophy, which ever and again continues to speak to us of what philosophy cannot depict in external form, namely the unconscious element in acting and producing, and its original idea with the conscious. Art is paramount to the philosopher precisely because it opens to him, as it were, the holy of holies, where burns in eternal and original unity, as if in a single flame, that which in nature and history is rent asunder, and in life and action, no less than in thought, must forever fly apart.[58]

Schelling rapidly revised this claim, arguing in his lectures on *The Philosophy of Art* just a couple of years later (1802–3) that philosophy is more parallel to art than subordinated to it, expressing in abstract or "ideal" form the same ultimate content that art expresses in more concrete or "real" form.[59] But it is obvious that the aesthetic theory of a philosopher who could make either of these claims cannot be well understood except as part of a much larger system. Equally obviously, we

---

Nenon (Bloomington: Indiana University Press, 1984); Manfred Frank, *Eine Einführung in Schellings Philosophie* (Framkfurt am Main: Suhrkamp Verlag, 1985); Andrew Bowie, *Schelling and Modern European Philosophie* (London: Routledge, 1993), which includes a chapter on Schelling's aesthetics; and Dale E. Snow, *Schelling and the End of Idealism* (Albany: State University Press of New York, 1996), which does not. A monograph on Schelling's aesthetics is Dieter Jähnig, *Schelling: Die Kunst in der Philosophie*, 2 vols. (Pfüllingen: Neske, 1966–69). Hans Feger provides background on Schelling's philosophy in general in *Poetische Vernunft: Ästhetik und Moral im Deutschen Idealismus* (Stuttgart: J.B. Metzler, 2007), ch. 8–10, and then focuses on Schelling's aesthetics in ch. 13–15. Briefer treatments include Engell, *Creative Imagination*, pp. 301–27; Frank, *Einführung in die frühromantische Ästhetik*, lectures 9–13; and Andrew Bowie, *Aesthetics and Subjectivity: From Kant to Nietzsche*, second edition (Manchester: University of Manchester Press, 2003), ch. 4; Dale Jacquette, "Idealism: Schopenhauer, Schiller and Schelling," in Berys Gaut and Dominic McIver Lopes, editors, *The Routledge Companion to Aesthetics*, second edition (London: Routledge, 2005), pp. 83–96; and Marie-Luise Raters, *Kunst, Wahrheit und Gefühl: Schelling, Hegel und die Ästhetik des angelsächsischen Idealismus* (Freiburg: Verlag Karl Albers, 2005), ch. 2.

[58] Quotations from F.W.J. Schelling, *System of Transcendental Idealism (1800) (STI)*, trans. Peter Heath, introduction by Michael Vater (Charlottesville: University Press of Virginia, 1978), p. 231. I have occasionally modified Heath's translation; here I have translated Schelling's *Organon* as "organon" rather than "organ." See F.W.J. Schelling, *System des transzendentalen Idealismus*, ed. Walter Schulz (Hamburg: Felix Meiner Verlag, 1957), p. 297.

[59] F.W.J. Schelling, *The Philosophy of Art (PA)*, ed. and trans. Douglas W. Stott (Minneapolis: University of Minnesota Press, 1989), p. 6. The German text of this work is in Schelling, *Ausgewählte Werke*, vol. II, pp. 181–565.

will not have space here to explicate adequately Schelling's philosophical system at any one moment of his career or the evolution of his philosophical system through his career. We will have to say just enough about Schelling's whole system at the time of his two most influential works on art, the two just referred to, to allow us to see how he transformed Kant's theory of the free play of our cognitive powers in aesthetic experience back into a theory of aesthetic experience as itself a form of cognition, and how he replaced Kant's positive view of the pleasure of aesthetic experience with an essentially negative view of it.

Schelling's *System of Transcendental Idealism* of 1800 completed his first philosophical system, in which he presented the parallel disciplines of "philosophy of nature" and "transcendental philosophy" as coinciding and culminating in the philosophy of art. In this system, written in response to Fichte's radicalization of Kant's original transcendental idealism by the replacement of the thing in itself with the self's own "positing" of its other, Schelling argued that the laws of nature on the one hand are the product of unconscious thought and the laws of human knowledge and action (including institutions) on the other are the product of conscious thought, while only art, as the product of both unconscious and conscious thought, reveals the unitary and active character of the thought that underlies all reality. That art reveals this is precisely why it is essentially cognitive, and that only art fully reveals this is why it is more cognitively valuable than even philosophy, which manifests more the conscious than the unconscious aspect of thought. Schelling expounded his philosophy of nature in two early works, the *Ideas for a Philosophy of Nature* of 1797 and the *First Outline of a System of the Philosophy of Nature* of 1799, and continued to expound it in works subsequent to the *System of Transcendental Idealism* as well.[60] But this brief review of the philosophy of nature from the Introduction to the *System* captures Schelling's central idea:

> If all *knowing* has as it were two poles that mutually presuppose and demand one another ... there must necessarily be *two* basic sciences ... The necessary tendency of all *natural science* is ... the move from nature to the intelligent.... The highest consummation of natural science would be the complete spiritualizing of all natural laws into laws of intuition and thought.

[60] F.W.J. Schelling, *Ideas for a Philosophy of Nature*, trans. Errol E. Harris and Peter Heath (Cambridge: Cambridge University Press, 1988); *First Outline of a System of the Philosophy of Nature*, trans. Keith R. Peterson (Albany: State University Press of New York, 2004); *System der gesammten Philosophie und der Naturphilosophie insbesondere* (1804), in Schelling, *Ausgewählte Schriften*, vol. 3, 141–588.

> The phenomena (the matter) must wholly disappear, and only the laws (the form) remain. Hence it is, that the more lawfulness emerges in nature itself, the more the husk disappears, the phenomena themselves become more mental, and at length vanish entirely.

Schelling illustrates this claim with the examples of optics, which he claims is "nothing but a geometry whose lines are drawn by light," which is of itself "of doubtful materiality," of magnetism, in which "all material traces are already disappearing," and of gravitation, "which even scientists have thought it possible to conceive of merely as an immediate spiritual influence," of which "nothing remains but its law."[61] No doubt the contemporary reader will object that the fact that the most general and fundamental laws of natural science can only be *grasped* by abstract acts of the human intellect hardly *makes* them into abstract acts of intellect in any sense, but this objection does not move an idealist who is committed to the claim that knowledge is possible only because of the underlying identity of the knower and the known:

> How both the objective world accommodates to representations in us, and representations in us to the objective world, is unintelligible unless between the two worlds, the ideal and the real, there exists a *predetermined harmony*. But this latter is unthinkable unless the activity, whereby the objective is produced, is at bottom identical with that which expresses itself in volition, and *vice versa*.[62]

Like Kant, Schelling thought that Leibniz's central idea of a preestablished harmony between representations and objects had to be revised, but instead of transforming it into a regulative principle as Kant ultimately did, Schelling sought a metaphysical foundation for it in the essentially mental nature of reality itself. After 1800, in his so-called identity philosophy, he would turn to Spinoza for inspiration, explaining the possibility of the cognitive correspondence between thought and nature by the metaphysical theory that they are both manifestations of an underlying absolute that is expressed in each, although as we will see that actually has only minor impact on the development of his philosophy of art.

So much for the philosophy of nature; on the other side, transcendental philosophy proceeds "from the subjective, as primary and absolute," to the objective that arises from this,[63] that is, it studies how the indisputably

---

[61] Schelling, *STI*, p. 6.
[62] Schelling, *STI*, pp. 11–12.
[63] Schelling, *STI*, p. 7.

subjective structures of human thought manifest or objectify themselves in human discourses and sciences, human actions and institutions. Here Schelling introduces an historical dimension, holding that human thought is actually "a *graduated sequence* of intuitions, whereby the self raises itself to the highest power of consciousness," and thus that transcendental philosophy must take the form of "a progressive history of self-consciousness, for which what is laid down in experience serves merely, so to speak, as a memorial and a document."[64] In these two brief comments, two important features of Schelling's thought are revealed. First, again revealing a preference for Leibniz over Kant, Schelling suggests that human thought takes the form of a gradual transition from intuitions to concepts, from more concrete to more abstract forms of thought, rather than that of a synthesis of intuitions and concepts; second, his claim that experience serves merely as a memorial and document of self-consciousness suggests that even with such things as human sciences and institutions, which are more obviously the products of thought than magnetism or gravitation, we are not always *self*-conscious, that is, conscious that these are in fact the products of our own thought, and that we need philosophy to make us conscious of that fact.

But it is central to Schelling's philosophy that even the products of human thought are never solely the products of conscious or self-conscious thought and intention, or voluntary actions, but always reflect unconscious thought and intentions as well. This fundamental fact is what, for the Schelling of 1800, art and only art reveals, and revealing that is the essentially cognitive function of art.

To prepare the way for his apotheosis of the role of art in the *System of Transcendental Idealism*, Schelling combines his philosophy of nature and his transcendental philosophy into the thesis that all nature, our own included, is the product of both unconscious and conscious thought, and that there is something contradictory about this. The contradiction is, or better, the contradictions are, although Schelling does not distinguish them, that the one and the same continuous process of thinking should be both unconscious and conscious, that it should be both ideal and real, that is, take the form of both mental representation and external object of representation, and that it should be both infinite and finite, that is, like a general concept that applies to indeterminately many objects and like a particular object to which a general concept applies. What we commonly call nature tends to line up with one side of these

---

[64] Schelling, *STI*, p. 2.

contrasts and what we commonly call thought with the other, but for Schelling we must be able to understand both sides of these contrasts as present in each of what we artificially distinguish as nature and thought. He argues that we can do this in two ways: first, inadequately, in a teleological view of nature that finds a way to incorporate not merely thought but also volition in our conception of nature, and then, more fully, in art, which we can experience as both a natural and an intentional product of both unconscious and conscious thought. Art thus offers a higher-level resolution of the underlying contradictions of existence than could natural beauty.

The task for uniting the two forms of thought conceived by Schelling to underlie nature on the one hand and our own knowledge and action on the other is to find something that makes manifest the "original identity of the conscious with the unconscious activity." He adds to Kant's characterization of teleological judgment his own identifications of that which is conscious with that which is intentional or purposive, and of that which is unconscious with that which is unintentional, in order to argue that the first form in which this identity is manifest is nature judged teleologically: "But now if all conscious activity is purposive, this coincidence of conscious and unconscious activity can evidence itself only in a product that is *purposive*, without *being purposively brought about*."[65] He does not reproduce Kant's argument that it is only the peculiar characteristics of organisms that force us to conceive of them *as if* they were internally purposive systems, a conception that in turn leads us to think of nature as a whole *as if* it were a purposive system for which we have to conceive of both an author and a final end, a purpose for the system as a whole. He just helps himself to the assumption that nature in general presents itself to us "as a product, that is, which although it is the work of unseeing mechanism, yet looks as though it were consciously brought about," or that it seems to us as if "in its mechanism, and although itself nothing but a blind mechanism," nature "is nonetheless purposive."[66] But Schelling's inadequate motivation of a teleological view of nature matters little, for he is insistent that such a view of nature does not reveal any connection between the purposiveness of nature and our *own* thought: "Nature, in its blind and mechanical purposiveness, admittedly represents to me an original identity of the conscious and unconscious activities, but it does

[65] Schelling, *STI*, pp. 213–14.
[66] Schelling, *STI*, p. 215.

not present this identity to me as one whose ultimate ground resides *in the self itself.*"[67] What he is looking for is something that will make manifest that the intellect that emerges unconsciously and nonpurposively in nature is in fact identical with our own conscious and purposive thought. Only art reveals that.

Schelling is looking for an intuition that "is to bring together that which exists separately in the appearance of freedom and in the intuition of the natural product, namely *identity of the conscious,* and the *unconscious* in the *self,* and *consciousness of this identity.*"[68] Drawing now on Kant's conception of genius as the gift of nature that allows an artist to create an object that can suggest a harmony between imagination and understanding that goes beyond anything implied by the determinate concepts that guide the intentional and voluntary aspects of the artist's creative process, Schelling finds this identity in the work of art, putting Kant's conception of genius as the source of art to his own use: "With the product of freedom, our product will have this in common, that it is consciously brought about; and with the product of nature, that it is unconsciously brought about."[69] A work of artistic genius is indisputably a product of human thought and human intentional action, yet at the same time it exceeds the conscious intentions of the artist in a way that must be attributed to nature, but to nature working with and through the conscious thoughts of the artist to determine the complete form, matter, and content of the object, and thus to unconscious as well as conscious thought. Further, in the work of art both the conscious and unconscious thought that begin within the artist result in an object that typically seems to exist independently of the artist but of course could not have come to exist without the artist, so what ordinarily may seem to be the insuperable gap between thought and object is breached, and the underlying identity of thought in both thinker and object is made manifest. Schelling sums all this up in the statements that "This unchanging identity, which can never attain to consciousness, and merely radiates back from the product, is for the producer precisely what destiny is for the agent, namely a dark unknown force which supplies the element of completeness or objectivity to the piecework of freedom, and ... is denominated by means of the obscure concept of *genius,*" while "The product we postulate is none

---

[67] Schelling, *STI,* p. 217.
[68] Schelling, *STI,* p. 219.
[69] Schelling, *STI,* p. 219.

other than the product of genius, or, since genius is possible only in the arts,[70] the *product of art*."[71]

Schelling does not pause in the crowning but brief final section of the *System of Transcendental Idealism* to persuade his reader of this analysis of the nature of artistic genius and its product by applying it to any example; that deficiency he will amply make up for in the lectures on *The Philosophy of Art*. But he does argue that in being experienced to resolve the alleged contradiction between the description of one and the same thing as both conscious and unconscious, voluntary and involuntary, the work of art will be experienced with an "infinite satisfaction" or "tranquility":

> The intelligence will therefore end with a complete recognition of the identity expressed in the product as an identity whose principle lies in the intelligence itself; it will end, that is, in a complete intuiting of itself. Now since it was the free tendency to self-intuition in that identity which originally divided the intelligence from itself, the feeling accompanying this intuition will be that of an infinite satisfaction [*Befriedigung*]. With the completion of the product, all urge to produce is halted, all contradictions are eliminated, all riddles are resolved.... The intelligence will feel itself astonished and *blessed* [*beglückt*] by this union, will regard it, that is, in the light of a bounty freely granted by a higher nature.[72]

For Schelling, the experience of art pleases because it resolves what is supposed to be a troubling paradox: this is the pleasure of relief from pain, or negative pleasure. Far from being an active, positive pleasure, this pleasure is experienced as a gift from without, something that we passively receive rather than ourselves produce, and it does not stimulate any one – audience or successive artists – to activity but rather stills all "urge to produce." It is passive as well as negative. And since tranquility is the only subjective response to the experience of art that Schelling mentions, there is no room in his account for the artistic arousal of the wide range of other human emotional states.

---

[70] On this point Schelling apparently just accepts Kant's position (*CPJ*, §47, 5:308–9), which, as we saw, was itself opposed to the position of Alexander Gerard that genius manifests itself in both natural science and the fine arts, although of course in specifically different ways; see Gerard, *An Essay on Genius* (London and Edinburgh: Strahan, Cadell, and Creech, 1774), Part III.

[71] Schelling, *STI*, p. 222. Schelling's conception of genius is discussed in Jochen Schmidt, *Die Geschichte des Genie-Gedankens in der deutschen Literatur, Philosophie und Politik 1750–1945*, 2 vols. (Darmstadt: Wissenschaftliche Buchgesellschaft, 1985), vol. 1, pp. 390–403.

[72] Schelling, *STI*, p. 221.

Schelling has thus transformed Kant's account of our positive pleasure in our free play with our own cognitive powers, which already excluded other emotions, into an account of relief from pain in the insight into the resolution of the fundamental paradox of metaphysics. Kant's idea that the imagination and the understanding are in harmony in aesthetic creation and experience has been transformed into the idea that unconscious and involuntary thought and conscious and voluntary thought reveal their identity in the work of art, but in that transformation the element of free play has been lost, the creativity of the imagination has been turned into metaphysical insight, and the positive feeling of life and activity that is the heart of Kant's account has been transformed into relief at the revelation of the solution to a theoretical problem.

Several additional features of Schelling's aesthetic theory in the *System of Transcendental Idealism* should be mentioned before we turn to the further developments of the lectures on *The Philosophy of Fine Art*. The account considered so far concerns primarily the cognitive content of aesthetic experience in the artist and the audience for a work of art and the affective dimension of that cognition. Schelling also offers brief accounts of the paradigmatic general categories of the objects of such experience, namely beauty in the work of art, sublimity in the work of art, and natural beauty. His account begins with a restatement of his thesis about the cognitive content of art: "The work of art reflects to us the identity of the conscious and unconscious activities" of thought. In spite of the fact that the work of art thus seems to overcome the alleged contradiction between the conscious and the unconscious, there is apparently some sense in which they remain ineluctably different, a point that Schelling makes by calling the "opposition" between them "an infinite one." On the basis of this lemma he then infers that "the basic character of the work of art is that of an *unconscious infinity* [synthesis of nature and freedom]. Besides what he has put into his work with manifest intention, the artist seems instinctively, as it were, to have depicted therein an infinity, which no finite understanding is capable of unfolding to the full."[73] This seems to be Schelling's way of deducing Kant's claim in his theory of aesthetic ideas that an inspired work of art conveys a rational idea through a wealth of harmonious material for the imagination in a way that cannot be "grasped and made distinct" by any determinate concept of the work or its content.[74] From the position that "Every aesthetic production

---

[73] Schelling, *STI*, p. 225.
[74] Kant, *CPJ*, §49, 5:315.

proceeds from the feeling of an infinite contradiction, and hence also the feeling which accompanies completion of the art-product" (or presumably the experience thereof) "must be one of an infinite tranquility," Schelling infers that "this latter, in turn, must also pass over into the work of art itself," and he therefore characterizes beauty as "the infinite finitely displayed" or "exhibited" (*dargestellt*): beauty is the manifestation in the work of the cognitive content of aesthetic experience accompanied with the affective [content] thereof, namely, satisfaction at the resolution of the contradiction between the infinite and the finite. In this context, an unmistakable allusion to Winckelmann's conception of the ideal of beauty emphasizes Schelling's conception of the passive rather than active nature of aesthetic pleasure: "Hence the outward expression of the work of art is one of calm, and of silent grandeur [*der stillen Größe*], even where the aim is to give expression to the utmost intensity of pain or joy."[75]

Schelling claims that beauty is the "basic feature of every work of art," because the resolution of the tension between the infinite, involuntary unconscious and the finite, intentional conscious is the gist of every aesthetic experience. But he then re-introduces the traditional distinction between the beautiful and the sublime as a distinction between kinds of beauty in his own sense, a distinction that does not concern the ultimate cognitive and affective character of the experience but the relation of the experience to its object. His claim is that "the difference ... consists simply in this, that where beauty is present, the infinite contradiction is eliminated in the object itself, whereas when sublimity is present, the conflict is not reconciled in the object itself, but merely uplifted to a point at which it is involuntarily eliminated in the intuition, and this, then, is much as if it were to be eliminated in the object."[76] The difference is presumably phenomenological: in the case of beauty in its narrower sense, not only does our experience seem to resolve the fundamental contradiction, but the object somehow also immediately presents itself to us intrinsically harmonious, whereas in the case of the sublime the object presents itself to us as riven by contradiction but nevertheless leads to the harmonious experience of beauty in its broader sense. Here Schelling seems to be drawing on Kant's claim that we can speak of beauty as if it were a property of the object[77] but that the sublime "should

---

[75] Schelling, *STI*, p. 225.
[76] Schelling, *STI*, p. 226.
[77] Kant, *CPJ*, §6, 5:211.

properly be ascribed only to the manner of thinking, or rather to its foundation in human nature,"[78] a claim that Kant makes because for him the essence of the experience of sublimity is a reflection on our own superiority over mere nature rather than a response to harmony within an object. For this reason Kant had thought of the experience of the sublime as primarily a response to nature rather than to art, although he has no trouble finding beauty in art as well as nature. But when Kant did, at least in his *Anthropology*, allow for the possibility of the sublime from art, he at least left the door open to the possibility that art might properly arouse a wider range of emotions than pleasure itself. There is no such opening in Schelling's account, where both the beautiful and the sublime produce just the state of tranquility. We will subsequently see how what is for Schelling perhaps the silent omission of other emotions from aesthetic response becomes the overriding goal of aesthetic experience for Schopenhauer.

While Kant had initially analyzed primarily natural beauty and then treated artistic beauty as a special and complicated case of beauty in general, Schelling emphasizes artistic beauty and treats natural beauty as the derivative case. Having treated teleological purposiveness in nature as something that bridges the gap between intention and the unintentional but does not bring out the specifically human character of intention, he does not ground an account of natural beauty in the experience of organisms, nor does he think of artistic beauty as the imitation of natural beauty. Instead, he says, "so far from the merely contingent beauty of nature providing the rule to art, the fact is, rather, that what art creates in its perfection is the principle and norm for the judgment of natural beauty"[79]: we find nature beautiful insofar as it seems to rise to the level of art rather than art beautiful insofar as it seems like nature. Here Schelling echoes Moses Mendelssohn's critique of Charles Batteux that beauty is not immediately given in nature but requires a human act of idealization and prepares the way for Hegel's even more aggressive rejection of the significance of natural beauty.

Finally, Schelling draws an inference that emphasizes the strictly cognitivist character of his interpretation of aesthetic experience. On his account, the essence of the experience of art is its cognitive content, its revelation of the resolution of the contradiction between the conscious and the unconscious, the finite and the infinite, and so on, and since

---

[78] Kant, *CPJ*, §30, 5:280.
[79] Schelling, *STI*, p. 227.

that content is essentially the same for all works of art, there really is no important difference among works of art:

> For if aesthetic production proceeds from freedom, and if it is precisely for freedom that this opposition of conscious and unconscious activities is an absolute one, there is properly speaking but one absolute work of art, which may indeed exist in altogether different versions, yet is still only one, even though it should not yet exist in its most ultimate form. It can be no objection to this view that it is not consistent with the very liberal use now made of the predicate "work of art." Nothing is a work of art which does not exhibit an infinite, either directly, or at least by reflection.[80]

This is not something that Kant ever would have said, for not only do different works of art take different ideas of reason as their themes, but since the essence of artistic beauty is the way in which the work of art freely plays with its theme – expressing the free play of the cognitive powers of its creator and stimulating a free play of those powers in its audience – there must be possible, at least in principle, an infinite number of genuine works of art rather than just one.[81]

The modification of this point is, however, one of the central accomplishments of Schelling's 1802–3 lectures on *The Philosophy of Fine Art*. These lectures are an early document of Schelling's transition to his "identity" philosophy, his replacement of his earlier, still Fichtean view that nature on the one hand and human theoretical and practical thought on the other are both manifestations of some more fundamental kind of thought, the unity of which is revealed only through art, with the more Spinozistic view that nature on the one hand and human thought on the other are both manifestations of some underlying subject that cannot be identified with either but can only be characterized as the "absolute" or "God."[82] This new standpoint leads to several important changes in Schelling's conception of art. For one, since the absolute can never be fully grasped by any human means, there is no need for him to suppose that one form of human thought and activity is the best way to grasp it, and he now treats philosophy and art as two different ways of grasping

---

[80] Schelling, *STI*, p. 231.
[81] To be sure, this implication of Kant's central conception of free play even in the case of art does not sit very well with his insistence that only classical works of art in dead languages can be the "models of beautiful art" (*CPJ*, §47, 5:310); this is a point at which Kant's preference for unanimity in taste overcomes his emphasis on free play, or his willingness to let taste "clip the wings" of genius prevails (*CPJ*, §50, 5:319).
[82] Schelling first pointed toward the new "identity" philosophy in the *Darstellung meines Systems der Philosophie* (1801) and *Fernere Darstellung aus dem System der Philosophie* (1802); see *Ausgewählte Schriften*, vol. 2, pp. 37–167.

the nature of reality, the former more abstract, intellectual, or "ideal," and the latter more concrete, intuitive, or "real." Further, again since there is no uniquely adequate way to grasp the absolute, although every form of human thought or activity is in some way an apprehension of the absolute, Schelling drops the insistence that in some sense there is only one work of art, and recognizes genuine variety among the media and genres of art as well as among particular works of art. Indeed, the bulk of the lectures consist in detailed description of the variety of the arts and of works of art. Finally, both since the absolute has now been identified with God and also because art is now understood as the more concrete rather than abstract way of apprehending the absolute, Schelling now introduces the idea that the characteristic content of art is the representation of *gods*, or the creation of mythology. This would prepare the way for the labors on a philosophy of mythology that occupied much of Schelling's later life.[83]

In spite of these changes, Schelling's underlying view that the significance of art lies in its cognitive content rather than in the free play of our cognitive powers with cognitive content remains fixed, and if anything his emphasis on the pleasure of aesthetic experience is even more diminished than previously – he goes from giving an account of aesthetic pleasure as negative satisfaction at the resolution of a paradox to barely mentioning it at all. He does preserve the idea that beauty manifests the underlying identity or as he now calls it "indifference" between opposites, now both the ideal and the real as well as freedom and necessity, and even goes so far as to say that in beauty *nature* appears to have played, but he does not say that *we* or our mental powers freely play with beauty, nor does he mention any special pleasure in play:

> Since our explanation of beauty asserts that it is the mutual informing of the real and the ideal to the extent that this informing is represented in reflected imagery, this explanation also includes the following assertion: beauty is the indifference, intuited within the real, of freedom and necessity. For example, we say a figure is beautiful in whose design nature appears to have played with the greatest freedom and the most sublime presence of mind, yet always within the forms and boundaries of the strictest necessity and adherence to law. A poem is beautiful in which the highest freedom

---

[83] See the *Philosophie der Mythologie* (1842), *Ausgewählte Schriften*, vol. 6, pp. 11–686, or Schelling, *Historical-critical Introduction to the Philosophy of Mythology*, trans. Mason Richey and Markus Zisselsberger with a foreword by Jason M. Wirth (Albany: State University Press of New York, 2007).

conceives and comprehends itself within necessity. Accordingly, art is an absolute synthesis or mutual interpenetration of freedom and necessity.[84]

Schelling certainly must be supposing that a human being and not something else in nature creates a poem, but precisely in this human case, though a reference to freedom remains, any reference to play disappears. And again there is no mention of pleasure at all, let alone any other emotions.

Thus the underlying cognitivism of Schelling's aesthetics does not radically change in *The Philosophy of Art*. However, one point about the treatment of the arts in these lectures is novel, and will also be crucial for understanding both Schopenhauer and Hegel. This is Schelling's view that although philosophy is primarily the intellectual or "ideal" form for representing reality and art the intuitive or "real" form – "Art is real and objective, philosophy ideal and subjective"[85] – the distinction between real and ideal appears within the arts as well. Thus although all art has a sensible, intuitive, and objective aspect, some arts are more sensible and objective than others and some more intellectual and subjective than others. In particular, Schelling maintains that "The *formative* [*bildende*] arts constitute the *real* side of the world of art,"[86] while "*Verbal* art is the *ideal* side of the world of art."[87] That is, poetry – Schelling conceives of the verbal arts as divided primarily into the poetic genres of lyric, epic, and drama – uses the sensible media of sound and imagery in order to present abstract ideas to us relatively directly, while in the formative arts such as architecture and painting the sensible qualities of the media are much more prominent in our experience and their intellectual content is less direct. Schelling's claim is actually that in each form of art "*all the forms of unity recur: the real, the ideal, and the indifference of the two,*"[88] but in each medium and genre of art the relation among these moments is different and one is more prominent than the other.

Schelling's classification of the arts is even more complicated than this initial characterization suggests. He divides the arts into three main groups rather than two: on one extreme, the most concrete or real of the arts, which include music and painting; on the other hand, the most ideal of the arts, the various forms of the verbal arts; but in the middle, the

[84] Schelling, *PA*, p. 30.
[85] Schelling, *PA*, p. 13.
[86] Schelling, *PA*, §72, p. 99.
[87] Schelling, *PA*, §73, p. 102.
[88] Schelling, *PA*, §87, 128.

"plastic" arts of architecture and sculpture, which involve more of a mix of the real and the ideal than either of the other two groups. Schelling groups music and painting together as the most real of the arts, because both depend upon the most immediate features of sense perception, such as the rhythm of sound, color, and line, and he classifies the verbal arts as the most ideal because they have the least direct relation to sense perception, conveying abstract ideas through words that suggest sensual imagery rather than directly presenting us with sensory experiences. Architecture and sculpture are put in the middle because they present us with objects that are both more real – not just sensible but also three-dimensional – than the imagery of poetry but at the same time, allegedly, better at suggesting abstract ideas to us than music or painting, thus more ideal than those. Sculpture, for example, "*as the immediate expression of reason, expresses its ideas particularly or even primarily by means of the human figure.*"[89]

But the most important point is that throughout all the details of his classification of the arts and his loving discussion of the details of particular media and works of art, Schelling always keeps his eye on the cognitive significance of art. So, for example, he says that "the primary demand that must be made of drawing" is "*truth*," although not "only that particular kind of truth attainable through faithful imitation of nature," but a truth that lies "at a deeper level than even nature has suggested and than the mere surface features of figures show."[90] Or about painting as a whole, which involves color and chiaroscuro as well as drawing,[91] he says that "painting is the art in which appearance and truth must be one, in which appearance must be truth and truth appearance."[92] Among the intermediate arts, for example, "Sculpture as such is an image of the universe."[93] And "the *essential nature* of poesy is the same as that of all art: it is the representation of the absolute or of the universe in the particular."[94] All art employs some more or less sensible medium to convey some truth more or less abstractly, and its essence always lies in some actual cognition rather than in a free play of our cognitive powers.

---

[89] Schelling, *PA*, §122, p. 183.
[90] Schelling, *PA*, §87, 131.
[91] Schelling, *PA*, p. 128.
[92] Schelling, *PA*, p. 139.
[93] Schelling, *PA*, §122, p. 182.
[94] Schelling, *PA*, p. 204. The division of the lectures into numbered paragraphs ceases before this point.

Through his recognition of the variety of arts and through his thesis that all the arts "intuit" ideas "objectively," in the form of "*real* or *objective* living and existing ideas" of the "gods" of mythology,[95] in which morally important ideas are personified, Schelling returns to a version of Kant's theory that the arts present a potentially infinite variety of aesthetic ideas, but a version from which the element of the free play of our cognitive powers with those ideas and the positive pleasure of such play has to a considerable extent disappeared. We will subsequently see that this cognitive interpretation of art together with the largely negative interpretation of aesthetic pleasure presented in Schelling's *System of Transcendental Idealism* are paralleled in the central themes of Schopenhauer's philosophy of art. But before we finally turn to Schopenhauer, we should not only take a look at the extraordinary influence of Schelling outside of academic aesthetics, but also note one last moment in Schelling's philosophical development that suggests that there are not merely parallels between the aesthetic theories of these two Idealists, but that for all of Schopenhauer's often expressed distaste for the trio of Fichte, Schelling, and Hegel, the philosophy of Schelling in fact must have had great influence on Schopenhauer. I refer here to the prominence of the concept of *will* in the further development of Schelling's philosophy, notably in the *Philosophical Investigations into the Essence of Human Freedom* of 1809. In this work, his only foray into moral philosophy, Schelling tackles the ancient problems of theodicy and free will on the basis of his identity philosophy. He is concerned with the questions of how the freedom of human beings is compatible with their being created by God and with how, supposing human freedom is possible, human beings who are essentially rational can freely choose evil, which is irrational – the problem that had plagued Kant throughout his many attempts to understand freedom of the will.[96] There are two stages to Schelling's solution to these problems. First, now clearly identifying God with that whose identity underlies all reality, he holds that in God the most basic ground of being must necessarily divide itself into two (for the sake of variety in existence) and must equally necessarily be united (in order to maintain identity), but that in man it must be possible for the ground of his being to divide itself without any guarantee that it must be reunited, precisely because that possibility is what marks the difference

---

[95] Schelling, *PA*, Introduction, p. 17.
[96] For clear evidence that Schelling is attempting to respond to Kant, see *Philosophical Investigations into the Essence of Human Freedom (EHF)*, trans. Jeff Love and Johannes Schmidt (Albany: State University of New York Press, 2006), p. 39.

between God and man: "Were now the identity of both principles in the spirit of man exactly as indissoluble as in God, then there would be no distinction, that is, God as spirit would not be revealed. The same unity that is inseverable in God must therefore be separable in man – and this is the possibility of good and evil."[97] Second, in a version of the doctrine of voluntarism, which treats God's will rather than intellect as the source of law, whether moral or otherwise, for the creation, Schelling treats God's will as the primary aspect of his being and the source of his reason, so while will and reason in God although different can never come apart, in man, will is more primary than reason but can also come apart from it: hence the possibility of irrational willing and evil. The crucial point in all of this for the history of aesthetics is that Schelling characterizes the ground of both divine and human being as will: "In this rising up (of freedom) the final empowering act was found through all of nature transfigured itself in feeling, intelligence, and, finally, in will. In the final and highest judgment, there is no other being than will. Will is primal being, to which alone all predicates of being."[98] And in all reality other than God, the possibility always remains that nonrational will that lies beneath all appearances, no matter how rational they seem, can break through:

> After the eternal act of self-revelation, everything in the world is, as we see it now, rule, order, and form; but anarchy still lies in the ground, as if it could break through once again, and nowhere does it appear as if order and form were what is original but rather as if initial anarchy had been brought to order. This is the incomprehensible base of reality in things, the indivisible remainder, that which with the greatest exertion cannot be resolved in understanding but rather remains eternally in the ground.[99]

In human beings, this ineliminable substratum of nonrational will expresses itself in irremediable "yearning"[100] and in an incessant struggle against our own capacity for a strictly rational use of our freedom: "For that reason the will reacts necessarily against freedom as that which is above the creaturely and awakens in freedom the appetite for what is creaturely just as he who is seized by dizziness on a high and steep summit seems to be beckoned to plunge downward by a hidden voice," or just as sailors were lured to their destruction against all reason by the songs of the sirens.[101]

[97] Schelling, *EHF*, p. 33.
[98] Schelling, *EHF*, p. 21.
[99] Schelling, *EHF*, p. 29.
[100] Schelling, *EHF*, p. 32.
[101] Schelling, *EHF*, p. 47.

Schelling thus introduces the idea of will as the ultimate reality that can sometimes break through to the surface of our experience. This idea will have a profound influence on the philosophy of Schopenhauer and through him on Nietzsche, and specifically on their aesthetics. But before we can turn to those figures, we will pause to examine the influence of Schelling on a variety of other, literary figures.

2

High Romanticism in the Shadow of Schelling

Schelling had an immediate and tremendous influence not only on fellow philosophers – as we shall soon see, both Schopenhauer and Hegel were deeply influenced by him, although in different ways – but also on more literary writers who indulged in theorizing in the first decades of the nineteenth century. Before we continue our survey of the major philosophical aestheticians of German idealism, a brief discussion of several of these writers who worked in the penumbra of Schelling in these decades is in order. We will consider first the German novelist "Jean Paul," whose theoretical work appeared in the first decade of the century. Then we will turn to the English poet and journalist Samuel Taylor Coleridge, whose chief work in philosophy and aesthetics appeared in the second decade of the century, and also take a brief look at the aesthetic attitudes expressed by fellow British Romantics William Wordsworth and Percey Bysshe Shelley, as well as several early essays on the philosopher John Stuart Mill. Finally, we will turn to the American Ralph Waldo Emerson, whose relevant works appeared in the next generation. We will find that these representatives of later Romanticism, as opposed to the "early Romanticism" represented by Friedrich Schlegel, largely share the cognitivist approach to art, the conception of art as the "organon of philosophy" of Schelling, although in the writings of the poets Wordsworth and Shelley we also find expressions of the view that the point of their poetic art is not just to afford insight into the nature of human emotions but to stir them. Surprisingly, the most unequivocal assertion that the point of poetry, and by implication art in general, is to arouse deeply felt human emotions comes from the utilitarian philosopher Mill.

1. JEAN PAUL

"Jean Paul," Johann Paul Friedrich Richter (1763–1825), was perhaps the most successful fiction writer in late eighteenth- and early nineteenth-century Germany, who in a long series of novels and stories combined the intellectual ambitions of idealism and early Romanticism with the love of the fantastic characteristic of later German Romantics such as E.T.A. Hoffmann.[1] Born in Bavaria, the son of a pastor, like so many other German intellectuals of the period, Richter was left poor owing to his father's early death. He went to Leipzig to study theology, but there, like Goethe before him, quickly turned to the study of literature. Again like so many others, he struggled to make a living as a tutor, and published several unsuccessful novels before achieving success with the novel *Die Unsichtbare Loge* (*The Invisible Lodge*) in 1793;[2] it was for this work that he adopted the pen name "Jean Paul," in honor of "Jean-Jacques," i.e., Rousseau. In 1798, Jean Paul moved to Weimar, where he was befriended by Herder, but his satirical and fantastical fiction did not earn the favor of Schiller or Goethe. In 1804, thus just a year after Schelling's lectures on the philosophy of art, Jean Paul published a theoretical work, the *Vorschule der Ästhetik* (*Preparatory School for Aesthetics*, revised in 1813).[3] Jean Paul had attacked Fichte in the appendix "Clavis Fichtiana" in his novel *Titan* the previous year,[4] but his own aesthetics has much affinity with Schelling's.[5]

Much of the *School for Aesthetics* is a poetics or theory of specific literary genres, but it begins with more general claims in aesthetic theory. In an obvious attack upon Kant, Jean Paul starts with an equation of the theory of free play as a form of "poetic nihilism" and a defense of the imitation

---

[1] Perhaps the best known of Jean Paul's novels is *Siebenkäs*, more fully *Blumen-, Frucht-, und Dornenstücke, oder Ehestand, Tod und Hochzeit des Armenadvokaten F. St. Siebenkäs* (1796–97), in Jean Paul, *Sämtliche Werke*, edited by Norbert Müller, fourth edition (Munich: Hanser, 1987), vol. II; *Flower, fruit, and thorn pieces; or, The wedded life, death, and marriage of Firmian Stanislaus Siebenkæs, parish advocate in the burgh of Kuhschnappel (A genuine thorn piece)*, translated by Alexander Ewing (London: G. Bell, 1897).

[2] Jean Paul, *Die Unsichtbare Loge*, in *Sämtliche Werke*, vol. I, pp. 1–469.

[3] Jean Paul, *Vorschule der Ästhetik*, *Sämtliche Werke*, vol. V, pp. 1–456; *Horn of Oberon: Jean Paul's School for Aesthetics*, translated by Margaret R. Hale (Detroit: Wayne State University Press, 1973). Hereafter *School for Aesthetics*.

[4] Jean Paul, *Titan*, in *Sämtliche Werke*, vol. III.

[5] A biography of Jean Paul is Günter de Bruyn, *Das Leben des Jean Paul Friedrich Richter* (Halle: Mitteldeutscher Verlag, 1975). For the philosophical context of his aesthetics, see Schmidt, *Genie-Gedankens*, pp. 430–50, and Götz Müller, "Jean Pauls Ästhetik im Kontext der Frühromantik und des deutschen Idealismus," in Jaeschke and Holzhey, *Früher Idealismus und Frühromantik*, pp. 159–73.

of nature and thus a cognitive approach to aesthetic theory. But, as for Schelling immediately before him and Hegel and others to follow, nature for Jean Paul hardly means mere physical reality, but rather physical reality as an expression of infinite, divine spirit:

> It follows from the lawless, capricious spirit of the present age, which would egotistically annihilate the world and the universe in order to clear a space merely for free *play* in the void, and which tears off the *bandage* of its wounds as a bond, that this age must speak scornfully of the imitation and study of nature.... He who scorns the universe respects nothing more than himself and at night fears only his own creation. Is not nature now spoken of as if this creation of a Creator, in which the painter himself is only a dot of color, were hardly fit to be the picture nail or the frame for some small painted creation of a creator. As if what is greatest were not precisely the infinite! If the scorners of reality would only first bring before our souls the starry skies, the sunsets, the waterfalls, the lofty glaciers, the character of a Christ, an Epaminondas, the Catos,... then indeed they would have produced the poem of poems and would have repeated God.[6]

Jean Paul's reference to the "starry skies," of course a famous phrase from Kant,[7] as well as to other stock images of the sublime, some of which were also used by Kant, might be meant to suggest that Kant should have organized his aesthetics around the experience of the sublime rather than around his theory of the experience of beauty as mere free play; but a fundamental difference would remain, namely that for Kant the experience of the sublime is ultimately an experience of the grandeur of our own theoretical and practical reason, while for Jean Paul the aim of poetry is the characterization both of ourselves and of nature in the ordinary sense as expressions of something beyond both, the universe as the manifestation of God.

While urging a cognitive approach to art, Jean Paul certainly recognizes the individuality of striking artistic accomplishments. Thus his account of genius is that it is a uniquely individual presentation of the universal truth of reality:

> Genius is distinguished by the fact that it sees nature more richly and more completely, just as man is distinguished from the half-blind and half-dead animal; with every genius a new nature is created for us, in that he further unveils the old one. Every poetic representation admired by successive ages is distinguished by some freshly sensuous individuality and manner of representation.[8]

---

[6] Jean Paul, *School for Aesthetics*, pp. 15–16.
[7] Kant, *Critique of Practical Reason*, 5:161.
[8] Jean Paul, *School for Aesthetics*, p. 12.

But his idea is not that the expression of human individuality is something that we enjoy for its own sake, but rather that it is a concomitant of the way in which the "absolute and infinity" are made perceptible:

> Whereas the other faculties and experience only tear leaves from the book of nature, imagination writes all parts into wholes and transforms all parts of the world into worlds. It totalizes everything, even the infinite universe. Hence its poetic optimism, the beauty of the figures who inhabit its realm, and the freedom with which beings move like sun in its ether. Imagination brings as it were the absolute and infinity of reason closer and makes them more perceptible to mortal man. To do this it uses much of the future and much of the past, its two creative eternities, because no other time can become an infinite or a whole.[9]

"Poetic optimism" is the opposite of "poetic nihilism": while the theory of free play supposedly denies the significance of anything beyond our individual selves and their pleasures, a theory of art as the presentation of the absolute and infinity in a sensible form celebrates the importance of something greater than us and our own importance only as part of that something greater. Jean Paul further stresses the revelatory, thus essentially cognitive character of genius in the conclusion to his detailed analysis of it:

> If, however, there are men in whom the instinct of the divine speaks more clearly and loudly than in others; if it teaches them to contemplate the earthly (instead of the earthly teaching them to contemplate it); if it provides and controls the perception of the whole; then will harmony and beauty stream back from both worlds and make them into *one* whole, for there is only *unity* before the divine and no contradiction in parts. That is genius; and the reconciliation of the two worlds is the so-called *ideal*. Only through *maps of heaven* can *maps of earth* be made; only viewed from above (for the view from below eternally divides heaven) does the whole sphere of heaven appear, and the sphere of earth itself will swim therein, small perhaps, but round and shining.[10]

Genius is a cognitive gift, the gift of perceiving the unity that lies beneath the diversity of the world as ordinarily perceived. Both this unity and the gift of perceiving it are of divine origin. Jean Paul's final image of the earth swimming within the whole sphere of heaven graphically expresses the theory that all of nature, including human nature, is only an expression of a greater, spiritual reality.

---

[9] Jean Paul, *School for Aesthetics*, p. 28.
[10] Jean Paul, *School for Aesthetics*, pp. 42–3.

Like everyone who thought about art in the late eighteenth and early nineteenth century, Jean Paul had to take up Winckelmann's celebration of the "noble simplicity and quiet grandeur" of Greek art. Following in the footsteps of Schiller's 1795 essay "On Naïve and Sentimental Poetry" and Schlegel's "On the Study of Greek Poetry" from the same year, he does this by accepting Winckelmann's characterization of Greek or "Classical" art but arguing that modern, "Romantic" art necessarily has a different character. Jean Paul focuses on Greek poetry, but calls it "plastic," thus extending to Greek poetry what Winckelmann had found in ancient sculpture and painting (and what Herder had argued was unique to sculpture). The four chief features of the "plastic" or objective quality of Greek poetry are "objectivity," that "all figures appear on earth fully of body and motion," while "modern forms float more like clouds in heaven, with immense but shifting contours that assume arbitrary shapes in each man's imagination";[11] "the *ideal* or the beautiful," which "always grasps the general ... and excludes the accidents of individuality";[12] "serene repose";[13] and finally, "moral grace."[14] Modern or "Romantic" poetry and art is paradigmatically the art of Christianity, but is anticipated by Platonic and Neo-Platonic philosophy[15] – Jean Paul thus quite rightly senses that Plato's otherwordliness cannot be read as the philosophical theory of classical Greek art but as its philosophical criticism. In contrast to classical art, modern (Romantic) art is essentially characterized by awareness of a gap between the finite and the infinite, and of longing to overcome that gap: "In place of serene Greek joy there appeared either infinite longing or ineffable bliss – perhaps without limit in time or space – the fear of ghosts which dreads itself – enthusiastic, introspective love – unlimited monastic renunciation."[16] Many forms of modern art try to overcome this gap, to reconcile the finite and the infinite, of course, but they can never do so by proceeding as if the gap did not exist in the first place. "Romantic poetry is presentiment of a greater future than finds room here below."[17] This is Jean Paul's version of Schiller's thesis that Greek art is "naïve" and modern art "sentimental," and that

---

[11] Jean Paul, *School for Aesthetics*, p. 47.
[12] Jean Paul, *School for Aesthetics*, pp. 49–50.
[13] Jean Paul, *School for Aesthetics*, p. 51.
[14] Jean Paul, *School for Aesthetics*, p. 53.
[15] Jean Paul, *School for Aesthetics*, p. 64.
[16] Jean Paul, *School for Aesthetics*, p.64.
[17] Jean Paul, *School for Aesthetics*, p. 61.

we moderns can never simply recapture the naïvety of Greek art, as Winckelmann seemed to think possible.

One feature that is distinctive in Jean Paul's poetics is his presentation of the humorous as a major category of modern, Romantic art, because he thinks of humor as the "inverted sublime" which "annihilates not the individual" (as does the ridiculous) "but the finite through its contrast with the idea." "In general, reason dazzles the understanding with light (e.g., by the idea of an infinite divinity), as a god dazzles, prostrates, and forcibly subverts finitude. Humor does the same; unlike persiflage, humor abandons the understanding and permits it to fall down piously before the idea. Therefore humor often delights even in contradictions and impossibilities."[18] Humor as opposed to mere satire is a distinctively modern phenomenon because it plays on our recognition of the gap between the finite and the infinite. But the fact that Romantic art in general is only a presentiment of a greater future, not a promise of it, and that in one of its most characteristic forms, the humorous, the understanding is prostrated and dazzled by the idea or the infinite rather than fully comprehending it, means that for Jean Paul the gap between the finite and the infinite can never be completely closed by Romantic art. Thus, although his image of light in the last quotation certainly suggests that Jean Paul is thinking within the framework established by Schelling – in Schelling's philosophy of nature, light is one of the paradigmatic expressions of the spiritual within the natural – Jean Paul does not think, as the Schelling of the *System of Transcendental Idealism* did, that art can succeed in accomplishing what philosophy itself could not, the final reconciliation of the finite and the individual. But neither is there any suggestion that he concludes, as in the next decade Hegel will, that art must be superseded by philosophy because philosophy can accomplish what art cannot. Rather, that for Jean Paul modern or Romantic art seems always destined to work within the gap between the finite and the infinite seems to express the modern condition in general. Thus, Jean Paul's position anticipates versions of cognitivist aesthetics that we will encounter much later in this work, such as that of Theodor W. Adorno's view of art's never-to-be-fulfilled promise of happiness, the view that art has a cognitive task that nothing else can fulfill but that art itself also cannot complete.

---

[18] Jean Paul, *School for Aesthetics*, pp. 88, 93.

2. COLERIDGE, WORDSWORTH, SHELLEY

Coleridge

Samuel Taylor Coleridge (1772–1834), one of thirteen children of an English vicar, was educated at the charitable school of Christ's Hospital in London and then at Jesus College, Cambridge. In 1795, he met William Wordsworth, and from 1795 to 1797, he lived near Wordsworth and his sister Dorothy in the English Lake District, writing what remain his most famous poems, "The Rime of the Ancient Mariner" and "Kubla Khan."[19] The former was published in a joint volume of *Lyrical Ballads* that first appeared in 1798 (with further editions in 1800 and 1802), after which the two men embarked on a trip to Germany; Coleridge would spend a year there, visiting German universities, learning German, and listening to lectures on German philosophy at Göttingen – thus he came close to the Jena Romantic circle but did not actually intersect it. At Göttingen, Coleridge learned about the philosophy of Kant, although Göttingen, with its British connections, had at least initially been a hotbed of criticism of Kant from an empiricist point of view; Coleridge reacted to Kant in ways similar to Schelling but before he became acquainted with Schelling's work, which happened only later.[20] Coleridge moved to Keswick in the Lake District in 1800, resuming his intimacy with Wordsworth and writing more poetry in these years (e.g., the "Ode to Deception"), but also forming the idea of writing a poetics, which would never quite come to fruition. He apparently read some Fichte as early as 1804,[21] and would accept Fichte's idea that spirit should be conceived of as essentially active rather than substantival, although he would also criticize Fichte's philosophy as degenerating into "a crude egoismus, a boastful and hyperstoic hostility to NATURE, as lifeless, godless, and altogether unholy."[22] At some point after his return from Malta, Coleridge became familiar with Friedrich Schlegel's 1808 *Lectures on Dramatic Art and Literature*, and certainly by 1810 he was familiar with a number of Schelling's, works, apparently including the *Ideas for a Philosophy of Nature* of 1797, the *System*

---

[19] On "The Rime of the Ancient Mariner," see Stanley Cavell, *In Quest of the Ordinary: Lines of Skepticism and Romanticism* (Chicago: University of Chicago Press, 1988), pp. 50–75.
[20] For an overview of Coleridge's acquaintance with both German and previous British philosophy, see Paul Hamilton, "The Philosopher," in *The Cambridge Companion to Coleridge*, ed. Lucy Newlyn (Cambridge: Cambridge University Press, 2002), pp. 170–86. On his relation to Schelling, see Raters, *Kunst, Wahrheit, und Gefühl*, pp. 113–39.
[21] Samuel Taylor Coleridge, *Biographia Literaria, with his Aesthetical Essays*, ed. J. Shawcross, 2 vols. (Oxford: Oxford University Press, 1907), Vol. I, p. xlvii.
[22] Coleridge, *Biographia Literaria*, vol. I, pp. 101–2.

of Transcendental Idealism of 1800, and the Munich Academy lecture on the plastic arts of 1807, although in *The Friend*, a philosophical work published that year, he criticized Schelling for having departed too much from Kant.[23] In 1807–8, Coleridge gave a series of lectures in London on "The Principles of Poetry," in 1810 he wrote a fragmentary "Essay on Taste," in 1811 he lectured on Shakespeare and Milton, and in 1812 and 1813 he again lectured on the principles of poetry, the second time in Bristol. In 1814, he published three essays on the "Principles of Genial Criticism," and then embarked on what would become the best known of his theoretical works, the *Biographia Literaria*, originally conceived of as an introduction to a collection of his poetry but which, since its publication in 1817, enjoyed a life of its own (it had enjoyed four British and three American editions before 1907, as well as numerous reprints).[24] In this work, a farrago of theory, criticism, anecdote, and autobiography that, had it been written in German could easily have been mistaken for one of Jean Paul's fictions, Coleridge claims that he had arrived at his central conceptions before becoming familiar with Schelling but openly acknowledges the affinity of his views with Schelling's. "In Schelling's "NATUR-PHILOSOPHIE," and the "SYSTEM DES TRANSCENDENTALEN IDEALISMUS, I first found a genial coincidence with much that I had toiled out for myself, and a powerful assistance in what I had yet to do," he writes. He openly acknowledges that there will be many similarities between his formulations and those of Schelling, as there are with those of Schlegel, but defends himself against "the charge of plagiarism" on the ground that "many of the most striking resemblances, indeed all of the main and fundamental ideas, were born and matured in my mind before I had ever seen a single page of the German philosopher."[25] Coleridge gave another course of lectures in 1818, from which an essay "On Poesy and Art" was published in his *Literary Remains*, completing his theoretical statements in aesthetics. A translation of Goethe's *Faust* (Part I) that he began in 1814 may have been published anonymously in 1821.[26]

---

[23] *Biographia Literaria*, vol. I, pp. xlix–xl.

[24] *Biographia Literaria*, vol. I, pp. xcvi–xcvii. For a brief account of the origins of *Biographia Literaria*, its contents, and its reception, see James Engell, "*Biographia Literaria*," in *Cambridge Companion to Coleridge*, pp. 59–74. For a fuller account, see Kathleen M. Wheeler, *Sources, Processes, and Methods in Coleridge's* Biographia Literaria (Cambridge: Cambridge University Press, 1980).

[25] Coleridge, *Biographia Literaria*, vol. I, p. 102.

[26] *Faustus: from the German of Goethe*, translated by Samuel Taylor Coleridge; edited by Frederick Burwick and James C. McKusick (Oxford: Clarendon Press, 2007). The standard edition of Coleridge's works is *The Collected Works of Samuel Taylor Coleridge*,

Coleridge wrote his chief works in aesthetics between 1810 and 1818, thus a decade later than Jean Paul, but stayed even closer to Schelling than Jean Paul had: he is not a modernist or post-modernist *avant la lettre* who thinks that art must always work within a gap between the finite and the infinite, but rather a confident idealist who believes that the imagination and its expression in art is precisely what bridges the gulf between the finite subject and the infinite spirit that is the ground of reality, more precisely that imagination is what makes known the identity between subject and object. Coleridge's central idea in aesthetics is that of the "primary" or "esemplastic imagination," "esemplastic" being a term he coined out of the Greek "εισενπλαττειν, to shape into one,"[27] and an adjective that actually renders his phrase redundant, since on his interpretation of the primary sense of "imagination" itself it also means the power to shape into one, an interpretation that he arrived at by thinking of the German term *Einbildungskraft*, "the power of imagining," as if it were actually *Einsbildungkraft*, the power of forming into one.[28] Coleridge also emphasizes the unifying character of aesthetic experience in his definition of its primary object, beauty: "The BEAUTIFUL, contemplated in its essentials, that is, in *kind* and not in *degree*, is that in which the *many*, still seen as many, becomes one.... The most general definition of beauty, therefore, is – that I may fulfill my threat of plaguing my readers with hard words – Multëity in Unity."[29] Considered in isolation, these characterizations of imagination and beauty could certainly be taken to suggest that the imagination is an essentially playful power of individual human beings to create forms or meanings or combinations of both that are not

---

Bollingen Series 75, general editor Kathleen Coburn, thus far 16 vols. (Princeton: Princeton University Press, 1969–2002). Works on Coleridge include John H. Muirhead, *Coleridge as Philosopher* (London: George Allen & Unwin, 1930); I.A. Richards, *Coleridge on Imagination* (London: Routledge & Kegan Paul, 1934); Walter Jackson Bate, *Coleridge* (London: Macmillan, 1968); and G.N.G. Orsini, *Coleridge and German Idealism: A Study in the History of Philosophy with Unpublished Materials from Coleridge's Manuscripts* (Carbondale: Southern Illinois University Press, 1969). Briefer treatments include René Wellek, *Immanuel Kant in England 1793–1838* (Princeton: Princeton University Press, 1931), pp. 63–135; M.H. Abrams, *The Mirror and the Lamp: Romantic Theory and the Critical Tradition* (Oxford: Oxford University Press, 1953), pp. 114–24, and *Natural Supernaturalism: Tradition and Revolution in Romantic Literature* (New York: W.W. Norton, 1971), especially pp. 256–77; and Engell, *Creative Imagination*, pp. 328–66.

[27] Coleridge, *Biographia Literaria*, vol. I, p. 107.
[28] See Shawcross's introduction to *Biographia Literaria*, vol. I, p. lxii.
[29] Coleridge, "On the Principles of Genial Criticism" (1814), in *Biographia Literaria*, vol. I, p. 232. See Engell, *Creative Imagination*, p. 357.

given, by nature or otherwise, and that have no cognitive value, reveal no deep truths, and thus to associate Coleridge with the new, originally Scottish approach to aesthetic experience as a form of mental play. In fact, however, Coleridge dismisses such a conception of imagination as mere "fancy," which "is indeed no other than a mode of Memory emancipated from the order of time and space" and "must receive all its materials ready made from the law of association."[30] In distinguishing fancy from imagination, Coleridge dismisses the Scottish-Kantian theory of aesthetic experience as free play. Instead, within his Schellingian metaphysics, the primary, esemplastic imagination is the way in which the fundamental unitary activity of the spirit that expresses itself as both subject and object, human consciousness and the nature and its ultimate ground of which the human is conscious, manifests itself in human experience, and art is the concrete human expression of imagination in this sense. Thus, for Coleridge, imagination is the deepest form of insight into the nature of reality, and art is the most effective form for the communication of this insight among human beings; in other words, for Coleridge as for Schelling, art is the organ of philosophy, grounded in cognition, although not without emotional effect.

Coleridge gives a concise statement of his Schellingian philosophy in Chapter XII of *Biographia Literaria*, "A Chapter of requests and premonitions concerning the perusal or omission of the chapter that follows,"[31] that referring to the surprisingly brief Chapter XIII in which he presents his central idea of the imagination as an organ of truth and its contrast to mere fancy as mere play with memories and associations. The central idea of Coleridge's philosophy is that subject and object, intelligence and nature, seem like opposites but must both manifest an underlying identity:

> Now the sum of all that is merely OBJECTIVE we will henceforth call NATURE, confining the term to its passive and material sense, as comprising all the phænomena by which its existence is made known to us. On the other hand the sum of all that is SUBJECTIVE, we may comprehend in the name of the SELF or INTELLIGENCE. Both conceptions are in necessary antithesis. Intelligence is conceived of as exclusively representative, nature as exclusively represented; the one as conscious, the other as without consciousness. Now in all acts of positive knowledge there is required a reciprocal concurrence of both, namely of the conscious being, and of that which is in itself unconscious. Our problem is to explain this concurrence, its possibility and its necessity.[32]

[30] Coleridge, *Biographia Literaria*, vol. I, p. 202.
[31] Coleridge, *Biographia Literaria*, vol. I, p. 160.
[32] Coleridge, *Biographia Literaria*, vol. I, p. 174.

The characterization of nature as unconscious in contrast to conscious intelligence is characteristically Schellingian, but the passage as a whole can be taken as a concise statement of the fundamental principle of German idealism: knowledge is possible only if the knower and the known, while superficially contrasted, are fundamentally identical.[33] After following Schelling in the view that this identity can be revealed in two different ways, either by explaining "how intelligence can supervene to" nature or how the latter "itself can grow into intelligence"[34] – Schelling's *Naturphilosophie* – or alternatively by explaining how "if the subjective is taken as the first" then "how there supervenes to it a coincident objective,"[35] Schelling's "transcendental idealism" – Coleridge then expounds the core of his philosophy in ten theses. First, he states, "Truth is correlative to being," and "Knowledge without a correspondent reality is no knowledge; if we know, there must be somewhat known by us," but yet "To know is in its very essence a verb active":[36] the identity between subject and object is something that in some sense must be created, is not simply static. Second, "All truth is either mediate, that is derived from some other truth or truths; or immediate and original,"[37] from which Coleridge infers the "scholium" that "a cycle of equal truths without a common and central principle" is "*inconceivable*" and the third thesis that "We are to seek therefore for some absolute truth capable of communicating to other positions a certainty, which it has not itself borrowed; a truth self-grounded, unconditional and known by its own light."[38] Thesis IV is that there can only be one such principle,[39] and the fifth thesis states that "Such a principle cannot be any THING or OBJECT" but "neither can the principle be found in the subject as a subject, contra-distinguished from an object,"[40] precisely because since either of these must be conceived of by contrast to the other it cannot be "self-grounded, unconditional and known by its own light." Instead (this is Thesis VI), "This principle ... manifests itself in the SUM or I AM;

---

[33] James Engell describes Coleridge's conception of imagination as that which identifies the perceiver and the perceived and thus creates the only possibility for a philosophy beyond the philosophies of pure objectivism and pure subjectivism; see *Creative Imagination*, pp. 333–5.
[34] Coleridge, *Biographia Literaria*, vol. I, p. 175.
[35] Coleridge, *Biographia Literaria*, vol. I, p. 176.
[36] Coleridge, *Biographia Literaria*, vol. I, p. 180.
[37] Coleridge, *Biographia Literaria*, vol. I, p. 180.
[38] Coleridge, *Biographia Literaria*, vol. I, p. 181.
[39] Coleridge, *Biographia Literaria*, vol. I, p. 181.
[40] Coleridge, *Biographia Literaria*, vol. I, p. 182.

which I shall hereafter indiscriminately express by the words spirit, self, and self-consciousness," understood however not by a simple contrast to the object of its consciousness or knowledge but rather as "a subject which becomes a subject by the act of constructing itself objectively to itself."[41] Self-consciousness is the model for knowledge in general because in a single act of self-consciousness there is consciousness of the self as both known and knower, the identity that must underlie all knowledge; thus, in the words of Thesis VII, "Only in the self-consciousness of a spirit is there the required identity of object and of representation … spirit in all the objects which it views, views only itself."[42] This also means that even in the knowledge of any object, there is always something beyond the object immediately known, thus that knowledge is never finite but always involves an element of the infinite (or so Coleridge argues in his Thesis VIII). And this step from the finite to the infinite means that the real object and subject of knowledge is more than the merely individual human being, but must be like God: thus, Thesis IX is that "We begin with the I KNOW MYSELF, in order to end with the absolute I AM. We proceed from the SELF, in order to lose and find all self in GOD."[43] Yet in the end – this seems to be the content of Thesis X, which suddenly rambles and does not indicate its point with capital letters – all of this is capable of being understood by or in "the fulness of the *human* intelligence"[44] and in particular is capable of being both understood and expressed by the human imagination, as long as that is understood to be more than mere fancy, or mere play with memories and associations.

This is the central claim of the brief but crucial Chapter XIII of *Biographia Literaria*, which Coleridge seems to have boiled down from a much longer text into a few pages that culminate with these assertions:

> The IMAGINATION then, I consider either as primary, or secondary. The primary IMAGINATION I hold to be the living Power and prime Agent of all human Perception, and as a repetition in the finite mind of the eternal act of creation in the infinite I AM. The secondary Imagination I consider as an echo of the former, co-existing with the conscious will, yet still as identical with the primary in the *kind* of its agency, and differing only in *degree*, and in the *mode* of its operation. It dissolves, diffuses, dissipates, in order to recreate …

Coleridge continues, in words already partially quoted:

---

[41] Coleridge, *Biographia Literaria*, vol. I, p. 183.
[42] Coleridge, *Biographia Literaria*, vol. I, p. 184.
[43] Coleridge, *Biographia Literaria*, vol. I, p. 186.
[44] Coleridge, *Biographia Literaria*, vol. I, p. 188.

FANCY, on the contrary, has no other counters to play with, but fixities and definites. The Fancy is indeed no other than a mode of Memory emancipated from the order of time and space; while it is blended with, and modified by that empirical phenomenon of the will, which we express by the word CHOICE. But equally with the ordinary memory the Fancy must receive all its materials ready made from the law of association.[45]

Against the background of the metaphysics expounded in the previous paragraph, what this means is that the primary human imagination is the way in which the human mind perceives its own essential nature, its identity with nature outside of it, and the foundation of both of these in one and the same spirit or God; the secondary imagination is the way that the human mind finds to express this cognition in art, inevitably partly dissolving and dissipating its profound sense of unity in order to incorporate it in something finite, a poem or a painting, but by that means also communicating or diffusing it to others; but the voluntary exercise of the fancy is a mere play with memories and associations that does not realize this cognitive vocation of art.[46] Thus Coleridge does not deny the existence of something that sounds like the free play of the imagination and understanding as Kant, inspired by Kames and Gerard, had understood it, but he denies that such play can be central to beauty and art.

Coleridge actually entertained something like a purely Kantian conception of beauty and taste – or, more strictly, the initial conception of beauty in the "Analytic of the Beautiful," to which, as we have seen, Kant himself added an indispensable element of intellectual content in the guise of the "aesthetic idea" in his theory of fine art – in the 1810 "Fragment of an Essay on Taste"[47] and the 1814 "Principles of Genial Criticism."[48] In the 1818 lecture "On Poesy or Art," however, he gives an account of art in the spirit of the core conceptions of *Biographia Literaria*. He begins this piece with what might seem like a purely subjectivist view of art, as a vehicle for the projection of human subjectivity onto a nature that is actually independent of humankind, though humankind might be one among its products. Thus he opens with the remark that "Art, used collectively for painting, sculpture, architecture, and music," but also including the "primary art," "writing," "is the mediatress between, and reconciler of, nature and man. It is, therefore, the power of humanizing nature, of infusing the thoughts and passions of man into every thing which is the

---

[45] Coleridge, *Biographia Literaria*, vol. I, p. 202.
[46] On the "levels of imagination" in Coleridge, see Engell, *Creative Imagination*, pp. 343–6.
[47] Coleridge, *Biographia Literaria*, vol. II, pp. 247–9.
[48] Coleridge, *Biographia Literaria*, vol. II, pp. 219–46, at pp. 233–9.

object of his contemplation; color, form, motion, and sound, are the elements which it combines, and it stamps them into unity in the mould of a moral idea."[49] The expression "stamps into unity" evokes Coleridge's conception of the "esemplastic imagination," but here it sounds as if this imagination, previously considered the vehicle of the profoundest metaphysical cognition, is now being reduced to a subjective faculty that paints or projects human perception and human emotion onto nature for the sake of human amusement. However, Coleridge quickly corrects any such impression. For he next maintains that nature itself must be understood as the primary product of mind, of course not the individual human mind but the mind of God, and that what art does is not to project merely subjective human thoughts and passions onto nature, but rather to recreate the unity of thought and nature:

> Nature is to a religious observer the art of God; and for the same cause art itself might be defined as of a middle quality between a thought and a thing, or, as I said before, the union and reconciliation of that which is nature with that which is exclusively human. It is the figured language of thought, and is distinguished from nature by the unity of all the parts in one thought or idea. Hence nature itself would give us the impression of a work of art, if we could see the thought which is present at once in the whole and in every part; and a work of art will be just in proportion as it adequately conveys the thought, and rich in proportion to the variety of parts which it holds in unity.[50]

Rather than projecting onto nature something that is in us but not outside us, art makes it possible for us to grasp in something concrete the wholeness and identity of subject and object that through philosophy we know only abstractly to be the truth of our relation to nature. In other words, as Schelling had done with his apotheosis of art in the *System of Transcendental Idealism*, here Coleridge suggests that art is the organ of philosophy. Art makes the central truth of philosophy intuitable: "We must imitate nature! yes, but what in nature, – all and every thing? No, the beautiful in nature. And what then is the beautiful? What is beauty? It is, in the abstract, the unity of the manifold, the coalescence of the diverse; in the concrete, it is the union of the shapely (*formosum*) with the vital." As Schlegel claimed that modern art must not imitate the superficial style of Greek art but its essence, indeed the essence of being Greek, namely the harmony between mankind and nature, so Coleridge

---

[49] Coleridge, *Biographia Literaria*, vol. II, p. 253.
[50] Coleridge, *Biographia Literaria*, vol. I, p. 255.

holds that art must not imitate the surface of nature but must capture the underlying harmony that creates nature itself: "If the artist copies the mere nature, the *natura naturata*, what idle rivalry!... Believe me, you must master the essence, the *natura naturans*, which presupposes a bond between nature in the higher sense and the soul of man." More fully, nature is itself the product of the act of intelligence, and art makes this fundamental fact about nature intuitable:

> In the objects of nature are presented, as in a mirror, all the possible elements, steps, and processes of intellect antecedent to consciousness, and therefore to the full development of the intelligential act; and man's mind is the very focus of all the rays of intellect which are scattered throughout the images of nature. Now to so place these images, totalized, and fitted to the limits of the human mind, as to elicit from, and to superinduce upon, the forms themselves the moral reflexions to which they approximate, to make the external internal, the internal external, to make nature thought, and thought nature, – this is the mystery of genius in the Fine Arts. Dare I add that the genius must act on the feeling, that body is but a striving to become mind, – that it is mind in its essence![51]

Here, older and newer ways of thought are being joined. As we saw earlier, the central idea of the theorist of imitation whom all later writers loved to scorn, namely Batteux, was actually that art should imitate the spirit of nature, not its mere letter; Coleridge is adopting that idea, but adding to it Schelling's idea, that nature itself is the product of spirit, although of course not of the secondary imagination of particular human artists.

Coleridge's account of genius in *Biographia Literaria* does introduce one strikingly novel image. There he says, quoting himself from his earlier work *The Friend*, which had circulated only by subscription, that

> To find no contradiction in the union of old and new; to contemplate the ANCIENT of days and all his works with feelings as fresh, as if all had then sprang forth at the first creative fiat; characterizes the mind that feels the riddle of the world, and may help to unravel it. To carry on the feelings of childhood into the powers of manhood; to combine the child's sense of wonder and novelty with the appearances, which every day for perhaps forty years had rendered familiar; ... this is the character and privilege of genius, and one of the marks which distinguish genius from talents.[52]

Coming upon this passage early in *Biographia Literaria*, one is struck above all by the image of the adult artist approaching the world with the open curiosity of the child. But coming back to it with the subsequent

---

[51] Coleridge, *Biographia Literaria*, vol. II, pp. 257–8.
[52] Coleridge, *Biographia Literaria*, vol. I, p. 59.

argument of this work and with the 1818 essay in mind, one realizes that genius lies first and foremost in feeling the riddle of the world and unraveling it, in other words, in the capacity for metaphysical insight, although to be sure achieving that insight must require shedding the habits and preconceptions of everyday life with which the adult is so typically saddled, and in that sense approaching the world with the freshness of a child – but with the reflective capacity of the adult as well. Coleridge likes Plato's image of *metempsychosis*, the idea of the *Meno* that education in the fundamental truths of any science, such as geometry, is recapturing knowledge that we had before we were even born, but lost consciousness of in the passage into bodily existence and must regain, but he does not take it literally any more than he thinks that Plato did.[53] The cognitive insight that is to be captured by genius and expressed through art is not literally the knowledge of a child, although it requires something childlike to discover it.

Coleridge is drawn to the Platonic image of coming to learn what in some sense we already know because it anticipates the structure of his own idea that in creating a work of art the artist is recreating mind's own creation of nature: "the man of genius"

> must out of his own mind create forms according to the severe laws of his intellect, in order to generate in himself that co-ordination of freedom and law ... which assimilates him to nature, and enables him to understand her. He merely absents himself for a season from her, that his own spirit, which has the same ground with nature, may learn her unspoken language in its main radicals ... – for this does the artist for a time abandon the external real in order to return to it with a complete sympathy with its internal and actual.[54]

Like Schelling, Coleridge transforms Kant's idea that a gift of nature allows the artistic genius to accomplish more than he intends into a conception of genius as the unconscious emerging into consciousness, which is in turn their conception of how intelligence itself arises in nature and thus of how the identity between the known and the knower is created. So Coleridge's conception of artistic genius is part and parcel of his artistic metaphysics.

For a work that was at least initially intended as the introduction to a volume of its author's own poetry,[55] the *Biographia Literaria* does not

---

[53] Coleridge, *Biographia Literaria*, vol. II, p. 121; "On Poesy or Art," vol. II, p. 259.
[54] Coleridge, "On Poesy or Art," vol. II, pp. 258–9.
[55] See Engell, "*Biographia Literaria*," pp. 59–61. Engell reports that Coleridge felt that Wordsworth had hijacked the privilege of writing the introduction to the *Lyrical Ballads*

often illustrate its lofty abstractions through the criticism of particular works of art. The central chapter on imagination is, however, followed by discussions of Shakespeare and especially Wordsworth that do somewhat bridge the gulf between Coleridge's metaphysics and his own experience of art. He begins his critical as well as appreciative account of Wordsworth with a list of his defects: inconstancy of style, "not seldom a *matter-of-factness* in certain poems," excessive drama in some poems, and then feelings, thought, and images that are sometimes too great for their subject.[56] But, their original friendship by no means forgotten, Coleridge concedes that these defects pale beside Wordsworth's excellences, which fulfill the conditions for genius in Coleridge's estimation: first, "an austere purity of language both grammatically and logically; in short a perfect appropriateness of the words to the meaning";[57] second, "a correspondent weight and sanity of the Thoughts and Sentiments, won – not from books, but – from the poet's own meditative observation";[58] third, "the sinewy strength and originality of single lines and paragraphs"; fourth, "the perfect truth of nature in his images and descriptions, as taken immediately from nature, and proving a long and genial intimacy with the very spirit which gives the physiognomic expression to all the works of nature";[59] fifth, "a meditative pathos, a union of deep and subtle thought with sensibility; a sympathy with man as man; the sympathy indeed of a contemplator ... from whose view no difference of rank conceals the sameness of the nature";[60] and "Last, and pre-eminently ... the gift of IMAGINATION in the highest and strictest sense of the word." "In the play of *Fancy*," Coleridge says, Wordsworth "is not always graceful, and sometimes *recondite*."[61] But fancy, remember, is mere play, the least significant form of imagination, and of little account; the imagination for which Coleridge praises Wordsworth,

---

from him – Wordsworth actually wrote the Preface for the second edition of *Lyrical Ballads* in 1800, revising it for yet another edition in 1802 – and when Wordsworth reprinted that introduction in a new edition of his *Poems* in 1815, Coleridge decided to write a similar introduction to a new volume of his own poems, which grew out of all proportion into the two volumes of *Biographia Literaria*, much larger than the collection of poems to which it was supposed to be the introduction and in the end was published on its own.

[56] Coleridge, *Biographia Literaria*, vol. II, pp. 97–109.
[57] Coleridge, *Biographia Literaria*, vol. II, p. 115.
[58] Coleridge, *Biographia Literaria*, vol. II, p. 118.
[59] Coleridge, *Biographia Literaria*, vol. II, p. 121.
[60] Coleridge, *Biographia Literaria*, vol. II, pp. 122–3.
[61] Coleridge, *Biographia Literaria*, vol. II, p. 124.

summing up his second, fourth, and fifth excellence (the first and third are stylistic virtues which almost any critic could praise in almost any poet), is nothing less than the esemplastic imagination, insight into the unity of human and nature as both products of underlying spirit. In a remarkable moment of one poet of imagination praising another poet of nature by citing a poetic naturalist, Coleridge sums up his appreciation of Wordsworth with a quotation from the *Travels* of the American botanist William Bartram (1739–1823):[62]

> "The soil is a deep, rich, dark mould, on a deep stratum of tenacious clay; and that on a foundation of rocks, which often break through both strata, lifting their backs above the surface. The trees which chiefly grow here are the gigantic black oak; magnolia magna-flora; fraxinus excelsior; platane; and a few stately tulip trees." What Mr. Wordsworth *will* produce, it is not for me to prophecy; but I could pronounce with the liveliest conviction what he is capable of producing. It is the FIRST GENUINE PHILOSOPHIC POEM.[63]

The image of the rocks pushing through the soil and of the tallest and most impressive trees then known of the American flora growing from both (the even taller firs and redwoods of the Pacific coast not yet being known, at least to Bartram) is the metaphor for the conscious subject emerging from and in turn reflecting back upon unconscious nature, the soil, and both being grounded in the underlying spirit, the rock; Bartram the naturalist, as if he were himself part of nature, offers the metaphor, but the poet, here Coleridge speaking of his friend Worsdworth, uses the metaphor self-consciously, illustrating the reflexive character of artistic genius that he has elsewhere described in abstractions. Here the voices of three authors coincide to make these abstractions concrete.

Whether Coleridge's own work would better be described as work of the esemplastic imagination or of fancy is beyond our concern here. Our aim has only been to show that even if in spite of the sometimes playful character of Coleridge's own poetry, his aesthetics is part and parcel of the aesthetics of truth rather than the aesthetics of play that dominated so much of post-Kantian aesthetics. We will see shortly that the same is true in the aesthetic thought of the first American writer who

---

[62] See William Bartram, *Travels through North and South Carolina, Georgia, East and West Florida*, etc. (Philadelphia, 1791), reprinted in *Travels and Other Writings*, ed. Thomas Slaughter (New York: Library of America, 1996), and Judith Magee, *The Art and Science of William Bartram* (University Park: Pennsylvania State University Press, 2007).

[63] Coleridge, *Biographia Literaria*, vol. II, pp. 128–9.

could move in the company of such as Friedrich Schlegel, Samuel Taylor Coleridge, and even Friedrich Schelling himself, namely Ralph Waldo Emerson. But before we turn to Emerson, we should take a brief look at the Preface to the *Lyrical Ballads* by Wordsworth, the reprinting of which provoked Coleridge to compose *Biographia Literaria*, and at the *Defence of Poetry* composed by another Romantic poet a few years later, namely Shelley.

Wordsworth

Our account of Coleridge has said nothing about the emotional impact of poetry or art more generally; that does not receive any attention in his theory of the imagination. William Wordsworth (1770–1850) was born in the Lake District, and after completing his education at St. John's College, Cambridge, and several years of travel, including the trip to Germany with Coleridge, he would spend the major part of his life there, much of the time as an officer in the British revenue service. Unlike Coleridge, he devoted almost all of his effort to poetry, having published his first poem even before he entered Cambridge. Apart from a *Guide to the Lakes* published in 1810, his Preface to the second edition of *Lyrical Ballads* in 1800, revised in 1802, is a rare piece of prose and his sole theoretical statement about his own art.[64] In this Preface, the emotional impact of poetry becomes the center of attention, although Wordsworth begins from a cognitivist premise. He starts by saying that the purpose of his poems is "to illustrate the manner in which our feelings and ideas are associated in a state of excitement ... to follow the fluxes and refluxes of the mind when agitated by the great and simple affections of our nature."[65] Thus far, poems are described as an instrument of knowledge, although knowledge of the course of human feelings, not of any metaphysical truth about them, about human nature more broadly, or about the relation of human being to nature. Wordsworth subsequently

---

[64] Discussions of Wordsworth's aesthetics include Abrams, *The Mirror and the Lamp*, pp. 103–14; Engell, *Creative Imagination*, pp. 265–76; Cavell, *In Quest of the Ordinary*, pp. 69–75; Theresa M. Kelley, *Wordsworth's Revisionary Aesthetics* (Cambridge: Cambridge University Press, 1988); Richard Eldridge, "Internal Transcendentalism: Wordsworth and 'A New Condition of Philosophy,'" in Eldridge, *The Persistence of Romanticism: Essays in Philosophy and Literature* (Cambridge: Cambridge University Press, 2001), pp. 102–23; and Raters, *Kunst, Wahrheit und Gefühl*, pp. 74–89.

[65] William Wordsworth, Preface to *Lyrical Ballads, with Pastoral and Other Poems* (1802), in Wordsworth, *The Major Works*, ed. Stephen Gill (Oxford: Oxford University Press, 1984), pp. 595–617, at p. 598.

argues that the poet can obtain the knowledge of human feelings that he expresses in his poems only by himself experiencing those feelings, although of course he cannot write poetry while in the immediate grip of powerful feelings, but must be able to write about what he has felt in a less passionate state than he was in when he originally experienced them. This leads to a famous passage:

> I have said that Poetry is the spontaneous overflow of powerful feelings: it takes its origin from emotion recollected in tranquillity: the emotion is contemplated till by a species of reaction the tranquillity disappears, and an emotion, kindred to that which was before the subject of contemplation, is gradually produced, and does itself actually exist in the mind.[66]

It has been a common charge in the two centuries since this was written that Wordsworth's inference is fallacious, because there is no logical necessity that a poet can find ways to successfully describe only what she herself actually felt; she might learn about some specific feelings from another source than her own experience, even another work of literature, but be so gifted that she can on that basis successfully evoke that feeling for others. But even though it is not necessarily so, it seems a matter of common sense that for the most part people, even poets who are gifted readers and imaginative writers, will best describe what they have actually felt; and Wordsworth is particularly concerned that emotions described on any other basis will have little impact on the audience for poetry.

Wordsworth initially describes the effect on the audience of the poet's expression of what has been recollected in tranquility as an improvement to the audience's own sensitivity to feelings, thus as a form of knowledge, and also as a form of stimulation, an almost Dubosian counter to "torpor":

> For the human mind is capable of being excited without the application of gross and violent stimulants; and he must have a very faint perception of its beauty and dignity who does not know this; and who does not further know, that one being is elevated above another, in proportion as he possesses this capability. It has therefore appeared to me, that to endeavour to produce or enlarge this capacity is one of the best services in which, at any period, a Writer can be engaged; but this service, excellent at all times, is especially so at the present day. For a multitude of causes, unknown to former times, are now acting with a combined force to blunt the discriminating powers of

---

[66] Wordsworth, Preface, p. 611.

the mind, and unfitting it for all voluntary exertion to reduce it to a state of almost savage torpor.[67]

This makes it sound as if a whole society is being dulled into a state of *ennui* – "by frantic novels, sickly and stupid German tragedies, and deluges of idle and extravagant stories in verse," Wordsworth fulminates – and that poetry coming from emotions genuinely felt has the best chance of raising the audience from its torpor. What will thereby be "produced" or "enlarged" in the audience is the capacity to feel emotions; but it is not clear at first that the point of this is anything other than what Wordsworth's initial comment about the purpose of his poems has suggested, namely, to allow the audience to know the emotions the poet herself has felt and then recollected in tranquility.

However, Wordsworth soon makes it clear that the point of poetry is to produce pleasure in its audience, indeed not just the negative pleasure of relief from boredom, but a positive pleasure, in particular a positive pleasure in sharing emotions both with the poet and with other human beings. Thus "The end of Poetry is to produce excitement in co-existence with an over-balance of pleasure,"[68] and the poet who successfully recollects in tranquility what she has previously felt in excitement both feels pleasure in that recollection of excitement and successfully communicates that pleasure as well as the emotions themselves to her reader. Thus Coleridge continues the famous passage previously quoted thus:

> In this mood successful composition generally begins, and in a mood similar to this it is carried on; but the emotion, of whatever kind and in whatever degree, from various causes is qualified by various pleasures, so that in describing any passions whatsoever, which are voluntarily described, the mind will upon the whole be in a state of enjoyment. Now, if Nature be thus cautious in preserving in a state of enjoyment a being thus employed, the Poet ought to profit by the lesson thus held forth to him, and ought especially to take care, that whatever passions he communicates to his Reader, those passions, if his Reader's mind be sound and vigorous, should always be communicated with an overbalance of pleasure.[69]

There is actually something Humean about Wordsworth's position, for his idea is that the formal features of poetry temper the most passionate emotions and transform them from something painful into something pleasurable: poetry uses "language closely resembling that of real

---

[67] Wordsworth, Preface, p. 599.
[68] Wordsworth, Preface, p. 609.
[69] Wordsworth, Preface, p. 111.

life, yet, in the circumstance of metre, differing from it so widely, [that] all these imperceptibly make up a complex feeling of delight, which is of the most important use in tempering the painful feeling which will always be found intermingled with powerful descriptions of the deeper passions."[70] But Wordsworth does not go as far as Hume did in suggesting that painful feelings are completely transmuted into pleasure, thereby losing all of their original character; and he also emphasizes that part of what pleases us in our experience of the feelings communicated to us by poetry is our knowledge that these feelings are shared by other human beings, perhaps the poet herself but more importantly other human beings in general: "the Poet binds together by passion and knowledge the vast empire of human society, as it is spread over the whole earth, and over all time."[71] Hume had noticed that we enjoy sharing our response to works of art, thus that those watching a play with others in a full theater enjoy it more than they would alone, but that would be true even if what were being enjoyed were purely formal features of the composition being performed; Hume had not emphasized that shareable feelings are the content of art, and that our pleasure in art arises from experiencing those feelings and knowing that they are shared.

Sometimes Wordsworth falls into the language of theories that do not place much emphasis on the arousal of emotion by poetry; thus in one remark that even Wolff could have made a century earlier, he simply says that "the Poet's art ... is an acknowledgement of the beauty of the universe."[72] But the stress on the emotional impact of real life on the poet and then of the poetry that the poet is thereby enabled to create is dominant in his account. He thus effects a synthesis between the aesthetics of truth and the aesthetics of emotional impact – by communicating the truth about emotions recollected in tranquility, the poet also communicates those emotions themselves, which both pleases her audience and also improves the audience's knowledge of the nature of human emotions. But there is no more suggestion in Wordsworth than there is in Coleridge that enjoyment of the sheer play of human imagination is any part of our enjoyment of poetry or any other art: what we admire in a poet is above all sincerity of feeling, not inventiveness or originality.

---

[70] Wordsworth, Preface, p. 611.
[71] Wordsworth, Preface, p. 606.
[72] Wordsworth, Preface, p. 605.

Shelley

The "Defence of Poetry" written in 1821 by Percey Bysshe Shelley (1792–1822) but published only a decade after his drowning the next year, starts off with a Coleridgean emphasis on the imagination, quickly gives that a cognitivist emphasis, and then, like Wordsworth's Preface, celebrates poetry as a communication of emotion from human to human, so should also be regarded as combining a cognitivist approach to art with a recognition of its emotional impact while not emphasizing the pleasure of imaginative play for its own sake. Shelley, from a much wealthier family than Coleridge or Wordsworth, had a meteoric career. After Eton, he went up to University College, Oxford, but was expelled in his first year because of his presumed association with a pamphlet on *The Necessity of Atheism*. He soon eloped to Scotland with one woman, but left her and their two children after three years to elope with Mary Godwin, the daughter of the feminist Mary Wollstonecraft and the political philosopher William Godwin, marrying her in 1816 after his first wife committed suicide. The pair moved to Italy in 1818, the same year Mary Shelley's *Frankenstein, or the Modern Prometheus* was published, and Shelley wrote most of his best known poetry in the four years that they lived together there before he drowned while sailing a new boat off the Ligurian coast. His wife published complete editions of his poetry and prose after his death.[73]

The "Defence of Poetry" begins by describing imagination as "mind acting upon ... thoughts so as to colour them with its own light, and composing from them as from elements, other thoughts, each containing within itself the principle of its own integrity." It is "το ποιειν or the principle of synthesis; and has for its objects those forms which are common to universal nature and existence itself."[74] In this definition Shelley takes a traditional conception of imagination – it combines previously given elements into representations of new and possibly unexperienced objects – but puts both his own stamp on this idea – the imagination colors the elements with which it works with the imaginer's "own light" or personality – as well as Coleridge's – namely, that the traditional combination

---

[73] Biographical data from Percy Bysshe Shelley, *The Major Works*, edited by Zachary Leader and Michael O'Neill (Oxford: Oxford University Press, 2003). "A Defence of Poetry" will be cited from this edition, where it appears at pp. 674–701. For discussion of Shelley's aesthetics, see Abrams, *Mirror and Lamp*, pp. 126–32, and Engell, *Creative Imagination*, pp. 256–64.
[74] Shelley, "Defence," *Major Works*, p. 674.

of given elements into new objects is a "synthesis" which gives to those objects their own "integrity." Shelley then makes imagination central to his conception of poetry, stating that "Poetry, in a general sense, may be defined to be 'the expression of the Imagination,'" and adds a thought that could have come from Giambattista Vico, that "Poetry is connate with the origin of man,"[75] something that humans naturally produce "even in the infancy of society."[76] Having started with this emphasis on imagination, however, Shelley turns to a cognitivist approach, and next states that "to be a poet," even in the infancy of society, "is to apprehend the true and the beautiful, in a word the good which exists in the relation, subsisting, first between existence and perception, and secondly between perception and expression."[77] In this statement, Shelley emphasizes not the capacity of imagination to invent something new, but rather the perception of something true, though truth about the moral relations of humans to one another and the world as well as truth about other facts, and he even subsumes successful expression, that is, an aesthetically satisfactory relation between the true content of a poem and the form in which that is communicated, under the rubric of truth as well as beauty. Or he suggests that beauty consists in truth in both relations – that between content and reality and the one between form and content. This dual conception of truth is also suggested in a further, fuller statement:

> Sounds as well as thoughts have relation both between each other and towards that which we represent, and a perception of the order of those relations, has always been found connected with a perception of the order of the relations of thoughts. Hence the language of poets has ever effected a certain uniform and harmonious recurrence of sound, without which it were not poetry, and which is scarcely less indispensable to the communication of its influence, than the words themselves without reference to that peculiar order.[78]

The imagination might seem to be poised to return to the stage when Shelley goes on to make a contrast between "a story and a poem," for it might be expected that he would distinguish them by distinguishing truth from invention. But in fact what he argues, entirely in the Aristotelian tradition, is that poetry expresses deeper and more universal truth than the superficial and accidental truth expressed by a mere story. Thus he

---

[75] Shelley, "Defence," *Major Works*, p. 675.
[76] Shelley, "Defence," *Major Works*, p. 676.
[77] Shelley, "Defence," *Major Works*, pp. 676–7.
[78] Shelley, "Defence," *Major Works*, p. 678.

argues "that a story is a catalogue of detached facts, which have no other bond of connection than time, place, circumstance, cause and effect," while poetry "is the creation of actions according to the unchangeable forms of human nature, as existing in the mind of the creator, which is itself the image of all other minds. The one is partial ... the other is universal."[79] Thus "A poem is the very image of life expressed in its eternal truth," and even if "Poetry is a mirror which makes beautiful that which is distorted," it does this not by inventing something that has never existed but by capturing the essence of that which does exist: beauty lies precisely in getting beyond meaningless superficial variety to the true essence of reality.

In these definitions, Shelley has if anything affirmed a more traditional aesthetics of truth than Coleridge. However, he soon effects a transition from the aesthetics of truth to the aesthetics of emotional impact much as Wordsworth had done. Here is the crucial passage: poetry

> awakens and enlarges the mind by rendering it the receptacle of a thousand unapprehended combinations of thought. Poetry lifts the veil from the hidden beauty of the world; it reproduces all that it represents, and the impersonations clothed in its Elysian light stand thenceforward in the minds of those who have once contemplated them, as memorials of that gentle and exalted content which extends itself over all thoughts and actions with which it co-exists.

Thus far, Shelley is talking about poetry as conveying truth colored by the beauty of its own form, which he has previously also subsumed under the rubric of truth. However, he now introduces the moral impact of poetry by talking about its moral benefit:

> The great secret of morals is Love; or a going out of our own nature, and an identification of ourselves with the beautiful which exists in thought, action or person, nor our own. A man to be greatly good, must imagine intensely and comprehensively; he must put himself in the place of another and of many others; the pains and pleasures of his species must become his own. The great instrument of moral good is the imagination; and poetry administers to the effect by acting upon the cause.[80]

Poetry acquaints its audience with the full range of human feelings, which is a cognitive accomplishment, but it does that by arousing those feelings in each of us who reads or hears it. Thus truth and emotional impact are inseparable: poetry conveys to us the truth about the feelings

---

[79] Shelley, "Defence," *Major Works*, pp. 679–80.
[80] Shelley, "Defence," *Major Works*, pp. 681–2.

of our fellows, on which our moral treatment of them depends, by conveying to us their feelings themselves. And the imagination is central to this accomplishment, but not the imagination as a faculty of invention, rather the imagination as a faculty of communication, that by which we put ourselves into the place of others and feel what they feel. Here Shelley is drawing on another eighteenth-century conception of the imagination, namely Adam Smith's conception, although the conception of imagination that is at the heart of his *Theory of Moral Sentiments* rather than that on which his theory of imitation was based. What is ultimately important about imagination for Shelley is that it is by means of the imagination of both the poet and his audience that emotion is communicated from one human being to another.

Shelley's emphasis on the moral benefit of such imagination might seem to moralize his conception of our response to poetry completely. He certainly emphasizes the moral benefits of the experience of poetry: "The imagination is enlarged by a sympathy with pains and passions so mighty that they distend in their conception the capacity of that by which they are conceived; the good affections are strengthened by pity, indignation, terror and sorrow; and an exalted calm is prolonged from the satiety of this high exercise,"[81] and "it were superfluous to explain how the gentleness and the elevation of mind connected with these sacred emotions can render men more amiable, and generous, and wise, and lift them out of the dull vapours of the little world of self."[82] However, Shelley also stresses the sheer pleasure of experiencing both the truths and the emotions that poetry conveys, independently of the beneficial effect of these on our conduct. "Poetry is ever accompanied with pleasure: all spirits on which it falls, open themselves to receive the wisdom which is mingled with its delight,"[83] so there is pleasure in the perception of truth, quite apart from the beneficial effects of knowing that truth; and there is pleasure in feeling the full range of human emotions, apart from the beneficial effect on our conduct of such feeling, as Shelley makes clear in his passing treatment of the paradox of tragedy:

> Our sympathy in tragic fiction depends on this principle: tragedy delights by affording a shadow of the pleasure which exists in pain.... The pleasure that is in sorrow is sweeter than the pleasure of pleasure itself.... Not that this highest species of pleasure is necessarily linked with pain. The

---

[81] Shelley, "Defence," *Major Works*, p. 684.
[82] Shelley, "Defence," *Major Works*, p. 690.
[83] Shelley, "Defence," *Major Works*, p. 680.

delight of love and friendship, the ecstasy of the admiration of nature, the joy of the perception, and still more of the creation of poetry is often wholly unalloyed.[84]

Some emotions are intrinsically pleasurable, of course, but even in the case of those that are not, the pleasure of experiencing the emotions of others, of not just knowing but actually feeling what they feel, colors and perhaps even outweighs the intrinsic painfulness of those emotions – perhaps that is what Shelley means by saying that "the pleasure that is in sorrow is sweeter than the pleasure of pleasure itself." For these two reasons, then – that there is pleasure in knowledge as such and pleasure in feeling what others feel, both apart from a direct influence on our conduct – Shelley can conclude that "The production and assurance of pleasure in this highest sense is true utility."[85] Utility ultimately depends upon pleasure, of course, so pleasure cannot be reduced to utility without circularity.

The mention of utility naturally brings us to utilitarianism, the characteristic British moral philosophy of the nineteenth century. Utilitarianism was pioneered by Hutcheson and Hume, each of whom, as we have seen, had a well-developed aesthetic theory as well; but of the three great later British utilitarians, namely Jeremy Bentham, John Stuart Mill, and Henry Sidgwick, the first dismissed aesthetics with the remark that "Prejudice apart, the game of push-pin is of equal value with the arts and sciences of music and poetry"[86] – utilitarianism only cares that people's preferences be satisfied, not what they are – while the last did not touch upon aesthetics at all. Only Mill, in whom the utilitarianism stamped upon him by Bentham and his own father, James Mill, was self-avowedly tempered by Coleridge, and who immortally reduced Bentham's position to the slogan that "push-pin is as good as poetry"[87] in his own attempt to distinguish between higher and lower pleasures, wrote directly on aesthetics. So we will turn to Mill before completing our survey of the penumbra of Schelling with an examination of the aesthetics of Ralph Waldo Emerson.

---

[84] Shelley, "Defence," *Major Works*, pp. 694–5.
[85] Shelley, "Defence," *Major Works*, p. 695.
[86] Jeremy Bentham, *The Rationale of Reward* (London: Robert Heward, 1830), p. 206.
[87] John Stuart Mill, "Bentham" (1838), in *Essays on Ethics, Religion, and Society, The Collected Works of John Stuart Mill*, ed. J.M. Robson, F.E.L. Priestly, and D.P. Dryer (Toronto: University of Toronto Press, 1969), pp. 75–115, at p. 113.

3. MILL

Son of the utilitarian philosopher and protégé of Jeremy Bentham, the Scotsman James Mill (1773–1836), John Stuart Mill (1806–73) was the subject, or victim, of the educational experiment aimed at producing a purebred utilitarian famously described in his *Autobiography*.[88] Such an education, Mill wrote, produced an attitude in which "the cultivation of feelings (except the feelings of public and private duty) was not in much esteem," in which "we did not expect the regeneration of mankind from any direct action on ... sentiments, but from the effect of educated intellect, enlightening the selfish feelings."[89] Coleridge eventually taught Mill the importance of feelings as well as intellect and calculation in moral and political life, and in an 1840 appreciation of Coleridge, Mill wrote that Coleridge provided an indispensable complement to Benthamite utilitarianism, teaching the importance of "restrained discipline" but also "the feeling of allegiance" and "a feeling of common interest among those who live under the same government."[90] Several years before this essay, however, and before his great *System of Logic* (1843) and major works in moral and political philosophy, including *Principles of Political Economy* (1848), *On Liberty* (1859), and *Utilitarianism* and *Considerations on Representative Government* (1861), Mill had written a pair of essays on poetry, in which he stressed the importance of the direct expression of emotion in genuine poetry and the emotional impact of such poetry on its reader. In these essays, published in 1833, he did not mention the name of Coleridge, and indeed they may be taken as a corrective to the absence of such an emphasis in Coleridge's own works of aesthetic theory. While Mill wrote these essays well before he was thirty, he reproduced them in his later essay collection *Dissertations and Discussions* (first published in 1859), and thus did not himself regard them as mere juvenalia. And even though these essays have not figured largely in the history of aesthetics, they are worth our attention because they point to an omission in Idealist aesthetics and to a factor the importance of which would eventually have to be restored in any complete account of aesthetic experience.[91]

---

[88] *The Autobiography of John Stuart Mill*, published posthumously in 1873; see *The Collected Works of John Stuart Mill*, vol. 1, *Autobiography and Literary Essays*, ed. John M. Robson and Jack Stillinger (Toronto: University of Toronto Press, 1981).

[89] Mill, *Autobiography* (Early Draft), in *Autobiography and Literary Essays*, p. 113.

[90] John Stuart Mill, "Coleridge," in *Essays on Ethics, Religion and Society*, pp. 133–5.

[91] On Mill's life, see, in addition to the *Autobiography*, Nicholas Capaldi, *John Stuart Mill: A Biography* (Cambridge: Cambridge University Press, 2004), and for our purposes

Mill starts these essays with the question "What is Poetry?" but he immediately makes plain that the answer to this question will not be formalistic, for example that poetry is merely "metrical composition"; indeed, what he means by poetry is not even limited to any specific form or genre of literature:

> That, however, the word poetry imports something quite peculiar in its nature, something which may exist in what is called prose as well as in verse, something which does not even require the instrument of words, but can speak through the other audible symbols called musical sounds, and even through the visible ones which are the language of sculpture, painting, and architecture; all this, we believe, is and must be felt, though perhaps indistinctly, by all whom poetry in any of its shapes produces any impression beyond tickling the ear.[92]

What Mill has in mind is something more like what would be called in German *Poesie* rather than what is called poetry, that is, verse, in English, and Mill thus makes it clear that his question "What is Poetry?" is equivalent to the question "What is art?" What he is about to argue distinguishes poetry from mere prose is therefore what distinguishes all art from other artifacts. The "distinction between poetry and what is not poetry," thus between art and non-art, is one, he trusts, felt and acknowledged by all who have any understanding of poetry or art whatever; the method of his argument is thus to be empirical, appealing to the feelings of all qualified judges – here there is no tincture of the *a priori* methodology of German Idealism, whatever other influence its English representative Coleridge might have had on Mill. But Mill's argument does not merely appeal to the feelings of qualified readers; the substance of his proposal is also that the primary aim of poetry and all art is to work upon the feelings of its audience. In the course of his argument, Mill will assume that genuine poetry is the expression of feelings that actually exist in the mind of the poet, as Wordsworth had ("emotion recollected

---

especially ch. 4, "The Discovery of Romance and Romanticism," pp. 86–132; for surveys of Mill's philosophy, see Alan Ryan, *J.S. Mill* (London: Routledge & Kegan Paul, 1974), and John Skorupski, *John Stuart Mill* (London: Routledge, 1989). Relevant monographs are F. Parvin Sharpless, *The Literary Criticism of John Stuart Mill* (The Hague: Mouton, 1967), and Colin Heydt, *Rethinking Mill's Ethics: Character and Aesthetic Education* (London: Continuum, 2006). A relevant article is Wendy Donner, "Morality, Virtue, and Aesthetics in Mill's Art of Life," in Ben Eggleston, Dale E. Miller, and David Weinstein, editors, *John Stuart Mill and the Art of Life* (New York: Oxford University Press, 2011), pp. 146–65.

[92] Mill, "Thoughts on Poetry and Its Varieties," Part I (originally in the *Monthly Repository*, January 1833), in Mill, *Autobiography and Literary Essays*, p. 343.

in tranquillity"), but what is fundamental to his conception is that poetry aims to produce feeling in its audience; and insofar as poetry or art is also concerned to convey truth or create beauty, it is genuinely poetic or artistic only insofar as it conveys "impassioned" truth[93] and beauty that "harmonizes" with some feeling which it has "a tendency to raise up in the spectator's mind ... a feeling of grandeur, or loveliness, or cheerfulness, or wildness, or melancholy, or terror."[94] Thus the premise of Mill's account, the basic claim that is to be confirmed from his or her own experience by each reader of Mill's essay, is that

> The object of poetry is confessedly to act upon the emotions; and therein is poetry sufficiently distinguished from what Wordsworth affirms to be its logical opposite, namely, not prose, but matter of fact or science. The one addresses itself to the belief, the other to the feelings. The one does its work by convincing or persuading, the other by moving. The one acts by presenting a proposition to the understanding; the other by offering interesting objects of contemplation to the sensibilities.[95]

Again, Mill makes it clear that what matters is not the outward form of a work, for example whether it is metrical or not, rhymed or not, but its intended effect: prose or non-art aims to produce conviction, whether its content is actually true or not, and poetry or art aims to move the emotions, even if its content, should it have content (as for example architecture usually does not), is also true. Mill uses the word "contemplation" in connection with poetry, but it is clear from what immediately precedes that by this he does not mean a purely cognitive attitude toward some truth, but rather the close attention to an object that is necessary for it to produce its emotional impact. Mill also says that poetry "is the delineation of the deeper and more secret workings of human emotion," which might be taken to mean that it is a medium for knowledge *about* emotions and thus that its aim is essentially cognitive even if its subject matter is emotional; but he immediately follows this with the statement that poetry "is interesting only to those to whom it recalls what they have felt, or whose imagination it stirs up to conceive what they could feel, or what they might have been able to feel had their outward circumstances been different."[96] Even when poetry does truly describe emotions, its aim is not, or not merely, to provide cognition about them, but to stimulate

---

[93] Mill, "Poetry and Its Varieties," Part I, *Autobiography and Literary Essays*, p. 348.
[94] Mill, "Poetry and Its Varieties," Part I, *Autobiography and Literary Essays*, pp. 343–4n.; this passage is from the 1833 version of the essay.
[95] Mill, "Poetry and Its Varieties," Part I, *Autobiography and Literary Essays*, p. 344.
[96] Mill, "Poetry and Its Varieties," Part I, *Autobiography and Literary Essays*, pp. 345–6.

experience of them. Mill also observes that the stimulation of emotion does not have to proceed by means of the "delineation" or description of emotion, even if it sometimes can; emotion may also be stimulated by description of an external object in a way that stirs the emotions of an audience. Thus, "If a poet describes a lion, he does not describe him as a naturalist would ... who was intent upon stating the truth, the whole truth, and nothing but the truth." Rather, "He describes him by imagery, that is, by suggesting the most striking likenesses and contrasts which might occur to a mind contemplating the lion, in the state of awe, wonder, or terror, which the spectacle naturally excites ... Now this is describing the lion professedly, but the state of excitement of the spectator really."[97] More precisely, it is describing the lion in a way aimed at producing the state of excitement, or the excitement of a particular emotion or range of emotions, in the spectator. Unlike Wordsworth and Shelley, who had forged a connection between poetry's conveying truth and its conveying emotion, Mill separates the two and argues that the aim of poetry is only its emotional impact. A decade after writing the essay we are discussing, Mill would write one of the nineteenth century's great works on philosophy of science; perhaps a thinker with his intimacy with science felt a stronger need to distinguish poetry from any vehicle of truth than the Romantic poet-philosophers had.

Be that as it may, having argued that poetry is aimed at stirring emotions rather than conveying truths, Mill is then faced with the problem of distinguishing between poetry and "eloquence" or oratory (or "propaganda," as R.G. Collingwood would add a century later), which also works by stirring the emotions of its audience. An obvious way of distinguishing between poetry and oratory would be to say that the latter aims to stir up emotions in its audience as a means to some end of the orator, as a way of motivating or manipulating its audience toward some action, while poetry aims at stirring emotions for the sake of the audience only, that is, for their enjoyment.[98] Mill takes a different tack, arguing that "Eloquence supposes an audience" while "the peculiarity of poetry appears to us to lie in the poet's utter unconsciousness of a listener."

> Poetry is feeling, confessing to itself in moments of solitude, and embodying itself in symbols, which are the nearest possible representations of the feeling in the exact shape in which it exists in the poet's mind. Eloquence is

---

[97] Mill, "Poetry and Its Varieties," Part I, *Autobiography and Literary Essays*, p. 347.
[98] So had Kant famously distinguished between poetry and oratory in *Critique of the Power of Judgment*, §51.

feeling pouring itself out to other minds, courting their sympathy or endeavouring to influence their belief, or move them to passion or action.[99]

Here Mill draws his distinction too strongly, making the poet's expression of his feeling for his own sake essential to poetry but the communication of his feeling to his audience accidental or incidental to his aims, and lumping together moving an audience to passion and to action as both characteristic of eloquence, when a distinction between moving an audience to passion and moving it to action might have been more germane to his original definition. Nevertheless, his distinction leads him to the memorable remark that "eloquence is *heard*, poetry is *over*heard,"[100] suggesting that the distinction between poetry and eloquence, art and non-art, lies not so much in the author's intentions as in the phenomenology of the audience's response: in art we are absorbed by an object and our emotional response to it, while with other sorts of objects we are always cognizant of the author's intentions regarding us.

Mill again overdraws his distinction when he states that "Poetry, accordingly, is the natural fruit of solitude and meditation; eloquence, of intercourse with the world";[101] surely many kinds of emotion are intimately connected with human intercourse with the world, and only an author who has had such intercourse can express these emotions and arouse them in his audience, whether or not he has any further aim in so doing. But apart from his exaggerations, what is important in Mill's account is his emphasis on the emotional aspect of the experience of art, so noticeably absent from the idealist philosophy of art since Kant. The emphasis on emotion is evident in Mill's account of beauty in the first edition of the essay, already mentioned. Mill takes up the topic of beauty precisely in order to controvert the view that "The direct aim of art as such, is the production of the *beautiful*"; this view would conflict with his own account of poetry because "as there are other things beautiful besides states of mind, there is much of art which may seem to have nothing to do with poetry or eloquence as we have defined them." As a possible counterexample to his own view, Mill refers to landscape painting, for example something by Claude Lorrain. He alludes to a traditional account of beauty on which such a painting presents "a beauty more perfect and faultless than is perhaps to be found in any actual landscape," but argues that such traditional criteria or components of

---

[99] Mill, "Poetry and Its Varieties," Part I, *Autobiography and Literary Essays*, pp. 348–9.
[100] Mill, "Poetry and Its Varieties," Part I, *Autobiography and Literary Essays*, p. 348.
[101] Mill, "Poetry and Its Varieties," Part I, *Autobiography and Literary Essays*, p. 349.

beauty as "unity, and wholeness, and æsthetic congruity" actually depend on "singleness of expression." Anticipating a common later objection to all expression theories of art, he concedes that "The objects in an imaginary landscape cannot be said, like the words of a poem or the notes of a melody, to be the actual utterance of a feeling," but insists, as we saw earlier, that there must nevertheless "be some feeling with which they harmonize, and which they have a tendency to raise up in the spectator's mind." "Even architecture," he adds, "to be impressive, must be the expression or symbol of some interesting idea"; if the emphasis in this clause were placed on the word "idea," this would sound like an idealist theory of art as cognition of an idea, of the kind that we have found in Schelling and will find in Hegel, but we should rather read the clause with the emphasis on "interesting," by which Mill in turn means emotionally interesting: what makes a thought expressed by architecture (or other non-verbal art) interesting and impressive is that it is "some thought, which has power over the emotions."[102] In this passage, Mill demonstrates that he does not entirely ignore either cognitive content or formal beauty as important features of art, but holds that they must be accompanied with emotional impact and constitute genuine art only insofar as they contribute to the emotional impact of the work. Mill also makes it clear here that it is the emotional impact on the audience that is the necessary feature of art, the occurrence of emotion in the artist being at best a causal condition for the creation of an object that can have such an impact on its audience. Were it to turn out that objects with emotional impact, whether verbal artifacts that have the linguistic form of expressing their author's state of mind or other sorts of artifacts that do not, could be created without the actual experience of emotion in their artists, that would not affect the status of such objects as art as long as they had emotional impact on their audience. Only that is the *sine qua non* of poetry or art, even if it is actually unlikely that art with an emotional impact on its audience could be produced by an artist who had not experienced the relevant emotion.

In his brief and early essays on poetry, Mill does not raise the question of why it should be important to us to experience emotions through the medium of poetry or other arts; perhaps the pleasure of so doing is supposed to be self-evident. He certainly does not argue, as Shelley had, that the experience of art has a direct benefit for our moral imagination. Since Mill did not devote any part of his later, more systematic work to

[102] Mill, "Poetry and Its Varieties," Part I, *Autobiography and Literary Essays*, pp. 353–4n.

aesthetics, he never directly addresses the question of the importance of the emotional experience of art. But perhaps Mill's most enduring work, the 1859 essay *On Liberty*, suggests a way he could have answered this question. In this work, deeply influenced by the posthumous publication of Wilhelm von Humboldt's essay on the limits of state action just a few years before,[103] Mill defends the most extensive possible liberty of thought and speech as the necessary condition for progress in the discovery of truth and for the appreciation of truth already discovered – a cognitivist argument for liberty, so to speak. But in the third chapter of the work, "Of Individuality, as One of the Elements of Well-Being," Mill argues that freedom in the development of individual character is a good in its own right, not just good as a means to the discovery of truth. The underlying assumption of this argument seems to be that (right-thinking) human beings approve of variety and individuality among human characters because they enjoy the spectacle of human variety. Mill puts the premise for his argument in aesthetic terms: "It is not by wearing down into uniformity all that is individual in themselves, but by cultivating it and calling it forth, within the limits imposed by the rights and interest of others, that human beings become a noble and beautiful object of contemplation; and as the works partake of the character of those who do them, by the same process human life also becomes rich, diversified, and animating."[104] If we assume that part of what we each enjoy in contemplating the full variety of human lives is the full variety of human emotions, then of course each of us has to have a way of experiencing that variety, which may extend well beyond the range of emotions that any one of us might otherwise enjoy in his or her own life apart from the experience of art. The expression of emotions in art might be a way, perhaps the best way, for us to experience the full range of human emotions and thus to be able to enjoy contemplating the full range of human variety. Mill does not quite make such an argument, but it would be consistent both with his early essays and with the centerpiece of his mature thought. Half a century later, as we will see in Volume 3, the British aesthetician Edward Bullough would

---

[103] Michael Forster shows how closely Mill follows von Humboldt's argument in "The Liberal Temper in Classical German Philosophy: Freedom of Thought and Expression," in *After Herder: Philosophy of Language in the German Tradition* (Oxford: Oxford University Press, 2000), pp. 244–80.

[104] Mill, *On Liberty*, chapter III, in *Collected Works of John Stuart Mill*, volume 18, *Essays on Politics and Society*, ed. J.M. Robson and Alexander Brady (Toronto: University of Toronto Press, 1977), p. 266.

make such an argument, and perhaps we may think of Mill as having anticipated it.

As we have seen thus far in this chapter, Coleridge developed an essentially cognitivist aesthetics from the philosophy of Schelling. Wordsworth, who was personally close to Coleridge, and Shelley, who had no personal contact with him but was clearly influenced by his poetics, began with Coleridge's aesthetics of truth but intimately connected the emotional impact of poetry to its truth, in Shelley's case truth in both content and form. It was left to the scientific philosopher Mill to emphasize the emotional impact of poetry, and under that as a general term, other kinds of art as well, almost exclusively. In turning now to Ralph Waldo Emerson, Mill's almost exact contemporary in America (although the American outlived his British counterpart by a decade), we also turn back to a more purely Coleridgean aesthetic.

4. EMERSON

In early nineteenth-century America, the need for texts in academic aesthetics, such as it was, as part of general courses in philosophy or rhetoric, was filled by American editions of the works of such Scottish writers as Lord Kames and Dugald Stewart. In the broader culture of the United States, the need for reflection on beauty and art, as on much else, was filled by the works of Ralph Waldo Emerson (1803–82).[105]

A thinker with a highly absorbent mind, Emerson was exposed early to many philosophical and intellectual traditions, including the Scottish tradition that was the basis of American collegiate education in philosophy at Harvard, where Emerson was an undergraduate and then a divinity student, as well as elsewhere, but also Neo-Platonism, mysticism, and

---

[105] The sole monograph devoted to Emerson's aesthetics focuses on Emerson's contact with artistic and literary culture in nineteenth-century America and his influence on it; see Vivian C. Hopkins, *Spires of Form: A Study of Emerson's Aesthetic Theory* (Cambridge, Mass.: Harvard University Press, 1951). Stanley Cavell's essays on Emerson are collected in *Emerson's Transcendental Etudes*, ed. David Justin Hodge (Stanford: Stanford University Press, 2003); see also Cavell, *Cities of Words: Pedagogical Letters on a Register of the Moral Life* (Cambridge, Mass.: Harvard University Press, 2004), pp. 19–34; another philosophical treatment is Russell B. Goodman, *American Philosophy and the Romantic Tradition* (Cambridge: Cambridge University Press, 1990). For biographies, see Gay Wilson Allen, *Waldo Emerson: A Biography* (New York: Viking, 1981), Robert D. Richardson, Jr., *Emerson: The Mind on Fire* (Berkeley and Los Angeles: University of California Press, 1995), and Lawrence Buell, *Emerson* (Cambridge, Mass.: Harvard University Press, 2003). For discussion of Emerson and Schelling, see Raters, *Kunst, Wahrheit und Gefühl*, pp. 139–59.

above all German Idealism, especially in the form given to it by Schelling and transmitted to the English-speaking world by Coleridge. According to some accounts, later in his career Emerson was also influenced by Hegel and the school of his American followers known as the St. Louis Hegelians,[106] but the "Transcendentalism" espoused in Emerson's first essay collection *Nature* (1836) and the *First* (1841) and *Second Series* (1844) of his *Essays* surely shows the influence of Schelling more than of Hegel in its conception of the unification of nature and human being rather than a conception of the sheer externalization of the human "spirit" in nature. Emerson's first book, *Nature*, includes a chapter on "Beauty," and the *Essays* include chapters on "Art" (*First Series*) and "The Poet" (*Second Series*), but none of these have the appearance of an academic treatise in aesthetics. Only in a second chapter on "Beauty" in the 1860 collection *The Conduct of Life* does Emerson offer anything that looks like an analysis of the concept of beauty; even here, however, Emerson begins by remarking that he is "warned by the ill fate of many philosophers, not to attempt a definition of Beauty," and says that he will rather only "enumerate a few of its qualities."[107] Yet this caution hardly precludes Emerson being seriously considered in a history of aesthetics; on the contrary, not only does it look back to Thomas Reid's observation on the manifold senses of the word "beauty" and kinds of beauty,[108] it also looks forward to the attack upon the possibility of definitions in aesthetics that would become characteristic of mid-twentieth-century Anglo-American aesthetics, although under the immediate influence of Wittgenstein rather than Emerson.[109] An account of Emerson belongs in the history of aesthetics because of his illustration of the aesthetics of German Idealism as well as because of his anticipation of this characteristic tendency of more recent aesthetics. He should also be noted because of his well-documented influence on the young Nietzsche, certainly a major figure in the history of aesthetics later in the nineteenth century: Emerson's remark in *Nature* that "The world thus exists to the soul to

---

[106] See Michael Moran, "Emerson, Ralph Waldo," in *Encyclopedia of Philosophy*, second edition, ed. Donald M. Borchert (Farmington Hills, Mich.: Thomson-Gale, 2006), vol. 3, p. 196.

[107] Ralph Waldo Emerson, *The Conduct of Life*, in *The Collected Works of Ralph Waldo Emerson*, Vol. VI, introduction by Barbara L. Packer, Notes by Joseph Slater, text edited by Douglas Emory Wilson (Cambridge, Mass.: Harvard University Press, 2003), p. 154.

[108] See Thomas Reid, *Essays on the Intellectual Powers of Man*, edited by Derek R. Brookes (University Park: Pennsylvania State University Press, 2002), Essay VIII, p. 575, and *Thomas Reid's Lectures on the Fine Arts*, edited by Peter Kivy (The Hague: Martinus Nijhoff, 1973), p. 40.

[109] See Volume 3, Part 4.

satisfy the desire of beauty"[110] could be a source for Nietzsche's famous remark in *The Birth of Tragedy* (1872) that "the existence of the world is justified only as an aesthetic phenomenon."[111]

Emerson, the son of a Unitarian minister in Boston, was, as already noted, educated at Harvard. By all accounts, he was undistinguished as an undergraduate student, but by the later 1820s he had already read widely among authors such as religious sages of all traditions from Confucius to Swedenborg and philosophers and social thinkers such as Leibniz, Montesquieu, Rousseau, Burke, Herder, and Madame de Staël's report on contemporary German literature and philosophy in *De l'Allemagne*.[112] After a few years as a schoolteacher, Emerson also became a Unitarian minister in Boston, but following the death of his first wife in 1831, after only two years of marriage, he gave up the ministry. His first resort after her death was a trip to Europe in 1833, during which he not only acquainted himself with Italian art but also met Wordsworth and Coleridge and became lifelong friends with Thomas Carlyle in England. Shortly after returning to his home in Concord, Massachusetts, he remarried, and also embarked on a career as a public lecturer throughout the United States. (with a further lecture tour to England in 1847–48) that would make him the most famous man of letters in nineteenth-century America; all of his books, which in addition to those already mentioned include *Representative Men* (1850), *English Traits* (1856), and *Letters and Social Aims* (1875), were based on his lectures. His career as a lecturer and writer made Emerson rich and famous as the "Sage of Concord."

Emerson's "Transcendentalism," enunciated in the works that first made him famous, *Nature*, the Harvard Phi Beta Kappa lecture "The American Scholar" (1837), and the Harvard Divinity School Address (1838), is the view that each human individual is part of a larger spiritual entity, which Emerson sometimes calls the "Over-Soul," and that this in turn comprises a unity with what we are so often inclined to conceive of as the opposite of the human soul, namely nature. Emerson succinctly expresses the first point in *Nature* when he states that "Man is conscious

---

[110] Emerson, *Nature*, in *The Collected Works of Ralph Waldo Emerson*, Vol. I, edited by Alfred R. Ferguson, introductions and notes by Robert E. Spiller (Cambridge, Mass.: Harvard University Press, 1971), p. 17.

[111] Friedrich Nietzsche, *The Birth of Tragedy and Other Writings*, ed. Raymond Geuss and Ronald Speirs, trans. Ronald Speirs (Cambridge: Cambridge University Press, 1999), p. 8. Actually, this remark comes the "Attempt at Self-Criticism" that Nietzsche added to the second edition of *The Birth of Tragedy* in 1886, suggesting that the influence of Emerson continued throughout Nietzsche's career.

[112] Moran, "Emerson, Ralph Waldo," p. 195.

of a universal soul within or behind his individual life, wherein, as in a firmament, the natures of Justice, Truth, Love, Freedom, arise and shine. This universal soul, he calls Reason: it is not mine or thine or his, but we are its."[113] Because of the "identity of the mind through all individuals," he who goes "down into the secrets of his own mind ... has descended into the secrets of all minds."[114] He expresses the second point in a remark such as that the "relation between the mind and matter is not fancied by some poet, but stands in the will of God, and so is free to be known by all men."[115] Because of the unity of mind or man and nature, nature reflects the human mind, but the human mind cannot exist except embedded in nature. In his early work, Emerson may emphasize the first of these facts more than the second, as when he writes that

> Sensible objects conform to the premonitions of Reason and reflect the conscience. All things are moral; and in their boundless changes have an unceasing reference to spiritual nature. Therefore is nature glorious with form, color, and motion, that every globe in the remotest heaven; every chemical change from the rudest crystal up to the laws of life; every change of vegetation ...; every animal function ... shall hint to man the laws of right and wrong ... This ethical character so penetrates the bone and marrow of nature, as to seem the end for which it was made.[116]

But he equally stresses the second fact, that humankind is essentially embedded in nature as well as nature reflecting the human mind, in only slightly later work such as the central essay on "The Over-Soul" in *Essays: First Series*. Here Emerson stresses that the unity that underlies all individuality is the unity of man and nature as well as the unity of diverse humans:

> The Supreme Critic on the errors of the past and the present, and the only prophet of that which must be, is that great nature in which we rest, as the earth lies in the soft arms of the atmosphere; that Unity, that Over-Soul, within which every man's particular being is contained and made one with all other.... We live in succession, in division, in parts, in particles. Meantime within man is the soul of the whole; the wise silence; the universal beauty, to which every part and particle is equally related; the eternal ONE.... We see the world piece by piece, as the sun, the moon, the animal, the tree: but the whole, of which these are the shining parts, is the soul.[117]

---

[113] Emerson, *Nature*, p. 18.
[114] Emerson, "The American Scholar," in *Collected Works*, Vol. I, pp. 66, 63.
[115] Emerson, *Nature*, p. 22.
[116] Emerson, *Nature*, pp. 25–6.
[117] Emerson, *Essays: First Series*, Essay IX, "The Over-Soul," in *The Collected Works of Ralph Waldo Emerson*, Vol. II, introduction and notes by Joseph Slater, text edited by Alfred R.

It is the bidirectionality of Emerson's Transcendentalism, the thought that nature gives rise to the most characteristic features of human thought but that human beings must also always recognize that they are at home only in nature, that marks the association of his thought with that of Schelling.

Emerson's language in these passages demonstrates that he conceives of our affinity with nature as expressed in aesthetic as well as ethical form: our responsiveness to natural beauty as well as our tendency to conceive of nature in ethical terms both mark our essential identity with nature and its with us. In the very first chapter of *Nature*, Emerson remarks that "The lover of nature is he whose inward and outward senses are still truly adjusted to each other; who has retained the spirit of infancy even into the era of manhood"[118] (a remark that surely reveals the influence of Coleridge's account of genius in *Biographia Literaria*), that is, one whose response to nature is aesthetic as well as ethical. Emerson then develops the themes that natural beauty is an expression of our identity with nature and that art is a vehicle through which this fundamental relationship is further expressed. Emerson continues the first chapter of *Nature* with the suggestion that natural beauty is found in the wilder, uncultivated, and untamed aspects of nature in the ordinary sense, our physical environment: "I am the lover of uncontained beauty. In the wilderness, I find something more dear and connate than in streets or villages. In the tranquil landscape, and especially in the distant line of the horizon, man beholds somewhat as beautiful as his own nature."[119] But he quickly moves to an identification of all of nature with beauty. Following the remark that "A nobler want of man is served by nature, namely, the love of Beauty," Emerson opens the third chapter of *Nature*, on "Beauty," with the remark that "The ancient Greeks called the world κοσμος, beauty. Such is the constitution of all things, or such the plastic power of the human eye, that the primary forms, as the sky, the mountain, the tree, the animal, give us a delight *in and for themselves*; a pleasure arising from outline, color, motion, and grouping."[120] But while this passage generalizes the objects that we may find beautiful in nature, to anything natural, it also suggests a restriction of natural beauty to what is in fact only the first of its three "aspects" or levels of importance. Emerson

Ferguson and Jean Ferguson Carr (Cambridge, Mass.: Harvard University Press, 1979), p. 160.
[118] Emerson, *Nature*, p. 9.
[119] Emerson, *Nature*, p. 10.
[120] Emerson, *Nature*, p. 12.

continues that "we may distribute the aspects of Beauty in a threefold manner." That "the simple perception of natural forms is a delight"[121] is only the first of these levels. The second level of beauty is the "presence of a higher, namely, ... spiritual element ... that which is found in combination with the human will," in other words, "Beauty is the mark God sets upon virtue":[122] beauty is the outward expression, in human action, but of course human action as itself part of nature, of virtue. Emerson also calls this kind of beauty "graceful," which seems a clear reference to Schiller's conception in "On Grace and Dignity" and perhaps a reference to Kames's account of gracefulness standing in turn beyond Schiller. Finally, Emerson holds that "There is still another aspect under which the beauty of the world must be viewed, namely, as it becomes an object of the intellect. Beside the relation of things to virtue, they have a relation to thought." Here Emerson refers to the beauty of order in nature as a whole, which can be taken in only by intellect, rather than the beauty of the forms of individual objects, which can be recognized by mere sense: "The intellect searches out the absolute order of things," and thereby "The beauty of nature reforms itself in the mind."[123] Here, with Platonic and Neo-Platonic as well as German Idealist antecedents in mind, Emerson holds that natural beauty is most deeply appreciated when it is interpreted as the reflection of the underlying order of nature. That an "intellectual" thought of such a metaphysical account of beauty is necessary for the deepest level of its reception is indicative of the fundamentally cognitivist character of Emerson's theory of beauty.

Thus far we have sampled Emerson's account only of natural beauty. But Emerson immediately turns to the beauty of art, arguing basically that art is a medium for capturing and transmitting the experience of natural beauty. He continues the chapter on "Beauty" in *Nature* with the remark that "The creation of beauty is Art," which might suggest that artistic beauty is a creation of the imagination rather than an imitation of something already present in nature and our experience of it, and indeed we will find some remarks in later writings that suggest such a view, which might count as an alternative to a purely cognitivist approach to artistic beauty. But here Emerson continues that "A work of art is an abstract or epitome of the world. It is the result or expression of nature, in miniature."[124] Artistic beauty is an expression of the beauty

[121] Emerson, *Nature*, p. 13.
[122] Emerson, *Nature*, p. 15.
[123] Emerson, *Nature*, p. 16.
[124] Emerson, *Nature*, pp. 16–17.

of nature, most fully understood, and as in general "Nothing is quite beautiful alone: nothing but is beautiful in the whole," so too in art "A single object is only so far beautiful as it suggests this universal grace." An artist is then one who produces artifacts that capture and communicate the beautiful order of nature:

> The poet, the painter, the sculptor, the musician, the architect, seek each to concentrate this radiance of the world on one point, and each in his several work to satisfy the love of beauty which stimulates him to produce. Thus is Art, a nature passed through the alembic of man. Thus in art, does nature work through the will of a man filled with the beauty of her first works.[125]

Here is where Emerson then continues with his remark that "The world thus exists to the soul to satisfy the desire of beauty." We can now see that it does this in two ways, most directly through the existence of objects in nature in the ordinary sense, that is, objects that are not human artifacts, as well as less directly, through its creation of human artists who are in turn capable of creating concentrated images of natural beauty in the first sense, as well as at several levels, the levels of mere form, of the graceful expression of virtue, and of order that must be understood intellectually.

Emerson develops these themes in the next chapter of *Nature*, on symbols and language, and in the chapters on "Art" in *Essays: First Series* and "The Poet" in *Essays: Second Series*. We can take a look at these chapters before returning to Emerson's later analysis of beauty in *The Conduct of Life*. In the essay on "Art," Emerson begins by stating the "in our fine arts, not imitation, but creation is the aim. In landscapes," for example, "the painter should give the suggestion of a fairer creation that we know." This might suggest that the aim of art is not to reproduce nature or in any other way render nature graphic or intelligible for us, but Emerson quickly corrects any such impression by continuing that "The details, the prose of nature he should omit, and give us only the spirit and splendor. He should know that the landscape has beauty for his eye, because it expresses a thought which is to him good."[126] This makes it clear that the creativity of the artist does not lie in offering any alternative to nature, but rather in having and communicating an insight into – a thought about – what is essential rather than accidental to nature. Emerson emphasizes this point some pages later when he says that "genius left to novices the gay and fantastic and ostentatious, and

---

[125] Emerson, *Nature*, p. 17.
[126] Emerson, "Art," in *Essays: First Series*, p. 209.

itself pierced directly to the simple and true ... the old, eternal fact I had met already in so many forms."[127] Art cannot simply be equated with an intellectual understanding of the underlying order of nature, the unity of man and nature, the unity among human beings, that is, the essential truths on the Emersonian worldview, but it plays a special role in getting us to recognize such truth:

> it has been the office of art to educate the perception of beauty. We are immersed in beauty, but our eyes have no clear vision. It needs, by the exhibition of single traits, to assist and lead the dormant taste. We carve and paint, or we behold what is carved and painted, as students of the mystery of Form. The virtue of art lies in detachment, in sequestering one object from the embarrassing variety. Until one thing comes out from the connection of things, there can be enjoyment, contemplation, but no thought.[128]

Here Emerson adapts the traditional, for example Kantian, terms of detachment and disinterested contemplation, but treats them as necessary conditions for appreciating the real truth about nature rather than as separating the creation and enjoyment of art – he clearly alludes to both – from the intellectual activity of understanding nature. Art has a special role for us, but within a primarily cognitive relation to the world.

Emerson also makes the Schellingian point that "man," by which he means both human beauty itself and human creativity, the human ability to present the beauty of both human and non-human nature in art, is itself an expression of a power within nature. He asks rhetorically "What is a man but nature's finer success in self-explication? What is a man but a finer and compacter landscape, than the horizon figures?"[129] Borrowing a favorite figure from Kant, we might say that for Emerson, art is the *ratio cognoscendi* of the essence of nature, but nature is the *ratio essendi* of art: art provides insight into the essence of nature, but it is the unity and coherence of nature that makes art possible. This bidirectional link between nature and art provides the foundation for Emerson's solution to what the eighteenth century had formulated as the problem of taste, and which, once again revealing his essentially cognitivist approach, Emerson formulates as the problem of the "universal intelligibility" of art: for Emerson, art, or at least successful art, "the work of genius," is universally intelligible because it gives expression to profound truths

---

[127] Emerson, "Art," *Essays: First Series*, p. 214.
[128] Emerson, "Art," *Essays: First Series*, pp. 210–11.
[129] Emerson, "Art," *Essays: First Series*, p. 209.

about nature that must be intelligible to all and does so in ways that are themselves natural, and thus also intelligible to all. Here Emerson relies on his conception of the "Over-Soul," explicated in a previous chapter of *Essays: First Series*,[130] or of the unity of all humans, as well as on his conception of the unity of humanity and nature. He writes:

> The reference of all production at last to an Aboriginal Power, explains the traits common to all works of the highest art, – that they are universally intelligible ... Since what skill is therein shown is the reappearance of the original soul, a jet of pure light, it should produce a similar impression to that made by natural objects. In happy hours, nature appears to us one with art; art perfected, – the work of genius. And the individual in whom simple tastes and susceptibility to all the great human influences overpowers the accidents of a local and special culture, is the best critic of art.... The best of beauty is ... a wonderful expression through stone or canvas or musical sound of the deepest and simplest attributes of our nature, and therefore most intelligible at last to those souls which have these attributes.[131]

On the basis of his Transcendentalist metaphysics and cognitivist approach to beauty in nature and in art, Emerson is as fully committed to the universal validity of judgments of taste as any eighteenth-century theorist, or even more so than some. Emerson has perhaps learned from Herder to reject the idea of Winckelmann that people at one time can simply recreate the beautiful art of another time – "Beauty will not come at the call of a legislature, nor will it repeat in England or America, its history in Greece. It will come, as always, unannounced, and spring up between the feet of brave and earnest men."[132] Thus moderns may better create images of shops and mills than of Olympian athletes. But Emerson also shares Herder's assumption, though on his own Schellingian, Transcendentalist grounds rather than on Herder's more naturalistic ground, that artistic beauty created at any time will be able to communicate its insight into the underlying truth about humanity's place in nature to audiences at any time.

Emerson returns to the theme of universal intelligibility in "The Poet," the first of the *Essays: Second Series*. Here Emerson emphasizes that poets, standing in for all artists, have gifts of both insight and expression that exceed those of other humans, but that what they understand and communicate is precisely through their work accessible to all:

---

[130] Emerson, "The Over-Soul," *Essays: First Series*, ch. IX, pp. 159–75.
[131] Emerson, "Art," *Essays: First Series*, p. 213.
[132] Emerson, "Art," *Essays: First Series*, p. 218.

the poet is the representative man. He stands among partial men for the complete man, and apprises us not of his wealth, but of the commonwealth.... He is isolated among his contemporaries, by truth and by his art, but with this consolation in his pursuits, that they will draw all men sooner or later. For all men live by truth, and stand in need of expression.... The poet is the person in whom these powers –

of sense and speech, insight and expression –

are in balance, the man without impediment, who sees and handles that which others dream of, traverses the whole scale of experience, and is representative of man, in virtue of being the largest power to receive and to impart.[133]

Here Emerson reproduces the twofold structure of the Kantian analysis of genius, with its emphasis on both the inventiveness and the expressiveness of genius, although Emerson's characterization of the first of these poles as "receptive" rather than creative again confirms the cognitivist character of his own approach.

Later in this essay, Emerson expands on the bold statement that "The poets are ... liberating gods,"[134] and in saying this he might seem finally to accept Kant's account that the essence of aesthetic experience and thus at least a necessary condition for art is the free play of the imagination within the constraints of the understanding's demand for unity rather than any form of intellectual insight. However, Emerson's thought in "The Poet" seems to be the same as his thought in the earlier essay on "Art," namely that the special gift of the artist is to liberate himself and thereby the rest of us from an excessive focus on the particulars in nature so that we can appreciate the essential truths about nature that lie behind or beneath its particulars; in other words, liberation from the particularity of the senses is a means to the appreciation of more important truth through beauty and art, not an end in itself. Thus Emerson continues that while the "emancipation" offered by poetry is "dear to all men," "the power to impart, as it must come from greater depth and scope of thought, is a measure of intellect. Therefore all books of the imagination endure, all which ascend to that truth, that the writer sees nature beneath him, and uses it as his exponent. Every verse or sentence, possessing this virtue, will take care of its own immortality."[135] The liberation that Emerson finds essential to art is the liberation of the intellect

---

[133] Emerson, "The Poet," *Essays: Second Series*, pp. 4–5.
[134] Emerson, "The Poet," *Essays: Second Series*, p. 19.
[135] Emerson, "The Poet," *Essays: Second Series*, pp. 19–20.

from its distractions and to the essential character of nature and mankind's relation to it and to each other.

In his most formal analysis of beauty, in the chapter on that topic in the 1860 collection *The Conduct of Life*, Emerson again emphasizes his cognitivist approach with the remarks that "Beauty is the form under which the intellect prefers to study the world"[136] and that "The question of Beauty takes us out of surfaces, to thinking of the foundations of things."[137] Here, however, Emerson recognizes multiple aspects of beauty, as earlier noted. First, he does not actually deny that the "forms and colors of nature" do contribute to our "sensuous delight" in natural beauty. Rather, he proposes that forms have "a new charm for us" or constitute a second aspect or level of beauty in our recognition of them "as a sign of some better health, or more excellent action" or "excellence of structure" either in what acts or in what is produced by action.[138] Emerson characterizes this second level of beauty with a variety of terms, all of which have a large role sooner or later in the history of aesthetics: "beauty must be organic" or "necessary," lying in structures essential to the well-being or proper functioning of its object, in "the soundness of bones that ultimate themselves in a peach-bloom complexion" or in "the real supporters of a house" that "honestly … show themselves,"[139] and "The line of beauty is the result of perfect economy" and "Veracity."[140] All of these qualities – organic functioning, soundness, honest, economy, veracity – can show themselves to particular advantage in the human form, and thus human form is the paradigmatic content of art, although its beauty also exceeds the beauty of art: "The felicities of design, or in works of nature, are Shadows or forerunners of that beauty which reaches its perfection in the human form. All men are its lovers."[141] But the beauty of sound human form is, so to speak, only the pinnacle of the second level of beauty. The highest level of beauty is beauty as the expression of moral character, or the expression of moral character that accompanies beauty in the first two senses. "And yet – it is not beauty that inspires the deepest passion. Beauty without grace is the hook without the bait. Beauty, without expression, tires."[142] Or, as Emerson concludes

---

[136] Emerson, "Beauty," in *The Conduct of Life*, p. 153.
[137] Emerson, "Beauty," *The Conduct of Life*, p. 154.
[138] Emerson, "Beauty," *The Conduct of Life*, p. 154.
[139] Emerson, "Beauty," *The Conduct of Life*, p. 155.
[140] Emerson, *The Conduct of Life*, pp. 156–7.
[141] Emerson, *The Conduct of Life*, p. 158.
[142] Emerson, *The Conduct of Life*, p. 159.

the essay, "beauty has a moral element in it, and I find the antique sculpture as ethical as Marcus Antoninus; and the beauty ever in proportion to the depth of thought."[143] First Emerson contrasts grace as the expression, presumably, of moral character, to beauty, but then he makes grace an element of beauty, thereby suggesting that the highest form of beauty is that which incorporates all three aspects of surface, form, and grace. In the end, then, Emerson's conception of the highest form of beauty is not far from Kant's conception of the "ideal" of beauty. But although it is only in connection with this third aspect of beauty that Emerson mentions passion as part of our response to beauty at all, thus potentially opening his analysis up to that aspect of aesthetic experience that Kant had struggled hard to exclude from his own account but that others such as Kames and among the Romantics both Wordsworth and Shelley had clearly recognized, at the same time Emerson also emphasizes yet again the essentially intellectualist cast of his conception of beauty: even the "moral element" is "depth of thought" rather than, for example, resolve or commitment. Even when he recognizes multiple aspects or layers of beauty, then, Emerson does not so clearly adopt multiple approaches to beauty: for him, beauty is above all the appearance of truth, of course in his particular Transcendentalist sense, and neither emotional impact nor the free play of the imagination are central to his account.

The long opening chapter of Emerson's final book, *Letters and Social Aims* of 1875, is titled "Poetry and Imagination," and through its emphasis on the latter might suggest a departure from the emphasis on both natural and artistic beauty as a vehicle of truth that is so prominent in his earlier work. But it is not clear when this material was actually written: after a fire at his home in 1872 precipitated his intellectual decline, this book was compiled out of older material by a friend, James Elliott Cabot, with general supervision but only minor intervention by Emerson, and Cabot stated that most of the essays in the volume, not excepting "Poetry and Imagination," were "written in great part long before,"[144] so the essay may have been contemporaneous with Emerson's earlier, not later, work. And be that as it may, while the essay does celebrate the centrality of imagination in successful poetry, presumably in the arts more generally, it also introduces a distinction, much like Coleridge's distinction, between imagination and mere "fancy" that treats the latter as

[143] Emerson, "Beauty," *The Conduct of Life*, p. 163.
[144] Ralph Waldo Emerson, *Letters and Social Aims*, in *The Complete Works of Ralph Waldo Emerson*, Vol. III, ed. Edward Waldo Emerson (Boston: Houghton Mifflin, 1904), Preface to First Edition, p. xi.

superficial play, or play with surfaces, and the former as "perception ... of a real relation between a thought and some material fact." The foremost requirement for poets and their poetry is therefore "veracity,"[145] and thus Emerson's approach to art even in this essay remains fundamentally cognitivist.

There may be a departure from Emerson's Schellingian Transcendentalism of forty years earlier in the fact that Emerson does not begin this essay by reasserting the essential identity of nature and human consciousness or thought, but instead begins from the premise that the human mind "projects" its thoughts on to nature, and uses natural objects as "symbols" of its own states. Emerson begins the section subtitled "Poetry" thus:

> The primary use of a fact is low; the secondary use, as it is a figure or illustration of my thought, is the real worth. First the fact, second its impression, or what I think of it. Hence Nature is called "a kind of adulterated reason." Seas, forests, metals, diamonds and fossils interest the eye, but 't is only with some preparatory or predicting charm. Their value to the intellect appears only when I hear their meaning made plain in the spiritual truth they cover. The mind, penetrated with its sentiments or its thoughts, projects it outward on whatever it beholds.[146]

In the last sentence of this passage, Emerson refers to both "sentiments" and "thoughts," which might suggest that poetry, or art more generally, expresses the emotions as well as the cognitions of artists and projects them on to natural objects that are then used as symbols or "imaginative expressions"[147] of those mental states, and that art can in turn arouse emotional impact as well as knowledge of truth in its audience. Such an emphasis on emotional impact would be a departure from Emerson's earlier work. But the singular "it" in the final clause would seem to refer back to the singular "meaning" in the previous sentence, and the term "meaning" could suggest that Emerson is still primarily thinking of the cognitive content of art as what is expressed or symbolized through the images of objects in nature, thus still thinking primarily of art as a vehicle of truth, although he is now emphasizing that nature is more the means for artistic expression than its object. In any case, as he continues he refers primarily to the meaning or truth expressed by art, for example when he says that "When some familiar truth or fact appears

---

[145] Emerson, "Poetry and Imagination," *Letters and Social Aims*, p. 29.
[146] Emerson, "Poetry and Imagination," *Letters and Social Aims*, p. 11.
[147] Emerson, "Poetry and Imagination," *Letters and Social Aims*, p. 12.

in a new dress, mounted as on a fine horse, equipped with a grand pair of ballooning wings, we can [not] enough testify our surprise and pleasure."[148] Thus when he adds that "Vivacity of expression" is the "high gift" of the poet and that "There is no more welcome gift to men than a new symbol," it is the vivacity or symbolization of "truth or fact," though truth about human thought rather than about nature outside of human beings, that he is talking about.

Having reaffirmed his commitment to truth as the content of art, Emerson does emphasize the creative character of imagination in the expression of such truth. He says that "All thinking is analogizing, and it is the use of life to learn metonymy. The endless passing of one element into new forms, the incessant metamorphosis, explains the rank which the imagination holds in our catalogue of mental powers."[149] Further, the "essential mark" of poetry "is that it betrays in every word instant activity of the mind, shown in new uses of every fact and image, in preternatural quickness or perception of relations."[150] But just as he stops short of elevating the emotional impact of art to an aspect of its creation or experience of equal importance to the discovery and communication of truth, likewise he stops short of recognizing sheer pleasure in the activity of the imagination as an aspect of art and our experience of it equal in importance to insight. He comes close, saying that "The act of imagination is ever attended by pure delight,"[151] but then draws back, next saying that "Whilst common sense looks at things or visible Nature as real and final facts, poetry, or the imagination which dictates it, is a second sight, looking through these, and using them as types or words for thoughts which they signify."[152] The cognitive content of art remains of paramount importance, not one of two or three equally important aspects. And thus Emerson's discussion of imagination culminates with his contrast between imagination and mere fancy, already mentioned:

> Imagination is central; fancy, superficial. Fancy relates to surface, in which a great part of life lies.... Fancy is a wilful, imagination a spontaneous act; fancy, a play as with dolls and puppets which we choose to call men and women; imagination, a perception and affirming of a real relation between a thought and some material fact. Fancy amuses; imagination expands and

---

[148] Emerson, "Poetry and Imagination," *Letters and Social Aims*, pp. 12–13.
[149] Emerson, "Poetry and Imagination," *Letters and Social Aims*, p. 15.
[150] Emerson, "Poetry and Imagination," *Letters and Social Aims*, p. 17.
[151] Emerson, "Poetry and Imagination," *Letters and Social Aims*, p. 18.
[152] Emerson, "Poetry and Imagination," *Letters and Social Aims*, p. 19.

exalts us. Fancy joins by accidental resemblance, surprises and amuses the idle, but is silent in the presence of great passion and action.[153]

Perhaps it would be fair to say that in this passage Emerson does recognize the importance of passion as well as true thought in art, although his view certainly seems to be that passion is aroused by true thought: imagination expands and exalts us by expressing a real relation between thought and some material fact. But, although there is no suggestion that Emerson has Kant in mind in this passage, he tacitly rejects Kant's idea that free play is central to the role of imagination in the creation and appreciation of art, and instead treats play like child's play, mere play with dolls and puppets. As we shall subsequently see, this interpretation of play was to become characteristic of many professional philosophers and aestheticians in the late nineteenth century and well into the twentieth century, and to constitute a continuing obstacle to the recognition that the free play of the imagination within but also with the limits of understanding and reason should count as at least one of the central elements of aesthetic experience.

Jean Paul, Coleridge, and Emerson remained largely in the shadow of Coleridge's conception of art as the organon of philosophy, a source of metaphysical insight, while Wordsworth and Shelley began from this premise, transmitted to them by Coleridge, but intertwined the emotional impact of art, or their particular art of poetry, with its truth; only Mill drew a strong contrast between truth and emotional impact and assigned art the task of producing only the latter. We can now turn from these figures to another philosopher who, also influenced by Schelling although he hated to admit it, likewise developed a highly intellectualistic account of aesthetic experience, and who did not merely ignore the passions in his account of such experience but rather argued that aesthetic experience can liberate us from the dolorous effects of passion. This philosopher is, of course, Arthur Schopenhauer.

---

[153] Emerson, "Poetry and Imagination," *Letters and Social Aims*, pp. 28–9.

3

The High Tide of Idealism

Schopenhauer, Hegel, and Schleiermacher

We have just seen that while Schelling's cognitivist approach to aesthetics excluded any place for the free play of the imagination and had little room for the emotional impact of art, and at least some of those within his penumbra, such as Emerson, retained his cognitivist approach, at least some others among the wide range of thinkers and poets to whom Schelling's influence was communicated by Coleridge, including Wordsworth, Shelley, and Mill, gradually found ways to combine emotion with truth in their conceptions of aesthetic experience. Now we return to the next two leading philosophers of German Idealism – Arthur Schopenhauer, almost as precocious as Schelling, and Hegel, older but slower to publish – and see that for all their differences they both accepted a strictly cognitivist approach to aesthetics and were as hostile as Kant himself had been to the emotional impact of art. In the final section of this chapter, we will see that one of their contemporaries in Berlin, the theologian Schleiermacher, took a less reductive approach to aesthetics, but his course on the subject did not have an immediate effect on the field. Instead, Hegel's aesthetics would dominate the subject in Germany for at least three decades following his death in 1830, while after that Schopenhauer's approach would influence not only the further development of aesthetics itself but a wide range of creative artists across Europe.

1. SCHOPENHAUER

Arthur Schopenhauer (1788–1860) generally expressed nothing but contempt for the trio of Fichte, Schelling, and Hegel, but at one point he conceded that "Schelling had once said 'willing is original and primary being.'"[1] It is difficult to imagine that Schopenhauer's own transformation of Kant's epistemology, metaphysics, and aesthetics into his theory that beauty in general and art in particular gives us cognition of the different "Platonic ideas" or types of "objectification" of the nonrational will as the ground of all reality, and by that very cognition of the general forms of the expression of the will distracts us from the incessant demands of our own particular wills, thereby at least temporarily bringing peace into our conflicted existence, was not profoundly influenced by Schelling's identification of the will as the ground of all being in the *Essence of Human Freedom*. But defending that historical conjecture will not be my task in this chapter. Rather, what will be argued here is that Schopenhauer exploits many of the central themes of Kant's aesthetics, notably Kant's concepts of disinterestedness, of genius, and of aesthetic ideas, but, like Schelling, transforms Kant's theory of the free play of our cognitive powers, even with aesthetic ideas, into a strictly cognitivist theory of the content of aesthetic experience – a transformation signaled by his use of the expression "Platonic ideas" instead of "aesthetic ideas" – and transforms Kant's theory of the positive pleasure of such free play into a theory of negative pleasure at our release from the incessant demands of our particular wills through the cognition of the general forms of the expression of the will in aesthetic experience. Unlike Schelling, however, Schopenhauer does at least sometimes recognize a positive rather than merely negative pleasure in aesthetic cognition, but this is a pleasure in cognition itself, and there is no hint in Schopenhauer that we take pleasure in the experience of any other emotions – the point of the experience of beauty is simply to free us from all other emotions. Thus Schopenhauer only barely hints at Kant's synthesis of the aesthetics of truth and the aesthetics of play, and excludes the emotional impact of art from his conception of aesthetic experience even more rigorously than Kant had done: for Schopenhauer, allowing emotion into aesthetic experience would not merely violate good taste, but would undermine the very point of this experience.

Schopenhauer was the son of a wealthy merchant from the German Hanseatic trading city of Danzig (present-day Polish Gdansk), who sent him to England to study business, but conveniently died and left the young man enough money to devote himself to philosophy without regular employment for the rest of his life. Free to pursue his own interests,

---

[1] Schopenhauer, "Fragments for the History of Philosophy," in *Parerga and Paralipomena*, trans. E.F.J. Payne (Oxford: Clarendon Press, 1974), vol. I, p. 132.

Schopenhauer first studied medicine and physiology at Göttingen – for an idealist, there would always be an unusual emphasis upon the physicality of the human condition in his philosophy – and then turned back to philosophy under the tutelage of the skeptical philosopher Gottlob Ernst Schulze (1761–1833) (known as "Anesidemus" after the title of his anonymous criticism of Kant through the vehicle of Kant's disciple Karl Leonhard Reinhold, a work published in 1792). Schopenhauer then went to Berlin to hear Fichte, who disappointed him, although his study of Plato under Scheiermacher (discussed later in this chapter) also put a permanent mark upon his work. Schopenhauer received his doctorate for his work *On the Fourfold Root of the Principle of Sufficient Reason* from Jena in 1813, too late to have heard Schelling in person, who had left for Würzburg and then Munich a decade earlier. Upon the publication of his *magnum opus*, *The World as Will and Representation* (late 1818, dated 1819, substantially expanded in 1844), Schopenhauer offered lectures as a *Privatdozent* at the university in Berlin. He offered them at the same time as Hegel's lectures, so attendance was very poor, but Schopenhauer persisted in announcing his lectures as long as he remained in Berlin, adding Hegel as well as Fichte to his list of enemies. He left Berlin for Frankfurt am Main during the cholera epidemic of 1831 (which would claim Hegel as one of its victims). He lived the life of a private scholar in Frankfurt, at first largely ignored, but eventually he enjoyed renown as *The World as Will and Representation* was taken up in the wave of pessimism that swept European intellectuals after the failed liberal revolutions of 1848. Schopenhauer became a seminal figure for many European intellectuals and writers, artists, and musicians, such as Friedrich Nietzsche, Richard Wagner, Thomas Mann, and Samuel Beckett, throughout the late nineteenth century and into the twentieth.[2]

---

[2] The literature on Schopenhauer is extensive. Two biographies are Rüdiger Safranski, *Schopenhauer and the Wild Years of Philosophy*, trans. Ewald Osers (Cambridge, Mass.: Harvard University Press, 1989), and David E. Cartwright, *Schopenhauer: A Biography* (Cambridge: Cambridge University Press. 2010). Most general treatments of Schopenhauer's philosophy include a treatment of his aesthetics: some of these are Georg Simmel, *Schopenhauer and Nietzsche* (1907), trans. Helmut Loiskandl, Deena Weinstein, and Michael Weinstein (Amherst: University of Massachusetts Press, 1986), ch. 5; Patrick Gardiner, *Schopenhauer* (Harmondsworth: Penguin Books, 1963), ch. 5; D.W. Hamlyn, *Schopenhauer* (London: Routledge & Kegan Paul, 1980), ch. 6; Ulrich Pothast, *Die eigentliche metaphysische Tätigkeit: Über Schopenhauers Ästhetik und ihre Anwendung durch Samuel Beckett* (Frankfurt am Main: Suhrkamp Verlag, 1982); Bryan Magee, *The Philosophy of Schopenhauer* (Oxford: Clarendon Press, 1983), ch. 8; Christopher Janaway, *Schopenhauer* (Oxford: Oxford University Press, 1994), ch. 6; Dale Jacquette, *The Philosophy of Schopenhauer* (Montreal and Kingston: McGill-Queen's University Press, 2005), ch. 5; and Julian Young, *Schopenhauer* (London: Routledge,

The general outlines of Schopenhauer's philosophy are much more widely known than those of Schelling's, and can be presented more briefly here. According to Schopenhauer, the general structures of conscious human thought – above all, the organization of our experience into space, time, causal relations among events, and intentional relations between desires and actions – are structures imposed by our own minds on the effects of an otherwise unknown substratum of reality on our own underlying reality. In this position, which the twenty-five-year-old already defended in *On the Fourfold Root of the Principle of Sufficient Reason*, Schopenhauer took himself to be the legitimate heir of Kant. Unlike Kant, however, in his *magnum opus*, The World as Will and Representation (Book I recapitulates this doctrine), Schopenhauer insisted that we could characterize the underlying reality that acts upon us and that acts within us as nonrational *will*; for Kant, we could infer that our own underlying reality is will, but a rational will or at least a will capable of rationality, yet we could make no inference at all about what underlies the rest of nature. Schopenhauer based this assertion upon the claims that we have a double knowledge of ourselves, through the cognitive representation in which our own bodies are like everything else in the world and through voluntary action in which we have a unique relation to our own bodies; that we recognize the latter to be more fundamental than the former, even though the former contains all the structures we think of as rational; and that we can extend this view to all of reality beyond ourselves. Thus in Book II of the *World as Will and Representation*, he writes:

> Whereas in the first book we were reluctantly forced to declare our own body to be mere representation of the knowing subject, like all other objects

---

2005), ch. 5 and 6. Papers on Schopenhauer's aesthetics can be found in Dale Jacquette, editor, *Schopenhauer, Philosophy, and the Arts* (Cambridge: Cambridge University Press, 1996); Günter Baum and Dieter Birnbacher, editors, *Schopenhauer und die Künste* (Göttingen: Wallstein Verlag, 2005); and Alex Neill and Christopher Janaway, editors, *Better Consciousness: Schopenhauer's Philosophy of Value* (Chichester: Wiley-Blackwell, 2009). Christopher Janaway, editor, *The Cambridge Companion to Schopenhauer* (Cambridge: Cambridge University Press, 1999), includes Cheryl Foster, "Ideas and Imagination: Schopenhauer on the Proper Foundation of Art," pp. 213–51, and Martha C. Nussbaum, "Nietzsche, Schopenhauer, and Dionyus," pp. 344–74. See also Michael Podro, *The Manifold in Perception: Theories of Art from Kant to Hildebrand* (Oxford: Clarendora Press, 1972). ch. VII; Schmidt, *Genie-Gedankens*, pp. 467–76; Lucien Krukowski, *Aesthetic Legacies* (Philadelphia: Temple University Press, 1992), ch. 2 and 5; Brigitte Scheer, *Einführung in die philosophische Ästhetik* (Darmstadt: Wissenschaftliche Buchgesellschaft, 1997), pp. 142–52; Schaeffer, *Art of the Modern Age*, pp. 182–208; Bowie, *Aesthetics and Subjectivity*, pp. 271–80; Feger, *Poetische Vernunft*, pp. 461–85; and Alexander Nehamas, *Only a Promise of Happiness: The Place of Beauty in a World of Art* (Princeton: Princeton University Press, 2007), pp. 5–13.

of this world of perception, it has now become clear to us that something in the consciousness of everyone distinguishes the representation of his own body from all others that are in other respects quite like it. This is that the body occurs in consciousness in quite another way, *toto genere* different, that is denoted by the word *will*. It is just this double knowledge of our own body which gives us information ... about what it is, not as representation, but as something over and above this, and hence what it is *in itself*.[3]

Then he goes on to state that we can use this "double knowledge" as the "key to the inner being of every phenomenon in nature":

> We shall judge all objects which are not in our own body ... according to the analogy of this body. We shall therefore assume that as, on the one hand, they are representation, just like our body ... so on the other hand, if we set aside their existence as the subject's representation, what still remains over must, according to its inner nature, be the same as what in ourselves we call *will*. If, therefore, the material world is to be something more than our mere representation, we must say that, besides being the representation, and hence in itself and of its inmost nature, it is what we find immediately in ourselves as will.[4]

Now it may seem natural to insist that once Schopenhauer has accepted Kant's distinction between representation or things as they appear and those things as they are in themselves, it is completely illegitimate of him to make any further claims about the real nature of the in-itself. But in fact Kant was willing to make a claim about the determinate nature of the in itself, at least about the human self as it is in itself, namely that the otherwise indeterminate concept of our real self can be made determinate through the concept of a rational will governed by the moral law.[5] Schopenhauer's departure from Kant lies not in his willingness to make any claim at all about the noumenal, but in the fact that he follows Schelling in insisting that our own underlying reality and by extension that of the rest of nature is thoroughly nonrational will, and that rationality is only one more superficial feature of appearance like spatiality, temporality, and causality which does not characterize will at its deepest

---

[3] Translations from Arthur Schopenhauer, *The World as Will and Representation* (*WWR*), trans. E.F.J. Payne, 2 vols. (Indian Hills, Colo.: Falcon's Wing Press, 1958), vol. I, §19, p. 103. All further citations from *WWR* will be from Volume I, the original portion of the work published in 1818 (dated 1819), so the reference to the volume will be omitted from subsequent notes.
[4] Schopenhauer, *WWR*, §19, p. 105.
[5] See Kant, *Groundwork for the Metaphysics of Morals*, section III, 4:452, and *Critique of Practical Reason*, 5:49, in *Practical Philosophy*, pp. 99, 179.

level. "Every person invariably has purposes and motives by which he guides his conduct; and he is always able to give an account of his particular actions. But if he were asked why he wills generally, or why in general he wills to exist, he would have no answer; indeed, the question would seem to him absurd. This would really be the expression of his consciousness that he himself is nothing but will."[6] For Schopenhauer, further, the nonrational nature of the will means that it never leads to a feeling of pleasure in the realization of our potential for rationality, what Kant called "contentment" or "moral feeling,"[7] but only to an endless striving that has no stable, unconditionally valuable goal and that therefore can never be completely satisfied. "Absence of all aim, of all limits, belongs to the essential nature of the will in itself, which is an endless striving ... human endeavours and desires ... buoy us up with the vain hope that their fulfillment is always the final goal of willing. But as soon as they are attained, they no longer look the same, and so are soon forgotten ... and are really, although not admittedly, always laid aside as vanished illusions."[8] The nature of the will that is the underlying reality of both ourselves and everything else in nature means that we are condemned to a painful cycle of frustration in which even the realization of our desires turns out to be nothing but the source of another unfulfilled desire, a cycle that would be ended by nothing but death. The will and rationality that for Schelling must be *able* to come apart in order to mark our difference from God *must* come apart for Schopenhauer, perhaps because for him there is no God to guarantee even the possibility of the reunion of these two contrary principles.

The first step of Schopenhauer's aesthetics, however, is to transform Kant's account of disinterestedness as a characteristic of aesthetic experience that allows us to make intersubjectively valid judgments of taste into the negative pleasure of at least a temporary respite from this cycle of frustration that is afforded by the experience of beauty. Schopenhauer's thought, presented in Book III of *The World as Will and Representation*, is that ordinarily we set ourselves on the possession of particular objects that we expect to fulfill desires, but that it is possible to so immerse ourselves in the perception of an object that we can actually forget our

---

[6] Schopenhauer, *WWR*, §29, p. 163.
[7] See *Critique of Practical Reason*, 5:118, and *Metaphysics of Morals*, Doctrine of Virtue, Introduction, section XII.a, 6:399, in *Practical Philosophy*, pp.528.
[8] Schopenhauer, *WWR*, §29, p. 164.

inevitably unsatisfying desire to possess or consume it, at least for a while. In such a state we

> devote the whole power of our mind to perception ... and let our whole consciousness be filled by the calm contemplation of the natural object actually present, whether it be a landscape, a tree, a rock, a crag, a building, or anything else. We *lose* ourselves entirely in this object ...; we forget our individuality, our will, and continue to exist only as pure subject, as clear mirror of the object.... Thus at the same time, the person who is involved in this perception is no longer an individual, for in such perception the individual has lost himself; he is *pure* will-less, painless, timeless *subject of knowledge.*[9]

This state of relief from the pain of particularized desire, clearly a negative form of pleasure, is achieved by perception, a form of cognition itself rather than a play with cognitive powers, although Schopenhauer's initial suggestion that it is achieved through the perception of particulars *qua* particulars is misleading; it is achieved through the cognition of the general form of the kind of expression of the underlying reality of will that the particular object is: "If, therefore, the object has to such an extent passed out of all relation to something outside it, and the subject has passed out of all relation to the will, what is thus known is no longer the individual thing as such, but the *Idea*, the eternal form, the immediate objectivity of the will at this grade."[10] The disinterested pleasure of Kant's free play of our cognitive powers with aesthetic ideas is transformed into relief at the liberation of the will from its unsatisfiable obsession with particulars through the cognition of the general forms or Platonic ideas of the expression of the will itself in aesthetic experience.

In this theory, Schopenhauer combines the idea that beauty in general, not just art, has cognitive content, not with Kant's idea of free play, as Kant had in his own theory of aesthetic ideas, but rather with Kant's hostility to emotion in aesthetic experience, and ends up with the view that aesthetic experience as a form of cognition frees us from all emotion other than our sense of relief at being so freed (which may be accompanied, as he later concedes, with a positive pleasure in knowing). The cognitive character of Schopenhauer's theory of ideas is further apparent in his specific theory of art, including his theory of genius as the source of art, his comments about the reception of art, and his classification of the arts as types of representations of the ideas – until he reaches music,

---

[9] Schopenhauer, *WWR*, §34, pp. 178–9.
[10] Schopenhauer, *WWR*, §34, p. 179.

which represents the will itself rather than any of its objectifications. Following his initial introduction of the theory of ideas as the objects of timeless, painless, will-less contemplation, Schopenhauer illustrates the contrast between the "different grades at which" the "objectivity" of the "will as thing-in-itself" appears, "i.e., the Ideas themselves, from the mere phenomenon of the Ideas in the form of the principle of sufficient reason, the restricted method of knowledge of individuals,"[11] with examples drawn from nature: the shape of particular clouds at particular moments is mere phenomenon, but the very fact that "as elastic vapour they are pressed together, driven off, spread out, and torn apart by the force of the wind" shows that "this is their nature, this is the essence of the forces that are objectified in them, this is the Idea."[12] (We have to take the identification of physical forces of the sort that are mentioned as the phenomenal expression or objectification of a thing-in-itself that is *will* as a leap of metaphysical faith: there can be no further evidence for it than the experience of will in our own cases that Schopenhauer earlier mentioned.) But in the ensuing sections, Schopenhauer makes it clear that the primary way in which we encounter Ideas and enjoy the benefits of contemplating them is through art, and here he makes clear the cognitive character of art and of our response to it:

> What kind of knowledge is it that considers what continues to exist outside and independently of all relations ... the true content of phenomena ... known with equal truth for all time, in a word, the *Ideas* that are the immediate and adequate objectivity of the thing-in-itself, of the will? It is *art*, the work of genius. It repeats the eternal ideas apprehended through pure contemplation, the essential and abiding element in all the phenomena of the world. According to the material in which it repeats, it is sculpture, painting, poetry, or music. Its only source is knowledge of the Ideas; its sole aim is communication of this knowledge.[13]

While natural things might occasionally suggest their own Ideas and dispose us toward contemplation, art actively and therefore presumably more reliably and frequently "plucks the object of its contemplation from the stream of the world's course, and holds it isolated before it."

Schopenhauer accordingly describes genius, the ability to create art, in strictly cognitive terms. Genius consists in the exceptional capacity for the recognition of timeless Ideas through the particularities of phenomena and in the exceptional capacity for the communication of such

---

[11] Schopenhauer, *WWR*, §35, p. 181.
[12] Schopenhauer, *WWR*, §35, p. 182.
[13] Schopenhauer, *WWR*, §36, pp. 184–5.

cognition. First, the heightened capacity for cognition: "Only through the pure contemplation ... which becomes absorbed entirely in the object, are the Ideas comprehended; and the nature of *genius* consists precisely in the preeminent ability for such contemplation ... the *gift of genius* is nothing but the most complete *objectivity*, i.e., the objective tendency of the mind ... Accordingly, genius is the capacity to remain in a state of pure perception, to lose oneself in perception." And "For genius to appear in an individual, it is as if a measure of the power of knowledge must have fallen to his lot far exceeding that required for the service of an individual will."[14] Second, the exceptional capacity for the communication of such cognition: while all people must have the capacity to contemplate the Ideas and through that contemplation to obtain relief from the demands of their will to some degree, otherwise the effect of art would be entirely lost on them, most people have the capacity to recognize or discover ideas to a "lesser and different degree" than the genius; and the genius in turn excels the rest of mankind not merely in the capacity to have such ideas but also in the capacity to retain them and convey them through a "voluntary and intentional work, such repetition being the work of art. "Through this he communicates to others the Idea he has grasped." The gift of the genius is the twofold gift of cognition and communication, although the latter can to some extent be acquired: "that he knows the essential in things which lies outside all relations, is the gift of genius and is inborn; but that he is able to lend us this gift, to let us see with his eyes, is acquired, and is the technical side of art."[15] The key point is not so much whether one aspect of genius is more innate than the other, however, but that it has these two aspects. In this regard, the structure of Schopenhauer's analysis of genius replicates that of Kant's, with the key difference that the element of play is missing from the experience of both the genius and the audience. For Kant, genius consisted in the ability to create a free play of the imagination with an idea and then to communicate that to the audience in a way that would allow the audience not just to apprehend the content of the artist's idea but also to enjoy a free play of their mental powers in some way analogous to but not fully determined by the free play of the artist – without that, the experience would not be an aesthetic experience for Kant. For Schopenhauer, however, although the genius must be *active* in plucking an idea out of the phenomena, he does not *play* with the idea, but simply

---

[14] Schopenhauer, *WWR*, §35, p. 185.
[15] Schopenhauer, *WWR*, §37, pp. 194–5.

contemplates it, and facilitates the contemplation of it in his audience, by means of which they are both, to some degree or other, transformed into will-less and therefore painless pure subjects of knowledge.

Throughout this cognitivist account, Schopenhauer's theme remains that aesthetic experience offers the negative pleasure of relief, although only momentary, from the incessant frustration of the will. In this regard, his theory remains parallel to Schelling's account of our pleasure in beauty as pleasure in the resolution of the paradox of being, although at least in Schelling's writings prior to the *Essence of Human Freedom*, for example in the apotheosis of art as the instrument and organon of philosophy in the *System of Transcendental Idealism*, there is no suggestion that the pleasure afforded by beauty is only temporary and might need to be supplanted by a moral resolution or attitude of some kind, as Schopenhauer will ultimately argue. (This is the subject of Book IV of the *World as Will and Representation*.) But there is a hint in Schopenhauer that aesthetic pleasure may have a positive side, a sheer pleasure in knowing that does not presuppose any antecedent frustration from which knowledge offers an escape. In §38 of *The World as Will and Representation*, Schopenhauer says that there are "*two inseparable constituent parts*" in the "aesthetic method of consideration," namely "knowledge of the object not as individual thing, but as Platonic *Idea* ...; and the self-consciousness of the knower, not as individual, but as *pure, will-less subject of knowledge*," and he then adds that the pleasure produced by contemplation of an aesthetic object arises sometimes more from one of these sources than the other.[16] Here he is alluding to his theory, again similar to Schelling's, that in the case of beauty the Idea presents itself to us (or at least to the genius) as if it were immediately in the object, whereas in the case of the sublime we are more conscious of a struggle to isolate the Idea out of the experience of the object. In the case of beauty, "that purely objective frame of mind is facilitated and favoured from without by accommodating objects,"[17] whereas in the case of the sublime "that state of pure knowing is obtained first of all by a conscious and violent tearing away from the relations of the same object to the will ... by a free exaltation, accompanied by consciousness, beyond the will and the knowledge related to it."[18] But in the opening paragraph of his discussion of the sublime, Schopenhauer does describe the "subjective part of aesthetic pleasure" as "that pleasure

---

[16] Schopenhauer, *WWR*, §38, pp. 195–6.
[17] Schopenhauer, *WWR*, §38, p. 197.
[18] Schopenhauer, *WWR*, §39, p. 202.

in so far as it is delight in the mere knowledge of perception as such."[19] Whether he intended it thus or not, this remark suggests that we might take pleasure in the contemplation of Ideas even if we did not need to be relieved from frustration by that contemplation. So here Schopenhauer hints at a return to the purely positive account of aesthetic pleasure characteristic of Kant and most other writers, including such contemporaries as Wordsworth, Shelley, and Mill, and to prepare the way for a return to this emphasis in subsequent aesthetics. But even Schopenhauer's suggestion of a positive pleasure in aesthetic experience remains firmly linked to his interpretation of this experience as an exceptional form of cognition rather than a free play with our cognitive powers that is not aimed at actual cognition. And of course there is no hint, as there was in those writers or will be in later writers such as Edward Bullough, that we could take positive pleasure in the experience of emotion as such.

Schopenhauer's theory of art as the genius's vehicle for the repetition and presentation of the Platonic Ideas leads him to a classification of the arts that is in some ways reminiscent of Schelling's detailed classification in the *Philosophy of Art* but that also departs from it in various ways. Schopenhauer's classification begins with architecture as the medium that, insofar as it is considered "merely as a fine art and apart from its provision for useful purposes," brings to "clearer perceptiveness some of those Ideas that are the lowest grades of the will's objectivity," such Ideas as "gravity, cohesion, rigidity, hardness," and so on, "those first, simplest, and dullest visibilities of the will."[20] Schelling, by contrast, began his classification with music, because it works with the most real of the ideal forms of representation, such as rhythm. Schopenhauer then mentions both horticulture and landscape and still-life painting as arts that present the Ideas of the objectification of the will in vegetable life, a form of its objectification that is more advanced than the mechanical forces presented by architecture but is still far from its objectification in human character and action.[21] From these arts, Schopenhauer advances to historical painting and sculpture, which present the outward forms of isolated manifestations of the will in human actions (§§45–49), and then to poetry, which reveals "that Idea which is the highest grade of the will's objectivity, namely the presentation of man in the connected series of his efforts and actions."[22] His discussion of poetry culminates with his own

---

[19] Schopenhauer, *WWR*, §39, p. 200.
[20] Schopenhauer, *WWR*, §43, p. 214.
[21] Schopenhauer, *WWR*, §44, pp. 218–19.
[22] Schopenhauer, *WWR*, §51, p. 244.

version of the conventional wisdom that tragedy is the "summit of poetic art": for Schopenhauer this is so because tragedy presents more effectively than any other art form "The unspeakable pain, the wretchedness and misery of mankind, the triumph of wickedness, the scornful mastery of chance, and the irretrievable fall of the just and the innocent."[23] Finally, Schopenhauer turns to music, which is for him the highest rather than the lowest of the arts, because it "is by no means like the other arts, namely a copy of the Ideas, but [is] a *copy of the will itself,* the objectivity of which are the Ideas. For this reason the effect of music is so very much more powerful and penetrating than is that of the other arts, for these others speak only of the shadow, but music of the essence."[24] Music is thus on a par with the other manifestations of the will rather than with the other arts as copies of the manifestations of the will; music is the art that crosses the Platonic barrier between art and other ordinary things by being a copy of reality itself rather than a copy of a copy of reality itself. From this point of view, Schopenhauer then interprets the different aspects of music as "copies" of different aspects of the will itself rather than of its objectifications: the deepest tones of harmony are a manifestation of inorganic forces; in "the whole of the ripienos ... between the bass and the leading voice singing the melody," he recognizes "the whole gradation of the Ideas in which the will objectifies itself," and finally in melody he recognizes "the highest grade of the will's objectification, the intellectual life and endeavour of man."[25]

Schopenhauer's accounts of both tragedy and music seem to present a paradox, indeed a version of the traditional paradox of tragedy: the contemplation of beauty, especially artistic beauty, is supposed to present us with timeless ideas the contemplation of which will release us from the frustration of our time-bound wills; but tragedy presents us with such affecting representations of human suffering, and music supposedly presents the will and all of its indifference to our own concerns to us with even greater directness, that it is difficult to see how we can take pleasure in these arts, except perhaps to the limited extent that Schopenhauer recognizes a positive pleasure in cognition as such – a form of pleasure, however, which he hardly emphasizes and does not seem adequate to account for the profundity of our pleasure in these arts. Schopenhauer recognizes the threat of this paradox and confronts it directly in his

---

[23] Schopenhauer, *WWR,* §51, p. 253.
[24] Schopenhauer, *WWR,* §52, p. 257.
[25] Schopenhauer, *WWR,* §52, pp. 258–9.

discussion of music. He writes that music "never expresses the phenomenon, but only the inner nature, the in-itself, of every phenomenon, the will itself."

> Therefore music does not express this or that particular gaiety and definite pleasure, this or that affliction, pain, sorrow, horror, gaiety, merriment, or peace of mind, but joy, pain, sorrow, horror, gaiety, merriment, peace of mind *themselves*, to a certain extent in the abstract, their essential nature, without any accessories, and so also without the motives for them.[26]

Schopenhauer's thought is that contemplation of the universal ideas always turns our attention away from the frustrating particularities of our personal situations, even when those universal ideas are themselves the ideas of pain, suffering, and so on. "It is just this universality" that Schopenhauer ascribes uniquely to music, although one would think that it could be achieved by tragedy as well, "that gives it that high value as the panacea of all our sorrows."[27] Music "reproduces all the emotions of our innermost being, but entirely without reality and remote from its pain."[28]

Schopenhauer's solution to what threatens to be the greatest paradox for art depends entirely on his theory of the redemptive power of the contemplation of universals, and thus confirms the thoroughly cognitivist and anti-emotional character of his aesthetic theory: knowledge of the essence even of our own emotions frees us from those emotions. He has transformed Kant's idea of the disinterestedness of aesthetic judgment into the idea of a literal release from painful self-interest through cognition, Kant's conception of the aesthetic ideas as that with which the mind plays in art into that which the mind knows in art, and Kant's conception of the genius as the one who can both more freely play with ideas than others yet communicate a sense of that free play to others into the conception of one who knows more readily than others and can communicate that knowledge and its ensuing benefit to others. Like Schelling, Schopenhauer has disrupted Kant's synthesis of the ancient idea of aesthetic experience as a form of knowledge and the novel idea of aesthetic experience as the free play of our mental powers and turned it back into the traditional theory of aesthetic experience as a heightened form of cognition alone, although, again like Schelling, his account of the cognition in aesthetic experience naturally reflects the innovations in his

---

[26] Schopenhauer, *WWR*, §52, p. 260.
[27] Schopenhauer, *WWR*, §52, p. 262.
[28] Schopenhauer, *WWR*, §52, p. 262.

account of cognition itself; and even more clearly than Schelling he has used his cognitivist account of aesthetics to reject the emotional impact of art. The strictly cognitivist approach to aesthetics would be continued by Hegel, who first lectured on aesthetics in Berlin the year after *The World as Will and Representation* was published.

2. HEGEL

In 1823, Georg Wilhelm Friedrich Hegel, professor of philosophy at the University of Berlin, concluded his popular lectures on the philosophy of art with the following statement:

> Art in its seriousness is for us something that is past. For us other forms are necessary in order to make the divine into an object. We require thinking. But art is an essential manner of the representation of the divine, and we must understand this form. It does not have as its object the agreeable nor subjective skillfulness. Philosophy has to consider what is truthful in art.[29]

The next time Hegel gave the course, which he then entitled "Philosophy of Art or Aesthetics," on the first day he said that "the highest determination of art is in its entirety something that is past for us ... the special representation [that is] art no longer has the immediacy for us that it had at the time of its greatest blossoming."[30] Hegel did not make these statements because he believed that for some contingent reason the fine arts of his time had all lost the creativity that they had enjoyed at earlier times. He certainly could not have believed that on any empirical grounds, for he grew up and lived in the German-speaking world that had produced the music of Mozart, Haydn and Beethoven, the poems, plays, and novels of Goethe and Schiller, the paintings of Caspar David Friedrich and the architecture of Karl Friedrich Schinkel, accomplishments that two centuries later still stand among the greatest moments in the history of German art and in some cases among the greatest of modern Western art. If Hegel had thought that art was now something of the past on any empirical grounds, he would have been a very poor critic. But Hegel was not making a contingent claim on empirical grounds; he

---

[29] Georg Wilhelm Friedrich Hegel, *Vorlesungen über die Philosophie der Kunst*, ed. Annemarie Gethmann-Siefert (Darmstadt: Wissenschaftlichebuchgesellschaft, 2003); hereafter *Lectures 1823*.

[30] Georg Wilhelm Friedrich Hegel, *Philosophie der Kunst oder Ästhetik. Nach Hegel. Im Sommer 1826 Mitschrift Friedrich Carl Hermann Victor von Kehler*, ed. Annemarie Gethmann-Siefert und Bernadette Collenberg-Plotnikov (Munich: Wilhelm Fink Verlag, 2004), hereafter *Lectures 1826*.

was asserting what he took to be a metaphysical necessity. He made this claim because he took art to be a form of cognition, one that is necessary in the development of cognition but also one that is ultimately inadequate for the complete realization of cognition and therefore ultimately has only historical significance as a stage in the development of cognition. As he put it himself in his *Encyclopedia of the Philosophical Sciences*, the handbook to his philosophical system as a whole, "Fine art is only a stage in liberation, not the highest liberation itself. – The true objectivity, which is now in the element of *thinking*, the element in which alone the pure spirit is for the spirit, in which liberation is joined with reverence, is lacking in the sensibly-beautiful of the work of art."[31] Nor did Hegel think that the inevitably superseded cognitive significance of art could be compensated for by an enduring pleasure in the free play of our mental powers with the work of art, independently of its cognitive content: he contemptuously rejected the "liveliness" of the experience of art as a mere "triviality," and explicitly rejected Kant's theory that the free play of our cognitive powers is the essence of all aesthetic experience and free play with ideas the essence of the experience of fine art. In Hegel's view, that art should in general "have the purpose of awakening agreeable sentiments through lively representations is something indeterminate, and agreeable sentiment ... something trivial,"[32] while Kant's specific theory that "The beautiful induces a free play of the powers of imagination," which "in the beautiful are not subjected to an abstract rule but appear to be operating freely" reduces aesthetic experience to something that "the artist has produced contingently and as a matter of luck ... as if were not in fact that which is true."[33]

As already suggested, Hegel also rejects the idea that it is a fundamental aim of art to arouse our emotions or expose us to the range of human emotions. After rejecting the idea that art aims to imitate nature, on the ground that this would be "superfluous," even "a presumptuous game,"[34] Hegel goes on to reject the view that the aim of art

---

[31] Georg Wilhelm Friedrich Hegel, *Enzyklopädie der philosophischen Wissenschaften im Grundrisse* (1830), ed. Wolfgang Bonsiepen and Hans-Christian Lucer, in Hegel, *Gesammelte Werke*, vol. 20 (Hamburg: Felix Meiner Verlag, 1992), §562, p. 548.
[32] *Lectures 1826*, p. 5.
[33] *Lectures 1826*, pp. 17–18.
[34] G.W.F. Hegel, *Aesthetics: Lectures on Fine Art*, trans. T.M. Knox, 2 vols. (Oxford: Clarendon Press, 1975), p. 42. This is a translation of the edition of Hegel's lectures that his student Hotho published in 1835, five years after Hegel's death. For discussion of the relation between this text and the lecture transcriptions thus far cited, see p. 124 below.

is supposed to consist in awakening and vivifying our slumbering feelings, inclinations, and passions of every kind, in filling the heart, in forcing the human being, educated or not, to go through the whole gamut of feelings which the human heart in its inmost and secret recesses can bear, experience, and produce, through what can move and stir the human breast in its depths and manifold possibilities and aspects, and to deliver to feeling and contemplation for its enjoyment whatever the spirit possesses of the essential and lofty in its thinking and in the Idea – the splendour of the noble, the eternal, and true: moreover to make misfortune and misery, evil and guilt intelligible, to make men intimately acquainted with all that is horrible and shocking, as well as with all that is pleasurable and felicitous.[35]

This is of course precisely what a variety of eighteenth-century philosophers from Du Bos to Heydenreich had thought was the aim of art, and that such contemporaries as Wordsworth and Shelley were including among the aims of art just as Hegel was preparing his own lectures. But Hegel rejects this view on the ground that while art does have the "ability to adorn and bring before perception and feeling every possible material," nevertheless, "confronted by such a multiple variety of content, we are at once forced to notice that the different feelings and ideas, which art is supposed to arouse or confirm, counteract one another, contradict and reciprocally cancel one another," indeed, "the more art inspires to contradictory [emotions] the more it increases the contradictory character of feelings and passions and makes us stagger about like Bacchantes."[36] Art has to seek a "higher and inherently more universal end" than the arousal of inevitably contradictory emotions, and this will be a kind of knowledge, but not knowledge about emotions, rather knowledge of something more essential about the nature of reality itself. Although on this point Hegel and Schopenhauer are diametrically opposed, since Schopenhauer, as we have seen, thinks that the fundamental truth about reality is that it is irrational, while for Hegel what is fundamental about reality is that it is rational, Hegel shares with Schopenhauer the inference that "Art by means of its representations, while remaining within the sensuous sphere, liberates man at the same time from the power of sensuousness."[37] He also makes the further inference that since it cannot be the aim of art to arouse emotions, it also cannot be the aim of art to educate or moralize us through the arousal of emotions; if art has any educational role at all, its "aim in teaching could

---

[35] Hegel, *Aesthetics*, p. 46.
[36] Hegel, *Aesthetics*, p. 47; "emotions" inserted in brackets by Knox.
[37] Hegel, *Aesthetics*, p. 49.

only consist in bringing into consciousness, by means of the work of art, an absolutely essential spiritual content."[38] Hegel thus rejects the conception of aesthetic education that had been offered by Heydenreich and Schiller as well as by Wordsworth and Shelley.

Hegel's unequivocal commitment to the aesthetics of truth further leads him to a complete rejection of the aesthetics of play and to a thorough dismissal of the importance of pleasure in our aesthetic experience of art and nature. Although he must have enjoyed many kinds of art in order to have acquired the extensive knowledge of the history of art that he demonstrably possessed, nowhere does he admit that the pleasure we take in art might be a sufficient reason for the importance that we grant it, and he explicitly argues against the importance of the experience of natural beauty, while rejecting the importance of art altogether as anything more than a medium for access to the history of the development of thought. Of course, the conclusions that Hegel draws from his cognitivist theory of art might seem like a *reductio ad absurdum* of this approach and a good argument for the play theory instead.

So far I have referred to Hegel's conception of the cognitive content of art only in the most general terms, as "thinking" or "thought," because the question of what he means by such terms, whether he means *human* thought or something more encompassing of which human thought is only a manifestation, is one of the most delicate and contested questions in Hegel interpretation. It should already be obvious that Hegel's aesthetics cannot be understood apart from his entire philosophical system, so we will need to make at least a few comments about that system and take a stance on this issue before we can consider his aesthetics in any detail. But first, a few words about Hegel's life and works are in order.

Hegel was born in Stuttgart in 1770, thus five years earlier than his friend Schelling and eighteen before his antagonist Schopenhauer.[39] Hegel entered the Tübingen Stift, the training school for ministers in the Duchy of Würtemburg, in 1788, where the precocious Schelling had already started; their age difference would not prevent them from becoming close friends and roommates, however, along with the future poet Friedrich Hölderlin. Hegel had no intention of becoming a minister, however, but unlike Schelling, who began a meteoric academic

---

[38] Hegel, *Aesthetics*, p. 50.
[39] For Hegel's life, see Terry Pinkard, *Hegel: A Biography* (Cambridge: Cambridge University Press, 2000). For Hegel's intellectual development, see H.S. Harris, *Hegel's Development: Toward the Sunlight, 1770–1801* (Oxford: Clarendon Press, 1972) and *Hegel's Development: Night Thoughts, Jena 1801–1806* (Oxford: Clarendon Press, 1983).

career immediately upon graduation from the Stift, Hegel floundered for years before becoming established in an academic career. He initially spent several years as a tutor, and was then invited to Jena in 1801 to lecture as a *Privatdozent* and co-edit a *Critical Journal of Philosophy* with Schelling, who had already been a professor for several years. During this period Hegel published his first significant works, essays on "The Difference between Fichte's and Schelling's System of Philosophy" and "Faith and Knowledge," a critical engagement with Kant's general philosophy, as well as an essay on "Natural Law" in which he first charged that Kant's categorical imperative is an "empty formalism" and set the stage for his own later social and political philosophy. During this period Hegel also worked on his first book, *The Phenomenology of the Spirit*. This was published in 1807 and might have led to a salaried professorship but for the disruption of the German universities (and German life in general) then caused by the French invasion led by Napoleon. Hegel had to take a job first in Bamberg as a newspaper editor (1807) and then (1808) as head of a *Gymnasium* in Nuremberg. The latter job did not prevent him from writing his biggest and most difficult work, the *Science of Logic* (1812–16), which finally earned him a professorship at Heidelberg. Once at Heidelberg, Hegel also published the first version of his *Encyclopedia of Philosophical Sciences* (1817, with further versions following in 1827 and 1830). After only two years at Heidelberg, Hegel was called to Berlin as the successor to Fichte, where he lectured with great renown until his sudden death in 1831. Whether because he was now at last securely established in Berlin, or because of the great demands of his lecturing (at least ten hours a week), or because he expected to have more time to prepare his works for publication, Hegel actually published little during his Berlin years – only his great work in political philosophy, *The Outlines of the Philosophy of Right*, in 1821. However, his devoted students took copious notes of his lectures, and it was on the basis of that material that his lectures on the history of philosophy, the philosophy of religion, and aesthetics were posthumously published.

Hegel lectured on aesthetics once during his Heidelberg years (from which no notes survive), and four times during his Berlin years, in 1821, 1823, 1826, and 1828–29. His student, Heinrich Gustav Hotho, who would himself enjoy a distinguished career first as a professor of aesthetics and then as an art historian and the curator of the engraving collection in Berlin, compiled three stout volumes of Hegel's *Aesthetics: Lectures on Fine Art* from a variety of sources, including his own detailed transcription of Hegel's lectures from 1823. This work, first published in 1835 and lightly revised in 1842, was long the basis for the study of Hegel's aesthetics, having been translated into French as early as 1840–52 and then twice into English, first by F.P.B. Osmaston in 1916–20 and in a far superior version by T.M. Knox in 1975.[40] Until recently, therefore, Hegel's aesthetics has been known through this text. However, the more recent publication of a number of the original lecture notes, especially Hotho's own notes from 1823 and those of F.C.H.V. von Kehler from 1826, have shown that Hotho made Hegel's course unduly repetitive, made the dialectical structure of Hegel's argument more rigid and complicated than it was in Hegel's own lectures, and imposed some of his own views upon the material. So we must now balance our knowledge of Hegel's *ipsissima verba* with our recognition of the historical influence of Hotho's version. But the lecture courses from 1823 and 1826 will be the primary source for what follows.[41]

[40] For references to these translations, see Hegel, *Aesthetics*, Vol. I, pp. vi–vii.
[41] Annemarie Gethmann-Seifert has been the editor responsible for the recent publication of the transcriptions of Hegel's courses, and her *Einführung in Hegels Ästhetik* (Munich: Wilhelm Fink Verlag, 2005) is based primarily on these notes, as is her earlier treatment in *Einführung in die Ästhetik* (Munich: Wilhelm Fink Verlag, 1995), pp. 202–32. All older work on Hegel's aesthetics has of course been based on Hotho's version, and some newer work continues that tendency. Monographs on Hegel's aesthetics include Jack Kaminsky, *Hegel on Art: An Interpretation of Hegel's Aesthetics* (Albany: State University Press of New York, 1962); William Desmond, *Art and the Absolute: A Study of Hegel's Aesthetics* (Albany: State University Press of New York, 1986); Stephen Bungay, *Beauty and Truth: A Study of Hegel's Aesthetics* (Oxford: Clarendon Press, 1987); Beat Wyss, *Hegel's Art History and the Critique of Modernity*, trans. Caroline Dobson Salzwedel (Cambridge: Cambridge University Press, 1999); and Benjamin Rutter, *Hegel on the Modern Arts* (Cambridge: Cambridge University Press, 2010). Collections of papers include William Maker, editor, *Hegel and Aesthetics* (Albany: State University Press of New York, 2000); Ursula Franke and Annemarie Gethmann-Seifert, editors, *Kulturpolitik und Kunstgeschichte: Perspektiven der Hegelschen Ästhetik*, Sonderheft des Jahrgangs 2005 der *Zeitschrift für Ästhetik und allgemeine Kunstwissenschaft* (Hamburg: Felix Meiner Verlag, 2005); and Stephen Houlgate, editor, *Hegel and the Arts* (Evanston: Northwestern University Press, 2007). Important essays elsewhere include Helmut Kuhn, "Die Vollendung der klassischen deutschen Ästhetik durch Hegel," in Kuhn, *Schriften zur Ästhetik*, ed. Wolfhart Henckmann (Munich: Kosel, 1966), pp. 15–144 (see also Gilbert and Kuhn, *History of Esthetics*, pp. 436–55); Dieter Henrich, "Zur Aktualität von Hegels Ästhetik," in *Hegel Studien*, Beiheft II (1974): 295–301, reprinted in Henrich, *Fixpunkte* (Frankfurt am Main: Suhrkamp Verlag, 2003), pp. 156–62, along with "Zerfall und Zukunft: Hegels Theoreme über das Ende der Kunst" (pp. 65–125) and "Kunst und Kunstphilosophie der Gegenwart" (126–55); Patrick Gardiner, "Kant and Hegel on Aesthetics," in Stephen Priest, editor, *Hegel's Critique of Kant* (Oxford: Clarendon Press, 1987), pp. 161–72; Paul Guyer, "Hegel on Kant's Aesthetics: Necessity and Contingency in Beauty and Art," in Guyer, *Kant and the Experience of Freedom*, pp. 161–83; Robert Wicks, "Hegel's Aesthetics: An Overview," in Frederick C. Beiser, *The Cambridge Companion to Hegel* (Cambridge: Cambridge University Press, 1993), pp. 348–77; Frederick Beiser, *Hegel* (London: Routledge, 2005), pp. 282–306; Michael Inwood, "Hegel," in Berys Gaut and Dominic McIver Lopes, *The Routledge*

We can now sketch the metaphysical background of Hegel's cognitivist view of art and of the diminished significance of art "for us" that it implies. Hegel shared Schelling's rejection of Fichte's "theory of science" of the 1790s that the human self is a pure thinker that "posits" its own other as an inadequate explanation of the contents of our knowledge, and shared Schelling's own rejection of his first system of transcendental idealism that thought is a force that manifests itself equally in both non-mental nature and human mental representation as a mysterious account of nature. But he also rejected the "identity philosophy" that Schelling was developing just at the time that he invited Hegel to Jena as diminishing the difference between nature and thought, the material and the mental.[42] Instead, Hegel developed a form of idealism that does not deny that matter exists independently of thought, but that holds that what is known, even about nature, is always ultimately the structure of thought itself, whether that is thought about nature, human manifestations and expressions of thought, or the underlying nature of thought or "Spirit" itself, which Hegel does not hesitate to identify with God, although a rather Neo-Platonic or Spinozistic God who is immanent in all other forms of thought rather than a transcendent God who is numerically distinct from his creation.[43] Hegel is not a subjective idealist like Berkeley, who *reduces* the material world to a stream of ideas in human minds that is lent continuity by the fuller stream of ideas in God's mind,

---

Companion to Aesthetics, second edition (London: Routledge, 2005). pp. 71–82; and Robert Pippin, "The Absence of Aesthetics in Hegel's Aesthetics," in Frederick C. Beiser, editor, *The Cambridge Companion to Hegel and Nineteenth-Century Philosophy* (Cambridge: Cambridge University Press, 2008), pp. 394–418. See also Scheer, *Einführung in die philosophische Ästhetik*, pp. 112–42, and Raters, *Kunst, Wahrheit und Gefühl*, ch. 3.

[42] On the relation between Hegel and Schelling, see Dieter Henrich, "Andersheit und Absolutheit des Geistes: Sieben Schritte auf dem Wegen von Schelling zu Hegel," in Henrich, *Selbstverhältnisse* (Stuttgart: Philipp Reclam jun., 1982), pp. 142–72; for Schelling's eventual response to Hegel, see Rolf-Peter Horstmann, "Zur Hegel-Kritik des späten Schelling," in Horstmann, *Die Grenzen der Vernunft: Eine Untersuchung zu Zielen und Motiven des Deutschen Idealismus* (Frankfurt am Main: Anton Hain, 1991), pp. 245–68.

[43] On the Spinozistic background to Hegel's metaphysics, see Frederick Beiser, *Hegel*, pp. 42–7. Beiser rightly argues that Hegel's mature conception of God cannot be simply identified with Spinoza's because of Hegel's adoption from Aristotle of a teleological conception of reality as purposive that Spinoza utterly rejected (pp. 65–71), but also notes that in his lectures on the history of philosophy, Hegel himself said that "When one begins to philosophize one must first be a Spinozist. The soul must bathe itself in the aether of this single substance, in which everything one has held dear is submerged" (pp. 46–7). For a defense of the traditional interpretation of Hegel's *Geist* as ultimately a conception of God, see Charles Taylor, *Hegel* (Cambridge: Cambridge University Press, 1975).

but an idealist who regards matter as ultimately *irrelevant* except insofar as it is conceived or modified by thought, human thought in the first instance but in the last analysis by human thought as itself a manifestation of thought as such or God. In such a metaphysics, the significance of art must be questionable because the *materiality* of the objects of the senses and imagination, whether that be the luminescence of marble or pigment or the sonority of music or words, is so essential to so much of our experience of art; for Hegel, the material dimension that is typically thought to be indispensable to art turns out to be a dispensable medium for thoughts that ultimately can be and have to be expressed in more purely intellectual form. In this regard one might well observe that for all of its innovation, Hegel's thought is actually deeply rooted in the rationalism of Leibniz and Wolff of a century earlier, whose firm hold on the German mind, it turns out, Kant had hardly weakened.

The recollection of Leibniz may serve as our entree to another key Hegelian notion, that of the "Absolute." This is in a way Hegel's version of Leibniz's idea that every genuine substance or monad ultimately expresses the entire universe, although from its own point of view. Kant had rejected the idea of a complete comprehension of all reality as an unattainable "idea of pure reason" that has at most "regulative" use in theoretical inquiry, but Hegel rejects Kant's rejection of the idea of complete comprehension, and resurrects it in his own conception of the "concept" (*Begriff*) or "Idea" (*Idee*). This becomes clear in Hegel's replacement of Kant's pairing of "intuitions" and "concepts" (*Anschauungen* and *Begriffe*) as the only "constitutive" sources of knowledge, to which "ideas" (*Ideen*) add only a "regulative" dimension, with a scheme in which both "intuition" and "representation" (*Anschauung* and *Vorstellung*) must be superseded by an all-inclusive "concept" (*Begriff*), "Idea" (*Idee*), or "thought" (*Denken*; Hegel uses all these terms interchangeably), which is nothing less than a completely comprehensive and thoroughly interconnected system of thought of precisely the kind that Kant had argued is never fully attainable and can at most provide a goal that we can approach asymptotically in the actual process of inquiry.[44] In his lectures on religion, for example, Hegel distinguishes "immediate intuition," "representation," and "thought." The last and highest of these forms of consciousness is

---

[44] On Hegel's rejection of Kant's distinction between intuitions and concepts, which was the keystone of Kant's critique of Leibnizian rationalism, see Paul Guyer, "Absolute Idealism and the Rejection of Kantian Dualism," in Karl Ameriks, editor, *The Cambridge Companion to German Idealism* (Cambridge: Cambridge University Press, 2000), pp. 37–66.

knowledge of what Hegel calls the "true" or the "absolute," the "ideal unity that comprehends in itself as all of its powers all determinacy, the world."[45] Hegel repeats this triad in the lectures on aesthetics, saying that "the first relation to the absolute spirit, intuition, is the immediate and therefore sensible knowledge of it. The second is the representing [*vorstellende*] conscious of the absolute spirit, the third the thinking [*denkende*] consciousness."[46] What for Kant was (apart from the special use of pure reason in morality) only an ideal but never attainable end point for theoretical inquiry becomes for Hegel both ultimate reality and the self-knowledge or self-consciousness thereof.

The reason Hegel mentions the triad of intuition, representation, and thought of the absolute in the lectures on religion is that he holds that art, religion, and philosophy are all three forms of "absolute spirit" or consciousness of the absolute, although art is consciousness of the absolute primarily through sensory intuition, religion is consciousness of the absolute in the form of less strictly sensory representations, but only philosophy is consciousness of the absolute as it really is, the interconnection of everything that is in all of its determinacy and yet thoroughgoing logic or generality. Thus Hegel says that all three have the same "content" but different "forms,"[47] thereby making indubitable the thoroughly cognitivist character of his aesthetics. In particular, "art rests on and arises from the interest in exhibiting the spiritual Idea for consciousness and in the first instance for immediate intuition," or for the senses, and through human action: the exhibition of truth in art is "brought forth by humans, made sensible and external," while its content is "the harmony [*Zusammenstimmung*] of the object with its concept, the idea," the "substantial, entirely universal elements, essences, powers of nature and of the spirit."[48] Here Hegel explicitly replaces Kant's free and harmonious play of the cognitive powers with the kind of actual harmony between object and concept that Kant excluded from aesthetic experience, although he keeps this harmony in the domain of the aesthetic by insisting that in art it is represented through or to immediate intuition. Art arises from the need, of human beings but also of spirit itself, to represent the absolute in sensory form. Since Hegel also equates spirit with God or the divine, he says that art arises from the need to

[45] Hegel, *Vorlesungen über die Philosophie der Religion*, Teil I, in *Vorlesungen*, ed. Walter Jaeschke (Hamburg: Felix Meiner, 1983), vol. III, p. 143.
[46] *Lectures 1826*, p. 33.
[47] *Religion*, vol. III, p. 143.
[48] *Religion*, vol. III, pp. 143–4.

represent the divine in sensory form: "Art is generated through the absolutely spiritual need that the divine, the spiritual idea, be an object for consciousness and in the first instance for immediate intuition."[49] This suggests that the artistic and the religious forms of the representation of the absolute cannot be completely separated, and indeed both the history of art that comprises much of Hegel's aesthetics and the history of religion that comprises much of his philosophy of religion ultimately tell much the same story of the emergence of an increasingly intellectual understanding of absolute spirit from initially immediate and sensory representations of it. However, while art "is not and cannot be without religion" and its "objective exhibition in sensible intuition of the image, of myths with religious content,"[50] ultimately religion is not bound to sensible imagery in the way that art is and begins the process of superseding art by more purely intellectual comprehension that ultimately leads to philosophy. The decreasing importance of art for religion as religion itself becomes increasingly intellectual is in fact the starting point for Hegel's thesis that art is ultimately something of the past:

> Beautiful art ... has its future in true religion. The restricted content of the idea [in art] makes the transition in and of itself into the infinite form of identical universality – the intuition, the immediate in knowledge that is bound to sensibility, makes the transition to a knowledge that communicates itself, to an existence that is itself knowledge, to *revelation*, so that the content of the idea has as its principle the free intelligence, and as absolute spirit is for the spirit.[51]

Spirit begins by seeking sensory representation of and to itself, but ultimately seeks to know itself as pure spirit or intellect, and thus the same force that, through human artists, creates art also finds art inadequate and seeks to supersede it: "The content is the abstract God of pure thought, or a search that looks around for itself restlessly and unreconciled in all [sensible] forms, in which it can never find its goal."[52] That goal can only be found in religion and then in philosophy.

Hegel repeats these premises in his lectures on the philosophy of art, and then constructs his famous division of the history of art into the "symbolic," "classical," and "romantic" "forms of art" (Hegel is careful to call these "forms" rather than "periods" because he recognizes that the

---

[49] *Religion*, vol. III, pp. 144–5n.
[50] *Religion*, vol. III, pp. 146–7.
[51] Hegel, *Enzyklopädie*, §563, p. 549.
[52] Hegel, *Enzyklopädie*, §561, p. 546.

real history of both art and religion is complex and that traits that might be paradigmatic for the art of one time and place can nevertheless be found in others, although perhaps less centrally). In the 1826 lectures, for instance, after some initial skirmishes with the theories of Kant and the Romantics, Hegel states his fundamental assumption that the function of art is to provide a concrete representation of the same content that is also represented by religion and philosophy:

> We can call the idea, the divine, the absolute in its concrete determination the spiritual in general. For the spiritual is the true, it is the spirit to which all points of view return as in their last result, in their truth. The idea is thus concrete, thus it is the spiritual and this is the true purpose, the ultimate purpose; that is then also the purpose of art. Its purpose is therefore the same as that of religion, of philosophy.[53]

But he quickly adds that while art represents spirit in forms accessible to the senses, "that which is called sensible reality is no reality in the sense of philosophy, rather in the sense of the spirit only that is true which is something in and for itself,"[54] that is, something that is understood in the form that it actually is – through and through intellectual. He repeats the point several lectures later when he says that "Art is only the intuiting consciousness of the absolute spirit, so that it presents it in an immediate, sensible manner, in the manner of an immediate formation"; "The form of religion is then the form of representation in general, where the absolute, the true, are given for representation in a subjective manner ... One can say that there is progress from art to religion, or that for religion art is only one side; art exhibits the truth, the spirit, in a sensible manner, religion adds the interiority of this intuiting, the piety, to it"; and finally there is philosophy, which "unmasks the spirit in and through itself; interiority no longer has the form of feeling, but of thinking, and philosophy is then the service of God that thinks and knows the content that in religion was the content of the heart."[55] Thus, as already suggested, the seed for the supersession of art is planted at the start of these lectures.

Hegel then further characterizes art by means of a contrast between the "idea" and the "ideal": the idea is, as we have already seen, the ultimate content of art, the concept or the absolute, but the ideal is this in its sensory representation. "The beautiful must be grasped not as mere idea,

---

[53] *Lectures 1826*, p. 24.
[54] *Lectures 1826*, p. 25.
[55] *Lectures 1826*, pp. 34–5.

but as ideal. The idea for itself is the true as such in its universality; the ideal is the truth at the same time in its reality in the essential determination of subjectivity.... The first determination is the idea in general, the second its formation [*Gestaltung*]. Idea and form [*Gestalt*]; the formed idea is the ideal."[56] We might say that Hegel's conception of the ideal is Kant's conception of the aesthetic idea, but with any trace of free play omitted from its sensuous aspect. It also leads to a historiography of art that is absent from Kant, and that provides the basis for the nineteenth-century discipline of art history,[57] for from here Hegel then argues that the relation between idea and ideal or content and form takes three forms in the history of art: the "symbolic," in which both the spiritual content of art and its sensible form are indeterminate and neither fully expresses the true nature of the idea or the absolute; the "classical," in which both the content and the form of art are determinate in their form and fully adequate to each other, but neither is completely adequate to the true nature of the absolute; and the "romantic," in which the idea or the self-understanding of the absolute is becoming more adequate but the sensible form for representing it is therefore necessarily becoming less adequate, and thus art is separating from more primitive religion and being replaced by more developed religion, on the way to being replaced by philosophy. Hegel defines these three forms clearly in the 1826 lectures. The symbolic form of art presents the "idea in its indeterminacy ... the idea that is not yet clear does not yet have the truthful form, its formation cannot yet yield the idea in a truthful way." In the classical form of art, "the form of art is the adequate image [*Einbildung*] of the idea, of the concept in appearance ... The concept is thus imagined [*eingebildet*] in the form that is proper to it.... The main thing is always that the suitability of the idea and its presentation is ... natural, the formation is in and for itself suitable for the concept." Finally, in the third form of art, romantic art, "the unification of classical art is again dissolved ... romantic art has attained the highest, and it is only defective because it makes evident the limitation of art. This defect consists in the fact that the absolute is made into an object in sensibly concrete form, that the spiritually concrete then comes forth in a sensible form, but the idea in its truth is only in the spirit" and thus cannot after all be grasped in sensible form.[58] "One can also say that in the third stage the spiritual

---

[56] *Lectures 1826*, p. 26.
[57] See Michael Podro, *The Critical Historians of Art* (New Haven: Yale University Press, 1983).
[58] *Lectures 1826*, pp. 27–9.

steps forth as spiritual, the ideal is free and sufficient in itself" (though perhaps Hegel should have said or even did say "idea" rather than "ideal" here). "As the spirit comes to be for itself, it is freed from the sensible form; the sensible is to it something indifferent and transitory, and the mind, the spiritual as spiritual, becomes the meaning of the sensible; the [sensible] form becomes again symbolic."[59] Romantic art is the form in which the progress of spirit to self-comprehension undermines the necessity and significance of art, although historically this is a very long process, beginning with the emergence of Christianity out of antiquity and continuing, so it seems, until shortly before or into Hegel's own time, thus comprising much of what most of us now think is great rather than necessarily self-destructive in the history of art.

By the indeterminacy of both content and form in symbolic art, Hegel means that the concept of the spirit that is the content of that art is both vague and opposed to rather than identified with spirit in its human manifestation, and that the sensible forms that are used to symbolize this vague content are themselves indeterminate and could mean any variety of things rather than uniquely and self-evidently signifying the one thing, spirit, that they are trying to symbolize. A symbol, Hegel argues, is different from a mere "sign" (*Zeichen*), because while the latter is supposed to refer to something entirely different from itself, a symbol is a "sensible existence that itself has the properties that it is supposed to signify." An eagle, for example, is not a merely arbitrary sign for bravery (as a red octagon is an arbitrary sign for the command "Stop!"), but is used as a symbol for strength because it is itself supposed to be strong. However, there is an indeterminacy in symbols because it is not self-evident "whether such a formation is a symbol or not, whether this sensible existence as it immediately presents itself is meant or something else," and if a symbol tried to make completely explicit that it is in fact a symbol as well as what it is a symbol of, then it would no longer be a symbol but would already be self-conscious thought.[60]

We can understand what Hegel means by these "forms of art" by looking at his paradigmatic examples of them. Hegel's paradigmatic examples of symbols in their twofold indeterminacy are, first, natural objects or phenomena taken to embody supernatural powers or significance, such as light in ancient Persian religion[61] or the egg or the lotus blossom

---

[59] *Lectures 1826*, p. 29.
[60] *Lectures 1826*, p. 70.
[61] See *Lectures 1826*, pp. 75–7.

in various ancient religions, which are symbols precisely because they can mean an indeterminate variety of things,[62] and instances of ancient religious architecture, such as the Tower of Babel or religious compounds that contain parts, such as the "twelve steps" and "seven columns" of some (unspecified) Egyptian temples that symbolize something, such as the twelve months of the year or the seven planets,[63] but do not succeed in representing something that is explicitly spiritual nor in self-evidently representing only a single content. Hegel insists that the indeterminacy of symbolic art is not merely an artifact of our own incomplete comprehension of something ancient and foreign, but is inherent to such art: "What its significance is can be clear for us only in part, as it was for those who [first] had the symbols."[64] Among symbolic art works, Hegel is particularly fascinated with the monuments of the ancient Egyptians (brought to prominence by the booty Napoleon brought back from his invasion of Egypt). "The Egyptians were the symbolic people.... In the Egyptian everything is symbol; a separated, self-sufficient interiority, which, however, because it is symbolic, has not gone so far as giving it a truly suitable form, which stands in essential connection to the inner."[65] The Egyptian architecture of death, for example, that is, the pyramids, represents the spiritual only indirectly, by representing death as if it were still self-conscious life. "The fixation of the spiritual first came to consciousness among them," but only by their making "the inner, as the soul, itself something concrete," and by representing and honoring death as if it were "perennial preservation."[66] Or by combining human and animal forms as in their representations of the gods, the Egyptians symbolized in some way the presence of spirit (represented by the human form) in nature (represented by the animal form).[67] But these symbols signify inadequate conceptions of the spirit, and do so by means of sensible forms that do not exhibit even these inadequate conceptions of the spiritual self-evidently and uniquely.

It is important to keep in mind, however, that although Hegel often presents architecture as the paradigmatically symbolic art, he by no means treats it as the exclusively symbolic art. On the contrary, he treats a wide range of surviving ancient materials, such as the theogony and

[62] *Lectures 1823*, p. 130.
[63] *Lectures 1823*, p. 131.
[64] *Lectures 1823*, p. 139.
[65] *Lectures 1823*, pp. 86–7.
[66] *Lectures 1823*, p. 85.
[67] *Lectures 1826*, p. 137.

mythology of the early Greeks (even though that is often accessible to us only through later, sometimes distorting media, such as Ovid's *Metamorphoses*) and the creation stories, sacred texts, and practices of various early religions such as Hinduism, Judaism, Zoroastrianism, and the like as symbolic arts.[68] Wherever, for example, "the subjective is superficial, a mishmash of personality and mere natural being [*Naturwesen*]," there we have the symbolic.[69]

The second of Hegel's forms of art is the classical. This is characterized by an anthropomorphic representation of the spirit, the representation of the divine in human form, and a sensible mode for the presentation of this conception, above all the sculptural representation of the human figure, that is fully adequate to this conception of the spirit. Greek sculptures of the gods in human form are thus the paradigmatic examples of classical art, although the transformation of the indeterminately symbolic Egyptian temple into the temple as the house for a god who is literally present in his or her own statue and the very direct interactions between gods and mortals in the Homeric epics are also prime examples of symbolic art. Whatever the specific medium, however, the anthropomorphic gods are the paradigmatic objects for classical art because they represent both the presence of spirit in nature and the superiority of spirit over mere nature. Thus Hegel writes that in classical art "significance has become self-sufficient for itself; and this self-sufficient significance is alone the spiritual, the truly inner, which is at the same time living, for itself, the universal, essential absolute that knows itself, so that it is free, self-sufficient." He continues:

> To classical art there belongs the elevation of the spirit over the immediately natural. [But] since the significance has become self-sufficient in free spirituality, it must also form itself, return to nature. But then the spiritual is dominant over the natural, so that the natural as such no longer has this peculiar self-sufficiency, but is ideal and therefore only expression, sign of the spirit. This form that is brought forth through the spirit has its significance immediately, this natural is immediately the expression of the spiritual. That is the human in general, the spiritual, individual, externally existing, that is the human form. It is an animal form, in which however there is something spiritual, and thereby is that which manifests this form the spiritual itself. The form now signifies nothing other than this meaning.[70]

---

[68] See *Lectures 1823*, pp. 119–53, and *Lectures 1826*, pp. 70–115.
[69] *Lectures 1826*, p. 81.
[70] *Lectures 1826*, p. 115.

Here Hegel executes a delicate maneuver: the anthropomorphism of Greek religion, which coincides perfectly with the capacity of Greek art, above all sculpture, for brilliant representation of the human form, allows for the precise rather than indeterminate and conflicted representation of the presence of spirit in nature, above all human nature, but at the same time of the superiority of spirit over mere nature. Precisely in the way that Greek sculpture practically makes marble come alive it shows the superiority of spirit, beginning with the spirit of the sculptor, over anything merely natural like mere marble.

The classical conception of the manifestation of spirit through humanity is perfectly manifested in the anthropomorphic representation of gods in human form, especially in sculpture but in other media as well. In classical art, spirit is not represented through vague and ultimately self-contradictory symbols such as animals or other aspects of subhuman nature, but through the form of the human being, who is clearly spiritual as well as natural. Thus Hegel states:

> The demotion of that which is animal and the distancing from the powers of nature pertains to the fact that the spiritual is established in its sublime, absolute right, and these ideals [of classical art] are evidence from the spirit ... the human form is what is essential to the formation.... It is a matter of deep insight to recognize that the spiritual, insofar as it exists, must have this and only this form, animation [*Lebendigkeit*] and human form. One can come upon all manner of appearance, but if it is to be truly known, then it must be understood in accordance with the concept that the external appearance, the existence of the spiritual can only be the human form.[71]

The content of classical art must be the gods in order for it to represent the spiritual, but the gods can only be represented as human given how far the self-understanding of spirit has progressed in the classical period. This means that the form that is available to classical art – the depiction of human form and human action by "artists, poets, prophets, sculptors, and the like"[72] – is perfectly suited to the content of classical art. This is the case in architecture too: the temple, which was previously an indeterminate symbol of the divine or spirit, now becomes a house for it, not merely symbolically, but literally, because the statue of the god that is housed by the Greek temple is not a symbol of the god but its literal presence.

---

[71] *Lectures 1826*, p. 123.
[72] *Lectures 1826*, p. 123.

The conflicts among the gods and the direct interactions between humans and gods that are the staples of classical art in its various media also express the very concrete conception of the spirit as not essentially different from the human spirit that has been attained in the classical conception. But while this is evidence of the perfection of classical art as such, it also reveals the limits of the classical self-conception of the spirit – as Plato had already implied in his argument that artistic representations of the gods behaving just like human beings should not be permitted in the ideal republic[73] – and insofar as the most perfect art turns out to be an adequate vehicle for an inadequate self-conception of the spirit, it reveals the inherent limitation of art as a vehicle for cognition. At first Hegel makes this point paradoxically:

> The Greek gods are not symbols, but are immediately expressive for themselves. Nothing is hinted at that is not manifest and clear in the exteriority [of classical art] ... The way and manner in which the form is determined is that it is the manifestation of the spiritual: anthropomorphistic character of classical art. That is no defect, rather without that classical art cannot be; it rather has the defect that its religion is not anthropomorphistic enough for the higher religion, for this requires a unification of the higher, abstract opposition ... the unification of divine and human nature must take place in a much more fundamental way, so that the human is not only the form of the divine, but is self-sufficient for itself, and therefore has the manner of contingent existence.[74]

What he appears to mean by this convoluted statement is that the anthropomorphic representation of the gods is inadequate not just because spirit is something grander than mere humankind, but also because even in the human being, spirit cannot be understood through the material, natural, bodily form of the human being: not merely in the case of the gods but in our own case the physical, which is the object of the senses and therefore the proper domain of art, is ultimately inessential, or at least insignificant. Hegel makes this point more directly in his discussion of the transition from classical art to romantic art: this transition is a "separation from the natural, which is demoted to something indifferent, something bad for which the spirit must have contempt." He continues:

> This is the point of view of the transition and at the same time the principle of the third sphere. It really contains the dissolution of art – since the

---

[73] Plato, *Republic*, Book II, 377–80.
[74] Hegel, *Lectures 1826*, p. 116.

manner of existence, the exhibition, is separated from the spiritual – the dissolution of the highest beauty, the dissolution of the standpoint where beauty as such is the highest. The sphere of spiritual beauty comes forth, which to be sure is burdened with this separation from the external and which either leaves this external outside ... or relates to it in a negative, injurious, painful manner.[75]

In order fully to comprehend itself, spirit must turn against the material and sensible altogether, thereby destroying not merely the possibility of beauty in art, although leaving open to art some other goal, but destroying art altogether, because having a material and sensible aspect is what defines art but at the same time what makes it possible for art to complete its task, as part of absolute knowing, of making spirit self-understood.[76]

This inference is the basis for Hegel's claim that the paradigmatic content of post-classical art is the central story of Christianity, in which the half-human, half-divine birth of Christ, his suffering, and his resurrection represent the transcendence of the spirit even in humans over their natural, bodily existence. This of course is not the explicit content of every post-classical work of art, but it is in Hegel's view the paradigmatic content of such art, and in his view even romantic art that does not have this as its content still has a distanced or alienated relation to the natural, bodily existence of the human being that was so fully accepted by the Greeks that they assigned the same form of existence even to their gods. Hegel expresses this view clearly and concisely in his lectures:

> Romantic art is the elevation of spirituality to itself. It is characterized by interiority and innerness, so that the spirit in itself becomes the reality that was otherwise present only in an external way. Nothing can be more *beautiful* than classical art, there is the ideal. The beauty of romantic art can only be that where the inner stands above matter, the external becomes free like the inner, the external becomes something indifferent, is to be overcome, is not in a position to be the true manner of manifestation. Romantic art becomes the pantheon which has destroyed all forms that still have something of sensible representation about them.... [Its first moment] is therefore preeminently the divine story itself, this conversion, reversal, which spirit turns against its naturalness and through which it liberates itself,

---

[75] Hegel, *Lectures 1826*, p. 133.
[76] Thus that modern art might be "saved" from Hegel's death sentence by assigning it some other task than the representation of spirit itself, as Robert Pippin has argued, is incompatible with Hegel's own understanding of the aims and nature of art; see Pippin, "What Was Abstract Art? (From the Point of View of Hegel)," in Houlgate, editor, *Hegel and the Arts*, pp. 244–70, e.g., p. 247. The rejection of the dematerialization of art by the latter-day Hegelian Benedetto Croce will be a large part of the story of early twentieth-century aesthetics, as we will see in Volume 3.

attains to its self-sufficiency.... Thus it is the religious as such, the absolute story of the self-comprehending spirit.... The first content of romantic art is thereby the religious story of Christ, emphasizing especially the suffering and the dying and the death of Christ.[77]

But even where the content of romantic art is not explicitly religious, it is spiritual and alienated from the body. Even the most modern form of romantic art, Hegel remarkably argues, namely the humorous, is characterized by a turn toward subjectivity that reduces the outward form to indifference.[78] Indeed, in both the classroom transcriptions of Hegel's lectures and the version edited by Hotho, Hegel's entire philosophy of art ends with a discussion of comedy, as if the attempt to represent spirit to the senses can ultimately be regarded only as comic: "comedy leads at the same time to the dissolution of art altogether. All art aims at the identity, produced by the spirit, in which eternal things, God, and absolute truth are revealed in real appearance and shape to our contemplation, to our hearts and minds. But ... comedy presents this unity only as its self-destruction."[79]

However, before he reaches this conclusion, Hegel presents a detailed account of romantic art. Just as architecture was the paradigmatic although not exclusive medium for symbolic art and sculpture was the paradigmatic although not exclusive medium for classical art, romantic art too has its paradigmatic although not exclusive medium, or in this case media: Hegel treats painting, music, and poesy (that is, creative literature in general rather than verse in particular) as paradigmatically romantic media of art because they are not as material, not as closely tied to their physical basis, as architecture and sculpture. Painting applies physical pigments to a physical surface, of course, but it creates an image that is more detached from its own physical components than is the image created by sculpture (as is evidenced by the fact that a two-dimensional painting can create a three-dimensional image while sculpture must be three-dimensional in order to create a three-dimensional image), and by means of this detachment it can "move towards subjectivity, for the spirit is essentially subjectivity as existing-for-itself, through which it opposes every substantial art."[80] Music uses physical instruments, including of course our own bodies, to create physical disturbances in the air surrounding us, but we do not focus on this as we listen to music and thus it seems to us as "if

---

[77] Hegel, *Lectures 1826*, p. 135.
[78] Hegel, *Lectures 1826*, p. 153.
[79] See Hegel, *Aesthetics*, p. 1236.
[80] Hegel, *Lectures 1823*, p. 248.

its effect almost no longer occurs through anything material." Instead, "the art in music lies on the subjective side," whether it be "on the one hand the art of the deepest sentiment or on the other that of strict, cold reason."[81] That is, music can appeal either to our emotions or to our intellect, but either way, so Hegel thinks, the physicality of its production and of our hearing it is virtually irrelevant to our comprehension of it, and so it falls into the realm of the spiritual rather than the physical – like Schopenhauer, Hegel strives to suppress the potential emotional impact of music. Finally, in poesy or the verbal arts, the content is the "entire wealth of representation, the spiritual existing by itself, that is in an element that belongs to the spirit itself," and the physical dimension of the spoken words themselves, the "tone" (as well as presumably the physical dimension of printed words) "is demoted to a mere means, is only a sign ... and this expression is entirely different from the content itself."[82]

Hegel divides poesy into three main forms – the epic, which gives the most physical description of agents and their actions, the lyric, which expresses "not the wealth of a world, but the particular sentiment, the particular judgment of the mind";[83] and finally the drama, which "can be considered as the most perfect stage of poesy and of art in general" because here the "object" is the "action" but the "subjectivity of the lyric unites itself with that."[84] The paradigmatic tragedy is, of course, the passion of Christ,[85] but in fact in the final hour of his lecture course Hegel actually left this point aside in order to focus on differences between ancient and modern tragedy – above all, like Herder fifty years earlier, on the difference between Sophocles and Shakespeare – and to argue that whereas ancient tragedy depicts the spirit through the clash of social forces, such as the clash between the laws of the *polis* and the laws of the family in *Antigone*, "the centre of romantic tragedy is the individual's sufferings and passions" – in *Hamlet*, for example, the royal status of the murdered king and his murderous usurper are just background machinery to set the background for Hamlet's "personal character," his "noble soul ... not made for this kind of energetic activity and full of disgust with the world and life."[86]

---

[81] Hegel, *Lectures 1823*, p. 262.
[82] Hegel, *Lectures 1823*, p. 270.
[83] Hegel, *Lectures 1823*, p. 297.
[84] Hegel, *Lectures 1823*, p. 298.
[85] See Hegel, *Aesthetics: Lectures on Fine Art*, tr. Knox, vol. II, p. 1223.
[86] Hegel, *Aesthetics.*, pp. 1225–6, punctuation modified. Hegel's contrast between ancient tragedy as focusing on the conflict of social forces and modern tragedy as focusing on individual

Especially in Hotho's posthumous compilation of Hegel's lectures, they are characterized by a wealth of fascinating illustrations and striking interpretations, above all in the second half on the individual media of art, and these often have great interest apart from his philosophical framework. Nevertheless, at least in the 1823 version of his lectures, Hegel ended his course by reminding his auditors once again, lest they had become carried away with his obvious passion about particular works of art from all periods, of his general thesis that "for us art in its seriousness is something past" (interestingly, although Hotho recorded this conclusion in his own transcription of Hegel's lectures in 1823, he did not include it in his posthumous compilation).[87] But space will not allow us to explore Hegel's detailed interpretation of works throughout the history of art any further. Instead, we can conclude this discussion of Hegel with some comments on his views on several of the standard topics of late eighteenth- and early nineteenth-century aesthetics.

One striking feature of Hegel's aesthetics is his rejection of the significance of natural beauty. For Kant, natural beauty had been the starting point of his analysis of aesthetic experience because the non-intentionally produced character of natural objects leaves maximal room for the free play of the human cognitive powers in response to them, and it was also in a way the end point of his analysis because the possibility that our cognitive powers could be pleased by the discovery of beauty in nature was a hint that our moral powers should also be able to realize their goal, the highest good, in nature. The beauty of art could be fit into a framework based on our experience of the beauty of nature because even in the case of an intentionally produced object with a rational content, it is still possible for our imagination to play freely with both the form and the content of the work of art; but natural beauty remained theoretically paradigmatic for Kant and sometimes, at least, even more morally significant.[88] Many other eighteenth-century authors, especially

---

conflicts goes back to his famous treatment of Sophocles' *Antigone* in the *Phenomenology of Spirit*, e.g., §§437, 464–9. Although Hegel's reading of the play finds its defenders, for example Stephen Houlgate, "Hegel's Theory of Tragedy," in his volume *Hegel and the Arts*, pp. 146–78, I do not find it very convincing in the face of Creon's obsessive projection of his own personal motivation by greed on to the other characters in the play.

[87] Hegel, *Lectures 1823*, p. 311.
[88] I have argued that since Kant regards genius as a "gift of nature," he ought to regard the existence of art itself as a natural phenomenon and as at least potentially as morally significant as natural beauty in the more usual sense, that is, beauty not produced by intentional human activity; see my "Nature, Art, and Autonomy" in *Kant and the Experience of Freedom*, pp. 229–74.

British authors from Joseph Addison to Archibald Alison, found beauty equally in nature and fine art. But Hegel rejects the significance of natural beauty because for him beauty is significant only as an expression, even if an ultimately inadequate one, of the spirit, and works of human art are more manifestly products of the spirit than anything in mere nature. This point is put in especially striking terms at the start of the posthumous version of the lectures:

> The beauty of art is *higher* than nature. The beauty of art is beauty *born of the spirit and born again*, and the higher the spirit and its productions stand above nature and its phenomena, the higher too is the beauty of art above that of nature.... Spirit alone is the *true*, comprehending everything in itself, so that everything beautiful is truly beautiful only as sharing in this higher sphere and generated by it. In this sense the beauty of nature appears only as a reflection of the beauty that belongs to spirit.[89]

In the 1826 version of Hegel's lectures, the attack upon natural beauty is quickly followed by the attack upon the view that the purpose of art is to "arouse agreeable sentiments through lively representations"[90] and then by the attack on Kant's theory of aesthetic response as the free play of our powers in response to objects as both inadequate accounts of the "beauty of art" (*das Kunstschöne*);[91] this attack comes later in Hotho's compilation, but it ultimately comes in the form of the criticism that in Kant's aesthetics the concept of free play is present only in the form of "abstract universality."[92] So for Hegel the rejection of the significance of natural beauty is part and parcel of his rejection of the play theory of aesthetic response in favor of his own version of the cognitive theory, his theory that beauty is an apprehension of the truth of the spirit that is possible only in art although it is only imperfectly possible in art.

Hegel's rejection of the significance of aesthetic responses to nature also requires a revision of the Kantian theory of the sublime. For Kant, even more than for many writers on the sublime before him, our experience of sublimity was paradigmatically a response to the magnitude and power of nature (specifically, the response that the magnitude and power of our own reason, especially practical reason, is in its own way even greater than that of nature), and at least in the *Critique of the Power of Judgment*, he mentioned man-made objects such as the pyramids of

---

[89] Hegel, *Aesthetics*, p. 2.
[90] Hegel, *Lectures 1826*, p. 4.
[91] Hegel, *Lectures 1826*, pp. 17–18.
[92] Hegel, *Aesthetics*, p. 60.

Giza and St. Peter's in Rome just to make the point that natural objects also will produce the desired response only when seen from the right distance.[93] Hegel, however, is not interested in nature as a source of the experience of sublimity at all, so instead he locates the sublime in symbolic art, specifically in the way in which the indeterminacy of both the conception of the spirit and the symbol that tries to refer to it leave the spirit hovering beyond our grasp: "the idea in its immeasurability appropriates the form, but as mishandled, as distorting. The idea ... appears as sublimity because in its form it at the same time indicates that its form is not suitable to it."[94] Thus for Hegel the experience of the sublime is not one of enduring moral importance, but a primitive experience that is left behind in the cognitive progress of art, which is in turn of course a progress toward its own supersession.

Finally, Hegel's dismissal of the importance of nature in aesthetic theory means that he must also revise Kant's theory of genius. For Kant, of course, genius was a gift of nature, the natural inspiration and talent that allows an artist to produce a work the greatness of which can be explained neither by the artist's antecedent conception of it nor by any of the rules of skill in the use of his medium which the artist has acquired through study and practice. For Hegel, however, it is not nature but the spirit that works through the artistic genius, and what creates a work of genius is not an inexplicable inspiration and talent that exceeds the conscious thought of the artist, but rather the depth of the artist's thought itself. Thus, for Hegel, "Self-sufficiency in the production, the freedom of the work, is that which is called genius. In the work of art the naturalness of talent plays a role, for the work of art has the element of sensible exhibition, the side of naturalness," but "in the deep thoughts of the artist thought must not suspend itself [*aufheben*], but rather must remain, so that thought forms itself, and just that, that thought forms itself in the artist, is what is more distinctive of artistic genius."[95] True to Hegel's cognitivist approach to aesthetics in general, genius is a heightened power for knowledge of the spirit, or for the self-comprehension of the spirit

---

[93] Kant, *CPJ*, §26, 5:252. In his early *Observations on the Feeling of the Beautiful and Sublime* (1764), however, Kant seems to allow that the pyramids and St. Peter's are as literally sublime as the vistas of nature that he takes as the only proper objects of this experience in the *Critique of the Power of Judgment*; see *Observations*, 2:210, in Immanuel Kant, *Anthropology, History, and Education*, ed. Günter Zöller and Robert B. Louden (Cambridge: Cambridge University Press, 2007), p. 25.
[94] Hegel, *Lectures 1826*, p. 27.
[95] Hegel, *Lectures 1826*, p. 63.

through the genius, which leads the way for others – until, of course, art has to be superseded by religion and philosophy.

The contrasts between Hegel's aesthetics and Kant's are clear. The relations between Hegel's approach to aesthetics and those of many others of his time are more complicated. Hegel's description of classical art as the most perfect form of art has sometimes been taken to align him with the celebration of classical art as the model for modern art by Winckelmann, while his lengthy discussion of romantic art has sometimes been taken to align him with the celebration of art as the highest form of insight by the German Romantics and their philosophical compatriot, the Schelling of the *System of Transcendental Idealism* who had made art the highest "organon" of philosophy. But it should be clear that in light of Hegel's thesis that for us art is something past that must be superseded by religion and that in turn by philosophy, he cannot accept either of these positions. For Hegel, the perfection of classical art is something that we can admire from afar but not recreate – this was in fact a point that had already been made by Schiller in his seminal essay on naïve and sentimental poetry – and romantic art cannot be an "organon" of philosophy because nothing that works through the senses, not even something that works through the senses as indirectly as poesy does, can fully grasp the spirit in all its determinacy. So both Neo-Classicism in aesthetics (and presumably in contemporary art itself) and Romanticism (likewise both in aesthetics and in contemporary art) must be rejected by Hegel, or regarded as moments in the history of art that were necessary in their own time but cannot provide serious models for the future.[96] In spite of his obvious affection for classical Greek art, which he shared with so many others of his time, and the powerful impact of Romanticism that had flourished in Jena just before Hegel's arrival in 1801, the combination of his cognitivism and his specific conception of the spirit prevents Hegel from accepting either Neo-Classicism or Romanticism as anything but historical phenomena.

Turning from Hegel's assessment of his predecessors to the continuing significance of Hegel's aesthetics, things become even more complicated. Many subsequent movements in the arts, such as color-field painting which reduces the painting to its picture-plane, music that

[96] For a brief discussion of Hegel's attitude toward Neo-Classicism and Romanticism, see Beiser, *Hegel*, pp. 298–306 and 34–49. For a more detailed assessment of Hegel's relation to his predecessors, see Helmut Kuhn, "Die Vollendung der klassischen deutschen Ästhetik durch Hegel," in his *Schriften zur Ästhetik*, pp. 15–144 (originally published in his *Die Kulturfunktion der Kunst*, volume I [Berlin, 1931]).

incorporates the very physical sounds of everyday life, or concrete poetry in which the shape of the print on the page is at least as important if not more important than the import of the words, could be interpreted as if they were intended to dispute Hegel's specific analyses of the various media of the arts and more generally his theory that art is something of the past in which there can be no further significant progress; and the invention of entirely new media of art since Hegel's time, such as photography, cinema, computer art, and so on would also seem to cast doubt on Hegel's thesis that art is something of the past.[97] But, as was mentioned at the outset, Hegel's theory was never intended as an empirical assessment that the art of the past had discovered all the possible media of art and done everything interesting in those media that could possibly be done.[98] Hegel's argument is rather an *a priori* argument that art must be superseded by religion but ultimately by philosophy that is based on the inadequacy of any material, sensible medium for the complete comprehension of the spirit. However, when one turns to the conception of philosophy that is the capstone of Hegel's theory of "Absolute Spirit" and thus of the entire system of philosophy, it is not clear that philosophy amounts to anything more than a comprehension of all the stages through which spirit had to pass on its way to self-knowledge. This would suggest that if not the further production then at least the continued contemplation of the history of art is actually *part* of philosophy, and thus may have greater significance than at first appears: if not the production of new art, then at least the contemplation of existing art would seem to be something that has great "seriousness" for us post-Hegelians after all. Further, if philosophy itself turns out to be nothing but the contemplation of the past of the spirit, then it is not clear that the *activity* of producing art can be replaced by any other genuinely productive activity, and that would seem to leave us in a strange position of enforced idleness and passivity. Unless it is clear how philosophy is supposed to be an ongoing form of activity, it is not clear how Hegel's theory leaves us with any opportunity for ongoing activity at all.

---

[97] Again, see Pippin, "What Was Abstract Art?"

[98] This is what makes Arthur Danto's appropriation of Hegel's conception of the "end of art" for the exposition of his theory that the specific project of pictorialism in painting had to come to an end after the development of photography and be replaced by some other purpose for painting, so strange, although Danto does try to keep his own approach on Hegelian territory by arguing that post-pictorial painting has actually become a form of philosophy. See Arthur C. Danto, *After the End of Art: Contemporary Art and the Pale of History*, Bollingen Series XXXV:44 (Princeton: Princeton University Press, 1997). We will return to Danto in Volume 3.

3. SCHLEIERMACHER

Hegel's lectures in Berlin and their publication shortly after his death had an enormous influence on the development not only of philosophical aesthetics but also of the discipline of art history in Germany in the following decades.[99] But not everyone was immediately converted to the Hegelian approach to art as only a way station in the progressive self-knowledge of the spirit. Hegel's colleague at the University of Berlin, the theologian-philosopher Friedrich Daniel Ernst Schleiermacher (1768–1834), lectured on aesthetics during the same years as Hegel did, but developed an approach in which the significance of art was not solely cognitive; instead, Schleiermacher conceived of art as a social practice involving the use of both our cognitive and practical capacities to express and communicate to one another both our emotions and the free play of our imagination or fantasy. In fact, although Schleiermacher did not name any of his predecessors or contemporaries in the surviving versions of his lectures, he was clearly resurrecting Kant's synthesis of the truth- and play-theories of aesthetics, and perhaps doing so in intentional opposition to Hegel's exclusively cognitive approach, while at the same time making room for the emotional impact of art as that which is communicated to its audience. Thus, Schleiermacher integrated into his aesthetics all three of the approaches that we have been chronicling. Because he saw the comprehension, expression, and communication of feeling as a constant in human life, further, Schleiermacher clearly felt no attraction at all to the idea that art for us is a thing of the past; for him it is rather an indispensable element in every form of human society. But Schleiermacher did not publish his lectures in his lifetime, and of all the aesthetic theories of early nineteenth-century Germany, his, the most comprehensive, had the least effect on his contemporaries and successors.

Schleiermacher was born into a Pietist pastoral family in Silesia, and intended for the church.[100] However, he defied his father in order to study

---

[99] See Podro, *The Critical Historians of Art*.
[100] The classical life of Schleiermacher is Wilhelm Dilthey, *Leben Schleiermachers* (Berlin: Georg Reimer, 1870). General accounts of Schleiermacher's philosophy are Manfred Frank, *Das Individualle-Allgemeine: Textstruktuierung und -interpretation nach Schleiermacher* (Frankfurt am Main: Suhrkamp Verlag, 1977); Günter Scholz, *Die Philosophie Schleiermachers* (Darmstadt: Wissenschaftliche Buchgesellschaft, 1984); and Christian Berner, *La Philosophie de Schleiermacher: Herméneutique, Dialectique, Ethique* (Paris: Editions du Cerf, 1995). The articles in Jacqueline Mariña, editor, *The Cambridge Companion to Friedrich Schleiermacher* (Cambridge: Cambridge University Press, 2005), cover Schleiermacher's philosophy and theology, and include a valuable bibliography,

at Halle, where the spirit of the Enlightenment represented by Christian Wolff had finally triumphed over Pietism, and where modern philological criticism of ancient texts was being pioneered by Friedrich August Wolf (1759–1824) and being applied to Biblical criticism by Johann Salomo Semler (1725–91), a student of Siegmund Jakob Baumgarten, the brother of Alexander Gottlieb. At Halle, Schleiermacher acquired a broad education in philosophy and the classics as well as in theology. After the usual few years as a tutor, he found a position as preacher at the Charité in Berlin (then the Prussian military hospital, now the university hospital of Berlin's medical school), and through the salon of Henriette Herz, the wife of the physician Marcus Herz who had been a student of both Kant and Mendelssohn, he came to know the leading intellectuals of Berlin, now including the relocated Friedrich Schlegel. With Schlegel he conceived of the project of translating all of Plato's dialogues into German, which became a major part of his life's work. During these first Berlin years, Schleiermacher published a *Theory of Social Conduct* and *On Religion: Speeches to its Cultured Despisers*[101] (both 1799), the first of which considered the relation of human individuals to each other and the second of which stressed the individual relationship to the divine rather than traditional theological issues. The focus on the feelings of the individual and his communication with others of and through his feelings would be a central theme in his later lectures on aesthetics. From 1804 to 1807, Schleiermacher was back in Halle as professor of theology, but university life in Halle was interrupted by Napoleon (as it was for Hegel in Jena in the same year) and Schleiermacher returned to Berlin, where he worked with Wilhelm von Humboldt on the foundation of the new university there, becoming professor at its inception in 1810 and remaining there for the rest of his life.

Schleiermacher first lectured on aesthetics in 1819, one year after Hegel arrived at the university but two years before he began to give his own lectures on aesthetics, and then lectured on the subject again in

---

but offer little coverage of his aesthetics. For discussions specifically on his aesthetics and hermeneutics (theory of interpretation), see Andrew Bowie, *Aesthetics and Subjectivity*, pp. 183–220, and *From Romanticism to Critical Theory*, pp. 104–37; Kristin Gjesdal, *Gadamer and the Legacy of German Idealism* (Cambridge: Cambridge University Press, 2009), pp. 155–84; and Michael N. Forster, *After Herder*, pp. 323–468, especially pp. 339–44. Suggestions for further reading can be found in Schleiermacher, *Hermeneutics and Criticism and Other Writings*, ed. Andrew Bowie (Cambridge: Cambridge University Press, 1998), pp. xxxiv–xxxvi.

[101] Friedrich Schleiermacher, *On Religion: Speeches to its Cultured Despisers*, trans. Richard Crouter (Cambridge: Cambridge University Press, 1988).

1825 and 1832–33 (one year after Hegel's death and one year before his own); he also lectured on aesthetics at the Royal Academy of Sciences in 1831 and 1832. A version of his lectures was posthumously published in his collected works in 1835, thus the same year as the first posthumous edition of Hegel's lectures.[102] But Schleiermacher's approach is very different from Hegel's, although like Hegel he focuses on artistic rather than natural beauty. He introduces his lectures with the Baumgartian point that "The name *aesthetics* signifies [the] theory of sentiment [*Empfindung*] and is thus opposed to logic."[103] However, although the emphasis on sentiment in the definition of the field might suggest that aesthetic experience is essentially passive, Schleiermacher immediately states that "As the beautiful is for the most part produced through human activity, so is the production and the reception of it. Productivity and receptivity differ only in degree." Here Schleiermacher introduces the terminology for the more recent distinction between "production" and "reception" aesthetics, that is, theories focusing on the experience of the artist and of the audience for art,[104] but only to stress that there is no fundamental distinction between them: the artist may lead the way in the clarification and communication of feeling, but through their stimulation by the work of the artist the audience will also engage in the activity of clarifying and communicating feeling rather than just passively appreciating the work of the artist. "If the beautiful is a free human production, then one must not seek it in the form of παθημα [passions], but in the form of action."[105] Not that art has nothing to do with passion, of course; rather it has everything to do with passion, but what it has to do with passion is to comprehend and communicate it, which takes activity on the part of both the artist and the audience. As we saw earlier, the idea that the activity of the artist and the audience are essentially similar

---

[102] There are two modern editions of Schleiermacher's lectures on aesthetics, *Friedrich Schleiermachers Ästhetik*, ed. Rudolf Odebrecht, Veröffentlichungen der Literatur-Archiv-Gesellschaft in Berlin, Vol. 4 (Berlin: Walter de Gruyter, 1931), and Friedrich Daniel Ernst Schleiermacher, *Ästhetik (1819/25)/Über den Begriff der Kunst (1831/32)*, ed. Thomas Lehnerer (Hamburg: Felix Meiner Verlag, 1984). The latter will be used here.
[103] Schleiermacher, *Ästhetik*, p. 3.
[104] See Wolfgang Iser, *The Act of Reading: A Theory of Aesthetic Response* (Baltimore: Johns Hopkins University Press, 1978); Robert Jauss, *Aesthetic Experience and Literary Hermeneutics*, trans. Michael Shaw (Minneapolis: University of Minnesota Press, 1982) and *Toward an Aesthetic of Reception*, trans. Timothy Bahti (Minneapolis: University of Minnesota Press, 1982); and Robert C. Holub, *Reception Theory: A Critical Introduction* (London: Routledge, 1984).
[105] Schleiermacher, *Ästhetik*, p. 4.

was implicit in Kant's analysis of genius, although Kant's exclusion of passions from aesthetics did not anticipate Schleiermacher's, because he denied the distinction that Kant drew between emotion and genuine aesthetic response. As we shall see later, Wilhelm Dilthey, Schleiermacher's biographer and his only real successor in nineteenth-century German aesthetics, would further develop the idea of the underlying identity of the activity of artist and audience.

Schleiermacher develops this theme in the first main part of the lectures, the "General Speculative" part as contrasted to the "Presentation of Individual Arts." Here Schleiermacher begins with a version of the Kantian distinction between our theoretical and practical capacities. In his words, "Opposition between being and consciousness. Ideality and reality. [The human] forms the real in his ideality: *cognizing* function. He forms his ideal in reality: *organizing* function. Through the latter he unites things with himself, through the former he unites himself with things."[106] That is, in more Kantian language, in knowledge we try to mold our ideas to the actual world, but in action we try to transform the world to conform to our ideals. Schleiermacher then adds that both of these functions must be applied to the third basic capacity of human beings for *feeling* (*Gefühl*), which is clearly related to Kant's introduction (following Mendelssohn) of the capacity for feeling as a third capacity between our theoretical and practical capacities, and also adds that in applying our cognizing and organizing faculties to feeling we come to understand and to establish relations between ourselves and the world and ourselves and each other.[107] The last is Schleiermacher's own distinctive theme, or at the very least a way of making Kant's thesis that our appreciation of the beautiful "prepares" us to love disinterestedly[108] a much more concrete thesis about the social role of art.

The application of our cognizing and organizing functions to our feelings and emotions takes the form of coming to understand them, moderating them, and creating forms for the expression of them which allow us to accomplish these aims and to communicate our results to others. Schleiermacher writes:

> What is identical between the artless and the artistic is the inner emotion [*Erregung*], and the externalizations [*Aeußerungen*] are the same. But the

---

[106] Schleiermacher, *Ästhetik*, p. 9.
[107] Schleiermacher, *Ästhetik*, p. 10.
[108] See Kant, *CPJ*, General Remark following §29, 5:267.

artless is without measure and rule (leaping for joy, storming around in rage, a scream of horror, etc.). The artistic has measure and succession and thereby becomes song and dance. Where there is measure and succession, however, there is an inner type, a prototype [*Urbild*], which precedes the production and comes between it and the emotion. The *art* is thus here the *identity of the inspiration* [*Begeisterung*] by means of which the externalization derives from the inner emotion and the *clarification* [*Besonnenheit*], by means of which it derives from the prototype.[109]

To be sure, Schleiermacher does not make the mere arousal of emotion the aim of art, or even the mere moderation of it. Rather, the key to both the production and the reception of art is moderation of it through coming to understand it and express it through a process of thought and action guided by a "prototype" or an image of a work, such as a dance, a song, or subsequently a painting, a statue, a poem, that is then developed in the process of creating and recreating a work of art – but a process that does not lose the original feeling either. Schleiermacher often puts this point by means of the almost untranslatable triad of *Erregung*, *Urbildung*, and *Ausbildung*,[110] literally, emotion, prototyping, and cultivation, but more reasonably something like feeling and emotion, having an image of how it might be shaped and communicated, and then finding and working within a suitable medium and form for its actual communication. This could be said to be a version of Kant's model of the aesthetic idea, with the modification that it is an emotion rather than an idea of reason that is being expressed and communicated through the work of art – without the emotion, there is nothing to be communicated on Schleiermacher's account. Schleiermacher's departure from Kant is of profound importance, but not complete, for he also stresses that every work of art, whatever its medium, involves an idea, something contributed by the understanding as the organizing function as the key to comprehending and expressing the emotion. Thus Schleiermacher is synthesizing the cognitive and the emotional approaches to aesthetic experience, and doing so even more explicitly than the British poets Wordsworth and Shelley were doing at the same time. He could be taken to be pointing the way to the theory of aesthetic experience as cognition *of* emotions that we will later find in both the Neo-Kantians and R.G. Collingwood, but Schleiermacher's stress on communication means that he is not losing sight of the fact that aesthetic experience for both

[109] Schleiermacher, *Ästhetik*, p. 11.
[110] Schleiermacher, *Ästhetik*, p. 12.

artist and audience involves the actual experience of emotions as well as understanding them.

Here we can see how Schleiermacher has connected the Kantian conception of the aesthetic idea to a non-Kantian recognition of the emotional impact of art, but we have not yet seen how he restores the Kantian conception of the free play of our mental powers to a central role in aesthetic theory, which it had been denied by Schelling, Schopenhauer, and Hegel. This is his next move. He says that "Nobody will deny that the prototype of art works lies in the domain of ... free play," but concedes that "most results of such play are to be sure insignificant." But what leads from an insignificant free play of ideas, untrammeled imagination or fantasy, to genuine aesthetic experience is that the play "be brought into the light of consciousness and that it demand presentation [*Darstellung*]."[111] Here Schleiermacher's argument becomes very quick, and we might wish that we could have been present at his lecture so that we could have asked him to amplify his claims, but his idea seems to be that while mere play may lead to an immediate feeling, the task of art is to transform that play and that feeling into a more articulate "mood" (*Stimmung*) and to find a means for preserving a sense of the free play and of the feeling that it arouses through an articulation and expression of that mood. He says that in order to find the "truly identical," presumably referring back to the identity between emotion and inspiration on the one hand and clarification and externalization on the other to which he had referred a few pages earlier,

> One must go back to the necessity of affection from without. This is the feeling. But music and mime do not proceed from the immediate feeling, but from the mood that arises from holding together the moments of affection. Just this however also determines the free play of fantasy ... One also cannot say exactly that music and mime as immediate expression of feeling are passive, and the intuiting [pictorial?] arts more active, for the former too relate only to the formed [*gehaltene*] feeling. For this attitude [*Haltung*] is the original willing-to-feel [*Fühlenwollen*], and thus music and mime are just as self-active [as the other arts]. The difference thus consists only in this, that all the arts are the expression of mood, as it is developed in ... objective activity, but music and mime borrow their expression from what is immediate in feeling, while the pictorial [*bildenden*] and verbal arts borrow theirs from the way in which the mood affects the free play of representations.[112]

---

[111] Schleiermacher, *Ästhetik*, p. 16.
[112] Schleiermacher, *Ästhetik*, p. 17.

We do not have room to pursue Schleiermacher's contrasts among the arts; what is important is just that he wants to combine the idea of the free play of the imagination and the feelings that are immediately associated with that with the clarifying and expressive functions of art. In this way he argues that art is the means for the comprehension and communication of the free play of our imagination and emotions, thus combining the truth- and play-theories of aesthetic experience in a way analogous to Kant's original synthesis of them in his theory of fine art, but through his model of communication adding that aesthetic experience involves the actual experience of emotions.

Schleiermacher returns to the centrality of play in art some pages later, and also follows Kant in suggesting that through the consciousness of the free play that is a central part of aesthetic experience we also become conscious of our freedom more generally. Thus he returns

> to the opposed approaches, one of which regards all art as holy, the other of which regards all art as play. Both can be right only if both are not strictly opposed. Art is play in contrast to the organizing activity which is work, and in contrast to the objective cognizing that is a task, a business ... in contrast to which art, not dependent on this opposition, is an occupation of the human being with himself, a play, and has no other object than this opposition itself.

Then he continues:

> In cognizing and forming the human being is conscious of the laws that he must necessarily follow and he has no determinate consciousness of whether they proceed more from the interior of the world or from his own interior. But in the case of art he has no doubt, and insofar as his free productions are symbols for that which he finds in knowledge, and in his images [*Bildungen*] in general the forms are borrowed from the domain of free art, so does he thereby first become conscious of his freedom. Hence art, although it is play, nevertheless stands by the side of both [knowing and organizing] and is their complement.[113]

In claiming that through art we obtain an awareness of our own freedom that stands alongside what we might get from our knowing and organizing capacities, or our theoretical and practical reason, Schleiermacher is clearly aligning himself with Kant's sense of the permanent significance of art rather than with Hegel's thesis that because cognition has progressed beyond what art can offer, art is for us something past, although also making consciousness of our freedom in aesthetic experience more

---

[113] Schleiermacher, *Ästhetik*, pp. 26–7.

prominent than Kant had done, for whom free play functioned more as an explanation of aesthetic pleasure than as its content.

Schleiermacher also returns to a more Kantian conception of genius than Hegel as well as Schelling and Schopenhauer before him had adopted. Following his original statement that art requires "*Erregung, Urbildung*, and *Ausbildung*," he argues that art can be "original" rather than "mechanical" and "receptive" only where there is "original inspiration," a "gift for invention," and "an organic disposition" for "execution."[114] Later in his lectures Schleiermacher says that "geniality" consists in "procreating mood, forming prototypification, and exhibiting execution" (*erzeugende Stimmung, gestaltende Urbildung, darstellende Ausführung*).[115] With these terms, he rejects Schopenhauer's idea that genius consists solely in a faculty of cognition that is more penetrating and quicker than that of other people, but also rejects Hegel's idea that genius is essentially the spirit working through particular individuals, another cognitivist conception of genius. For Schleiermacher genius consists in a gift for inspiration, invention, and communication that is greater in degree than what other people have, although of course not completely different in kind, since as we saw it was the original premise of his lectures that aesthetic production and aesthetic reception differ only in degree, not in kind, and that the audience for art must be capable of re-experiencing and recreating for themselves what artists also experience and create.

Finally, we may note that following his original interest in the relations of human beings both to each other and to the divine, Schleiermacher argues that there are two "styles" in art, the "religious or holy" and the "social" (indeed, even the "erotic").[116] The former express our feelings about the divine, the latter about ourselves. He argues that these two styles are found in every branch of art: in architecture we have buildings for worship and pleasure, in mime gestures for the accompaniment of religious processions and of masquerades, in music both liturgy and opera, and so on. However, not only does he think that both of these styles of art are independently necessary for human beings – thus rejecting Hegel's view that all art is essentially religious art – he also thinks that they come together in the central activity of celebration or festival (*Fest*). In the festival or "festival life" (*Festleben*), human beings celebrate and cement both their relation to God and their relation to each other.

---

[114] Schleiermacher, *Ästhetik*, pp. 12–13.
[115] Schleiermacher, *Ästhetik*, p. 44.
[116] Schleiermacher, *Ästhetik*, pp. 22–3.

"All religious festival life, all cult is only the interaction of spontaneity and receptivity, the production and enjoyment of both domains," the religious and the social. While hardly denying the religious significance of art that was so central to Hegel, Schleiermacher insists that art has an active as well as an intellectual component, and that it serves to create solidarity among human beings as well as to relate them individually to the divine. Schliermacher's conception of "festival life" would later be taken up by the twentieth-century philosopher of hermeneutics Hans-Georg Gadamer, who, as we will later see, himself uses it to effect a synthesis between the Kantian conception of free play and the purely cognitivist aesthetics that Gadamer learned from his mentor Martin Heidegger.

Schleiermacher thus recreated the synthesis represented by Kant's conception of aesthetic ideas of the free play of imagination with the organizing role of a concept in aesthetic experience, while adding to this synthesis the third element of the actual *Erregung* or arousal of emotion as what is shaped and communicated by the production and reception of art. His approach to aesthetics could thus have set the stage for a major advance in the field, but neither his lectures nor their posthumous publication had the same impact as Hegel's did in the decades immediately following their deaths or as Schopenhauer's book would have after that. As already mentioned, it is only in the work of his biographer Dilthey at the end of the century that anything like Schleiermacher's threefold synthesis of approaches to aesthetic experience would be revived. What we will next see, however, is that while the aestheticians most influenced by Hegel did not overturn his rejection of the idea of free play, they did begin to look for ways to accommodate the emotional impact of art in their own theories.

4

In the Wake of Hegel

While Schelling had broad impact on the thought of literary writers during the first part of the nineteenth century, the aesthetics of Hegel had the greatest influence on the development of academic aesthetics in Germany during the three decades following his death in 1831 – the span of a generation, what we might call the post-Hegelian generation. The leading figures of this generation were Friedrich Theodor Vischer, Karl Rosenkranz, and Hermann Rudolf Lotze, and what is common to all of them is that they made at least tentative efforts to find room for the approaches that Hegel's single-mindedly cognitivist approach to aesthetics had excluded, namely the Kantian idea of the free play of imagination and the ultimately Dubosian recognition of the emotional impact of art. But before we turn to these figures, we will briefly consider one who was more of a contemporary of Hegel, K.W.F. Solger, who, like Hegel, adopted an essentially cognitivist approach to aesthetics but who, unlike Hegel, did not think that the cognitive limits of art needed to be remedied by higher forms of knowledge such as religion and philosophy, because for him the content of art is essentially religious. Yet at the same time he claimed that art is essentially ironical, that it promises a reconciliation of our spiritual and material natures that it can never fully deliver, and in this sense Solger's theory points the way toward the twentieth-century aesthetics of Theodor W. Adorno, whose own cognitivist approach to art is that it holds out to us what we might call the logical possibility of a fully reconciled life while at the same time revealing the real impossibility of such a life. In his own time, Solger's lectures were immediately overshadowed by Hegel's, but in the long run they may have had at least one important reverberation in the following century.

1. SOLGER

Along with the lectures by Hegel and Schleiermacher, yet another set of lectures on aesthetics was delivered in Berlin in 1819 by Karl Wilhelm Ferdinand Solger (1780–1819), also a professor at the university.[1] Solger had studied jurisprudence at Halle from 1799–1802, but spent 1801–2 listening to Schelling at Jena. He then came to Berlin as a government employee, but after hearing Fichte lecture in 1804, he gave up his position to devote himself to philosophy. He became a professor at the university in 1811, and was active in securing Hegel's appointment as Fichte's successor in 1818. But he died the next year, and thus his 1819 lectures on aesthetics, which had been preceded by an 1815 book *Erwin, Four Dialogues on Beauty*, were his last work (they were posthumously published in 1829, the same year as Hegel's last lectures on aesthetics).

Solger was influenced by Fichte, but more so by Schelling and by his close association with some of the German Romantics, especially Ludwig Tieck. But through these influences he was led to an aesthetics that is in many ways similar to Hegel's, and in Hotho's version of his lectures Hegel referred to him respectfully, saying that he "was not content," like the other Romantics, "with superficial philosophical culture; on the contrary, his genuinely speculative inmost need impelled him to plumb the depths of the philosophical Idea. In this process he came to the dialectical moment of the Idea ... to the activity of the Idea in so negating itself as infinite and universal as to become finitude and particularity, and in nevertheless cancelling this negation in turn and so re-establishing the universal and infinite in the finite and particular. To this negativity Solger firmly clung."[2] This may not initially seem to be a fair assessment, but in the end it is correct. Solger was essentially a philosopher of religion: he conceived of God as the unification of all opposites, of our own "higher self-consciousness" as consciousness that in spite of our difference from God we are also united with God, and of beauty, in nature but especially in art, as the revelation of God and our higher self-consciousness in sensible form. Nevertheless, he concludes that art does not fully unify the

---

[1] For information on Solger's career, see Hermann Fricke, *K.W.F. Solger: Ein Brandenburgisch-Berlinisches Gelehrtenleben an der Wende vom 18. zum 19. Jahrhundert* (Berlin: Hauder & Spener, 1972). Wolfhart Henckmann has published several articles on Solger's aesthetics, including "Die geistige Gestalt K.W.F. Solgers," *Philosophisches Jahrbuch* 81 (1974): 172–86, and "Symbolische und Allegorische Kunst bei K.W.F. Solger," in Jaeschke and Holzhey, editors, *Frühe Idealismus und Frühromantik*, pp. 214–40.
[2] Hegel, *Aesthetics: Lectures on Fine Art*, trans. Knox, vol. I, p. 68.

sensible world and the higher world, but renders the real world "nugatory," and is in this sense inevitably "ironic," although he emphasized that this irony has nothing to do with "common mockery, which finds nothing noble in man."[3] He thereby appears to hold, like Hegel, that art has an essentially cognitive function, that of revealing the presence of the universal, the Idea, or the divine in the particular and actual, yet that it is also incapable of fully doing that, of reconciling the gap between the particular and the universal, the real and the ideal. This is what Hegel means by claiming that Solger "firmly clung" to negativity. Unlike Hegel, however, Solger does not hold that the limits of art can be overcome by philosophy.

Solger began his lectures with a brief review of the prior history of aesthetics, focusing especially on Baumgarten and Kant. He held that Baumgarten's conception of beauty as "sensible perfection" and Kant's conception of it as "merely the general form of purposiveness"[4] were unsuccessful attempts to combine opposites at the level of common sense, in which "two entirely opposed elements," especially the material character of imagination and moral ideas of reason, "lie in indissoluble conflict,"[5] rather than a genuine recognition of the "higher self-consciousness" in which opposites really are combined. Where Kant thought he had successfully described a free play of our cognitive powers, especially in the case of fine art where our imagination plays with rational ideas to yield aesthetic ideas, Solger charged that he had merely "displayed a vacillation between empiricism and rationalism."[6] Schelling, however, more than Kant and Fichte as well, "assessed the *subjective* and the *objective* more equally," and found in thought generally but in art in particular "an interplay (*Wechselspiel*) between the subjective or conscious and the objective or unconscious activity," a combination also represented by Schelling's term "intellectual intuition," which combines the sensible and the intellectual.[7] Thus Solger dismissed Kant's "free play" while being more hospitable to Schelling's "interplay," but in fact the idea of aesthetic experience as free play has virtually no role in his aesthetics. Aesthetic experience is an entirely serious business in which the divine in itself and the divine in us are revealed to us.

[3] Karl Wilhelm Ferdinand Solger, *Vorlesungen über Ästhetik*, ed. K.W.L. Heyse (Berlin, 1829, facsimile edn.: Karben: Verlag Petra Wald, 1996), p. 125.
[4] Solger, *Vorlesungen*, pp. 32–3.
[5] Solger, *Vorlesungen*, p. 35.
[6] Solger, *Vorlesungen*, p. 38.
[7] Solger, *Vorlesungen*, pp. 40–1.

This conception of the aesthetic is manifested in Solger's comparison between the "standpoint of *religion*" and the "standpoint of the *beautiful*." In the former standpoint, the "highest consciousness is something universal that can present itself in reality only successively. If this highest life itself becomes the center-point of our consciousness, then we must, insofar as we negate ourselves as something real, perceive the presence in us of the highest, universal life, or perceive our own consciousness as a manifestation of the divine consciousness. Our own individuality is merely an externalization of the divine presence." But if we preserve a sense of "the entire world of reality as the complete image [*Abbild*] of the highest consciousness," if we "see the world of reality as the revelation of the divine life," then we occupy the standpoint of the beautiful.[8] The "secret of art," he continues, is this:

> We must recognize in the beautiful a living unfolding, an effect of the divine presence, through which every concept creates its own existence. The concept must be individually alive [*lebendig*], and conversely the individual object must not appear as abstracted from the universal concept, but as the immediate presence of the concept, as the concept itself in its particularity. Both sides must let themselves be dissolved in the third moment of relation; the point of reflection must be sublated in its entire completeness.[9]

The sensible and imaginative elements on the one hand and the intellectual and moral elements on the other, which Kant had failed genuinely to combine, are fully combined for Solger because the experience of beauty is in fact a revelation of divinity and its presence in the world outside of us and in ourselves. The effect of beauty, in turn, is "that it produces the feeling of unity within ourself, of consolation, of complete satisfaction."[10] It is striking that Solger makes this claim just after the publication of Schopenhauer's philosophy of art in *The World as Will and Representation* the previous winter, although while for Schopenhauer the calming effect of aesthetic experience was grounded in the contemplation of the thoroughly nonreligious Platonic Ideas, for Solger it is grounded in the recognition of beauty as a revelation of divinity. However, Solger makes no mention of Schopenhauer.

For Solger artistic beauty is a revelation of the divine and of our identity with it, whether the explicit content of art is religious or secular,

---

[8] Solger, *Vorlesungen*, p. 68.
[9] Solger, *Vorlesungen*, p. 69.
[10] Solger, *Vorlesungen*, p. 76.

and a good part of his lectures is given over to an exposition of "divine beauty" and "earthly beauty" as the two main forms of beauty in general as the "matter of art."[11] In this part of his work he has many interesting ideas about religious art and secular art, the latter epitomized for him, as it would be for Hegel as well, by Shakespeare's tragedies, above all *Hamlet*, *Macbeth*, and *Romeo and Juliet*. We will have to pass Solger's illustrations by, however, in order to comment on his account of artistic production. While he recognizes that art is an "activity" that brings about "the unification of the idea with the appearance,"[12] and therefore stresses that all forms of art must have a genuinely technical side as well as an intellectual or content-oriented one, but also that these two sides must genuinely come together so that the technical side does not appear to be a merely "mechanical" vehicle for the expression of the content,[13] he nevertheless stresses that the idea that is the content of the work of art is *revealed to* rather than *invented by* the artist, and thus that the artist's work is that of *unfolding* the idea that is revealed to him in a sensible medium rather than *creating* a vehicle for the expression of an idea, and in the course of doing that, himself refining the idea he is exploring. Thus he says that as far as its "theoretical side," that is, its content, is concerned, "The revelation of the idea constitutes the entire consciousness of the artist as its enduring quality, and this enduring quality we call *genius*."[14] To be sure, we should not think that the artist is completely conscious of the full content and ramifications of the idea that animates his work as he starts the technical process of its physical production,[15] but nevertheless Solger speaks throughout of the idea that is at the heart of a work, whether it is ultimately an idea of the unity of God or of our unity with God, as revealing itself to the artist in the course of his work rather than as being created by the artist. Here again Solger shares the cognitive approach of his teacher Schelling and his colleague Hegel.

But for all of his emphasis that the content of artistic beauty is the unity of the world and of ourselves with God and its form the unification of the technical with the theoretical, Solger does not allow that art can

---

[11] Solger, *Vorlesungen*, pp. 136–80.
[12] Solger, *Vorlesungen*, p. 91.
[13] Solger, *Vorlesungen*, p. 121.
[14] Solger, *Vorlesungen*, p. 119.
[15] Solger, *Vorlesungen*, p. 113.

fully succeed in reconciling the spiritual and the material. This is his conception of "irony." Solger writes:

> The genuine work of art develops, as a plant from its seed, through quiet and still activity. The other side of the spiritual activity of the artist [however], in which it comes to completion, is that it dissolves reality. The artist must negate [*vernichten*] the real world, not merely insofar as it is appearance [*Schein*], but insofar as it is itself expression of the idea. This mood of the artist, through which he posits the real world as nugatory [*das Nichtige*], we call artistic *irony*. No work of art can arise without this irony, which with inspiration constitutes the centerpoint of artistic activity. It is the mood through which we notice that reality is the unfolding of the idea, but that is in and for itself nugatory and first becomes truth again only when it dissolves in the idea.[16]

Art necessarily has a technical, material side, but, like Hegel, Solger ultimately believes that the material world is irrelevant to the real truth about the divine, and so art is doomed to fall short of its mission by its own inescapable limitation. This is the irony of art, and Solger's theory of the irony of art is his counterpart to Hegel's theory of the end of the significance of art, although Solger does not put his view in historical terms and does not suggest that the irony of art can and will be made good by superior means of absolute knowledge. The point remains, however, that the combination of a purely cognitive approach to art with the view that what is to be known is ultimately entirely spiritual in nature inevitably condemns art to inadequacy in one way or another.

We can now turn from this contemporary and colleague of Hegel, who developed a view so close although not identical to Hegel's, to several of the students of Hegel. Numerous students and followers of Hegel published their own systems of aesthetics, some even before Hegel's lectures were published, including Hotho himself (1829), Christian Hermann Weisse (*System der Ästhetik als Wissenschaft von der Idee der Schönheit*, Leipizg, 1830), and Arnold Ruge, the left-Hegelian and early supporter of Karl Marx (*Neue Vorschule der Ästhetik*, Halle, 1837). But three of the most interesting and influential of these post-Hegelian aestheticians are Friedrich Theodor Vischer, Karl Rosenkranz, and Hermann Rudolf Lotze. They begin to find room within a recognizably Hegelian framework for the approaches to aesthetics that Hegel had rejected.

---

[16] Solger, *Vorlesungen*, p. 125.

2. VISCHER

Georg Lukács called Friedrich Theodor Vischer (1807–87) the most important post-Hegelian aesthetician.[17] Like Hegel himself, Vischer was a Stuttgarter and attended the Tübingen Stift with the intention of pursining a career in the ministry; among his friends were David Friedrich Strauss (1808–74), shortly to achieve notoriety for an historical work denying the divinity of Jesus,[18] and the poet Edward Mörike (1804–75), first a pastor but later professor of literature at Tübingen. After brief service as a minister himself, however, Vischer took a Ph.D. in philosophy and aesthetics and launched an academic career. He began teaching aesthetics and literature in Tübingen as a *Privatdozent*, became associate professor in 1837, and was appointed professor of philosophy in 1844. But from 1845 to 1847, he was suspended from teaching, supposedly on account of his pantheism, and in 1848 he was a member of the short-lived all-German liberal parliament in Frankfurt. In 1855, he moved to the university in Zürich, but in 1866 he returned to Tübingen as professor and also began teaching at the Stuttgart Polytechnic. In addition to his philosophical writings, Vischer published widely in many media; among his nonphilosophical works are a parodic *Faust, Part III*, and a novel *Auch Einer* (1879), an exploration of the "mischief of objects." In the style of Goethe, he also published marvelous travelogs based on his visits to Italy and Greece, and he wrote on the sociology of fashion as well.[19]

---

[17] See Willi Oelmüller, *Friedrich Theodor Vischer und das Problem einer nachhegelschen Ästhetik* (Stuttgart: Kohlhammer, 1959), p. 7. This remains the most valuable monograph on Vischer; for an older one, see Ewald Volhard, *Zwischen Hegel und Nietzsche: Der Ästhetiker Friederich Theodor Vischer* (Frankfurt am Main: Kohlhammer, 1932). The source of Lukács's remark is "Karl Marx und Friedrich Theodor Vischer," Werke, vol. 10 (Neuwied/Berlin: Luchterhand, 1969). Other brief treatments are Pochat, *Geschichte der Ästhetik*, pp. 567–74, and Egbert Witte, *Logik ohne Dornen: Die Rezeption von A.G. Baumgartens Ästhetik im Spannungsfeld von logischem Begriff und ästhetischer Anschauung* (Hildesheim: Georg Olms Verlag, 2000), pp. 152–62. Francesca Iannelli, *Das Siegel der Moderne: Hegels Bestimmung des Hässlichen in den Vorlesungen zur Ästhetik und die Rezeption bei den Hegelianern* (Munich: Wilhelm Fink Verlag, 2007), pp. 268–91, focuses exclusively on Vischer's treatment of the ugly, not an especially prominent topic in his aesthetics.

[18] David Friedrich Strauss, *Das Leben Jesu kritisch bearbeitet* (Tübingen: Osiander, 1835–36), translated into English by Marian Evans (George Eliot), *The Life of Jesus, Critically Examined*, 3 vols. (London: Chapman Brothers, 1846).

[19] Vischer's occasional writings are collected in a six-volume set, *Kritische Gänge*, edited by his son Robert (whom we will come to in his own right later), second edition (Munich: Meyer & Jessen Verlag, 1922). A selection of this material has recently been published as Friedrich Theodor Vischer, *Kritische Skizzen*, edited by Hermann Bausinger (Tübingen: Klöpfer & Meyer, 2009); several of Vischer's essays on fashion have been republished

Vischer's ideas initially were close to those of Hegel, but his views developed over his long career. He ended up with a position that was in some ways more Kantian than Hegelian, but which clearly made room for an emotional aspect of aesthetic experience, and indeed treated aesthetic properties as projections of human emotions onto the forms of objects, the position his son Robert and others such as Theodor Lipps would refer to as "empathy" (*Einfühlung*). Vischer's first major work in aesthetics was *Über das Erhabene und Schöne* (*On the Sublime and the Beautiful*, 1837), but his *magnum opus* was his six-volume *Aesthetik oder Wissenschaft des Schönen* (*Aesthetics or the Science of the Beautiful*), which he began during the two years in which he was prohibited from teaching and which was published from 1846 to 1857.[20] A single volume based on his lectures from 1860 onward was edited by his son under the name *Das Schöne und die Kunst*, "The Beautiful and Art,"[21] and the volumes of his essays, collected under the title *Kritische Gänge* ("Critical Paths"), also reached six volumes.[22] Vischer composed his original *Aesthetik* as a handbook for his lectures divided into short numbered paragraphs followed by often much longer notes in which he revealed his remarkable erudition and engaged in detailed criticism of his philosophical predecessors as well as illustration of his claims from throughout the history of the arts. The general spirit of the work is certainly Hegelian, and is based on what sounds like a Hegelian conception of the "Idea" or "absolute Spirit." But Vischer marks his independence from Hegel from the outset, by beginning with the argument that aesthetics must be defined as the science of the beautiful, not as the science of art, and that it must be shown by argument that art is the highest form of the beautiful;[23] indeed, Vischer devotes a considerable section of his work to the beauty of nature, from the beauty of inorganic nature to the beauty of the human body, as the "one-sided existence of beauty" in which its objective but not yet its subjective element is exhibited.[24] Vischer also pointedly departs from Hegel

as Friedrich Theodor Vischer, *Mode und Cynismus*, edited by Michael Neumann (Berlin: Kulturverlag Kadmos, 2006).

[20] Friedrich Theodor Vischer, *Aesthetik oder Wissenschaft des Schönen*, eight volumes (Reutlingen and Leipzig: Karl Mäcken's Verlag, 1846–57); second edition edited by Robert Vischer, six volumes (Munich: Meyer and Jessen Verlag, 1922–23).

[21] Friedrich Theodor Vischer, *Das Schöne und die Kunst: Eine Einführung in die Aesthetik*, edited by Robert Vischer (Stuttgart: Cotta, 1898).

[22] Friedrich Theodor Vischer, *Kritische Gänge*, edited by Robert Vischer, second edition, six volumes (Munich: Meyer & Jessen, 1922).

[23] Vischer, *Aesthetik*, §1, vol. I, p. 1.

[24] Vischer, *Aesthetik*, §§232–378, Vol. II, pp. 1–356.

in a protracted argument that although much art has religious content, art is actually superior to religion for the presentation of the idea precisely because of its immediacy, its grasp on our senses, which for Hegel had made art inferior to religion as a vehicle for absolute knowledge.[25] And Vischer returned to eighteenth-century practice by recognizing the sublime and even the comic as separate aesthetic categories, rather than subsuming all aesthetic properties under beauty, as Hegel had done. Most importantly for our purposes, however, Vischer defended Kant's conception of aesthetic experience as the free play of our mental powers against Hegel and others who had denigrated it by arguing that, although Kant had failed to recognize that his own conception of "inner purposiveness" (as Vischer calls it) is actually a conception of the manifestation of the objective existence of the Idea or spirit in the *content* of beauty,[26] his conception of the free play of our mental powers – although it needs to be expanded to include our practical as well as our theoretical faculties – is a sound and indispensable description of our *experience* of beauty, its subjective rather than objective side.[27] Thus, Vischer tries to reconcile Hegel and Kant, which is to say he tries to combine the truth-theory of aesthetics with the play-theory, as indeed Kant himself had attempted to do in his theory of fine art and its "aesthetic ideas." And in his later work, as already suggested, Vischer went even further than this and made room for emotion in aesthetic experience, indeed coalesced the Kantian conception of form as the proper object of taste with the idea of the projection of emotion onto aesthetic objects in both nature and art.

In the *Aesthetik*, Vischer conceives of the "absolute Idea" as "the unity of all opposites, which come together in the highest opposition, that between subject and object, which sublates itself through the divided but then reunited activity of knowing and willing," which "cannot as such come to appearance at any single point of time and space but realizes itself in all spaces and in the endless course of time through a continually self-renewing process of movement."[28] Vischer says that "this highest unity is not merely a formal concept" and that in using this conception "aesthetics supports itself on metaphysics," but his concept of the absolute Idea certainly seems more abstract than Hegel's, for he does not explicitly identify it with mind, whether human or superhuman, and in spite of his own origins as a theologian he certainly does not explicitly

---

[25] See for example Vischer, *Aesthetik*, §5, vol. I, p. 21.
[26] Vischer, *Aesthetik*, §43, vol. I, p. 128.
[27] Vischer, *Aesthetik*, §75, vol. I, p. 203.
[28] Vischer, *Aesthetik*, §10, vol. I, p. 45.

identify the Idea with God. Rather, the Idea is real in a twofold way, "in the general, eternal course of the world and in the comprehending spirit of what thinks [*das Denkenden*],"[29] but there is no suggestion that the former reduces to the latter. Moreover, Vischer explicitly distinguishes his position from Hegel's by insisting that among the opposites that are united but not dissolved in the absolute Idea are necessity and contingency: contingency must be recognized to be a complement to necessity, not simply eliminated. He says that "It is the deficiency of the Hegelian system, not that it has no place for the contingent, but that it momentarily includes it only as a way of considering things from the point of view of 'bad finitude,' in order to immediately dissolve it in the representation of consideration in thought,"[30] whereas on his view contingency should be recognized as a permanent feature of reality along with necessity. Part of the function of beauty, in turn, is to capture the appearance of necessity in the contingent, not just to present necessity – necessary forms, necessary laws, and so on – through contingent materials that are as it were made irrelevant by their own content. Indeed, for this reason, even though Vischer recognizes philosophy to be a superior medium to art for the comprehension of the Idea, art's representation of the presence of both necessity and contingency in the "continually self-renewing process of movement" that constitutes the Idea means that in his view it can no more be superseded by philosophy itself than it could be superseded by religion.

Having defined the Idea, Vischer then argues that it must present itself "in the form of immediacy or intuition,"[31] and then that the "appearance" (*Erscheinung*) of the Idea to sensible intuition is beauty. But he also argues that "since the Idea can never be present in any single being," the thought that it is "completely realized" in any particular object is "a mere illusion" (*bloßer Schein*),[32] so the beautiful will always be an object (or an object that represents an object) that *suggests* something greater than itself, the Idea with all of its reconciliation of opposites, without ever fully realizing it. Thus the beautiful is an intimation of the Idea or perhaps, to borrow a term that would later become popular, a promise of the Idea.[33] The beautiful "is a sensible particular that appears to be

[29] Vischer, *Aesthetik*, §10, vol. I, p. 48.
[30] Vischer, *Aesthetik*, §41, vol. I, p. 120.
[31] Vischer, *Aesthetik*, §10, vol. I, p. 48.
[32] Vischer, *Aesthetik*, §13, vol. I, pp. 51–2.
[33] The characterization of the beautiful as a "promise of happiness" was introduced by Charles Baudelaire. For a recent discussion of this topic, see Nehamas, *Only a Promise of Happiness*, which will be discussed in the Epilogue in Volume 3.

a pure expression of the Idea, so that in the latter there is nothing that does not sensibly appear and nothing sensibly appears that is not a pure expression of the idea."[34] Now the fact that a sensible particular can only intimate and never fully realize the Idea may be precisely why Hegel held that art must be superseded by religion and then philosophy, but for Vischer, who sides explicitly with Schelling on this point,[35] the Idea needs sensible presentation, and if we interpret this to mean that we ourselves are ineluctably sensible as well as intellectual creatures who need to represent reality by means of our senses as well as our intellect, then Vischer would in fact also be siding with Kant.

Vischer also distinguishes his aesthetics from the theological aesthetics of Hegel by arguing that since the highest presentation of the Idea is as "self-consciousness" and "personality," the "highest content of the beautiful" must also be personality,[36] although personality that is particular as well as universal, and thus human personality, not divine personality. But since this personality must also be universal as well as particular, he argues that the highest form of beauty concerns not so much individual personality as the "ethical world" (*sittliche Welt*) of the human species in its various kinds and individuals; thus "the most worthy content of the beautiful lies in the ethical powers of public life."[37] By means of this argument Vischer prepares the way for his detailed interpretation of the arts, including the arts of his own day such as the novel and novella, as by no means consisting exclusively in but as culminating in the representation of the social life of human beings (which is why Lukács so admired him, as will be evident from our discussion of Lukács in Volume 3). From this Vischer further infers that since the Idea itself is the "self-realizing moral end" of humankind, the content of the beautiful is ultimately identical with this.[38] Yet at the same time, well aware of the eighteenth-century and especially Kantian conception of the disinterestedness of the judgment of the beautiful, he wants to avoid a reduction of the beautiful to the good, and especially any praise for didactic art. He does this by arguing that while the problem with religion is that it presents the good as something that already exists but entirely apart from us,[39] and the problem with ordinary morality is that it presents the good as something

---

[34] Vischer, *Aesthetik*, §14, vol. I, pp. 52–3.
[35] Vischer, *Aesthetik*, note to §13, vol. I, p. 52.
[36] Vischer, *Aesthetik*, §19, vol. I, p. 72.
[37] Vischer, *Aesthetik*, §20, vol. I, p. 75.
[38] Vischer, *Aesthetik*, §22, vol. I, p. 77.
[39] Vischer, *Aesthetik*, §24, vol. I, p. 81.

that we are always striving for but that is never attainable in our actual existence, the beautiful presents the possibility of a harmonious existence in reality,[40] of course not suggesting that all the contradictions of life are already fully resolved but at the same time not presenting them as resolvable only in an indefinite future or indeed in an afterlife. To borrow a later phrase, the beautiful is only a promise of happiness, but it is least more of a genuine promise of happiness than religion and ordinary morality have to offer.[41]

Let us turn now from Vischer's internecine battle with Hegel to his rehabilitation of Kant. Vischer observes that Kant characterized the "unity which combines the manifold in that which is perfect" as an "end in the sense of Wolff," but that while Wolff's conception of an end remained completely external, "Only Kant himself grasped the concept of an end in its depth." In his critique of teleological judgment, Vischer holds, Kant conceived of the end as an understanding that is "active" and "constructive" in the object itself, but that because of his inclination toward "subjective idealism" he insisted on interpreting the self-realizing end in both teleology and aesthetics as something subjective, something that exists only in our response to the beautiful and the organic, not something genuinely internal to them. But there was in his view nothing in Kant's conception of purposiveness itself that necessitated his subjectivism, so Kant could have led the way to a more satisfactory conception of the Idea as manifesting itself in beauty.[42] Independent of this claim, however, and more convincing, is Vischer's argument that Kant's conception of the free play of our cognitive powers is a correct description of what is properly subjective in beauty, namely our experience of it, and moreover that Kant is correct in emphasizing the pleasure in this experience, something largely neglected by Hegel and the idealists of the previous generation (again excluding Schleiermacher). Thus Vischer writes:

> The aesthetic disposition (*Stimmung*) in the subject is as a reflection (*Reflex*) of the object also considered in itself a pure mean of the opposed forms of its activity. This mean is determined by Kant as a free play and the pleasure that is connected with it as a pure satisfaction, i.e., as one that excludes every *interest*.... The beautiful is therefore not to be confused with the *interesting*.

[40] Vischer, *Aesthetik*, §56, vol. I, p. 158.
[41] Oelmüller argues that Vischer gives up this optimistic view of aesthetic experience in his later works (*Vischer und das Problem*, pp. 183–6). The interpretation of *Das Schöne und die Kunst* to be offered will suggest that in his later career Vischer gives up Hegelian metaphysics but not the underlying optimism of his aesthetics.
[42] Vischer, *Aesthetik*, §43, vol. I, pp. 128–31.

All satisfaction of this unfree sort can be called with Kant pathological, but free, aesthetic satisfaction can be called contemplative.[43]

Vischer endorses Kant's interpretation of aesthetic experience. He says that it was a mistake for Kant to limit the free play to our *cognitive* powers alone, and that Kant "would have done well to take it in a wider sense" that would include the free play rather than normal, rule-bound activity of our *practical* powers as well, but that with this correction having been made, Kant was quite right to characterize our experience of the beautiful as a free play; his only mistake was to take this as exhausting what we can say about the beautiful, without realizing that this free play is the subjective "reflection" of the manifestation of the Idea in beautiful objects, which is after all itself always a harmonious but never completely resolved interaction between the universal and the particular, the necessary and the contingent, in objects, to which it is entirely appropriate for us to respond with a free play of all of our mental powers. In this context, Vischer also invokes Schiller, whom he thinks deepened Kant's notion of play in his notion of the "play-drive" as reconciling the "form-drive" and the "matter-drive" while successfully combining it with an account of the objective content of beauty as the appearance of freedom itself.[44] Vischer thus argues against all those who would criticize the Kantian conception of play as "too contemptible" that it can be successfully combined as an account of the experience of the beautiful with a proper account of the Idea as the content of the beautiful. Like so many other readers before and since, Vischer concentrates more on Kant's Analytic of the Beautiful than on his later account of fine art,[45] and so he might be criticized for having failed to see that in his concept of aesthetic ideas Kant himself had anticipated at least some aspects of Vischer's own approach.

From his premise that the absolute Idea reconciles the difference between the subject and the object without erasing it, Vischer constructed an elaborate system of natural and artistic beauty. Thus, he first divides beauty in general into a more subjective side, which includes the sublime and the comic (and the sublime itself includes a subjective sublime, an objective sublime, and a "sublime of the subject-object, or the tragic"); a more objective side, namely natural beauty; and then a form that brings out both the subjective and the objective, namely the beauty of art. The arts are in turn divided into the more objective ones, namely

---

[43] Vischer, *Aesthetik*, §75, vol. I, p. 203.
[44] Vischer, *Aesthetik*, §75, vol. I, pp. 204–7.
[45] *CPJ*, §§43–53.

architecture, sculpture, and painting; a more subjective one, namely music, which he conceives of as primarily an art for the expression of emotion through sound; and finally an art form that combines the objective and the subjective, namely literature. But even within the latter there is again a division among the most objective form, namely the epic; the most subjective form, the lyric; and finally the objective-subjective form, the drama (Vischer subsumes modern prose forms under all of these traditional poetic categories). Vischer illustrates these categories with a wealth of illuminating examples, much in the spirit of Hegel.

Thus far we have seen how Vischer synthesizes a metaphysical approach to art inspired by Hegel with a concession that Kant had gotten something right about the phenomenology of aesthetic experience, but we have not seen much reference to the emotional impact of art. Not surprisingly, this aspect of aesthetic experience becomes more prominent in Vischer's account of literature than it was in his accounts of the other arts. He describes lyric poetry as the product of "the poetic fantasy that presents itself from the standpoint of one who feels [*der empfindenden*]," a form in which "the subject expresses himself, his mood" and carries over "his own thoughts ... and movements of will into the atmosphere of mood [*Stimmungs-Atmosphäre*]."[46] "The lyrical subject introduces to us outer objects that tell and depict a story ... while it sets its and our fantasy into a determinate condition."[47] Here Vischer reveals that the experience of art has an effect on the mood as well as the thought of the audience: an "atmosphere" is more emotional than intellectual.[48] The emotional impact of art on its audience is even more explicit in Vischer's contrast between modern and ancient drama. "*Classical* tragedy takes place on mythic-heroic ground," and its "characters are more types than individuals,"[49] commented upon by a chorus that blends music into the drama. But modern tragedy deals with a wealth of individual characters, from high to low – of course Vischer has Shakespeare in mind – and the chorus is dropped, thus combination between drama and music is replaced with a combination between tragedy and comedy. And what is crucial about the disappearance of the chorus is that the response of an

---

[46] Vischer, *Aesthetik*, §885 (vol. 5, pp. 1324–5).
[47] Vischer, *Aesthetik*, pp. 1326–7.
[48] The contemporary German aesthetician Gernot Böhme has based his theory on the concept of "atmosphere," anticipated if not influenced by Vischer, whom he does not mention. See Böhme, *Aisthetik: Vorlesungen über Ästhetik als allgemeine Wahrnehmungslehre* (Munich: Wilhelm Fink Verlag: 2001).
[49] Vischer, *Aesthetik*, §905, vol. 5, p. 1408.

"ideal observer" within the work to the characters and events it depicts is replaced by the "actual feelings of the empirical observer," that is, the real audience: this is "the subjective echo of the multitude of persons involved and of their deepened, more variegated mental life [*vielsaitigeren Gemüthsleben*]."[50] The characters of modern drama are depicted as having a full range of both intellectual and emotional life, and their audience hears an "echo" of that, or experiences some of it for themselves.

So at least with regard to some forms of modern art, Vischer recognizes that the experience of the audience will be emotional as well as intellectual and imaginative. In his later lectures, Vischer's Hegelian metaphysics fades away, his appreciation of Kant becomes more pronounced, but most importantly he suggests that there may be an emotional dimension to the experience of any form of beauty, indeed that beauty must be regarded as form but as also the projection of our emotional responses on to objects: experiencing objects as embodying our own emotions replaces the Hegelian conception of beauty as the sensible appearance of the Idea. This dimension of aesthetic experience is what Vischer calls *Einfühlung*, and represents a decided turn away from the metaphysical cognitivisms of Hegel, Schelling, and Schopenhauer.[51]

Robert Vischer edited *Das Schöne und die Kunst* after his father's death on the basis of Friedrich Theodor's own lecture notes, which were apparently just sketches, although much worked-over, and several student transcriptions of his classes, including some of his own, dating from 1866 to 1883. Vischer begins the lectures with the statement that "the value that the object of aesthetics, the beautiful, has over the content of the sciences, and the real ground of its incomparable effect, lies in the fact that it has immediately comprehensible significance [*Bedeutung*], which is just as present to sense and nerve [*Sinn und Nerv*] as to spirit and mind [*Geist und Gemüt*].[52] Vischer's assertion of the equal importance in aesthetic experience of the sensory and the intellectual makes it clear from the outset that he is now distancing himself from Hegelianism, and his inclusion of both "sense" and "nerve" on the sensory side makes it clear that emotion ("nerve") will be as important as perception ("sense") in his

[50] Vischer, *Ästhetik*, §907, vol. 5, p. 1416.
[51] On Vischer's response to Schopenhauer and the early work of Nietzsche, as well as his disgust at what had become, at the hands of Richard Wagner, of his own suggestion that the *Nibelungenlied* might make good material for an opera, see Oelmüller, *Vischer und das Problem*, pp. 188–206.
[52] Vischer, *Das Schöne und die Kunst*, edited by Robert Vischer (Stuttgart: Cotta, 1898), pp. 3–4.

account. Vischer then continues in a way that sounds Schopenhauerian for a moment, but is clearly moving in the direction of Kant. Like Kant, he emphasizes the disinterestedness of aesthetic experience, although he will not introduce that terminology until later: "What life, the state, society, the law demands, does not weigh upon us" in the aesthetic sphere; the aesthetic "charms, strengthens, elevates [us] without any practical relation. It releases us from the stress and coercion [*Drang und Zwang*] of the ought, for it presents the final end of the world as attained and shows life in the splendor of perfection." Vischer describes the effect of this presentation in terms that are momentarily Schopenhauerian – "This release from the pain of unattained ... ends" – but then turn Kantian – "is essentially a unification." In particular, this "release is also in the intuiting subject a unification of [its] powers." And then his account takes a Schillerian turn as well: "The beautiful, I have said, produces a whole again out of the divided human being."[53] The idea is that aesthetic experience involves the harmonious activity of all of our powers, and this has a beneficial effect on the person, unifying what is otherwise divided. Vischer is explicit that this is not just a precondition for the artist, but a result for the audience, the "intuiting subject," as well.

Later in the work, Vischer will make his increasing affinity with Kant even clearer by describing his theory of beauty as one of "interestless interest."[54] But he has also already suggested that his view goes beyond Kant because the unification in aesthetic experience involves all our powers, "nerve" as well as "sense," and the focus of his lectures is the emotional impact of various forms and our projection of that emotional impact back on to the forms of objects. Vischer states that "aesthetic intuition is not directed to the *what*, but only to the *how*, not to the *matter* [*Stoff*] but to the *form*. Form is the ordering of the matter into unity in multiplicity, thus harmony. It is not itself matter, only the collective effect [*Gesamtwirkung*] of all the parts of the matter, in this sense only surface, thus *sensible-nonsensible* [*sinnlich-unsinnlich*]."[55] This sounds like a traditional definition of form, and it would seem that Vischer's theory has now become the Kantian theory, indeed the theory of the "Analytic of the Beautiful," indeed perhaps the Schopenhauerian version of the Kantian theory, that what provides us with release from the unsatisfied ends of state, society, and so on, is the focus of our attention solely on the

---

[53] Vischer, *Das Schöne und die Kunst*, p. 4.
[54] E.g., Vischer, *Das Schöne und die Kunst*, pp. 61, 83.
[55] Vischer, *Das Schöne und die Kunst*, p. 48.

relations among the aspects of the objects before us without any regard to the significance of the aspects so related. But it is clear that Vischer is taking a different path as soon as he illustrates what he has in mind by an account of our experience of a beautiful landscape (by which he seems to have in mind an actual scene in nature, not a painting thereof). We abstract from the matter itself in the sense that "we do not ask what is the content [*Gehalt*] of the stone, the water, the plants," but instead respond to the way in which the air and light and our perspective on these things "affect us with a mood [*so stimmungsvoll ... wirken*]."[56] Thus form is not a relation among things that we could capture with a mathematical formula, but that in the appearance of objects that we capture with a mood. Vischer rejects the kind of formalism that he associates especially with Herbart and his student Robert Zimmermann (1824–98),[57] who says, "it is indifferent, what the matter of the part that are put together is *in itself*, only the *relation* matters,"[58] and instead writes that while "matter is 1. sensible material, 2. the object, as it lies before us before being seen (the subject), 3. the living content [*Lebensgehalt*] in this object, the beautiful abstracts from 1 and 2 but not from 3"[59] – the beautiful does *not* abstract from the living content of the object, or from its effect on our emotions. He continues: "So does the inner essence and life of the object, as it is, reveal itself in its form, according to the way in which [*nachdem*] the spirit of the apprehender (of the observer and of the artist) has laid itself in that and made it into its own property."[60] Everything depends here on precisely how the little word "*nachdem*" should be understood, but Vischer's meaning seems to be that there is not a one-way passage of mood or emotional impact from object to subject, but rather an interchange, in which the form of the object stimulates a certain mood or emotion in an artist making an artwork about it or in an audience responding to either a natural object or a work of art, which is then transposed back onto the object, so that mood seems to be essential to the object itself. The pleasure in such an intuition is a "pure unity of ideal and sensible pleasure," and for us to be able to experience objects in such a way we must exclude our ordinary interests in using them for specific ends, thus

---

[56] Vischer, *Das Schöne und die Kunst*, p. 49.
[57] Vischer, *Das Schöne und die Kunst*, pp. 56–60; see Robert, Edler von Zimmermann, *Aesthetik* (Vienna: W. Braumüller, 1858–65), and *Studien und Kritiken zur Philosophie und Aesthetik* (Vienna: W. Braumüller, 1870).
[58] Vischer, *Das Schöne und die Kunst*, p. 58.
[59] Vischer, *Das Schöne und die Kunst*, p. 61.
[60] Vischer, *Das Schöne und die Kunst*, p. 61.

there must reign "interestless interest (play)."[61] The Kantian provenance of these terms could not be more clear, but what Vischer is arguing is that the Kantian state of disinterested mental play with the appearance of an object is only the precondition for the emotional response to and the projection of that emotional response back on to the object, which are the core of aesthetic experience and aesthetic qualities.

Vischer describes the triggering of mood or emotion by objects and our projection of that mood back onto objects as "a peculiar kind of symbolism [*Symbolik*], an unconscious empathy [*Einfühlens*] of the soul,"[62] but he uses many other terms for this phenomenon as well. He says that "the spirit" – although here he means the human spirit, nothing more – "sinks itself into a given object and creatively transforms it,"[63] that form is "penetrated by free life,"[64] that a work of art is "something magically ensouled [*ein zaubrisch Beseeltes*],"[65] that "we lend our soul" to a natural or artistic work "and without this symolism would never call" it "beautiful,"[66] that beauty is something that "especially arouses [*anregen*] us,"[67] and that "In the beautiful we must always start from the form, but we feel in it something inner."[68] Beautiful objects touch our emotions, not just our senses; thus, for example, "In the magnificent materials, the glowing and shimmering velvet, silk, gold, silver that are imitated in the paintings of Metsu, Terborch, Netscher and other Dutch painters, there lie wonderful charms, that are not merely sensory, but arouse our emotions in such a special way that it cannot be described," and likewise in nature, "we hear threatening spirits in a storm, and even milder noises, such as the murmuring of a stream, the gentle blowing of the wind in the trees, speak to us. Through these impressions on the senses we at the same time feel impressions on our souls."[69] "Everything beautiful moves us, touches us deeply,"[70] and we project this back onto the objects that so move us. Vischer's followers would prefer his term "empathy" (*Einfühlung*) for this response, but perhaps his own favorite was

---

[61] Vischer, *Das Schöne und die Kunst*, p. 61.
[62] Vischer, *Das Schöne und die Kunst*, p. 61.
[63] Vischer, *Das Schöne und die Kunst*, p. 65.
[64] Vischer, *Das Schöne und die Kunst*, p. 66.
[65] Vischer, *Das Schöne und die Kunst*, p. 66.
[66] Vischer, *Das Schöne und die Kunst*, p. 74.
[67] Vischer, *Das Schöne und die Kunst*, p. 76.
[68] Vischer, *Das Schöne und die Kunst*, pp. 76–7.
[69] Vischer, *Das Schöne und die Kunst*, p. 76.
[70] Vischer, *Das Schöne und die Kunst*, p. 82.

"ensoul," as when he speaks of our "ensouling all of nature" (*Beseelung der ganzen Natur*).[71]

Vischer recognizes that his insistence that beautiful objects must touch and move us, cause an emotional response that we then project back on to them as the very content of their beauty, could seem to threaten the Kantian conception of the disinterestedness of aesthetic response that he has explicitly endorsed. He agrees with Kant, and, he explicitly adds, Goethe and Schiller, that "theoretical interest, the interest of use, moral, political, and religious interest," all "wishing or willing, desiring or aversion in relation to the existence" of beautiful objects must be "absolutely excluded" from our properly aesthetic response to them.[72] How is this requirement to be reconciled with the fact that "the beautiful will *touch*" us? Vischer's answer is analogous to the answer that Schopenhauer gave in the case of music: "The beautiful says to us something about the content [*Gehalt*] of life, it is an appearance, a seeming, in which content [*Inhalt*] appears; only it is not the individual case, not an empirical truth that it puts before the soul, but it is always an inner and general truth."

> In the beautiful we let everything please us: images from ancient mythology, gods, genies.... We Protestants allow the approach of the Catholics to please us and we do not struggle against it. We are charmed by the view of Raphael's Sistine Madonna, like everyone, but it does not occur to us to believe in the Maria myth. We know that here the ancient mythical belief in female deities has had an effect on Christianity. But we do not ask about that when we see the Sistine Madonna. There it is not a matter of the truth of the Catholic belief in the mother of God, but of an inner, universal truth. We see the woman, who as a mother remains as pure as a virgin, the elevated image of motherly purity, the most noble virginity. That is the universal, the inner truth, that we here experience[73] –

that is to say, both know and feel. In other words, Vischer's conception of the disinterestedness of aesthetic response is really the original, Shaftesburian, even Neo-Platonic conception: our sense of beauty is not a response to some abstract form that has nothing to do with the whole range of human ideals, hopes, passions, and so on; our sense of beauty has everything to do with all of that, it is a response that unifies all of our human powers and feelings, but beautiful objects, many of them made in very different context and belief systems than our own, can only have their full effect on us if we leave the particularities of our own beliefs

---

[71] Vischer, *Das Schöne und die Kunst*, p. 90.
[72] Vischer, *Das Schöne und die Kunst*, p. 82.
[73] Vischer, *Das Schöne und die Kunst*, p. 83.

and interests aside. If we focus on the general rather than the particular, then we can even enjoy ideas and feelings that would be disturbing if we personalized them, connected them specifically to our own interests and beliefs. We can enjoy in general what we might not enjoy in particular. Of course, Vischer's view is not the same as Schopenhauer's, which is that by focusing on the "Platonic Form" even of the terrifying or frustrating, we will be relieved from our own particular terrors or frustrations and enter into the negative state of relief from pain; his view clearly is that there is a positive pleasure in experiencing the full range of human emotions and in experiencing art and even nature as ensouled by them, a pleasure that we can often experience only if we set our own personal interests aside.

In moving from Vischer's *Aesthetik* to his later lectures, we have traversed several decades and entered into the period in which his idea of empathy or ensoulment became the slogan of a whole school of aestheticians. Before we see what some of those writers added to Vischer's idea, however, let us turn the clock back and see what followed his earlier work. For there were further developments within Hegelian aesthetics before it was displaced by newer trends, and many of those newer trends also need to be discussed before we can look back to the later development of the idea of empathy. The next Hegelian that we can consider is Karl Rosenkranz.

3. ROSENKRANZ

Even though he himself worried that he was merely an epigone of Hegel, Karl Rosenkranz (1805–79), was also an innovator in the Hegelian tradition. His innovation was not merely an extended analysis of the "aesthetics of the ugly" in his book of that name (1853), but the foundation of that analysis on a conception of the Idea as freedom that led to the argument that just as in the moral sphere an unavoidable concomitant of freedom is the possibility of evil, so in the aesthetic sphere an unavoidable concomitant of beauty as the sensible expression of freedom is the possibility of ugliness as the distorted expression of freedom. Unlike Vischer, Rosenkranz restricted his analysis to the objects of aesthetic experience rather than to the subjective side of aesthetic experience itself, so his emphasis on freedom as the ultimate source of both beauty and ugliness did not lead him to a renewed appreciation of Kant's conception of the free play of our cognitive powers as the basis of aesthetic experience or to Vischer's emphasis on the emotional experience of natural and artistic beauty. His account of aesthetic experience remains purely cognitivist. Nevertheless, his emphasis on freedom within the Hegelian, cognitivist approach to aesthetics, while explicitly aimed at broadening Hegel's conception of aesthetic qualities, what can be presented or represented, might also prepare the way for a broader conception of aesthetic experience itself.

Rosenkranz began his university studies at Berlin in 1824, but was influenced more by Schleiermacher than by Hegel while he was there. Only after transferring to Halle in 1826 did he begin an intensive study of Hegel. Displaying the combination of interests that would remain with him throughout his career, he earned his doctorate at Halle in 1828 for a work on German literature in the Middle Ages, but earned his habilitation only eight months later with a work on Spinoza. He became a professor at Halle in 1831, but moved to Königsberg in 1834 to take over the chair once held by Kant – the chair for which Kant had had to wait until he was forty-six, but that Rosenkranz enjoyed at age twenty-eight. He spent the rest of his extraordinarily productive career in Königsberg, where he produced the first collected edition of Kant's works and an accompanying *History of the Kantian Philosophy* (1840), a study of Schelling (1843), biographies of Hegel (1844 and 1870), Goethe, and Diderot, as well as systematic works such as *Psychology or the Science of Subjective Spirit* (1837), a *System of Science* (1850), and a *Science of Logical Ideas* (1858–59). He also published poetry and political writings, and was active in the short-lived liberal Prussian government in 1848–49, including a stint as Minister of Culture.[74]

But the work for which Rosenkranz is best remembered is the *Aesthetics of the Ugly*, distinguished among works in the Hegelian school for the clarity, indeed elegance, of its style as well as for its originality. The thesis of the work is that the ugly is the negation of the beautiful, although since the beautiful itself and therefore the ugly as well are both products of freedom, in the broadest possible sense of a force at work in nature as well as in intentional human conduct, there is no dialectical necessity that the ugly exist, and moreover, in the form of the comic, the ugly can be transformed back into the beautiful; the comic is thus for Rosenkranz the most complex and interesting, one might say the most redemptive form of art, and what was for him the greatest work of comic art, namely

---

[74] Work on Rosenkranz includes Holger Funk, *Ästhetik des Häßlichen: Beiträge zum Verständnis negativer Ausdrucksformen im 19. Jahrhundert* (Berlin: Agora Verlag, 1983); Werner Jung, *Schöner Schein der Häßlichkeit oder Häßlichkeit des schönen Scheins* (Frankfurt am Main: Athenäum, 1987); and Iannelli, *Das Siegel der Moderne*, pp. 249–59.

Don Quixote, may have been the greatest work of art of all.[75] Thus, while for Hegel the comic represented the end of art, for Rosenkranz the possibility of the comic is nothing less than the apotheosis of art.

Rosenkranz begins *The Aesthetics of Ugliness* with an analysis of the ugly in nature, the ugly in spirit, and the ugly in art. Ugliness in nature results when the free development of natural objects, including nonorganic objects such as crystals but paradigmatically organisms, that is, their development toward the ideal form for their type or species, is distorted by external forces such as agents of disease or harshness of environment. Ugliness in spirit results when the free, self-determining will chooses evil instead of goodness and purity, thus, "The cause of evil and the ugliness that is transmitted to the external appearance of a human being by it is his freedom, not a transcendental essence outside of him."[76] Rosenkranz points out that it is natural for the beauty of the will, that is, its goodness and purity, to have a beautifying effect on the outward appearance and deportment of a person, and natural for us to expect that, and likewise natural for ugliness or evil in the will to have an ugly effect on outward appearance, but the ethical and the aesthetic properties are not identical, and in particular not all ugliness in human appearance is a sign of moral evil – it can also be a product of interference with the unhindered development of the human organism that would otherwise produce natural beauty. Finally, ugliness in art is a possibility just because art is the appearance of the spirit and the spirit is freedom itself, which means that it cannot be necessitated to produce beauty but can also produce ugliness; moreover, insofar as art is not just the appearance or sensible manifestation of the spirit but also the representation or depiction of it, it would not be complete unless it could represent all the expressions of freedom, the misuse or perversion of freedom as well as its optimal use. Rosenkranz writes:

> The realm of the ugly is ... as great as the realm of sensible appearance in general.... Since the ugly is [the negation] of the beautiful, it can be the negation of each of its forms, generated by the necessity of nature or by the freedom of the spirit.... In order for the beautiful to be enjoyed in and for itself, the spirit must produce it ... Thus arises art. It is externally connected with human needs, but its true ground remains the longing of spirit for the pure, unmixed beautiful.

---

[75] See the trenchant analysis of *Don Quixote* that concludes the first section of the *Ästhetik des Häßlichen* (Königsberg: Gerüder Bornträger, 1853) ed. Dieter Kliche (Leipzig: Reclam Verlag, 1996), pp. 57–9.
[76] Rosenkranz, *Häßlichen*, p. 32.

> But if the production of the beautiful is the task of art, must it not appear to be the greatest contradiction if we see that art also produces the ugly?[77]

No, Rosenkranz answers, because it is inherent in the freedom of the spirit that it be able to produce ugliness as well as beauty and necessary to a complete representation of the spirit that its capacity to produce ugliness as well as beauty be truly represented. The possibility, indeed the necessity, of ugliness in art is not just that it serves to highlight beauty by its contrast, but "must lie deeper than in that external relation of reflection":

> It lies in the essence of the Idea itself. The sensible element is necessary for art – and this is its limit in comparison with the freedom of the good and the true – but in this element the appearance of the idea will and should express itself in its totality. It belongs to the essence of the idea to leave the existence of its appearance free and thereby to establish the possibility of the negative.... If nature and spirit are to be presented in their full depth, then the naturally ugly, the evil and the diabolical cannot be lacking.... For this reason, therefore, to depict the appearance of the idea in its totality, art cannot avoid offering an image of the ugly.[78]

Rosenkranz argues, in traditional Hegelian fashion, that spirit or idea needs to present itself to the senses, but adds that it needs to do so freely, and therefore needs to do so through art, a free production of human beings, as well as in other forms that do not pass through human freedom. But then, just because art is freely produced, it is possible for it to be ugly as well as beautiful. Moreover, since the task of art is to depict (*schildern*) spirit – Rosenkranz is still working with a fundamentally mimetic conception of art – and spirit can freely manifest itself in natural and moral ugliness as well as beauty, art must be able to depict these too. Rosenkranz's argument works at two levels: as a *product* of freedom, art must be capable of producing ugliness as well as beauty, and as a *representation* of freedom, art must be capable of representing ugliness as well as beauty.

It might be objected to this analysis that art does not simply copy nature, but that it idealizes nature, and that since idealization produces beauty, truly successful art must be beautiful. Rosenkranz answers this objection by agreeing that art always depicts the essential rather than the accidental, the true rather than the merely "empirical," but that this is the case in art's representation of the ugly as well as the beautiful.

---

[77] Rosenkranz, *Häßlichen*, p. 35.
[78] Rosenkranz, *Haßlichen*, pp. 37–8.

Rosenkranz's view that art must exclude the accidental seems more conventional than Vischer's view that the task of art is to represent the contingent as well as the necessary, but he puts this conventional premise to use in his unconventional defense of the possibility of the representation of ugliness in art:

> It is true that art also idealizes the ugly, i.e., it must treat it in accordance with the general laws of the beautiful that it injures through its existence; art must not hide the ugly, dress it up, falsify it, distort it with alien decoration, but must form it, without injury to truth, in accordance with the measure of its aesthetic significance. This is necessary, for art proceeds in this way with all reality. The nature that art presents to us is the real but not the common, empirical nature. It is nature as it would be if its finitude allowed it such perfection. And likewise the history that art gives us is the real and yet not the common, empirical history.... In the common reality there is never any lack of the most enraging and repulsive uglinesses; art is not to take these up without anything further. It must put the ugly before us in its negative essence, but it must do this with the same ideality with which it treats the beautiful. It must leave out of its content everything that belongs merely to the contingent existence of the ugly.... It must bring out those determinations and forms that make the ugly into the ugly.[79]

Rosenranz's aesthetic cognitivism is, so to speak, an essentialist cognitivism, a theory that art represents the essences rather than the accidents of things (a precedent for this is of course Schopenhauer's theory of the Platonic Ideas as the content of natural and artistic beauty), and thus the depiction of the ugly is possible for art precisely insofar as art depicts the essence of ugliness.

The multiple levels of Rosenkranz's analysis of the possibility of ugliness in art are also evident in the "Division" that concludes the introductory section of his book. Here he says that "The first requisite for beauty is ... the need for boundaries," and that "The negation of this general unity of form is thus formlessness"; thus the first form of ugliness is formlessness.[80] He immediately points out that at the most abstract ("metaphysical") level everything has some form, so from that point of view there is no such thing as formlessness; the formlessness of an ugly work of art must therefore be a "relative" formlessness, and this turns out to be a form that "contradicts" or is inappropriate to the content of the work of art. "Thus the beautiful demands unity of content and form in certain relationships."[81] The second demand of beauty is truthfulness to nature,

---

[79] Rosenkranz, *Häßlichen*, p. 41.
[80] Rosenkranz, *Häßlichen*, p. 50.
[81] Rosenkranz, *Häßlichen*, p. 51.

but since this must be idealized nature, not common nature with all of its accidents, the beautiful demands "correctness" or the representation of objects in accordance with the laws of nature, and the ugly is what violates these laws: "The beautiful cannot do without this correctness. Thus if a form violates the lawfulness of nature, from such contradiction there arises unmistakable ugliness."[82] But beyond or, better, beneath formlessness and incorrectness, the real source of ugliness lies in the freedom that expresses itself as beauty but that also includes the possibility of its own perversion:

> Formlessness was thus the first and incorrectness the second main form of the ugly. But there remains that form that really contains the ground for both, the internal malformation that also manifests itself as exterior disharmony and unnaturalness, because it is turbid and confused itself. For beauty freedom is the true content, freedom in the general sense, under which is understood not only the ethical freedom of the will but also the spontaneity of intelligence and the free movement of nature. The unity of form and its individuality become perfectly beautiful only through self-determination....
>
> The principle of the ugly, however, is constituted by unfreedom, from which the individual aesthetically or rather unaesthetically characteristic flows; unfreedom taken in the general sense that includes not merely art but also nature and life in general. Unfreedom as the lack of self-determination or as the contradiction of self-determination with the necessity of the essence of a subject generates that which is ugly in itself, which comes to appearance in the incorrect and the formless.... True freedom is in all ways the mother of the beautiful, unfreedom that of the ugly.[83]

Rosenkranz's term "unfreedom" is vague, but it should not be taken to mean the absence of freedom; at least in the case of art, it means rather the willful misuse of freedom, the use of freedom in contradiction to both the laws of nature and the law for the will, that is, the moral law. Rosenkranz thus seems to mean that ugliness in art manifests itself in the content of the work, in the misrepresentation of the real laws of nature and in tension between the content and the form of the work, but that more generally it arises from the misuse of the freedom of the artist in the production of the work. Again, then, beauty seems to be both the expression of the freedom of the spirit in the artist and the representation of freedom in all the expressions of the spirit, and ugliness can arise from the same freedom of the spirit in the artist as well

---

[82] Rosenkranz, *Häßlichen*, p. 52.
[83] Rosenkranz, *Häßlichen*, pp. 54, 56.

as from the content of the work, its representation of ugly manifestations of the freedom of the spirit in all its form. There seems to be a difference between these two forms of ugliness that Rosenkranz does not mention, however, namely that ugliness as part of the content of art seems necessary to its mission of representing the manifestation of the spirit but ugliness as a result of the misuse of the freedom of the artist in the production of the work seems merely unfortunate although perhaps also inevitable.

Rosenkranz's work includes an interesting commentary on the possibility for ugliness in different media of art, in which he argues that where the freedom of the artist is constrained by both the non-artistic purpose of his work and the cost of its materials and production – as is almost always the case in architecture and often the case in sculpture (which is often part of a larger architectural program or has a specifically celebratory or memorial function) – there is less room for freedom and therefore for ugliness as well, but that in arts that are not so constrained by function and in which the costs of materials and production are lower – such as painting, music, and literature – there is also more room for the misuse of freedom, and therefore for ugliness.[84] The bulk of the book is then taken up with detailed analyses of formlessness, incorrectness, and disfiguration or malformation. In the last of these sections, he analyzes in turn the vulgar, the repulsive, and caricature, and then makes the argument that caricature is the most important form of ugliness because it is the contrast to the ideal of beauty, but also such a direct expression of freedom that it allows for the reemergence of beauty. The details of Rosenkranz's analyses are fascinating. But for our story the interest of his work is his emphasis on the freedom of the spirit in general as the object that is portrayed through ugliness in art (in one sense) and the freedom of the artist himself as a source of ugliness in art (in another sense). In spite of this emphasis on freedom throughout his account, however, Rosenkranz remains within a cognitivist approach to art and does not recognize the free play of our mental powers as the source of the pleasure of aesthetic experience in both artist and audience. Nor does he give any special attention to the emotions that might be aroused by either beauty or ugliness or by the depiction of either.

[84] Rosenkranz, *Häßlichen*, pp. 44–8.

4. LOTZE

The idea of aesthetic experience as a free play of our mental powers would, however, play a central role in the work of Hermann Rudolf Lotze (1817–81). Lotze was a transitional figure between the idealism of the first half of the nineteenth century and some of the most important movements at the end of the century, including both Neo-Kantianism and American pragmatism. In an essay on "The Concept of Beauty" from as early as 1845, thus contemporaneous with the early work of Vischer, he said that "the thoughtful contemplation of the beautiful owes more to Kant, who found beauty in the suitability of the relations of the object to the play of our cognitive faculties, than is now customarily acknowledged."[85] Lotze went further than Vischer in his appreciation of the concept of free play, regarding it not merely as a good description of the subjective side of aesthetic experience but as absolutely essential to the comprehension of the beautiful. But he also argued that it could be regarded as the basis for the value of beauty only if the play of our mental faculties was itself of value. That this is so, however, he is prepared to argue: in his view, the free play of our mental powers has both intrinsic value as part of our harmonious life and relative or more precisely representative value as an intimation of our place in a harmonious universe. In this way Lotze may be regarded as developing Kant's claim, in his analysis of "intellectual interest" in the beautiful, that (natural) beauty gives us a "sign" of a correspondence between nature and our own purposes[86] into a theory of the objective value of beauty that is part of a theory of the objective value of the universe. Unlike Kant, Lotze also applies his version of the theory of our "intellectual interest" in beautiful to art.[87]

Lotze studied both medicine and philosophy at Leipzig, where he came under the influence of the Hegelian aesthetician Christian Hermann Weisse, and earned doctorates and teaching qualifications in both fields. He actually began as an instructor in medicine before he

---

[85] Hermann Rudolf Lotze, *Über den Begriff der Schönheit* (1845) ("On the concept of the Beautiful"), reprinted in his *Kleinere Schriften*, vol. 1 (Leipzig: S. Hirzel, 1885), pp. 291–341, at p. 295.

[86] Kant, *CPJ*, §42, 5:300.

[87] Little of the literature on Lotze focuses on his aesthetics. The only recent monograph on Lotze is Reinhard Pester, *Hermann Lotze–Wege seines Denkens und Forschens: Ein Kapitel deutscher Philosophie- und Wissenschaftsgeschichte im 19 Jahrhundert* (Würzburg: Könighausen & Neumann, 1997).

switched to philosophy, and made his name by criticizing the prevailing approach to medicine based on Schelling's philosophy of nature in favor of a more empirically grounded approach. Even after he devoted his efforts fully to philosophy, his thought was always marked by an emphasis on the place for empirical research within a speculative, teleological metaphysical framework. (This was certainly a reason for his influence on William James and George Santayana, whose first work was a study of the philosophy of Lotze published in 1889.)[88] Lotze began teaching philosophy in Leipzig, where he published a *Metaphysics* in 1841 and a *Logic* in 1843. In 1844 he was appointed as professor in Göttingen, where he would remain until 1881, when he was called to the university in Berlin, although he died a few months after starting his appointment there. During his Göttingen years, Lotze published a three-volume version of his system, the *Microcosmos* (1856–64, translated into English in 1885),[89] and then started another version of it with more detailed volumes on logic and metaphysics, which were translated into English by the British idealist philosopher and aesthetician Bernard Bosanquet.[90] Lotze did not live to complete the third part of his final system, which would have included aesthetics, but aesthetics was central to his thought from the outset, and his views are well represented in the essay on the concept of beauty, already mentioned; another long essay from 1847, "On the Conditions of Beauty in Art";[91] and in *Fundamentals of Aesthetics*, one of a series of posthumously published outlines of his lecture courses based on Lotze's own dictation.[92] Lotze also published an important *History of Aesthetics in Germany* that covers figures from Baumgarten to Herbart in its first book, but in its second book provides a "history of individual aesthetic concepts," making the work more of a systematic treatise than might first appear.[93]

---

[88] George Santayana, *Lotze's System of Philosophy*, ed. Paul Grimley Kuntz (Bloomington: Indiana University Press, 1971).

[89] Hermann Lotze, *Microcosmus: An Essay concerning Man and his relation to the World*, trans. Elizabeth Hamilton and E. E. Constance Jones, 2 vols. (Edinburgh: T. Clark, 1885).

[90] Hermann Lotze, *Logic, in Three Books, of Thought, of Investigation, and of Knowledge*, translated by Bernard Bosanquet, second edition (Oxford: Clarendon Press, 1888).

[91] Lotze, *Über Bedingungen der Kunstschönheit* (1847) ("*Conditions*"), in *Kleinere Schriften*, vol. 2 (Leipzig: S. Hirzel, 1886), pp. 205–72.

[92] Lotze, *Grundzüge der Ästhetik: Diktate aus den Vorlesungen* (Berlin: Alexander Verlag, 1990) ("*Fundamentals*"). In the case of aesthetics, this volume included the first nine chapters, comprising all of the general theory plus the chapters on music and architecture, from 1865, and the final three chapters on sculpture, painting, and literature from 1856.

[93] Hermann Lotze, *Geschichte der Ästhetik in Deutschland* (Munich: Cotta, 1868).

The central idea of Lotze's system is that the universe is purposive, that its purposes are expressed and achieved through natural laws that must be gleaned from empirical research and not deduced *a priori* as in his opinion earlier idealists had attempted to do, but that the infinite extent and complex but harmonious interrelations of empirical phenomena can never be completely captured by the laws that we can discover. The free but harmonious play of our own mental powers in our experience of beauty is of central importance and value because it is not only an instance of the harmonious purposiveness of the universe as a whole but also an intimation of the vastness and the purposiveness of the universe that goes beyond anything that patient scientific research, indispensable as it is, can ever offer us. He gives us a concise statement of this general theory and of the significance of beauty, in particular art, for the representation of it, in the 1847 essay on beauty in art:

> Our sensible observation of the world sees three powers intertwined in the course of things: universal laws of coming-to-be and passing-from-being, exceptionless for every individual form of succession, from the eternal fate of appearances; subjected to them is a fullness of living reality, which overlay these stiff limits with wonderful inborn drives of formation and internal liveliness; and in these we believe that we sometimes finally detect more clearly the traces of an ordering thought, which leads the connectionless noise of appearances to a common goal. This goal-directed movement does not form of the sense of the course of the world by itself, but the meaning of the latter lies precisely in the fact that this gradual progress includes within itself those contradictory powers, the never-progressing laws and the wilful liveliness of things. If art is to give us an image of this entire course of the world in its works, then none of these features can be lacking from it, and its procedures must leave every space for the development of this meaning. Now if the individual features stand before the eyes of the experience of life only as riddles, the unification of which through a common solution can occupy the entire power of a human heart, then art also should not set out from a well-known and certain solution of all the questions that force themselves upon one here, but it is this solution itself.[94]

Now while it clearly suggests the general form of Lotze's metaphysics and the importance of the inexhaustible wealth of empirical reality within it, which Lotze took to distinguish his philosophy from that of Schelling and Hegel, this passage could also suggest that he continued the purely cognitive approach to aesthetics that they had adopted. That conclusion would be wrong, however. Rather, Lotze's view is that the free play of our mental powers is the core of our experience of beauty, including artistic

---

[94] Lotze, *Conditions*, vol. 2, p. 219.

beauty, but that this free play must be recognized as valuable precisely because it is both an instance and a representation of the purposive harmony of the world in all its fullness and complexity. Lotze thus offers his own synthesis of the approaches to aesthetic experience as a form of free play and as a form of cognition: While for Kant the fact that aesthetic experience is an experience of free play allowed it to become a symbol of the morally good, for Lotze this fact is what allows aesthetic experience to offer insight into the purposiveness of the world that is beyond the grasp of our scientific methods.

Lotze makes this clear in the discussion of Kant with which he began both his early essays on aesthetics and his lecture course twenty years later. He begins the latter with Kant's distinction between the agreeable, the beautiful, and the good, arguing that what is crucial to the beautiful is not so much that it pleases universally, unlike the former, yet without a concept, unlike the latter,[95] but that it pleases because of our mental *activity* in the free play of the faculties. With regard to the distinction between the agreeable and the beautiful in particular, he writes:

> A more correct distinction between them would be that those impressions seem "merely agreeable" to us that we *merely suffer* [*erleiden*] through stimuli, without being conscious of exercising an activity through which their apprehension is first completed. "Beauty" by contrast can only pertain to those impressions whose apprehension does not consist in an unanalyzable well-being, but arises from a manifold of relating, connecting, comparing activities of our power of representation or imagination. It is consistent with this that the "agreeable" pertains primarily to sensibility, and indeed to its *simple* impressions, while "beauty" pertains to the objects of the *higher* faculties of the spirit [*Geist*] and to *composite* sensible impressions, whose *whole* content cannot be grasped *merely* by the senses, but only through an additional reconstruction of the interconnection of their manifold through the imagination.[96]

Lotze thus takes Kant's idea of free play to be indispensable to the analysis of the experience of beauty. He also takes it to be incomplete, because "We must demand that that which is called 'beautiful' insofar as it has an effect upon us also have, considered in itself, an *unconditional* value, which justifies our aesthetic pleasure and our honor of it, i.e., we demand an *objective significance* of the beautiful."[97] Yet, he immediately adds, "Such a justification is not entirely lacking in Kant's point of view."

---

[95] Lotze, *Fundamentals*, §3, p. 7.
[96] Lotze, *Fundamentals*, §5, p. 9.
[97] Lotze, *Fundamentals*, §9, p. 12. See also "Concept," pp. 296–8.

In an unmistakable allusion to Kant's analysis of our intellectual interest in beauty, he explains:

> For the *individual* "beautiful object" beauty in general remains merely a form of how it appears to us; and without a doubt it *can* appear to us as beautiful through a *contingent* correspondence between some properties of it that are in themselves quite insignificant and the habits of our apprehending activity. Only that reality is so ordered *in general* that such a friendly concomitance between the forms of things and the needs of the life of the spirit is *possible* is a *general* fact of the world-order that we must cherish as an *infinite* good. And each individual object that through [its] forms (no matter how contingent they may be *in themselves*) reminds us of this universal being-for-each other of things and of the world of spirit has, as a testimony to that goodness, the objective value on account of which it also appears as beautiful *in itself*.[98]

Lotze's view is that our harmonious mental activity, or as he also calls it "elasticity," is not only pleasurable but also valuable as part of the purposive harmony of the world as a whole, and that beautiful objects are valuable both because they induce this pleasurable activity and also represent the harmony of the world as a whole. Lotze considers the objection that this approach might conflate the beautiful with the good, but he responds that while the good concerns our actions in particular, the sense of value that we get from the experience of the beautiful extends over the whole of our being and spreads itself onto objects as well.[99] Lotze also addresses this point by resurrecting another Kantian idea, namely that the beautiful offers us a bridge between the realm of nature and the moral realm of the spirit. Coming at the point from the opposite side, that is, from the question of how the mere play of mental powers could have any moral significance at all, he writes in the essay on the concept of beauty:

> The appearances of that liveliness, of the constant flow of alterations or of sudden interruptions and violent new beginnings, in short all those forms of transition, of coalescence and opposition, which run through all the arts as important means of presentation, reawake the recollection of a special moral condition of the soul and of its value. The power of the ruling efforts however concern not only the course of representations and feelings; it also manifests itself through inborn necessity in outer bodily motions, which throw a bridge from the spiritual values of thought to sensible presentation.[100]

---

[98] Lotze, *Fundamentals*, §9, p. 12.
[99] Lotze, *Fundamentals*, §13, p. 15.
[100] Lotze, "On the Concept of the Beautiful," p. 299.

For Lotze, the possibility of real interaction between body and mind through which the spiritual purposes of the universe are realized is essential, and art is a crucial medium for this interaction as well as a reminder of its possibility. "Without being related to any purpose the fulfillment of which ... would be insignificant in comparison to the world as a whole and the sense of the world-course," the beautiful, "partly in the movements of a mind, partly in the forms of that which exists," exhibits the "peaceful result" of both.[101]

On this general basis, Lotze, like other nineteenth-century thinkers, builds a classification of the particular arts, although not in such detail as Hegel or Vischer. Indeed, he derives the necessity of a variety of art forms from the infinite multitude and complexity of the world that the arts represent for us: since the world is so multiform, there must also be a variety of ways of experiencing and representing its harmoniousness, thus a variety of arts. Lotze denies that there can be any single "ideal of beauty" and insists upon the multiplicity of the ways in which beauty may appear:

> Precisely because beauty is not an appearance, but the sense of a general occurrence, the whole wealth of its depth is exhausted only if we consider the infinite multiplicity of its forms of externalization. Just as every external circumstance that forces a soul to the development of an activity does not alter this soul but rather enriches it through the reality and the recollection of a deed the possibility of which lay within it, so does the beautiful of beauty, if we may speak like this, consist not as much in a simple concept of its determination as in the infinite multiplicity of its confirmation through the course of appearances.[102]

There can be no single ideal of beauty, for beauty "is the sense of the entire cosmos with all of its blessedness, suddenly coming to appearance in some particular, which through its evocative features decisively places itself in the interconnection of this world and on all sides resonates through gentle but recognizable relations with the totality of the fullness and of the wealth of which it is a part."[103]

Among the different media of art, Lotze pays particular attention to architecture, music, and painting. One passage from his treatment of landscape painting will have to suggest his approach as a whole:

> We place ourselves in a twofold way into the gentle waves of the spirit of nature that we here admire. For first we coalesce with every individual form

---

[101] Lotze, "The Concept of the Beautiful," p. 304.
[102] Lotze, "The Concept of the Beautiful," p. 319.
[103] Lotze, "The Concept of the Beautiful," p. 334.

and its internal conditions; we feel the fresh force of the vegetation ... we sense the silent rest of the massive layers of sandstone or the thrusting power of elevated basalts tumbled upon one another, the restless motion, finally, with which the sea struggles against its banks. But a second, greater pleasure lies in the apprehension of the relations and affinities that everywhere penetrate this manifold life ... so from the picture as from nature itself our imagination sways over the outline of the land ... of the mountain ... of the valleys, and the manifold feelings of constant forward motion, sudden leaps or ... free turnings, lovely enclosures or wide vistas come together into a total intuition of the life that announces itself in the entire region.[104]

Here we have a concrete instance of the abstract idea that there is a harmony between the free play of our mental powers and the harmony of the larger universe of which we are a part that is the core of Lotze's aesthetics.

Lotze thought that his theory gave due weight to the infinite wealth of nature and its contingency at least relative to any laws that we can formulate in a way that the views of other idealists, especially his contemporary Vischer, did not.[105] Since, as we saw, Vischer himself thought that he had given fuller credit to contingency and the necessity of its represention in art than Hegel had, this criticism of Vischer may not have been entirely fair. But there can be no question that Lotze more fully rehabilitated Kant's idea of the free play of the faculties itself as well as his idea that the occurrence of this free play is a sign that we are at home in the world – as illustrated by his approach to landscape painting – than any of his immediate predecessors or contemporaries did. Lotze may thus have opened the way for the renewed emphasis on the aesthetics of play in the later nineteenth-century theories that we will encounter in subsequent chapters. On the other hand, Lotze did not explicitly emphasize the emotional dimension of our response to nature or art as Vischer had, let alone allow such emotional response to become transformed into beauty itself. Thus, although Lotze had resurrected Kant's conception of play and Rosenkranz had emphasized the idea of freedom as both the source and the object of art, while Vischer had emphasized the emotional side of aesthetic experience, a full synthesis of the three approaches to aesthetic experience, though hinted at by Schleiermacher, had not yet appeared in German aesthetics by the end of the period of Hegel's greatest influence, around 1860.

---

[104] Lotze, "The Conditions of Beauty in Art," p. 253.
[105] See Lotze, *Fundamentals*, §17, pp. 19–20, where he explicitly refers to Vischer.

We could now turn to German aesthetics in the remaining decades of the nineteenth century to see if and when such a threefold synthesis finally reemerges. But instead of doing that immediately, we will first turn our attention to developments elsewhere, primarily in Great Britain, and then return to the German scene in the third part of the present volume.

PART TWO

(MOSTLY) BRITISH AESTHETICS IN THE SECOND HALF OF THE NINETEENTH CENTURY

In Part One of this book, we have seen how the leading aestheticians of German Idealism, Schelling, Schopenhauer, and Hegel, all adopted a cognitivist approach to aesthetics, supposing that the goal of aesthetic experience and particularly of art was to provide insight into the nature of reality, either for its own sake, as in Schelling and Hegel, or as a means to relief from the pain of ordinary life, as in Schopenhauer. We also saw how for Hegel the supposition that art aims at delivering metaphysical truth is its justification but also its own death sentence. We then saw how many of those influenced by these philosophers struggled to escape from the restrictions and consequences of their positions. Schelling's influence was transmitted to England through Coleridge, but Wordsworth, personally close to Coleridge, Shelley, Emerson in the United States, and even John Stuart Mill, on whom the influence of Coleridge ameliorated the utilitarianism bequeathed to him by Bentham and his own father, sought ways to make room for the emotional impact particularly of art in their own aesthetics. Among German aestheticians after Hegel, there were similar struggles with the confines of his reductive approach to aesthetics, and while Rosenkranz, for example, aimed to broaden Hegel's approach to the cognitive value of art, Vischer over the course of his long career, devoted almost exclusively to aesthetics, sought to make room for both the Kantian idea of aesthetic experience as the free and harmonious play of our mental powers and the non-Kantian idea of the emotional impact of aesthetic experience of both nature and art. Lotze too sought for at least some common ground between Kantian and Hegelian aesthetics.

At this point, we could continue the story of the development of German aesthetics in the second half of the nineteenth century, which was largely a response to these developments in Germany in the first half of the century, unlike German aesthetics in the latter part of the eighteenth century, which, as we saw in Volume 1, was very much a response to the French and British aesthetics of the middle part of that century as well as to the domestic development of aesthetics from Wolff to Meier. But to avoid too much disruption to chronology, as well as to introduce a little variety into our narrative, at this point instead of now continuing the history of German aesthetics we will turn to developments outside of Germany beginning around the 1840s, thus after the earlier works of Emerson and Mill and at the same time as the earlier works of Vischer and Lotze considered in the last chapter. As the title of this part suggests, we will focus primarily on the development of aesthetics in Britain from the 1840s to the 1890s, but will also consider at least some developments in France in this period as well. After this, we will return to Germany for the final part of the present volume, with some consideration of the influence of late nineteenth-century German aesthetics in Britain and the United States as well.

Yet the development to be traced in the present part has a certain similarity to the narrative arc of German aesthetics in the first part of the century. Just as the German Idealists adopted an exclusively cognitivist approach to aesthetics that then had to be broadened to allow room for the other approaches that had been identified in the previous century, so outside of Germany we will also see a development from an essentially cognitivist approach to a more multi-sided approach. In this case we will see that the dominant aesthetics of mid-nineteenth century Britain, the aesthetics of John Ruskin, himself not a professional philosopher of course but the inescapable critic of art and society of his time and place, is above all an aesthetics of truth and truthfulness, but that in this case the immediate response was not simply an attempt to amplify his approach but an attempt to reject it completely: the movement of aestheticism or "art for art's sake" that emerged in later nineteenth-century Britain, although with some French and even American antecedents, can be considered a violent rejection of Ruskin's approach to aesthetics. We will then see that this movement itself produced responses, equally violent in the case of the Russian Leo Tolstoy, who might be regarded as having combined a narrow interpretation of the aesthetics of truth with an equally narrow interpretation of the aesthetics of emotional impact in his 1896 tract *What is Art?*, and more irenic in the case of the British Neo-Hegelian Bernard Bosanquet. The latter's career bridges the divide between the nineteenth and twentieth centuries, however, and so once we have considered his work we will interrupt the flow of our narrative yet again to return to the further development of German aesthetics in the last third of the nineteenth century. In Volume 3, we will resume the story of the development of British aesthetics in the twentieth century, continue the history of German aesthetics, but also turn to a new scene, namely the United States, where we will consider the development of aesthetics from the first book of George Santayana until the end of the twentieth century. Santayana's book *The Sense of Beauty* appeared in 1896, the same year as Tolstoy's work, but introduces ideas that will only be more fully developed in the next century, and so we will count him as belonging to the twentieth century while Tolstoy still counts as part of the nineteenth.

5

Ruskin

1. RUSKIN, TURNER, AND TRUTH

The most significant figure in nineteenth-century British aesthetics was not a professor of philosophy, nor a professor of any kind at all until late in his career, when John Ruskin (1819–1900), art critic and social critic, became the first Slade Professor of Fine Art at Oxford. But the history of aesthetics can hardly be told without an account of Ruskin, who, although he only occasionally mentioned names from the British and German philosophical aesthetics of the eighteenth and early nineteenth centuries, clearly drew much while rejecting some from these traditions, and who would in turn become both an influence on and target for much of British aesthetics into the twentieth century. The works that made Ruskin's name – the five volumes of *Modern Painters* (1843–60), the *Seven Lamps of Architecture* (1849), and the three volumes of *The Stones of Venice* (1851–53) – were, as their titles suggest, works of description and criticism focused on the fine arts of painting and architecture, indeed, in the case of the last-named work even travel literature, but they also had a theoretical dimension that aligned Ruskin squarely with the philosophical aesthetics that, as we have seen, dominated the first half of the nineteenth century, the aesthetics of truth. As already suggested, Ruskin's version of the aesthetics of truth would then produce a powerful reaction, in the first instance the movement known as aestheticism or "art for art's sake," which does not so much try to amplify Ruskin's theory as to undercut the need for aesthetic theory altogether, arguing that aesthetic experience is a domain of pleasure that needs no explanation or justification from other areas of human experience.

Modern Painters, the first volume of which Ruskin published at the age of twenty-four, began as a brief in behalf of the English landscape painter

Joseph Mallord William Turner (1775–1851), to whose work and person Ruskin had been introduced at a very early age by his father. Ruskin defended Turner's work on the grounds that it contained more of both truth and beauty than anything else that had yet been done. Ruskin began the Preface to the work with these words:

> The work now laid before the public originated in indignation at the shallow and false criticism of the periodicals of the day on the works of the great living artist to whom it principally refers. It was intended to be a short pamphlet ... I now scarcely know whether I should announce it as an Essay on Landscape Painting, and apologize for its frequent reference to the works of a particular master; or, announcing it as a critique on particular works, apologize for its lengthy discussion of general principles.... But when *public* taste seems plunging deeper and deeper into degradation day by day, and when the press universally exerts such power as it possesses to direct the feeling of the nation more completely to all that is theatrical, affected, and false in art; while it vents its ribald buffooneries on the most exalted truth, and the highest ideal of landscape, that this or any other age has ever witnessed, it becomes the imperative duty of all who have any perception or knowledge of what is really great in art, and any desire for its advancement in England, to come fearlessly forward, regardless of such individual interests as are likely to be injured by the knowledge of what is good and right, to declare and demonstrate, wherever they exist, the essence and authority of the Beautiful and the True.[1]

This passage suggests that the painting of Turner is to be defended as realizing more fully than any other work the separate desiderata of beauty and truth, and one might infer from this that Ruskin belongs in the tradition of those who, like Kant, separated the value of truth as the content of art from the value of our free play with the beauty of its form while also recognizing that the best art is a synthesis of both of these values. However, although in his general statements of principles for both painting and architecture, Ruskin does separate truth and beauty, his account of beauty itself turns that into a vehicle for a certain kind of truth, so his aesthetics as a whole is dominated by the aesthetics of truth. At the same time, Ruskin clearly distinguishes a number of different kinds of truth in art, and although metaphysical truth is one of the kinds of truth that art can deliver, Ruskin certainly does not interpret art as a vehicle of metaphysical truth that might be better delivered by other means, as Hegel had. Further, Ruskin also adds to the multiple kinds of truth that art can realize *truthfulness* or sincerity as a property of both artists and artworks.

[1] John Ruskin, *Modern Painters, Volume I – Of General Principles and of Truth.* Boston: Estes and Lauriat, n.d., pp. 5–6.

Here he emphasizes a value that a later writer such as Leo Tolstoy will celebrate, although Ruskin certainly does not anticipate Tolstoy in making sincerity the sole value of art. Rather, what is distinctive of Ruskin's aesthetics among nineteenth-century theories is the variety of forms of truth and truthfulness that it recognizes; the challenge in reading Ruskin is to understand all that he means by truth.

This was long ago recognized by one of Ruskin's most sympathetic readers. Referring to a passage in *The Stones of Venice* in which Ruskin comments on the irony of the proximity of the seat of the often sinful government of Venice to St. Mark's Cathedral, Marcel Proust wrote:

> This passage from *The Stones of Venice* is of great beauty, rather difficult though it be to give an account of the reasons for this beauty. It seems to us that it rests on something false and we feel some scruples in giving in to it.
>
> And yet there must be some truth in it. Properly speaking, there is no beauty that is entirely deceitful, for aesthetic pleasure is precisely what accompanies the discovery of a truth. To what kind of truth may correspond the very vivid pleasure we experience when reading such a page is rather difficult to say.[2]

What Proust writes about Ruskin's own prose is true of the object of that prose, namely aesthetic pleasure itself: it is essentially connected to truth, but to truth understood in a way that will bring out what is distinctive about aesthetic experience yet without simplifying that experience.

Ruskin was the only child of devoted parents, both of whom took a great interest in his education in art as well as religion. His mother was a pious Evangelical who hoped to make a minister out of her son, and as we will see there is a strong religious dimension in Ruskin's early writing, and a religious tone that remained strong even after his eventual loss of faith. His father was a Scottish-born wine merchant, one of the original founders of the sherry firm of Pedro Domecq, and when he went on sales trips to the great houses of England he took along his son, who was thus exposed early to the private art collections of the nation. From John's sixth year on, the prospering family also took annual trips to see the landscape, architecture, and paintings of Europe, above all France, Switzerland, and Italy, and Ruskin gained a great knowledge of and love for both natural and painted landscape on these trips. His father also began his own small collection of art, especially of Turner, and Ruskin

---

[2] Marcel Proust, *On Reading Ruskin: Prefaces to* La Bible d'Amiens *and* Sésame et les Lys. Trans. and ed. Jean Autret, William Burford, and Phillip J. Wolfe (New Haven and London: Yale University Press, 1987), pp. 52–3.

met the famous artist when he was still quite young, indeed wrote his first defense of Turner when he was just seventeen, although the artist himself deterred him from publishing it then. At the same age, after being educated primarily at home, Ruskin (accompanied by his mother) went up to Oxford, where, after a promising start as the winner of a prestigious poetry prize, he had to take time off on account of illness, and graduated, without distinction, only six years after entrance. However, no sooner had he finally graduated than he published the first volume of *Modern Painters* under the anonymous title of "A Graduate of Oxford," and his extraordinary literary career was under way. The posthumous collection of Ruskin's published works eventually ran to thirty-nine stout volumes.[3] In addition to the three works already mentioned, Ruskin's works directly pertaining to art include *Pre-Raphaelism* (1851), *Giotto and his works in Padua* (three parts, 1853–60), *Lectures on Architecture and Painting* (1854–55), catalogues of the works of Turner bequeathed to the National Gallery of Britain (1857–58, 1881) and to the Fitzwilliam Museum (1861), *The Political Economy of Art* (1857, expanded in 1880 as *A Joy Forever*), *The Elements of Drawing* (1857), *Lectures on Art* (1870), and *The Laws of Fésole* (four parts, 1877–78). His works of social criticism written after 1860, following his final loss of religious faith in 1858, include *Unto this Last* (1862), *Sesame and Lilies* (1865), *Fors Clavigera* (1871–84), *Munera Pulveris* (originally "Essays on Political Economy") (1872), and *The Storm Cloud of the Nineteenth Century* (1884); he also wrote numerous works on the geology, botany, and natural history of both Britain and the Alps, numerous travel works on Italy and Britain, a study of Greek mythology, *The Queen of the Air* (1869), and the autobiography *Praeterita* (three volumes, 1885–89).[4] Ruskin never had to work for a living, and following the death of his father in 1864, he became wealthy; his only formal employment was as the Slade Professor at Oxford, a position that he held, with interruptions for bouts of mental illness between 1879 and 1883, from 1869 until 1885, when he finally resigned in protest at the introduction of vivisection into scientific instruction at the university. But in spite of his wealth, Ruskin was unhappy in love, first entering an allegedly unconsummated marriage in 1848 that ended in 1854 when his wife left him for the painter J.E. Millais, and then falling in love with

---

[3] E.T. Cook and Alexander Wedderburn, eds., *The Library Edition of the Works of John Ruskin* (London: George Allen, 1903–12).

[4] A compendious although still "select" bibliography of Ruskin's works is provided in Ruskin, *The Seven Lamps of Architecture*, introduction by Sir Arnold Lunn (London: Dent, 1956), pp. xii–xiv.

a ten-year-old girl, Rose La Touche, a student at a school that Ruskin was sponsoring. Ruskin proposed to her when she turned eighteen, but she would herself die insane, at age twenty-seven, without ever having agreed to marry her nearly thirty years older suitor. Ruskin suffered increasingly from bouts of mental illness in his later years, and after his final breakdown in 1888 lived as an invalid, with only occasional periods of lucidity, at his estate in the Lake Country, under the care of his cousin Joanna Severn. He died in 1900, the sad final chapter of his life thus paralleling the nearly simultaneous breakdown and eventual death of Friedrich Nietzsche, although Ruskin enjoyed twenty-five more years of productivity than did Nietzsche.[5]

As noted, Ruskin began *Modern Painters* with the claim that the work of Turner manifested both truth and beauty to an unparalleled degree. In his formal statement of general principles, however, Ruskin distinguishes five sources of "greatness in art": "ideas of power," "ideas of imitation," "ideas of truth," "ideas of beauty," and "ideas of relation."[6] This list is somewhat misleading, however, for power is a general source of value that is not restricted to art, while imitation, although it would seem to be closely related to truth, is dismissed by Ruskin as of no great value. This leaves truth, beauty, and relation as the distinctive sources of value for art, but both beauty and relation turn out, on closer analysis, to be forms of truth. So the distinctive sources of greatness in art are all forms of truth, although by no means all the same sort of truth.

Power is the "excellence" by means of which "difficulty" is overcome, so to "prove a work excellent" in this regard "we have only to prove the difficulty of its production."[7] Ruskin is explicit that whether a work that

---

[5] Ruskin has been well-treated by biographers, from *The Life of John Ruskin* by W.G. Collingwood, the father of the philosopher R.G. Collingwood who will be a central figure later in this narrative (London: Methuen & Co., 1893), to the magisterial work by Tim Hilton, *John Ruskin: The Early Years* (New Haven and London: Yale University Press, 1985), and *John Ruskin: The Later Years* (New Haven and London: Yale University Press, 2000). For a survey of Ruskin's intellectual career, see also John D. Rosenberg, *The Darkening Glass: A Portrait of Ruskin's Genius* (New York: Columbia University Press, 1961). Works on Ruskin's aesthetics include George P. Landow, *The Aesthetical and Critical Theories of John Ruskin* (Princeton: Princeton University Press, 1971), and Elizabeth K. Helsinger, *Ruskin and the Art of the Beholder* (Cambridge, Mass.: Harvard University Press, 1982). A brief survey is George P. Landow, *Ruskin* (Oxford: Oxford University Press, 1985); I have drawn on pp. 1–3, 92–95 for the brief account of Ruskin's life here. See also Raters, *Kunst, Wahrheit und Gefühl*, pp. 260–89.

[6] Ruskin, *Modern Painters* I, Synopsis of Contents, p. 57, and Part I, Section I, chapters II–VII, pp. 85–106.

[7] Ruskin, *Modern Painters* I, p. 88.

demonstrates power "be useful or beautiful is another question," that is, there is nothing distinctively aesthetic about the manifestation of power. As he also puts it, "the nature and effects of ideas of power ... are independent of the nature or worthiness of the object from which they are received," so "whatever has been the subject of a great power, whether there be intrinsic and apparent worthiness in itself or not, bears with it the evidence of having been so, and is capable of giving the ideas of power, and the consequent pleasures, in their full degree."[8] Ruskin's point is simply that there is something admirable and pleasing about the display of human power – he is not talking about the power of nonhuman nature or of the divine here, although as we will shortly see, both of those powers do play a large role in his aesthetics – and that our pleasure in the power manifested in a work is independent of its other sources of pleasure. His suggestion that we are capable of enjoying the manifestation of power in a work in "full degree" independent of the other values of the work is misleading, however, for Ruskin goes on to argue that "men may let their great powers lie dormant, while they employ their mean and petty powers on mean and petty objects; but it is physically impossible to employ a great power, except on a great object."[9] Presumably this means that there is no logical impossibility in devoting great effort to trivial (or even bad) ends, but that it is psychologically impossible for human beings to devote their greatest effort to something that does not seem worthy of that effort on independent grounds. So Ruskin's position seems to be that the power – the effort as well as the skill – devoted to a work of art is something that we admire for its own sake, just as we admire such power when manifested in other forms of human work, but that we cannot expect to find the greatest manifestations of such power, and thus the greatest pleasure in it, except in works that have other sources of value to a high degree, and thus, in the case of works of art, except in works that manifest the other sources of specifically aesthetic value to a high degree.

Is imitation such an independent source of genuinely and uniquely aesthetic value? Ruskin dismisses ideas of imitation and the pleasure in them as "the most contemptible which can be received from art," as no better than "the mean and paltry surprise which is felt in jugglery."[10] This is because he defines imitation as "anything look[ing] like what is not,

---

[8] Ruskin, *Modern Painters* I, pp. 86–7.
[9] Ruskin, *Modern Painters* I, p. 87.
[10] Ruskin, *Modern Painters* I, pp. 92–3.

the resemblance being so great as *nearly* to deceive," which produces "a kind of pleasurable surprise, and agreeable excitement of mind, exactly the same in its nature as that which we receive from juggling."[11] The pleasure that we take in imitation in this sense can perhaps be understood as the pleasure in being threatened with deception but of being able to resist it, a pleasure that is (to borrow terms from Edmund Burke, whom Ruskin mentions in this chapter) negative rather than positive, and also, we might say, a pleasure that turns us toward ourselves, that is, toward an admiration of our own cleverness in resisting the deception, rather than toward what ought to be the object of our attention, the work of art and its genuine merits as well as what is represented by the work of art, the glory of nature itself. Ruskin makes the latter point in stating that "Ideas of imitation are contemptible ... because not only do they preclude the spectator from enjoying inherent beauty in the subject, but they can only be received from mean and paltry subjects because it is impossible to imitate anything really great. We can 'paint a cat or a fiddle, so that they look as if we could take them up;' but we cannot imitate the ocean, or the Alps"[12] (classical examples, of course, of the sublime rather than the beautiful). By "subject" in this sentence Ruskin appears to mean not the work of art but its subject, for example, in the case of a painting of the Alps, the Alps themselves, and then his first point here is that the self-directed pleasure we take in escaping from actually being deceived distracts us from the proper admiration of what is actually depicted; his second point would be that given the impossibility of being even nearly deceived into taking a painting of the Alps for the Alps themselves, the kind of imitation he is attacking could hardly be the source of our pleasure in such a painting. Finally, Ruskin objects that the kind of skill required for such imitative work is not real power, but "requires nothing more for its attainment than a true eye, a steady hand, and moderate industry – qualities which in no degree separate the imitative artist from a watch-maker, pin-maker, or any other neat-handed artificer,"[13] so this sort of imitation blocks the possibility of our enjoyment of real power in a work of art, which, although it is not a source of pleasure that is unique to art, is a genuine source of pleasure in art.

Ruskin's comparison of the imitative artist to a pin-maker cannot but put one in mind of Adam Smith's famous example of the manufacture of pins in *The Wealth of Nations*, and at least suggests that Smith's analysis of

[11] Ruskin, *Modern Painters* I, Part I, §1, ch. IV, §2, p. 91.
[12] Ruskin, *Modern Painters* I, Part I, §1, ch. IV, §5, p. 93.
[13] Ruskin, *Modern Painters* I, Part I, §1, ch. IV, §6, p. 94.

imitation, in which what we admire in imitation is the fact that an object can be successfully represented in a medium that would not appear to be naturally well-suited for that purpose, might be Ruskin's unstated target here. One might also question Ruskin's dismissal of the pleasures of near-deception in light of the success of *trompe l'oeil* painting, especially in the United States by such painters as William Harnett and John Frederick Peto, not long after Ruskin wrote these words. But perhaps Ruskin suggests that our pleasure in such paintings is not in their mere verisimilitude, but in something else, perhaps in the mood of nostalgia created by the depicted objects. For present purposes, however, the important question is, if the kind of imitation that Ruskin has here dismissed is not the kind of truth in art that he is celebrating, then what is?

Ruskin begins his chapter "Of Ideas of Truth" with the straightforward explanation that "The word truth, as applied to art, signifies the faithful statement, either to the mind or senses, of any fact of nature."[14] This suggests the classical definition of truth as *adequatio rei et intellectus*, the adequacy of a representation to its object. But interpretation is needed to accommodate the fact that the art with which Ruskin is primarily concerned, namely painting, deals with images, not statements, indeed that the genre of painting with which he is particularly concerned, namely landscape painting, does not typically carry a readily verbalizable message, as perhaps some other genres of painting, such as historical painting, might be thought to do. Interpretation will also be needed to prevent this definition of truth from collapsing the truth of painting back into the kind of *trompe l'oeil* imitation that Ruskin has just dismissed. In fact, the theme that Ruskin will develop under the rubric of truth, which will occupy the first volume of *Modern Painters* and half of the second, is that painting should not represent its object in a mechanically imitative way but rather that it should suggest to the viewer what it is like to *experience* the object. What Ruskin has in mind here might be thought of as a phenomenological sense of truth: truth in painting is not a correspondence between an image and an object that might be analogized to the truth of a statement about a fact, but is rather a correspondence between the experience afforded by a painting and the experience afforded by an actual view of its subject. Once we have developed this theme, however, we will also see that phenomenological truth is only the first sort of truth that Ruskin finds in art.

---

[14] Ruskin, *Modern Painters* I, Part I, §1, ch. V, §5, p. 94.

Ruskin's initial chapter on truth concentrates on the difference between what he means by imitation and what he means by truth. The difference between the two is summed up in the following points. First, "Imitation can only be of something material, but truth has reference to statements both of the qualities of material things, and of emotions, impressions, and thoughts. There is a moral as well as material truth, – a truth of impression as well as of form, – of thought as well as of matter; and the truth of impression and thought is a thousand times the more important of the two."[15] This brief passage really anticipates the gist of Ruskin's full account of both truth and beauty, for as he continues it will become clear that what he means by truth in art is the recreation and communication of our impressions or experiences of nature, while what he means by beauty is not a superficial aspect of the forms of works of art but rather the communication of the underlying order and divine source of nature – the truth of thought rather than of impression, what we might conceive of as metaphysical rather than phenomenological truth. That will emerge only later, however. For now, Ruskin continues his attack on mere imitation. His next point is that "Truth may be stated by any signs or symbols which have a definite signification in the minds of those to whom they are addressed, although such signs be themselves no image or likeness of anything";[16] in other words, truth is not an isomorphic relation between sign and signified, but rather a question of whether a work can in any way communicate a veridical experience or thought of its subject to its audience. With this brief remark, Ruskin anticipates the attack upon the idea that successful artistic depiction is a matter of resemblance that would be developed by the art historian Ernst Gombrich and the philosopher Nelson Goodman in the middle of the twentieth century.[17] Third, Ruskin maintains that imitation is inimical to concentrated attention to an object or to our impression or thought of it, because "an idea of imitation requires the resemblance of as many attributes as we are usually cognizant of in [the] real presence" of an object, while "an idea of truth" as he conceives of it "exists in the statement of *one* attribute of anything."[18] Here Ruskin continues to talk about

---

[15] Ruskin, *Modern Painters* I, Part I, §1, ch. V, p. 95.
[16] Ruskin, *Modern Painters* I, Part I, §1, ch. V, p. 95.
[17] For Gombrich, see *Art and Illusion: A Study in the Psychology of Pictorial Representation*, Bollingen Series XXXV:5 (Princeton: Princeton University Press, 1960), Part One; for Goodman, see *Languages of Art* (Indianapolis: Bobbs Merrill, 1968), to be discussed in Volume 3.
[18] Ruskin, *Modern Painters* I, Part I, §1, ch. V, p. 96.

truth as a property of statements, but the requirement of focus that he suggests will be central to the phenomenological conception of truthful impression that he actually develops. Finally, Ruskin insists "on the last and greatest distinction between ideas of truth and of imitation – that the mind, in receiving one of the former, dwells upon its own conception of the fact, or form, or feeling stated, and is occupied only with the qualities and character of that fact or form, considering it as real and existing, being all the while totally regardless of the signs or symbols by which the notion of it has been conveyed."[19] In enjoying mere imitation, we must be conscious of both the signified and the sign – on Adam Smith's account, we must be conscious of the disparity between the sign and the signified which makes the successful representation of the latter by the former a feat, on Ruskin's account we must become conscious of the difference between what is signified and the mere sign in order to escape from the deception to which we almost succumb – but in enjoying artistic truth, the sign disappears from our consciousness, leaving us with something like an impression of nature itself. Our experience of nature is immediate, without consciousness of any of the machinery by which it may be effected, such as retinal images; in the case of art our focus should also be on the experience that is produced and not on the device that produces it. Since immediacy is a characteristic of our experience of nature, it must also be a feature of the phenomenological truth of art.

In the extended discussion of truth in art that, as already noted, occupies most of the first and half of the second volume of *Modern Painters*, it becomes even clearer that what Ruskin really intends by this rubric is the truth of impression, or phenomenological truth. But Ruskin's idea is perhaps best epitomized in a passage on "Turnerian Topography" in the fourth volume of *Modern Painters*. Here Ruskin first gives a sarcastic account of the mechanical procedure of ordinary painters, who make sure they have enough ruins in the background and figures in the foreground to make their paintings "generally interesting ... all this being, as simply a matter of recipe and practice as cookery," and then contrasts this to the work of the "artist who has real invention" – that is, Turner – who first "receives a true impression from the place itself, and takes care to keep hold of that as his chief good ... and then sets himself as far as possible to reproduce that impression on the mind of the spectator of his picture." The artist's experience of his subject is not a momentary glimpse of it: "this impression on the mind never results from the mere

---

[19] Ruskin, *Modern Painters* I, Part I, §1, ch. V, p. 99.

piece of scenery which can be included within the limits of the picture. It depends on the temper into which the mind has been brought, both by all the landscape round, and by what has been seen previously in the course of the day"; but this is of course true of any real experience of objects outside of some artificial setting like a cognitive psychology laboratory. Ruskin then continues, still using the language of "facts" which seems best suited to the conception of truth as correspondence between statements and facts:

> Any topographical delineation of the facts, therefore, must be wholly incapable of arousing in the mind of the beholder those sensations which would be caused by the facts themselves, seen in their natural relations to others. And the aim of the great inventive landscape painter must be to give the far higher and deeper truth of mental vision, rather than that of the physical facts, and to reach a representation which, though it may be totally useless to engineers or geographers, and when tried by rule and measure, totally unlike the place, shall yet be capable of producing on the far-away beholder's mind precisely the impression which the reality would have produced, and putting his heart into the same state in which it would have been, had he verily descended into the valley from the gorges of Airolo [a specific landscape painted by Turner].[20]

By "higher and deeper" truth Ruskin here means phenomenological rather than, say, cartographical truth, although he also could have used these terms for the metaphysical sense of truth that we will encounter in his subsequent treatment of beauty.

Ruskin organizes his detailed discussion of the truth of impressions first around the "general truths" of the means used in all painting, namely the truths of tone, color, chiaroscuro, and space,[21] and then around the main classes of objects depicted in landscape, namely the truth of skies,[22] the truth of earth (or of geology and topography), the truth of water, and the truth of vegetation.[23] In all of these sections, his aim is to show how veridical experiences of the objects of painting can be created through the means of painting. There is no room here for a discussion of Ruskin's immensely detailed account of these forms of truth, which contrasts many of Turner's works to the vast range of paintings from the thirteenth to the nineteenth centuries already known to the still only

---

[20] Ruskin, *Modern Painters* IV, LE 6.32–9, cited from John Ruskin, *Selected Writings*, ed. Dinah Birch (Oxford: Oxford University Press, 2004), pp. 86–8; the last passage is also cited by Landow, *Ruskin*, p. 32.
[21] *Modern Painters* I, Part II, section II, chs. I–V.
[22] Ruskin, *Modern Painters* I, Part II, section III, chs. I–V.
[23] Ruskin, *Modern Painters* II, Part II (continued), sections IV–VI.

twenty-seven-year-old Ruskin. But several passages from his chapter on "The Truth of Space" can illustrate his approach throughout this wealth of material. The first emphasizes in general terms Ruskin's conception of truth as truthful impression, or his view that the aim of truth in painting is the aim of capturing not nature itself but the character of our impressions of nature, with all the ways in which those are both precise and not, self-contained yet reaching beyond themselves. It also suggests the character of Ruskin's argument for the superiority of Turner's landscapes even over those traditionally regarded as the greatest:

> Nothing can be true which is either complete or vacant; every touch is false which does not suggest more than it represents, and every space is false which represents nothing.
>
> Now, I would not wish for any more illustrative or marked examples of the total contradiction of these two great principles, than the landscape works of the old masters, taken as a body: – the Dutch masters furnishing the cases of seeing everything, and the Italians of seeing nothing. The rule with both is indeed the same, differently applied. "You shall see the bricks in the wall, and be able to count them, or you shall see nothing but a dead flat;" but the Dutch give you the bricks, the Italians the flat. Nature's rule being the precise reverse – "You shall never be able to count the bricks, but you shall never see a dead space."[24]

The last is what our ordinary experience of nature is like (here taking the built environment as part of nature), and the aim of truth in art is to capture that.

The second passage exhibits Ruskin's conception of truth through a specific example:

> Perhaps the truth of this system of drawing is better to be understood by observing the distant character of rich architecture, than of any other object. Go to the top of Highgate Hill on a clear summer morning at five o'clock, and look at Westminster Abbey.[25] You will receive an impression of a building enriched with multitudinous vertical lines. Try to distinguish one of those lines all the way down from the one next to it: You cannot. Try to count them: You cannot. Try to make out the beginning of or end of any one of them: You cannot. Look at it generally, and it is all symmetry and arrangement. Look at it in all its parts, and it is all inextricable confusion. Am not I, at this moment, describing a piece of Turner's drawing, with the same words by which I describe nature.... Turner, and Turner only, would follow and render on the canvas that mystery of decided line, – that distinct, sharp, visible, but unintelligible and inextricable richness, which, examined

---

[24] Ruskin, *Modern Painters* I, Part II, section II, ch. V, §5, p. 301.
[25] This might still have been possible in 1843; one could hardly do it now.

part by part, is to the eye nothing but confusion and defeat, which, taken as a whole, is all unity, symmetry, and truth.[26]

It may not be entirely fair of Ruskin to attribute the achievement of such phenomenological truth only to his contemporary Turner and not to any Dutch master – Ruskin certainly captures the experience I had the first time I saw Vermeer's incomparable *View of Delft* in the Mauritshuis in the Hague. But the point remains: truth in painting is phenomenological truth to what would be our experience of its subject, not any form of truth that is independent of the phenomenological character of experience. It is like what Baumgarten called "aesthetic truth" or verisimilitude, something felt to be true by the senses rather than known to be true by the intellect.

We must now turn from Ruskin's discussion of what he labels truth to his discussions of beauty and relation as sources of pleasure and value in art, and show that he conceives of these too as forms of truth. Ruskin begins his account of beauty with a definition of beauty that makes it sound as if it has nothing to do with truth and can be apprehended without the involvement of anything beyond the external senses: "Any material object which can give us pleasure in the simple contemplation of its outward qualities without any direct and definite exertion of the intellect, I call in some way, or in some degree, beautiful." There seems to be no room for thought here: "Why we receive pleasure from some forms and colors, and not from others, is no more to be asked or answered than why we like sugar and dislike wormwood. The utmost subtilty of investigation will only lead us to ultimate instincts and principles of human nature, for which no father reason can be given than the simple will of the Deity that we should be so created."[27] However, this initial, strictly noncognitivist account of beauty, so reminiscent of Hume's limited definition of the sources of beauty in "Of the Standard of Taste," which leaves no room for a free play of higher mental capacities with the beautiful object, but seems to make beauty into a stimulus of a purely physiological response, is immediately qualified:

> Observe, however, I do not mean by excluding direct exertion of the intellect from ideas of beauty, to assert that beauty has no effect upon nor connection with the intellect. All our moral feelings are so interwoven with our intellectual powers, that we cannot affect the one without in some degree addressing the others; and in all high ideas of beauty, it is more than

---

[26] Ruskin, *Modern Painters* I, section II, ch. V, §12, pp. 307–8.
[27] Ruskin, *Modern Painters* I, Part I, §1, ch. VI, §1, p. 100.

probable that much of the pleasure depends on delicate and untraceable perceptions of fitness, propriety, and relation, which are purely intellectual, and through which we arrive at our noblest ideas of what is commonly and rightly called "intellectual beauty."[28]

Ruskin gestures toward his initial characterization of beauty with his remark that no exertion of the intellect is involved in the response to beauty, which makes this response at least analogous to a purely sensory response in involving no voluntary activity of thought – Ruskin's model of beauty in this passage seems reminiscent of Hutcheson's account of our response to beauty as immediate and involuntary, and in that regard like a sense, even though this response is a "reflex" response to sense perceptions and not itself a sense perception. But even this characterization of our response to beauty as intellectual but immediate does not reveal what Ruskin means by "high ideas of beauty." His full account, presented in the second volume of *Modern Painters*, is that our response to beauty is a *theoretic* but not merely *intellectual* response; it is nothing less than a response to the *moral* significance of various formal and relational properties of objects, a significance that at least in the earlier stages of Ruskin's career depends on the recognition or interpretation of the divine origin of the elements of beauty, even if this recognition or interpretation does not require an "exertion" of the intellect.

Ruskin's elaboration of his initial account of the "ideas of beauty" thus begins with a discussion of the "theoretic faculty" that distinguishes our response to beauty from a merely sensual or a merely intellectual response:

> The term "æsthesis" properly signifies mere sensual perception of the outward qualities and necessary effects of bodies ... But I wholly deny that the impressions of beauty are in any way sensual, – they are neither sensual nor intellectual, but moral, and for the faculty for receiving them, whose difference from mere perception I shall immediately endeavor to explain, no term can be more accurate or convenient than that employed by the Greeks, "theoretic," which I pray permission, therefore, always to use, and to call the operation of the faculty itself Theoria.[29]

Ruskin's argument is that beauty is ultimately of moral significance, but to make this argument he first has to distinguish his conception of morality from anything merely utilitarian. He starts his argument by arguing that the "Utilitarians" (he uses this term as the name of a party,

---

[28] Ruskin, *Modern Painters* I, Part I, §I, ch. VI, §4, pp. 101–2.
[29] Ruskin, *Modern Painters* II, Part III, section I, ch. II, §1, p. 201.

but mentions no individuals) have not even understood the true nature of utility. His critique of utilitarianism reveals the premise for his own account of beauty, even though the traditional conception of the beauty of utility, as found for example in Hume, will be fundamentally transformed in Ruskin's account:

> Men in the present century understand the word Useful in a strange way ... it will be well in the outset that I define exactly what kind of utility I mean to attribute to art ...
>
> That is to everything created, pre-eminently useful, which enables it rightly and fully to perform the functions appointed to it by its Creator. Therefore, that we may determine what is chiefly useful to man, it is necessary first to determine the use of man himself.
>
> Man's use and function (and let him who will not grant me this follow me no farther, for this I propose always to assume) is to be the witness of the glory of God, and to advance that glory by his reasonable obedience and resultant happiness.
>
> Whatever enables us to fulfill this function, is in the pure and first sense of the word useful to us. Pre-eminently therefore whatever sets the glory of God more brightly before us. But things that only help us to exist, are in a secondary and mean sense, useful.[30]

Although Ruskin will preserve a distinction between "typical" and "functional" beauty in the account to follow, this passage (which could have been written by Christian Wolff a century earlier) shows that anything that is useful to us in any ordinary sense is only a means to the support of our theoretical capacity, and that the latter is in turn led through its recognition of beauty in nature to a recognition and glorification of God. This is the sense in which the faculty for beauty is "theoretic" but "high ideas of beauty" are ultimately "moral" rather than merely "intellectual." This comes out in stages in his further elaboration of his conception of our "theoretic faculty." First, he distinguishes between the merely useful and that which is more properly theoretical by distinguishing between mere craft or technology and pure science:

> All science and all art may be divided into that which is subservient to life, and which is the object of it. As subservient to life, or practical, their results are, in the common sense of the word, useful. As the object of life or theoretical, they are, in the common sense, useless; and yet the step between practical and theoretic science is the step between the miner and the geologist, the apothecary and the chemist ... so that the so-called useless part

---

[30] Ruskin, *Modern Painters* II, Part III, section 1, ch. I, §§3–4, pp. 192–3.

of each profession does by the authoritative and right instinct of mankind assume the superior and more noble place.

However, the merely intellectual contemplation of the laws of geology and chemistry in their own right is still not the real end or "use" of mankind; that is realized only in the recognition of the glory of the God who is the ultimate source of these laws:

> [A]ll the great phenomena of nature, the knowledge of which is desired by the angels only, by us partly, as it reveals to farther vision the being and the glory of Him in whom they rejoice and we live, dispense yet such kind influences and so much of the material blessing as to be joyfully felt by all inferior creatures, and to be desired by them with such single desire as the imperfection of their nature may admit.[31]

The value of apothecary, for example, depends upon the value of the contemplation of the laws of chemistry that it makes possible, rather than, as the "Utilitarian" might assume, the converse, but the value of the contemplation of the laws of chemistry in turn is that they reveal to us the nature of their divine source. Ruskin then uses the same twofold structure for his account of beauty: beautiful objects please us through the recognition of various formal and relational properties, but those in turn ultimately please us only insofar as we recognize or interpret them as products of their divine source. Our response to beauty is thus far more cognitive than sensual, but it also depends not merely upon the cognition of formal features or relations but upon the further recognition of their source, and is in that regard not merely "intellectual" but "moral." Thus Ruskin concludes, "the mere animal consciousness of the pleasantness I call æsthesis; but the exulting, reverent, and grateful perception of it I call theoria. For this, and this only, is the full comprehension and contemplation of the beautiful as a gift of God, a gift not necessary to our being, but added to, and elevating it."[32] The first stage of the experience of beauty may be the sensual and intellectual apprehension of material, formal, and relational features of objects, but the experience of beauty is complete only with the comprehension of the moral significance of the existence of those features. At this stage of his career there seems to be no distinction between the moral and the religious for Ruskin.

This structure is at work throughout Ruskin's detailed account of beauty. Rejecting what he takes to be Archibald Alison's indiscriminate

---

[31] Ruskin, *Modern Painters* II, Part III, section I, ch. I, §8, pp. 198–9.
[32] Ruskin, *Modern Painters* II, Part III, section I, ch. II, §6, p. 205.

associationism, in which beauty can be created by any pleasing association, Ruskin actually returns to more standard eighteenth-century models by dividing beauty into two specific varieties:

> By the term beauty, then, properly are signified two things. First, that external quality of bodies already so often spoken of, and which, whether it occur in a stone, flower, beast, or in man, is absolutely identical, which, as I have already asserted, may be shown to be in some sort typical of the Divine attributes, and which, therefore, I shall, for distinction's sake, call typical beauty; and, secondarily, the appearance of felicitous fulfillment of function in living things, more especially of the joyful and right exertion of perfect life in man. And this kind of beauty I shall call vital beauty.[33]

In each kind of beauty, surface features of objects must be interpreted as expressions of deeper truths about nature or humanity in order to complete the experience of beauty. In the case of typical beauty, what is to be interpreted are traditionally recognized formal elements of beauty. Ruskin's list of these elements includes infinity, exemplified, for instance, by "subtilty and constancy of curvature in all natural forms whatsoever";[34] unity, by which he means interrelation among things, "so that there is not any matter, nor any spirit, nor any creature, but is capable of an unity of some kind with other creatures, and in that unity is its perfection and theirs, and a pleasure also for the beholding of all other creatures that can behold";[35] repose, "either a simple appearance of permanence and quietness, as in the massy forms of a mountain or rock, accompanied by the lulling effect of all mighty sight and sound ... or else ... repose proper, the rest of things in which there is vitality or capability of motion actual or imagined";[36] symmetry, the "opposition of one part to another and a reciprocal balance obtained" between them "in all perfectly beautiful objects";[37] purity, found in light and color but also in "every healthy and active organic frame," for example "the young leaves when first their inward energy prevails over the earth, pierces its corruption, and shakes its dust away from their own white purity of life";[38] and finally moderation, such as "chasteness, refinement, or elegance" and "finish, exactness, or refinement, which are commonly desired in the works of men, owing both to their difficulty of accomplishment and consequent expression

---

[33] Ruskin, *Modern Painters* II, Part III, section I, ch. III, §17, p. 219.
[34] Ruskin, *Modern Painters* II, Part III, section I, ch. V, §15, p. 237.
[35] Ruskin, *Modern Painters* II, Part III, section I, ch. VI, §2, p. 241.
[36] Ruskin, *Modern Painters* II, Part III, §1, ch. VII, §2, p. 257.
[37] Ruskin, *Modern Painters* II, Part III, section I, ch. VIII, §1, p. 263.
[38] Ruskin, *Modern Painters* II, Part III, section I, ch. IX, §8, p. 271.

of care and power ... and from their greater resemblance to the working of God."[39] The last element of typical beauty, moderation, seems to be a merit of works of art, whereas the preceding elements appear to be features of nature that can in turn be captured in artistic representations of nature. But what is important to Ruskin's conception of beauty is that all of these features are not enjoyed, whether sensually or intellectually, only for their own sake, but are interpreted as "types," that is, signs, or in the case of nature rather than its artistic representation, effects, of attributes of God. Thus, Ruskin interprets infinity as "the type of divine incomprehensibility,"[40] unity (under which rubric he also discusses proportion) as "the type of the divine comprehensiveness",[41] repose as "the type of divine permanence,"[42] symmetry as "the type of divine justice,"[43] purity as "the type of divine energy,"[44] and, finally, moderation as the "type of government by law," "that acting of God with regard to all his creation, wherein, though free to operate in whatever arbitrary, sudden, violent, or inconstant ways he will, yet he, if we may reverently so speak, restrains in himself this omnipotent liberty, and works always in consistent modes, called by us laws."[45] Ruskin does not claim that his has "enumerated all the sources of material beauty," but he does take it to be adequate "to show, in some measure, the inherent worthiness and glory of God's works." Understood as signs thereof, the pleasures of beauty can even be called "visionary pleasures," and in them can be found "cause for thankfulness, ground for hope, anchor for faith, more than in all the other manifold gifts and guidances, wherewith God crowns the years, and hedges the paths of men."[46] Beauty understood this way clearly cannot be merely sensual nor an object for the mere play of our mental powers, but represents a profound form of cognition.

Ruskin's second main kind of beauty is "vital beauty," the beauty of living things (although any boundary between this and typical beauty has already been breached at least once by the beauty of purity). Vital beauty is divided into three subspecies – relative vital beauty, generic vital beauty, and vital beauty in human beings – and again, these seem

[39] Ruskin, *Modern Painters* II, Part III, section I, ch. X, §§1, 3, p. 272.
[40] Ruskin, *Modern Painters* II, Part III, section I, ch. V, p. 228.
[41] Ruskin, *Modern Painters* II, Part III, section I, ch. VI, p. 240.
[42] Ruskin, *Modern Painters* II, Part III, section I, ch. VII, p. 256.
[43] Ruskin, *Modern Painters* II, Part III, section I, ch. VIII, p. 263.
[44] Ruskin, *Modern Painters* II, Part III, section I, ch. IX, p. 266.
[45] Ruskin, *Modern Painters* II, Part III, section I, ch. X, p. 271 and §6, pp. 274–5.
[46] Ruskin, *Modern Painters* II, Part III, section I, ch. XI, §§1, 4, pp. 277, 279.

to be categories of beauty that can be realized by both natural objects, in this case organisms, and their artistic representation. Relative vital beauty, in spite of its misleading name, is the beauty of a healthy individual, our pleasure in it "the pleasure afforded by every organic form ... in proportion to its appearance of healthy vital energy; as in a rose-bush, setting aside all considerations of gradated flushing of color and fair folding of line, which it shares with the cloud or the snow-wreath," and which would be instances of typical beauty, "we find in and through all this, certain signs pleasant and acceptable as signs of life and enjoyment in the particular individual plant itself."[47] Generic vital beauty is what is manifested in an individual insofar as it realizes "The perfect *idea* of the form and condition in which all the properties of the species are fully developed," and insofar as a work of art represents such beauty it is "ideal," although "Ideal works of art ... represent the result of an act of imagination," because actual instances of natural species never fully realize the idea of that species.[48] Vital beauty in man is more complex than either of these, not merely because the variety of human form and physiognomy is so much greater than that in any other single biological species, but because vital beauty in man is the visible expression of virtue, and there are not only a myriad of ways in which humans can be vicious but also a myriad of ways in which virtue can be expressed – so there can be no simple rule for the depiction of human virtue (here Ruskin discusses at length the challenge of portraiture). But this is all the more reason why the recognition of human vital beauty whether in a living person or in a portrait must be an act of insight that engages all of our cognitive powers, and hardly a mere sense-perception or even a rule bound act of intellection.

That Ruskin's aesthetics is based on truth becomes even clearer as he turns from the "theoretic" to the "imaginative faculty." Imagination is needed for art because "those sources of pleasure which exist in the external creation ... in any faithful copy ... must to a certain extent exist also," but these "sources of beauty ... are not presented by any very great work of art in a form of pure transcript. They invariably receive the reflection of the mind under whose shadow they have passed, and are modified or colored by its image," this modification being "the Work of the Imagination."[49] Imagination is divided into three functions, "imagination

---

[47] Ruskin, *Modern Painters* II, Part III, section I, ch. XII, §4, p. 283.
[48] Ruskin, *Modern Painters* II, Part III, section I, ch. XIII, §2, pp. 293–4.
[49] Ruskin, *Modern Painters* II, Part III, section II, ch. I, §1, p. 334.

associative," "imagination penetrative," and "imagination contemplative." The first of these is the artist's power to grasp parts and form them into a whole that is more illustrative of the real experience of nature than is any mere transcription of nature. This is more than mere skill at composition (Ruskin criticizes Dugald Stewart for reducing imagination to composition),[50] for "in composition the mind can only take cognizance of likeness or dissimilarity, or of abstract beauty among the ideas it brings together,"[51] but the imagination associative is not limited to mechanically tracing patterns as it finds them in nature: it "is never at a loss, nor ever likely to repeat itself; nothing comes amiss to it, but whatever rude matter it receives, it instantly so arranges that it comes right; all things fall into their place and appear in that place perfect, useful, and evidently not to be spared."[52] (Of course no artist has had the gift of imagination associative more than Turner.)[53] Yet although the imagination associative grasps unities that are greater than those that nature presents, at least to causal observation, Ruskin interprets what we might regard as the idealization of natural connections as recognition of the deeper truth about the organization and unity of nature: "Let it be understood once for all, that imagination never designs to touch anything but truth, and though it does not follow that where there is the appearance of truth, there has been imaginative operation, of this we may be assured, that where there is appearance of falsehood, the imagination has had no hand."[54]

Imagination penetrative, the middle but highest of the three functions of the imagination, is described as directly penetrating beneath a superficial image of nature:

> It never stops at crusts or ashes, or outward images of any kind, it ploughs them all aside, and plunges into the very central fiery heart, whatever semblances and various outward shows and phases the subject may possess, go for nothing, it gets within all fence, cuts down to the root, and drinks the very vital sap of that it deals with ... it looks not in the eyes, it judges not by the voice, it describes not by outward features, all that it affirms, judges, or describes, it affirms from within.[55]

In this flood of metaphor, it is hard to see exactly what the object of the imagination penetrative is, but it seems to be deep truth of every kind:

---

[50] Ruskin, *Modern Painters* II, Part III, section II, ch. II, §3, p. 341.
[51] Ruskin, *Modern Painters* II, Part III, section II, ch. II, §6, p. 243.
[52] Ruskin, *Modern Painters* II, Part III, section II, ch. II, §15, p. 350.
[53] Ruskin, *Modern Painters* II, Part III, section II, ch. II, §20, pp. 353–4.
[54] Ruskin, *Modern Painters* II, Part III, section II, ch. II, §22, p. 355.
[55] Ruskin, *Modern Painters* II, Part III, section II, ch. III, §3, p. 358.

deep truth about the laws and energies of nature, deep truths about the passions and motivations of humans – "the heart and inner nature"[56] – and deep truths about the divine that lies behind all that. What Ruskin stresses is rather that although this form of insight is not rule-driven or inferential, it is nevertheless "the highest intellectual power of man. There is no reasoning in it, it works not by algebra, nor by integral calculus, it is a piercing ... mind's tongue that works and tastes into the very rock heart, no matter what be the subject submitted to it ... whatever utmost truth, life, principle, it has laid bare, and that which has no truth, life, nor principle, dissipated into its original smoke at a touch."[57] The imagination penetrative, whether it works with paint or words, gets beneath surfaces, and what it finds can only be described as truth: "there is in every word set down by the imaginative mind an awful under-current of meaning, and evidence and shadow of the deep places out of which it has come."[58] "In all these instances ... the virtue of the imagination is its reaching, by intuition and intensity of gaze (not by reasoning, but by its authoritative and opening power,) a more essential truth than is seen at the surface of things."[59] "The life of the imagination is in the discovering of truth."

Finally, imagination contemplative, although its name might seem to suggest passivity, is the function of imagination by which the truths grasped by the imagination penetrative and the connections among them grasped by the imagination associative are fixed in memorable form. Here Ruskin's first examples are from poetry rather than painting, and that the following passage appears in a discussion of Milton's rendition of Death, not as a condition but as an agent, and Satan, a force of evil not visible to humans, explains his contrast between the immaterial subject and more material images of the imagination contemplative; but what is crucial is the idea that the latter is the function of imagination by which truths once grasped are fixed and thereby enabled to be communicated: "depriving the subject of material and bodily shape, and regarding such of its qualities only as it chooses for particular purposes, it forges these qualities together in such groups and forms as it desires, and gives to their abstract being consistency and reality, by striking them as it were with the die of an image belonging to other matter."[60] Turning

---

[56] Ruskin, *Modern Painters* II, Part III, section II, ch. III, §7, p. 360.
[57] Ruskin, *Modern Painters* II, Part III, section II, ch. III, §4, p. 358.
[58] Ruskin, *Modern Painters* II, Part III, section II, ch. III, §5, p. 359.
[59] Ruskin, *Modern Painters* II, Part III, section II, ch. III, §29, p. 383.
[60] Ruskin, *Modern Painters* II, Part III, section II, ch. IV, §4, p. 389.

to the visual arts, he seems to reverse direction, and to suggest that the imagination contemplative fixes the immaterial meaning behind the material surface. This passage seems to combine the functions of imagination both penetrative and contemplative: "it is of no small importance to prove how in all cases, the imagination is based upon, and appeals to, a deep heart feeling; and how faithful and earnest it is in contemplation of the subject matter, never losing sight of it, or disguising it, but depriving it of extraneous and material accidents, and regarding it in its disembodied essence."[61] But perhaps this is exaggerated; a few pages later, Ruskin may suggest more clearly what he means when he says of the greatest painters that "they all paint the lion more than his mane, and the horse rather than his hide":[62] the essence sought and found by the imagination contemplative need not be immaterial, but is always free from the merely accidental.

Ruskin sums up his treatment of the imagination by appeal to truth: "in all its three functions" the imagination is "associative of truth, penetrative of truth, and contemplative of truth; and having no dealings nor relations with any kind of falsity."[63] The imagination is the faculty for discerning and communicating beauty, so beauty is a function of truth. Though we might ordinarily think of beauty as superficial or subjective, for Ruskin beauty is not the truth of appearance that he first discussed under the rubric of truth, but truth about what lies behind appearance, and about the further source of even that: beauty is essential and ultimately metaphysical or theological. What is grasped by imagination and understood in beauty is not always propositional in nature, although presumably in some cases, such as those of the divine attributes grasped in typical beauty, what is grasped could readily be given propositional form. In other cases, the truths of "heart" to which Ruskin often refers, it might be more difficult to give propositional form to the truth that is grasped in beauty. So it would be misleading to try to reduce Ruskin's conception of beauty to a single form of truth. But in a general way, it should not be too misleading to say that his account of beauty adds a metaphysical dimension to the initially merely phenomenological conception of truth that he had discussed under the rubric of truth.

The last of Ruskin's five sources of pleasure in art is "ideas of relation," a term that he says he uses "as one of convenience than as adequately

---

[61] Ruskin, *Modern Painters* II, Part III, section II, ch. V, §7, p. 396.
[62] Ruskin, *Modern Painters* II, Part III, section II, ch. V, §11, p. 399.
[63] Ruskin, *Modern Painters* II, Part III, section II, ch. IV, §22, p. 406.

expressive of the vast class of ideas" he intends "to be comprehended under it, namely, all those conveyable by art, which are the subjects of distinct intellectual perception and action, and which are therefore worthy of the name of thoughts."[64] Under this head, he says, "must be arranged everything productive of expression, sentiment, and character, whether in figures or landscapes." Under this rubric Ruskin thus intends to capture the dimension of our experience of art that earlier theorists had tried to capture through the concept of the association of ideas. As the organization of *Modern Painters* drifted away from its original plan – the third volume, which is titled simply "Of Many Things," marks the breakdown of the original organization – Ruskin did not end up writing a detailed section on ideas of relation as he had done for truth and beauty in volumes I and II. But as will become evident especially in his writings on architecture, to which we can now begin to turn, one of the things that he clearly had in mind for this dimension of aesthetic experience is the historical associations suggested by works of art, the way in which we interpret both the meanings originally intended by their authors but also, and equally important, the many historical associations works pick up along their historical way from original creation to contemporary reception. Buildings, for example, acquire relations or associations to events that take place within them, whether originally intended or not, as well as to events they witness, whether foreseen or not, and all of these become part of the meaning of the objects for later generations. In *The Seven Lamps of Architecture*, published in 1849 (thus in the interval between the second and third volumes of *Modern Painters*), Ruskin describes this dimension of aesthetic experience under the rubric "The Lamp of Memory." Historical associations can color our experience of nature; thus Ruskin describes his experience of a favorite spot in the Alps by writing that "Those ever springing flowers, and ever flowing streams had been dyed by the deep colours of human endurance, valour, and virtue; and the crests of the sable hills that rose against the evening sky received a deeper worship, because their far shadows fell eastward over the iron wall of Joux, and the four-square keep of Granson" (where the Swiss Confederates defeated Charles the Bold of Burgundy in 1476, a key victory for the cause of Swiss independence).[65] But the recollection of human history is better preserved by monumental works of human hands, although of course it is preserved in human words as well:

[64] Ruskin, *Modern Painters* I, Part I, section I, ch. VII, §1, p. 104.
[65] Ruskin, *Seven Lamps of Architecture*, ch. VI, section I, p. 181.

> It is as the centralisation and protectress of this sacred influence, that Architecture is to be regarded by us with the most serious thought. We may live without her, and worship without her, but we cannot remember without her. How cold is all that history, how lifeless all imagery, compared to that which the living nation writes, and the uncorrupted marble bears! – how many pages of doubtful record might we not often spare, for a few stones left one upon another! The ambition of the old Babel builders was well directed for this world: there are but two strong conquerors of the forgetfulness of men, Poetry and Architecture; and the latter in some sort includes the former, and is mightier in its reality: it is well to have, not only what men have thought and felt, but what their hands have handled, and their strength wrought, and their eyes beheld ... it is in becoming memorial or monumental that a true perfection is attained by civil and domestic buildings; and this partly as they are, with such a view, built in a more stable manner, and partly as their decorations are consequently animated by a metaphorical or historical meaning.[66]

We might take Ruskin's disjunction between metaphorical and historical meaning to suggest the distinction between meanings originally intended in the design and construction of buildings and monuments and associations accrued in the course of their subsequent history. Perhaps some instances of the former could be subsumed under one of the categories of truth we have already found in Ruskin: for example, the intended meanings of works of religious architecture may well be cases of what Ruskin has in mind as moral or metaphysical truth. But the accrued historical associations of buildings and monuments seem to fall into a different category: they suggest neither phenomenological truths about our sensory experience of objects nor metaphysical truths about what might lie behind appearances, but historical truths about human ambitions, accomplishments, failures – the whole range of human actions. Thus we might find under Ruskin's rubric of ideas of association a third form of truth, historical truth, to add to phenomenological and metaphysical truth. Ruskin's remarks about the relations between architecture and poetry suggest what might be particularly aesthetic about the historical associations of art: we may need the information conveyed by poetry or other verbal sources to interpret the historical significance of a physical artifact, whether ruined or intact, but we need the physical object and its impact upon our senses to make that historical significance fully alive for us. This suggests that for Ruskin the aesthetic dimensions lies in the interaction between sense perception and intellectual or moral

---

[66] Ruskin, *Seven Lamps of Architecture*, ch. VI, sections II–III, pp. 181–2.

cognition, although as elsewhere there is no suggestion that this interaction should be understood as a form of play.

2. TRUTH AS SINCERITY

Yet a fourth conception of truth that is central to Ruskin's aesthetics is that of truthfulness or sincerity, a category that he applies both to artists and to works of art. Part of what Ruskin has in mind is straightforward: if the merits of works of art are any or all of the forms of truth we have so far distinguished, that is, phenomenological, moral and metaphysical, and historical truth, then of course the artist who is to create successful works of art must be committed to the discovery and communication of truth in these several forms. Thus Ruskin writes at the outset of his discussion of Truth in *Modern Painters* I:

> We shall ... find that no artist can be graceful, imaginative, or original, unless he be truthful; and that the pursuit of beauty, instead of leading us away from truth, increases the desire for it and the necessity of it tenfold; so that those artists who are really great in imaginative power, will be found to have based their boldness of conception on a mass of knowledge far exceeding that possessed by those who pride themselves on its accumulation without regarding its use[67] –

and presumably to be acquired only by means of an exceptional commitment to the pursuit of truth. Ruskin also applies this requirement of truthfulness to his own work as a critic, even though he is also an advocate:

> I shall endeavor ... to enter with care and impartiality into the investigation of the claims of the schools of ancient and modern landscape to faithfulness in representing nature. I shall pay no regard whatsoever to what may be thought beautiful, or sublime, or imaginative. I shall look only for truth: bare, clear, downright, statement of facts; showing in each particular, as far as I am able, what the truth of nature is, and then seeking for the plain expression of it, and for that alone[68] –

and finding that, of course, above all in the works of Turner. What Ruskin means here by disregarding "what may be thought beautiful, or sublime, or imaginative" is not that he is disregarding beauty, sublimity, and imaginativeness themselves, for his argument is precisely that these are constituted by various forms of truth; he means rather that he will disregard

---

[67] Ruskin, *Modern Painters* I, Part II, section I, ch. I, §9, p. 126.
[68] Ruskin, *Modern Painters* I, Part II, section I, ch. I, §10, p. 127.

received opinion, accepting as true in any of the aesthetically relevant senses only what his own experience confirms to be true. In this regard, his commitment to truthfulness is not different from that of any sincere scientist.

Ruskin develops this theme more fully in a chapter on "The Real Nature of Greatness of Style" in *Modern Painters* III. Here he argues that "great" or "high" art requires "Choice of Noble Subject,"[69] for example, "sacred subjects, such as the Nativity, Transfiguration, Crucifixion," but only, he qualifies, "if the choice be sincere" – that is, an artist who paints these things without himself believing in them cannot produce great art; "Love of Beauty";[70] "Sincerity";[71] and "Invention," that is, "it must be produced by the imagination."[72] What he has to say about "love of beauty" and "sincerity" in this chapter deserves special comment. About the former, he says that "The second characteristic of the great school of art is, that it introduces in the conception of its subject as much beauty as is possible, consistently with truth," and then immediately adds a lengthy footnote in which he argues against the popular (or Neo-Platonic or Romantic) identification of truth with beauty: Only "People with shallow powers of thought, desiring to flatter themselves with the sensation of having attained profundity ... who desire to be thought philosophical, declare that 'beauty is truth' and 'truth is beauty.'"[73] Ruskin explains his rejection of this identification by claiming that "truth and beauty are entirely distinct, though often related things. One is a property of a statement, the other of objects." This conforms to modern usage of the term "truth," but seems to belie everything that Ruskin has said about both truth and beauty in the first two volumes of *Modern Painters*. It does not, however, because Ruskin holds that through a work of art the artist makes a statement:

> The painter asserts that this which he has painted is the form of a dog, or a man, or a tree. If it be *not* the form of a dog, a man, or a tree, the painter's statement is false; and therefore we justly speak of a false line, or false color; not that any line or color can in themselves be false, but they become so when they convey a statement that they resemble something which they do *not* resemble.[74]

---

[69] Ruskin, *Modern Painters* III, Part IV, ch. III, §5, p. 43.
[70] Ruskin, *Modern Painters* III, Part IV, ch. III, §12, p. 49.
[71] Ruskin, *Modern Painters* III, Part IV, ch. III, §16, p. 52.
[72] Ruskin, *Modern Painters* III, Part IV, ch. III, §21, p. 56.
[73] Ruskin, *Modern Painters* III, Part IV, ch. III, §12, p. 49n.
[74] Ruskin, *Modern Painters* III, Part IV, ch. III, §12, p. 49n.

Ruskin is not retracting what he has previously said about the importance of either truth to experience or beauty as moral or metaphysical truth in this passage, but is only using "beauty" in a restricted and perhaps more ordinary sense, to mean superficial, merely sensory beauty, and what he is arguing now is that beauty in this sense cannot be placed above truth or beauty in the deeper sense in truly great art. He is talking about beauty in the superficial sense when he continues:

> For although truth and beauty are independent of each other, it does not follow that we are at liberty to pursue whichever we please. They are indeed separable, but it is wrong to separate them; they are to be sought together in the order of their worthiness; that is to say, truth first, and beauty afterwards. High art differs from low art in possessing an excess of beauty in addition to its truth, not in possessing an excess of beauty inconsistent with truth.[75]

There is no serious contradiction between Ruskin's subordination of surface beauty to truth here and his identification previously of a deeper sense of beauty with moral and metaphysical truth.

Ruskin's elaboration of the requirement of sincerity for great or high art also requires comment. We would ordinarily think of this as a character trait, the commitment of a person to tell only truth and not to withhold truth from another who should know it, and something like that was what Ruskin required of artists and himself in *Modern Painters* I. Ruskin, however, adds a quantitative dimension to sincerity: it is the pursuit of maximal possible truth in any work, thus it is "characteristic of great art that it includes the largest possible quantity of Truth in the most perfect possible harmony." No work of art can present all possible truths, however, not even about its chosen subject matter, but sincerity is demonstrated in revealing as much truth as possible as is harmonious with the full aim of the work.

> The inferior artist chooses unimportant and scattered truths; the greatest artist chooses the most necessary first, and afterwards the most consistent with these, so as to obtain the greatest possible and most harmonious *sum*. For instances, Rembrandt always chooses to represent the exact force with which the light on the most illumined part of an object is opposed to its obscurer portions. In order to obtain this, in most cases, not very important truth, he sacrifices the light and color of five sixths of his picture ... Veronese, on the contrary, chooses to represent the great relations of visible things to each other, to the heaven above, and to the earth beneath them.... All this, moreover, he feels to be harmonious, – capable of being

---

[75] Ruskin, *Modern Painters* III, Part IV, ch. III, §12, p. 50n.

joined in one great system of spacious truth. And with inevitable watchfulness, inestimable subtlety, he unites all this in tenderest balance ... restraining, for truth's sake, exhaustless energy, reining back, for truth's sake, his fiery strength; veiling, before truth, the vanity of brightness; penetrating, for truth, the discouragement of gloom ... subduing all his powers, impulses, and imagination, to the arbitrament of a merciless justice, and the obedience of an incorruptible verity.[76]

Ruskin does not deny the brilliance of Rembrandt, his "magnificent skill and subtlety" and "picturesque and forcible expression." But Rembrandt is not committed to revealing as much truth as is possible in a work, and that is what sincerity as Ruskin understands it requires.

Ruskin sums up his account of the qualities required for greatness of artistic style with the claim that "the sum of them is simply the sum of all the powers of man."

> For as (1) the choice of the high subject involves all conditions of right moral choice, and as (2) the love of beauty involves all conditions of right admiration, and as (3) the grasp of truth involves all strength of sense, evenness of judgment, and honesty of purpose, and as (4) the poetical power involves all swiftness of invention, and accuracy of historical memory, the sum of all these powers is the sum of the human soul. Hence we see why the word "Great" is used of this art.[77]

It would be hard to find a passage that epitomizes the Victorian seriousness of Ruskin's aesthetics better than this.

Before we leave the subject of sincerity, however, we must turn back to Ruskin's work on architecture, where he introduces sincerity as a quality of the work rather than the artist. Ruskin's writing on architecture was his earliest vehicle for social criticism because architecture is "distinctively political,"[78] that is, in most of its forms produced by and for a polity of some kind or other, and because like every other form of political activity it is exposed to the tension between the higher and lower aims of human societies. Moral and political considerations are thus interwoven with aesthetic considerations throughout this work. This is immediately evident in *The Seven Lamps of Architecture*, which aims to show "how every form of noble architecture is in some sort the embodiment of the Polity, Life, History, and Religious Faith of nations."[79] The "seven lamps" are the

---

[76] Ruskin, *Modern Painters* III, Part IV, ch. III, §16, pp. 52–3.
[77] Ruskin, *Modern Painters* III, Part IV, ch. III, §24, p. 59.
[78] Ruskin, *Seven Lamps of Architecture*, Introductory, p. 2.
[79] Ruskin, *Seven Lamps of Architecture*, ch. VII, p. 203.

sources of value in architecture. Some of them are familiar from Ruskin's treatment of painting; others are even more directly moral and political than the former, which is part of the reason why there are seven sources of value in architecture but were only five for painting. The complete list of the "lamps" is Sacrifice, Truth, Power, Beauty, Life, Memory, and Obedience. By "sacrifice" Ruskin means the expenditure of effort and wealth in building as an expression of honor and reverence; by "power" the achievement of sublimity and majesty through architectural means; by "beauty" the pleasing imitation of natural forms, in structural elements like columns that capture the spirit of tree trunks, but even more so in ornamentation, such as capitals and tracery that capture the essence of foliage; by "life," particularly "the vivid expression of the intellectual life which has been concerned in [the] production" of the works of architecture;[80] by "memory," as we have already seen, the record of human history embodied in works of architecture and even in their ruins; and by "obedience" "that principle ... to which Polity owes its stability, Life its happiness, Faith its acceptance, Creation its continuance"[81] – the freely self-imposed restraint, or balance between liberty and self-constraint, that makes all human institutions possible, and which is both reflected in successful buildings as works of art and facilitated by them as objects with social, political, and liturgical functions. In discussing the "Lamp of Obedience," Ruskin stresses the value of tradition rather than originality for the health of society, and here he seems his most conservative: thus he suggests that for his own time there are only four historical styles that can be used without vulgarity, namely the "Pisan Romanesque," the "early Gothic of the Western Italian Republics," the "Venetian Gothic," and the "English earliest decorated,"[82] that is, English Gothic before the Perpendicular period. These recommendations were certainly not without influence on the historicist architectural movements of the mid- and later nineteenth century. But the most influential of Ruskin's "lamps," as well as the one most germane to our present theme, is the lamp of "truth." Here what Ruskin means is that architecture must be truthful or non-deceitful, that it must not pretend to be other than what it is – in other words, that it must be sincere, or like sincerity as a quality of the conduct and character of a person.

---

[80] Ruskin, *Seven Lamps of Architecture*, ch. V, p. 151.
[81] Ruskin, *Seven Lamps of Architecture*, ch. VII, p. 203.
[82] Ruskin, *Seven Lamps of Architecture*, ch. VII, p. 213.

Ruskin begins the discussion of truth in architecture with a moral premise: what does "the largest sum of mischief in the world" is not "calumny nor treachery," because they are readily recognized and resisted; rather,

> it is the glistening and softly spoken lie; the amiable fallacy; the patriotic lie of the historian, the provident lie of the politician, the zealous lie of the partisan, the merciful lie of the friend, and the careless lie of each man to himself, that cast the black mystery over humanity, through which we thank any man who pierces, as we would thank one who dug a well in a desert; happy, that the thirst for truth still remains with us, even when we have willfully left the fountains of it.[83]

Architecture, like other art forms, can be directly used for the lies and pretenses of an insincere or self-deceitful regime, religion, or individual, and of course that should be avoided. But what is also to be avoided, in order to promote rather than injure our fragile commitment to truthfulness, is deceitfulness about the nature of building itself:

> In architecture another and a less subtle, more contemptible, violation of truth is possible; a direct falsity of assertion respecting the nature of material, or the quantity of labour. And this is, in the full sense of the word, wrong; it is as truly deserving of reprobation as any other moral delinquency; it is unworthy alike of architects and nations; and it has been a sign, wherever it has widely and with toleration existed, of a singular debasement of the arts; that it is not a sign of worse than this, of a general want of severe probity, can be accounted for only by our knowledge of the strange separation which has for some centuries existed between the arts and all other subjects of human intellect, as matters of conscience.[84]

Of course, Ruskin, as is evident from all that we have seen, is opposed to the "strange separation ... between the arts and all other subjects of human intellect," so he cannot tolerate deceitfulness in the arts: were the barrier between the arts and all other subjects of human intellect – and conduct – to be removed, then deceitfulness in the arts would inevitably lead to deceitfulness elsewhere. In an aesthetically ideal world where the practice of the arts is unified with all our other practices, there must instead be sincerity or honesty in the arts to foster sincerity and honesty everywhere else.

There are three main varieties of "Architectural Deceits" that Ruskin proscribes:

---

[83] Ruskin, *Seven Lamps of Architecture*, ch. II, p. 30.
[84] Ruskin, *Seven Lamps of Architecture*, ch. II, pp. 33–4.

1st. The suggestion of a mode of structure or support, other than the true one; as in pendants in late Gothic roofs.

2nd. The painting of surfaces to represent some other material than that of which they actually consist (as in the marbling of wood), or the deceptive representation of sculptured ornament upon them.

3rd. The use of cast or machine-made ornaments of any kind.

Now, it may be broadly stated, that architecture will be noble in exactly the degree in which all these false expedients are avoided.[85]

A detailed discussion of Ruskin's elaboration of these three forms of architectural deceit is beyond our present purview, but several points are worthy of note here.[86] First, Ruskin's discussion of deceitfulness and sincerity in modes of support casts light on the historicism suggested in the "Lamp of Obedience": Ruskin is cautious about the use of iron in styles of architecture that have been "practised for the most part in clay, stone, or wood," even though he recognizes that "there appears no reason why iron should not be used as well as wood; and the time is probably near when a new system of architectural laws will be developed, adapted entirely to metallic construction." Nevertheless, he argues, "every idea respecting size, proportion, decoration, or construction, on which we are at present in the habit of acting or judging, depends on presupposition of such materials" as clay (brick), stone, and wood; in other words, our expectations about how buildings should look are based on traditional materials, and so while they will in due course change, they cannot be expected to change overnight – for the present, therefore, that is, in Ruskin's own present, "metals may be used as a *cement*, but not as a *support*."[87] Of course, the possibilities of the use of metal for support in buildings was to develop rapidly after Ruskin wrote but before he died, along with associated technologies such as elevators, plumbing, and lighting, and expectations about what the proper size, proportion, decoration, and construction should be would change along with them, whether as rapidly or more rapidly than Ruskin expected, and Ruskin's insistence on honesty in the expression of the structure of buildings would become a core value of architecture in the twentieth century while the outward forms of buildings adhering to this value departed

---

[85] Ruskin, *Seven Lamps of Architecture*, ch. VII, pp. 34–5.
[86] For discussion of Ruskin from the vantage point of architectural theory, including a discussion of this passage, see Hanno Walter Kruft, *A History of Architectural Theory from Vitruvius to the Present*, trans. Ronald Taylor, Elsie Callander, and Antony Wood (New York: Princeton Architectural Press, 1994), pp. 331–4.
[87] Ruskin, *Seven Lamps of Architecture*, ch. II, §X, pp. 40–1.

radically from anything Ruskin knew. Historically, Ruskin's own predilection toward early historical styles in the "Lamp of Obedience" would give way to his requirement of structural honesty in the "Lamp of Truth," and given the primacy of truth in Ruskin's aesthetics that seems like the appropriate outcome.

The second point to be noted is Ruskin's attitude toward ornament. "Ornament," he says, "has two entirely distinct sources of agreeableness: one, that of the abstract beauty of its forms, which, for the present we will suppose to be the same whether they come from the hand or the machine; the other, the sense of human labour and care spent upon it." In the name of truth, he argues that the "true delightfulness" of ornament "depends upon discovering in it the record of thoughts, and intents, and trials, and heart-breakings – of recoveries and joyfulness of success … and in that is the worth of the thing, just as much as the worth of anything else we call precious." For this reason Ruskin argues that "our consciousness of its being the work of poor, clumsy, toilsome man" makes ornament far more pleasurable than the greater formal excellence that might be achieved by machine or, for that matter, by nature, as when "a cluster of weeds growing in a cranny of ruin … has … a beauty in all respects *nearly* equal, and, in some, immeasurably superior, to that of the most elaborate sculpture of its stones."[88] The premise of Ruskin's argument here is that just as a building should reveal rather than hide the true nature of its construction and support, so should it reveal rather than hide the fact that it is the work of human hands; we will value truthfulness about this fact, as well as the fact itself, more than we value the greater formal beauty possible in machine-made ornamentation. Ruskin's thought here is entirely consistent with his valuation of truth over superficial beauty, that is, beauty insofar as it does not itself consist in truth, in his chapter on "Greatness of Style" in *Modern Painters* III. Ruskin's attack upon superficial ornament would be taken up in the cause of twentieth-century modernist architecture by Adolf Loos, in his famous 1908 essay "Ornament and Crime,"[89] although Loos would not complement his attack upon superficial ornament – the decorated stucco tacked on to late nineteenth-century Vienna apartment houses – with a valorization of handmade ornament instead, as Ruskin did. (In

---

[88] Ruskin, *Seven Lamps of Architecture*, ch. II, §XIX, p. 53.
[89] Adolf Loos, *Ornament and Crime and Other Essays*, trans. Michael Mitchell (Riverside, Calif.: Ariadne Press, 1998), pp. 167–76.

fact, the plain exteriors of Loos's buildings, mostly residences, were complemented by rich materials and oriental carpets in the interiors.)

This discussion of architectural ornament in *The Seven Lamps of Architecture* prepares the way for one of the most famous passages in all of Ruskin's work, his chapter on "The Nature of Gothic" in the second volume of *The Stones of Venice* (1853). In this passage, Ruskin praises the irregular exuberance of Gothic decoration in contrast to the exact regularity of the decorative elements in ancient Greek or Renaissance buildings because it is, he supposes, the concomitant and expression of treating the laborers, the stonemasons and sculptors, as free men who have minds of their own and the right to express them rather than as slaves. Ruskin writes:

> You must either make a tool of the creature, or a man of him. You cannot make both. Men were not intended to work with the accuracy of tools, to be precise and perfect in all their actions. If you will have that precision out of them, and make their fingers measure degrees like cog-wheels, and their arms strike curves like compasses, you must unhumanize them. All the energy of their spirits must be given to make cogs and compasses of themselves. All their attention and strength must go to the accomplishment of the mean act.... On the other hand, if you will make a man of the working creature, you cannot make a tool. Let him but begin to imagine, to think, to try to do anything worth doing; and the engine-turned precision is lost at once. Out come all his roughness, all his dullness, all his incapability ... but out comes the whole majesty of him also.[90]

The phrase "engine-turned precision" indicates that Ruskin's argument is aimed as much at the modern industrial economy as at the architecture of Greece, the Renaissance, and the Greek and Renaissance Revivals of the eighteenth and earlier nineteenth centuries: to get precise ornamentation, e.g., dentilation or egg-and-dart moldings, you must either turn men into machines or produce the ornamentation by machines. The latter might not seem objectionable, might indeed seem to free men up for the free pursuit of their other activities (that is at least what the young Marx, in the manuscripts written a few years before, seems to have hoped), but Ruskin's view is the opposite: the workers who operate modern machinery must become as machine-like as their machines. Thus he writes, in a passage that once again must be aimed at Adam Smith, but is also clearly reminiscent of the sixth of Schiller's letters *On the Aesthetic Education of Mankind*:[91]

---

[90] Ruskin, *The Stones of Venice* II, ch. VI; cited from Ruskin, *Selected Writings*, ed. Philip Davis (London: J.M. Dent, 1995), p. 196.
[91] Friedrich Schiller, *On the Aesthetic Education of Man: In a Series of Letters*, ed. and trans. Elizabeth M. Wilkinson and L.A. Willoughby (Oxford: Clarendon Press, 1967), pp. 30–43.

We have much studied and much perfected, of late, the great civilized invention of the division of labour; only we give it a false name. It is not, truly speaking, the labour that is divided; but the men: – Divided into mere segments of men – broken into small fragments and crumbs of life; so that all the little piece of intelligence that is left in a man is not enough to make a pin, or a nail, but exhausts itself in the making the point of a pin or the head of a nail. Now it is a good and desirable thing, truly, to make many pins in a day; but if we could only see with what crystal sand their points were polished, – sand of human soul, much to be magnified before it can be discerned for what it is – we should think there might be some loss in it also.... And all the evil ... can be met only by a right understanding, on the part of all classes, of what kinds of labour are good for men, raising them, and making them happy; or by a determined sacrifice of such convenience, or beauty, or cheapness as is to be got only by the degradation of the workman; and by equally determined demand for the products and results of healthy and ennobling labour.[92]

Ruskin's reference to "cheapness" is necessary to save his argument from the objection that hand labor is only a necessary, not a sufficient condition of freedom, for people can be made to do hand work under conditions that are as degrading as feeding a machine all day (for instance, small children being made to spend their time knotting carpets). But that point only makes clear that what is at issue for him is freedom, not beauty, or at least not superficial beauty: given the connection between moral truth and the deeper kind of beauty that was his concern in Part III of *Modern Painters*, surely he can claim that deep beauty is not inconsistent with moral value, in this case the moral value of individual freedom and self-expression, but is rather an expression of it. The celebration of individual freedom that is "The Nature of Gothic" is thus part and parcel of Ruskin's conception of beauty as moral truth. Ruskin's emphasis on hand work as an expression of an individual freedom would be taken up in the "Arts and Crafts" movement in English architecture and decoration, led by William Morris (1834–96), for whom reading *The Stones of Venice* was a decisive moment in his education. Although both Ruskin and Morris alternately became political socialists, paradoxically their emphasis on the freedom and dignity of hand work led to the creation of homes and furnishings available only to the quite well-off.[93]

[92] Ruskin, *The Stones of Venice* II, Ch. I; *Selected Writings*, pp. 198–9.
[93] Like Ruskin, Morris was a prolific writer, as well as designer, manufacturer, and publisher of the beautiful Kelmscott Press books. His collected works were published in twenty-four volumes, *The Collected Works of William Morris*, edited by May Morris (London: Longmann, Green and Co., 1910–15). A modern edition of his Utopian novel, which also includes his preface to Ruskin's "Nature of Gothic," is *News from Nowhere and Other*

3. CONCLUSION, WITH AN EXCURSUS ON ARNOLD

Ruskin ultimately emphasizes freedom in art, but particularly the expression of freedom as a moral value. His position is thus not a return to the view that the pleasure of the free play of our powers, especially our powers of imagination, is the primary source of aesthetic pleasure, and thus not a challenge to the dominant value of truth in his theory of our pleasure in the beauties of nature and art; his view is rather that room for the free play of the imaginative power of individual artisans and craftsmen is a measure of the moral health of a society, not an end in its own right. For Ruskin, freedom is the most fundamental moral value, and the expression of the value of freedom is the most important truth that art can convey. And while we no doubt have deep emotional associations with the expression of freedom, Ruskin does not make them explicit, nor does he explain how other emotions would enter into our response to art. Complex as his view of artistic truth is, his aesthetic theory still remains within the confines of the cognitivist approach to truth. For the synthesis either of the theory of free play or of emotional impact as the fundamental source of aesthetic value in their own right in British aesthetics, we will have to wait.

It might seem that we need not have to wait very long, for another eminent Victorian, the poet and critic Matthew Arnold (1822–88). Son of Thomas Arnold, the famous Headmaster of Rugby School, Matthew was educated there and then at Balliol College, Oxford, where he studied from 1841 to 1844. His early years at Oxford thus overlapped with Ruskin's later years there, and in 1843 Arnold won the Newdigate Prize in poetry that Ruskin had won several years earlier. But their subsequent careers were very different, not just because Arnold made an early and enduring mark as a poet that Ruskin never did – his "Dover Beach" (1867), for example, is still one of the best known poems in English – but also because, lacking Ruskin's personal fortune, he had to make a career. He did find one as a national Inspector of Schools, in which post he spent much of his adult life. Consequently, much of his prose work concerned education, and then more broadly social and cultural criticism. His best known work in this vein is *Culture and Anarchy* (1869),

---

Writings (London: Penguin, 1993). Works on Morris include Paul Thompson, *The Work of William Morris* (London: Heinemann, 1967); E.P. Thompson, *William Morris: Romantic to Revolutionary*, revised edition (New York: Pantheon, 1977); and Peter Stansky, *Redesigning the World: William Morris, the 1880s, and the Arts and Crafts* (Princeton: Princeton University Press, 1985).

in which he defined culture as "*a study of perfection*," where perfection is "a harmonious expansion of *all* the powers which make the beauty and worth of human nature, and is not consistent with the overdevelopment of any one power at the expense of the rest," and where "culture seeks the determination of this question" – what human perfection actually is – "through *all* the voices of human experience which have been heard upon it, of art, science, poetry, philosophy, history, as well as of religion, in order to give a greater fulness and certainty to its solution."[94] The book is essentially a brief for the importance of culture in this broad sense in contrast to narrowly scientific or practical education, and as such it remains of enduring importance; it does not, however, offer any detailed analysis of the nature of poetry or the arts more broadly as part of culture. In other works, however, Arnold did say more about his own chosen art, and in particular in an essay on "The Function of Criticism at the Present Time" published in 1864 and then used as the introduction to his *Essays in Criticism* in 1865, he seems to point toward the free play tradition in aesthetics and thus to precisely what has here been argued was missing from Ruskin's approach to aesthetics. In this essay, Arnold says that "creative literary genius does not principally show itself in discovering new ideas, that is rather the business of the philosopher,"[95] and instead, not only using but appearing to endorse the language of the free play tradition of eighteenth-century aesthetics, he suggests that the foundation of creative literary genius is instead the "disinterested love of a free play of the mind on all subjects, for its own sake," and that both art and also "criticism, real criticism, is essentially the exercise of this very quality."[96] However, not only does Arnold not offer any further account of the pleasure of the free play of the mind for its own sake; on the contrary he goes on to suggest that the value of free play is rather "the creating of a current of true and fresh ideas."[97] In other words, his view seems to be that the value of criticism and by implication of art itself is after all cognitive, the discovery and communication of truth, and that free play is only a necessary stage in the discovery of truth – a view not that different from that underlying John Stuart Mill's nearly contemporary argument in *On Liberty*.

---

[94] Matthew Arnold, *Culture and Anarchy and other writings*, ed. Stefan Collini (Cambridge: Cambridge University Press, 1993), pp. 59, 61–2.
[95] Arnold, *Culture and Anarchy and other writings*, p. 28.
[96] Arnold, *Culture and Anarchy and other writings*, p. 35.
[97] Arnold, *Culture and Anarchy and other writings*, p. 38.

This impression is only confirmed by Arnold's later essay on "The Study of Poetry" (1880). Here Arnold places himself squarely in the Aristotelian and thus cognitivist tradition, saying that "as to the substance and matter of poetry" we should guide ourselves by "Aristotle's profound observation that the superiority of poetry over history consists in its possessing a higher truth and a higher seriousness." Thus, "the substances and matter of the best poetry acquire their special character from possessing, in an eminent degree, truth and seriousness." In this essay, which is essentially a Humean argument that one can learn to judge the merits of poetry only from intimate acquaintance with its best examples, Arnold goes on to argue that the best is distinguished by the quality of its "diction" and "movement" as well as by the truth of its content, but he is not arguing for a separate source of pleasure in poetry, and thus for an at least twofold rather than monistic cognitivist approach to poetry or art more generally. Rather, his argument is that quality of truth and quality of diction are necessarily interdependent, thus that "So far as high poetic truth and seriousness are wanting to a poet's matter and substance, we may be sure, will a high poetic stamp of diction and movement be wanting to his style and manner. In proportion as this high stamp of diction and movement, again, is absent from a poet's style and manner, we shall find, also, that high poetic truth and seriousness are absent from his substance and manner."[98] Arnold does not explain the causal assumptions on which these "dry generalities" rest, but we may safely assume that he thinks a clear insight into truth is the foundation of great poetry and brings clear expression in its train, not that a gift for distinctive expression by itself necessarily leads to the discovery of important truth.

Thus, in spite of the tantalizing hint of his essay on "The Function of Criticism," Arnold, like his great peer Ruskin, remains firmly within the cognitivist tradition in aesthetics. The ensuing movement of "art for art's sake" or "aestheticism," which in the realm of visual arts may be considered a response to Ruskin, may in more general form also be considered a response to Arnold. As we shall now see, the immediate response to these great cognitivists was not an amplification of their approach by means of the recognition of the elements of free play and emotional impact in our experience of art, but rather the rejection of their moralistic version of cognitivism altogether with the idea of "art for art's sake," an approach that eschewed the explanation of the value of aesthetic

---

[98] Matthew Arnold, "The Study of Poetry," cited from the Poetry Foundation at http://www.poetryfoundation.org/learning/essay/237816?page=4.

experience in terms of any other theoretical or practical values. Or at least that is what may initially seem to be the impetus of this movement. For what we shall see in the next chapter is that the greatest proponents of this approach, Walter Pater and Oscar Wilde, are more subtle thinkers than they may at first appear, and that they do not reject the moral and cultural ambitions of Ruskin's and Arnold's cognitivism but instead aim to embed those ambitions in a broader conception of the sources of our pleasure in art.

6

Aestheticism

The Aestheticist Movement

One of the characteristic cultural movements of the nineteenth century was "aestheticism," the movement captured by the slogans "*l'art pour l'art*" or "art for art's sake." In large part, this was a movement of artists and writers rather than of professional philosophers, yet it responded to the moralism not only of John Ruskin, but also of some more academic aesthetics early in the century, and it prepared the way for some of the more academic aesthetics of the end of the century and the beginning of the next, especially in Britain. So it cannot be overlooked here.

In its earlier phase, the aestheticist movement did not offer a positive theory of what aesthetic experience or art is, but rather protested against other, especially moralistic accounts of what the function of art is – the slogan "art for art's sake" does not explain what art is, but only implies that it is not for the sake of something else, for example, morality, religion, the state, or metaphysics. In other words, the slogan "art for art's sake" was the banner of a protest movement, not the name of a philosophical theory. But as we previously saw, an academic aesthetician in mid-century such as Friedrich Theodor Vischer also emphasized that beauty was not for the sake of religion, state, or society, without denying the possibility of a theory of beauty, so an insistence upon the autonomy of aesthetic experience and art from societal constraints does not necessarily lead to a rejection of serious aesthetic theory. And, later in the aestheticist movement, obviously in the works of the Oxford classicist and critic Walter Pater, the theory of beauty that was offered was broader rather than narrower, and suggested the possibility for a comprehensive rather than reductive approach to aesthetic theories. Perhaps a bit more beneath the surface, the theoretical writings of Oscar Wilde implied that aesthetic pleasure was not a distinct phenomenon cut off from other human concerns and emotions, but that in fact art is a vehicle for the communication of the deepest human emotions. It was rather some British art theorists of the beginning of the twentieth century, particularly Clive Bell and others associated with the Bloomsbury group in literature and painting, who isolated aesthetic response from other human interests and thus closed the door to a comprehensive and integrative approach to aesthetic experience that Pater and Wilde had actually opened under the banner of aestheticism. But we will return to those reductionists in the next volume; for now, we will begin with the earlier aestheticists and then see how different were the views of Pater and Wilde in spite of some similar language.

1. MORALISM AND "ART FOR ART'S SAKE": FROM COUSIN TO BAUDELAIRE

A protest movement is a protest against something, of course, and one way to begin the examination of the aestheticist movement is by seeing what it was protesting. Aestheticism actually began in France, rather than Britain, or at least the slogan "art for art's sake" first appears in French literature, so we can begin by adding to our previous discussion of Ruskin a French example of the kind of thinking about aesthetic experience and art against which the slogan was a protest.

Cousin

This is the example of the French "eclectic" philosopher, Victor Cousin (1792–1867), professor at the Sorbonne for most of his career (except during the years 1821–28 when he was stripped of his position for political reasons) and from 1830 until his death a member of the *Académie française*.[1] Cousin was early influenced by Scottish common-sense philosophy, above all by Reid, and later came to know the work of both Hegel and Schelling, all of whose views influenced his own. His vast output included a thirteen-volume translation of Plato, editions of Proclus and Descartes, numerous works on all periods of the history of philosophy including monographs on Locke and the Scottish philosophy, and several presentations of his own philosophy, including *Fragments philosophique* (1826) and the lectures *Du vrai, du beau, et du bien*. The latter work, although published in both French and English in 1854, thus late

---

[1] The only work on Cousin's aesthetics is Frederic Will, *Flumen historicum: Victor Cousin's Aesthetic and its Sources* (Chapel Hill: University of North Carolina Press, 1965).

in Cousin's life, was a revision of lectures he had given in Paris during the first phase of his teaching from 1815 to 1821, and thus represents the thought of the early nineteenth century published just in time to stimulate the reaction of the middle and later parts of the century.

In the first part of this work, on "The True," Cousin draws on both Reid and Kant to argue for the existence of universal and necessary truths at the foundation of all knowledge, but argues against what he takes to be Kant's pure rationalism and skepticism that these principles necessarily apply to concrete and real objects. With appeals to Plato, St. Augustine, Descartes, Malebranche, Leibniz, and others, he argues that God is the "principle of principles,"[2] that God's "thoughts are truths, eternal as himself, which are reflected in the laws of the universe, which the reason of man has received the power to attain," thus that "Truth is the offspring, the utterance ... the eternal word of God."[3] He then develops a theory of the beautiful deeply influenced by Reid, and thus through him if not directly by Shaftesbury, according to which beauty is an objective property of the world that is perceived by the mind of man and is in turn an expression of the mind of God. Thus far, Cousin's approach belongs firmly within the cognitivist tradition.

Cousin begins with a "psychological analysis"[4] of beauty in which, following eighteenth-century models, he stresses the distinction between the enjoyment of the beautiful and that of mere "agreeable sensation,"[5] and emphasizes that judgments of beauty, unlike mere judgments of agreeableness, claim universal rather than idiosyncratic validity. But unlike both Kant and the Scots, at least before Reid, he asserts that such intersubjective validity is possible only on the authority of reason, that "when we say: this is true, this is beautiful, it is no longer the particular and variable impression of our sensibility that we express, it is the absolute judgment that reason imposes on all men."[6] He also insists that "The sentiment of the beautiful is so far from being desire, that each excludes the other.... It is the property of beauty not to irritate and inflame desire, but to purify and ennoble it."[7] He does not offer a detailed explanation of the role of reason in the experience of beauty, but true to his attempt

---

[2] Victor Cousin, *Lectures on the True, the Beautiful, and the Good*, trans. O.W. Wight (New York: Appleton, 1873), p. 75.
[3] Cousin, *The True, the Beautiful, and the Good*, p. 101.
[4] Cousin, *The True, the Beautiful, and the Good*, p. 125.
[5] Cousin, *The True, the Beautiful, and the Good*, p. 126.
[6] Cousin, *The True, the Beautiful, and the Good*, p. 128.
[7] Cousin, *The True, the Beautiful, and the Good*, p. 132.

to combine the insights of both rationalism and empiricism, he does say that "When we have before our eyes an object whose form is perfectly determined, and the whole easy to embrace ... each of our faculties attaches itself to this object, and rests upon it with an unalloyed satisfaction. Our senses easily perceive its details; our reason seizes the happy harmony of all its parts."[8] So to some extent Cousin's emphasis on reason is only a verbal difference with previous aestheticians, who described aesthetic experience as an immediate grasp of harmony but attributed it to an *analogon rationis* (as in Baumgarten) or the imagination working in harmony with understanding (as in Kant) rather than to reason alone. Cousin reveals this affinity when he adds that "In order to complete the study of the different faculties that enter into the perception of beauty, after reason and sentiment, it remains to us to speak of a faculty not less necessary, which animates and vivifies them, – imagination,"[9] although he offers no explanation of what the imagination is beyond insisting that it is more than mere memory. He seems forced to recognize the role of imagination in aesthetic experience in order to mark some difference between the perception of the true and that of the beautiful, and thus at least to open the door to adding the idea of play to the idea of truth in the explanation of our experience of beauty. Nevertheless, he remains more interested in what the beautiful has in common with the true, namely dependence upon reason, than in what distinguishes the two.

In any case, any hint of a *rapprochement* between the theories of aesthetic truth and aesthetic play quickly disappears when Cousin turns from the "psychological analysis" of the experience of beauty to "The Beautiful in Objects."[10] Here, tacitly following the third part of Burke's *Philosophical Enquiry into the Origin of Our Ideas of the Sublime and Beautiful,* he first argues that the objective basis of beauty lies neither in fitness to an end nor in proportion alone,[11] and claims rather that "The most probable theory of the beautiful is that which composes it of two contrary and equally necessary elements, unity and variety," thus of "order, proportion, symmetry even," yet combined with diversity, for example, "How many shades in the color, what richness in the least details!"[12] But he then shows his interest in what unifies the beautiful with the true and ultimately the good rather than in what separates them by arguing for a

---

[8] Cousin, *The True, the Beautiful, and the Good,* pp. 132–3.
[9] Cousin, *The True, the Beautiful, and the Good,* p. 134.
[10] Cousin, *The True, the Beautiful, and the Good,* p. 140.
[11] Cousin, *The True, the Beautiful, and the Good,* pp. 141–2.
[12] Cousin, *The True, the Beautiful, and the Good,* p. 143.

scale of beauties in which "Unity and variety are applied to all orders of beauty." This scale begins with "sensible objects," the "colors, sounds, figures, movements" of which "are capable of producing the idea and the sentiment of beauty," in other words, what we call "physical beauty," but then rises "from the world of sense ... to that of mind, truth, and science," where we find "beauties more severe, but not less real," the "intellectual beauty" of the "universal laws that govern bodies, those that govern intelligence," and even of "the great principles that contain and produce long deductions," and finally reaches "the moral world and its laws," where in "the idea of liberty, virtue, and devotedness, here the austere justice of an Aristides, there the heroism of a Leonidas ... we shall certainly find a third order of beauty ... to wit, moral beauty."[13] Nor does Cousin content himself with asserting a structural similarity between the beautiful on the one hand and the true and the good on the other, namely that they are all forms of harmony or unity amidst variety that are recognized by reason even if in the case of the beautiful the imagination is also somehow involved. Rather, he seeks "the unity of these three sorts of beauty" and asserts "that they resolve themselves into one and the same beauty, moral beauty, meaning by that, with moral beauty properly so called, all spiritual beauty."[14] Drawing explicitly on Winckelmann and implicitly on Kant's concept of the "ideal of the beautiful," Cousin argues that what we admire in a statue is "the character of divinity stamped upon" it and that what we admire in a living human being is the "beauty of the soul" that underlies the beauty of the face.[15] Thus he concludes that "Physical beauty is ... the sign of an internal beauty, which is spiritual and moral beauty; and this is the foundation, the principle, the unity of the beautiful."[16] Beyond that, Cousin argues that "above real beauty, is a beauty of another order – ideal beauty," which "resides neither in an individual, nor in a collection of individuals," but in God.

> God, being the principle of all things, must for this reason be that of perfect beauty, and, consequently, of all natural beauties that express it more or less imperfectly; he is the principle of beauty, both as author of the physical world and as father of the intellectual and moral world.[17]

---

[13] Cousin, *The True, the Beautiful, and the Good*, pp. 143–4.
[14] Cousin, *The True, the Beautiful, and the Good*, p. 145.
[15] Cousin, *The True, the Beautiful, and the Good*, pp. 146–7.
[16] Cousin, *The True, the Beautiful, and the Good*, p. 149.
[17] Cousin, *The True, the Beautiful, and the Good*, p. 150.

Physical beauty, whether in the human being or the artistic representation of the human being, is an expression of moral beauty, and both physical beauty and moral beauty are ultimately grounded in and refer us to God. The door seems to have been shut after all to any theory that would emphasize anything as unimportant as free play in aesthetic experience.

Gautier

It is easy to imagine how such a doctrine could have appealed to many, especially when published in the central decade of the period we call "Victorian."[18] It is equally easy to imagine how such an expression of traditional piety could have triggered a vehement rejection. The early use of the slogan "art for art's sake" actually expresses disdain for recent utilitarian accounts of the value of art as well as for a view such as Cousin's.[19] The expression may have been previously used by Benjamin Constant in his diary in 1803–4, but was popularized by the 1834 Preface to the 1835–36 novel *Mademoiselle du Maupin* by Théophile Gautier (1811–72), who would have a diverse career as a poet, playwright, novelist, and critic, his other accomplishments include the libretto for the ballet *Giselle*, and Baudelaire's *Les Fleurs du Mal* would be dedicated to him.[20] Actually, the precise words "art for art's sake" (or "*l'art pour l'art*") are not to be found there, but the thought certainly is. The novel is a story of sexual ambiguity, loosely based on a seventeenth-century figure, in which a chevalier and his mistress both fall in love with the same, cross-dressing woman,

---

[18] For a recent critique of the assumed conservatism of "Victorian" aesthetics, however, see Rachel Teukolsky, *The Literate Eye: Victorian Writing and Modernist Aesthetics* (Oxford: Oxford University Press, 2009).

[19] While rejecting a clear distinction between aestheticism on the one hand and cognitivism and/or moralism on the other in the Victorian period, Teukolsky accepts a traditional genealogy of the idea of aestheticism, tracing it back to a supposed assertion of the "autonomy of art" by Kant (*The Literate Eye*, p. 8). But while Kant asserted the autonomy of *aesthetic judgment*, he never maintained the autonomy of *art*, claiming instead that "If the beautiful arts are not combined ... with moral ideas, which alone carry with them a self-sufficient satisfaction, then ... their ultimate fate" is to make "the spirit dull, the object by and by loathsome, and the mind ... dissatisfied with itself" (*Critique of the Power of Judgment*, §53, 5:326). Nineteenth-century aestheticism cannot be considered "a neo-Kantian philosophy in which art's only function [is] to exist in and of itself" (Teukolsky, *The Literate Eye*, p. 8).

[20] See John Wilcox, "The Beginnings of *L'art pour L'art*," *Journal of Aesthetics and Art Criticism* 11 (1953): 360–77, at p. 360, cited by Crispin Sartwell, "Art for Art's Sake," in *Encyclopedia of Aesthetics*, ed. Michael Kelly, 4 vols. (New York: Oxford University Press, 1998), vol. I, pp. 118–21, at pp. 118–19.

one thinking she is a woman and the other that she is a man, who is in turn accompanied by a cross-dressing page. It may well be imagined that the author of such a racy novel (it would not be translated into English for more than forty years) might have thought that it needed to be preceded by an apologia in the bourgeois France of Louis-Philippe. Clearly operating on the premise that the best defense is a good offense, Gautier attempts to undercut those who would object to his work on moral grounds, whether traditional Christian morality or modern utilitarianism, and then for good measure attacks all journalistic criticism as well. He lampoons the "current affectation" for Christianity, objecting to the hypocrisy of people who "pretend to be St. Jerome, just as they used to pretend to be Don Juan," who "talk about the sanctity of art, the noble mission of the artist, the poetry of Catholicism … the painters of the Angelic School, the Council of Trent, the progress of civilization and a thousand other fine things."[21] He then attacks "utilitarian critics," who object to a book if it contains "Not one word about the needs of society, nothing that is a civilizing or progressive influence," and thus cannot be applied "to the moralization and well-being of the poorest and most numerous classes" of society.[22] In this case, Gautier goes beyond the accusation of hypocrisy to suggest three arguments against the moralistic assumption that works of art should make direct contributions to increasing utility in society. First, he notes that works of art do not determine the moral condition of the society in which they are made, but reflect it: "Pictures are created according to the model, not the model according to the picture.... Trees bear fruit, fruit doesn't bear trees … Books are the fruits of manners."[23] Second, Gautier suggests that utilitarianism is an inadequate moral theory because utility is always relative to some particular way of life, but the value of life itself cannot be explained by utility: "Does anything exist on this earth of ours, in this life of ours, which is absolutely useful? In the first place there is very little use in our being on earth and alive."[24] In other words, it cannot be utility that gives meaning to human life; utility is what is useful to the pursuit of a meaning in life that comes from some other source (if we are to speak of the "meaning of life" at all). And finally, Gautier observes that it takes very little to satisfy basic human needs – "Soup and a bit of meat twice a day," "a hollow

---

[21] Théophile Gautier, *Mademoiselle du Maupin*, trans. Helen Constantine (London: Penguin Books, 2005), p. 5.
[22] Gautier, *Mademoiselle du Maupin*, p. 20.
[23] Gautier, *Mademoiselle du Maupin*, p. 19.
[24] Gautier, *Mademoiselle du Maupin*, p. 20.

cube, seven or eight feet square, with a hole to breathe through," and a blanket, all of which could be had for "twenty-five sous a day." Beauty is what adds pleasure to life rather than what satisfies basic needs:

> Nothing that is beautiful is indispensable to life. If you did away with flowers, the world would not suffer in any material way. And yet who would wish there not to be flowers? I could do without potatoes more easily than roses and I think there is only one utilitarian in the world capable of tearing out a bed of tulips to plant cabbages.... The only things that are really beautiful are those which have no use.[25]

After this somewhat ill-considered outburst (of course, without flowers there would be little food, though it is true that many of the most showy flowers, natural or cultivated, do not produce food), Gautier launches a general attack upon the surfeit of criticism in popular publications, arguing that "Reading the journals prevents people from having real savants and real artists; it's like a daily excess which causes you to arrive all enervated and fatigued on the couch of the Muses, those harsh and difficult women who want their lovers to be vigorous and fresh. The journal is killing the book ... just as artillery killed courage and muscular strength."[26] Reading about books or other forms of art becomes a substitute for directly experiencing the art, both occupying the time that might be spent with the latter and making the reader too lazy for the real thing. With such a general attack upon criticism, of course, Gautier can defang any particular attacks upon his own work (never mind the reams of criticism he would write in his own subsequent career).

Poe

In this bit of polemic, Gautier hints at some sound reasons why it should not be piously assumed that all valuable art is in the service of moral or religious goals, as Cousin for example did, but he does not offer a positive account of what beauty is or do more than hint that the intrinsic pleasure that we take in beauty is a sufficient account of its value. Gautier's close contemporary, the American poet and fabulist Edgar Allan Poe (1809–49), had somewhat more formal education than Gautier – a year at the University of Virginia and a semester at the U.S. Military Academy at West Point – and some more exposure to British aesthetic theory of the preceding century, then a part of the American college curriculum.

---

[25] Gautier, *Mademoiselle du Maupin*, pp. 20–1.
[26] Gautier, *Mademoiselle du Maupin*, p. 36.

Thus he not only came closer to formulating the slogan "art for art's sake," but expressed his position within a more traditional philosophical framework. During his abbreviated career, Poe supported himself not only with his poems and stories, but with a vast number of book reviews and a few more general essays on poetry and poetics. In the first of these pieces, the "Letter to B –" published as the preface to his second volume of *Poems* in 1831, Poe, in a passage that could easily have been written by Beattie half a century earlier, rejects the view that the primary purpose of poetry is instruction about some important truth in favor of the view that its purpose is pleasure and that insofar as it engages in instruction, that is only because under some circumstances instruction can be pleasurable. At all of twenty-two, but not hesitating to oppose the biggest names in philosophy as well as poetry, Poe writes:

> Aristotle, with singular assurance, has declared poetry the most philosophical of all writing – but it required a Wordsworth to pronounce it the most metaphysical. He seems to think that the end of poetry is, or should be, instruction – yet it is a truism that the end of our existence is happiness; if so, the end of every separate part of our existence – every thing connected with our existence should still be happiness. Therefore the end of instruction should be happiness; and happiness is another name for pleasure; – therefore the end of instruction should be pleasure: yet we see the above mentioned opinion implies precisely the reverse.[27]

Unlike Gautier, Poe is willing to work within a utilitarian framework, affirming that happiness or pleasure is our most fundamental value and goal, but he then argues that poetry contributes directly to this goal and need not be justified by any putative facilitation of some other means to this goal. As he puts it a few pages later, "A poem, in my opinion, is opposed to a work of science by having, for its *immediate* object, pleasure, not truth."[28] No doubt the acquisition of truth through science can yield pleasure in various ways – directly, through our sheer pleasure in knowing, and indirectly, through its contribution to the technological amelioration of our living conditions – but poetry need not depend upon the pleasures of truth for its own pleasure; that is immediate.

In "The Philosophy of Composition," an essay written fifteen years later to explain "the precision and rigid consequence" of his famous poem "The Raven," Poe maintains that the specific way in which a poem

---

[27] Edgar Allan Poe, *Essays and Reviews*, ed. G.R. Thompson (New York: Library of America, 1984), p. 7. A rare discussion of Poe in the context of the history of aesthetics is in Raters, *Kunst, Wahrheit, und Gefühl*, pp. 159–73.
[28] Poe, *Essays and Reviews*, p. 11.

pleases is by "intensely excit[ing], by elevating, the soul," and that anything that does not do this, such as many stretches in a long composition like *Paradise Lost*, even if it has the outward structure of poetry, is really prose, not poetry at all.[29] He continues that when people "speak of Beauty, they mean, precisely, not a quality that is presupposed, but an effect – they refer, in short, to that intense and pure elevation of *soul – not* of intellect, or of heart." "The object, Truth, or the satisfaction of the intellect, and the object Passion, or the excitement of the heart," Poe argues, are "far more readily attainable in prose" than in poetry, and require a precision (for truth) and a "homeliness" (for passion) that are "absolutely antagonistic to that Beauty which … is the excitement, or pleasurable elevation, of the soul."[30] Poe's distinction between passion as the "excitement of the heart" and beauty as the "elevation of the soul" is far from clear, but it does seem likely that he is writing here against the background of such eighteenth-century distinctions as Kames's distinction between passion and emotion, that is, between an affective state that leads to desire and action – passion – and one that does not – the elevation of the soul rather than the excitement of the heart. So here Poe is continuing into the nineteenth century the eighteenth-century division of the mind into intellect and conation or will on the one hand and the special province of aesthetic experience on the other hand, a division he could have been familiar with in writers such as Hutcheson or Kames. Poe would come to be seen as the avatar of literary modernism, but his aesthetic theory, such as it is, is deeply rooted in the eighteenth-century alternative to an aesthetics of truth.

The continuity of Poe's thought with eighteenth-century aesthetics is also evident in a detailed essay on poetics from 1848, "The Rationale of Verse": here Poe illustrates with detailed examples how harmony, "equality,"[31] and rhyme realize the abstract "Principle of Variety in Uniformity" and thus account for our "undeniable" "enjoyment" of poetry.[32] But the character of Poe's thought is most apparent in "The Poetic Principle," published only after his death, in 1850. Here, although Poe still does not use the generic slogan "art for art's sake," he deploys a specific application of it, championing the idea of "a poem simply for the poem's sake." He opposes his conception of the intrinsic dignity or value of the poem – or work in any other medium of art, insofar as it shares the

---

[29] Poe, *Essays and Reviews*, p. 15.
[30] Poe, *Essays and Reviews*, p. 16.
[31] Poe, *Essays and Reviews*, p. 33.
[32] Poe, *Essays and Reviews*, pp. 34, 33.

"Poetic Sentiment"[33] – to what he calls "the heresy of *The Didactic*," a heresy that lies in the supposition that art has value only insofar as it offers instruction in truth – a heresy with which Poe in particular taxes Henry Wadsworth Longfellow, the leading "establishment" poet of the United States at the time.[34] Thus Poe writes:

> Every poem, it is said, should inculcate a moral; and by this moral is the poetical merit of the work to be adjudged. We Americans, especially, have patronised this happy idea; and we Bostonians have taken it into our heads that to write a poem simply for the poem's sake, and to acknowledge such to have been our design, would be to confess ourselves radically wanting in the true Poetic dignity and force: – but the simple fact is, that, would we but permit ourselves to look into our own souls, we should immediately there discover that under the sun there neither exists nor *can* exist any work more thoroughly dignified – more supremely noble than this very poem – this poem *per se* – this poem which is a poem and nothing more – this poem written solely for the poem's sake.[35]

No more than Karl Philip Moritz had done a half century earlier when he introduced the idea of the "internal purposiveness" of a work of art does Poe actually explain what it means to write a poem for the poem's sake, and while we know what it means for one purposive agent to do something for the sake of another purposive agent, that is, to make the end of the other her own end, it is by no means obvious what it would mean for a human agent to perform an action – write a poem or produce another work of art – for the sake of something that is not an agent at all, namely, the poem or work of art itself. But as Poe continues, it becomes clear that this talk of the poem for the poem's sake does not really impute an end or goal to the poem itself, but is rather a colorful way of saying for which of our *own* human ends poetry or art more generally should be created: not for our end of discovering truth, which is of course our proper end in the pursuit of science, nor for the end of arousing or controlling our passions, which may be our proper end in the pursuit of morality, but for the end of achieving an elevated state of the soul and in that state enjoying "supernal Loveliness."[36] Poe makes this clear by once again "Dividing the world of mind into its three most immediately obvious distinctions" and revealing that to write a poem for the poem's own sake is actually

---

[33] Poe, *Essays and Reviews*, p. 77.
[34] See the long polemic against Longfellow conducted from 1842 to 1845 at Poe, *Essays and Reviews*, pp. 670–777.
[35] Poe, *Essays and Reviews*, pp. 75–6.
[36] Poe, *Essays and Reviews*, p. 77.

to serve one aspect of our own minds rather than either or both of the other two. If we make this division, Poe writes,

> we have the Pure Intellect, Taste, and the Moral Sense. I place taste in the middle, because it is just this position, which, in the mind, it occupies. It holds intimate relations with either extreme; but from the Moral Sense is separated by so faint a difference that Aristotle has not hesitated to place some of its operations among the virtues themselves. Nevertheless, we find the *offices* of the trio marked with a sufficient distinction. Just as the Intellect concerns itself with Truth, so Taste informs us of the Beautiful while the Moral Sense is regardful of Duty. Of this latter, while Conscience teaches the obligation, and Reason the expediency, Taste contents herself with displaying the charms: – waging war upon Vice solely on the ground of her deformity – her disproportion – her animosity to the fitting, to the appropriate, to the harmonious – in a word, to Beauty.[37]

This passage both makes clear that Poe's slogan "the poem for the poem's sake," revolutionary as it may sound, is actually founded upon the traditional distinction of the mind into the three departments of intellect, moral sense, and taste, but also reveals that in spite of its fundamental independence from knowledge of truth on the one hand and the demands of morality on the other, the experience of beauty can be brought into close connection with either without losing what is distinctive about it: we saw earlier that Poe allows that the pleasure of instruction in truth can contribute to the pleasure in beauty without being identical to it, and here he allows that beauty can be found in the harmonious character of what is morally appropriate without being reduced to the latter.

Poe continues to explore the difference but close connection between beauty and truth on the one hand and the passions characteristic of morality and the elevation of soul characteristic of beauty in the concluding pages of "The Poetic Principle," and here again shows how deeply rooted in tradition his thought actually is. Here he claims again that the "Human Aspiration for Supernal Beauty ... is always found in *an elevating excitement of the soul*," which is "quite independent of that passion which is the intoxication of the Heart" on the one hand and "of that Truth which is the satisfaction of the Reason" on the other. Yet what "supernal beauty" produces is "Love," which is not so easy to distinguish from "passion." Poe has to appeal to mythology to suggest the difference he is trying to capture: "Love, on the contrary – Love – the true, the divine Eros – the Uranian, as distinguished from the Dionæan Venus – is unquestionably

[37] Poe, *Essays and Reviews*, p. 76.

the purest and truest of all poetical themes." The difference between mere passion and the elevation of the soul in genuine aesthetic experience can be expressed in these terms, or perhaps captured by an enumeration of objects of genuine taste, beauties that appeal not to personal passion or desire but to something higher and more general. The person with true taste "recognises the ambrosia which nourishes his soul" in such things as "the bright orbs that shine in Heaven – in the volutes of the flower – in the clustering of low shrubberies – in the waving of the grain-fields – in the slanting of tall, Eastern trees – in the blue distance of the mountains" and so on, that is, in things that cannot be objects of personal, especially sexual passion and desire, and he – of course, he – "feels it in the beauty of woman – in the grace of her step – in the lustre of her eye – in the melody of her voice," even "in the harmony of the rustling of her robes,"[38] only after and in the same manner as he has experienced the impersonal, sexless, and passionless beauty of the heavenly bodies, mountains, and flowers. Mere passion and the love of beauty – or the beauty of love – are closely related, but on a different plane.

In this final passage, Poe also returns to the relation between beauty and truth, once again insisting that they are different although they can be related. Here what he suggests is that we can have knowledge that some harmony obtains, as we can have knowledge that any other fact obtains, but that what pleases us in the aesthetic experience is not the knowledge that this harmony exists but simply and immediately the harmony itself: "if, to be sure, through the attainment of a truth, we are led to experience a harmony where none was apparent before, we experience, at once, the true poetical effect – but this effect is referable to the harmony alone, and not in the least degree to the truth which merely served to render the harmony manifest."[39] Knowledge and the experience of beauty may be simultaneous, as it were, but their objects are still different: one, harmony itself, the other, the fact that such harmony exists and whatever else might follow from that for the intellect.

Baudelaire

Poe, then, came closer than did Gautier to formulating the principle "art for art's sake" in order to express the independence of art from the demands of morality as well as knowledge that Gautier also prized. In so doing, however, he also revealed that this modern-sounding slogan

[38] Poe, *Essays and Reviews*, p. 93.
[39] Poe, *Essays and Reviews*, p. 93.

is but a way of expressing the alternative to an aesthetics of truth that eighteenth-century philosophers beginning with the Scots and then following them some German thinkers had already entertained. Poe did not talk in terms of the aesthetics of play or free mental activity, however, rather using only the traditional terminology of harmony and unity amid variety. Nor does Poe's admirer in France, the Parisian poet and critic Charles Baudelaire (1821–67), explicitly develop an aesthetics of play: he too works within what is still essentially the same eighteenth-century framework within which Poe worked, indeed to a considerable extent his theoretical writings consist of a translation of Poe's "Poetic Principle" – with one exception, however, namely that he transforms the eighteenth-century requirement of "variety" for beauty, still accepted by Poe, into the requirement of "strangeness." In so doing, Baudelaire draws the boundary between the beautiful on the one hand and the true and the good on the other more firmly than Poe had done, and thus says even more emphatically than Poe that "poetry has no other aim or object but herself; she can have no other, and no poem will be as great, as noble, as supremely worthy of the name as one that has been written for the sole pleasure of writing a poem."[40] This statement, it may be noted, unlike Baudelaire's earlier statement about Poe that "True poet that he was, he held that the aim and object of poetry is of the same nature as its principle, and that it ought to have nothing else in view but itself,"[41] not only makes it sound as if a poem or work of art is itself a goal-directed agent of some kind for whose sake something (its own composition) could be done; rather, although its first clause ("poetry has no other aim or object but herself") is in that vein, the second clause (" ... written for the sole pleasure of writing a poem") clearly asserts that it is for the *human* end of pleasure that a poem is written (of course, by a human), as contrasted to any other *human* end such as the acquisition of truth or the achievement of morality. Poetry for its own sake – the closest that Baudelaire comes to the slogan "art for art's sake" – means nothing more mysterious than that poetry should be written for the sake of pleasure rather than for the sake of truth or morality. It is in the same spirit that Baudelaire quotes the famous remark by the novelist Stendahl (Henri-Marie Beyle, 1783–1842) that "Beauty is nothing else but a promise of happiness."[42]

[40] Charles Baudelaire, "Further Notes on Edgar Poe," in *The Painter of Modern Life and Other Essays*, trans. and ed. Jonathan Mayne (London: Phaidon, 1965), p. 107.
[41] Baudelaire, "Edgar Allan Poe: His Life and Works," in *The Painter of Modern Life*, p. 79.
[42] Baudelaire, *The Painter of Modern Life*, p. 3. The editor of Baudelaire provides references to two works of Stendahl for this quotation, *De l'Amour* (1822), ch. XVIII, and *Histoire de la Peinture en Italie* (1817), ch. 110.

What Baudelaire actually says about Stendahl's own slogan is somewhat strange; he follows his quotation of it with the statement that "This definition doubtless overshoots the mark; it makes Beauty far too subject to the infinitely variable ideal of Happiness; it strips Beauty too neatly of its aristocratic quality: but it has the great merit of making a decided break with academic error."[43] Presumably the "academic error," the break from which Baudelaire praises, is the identification of the beautiful with the morally good rather than with what makes us happy, the identification promulgated in his Parisian lectures by Cousin at the same time that Stendahl was making his statement; but what is strange is that Baudelaire criticizes Stendahl for his association of beauty with the "infinitely variable ideal of Happiness" when it is precisely the infinite variability of beauty itself that Baudelaire himself praises and ultimately identifies with its strangeness. Baudelaire asserts the variety and in turn the strangeness of beauty in a review of the art displayed in the 1855 *Exposition Universelle* in Paris, where he objects to any attempt to find rules for beauty:

> Anyone can easily understand that if those whose business it is to express beauty were to conform to the rules of the pundits, beauty itself would disappear from the earth. since all types, all ideas and all sensations would be fused in a vast, impersonal and monotonous unity, as immense as boredom or total negation. Variety, the *sine qua non* of life, would be effaced from life. So true is it that in the multiple productions of art there is an element of the ever-new which will eternally elide the rules and analyses of the school! That shock of surprise, which is one of the great joys produced by art and literature, is due to this very variety of types and sensations....
>
> With all due respect to the over-proud sophists who have taken their wisdom from books, I shall go even further, and however delicate and difficult of expression my idea may be, I do not despair of succeeding. *The Beautiful is always strange*. I do not mean that it is coldly, deliberately strange, for in that case it would be a monstrosity that had jumped the rails of life. I mean that it always contains a touch of strangeness, of simple, unpremeditated and unconscious strangeness, and that it is this touch of strangeness that gives it its particular quality as Beauty.[44]

The inclusion of novelty among the sources of beauty was not a novelty, of course; that had been one of the three chief "pleasures of the

---

[43] Baudelaire, *The Painter of Modern Life*, pp. 3–4.
[44] Baudelaire, "Exposition Universelle I," from Jonathan Mayne, ed., *Art in Paris 1845–1862: Salons and Other Exhibitions Reviewed by Charles Baudelaire* (London: Phaidon, 1964), pp. 121–8, reprinted in Charles Harrison, Paul Wood, and Jason Gaiger, *Art in Theory: 1815–1900* (Oxford: Blackwell, 1998), pp. 485–9, at p. 487.

imagination" for Joseph Addison in 1712, and had been included in many subsequent lists of aesthetic categories, notably Alexander Gerard's in 1759. What is novel is Baudelaire's transformation of the traditional category of novelty into that of strangeness as well as his suggestion that it is the touch of strangeness alone that gives a work its beauty. Baudelaire does not explain why the variety expected in a beautiful work must take the form of strangeness, nor does he offer an example of what he means by strangeness that is yet not monstrous, although examples are readily to be found in his own poetry or in the exoticism that swept through so many forms of art in the second half of the nineteenth century, not merely poetry but also painting, architecture, and music.

Not only does Baudelaire not explain the necessity of strangeness; for that matter, he does not explain the necessity of variety itself as a condition of beauty. He only hints that variety is necessary to avoid boredom – thus revealing the continuing influence on French thought of Du Bos's foundational *Critical Reflections* of 1719 – and indeed that is in some way necessary for life itself. But he does not explain why variety is the *sine qua non* of life. We find more by way of an explanation of this assertion in the work beginning in the next decade of the author who seems to have been the first to speak entirely generally of "the love of art for its own sake,"[45] the Oxford don and man of letters Walter Pater. As we shall see, however, Pater does not use this expression to express a view that separates the value of art from all other human values, but rather one that prizes art because it integrates human values.

2. "THIS HARD, GEM-LIKE FLAME": PATER

Walter Pater (1839–94) spent his career as a Fellow of Brasenose College, Oxford, but his only book of the sort that might have been expected from a scholar occupying such a position is *Plato and Platonism: A Series of Lectures*, published in 1868, just a year before his death.[46] Otherwise, his reputation in his own lifetime was and has remained founded on three slender collections of essays – *The Renaissance*, which was first published in 1873 and went through three further editions in his lifetime,[47]

---

[45] Walter Pater, *The Renaissance: Studies in Art and Poetry*, ed. Adam Philips (Oxford: Oxford University Press, 1986), "Conclusion" (1868), p. 153.
[46] Walter Pater, *Plato and Platonism: A Series of Lectures* (London: Macmillan, 1893; reprinted New York: Macmillan, 1903).
[47] Pater removed the 1868 conclusion of *The Renaissance* from the next (1873) edition, but then restored it to subsequent editions.

Imaginary Portraits in 1887,[48] and *Appreciations*, a collection of reviews, in 1889, as well as one completed novel, *Marius the Epicurean: His Sensations and Ideas*,[49] published in 1885, and one uncompleted novel, *Gaston de Latour*, published posthumously in 1897.[50] Two other posthumous volumes were *Greek Studies* and *Miscellaneous Studies*. In spite of this slender output, which did not include a systematic work in philosophical aesthetics, Pater may be considered the most significant British writer on aesthetic topics between Ruskin and the turn of the twentieth century.[51]

As noted at the end of the previous section, Pater did explicitly use the expression "the love of art for its own sake," and has been regarded as the preeminent advocate of the complete independence of aesthetic experience and thus of art from the demands of knowledge on the one hand and of morality on the other, thus the independence of aesthetic experience from truth about either theoretical or practical matters. His famous statement, a page before his introduction of the phrase "the love of art for its own sake" in the penultimate sentence of the original conclusion to *The Renaissance*, that "To burn always with this hard, gem-like flame, to maintain this ecstasy, is success in life,"[52] as well as the final sentence of the introduction, "For art comes to you proposing frankly to give nothing but the highest quality to your moments as they pass, and simply for those moments' sake,"[53] certainly seem to confirm the view that Pater advocates the independence of aesthetic experience from all other sources of value in human life, and indeed the supremacy of the value of aesthetic experience over all other forms of value. These statements seem to justify such a statement as that "the achievement of Pater is precisely to purify the aesthetic vision represented so intensely by Ruskin of its inconvenient moral bias."[54] However, such an interpretation is a

---

[48] Walter Pater, *Imaginary Portraits, with The Child in the House and Gaston de Latour*, with introduction by Bill Beckley (New York: Allworth Press, 1997).

[49] Walter Pater, *Marius the Epicurean*, ed. Michael Levey (London: Penguin, 1985). Levey is also the author of a biography, *The Case of Walter Pater* (London: Thames and Hudson, 1978).

[50] The existing chapters of *Gaston de Latour* are reprinted in the 1997 edition of *Imaginary Portraits*.

[51] A monograph on Pater's aesthetics is Carolyn Williams, *Transfigured World: Walter Pater's Aesthetic Historicism* (Ithaca: Cornell University Press, 1989). A monograph on Pater's aesthetics is Kenneth Daley, *The Rescue of Romanticism: Walter Pater and John Ruskin* (Athens: Ohio University Press, 2001), and a collection of essays is Elicia Clements and Leslie J. Higgins, *Victorian Aesthetic Conditions: Pater Across the Arts* (Basingstoke: Palgrave Macmillan, 2010).

[52] Pater, *The Renaissance*, p. 152.

[53] Pater, *The Renaissance*, p. 153.

[54] Stephen Bann attributes this interpretation, without further information, to Harold Bloom, in his entry on Pater in Kelly, *Encyclopedia of Aesthetics*, Vol. 3, pp. 445–7, at 447.

simplification of Pater's position. His conception that art should be valued for "its own sake" and for the sake of the "moments" of our intense experience of it is not meant to separate our experience of art from other sources of value in our lives, but rather expresses his view that in the experience of art all of the sources of value in our lives can come together most fully and completely. Pater employs the language of aestheticism, but his aesthetics is integrative rather than reductive.

The compatibility between Pater's idea of art for art's sake and his conception of the integrative rather than divisive character of aesthetic experience is evident in a comment in his description of Plato's aesthetics in *Plato and Platonism*, where Pater writes:

> Art, as such, as Plato knows, has no purpose but itself, its own perfection. The proper art of the Perfect City is in fact the art of discipline. Music, all the various forms of fine art, will be but the instruments of its one overmastering social or political purpose, irresistibly conforming its so imitative subject units to type.[55]

Pater himself does not accept Plato's assumption that the perfection of art consists in the perfection of its contribution to societal discipline, but he does accept the idea that the perfection of art in its own terms includes rather than excludes a connection to morality. No more than Poe, to be sure, does Pater think that successful art is didactic. On the contrary – and here is Pater's substantive advance beyond such writers as Gautier, Poe, and Baudelaire, that is, his advance beyond simply generalizing the formula "poetry for poetry's sake" into the formula "art for art's sake" – he thinks that successful art results from and produces a free play of all our mental powers that he sums up in the superficially contradictory phrase "imaginative reason."[56] Unlike his predecessors in the aestheticist movement, then, Pater does not just distance himself by rejecting the subordination of aesthetic experience to truth and especially to moral truth, but positively aligns himself with the conception of aesthetic experience as free play, while also emphasizing that such free play involves all of our powers, thus includes a connection to morality. Precisely what form that connection should take we will now see.

Pater's view is that aesthetic experience is concrete and complex, transcending traditional boundaries among domains of human concern and especially the supposed boundary between form and content,

---

[55] Pater, *Plato and Platonism*, pp. 248–9.
[56] Pater, "The School of Giorgione," *The Renaissance*, p. 83.

and that the objects of such experience and such experience itself can only be produced by a free play among our various sensory and intellectual capacities. He opens the Preface to *The Renaissance* by abjuring any attempt to "define beauty in the abstract, to express it in the most general terms, to find some universal formula for it," and argues instead that "To see the object as in itself it really is, has been justly said to be the aim of all true criticism whatever." He amplifies this point in a way that suggests an assertion of subjectivism, that is, that each person's response to any beautiful object is necessarily idiosyncratic: "in æsthetic criticism the first step towards seeing one's object as it really is, is to know one's own impression as it really is, to discriminate it, to realise it distinctly.... What is this song or picture, this engaging personality presented in life or in a book, to *me*? What effect does it really produce on me?"[57] But an assertion of subjectivism is not Pater's chief point; his point is rather that aesthetic experience is always an engagement between an object in all its concreteness and a subject in all of his or her concreteness; no doubt some variation in aesthetic response among different subjects is therefore to be expected, because both objects and subjects in their full concreteness will inevitably differ from one another in some regard or another, but that those differences will lead to significant disagreements among subjects about the features or merits of any particular aesthetic objects is not any part of Pater's argument. What is part of his argument is that the individuality of particular works of art as well as of the several art forms must be fully recognized by "æsthetic criticism" or theory. The preface stresses the individuality of different works of art:

> The æsthetic critic, then, regards all the objects with which he has to do, all works of art, and the fairer forms of nature and human life, as powers or forces producing pleasurable sensations, each of a more or less peculiar or unique kind.... To him, the picture, the landscape, the engaging personality in life or in a book, *La Gioconda*, the hills of Carrara, Pico of Mirandola, are valuable for their virtues, as we say, in speaking of a herb, a wine, a gem; for the property each has of affecting one with a special, a unique, impression of pleasure.... Our education becomes complete in proportion as our susceptibility to these impressions increases in depth and variety.[58]

One noteworthy feature of Pater's aestheticism is that we are here enjoined to regard objects of nonhuman nature (the hills of Carrara),

---

[57] Pater, *The Renaissance*, p. xxix.
[58] Pater, *The Renaissance*, p. xxx.

human beings (Pico de Mirandola), and works of art, whether representations of particular human beings (*La Gioconda*) or not (just pictures), equally as "powers or forces producing pleasurable sensations": this might seem to undercut the importance of cognitive and moral stances toward nature and human beings, but it need not, because, as has already been suggested, aesthetic experience on Pater's account includes rather than excludes these crucial human attitudes.

As already remarked, the preface to *The Renaissance* stresses the concreteness and therefore the individuality of particular works of art (as well as of particular locales in nature and particular people themselves), and therefore requires of the critic or appreciator more generally not "a correct abstract definition of beauty for the intellect" nor any sort of determinate rule for aesthetic appreciation and judgment, but rather "a certain kind of temperament, the power of being moved by the presence of" particular beautiful objects. Such a critic will "remember always that beauty exists in many forms. To him all periods, types, schools of taste, are in themselves equal."[59] In the central essay on "The School of Giorgione" in the body of the text, Pater stresses the point that each art form has its own powers and potentials, and thus argues against general rules for beauty ranging over the several arts as well as against such rules ranging over particular works:

> Each art, therefore, having its own peculiar and untranslatable sensuous charm, has its own special mode of reaching the imagination, its own special responsibilities to the material. One of the functions of aesthetic criticism is to define these limitations; to estimate the degree in which a given work of art fulfils its responsibilities to its special material; to note in a picture that true pictorial charm, which is neither a mere poetical thought or sentiment, on the one hand, nor a mere result of communicable technical skill in colour or design, on the other; to define in a poem that true poetical quality, which is neither descriptive nor meditative merely, but comes of an inventive handling of rhythmical language, the element of song in the singing; to note in music the musical charm, that essential music, which presents no words, no matter of sentiment or thought, separable from the special form in which it is conveyed in us.[60]

"Pictorial charm," "true poetical quality," and "musical charm, that essential music," do not work in the same way, so there can be no general

---

[59] Pater, *The Renaissance*, p. xxx.
[60] Pater, "The School of Giorgione," *The Renaissance*, p. 83. Pater adds in a footnote that Lessing's differentiation between the means of representation available to sculpture and poetry is an anticipation of his own more general claim.

rules for beauty that efface the boundaries between pictures, poems, and music. Now if this claim were taken to imply that there *are* general rules for achieving pictorial charm within the domain of pictures, poetical quality within the domain of poems, and musical charm within the domain of music, then it would seem to contradict Pater's earlier point that there can be no abstract definition of beauty because each work of art (or beauty of nature or beautiful person) is a concrete individual. But Pater clearly intends to exclude such a contradiction precisely by asserting that true pictorial charm cannot be reduced to "a mere result of communicable technical skill in color or design" and that "true poetical quality" requires an "inventive handling" of rhythm and other aspects of poems; this implies that individuality within the various media of art is an ineluctable aspect of genuine beauty, although of course each art has its own characteristic media within which individuality can be achieved.

Pater might again seem to undercut this conclusion when, a page later, he makes the famous statement that "*All art constantly aspires towards the condition of music.*"[61] But the point that Pater is making here is compatible with the existence of fundamental differences among the means and ends of the different media of art. What Pater takes to be particularly characteristic of music – and here he must be thinking especially of instrumental music without a verbal text or program – is that it effaces the customary distinction between form and content, instead achieving whatever particularity of expression of mood or thought it strives for through its use of the formal devices of melody, harmony, rhythm, and so on. Thus he states:

> It is the art of music which most completely realises this artistic ideal, this perfect identification of matter and form. In its consummate moments, the end is not distinct from the means, the form from the matter, the subject from the expression; they inhere in and completely saturate each other; and to it, therefore, to the condition of its perfect moments, all the arts may be supposed constantly to tend and aspire. In music, then, rather than in poetry, is to be found the true type or measure of perfected art.[62]

Although the ideal fusion of form and matter is most readily found in music, however, other arts can at least aim for such a fusion, each in its own way:

> For while in all other kinds of art it is possible to distinguish the matter from the form, and the understanding can always make this distinction, yet it is the constant effort of art to obliterate it. That the mere matter of a poem,

---

[61] Pater, "The School of Giorgione," *The Renaissance*, p. 86.
[62] Pater, "The School of Giorgione," *The Renaissance*, p. 88.

for instance, its subject, namely, its given incidents or situations – that the mere matter of a picture, the actual circumstances of an event, the actual topography of a landscape – should be nothing without the form, this mode of handling, should become an end in itself, should penetrate every part of the matter: this is what all art constantly strives after, and achieves in different degrees.[63]

Perhaps this aspiration that every work of art should achieve the musical goal of effacing the distinction between form and content, though not by musical means but by its own means, may be seen as a corollary of the requirement of concreteness in aesthetic experience and its objects: the concrete object presents itself in experience as a fully integrated unity, although of course in subsequent reflection upon that experience a distinction between form and content can no doubt always be drawn.

As suggested earlier, in Pater's view aesthetic experience can efface the boundaries among what are ordinarily regarded as the different domains of human concern as well as the usual boundary between form and content. As in the latter case, the effacement of the usual boundaries among different human concerns and activities should be regarded as an aspiration of art that is by no means always achieved, but that is achieved by the most successful art. Pater suggests this point in his initial explanation of what is distinctive about the Renaissance, or more generally renaissances, since he writes not only about the Italian Renaissance of the fifteenth century but also about what some have called the renaissance of twelfth-century France[64] and about some other historical moments that might be considered renaissances as well. Here is what he says:

The various forms of intellectual activity which together make up the culture of an age, move for the most part from different starting-points, and by unconnected roads. As products of the same generation they partake indeed of a common character, and unconsciously illustrate each other; but of the producers themselves, each group is solitary, gaining what advantage or disadvantage there may be in intellectual isolation. Art and poetry, philosophy and the religious life, and that other life of refined pleasure and action in the conspicuous places of the world, are each of them confined to its own circle of ideas, and those who prosecute either of them are generally little curious of the thoughts of others. There come, however, from time to time, eras of more favorable conditions, in which the thoughts of men draw nearer together than is their wont, and the many interests of the intellectual world combine in one complete type of general culture. The fifteenth

---

[63] Pater, "The School of Giorgione," *The Renaissance*, p. 86.
[64] See Charles Homer Haskins, *The Renaissance of the Twelfth Century* (Cambridge, Mass.: Harvard University Press, 1927).

century in Italy is one of these happier eras, and what it is sometimes said of the age of Pericles is true of that of Lorenzo: – it is an age productive in personalities, many-sided, centralized, complete. Here, artists and philosophers and those whom the action of the world has elevated and made keen, do not live in isolation, but breathe a common air, and catch light and heat from each other's thoughts.[65]

The sharp boundaries between knowledge, action, and aesthetic experience that Hutcheson and Kant seem to have suggested and that even such more modern figures as Poe and Baudelaire still accepted turn out to be characteristic of some, even many periods of history, but not of history's finest hours. In those periods, science, morality, and art inspire one another, or even join in the person of a single human being, such as Leonardo da Vinci, who naturally has his own chapter in *The Renaissance*.

This is not yet to say that the aesthetic is somehow higher or more valuable than the scientific or the moral. But if what is characteristic of the aesthetic is concreteness and individuality, or the integration of experience, then it may be by means of the aesthetic achievement of unity that all of the domains of human experience are integrated; such integration may be something that is possible only through art. This is at least suggested by Pater's attribution of artistic creation and aesthetic appreciation to a free but also coherent play of all of our powers, something that can be captured only by the superficially paradoxical expression "imaginative reason" that Pater adopts from Matthew Arnold.[66] Pater first introduces the terminology of free play in his opening chapter on the French renaissance of the twelfth century, speaking both specifically of the poetry of the period and then more generally of the cast of mind of one of the heroes of this essay, Peter Abelard (1079–1142). Pater writes,

> In that poetry, earthly passion, with its intimacy, its freedom, its variety – the liberty of the heart – makes itself felt; and the name of Abelard, the great scholar and the great lover, connects the expression of this liberty of the heart with the free play of human intelligence around all subjects presented to it, with the liberty of the intellect, as that age understood it.[67]

---

[65] Pater, *The Renaissance*, pp. xxxii–xxxiii.
[66] The phrase comes from Arnold's 1864 essay "Pagan and Medieval Religious Sentiment," where he writes that "the main element of the modern spirit's life is neither the senses and understanding, nor the heart and imagination; it is the imaginative reason" (cited from Pater, *The Renaissance*, p. 166).
[67] Pater, "Two Early French Stories," *The Renaissance*, p. 2.

Here Pater describes the state of mind that he admires as one in which both passion and thought are free from external constraints and free to interact with each other. He does not explicitly include the senses in this description, and thus does not yet explicitly generalize his idea beyond the case of poetry to arts that involve the senses more directly. But he alludes to the senses on the next page when he describes the spirit of this early renaissance as moving from the side of the Seine into the "early literature of Italy" and "even in Dante" "with its qualities already well defined, its intimacy, its languid sweetness, its rebellion, its subtle skill in dividing the elements of human passion, its care for physical beauty, its worship of the body";[68] and at the end of the first essay, Pater describes Abelard's admirable cast of mind in general terms that do not explicitly include a role for the senses and imagination but also do not exclude it: "The opposition of the professional defenders of a mere system to that more sincere and generous play of the forces of the human mind and character, which I have noted as the secret of Abelard's struggle, is indeed always powerful."[69] Here what Pater has in mind as the ideal form of human experience is the free play of all our powers of mind independent of the constraints of "system" or any arbitrary and conventional rules.

Pater returns to the idea of play in a complicated passage in "The School of Giorgione" in which he connects the idea of play as moments of heightened life to his theme that all art aspires to the condition of music in order to arrive at a characterization of the art of this school:

> In these then, the favourite incidents of Giorgione's school, music or the musical intervals in our existence, life itself is conceived as a sort of listening – listening to music, to the reading of Bandello's novels,[70] to the sound of water, to time as it flies. Often such moments are really our moments of play, and we are surprised at the unexpectedness of what may seem our least important part of time; not merely because play is in many instances that to which people really apply their own best powers, but also because at such times, the stress of our servile, everyday attentiveness being relaxed, the happier powers in things without are permitted free passage, and have their way with us. And so, from music, the school of Giorgione passes often to the play which is like music; to those masques in which men avowedly do but play at real life.[71]

---

[68] Pater, "Two Early French Stories," *The Renaissance*, p. 3.
[69] Pater, "Two Early French Stories," *The Renaissance*, p. 17.
[70] Matteo Bandello (1480?–1562) published four volumes of *Novelle* from 1554 to 1573, the later volumes, obviously, posthumously (see Pater, *The Renaissance*, p. 167).
[71] Pater, "The School of Giorgione," *The Renaissance*, pp. 96–7.

In the opening sentence of this passage, Pater characterizes the aesthetic condition as one that we may enjoy in response either to real life – listening to the sound of water – or to art – listening to music or to the reading of novellas – but in the remainder he describes play first as a phenomenon of real life, which can then be recaptured by art. His characterization of play also moves from passivity – listening to water, allowing free passage to the "happier powers in things" and letting them "have their way with us" – to activity, applying our "own best powers." Here Pater reconstructs Kant's synthesis of what started out as two separate ideas in eighteenth-century aesthetics, the idea that aesthetic experience takes place in a space freed from the ordinary concerns of life or "everyday attentiveness" that was suggested in the idea of disinterestedness first introduced by Shaftesbury and Hutcheson and the idea of aesthetic experience as an especially pleasurable form of mental activity stressed by such as Gerard and Kames. Kant recognized that in the absence of the satisfaction of an ordinary practical interest, our pleasure in beauty could be explained only by the free activity of our own cognitive powers, and Pater's account of play makes a similar transition from a negative to a positive characterization of it.

To be sure, Pater himself does not mention Kant in *The Renaissance*, but its final essay concerns another German of Kant's time, namely Johann Joachim Winckelmann, and it is perhaps not surprising that Pater uses Kantian language in characterizing Winckelmann's aesthetic experience. Describing Winckelmann's first protracted experience of Greek art in the Saxon royal collections at Dresden, Pater says that "Winckelmann here reproduces for us the earlier sentiment of the Renaissance."

> On a sudden the imagination feels itself free. How facile and direct, it seems to say, is this life of the senses and the understanding, when once we have apprehended it! Here, surely, is that more liberal mode of life we have been seeking so long, so near to us all the while.... Here, then, in vivid realisation, we see the native tendency of Winckelmann to escape from abstract theory to intuition, to the exercise of sight and touch. Lessing, in the *Laocoon*, has theorised finely on the relation of poetry to sculpture; and philosophy may give us theoretical reasons why not poetry but sculpture should be the most sincere and exact expression of the Greek ideal. By a happy, unperplexed dexterity, Winckelmann solves the question in the concrete. It is what Goethe calls his *Gewahrwerden der griechischen Kunst*, his *finding* of Greek art.[72]

---

[72] Pater, "Winckelmann," *The Renaissance*, pp. 118–19.

Here Pater describes Winckelmann's aesthetic experience, which the rest of us would be lucky to share, as a facile – that is, not superficial but easy, unconstrained – cooperation between the senses and the understanding, and equates this with the freedom of the imagination. The freedom of the imagination is thus negative, that is, freedom from constraint, but also positive, that is, a "liberal mode of life" or activity. Pater also takes the opportunity to return to his opening theme that aesthetic experience is concrete rather than abstract and to praise Winckelmann over Lessing for the concreteness rather than abstraction of his experience and his writing about it. Perhaps one thinks that abstractions leave room for the free play of the mind precisely because they do not specify all the details of particular objects, while concreteness might seem to tie the mind down to the details of a given object; but Pater associates abstractness with rules, thus with constraint, and by contrast finds room to play in the richness of detail of the concrete.

Pater returns to the theme of play later in the essay on Winckelmann, and there gives perhaps his most explicit account of the free play between imagination and reason, between our sensory and intellectual powers, that is captured in his borrowed phrase "imaginative reason." Here he does not move from play as a feature of life in general to play as what is characteristic of aesthetic experience, but rather suggests that the free play of our powers in art creates new possibilities for human life in general:

> The basis of all artistic genius lies in the power of conceiving of humanity in a new and striking way, of putting a happy world of its own creation in place of the meaner world of our common days, generating around itself an atmosphere with a novel power of refraction, selecting, transforming, recombining the images it transmits, according to choice of the imaginative intellect. In exercising this power, painting and poetry have a variety of subjects almost unlimited.[73]

Here Pater employs the typical eighteenth-century characterization of the activity of the imagination – it selects, transforms, and recombines images and ideas given to it by the senses and the intellect from ordinary life – but adds that the new ideas so created are not simply ideas of an alternative reality, but can be ideas of a better reality to which we can aspire. This is perhaps the real force of his transition from speaking of a free play *between* imagination and reason to a single, integrated imaginative reason or intellect.

[73] Pater, "Winckelmann," *The Renaissance*, p. 137.

That the free play of the imaginative reason or intellect ultimately leads to ideas of a better and happier world reveals that Pater's idea of art for art's sake is certainly not incompatible with the idea that aesthetic experience can play a role in envisioning and at least to that extent realizing a better world, thus that aesthetic experience is not unconnected to moral ideals. As his later discussion of Plato's aesthetics suggests, he does not object to Plato's idea that the perfection of art can serve the perfection of life, but objects only to Plato's particularly rigid, joyless image of a better life for human beings. That Pater objects not to any connection between art and morality but only to the subservience of art to the rigid constraint of particular moralities is in fact clear throughout *The Renaissance*. Pater praises renaissance art for breaking with the particular, constraining morality of its time, but precisely because it can do so in the hope of a new and better way of living, art need not break with morality in general; rather it can have a moral inspiration, and does so at the moments of its renaissance:

> One of the strongest characteristics of that outbreak of the reason and the imagination, of that assertion of the liberty of the heart, in the middle age, which I have termed a medieval Renaissance, was its antinomianism, its spirit of rebellion against the moral and religious ideas of the time. In their search after the pleasures of the senses and the imagination, in their care for beauty, in their worship of the body, people were impelled beyond the bounds of the Christian ideal; and their love became sometimes a strange idolatry, a rival religion.[74]

To free art and, through art, life from the constraints of Christianity is not to free art from morality in general, but from a particular morality, one that has often enlisted art in its own cause but which may be found hostile to the aesthetic impulse as such, that is, to the aspiration to the freedom of the imagination. Of course, the freedom of imagination, or at least some particular form of it, can become a shibboleth or idol itself, and thus the rejection of one religion runs the risk of degenerating into just another religion. But, Pater's implication seems to be that at its best art can achieve freedom without collapsing into constraint and point the way to a life that does so as well, and this is clearly a moral ideal for him even if it is not identical to the goal of this or that particular, conventional morality.

If the moral goal of art becomes too particular and too explicit, too much of an abstraction, that can undermine the concrete unity of form

---

[74] Pater, "Two Early French Stories," *The Renaissance*, p. 16.

and content to which art properly aspires. That is always a risk for art with a moral impetus, and perhaps more of a risk for some media of art than for others, but it is not an inevitability. Thus Pater writes:

> Poetry ... works with words addressed in the first instance to the pure intelligence; and it deals, most often, with a definite subject or situation. Sometimes it may find a noble and quite legitimate function in the conveyance of moral or political aspiration, as often in the poetry of Victor Hugo. In such instances it is easy enough for the understanding to distinguish between the matter and the form, however much the matter, the subject, the element which is addressed to the mere intelligence, has been penetrated by the informing, artistic spirit. But the ideal types of poetry are those in which this distinction is reduced to its *minimum*; so that lyrical poetry, precisely because in it we are least able to detach the matter from the form, without a deduction of something from that matter itself, is, at least artistically, the highest and most complete form of poetry.[75]

So not only are some media of art more susceptible to the separation of content from form in the name of some moral or political ideal; even within a particular medium, such as poetry, some specific forms (perhaps drama) are more susceptible to this risk and others (here lyric) are more resistant to it. But just as all art can aspire to the condition of beauty, that is, to a complete synthesis of form and content, so all art can at least aspire to complete freedom of the imaginative reason or intellect from the constraints of the morality of its time and place. But that aspiration, again, itself seems to be inspired by a moral ideal of the value of freedom itself. So Pater's idea of art for art's sake does not cut art off from all connection to morality, but rather connects it to a particularly generous conception of morality.

Unlike others typically regarded as part of the aestheticist movement, then, Pater does not explicitly reject the moral significance of art; on the contrary, his view that the best art involves all our faculties makes room for the idea that the free play of imagination in art involves our practical as well as theoretical capacities. Pater's idea that the best art involves all our faculties also at least implies that our response to such art must involve our capacity to feel emotions as well as our other capacities of sense, imagination, and thought. Thus, from his study in Brasenose College, Pater suggested the possibility of a comprehensive approach to aesthetics. The last great figure of nineteenth-century British aestheticism, Oscar Wilde, did not overtly endorse such a comprehensive approach to aesthetic experience as Pater had; but far from suggesting

[75] Pater, "The School of Giorgione," *The Renaissance*, p. 87.

that our pleasure in artistic beauty has nothing to do with any other human interest, he actually implied that art concerns the deepest human emotions. He and Pater thus at least together offered the possibility of a comprehensive approach to the experience of beauty as involving our sensory, intellectual, and emotional capacities. We will subsequently see that this possibility was by no means immediately exploited in British aesthetics. But first, Wilde.

3. WILDE

The celebrity with the marvelous name Oscar Fingal O'Flahertie Wills Wilde (1854–1900) was the son of Sir William Wilde, a prominent Anglo-Irish surgeon and philanthropist, and his wife Lady Jane Francesca née Elgee. He was born in Dublin and took his first degree there, at Trinity College (1871–74). He then went to Magdalen College, Oxford, where he graduated with double firsts in classical moderations and *Litterae humaniores* (1874–78). While at Oxford, he was exposed to the work and influence of Ruskin and Pater, both active there at the time. He also developed a reputation as an aesthete for his personal style of dress and the décor of his rooms, for which he may have taken some punishment from more conventional students. But his reputation as well as his wit led to his first career as a poet, as the target of Gilbert and Sullivan's *Patience* (1881), and a successful lecturer on the aestheticist movement in Britain and the United States (1882–86). In 1884 he married Constance Lloyd, the daughter of a prominent London barrister, with whom he shortly had two sons. Soon thereafter, however, he began a series of homosexual affairs. Professionally, he gave up lecturing and focused on writing and reviewing, and also edited a magazine, *The Woman's World*, for several years (1887–89). Following that, he wrote his most important works: the essay "The Soul of Man under Socialism" (1891); the four essays included in the volume *Intentions* in 1891, namely "The Decay of Lying," "Pen, Pencil, and Poison," "The Critic as Artist" (in two parts), and "Masks"; his only novel, *The Picture of Dorian Gray*; and his series of successful, still often performed plays, *Lady Windermere's Fan* (1891), *A Woman of No Importance* (1892), *An Ideal Husband* (1893), and finally *The Importance of Being Earnest* (1894). *Salomé*, written in French in 1891, was banned from the British stage; Richard Strauss's daring and dissonant opera of 1905 was based on Wilde's play, and while widely successful in Europe, also suffered from censoriousness if not censorship, lasting only one night in its initial production at New York's Metropolitan Opera.

These few years of brilliance were quickly followed by disaster. Wilde's unsuccessful libel suit against the Marquess of Queensbury, the pugnacious father of Wilde's young companion Lord Alfred Douglas, led to Wilde's own prosecution and conviction for homosexual conduct, then still of course criminalized, and to his imprisonment from 1895 to 1897. Upon his release, he moved to Paris (having chosen not to when he still had time to do so before the trial) and, though now penniless, lived openly as a homosexual. But he did not have long to enjoy his freedom, dying of cerebral meningitis in 1900. His letter to Lord Douglas from Reading Gaol, *De Profundis*, was first published posthumously in 1905, but waited until 1962 for a full edition.

Wilde was regarded and, as already noted, caricatured as a leading advocate of the idea of "art for art's sake." It is certainly not difficult to find statements in his works that support this assessment of his position. In "The Decay of Lying," for example, we find such statements as "Art never expresses anything but itself ... and it is this, more than that vital connection between form and substance, on which Mr. Pater dwells, that makes music the type of all the arts."[76] This is repeated in the character Vivian's summary of his new aesthetics as "Art never expresses anything but itself. It has an independent life, just as Thought has, and develops purely on its own lines."[77] It having been argued throughout that art should not imitate nature or real life but should describe something better, thus that it is actually a form of lying, Wilde's character also asserts that "The only form of lying that is absolutely beyond reproach is Lying for its own sake, and the highest development of this is ... Lying in Art. Just as those who do not love Plato more than Truth cannot pass beyond the threshold of the Academe, so those who do not love beauty more than Truth never know the inmost shrine of Art."[78] However, these words are spoken by a character in a dialogue, as indeed are all the words of the following essay "The Critic as Artist," and thus cannot automatically be assumed to represent Wilde's own view without qualification; indeed, his substitution of "lying" for "art" in the phrase "Lying for its own sake" may be meant as a parody of the idea of "art for art's sake" rather than as a straightforward assertion of it. A careful reading of both "The Artist

---

[76] Oscar Wilde, "The Decay of Lying," in *Intentions* (London: Oscar, McIlvaine, 1891), reprinted in *The Artist as Critic: Critical Writings of Oscar Wilde*, ed. Richard Ellmann (New York: Random House, 1969; reprinted Chicago: University of Chicago Press, 1982), pp. 313–14.
[77] Wilde, "The Decay of Lying," *The Artist as Critic*, p. 319.
[78] Wilde, "The Decay of Lying," *The Artist as Critic*, p. 318.

as Critic" and *Dorian Gray* may suggest that while art's search for beauty should certainly be free from constraint by truth if that is superficially understood as the mere imitation of nature and equally free from the superficial constraint of conventional morality, art's deepest mission may be to allow its audience to experience and understand the deepest and finest human emotions, and that the most profound form of immorality may be to confuse superficial images of beauty, of the kind that art can all too easily make, with the grounds for true love.

The argument of "The Decay of Lying," to be sure, does not reach such a conclusion. The dialogue takes the arch form of Wilde's main character Vivian reading his own essay titled "The Decay of Lying: A Protest"[79] to his friend Cyril while interrupting himself with lengthy comments on it. Vivian attacks contemporary naturalists, above all Zola, for describing characters whose lives are "absolutely without interest," and asserts instead that "In literature we require distinction, charm, beauty, and imaginative power."[80] Departing from the reading of his essay, Vivian then, as we previously saw Gautier, Poe, and Baudelaire do, maintains generally that "As long as a thing is useful or necessary to us, or affects us in any way, either for pain or for pleasure, or appeals strongly to our sympathies, or is a vital part of the environment in which we live, it is outside the proper sphere of art."[81] Returning to his script, Vivian then states that

> Art begins with abstract decoration, with purely imaginative and pleasurable work dealing with what is unreal and non-existent. This is the first stage. Then life becomes fascinated with this new wonder, and asks to be admitted into the charmed circle. Art takes life as part of her rough material, recreates it, and refashions it in fresh forms, is absolutely indifferent to fact, invents, imagines, dreams, and keeps between herself and reality the impenetrable barrier of beautiful style, of decorative or ideal treatment.[82]

Some pages later, Vivian returns to his script, continuing his attack on any theory that art creates beauty by imitating the beauty of nature: "Art finds her own perfection within, and not outside of, herself. She is not to be judged by an external standard of resemblance. She is a veil, rather than a mirror."[83] His claim is that "Life imitates Art far more than Art imitates Life,"[84] that our conceptions and perceptions of natural beauty

---

[79] Wilde, "The Decay of Lying," *The Artist as Critic*, p. 293.
[80] Wilde, "The Decay of Lying," *The Artist as Critic*, p. 296.
[81] Wilde, "The Decay of Lying," *The Artist as Critic*, p. 299.
[82] Wilde, "The Decay of Lying," *The Artist as Critic*, p. 301.
[83] Wilde, "The Decay of Lying," *The Artist as Critic*, p. 306.
[84] Wilde, "The Decay of Lying," *The Artist as Critic*, p. 311.

are determined by ideals of beauty created by art rather than those ideals of beauty being provided by nature. Thus, "At present, people see fogs" – see them at all, as well as seeing them as beautiful – "not because there are fogs, but because poets and painters have taught them the mysterious loveliness of such effects. There may have been fogs for centuries in London," but "They did not exist till Art invented them";[85] and, conversely, to see a Turneresque sunset as beautiful "is a distinct sign of provincialism of temperament" once Turner is no longer "the last note in art."[86] Vivian's view is that through our own powers of imagination art creates decorative forms and styles for the representation of nature, and that our perception of beauty in nature is dependent upon the creation of such forms and styles by art rather than vice versa. This is what leads up to his first assertion that "Art never expresses anything but itself."

Vivian then sums up his argument to Cyril with three doctrines, a corollary, and a "final revelation." The first doctrine follows his second assertion that "Art never expresses anything but itself," and consists in the affirmation of the independence of art from the conventions of its time: "It is not necessarily realistic in an age of realism, nor spiritual in an age of faith. So far from being the creation of its time, it is usually in direct opposition to it." His second doctrine is that "All bad art comes from returning to Life and Nature, and elevating them into ideals"; rather, he holds, "Life and Nature may sometimes be used as part of Art's rough material, but before they are of any real service to art they must be translated into artistic conventions. The moment Art surrenders its imaginative medium it surrenders everything."[87] Then comes Vivian's third doctrine, that "Life imitates Art far more than Art imitates Life. This results not merely from Life's imitative instinct, but from the fact that the self-conscious aim of Life is to find expression, and that Art offers it certain beautiful forms through which it may realize that energy." The corollary of this is "that external Nature also imitates Art. The only effects that she can show us are effects that we have already seen through poetry, or in paintings." And all of this leads to the revelation that "Lying, the telling of beautiful untrue things, is the proper aim of Art."[88] Vivian's position is thus that the human imagination creates beautiful forms and styles in art that beautify our representations of nature and that even

---

[85] Wilde, "The Decay of Lying," *The Artist as Critic*, p. 312.
[86] Wilde, "The Decay of Lying," *The Artist as Critic*, p. 313.
[87] Wilde, "The Decay of Lying," *The Artist as Critic*, p. 319.
[88] Wilde, "The Decay of Lying," *The Artist as Critic*, p. 320.

transform our experience of nature itself, but that since these forms and styles are not found in nature they cannot be considered true to nature and their use must instead be considered as a form of lying. In all of this, Wilde seems to be celebrating the freedom of imagination in art above any other possible value in it, thus to be confirming the customary understanding of aestheticism rather than suggesting a more comprehensive approach to aesthetic experience.

That the creation of beauty requires human powers of selection and imagination and that the experience of such beauty is intrinsically pleasurable, requiring no external justification, certainly seem to be part of Wilde's own view, and will be further developed in "The Critic as Artist": what that title means is precisely that the exercise of intellectual powers that we might typically think of as characteristic only of criticism is essential to the production of art because art is not a mere imitation of nature, thus artistic beauty is not a mere imitation of natural beauty. That the creation of beauty in art and the perception of nature through the forms created by art are a lie is equally clearly a provocation, because the beautification of nature or its perception is not an assertion that nature is something that it is not; it is not an assertion at all. This provocation seems to be a pose of the character Vivian, and not a commitment on Wilde's own part; it is in any case not part of the argument of the following "Critic as Artist." But more than simply dropping the equation of beautification with lying, the "Critic as Artist" goes beyond developing a purely formalistic account of artistic beauty and of the transformation of our perception of nature by art. Instead, it suggests that an even deeper source of our pleasure in art is the access it offers us to the deepest and finest human feelings and emotions. This suggests that there is a connection between beauty and truth after all – not between beauty and truth about metaphysical ideas but between beauty and the truth about our own experience. And if the lesson of *Dorian Gray* is that the deepest form of immorality is to settle for superficial beauty and pleasure instead of seeking a life of deeper and finer feelings, then beauty will turn out to be intertwined with morality as well as with truth, not independent of and irrelevant to both of those. Wilde's version of "art for art's sake" may turn out to be that art must be allowed to "follow its own lines" independent of conventions about truth and morality, but that by doing so it is ultimately linked to truth and beauty as such.

The two-part essay "The Critic as Artist" names one of its speakers "Ernest," a name that might suggest that the views presented by this speaker are the author's own. However, this may be a trick, for it is not the interventions of "Ernest" but the impassioned speeches of "Gilbert" that appear to have authorial authority. Ernest seems to advocate a conception of beauty in art independent of all other human concerns, as when he asks, "Why cannot the artist be left alone, to create a new world if he wishes it, or, if not, to shadow forth the world we already know, and of which, I fancy, we would each one of us be wearied if Art, with her fine spirit of choice and delicate instinct of selection, did not, as it were, purify it for us, and give to it a momentary perfection?"[89] Even Gilbert can seem to advocate art for art's sake when he praises Aristotle's *Poetics* for treating art "not from the moral, but from the purely æsthetic point of view." The latter remark precedes a subtle restatement of Aristotle's own famous enumeration of the elements of a tragedy. Aristotle's definition concludes with the claim that a tragedy should present "incidents arousing pity and fear, wherewith to accomplish its catharsis of such emotions."[90] Gilbert, however, speaks thus:

> Aristotle, like Goethe, deals with art primarily in its concrete manifestations, taking Tragedy, for instance, and investigating the material it uses, which is language, the subject matter, which is life, the method by which it works, which is action, the conditions under which it reveals itself, which are those of theatric presentation, its logical structure, which is plot, and its final æsthetic appeal, which is to the sense of beauty realized through the passions of pity and awe. That purification and spiritualizing of the nature which he calls καθαρσις is, as Goethe saw, essentially æsthetic, and is not moral, as Lessing fancied.[91]

While exactly what Aristotle meant by catharsis continues to be debated after more than two millennia,[92] this intimation that the point of tragedy's evocation of pity and fear is a purely aesthetic gratification of the "sense of beauty," nothing moral, surely goes beyond any plausible interpretation of Aristotle's text, and would seem to be explicable only by aestheticism's own separation of beauty from everything necessary and useful, its interpretation of the slogan "art for art's sake" as meaning that art is created for the experience of beauty alone. However, interpreting

---

[89] Wilde, "The Critic as Artist," Intentions, www.wilde-online.info/the-critic-as-artist.html, p. 3.
[90] Aristotle, *Poetics*, ch. 6 (1449b20–30); translation by Ingram Bywater from *The Complete Works of Aristotle*, ed. Jonathan Barnes (Princeton: Princeton University Press, 1984), vol. II, p. 2320.
[91] Wilde, "Critic as Artist," wilde-online, p. 9.
[92] See Alexander Nehamas, "Pity and Fear in the *Rhetoric* and *Poetics*," and Jonathan Lear, "Katharsis," both in Amélie Oksenberg Rorty, *Essays on Aristotle's Poetics* (Princeton: Princeton University Press, 1992), pp. 291–314 and 315–40.

Wilde's stance in this essay as endorsing such a version of aestheticism is too simple. For Gilbert begins his speech on Greek art criticism with the claim that "our primary debt to the Greeks" is to their recognition that the "two supreme and highest arts are"

> Life and Literature, life and the perfect expression of life. The principles of the former, as laid down by the Greeks, we may not realize in an age so marred by false ideals of our own. The principles of the latter, as they laid them down, are, in many cases, so subtle that we can hardly understand them. Recognizing that the most perfect art is that which most fully mirrors man in all his infinite variety, they elaborated the criticism of language, considered in the light of the mere material of that art, to a point to which we, with our accentual system of reasonable or emotional emphasis, can barely if at all attain; studying, for instance, the metrical movements of a prose as scientifically as a modern musician studies harmony and counterpoint, and, I need hardly say, with much keener æsthetic instinct.... Even the work of Mr. Pater, who is, on the whole, the most perfect master of English prose now creating amongst us, is often far more like a piece of mosaic than a passage in music, and seems, here and there, to lack the true rhythmical life of words and the fine freedom and richness of effect that such rhythmical life produces.[93]

Here Gilbert praises the high level of formal refinement developed in Greek literature and promoted by Greek literary theory not for its own sake, not because it gratifies some entirely detached sense of beauty, but rather because it is what allowed Greek literature to "most fully mirror man in all his infinite variety." Wilde's interpretation of Aristotle's *Poetics*, in other words, is not a perversion of Aristotle's concept of catharsis into a late nineteenth-century doctrine of aesthetic formalism, but rather a claim that artistic beauty lies in the use of formal devices to effect an experience of pity and fear and all the other infinite variety of human emotions; beauty is not contrasted to the representation or even arousal of emotions, but intimately connected to it.

Sometimes Gilbert's argument seems to be that art must be an alternative to ordinary life because such life is sordid, not beautiful. Thus he says of the critic that

> He will always be showing us the work of art in some new relation to our age. He will always be reminding us that great works of art are living things – are, in fact, the only things that live. So much, indeed, will he feel this, that I am certain that as civilization progresses and we become more highly organized, the elect spirits of each age, the critical and cultured spirits, will grow

[93] Wilde, "Critic as Artist," wilde-online, pp. 7–8.

less and less interested in actual life, and *will seek to gain their impressions almost entirely from what Art has touched.* For Life is terribly deficient in form. Its catastrophes happen in the wrong way and to the wrong people. There is grotesque horror about its comedies, and its tragedies seem to culminate in farce.[94]

This is followed by a suggestion that through art we can experience emotions that are not only more refined than those of the more grotesque levels of vulgar life, but that are free of the pains of ordinary life altogether. Thus, once again appearing to twist Aristotle's meaning, Gilbert expostulates that

> Art does not hurt us. The tears that we shed at a play are a type of the exquisite sterile emotions that it is the function of Art to awaken. We weep, but we are not wounded. We grieve, but our grief is not bitter. In the actual life of man, sorrow, as Spinoza says somewhere, is a passage to a lesser perfection. But the sorrow with which Art fills us both purifies and initiates, if I may quote once more from the great art-critic of the Greeks. It is through Art, and through Art alone, that we can realize our perfection; through Art, and through Art only, that we can shield ourselves from the sordid perils of actual existence.

This position leads Gilbert to accept Ernest's inference that "there is something radically immoral" in art, an inference that he affirms by stating that "emotion for the sake of emotion is the aim of art, and emotion for the sake of action is the aim of life, and of that practical organization of life that we call society … which is the beginning and basis of morals."[95] The sterility of the emotions aroused by art is precisely that they are free from any disposition to action and thus any significance for morality, which can hardly have been what Aristotle intended.

However, Gilbert puts his position in a different light several pages later when he maintains that art "can lead us away from surroundings whose beauty is dimmed to us by the mist of familiarity, or whose ignoble ugliness and sordid claims are marring the perfection of our development. It can help us to leave the age in which we were born, and to pass into other ages … It can teach us how to escape from our experience, and to realize the experiences of those who are greater than we are."[96] Here the suggestion is that the point of art is not to transpose us into a domain of beauty disconnected with the emotions of real life altogether, but rather to liberate us from the constraints of our own limited

---

[94] Wilde, "Critic as Artist," wilde-online, p. 24.
[95] Wilde, "Critic as Artist," wilde-online, pp. 27–8.
[96] Wilde, "Critic as Artist," wilde-online, p. 30.

and usually petty lives and put us into contact with human emotions far greater than we can ordinarily experience. Gilbert strengthens this suggestion a page later when he appropriates the famous expression of Matthew Arnold that great art, conveyed to us with the accompaniment of great criticism, exposes us to "the dreams, and ideas, and feelings of myriad generations"; the "true man of culture" is one to whom "no form of thought is alien, no emotional impulse obscure," and who has learned through art and its criticism "'the best that is known and thought in the world'" and "lives – it is not fanciful to say so – with those who are the Immortals."[97] The distance between Wilde and the paradigm of high Victorianism may not be as great as it sometimes seems.

To be sure, Wilde tries to maintain distance between his own position and any conventional moralism by having Gilbert insist that "what the critical spirit can give us" is "the contemplative life, the life that has for its aim not *doing* but *being*, and not *being* merely, but *becoming*," and by invoking the authority of Aristotle's recommendation of the "theoretical life" as the highest good.[98] But the aim of his argument ultimately seems to be not to assert that exposure to the greatest emotions of humankind through art can and should never have any impact on action at all, but rather to distance himself from the "philanthropists and sentimentalists of our day, who are always chattering to one about one's duty to one's neighbor,"[99] to make sure that aesthetic experience does not lead one to become a "prig."[100] In other words, what he wants to separate the aesthetic from is not morality as such, but moralism, a real danger in Victorian England as Wilde was soon to learn. Anti-moralism rather than anti-morality may also be the lesson of Wilde's position on individualism, a central theme in his theory of criticism as well as in his famous essay "The Soul of Man under Socialism." One might suppose that Wilde's emphasis on exposure to the greatest human emotions and to "the best that is known and thought in the world" through art would lead to an emphasis on the universal validity of aesthetic judgments: since the greatest emotions that have ever been felt by any human beings should

---

[97] Wilde, "Critic as Artist," wilde-online, p. 30; the phrase "the best that is known and thought in the world" comes from Matthew Arnold's essay "The Function of Criticism at the Present Time," *Essays in Criticism: First Series* (London: Macmillan, 1865); in Matthew Arnold, *Poetry and Prose*, ed. John Bryson (Cambridge, Mass.: Harvard University Press, 1970), p. 372.
[98] Wilde, "Critic as Artist," wilde-online, pp. 30–1.
[99] Wilde, "Critic as Artist," wilde-online, p. 32.
[100] Wilde, "Critic as Artist," wilde-online, p. 31.

presumably be valid for all, so the works of art that most successfully convey them, it might seem, should be valid, be the most beautiful, for all. However, Gilbert emphasizes the role of the individual in the critical reception of art: "it is only by intensifying his own personality that the critic can interpret the personality and work of others, and the more strongly this personality enters into the interpretation the more real the interpretation becomes, the more satisfying, the more convincing, and the more true."[101] If the interpretation of a work of art is necessarily an interaction between the work (or its original artist) and the critic (or audience in general), then, it would seem, each interpretation must be at least partially determined by the individual interpreter, and thus be necessarily even if only partially idiosyncratic. However, the point may rather be that it is only by being genuinely personal rather than conventional that the interpreter can obtain a valid experience of a work that does not, after all, come from himself: "the æsthetic critic rejects those obvious modes of art that have but one message to deliver, and having delivered it become dumb and sterile, and seeks rather for such modes as … by their imaginative beauty make all interpretations true and no interpretation final."[102] What is vital is to avoid convention in interpretation and indeed in art itself, for only so can an individual at one time open herself to the great art of all times and thus to the greatest that has been and will be felt as well as known and thought at all times. Finality may be lost along with conventionality, but that is only because by being individual rather than conventional one opens oneself up to the infinite variety of mankind.

This also seems to be the lesson of the final discussion of criticism in "The Critic as Artist." Here Ernest proposes that "a critic should above all things be fair," "rational," and "sincere." Gilbert argues against the first proposition that "The man who sees both sides of a question, is a man who sees absolutely nothing at all. Art is a passion, and, in matters of Art, Thought is inevitably colored by emotion, and so is fluid rather than fixed." Against the second proposition Gilbert argues that in order to experience art fully one must experience it "beyond all other things in the world," that is, beyond reason. And against the third, he argues that "The true critic will, indeed, always be sincere in his devotion to the principle of beauty, but he will seek for beauty in every age and in each school, and will never suffer himself to be limited to any settled custom

---

[101] Wilde, "Critic as Artist," wilde-online, p. 23.
[102] Wilde, "Critic as Artist," wilde-online, p. 21.

of thought, or stereotyped mode of looking at things."[103] The last objection sums up all three: the true critic, that is, the true appreciator of art, must be open to the full range of human emotions rather than being passionless, locked into a single conception of reasonableness, and trapped within a single point of view. What is needed instead of these high-sounding but actually confining limitations is rather "a temperament exquisitely susceptible to beauty, and to the various impressions that beauty gives us."[104] But what such a temperament makes possible is precisely openness to "a richer experience, or a finer susceptibility, or a newer mode of thought," the transformation into something finer and greater of "acts and passions that with the common would be commonplace, or with the uneducated ignoble, or with the shameful vile."[105] This is "dangerous," to be sure, but nothing great is achieved without danger. To return to the starting point of the argument, the truly critical temperament, true susceptibility to the beauty of art, makes possible catharsis in the sense of initiation into "noble feelings of which [one] might else have known nothing, the word καθαρσις having, it has sometimes seemed to me, a definite allusion to the rite of initiation, if indeed that be not, as I am occasionally tempted to fancy, its true and only meaning here."[106] But that is true only if initiation here means not initiation into an esoteric religious rite but rather initiation into the full variety of the greatest human emotions.

In his penultimate speech in "The Critic as Artist," Gilbert claims that aesthetic experience is "higher" than morality:

> The artistic critic, like the mystic, is an antinomian always. To be good, according to the vulgar standard of goodness, is obviously quite easy. It merely requires a certain amount of sordid terror, a certain lack of imaginative thought, and a certain low passion for middle-class respectability. Æsthetics are higher than Ethics. They belong to a more spiritual sphere. To discern the beauty of a thing is the finest point to which we can arrive. Even a colour-sense is more important, in the development of the individual, than a sense of right and wrong. Æsthetics, in fact, are to Ethics in the sphere of conscious civilization, what, in the sphere of the external world, sexual is to natural selection. Ethics, like natural selection, makes existence possible. Æsthetics, like sexual selection, fill it with new forms, and give it progress, and variety and change. And when we reach the true

---

[103] Wilde, "Critic as Artist," wilde-online, p. 36.
[104] Wilde, "Critic as Artist," wilde-online, p. 31.
[105] Wilde, "Critic as Artist," wilde-online, p. 46.
[106] Wilde, "Critic as Artist," wilde-online, p. 9.

culture that is our aim, we attain to the perfection of which the saints have dreamed.[107]

Wilde clearly enjoyed tweaking Victorian sensibilities, by having his character imply that it is harder to create beauty than to be good – although he carefully says that what is easy is to be good according to a vulgar standard, not to be good *tout court*, and his dismissal of compliance with moral standards out of terror of punishment is no different from the contempt for morality if motivated by nothing more than hope of divine reward and fear of divine punishment evinced by Enlightenment thinkers from Shaftesbury to Kant – and by linking the beauty prized by aesthetics directly with sexuality (although Burke had also done this a century earlier). Even when testifying in his own voice in his libel suit against the Marquess of Queensbury, he asserted that no "book or work of art ever had any effect whatever on morality," agreed that he did "not consider the effect in creating morality or immorality," and objected only to the opposing counsel's assertion that his claim not to care about morality in his artistic work was a "pose."[108] But it is difficult not to read Wilde's *chef d'oeuvre*, *The Picture of Dorian Gray*, as a moralistic although not didactic work. The point of the book is surely that it is fatal to mistake the pleasures of art and outward beauty for the deepest springs of human happiness. The action of the novel is begun by Dorian Gray's foolish wish that he himself should enjoy the permanent beauty of a work of art while his portrait rather than his own visage suffers the inevitable damage of even ordinary life (for at that point he does not foresee the life of extraordinary corruption that he will come to live). Presented with his first opportunity for a morally significant choice, he reveals his preference for the artificial beauty of the fictional characters the actress Sybil Vane portrays over the possibility of genuine love for the real human being that she is, and that is when his portrait begins to change. After a lifetime of sins, including his murder of the artist and once friend who had painted the portrait, all of which had corrupted the portrait but none of which had marred his own beauty, he attempts to destroy the record of his immorality by slashing the portrait, only for it to turn out that his own beauty was merely a fiction after all and that he has plunged the knife into his own heart, in his own body that bears the record of his every misdeed, and that the superficial beauty of the artistic image is intact after all. It is difficult to see this novel as a work that places art above morality rather

---

[107] Wilde, "Critic as Artist," wilde-online, pp. 15–6.
[108] "Oscar Wilde on the Witness Stand," *The Artist as Critic*, p. 436.

than as a tale about morality: while through the characters of his essays Wilde has argued that art can offer access to deeper and greater human feelings and thoughts than we experience in our quotidian existence and that contemplation of these need have no immediate effect on our actions, through his novel he has surely argued that even if art can add a level of pleasure and meaning to life beyond what morality has to offer, the beauty of art certainly cannot compensate for immorality.

Far from being an aesthete who believed in the independence of art and aesthetic experience from every other human concern, Wilde in fact conceived of art as a medium for the fullest exercise of human imagination, the communication of the broadest possible range of human emotions, and for the exploration of the deepest truths about morality rather than for the celebration of superficial social conventions. He thus did not take the slogan "art for art's sake" as the banner of a reductive or isolationist approach to aesthetic experience, but rather took it to express the power that art can have precisely when it fully exploits all these possibilities. Thus, like the German academic Vischer and the Oxford don Pater, the "aesthete" Wilde actually understood the claim of autonomy for art to be justified by art's potential for comprehending rather than isolating human concerns.

Neither Pater let alone Wilde were philosophy professors. The leading British academic philosopher of their time writing on aesthetics, Bernard Bosanquet, who published his *History of Æsthetic* the year after Wilde published his essays, wrote from within the framework of the Neo-Hegelianism that dominated Oxford in the later nineteenth century, the Oxford of Benjamin Jowett and T.H. Green, but advocated a broader conception of aesthetic experience than Hegel himself had accepted, one that came close to the breadth of spirit we have found in Pater and Wilde. A few years later, however, the great Russian novelist Leo Tolstoy reacted violently against a much narrower conception of aestheticism than he could have found in Pater, Wilde, or Bosanquet, none of whom he cites in his otherwise wide-ranging catalogue of recent aestheticians, and promulgated a correspondingly narrow moralism as an alternative to that aestheticism as he narrowly conceived it. In the next chapter, we will first consider Bosanquet's broadening of Hegelian aesthetics, and then conclude our survey of aestheticism with a look at Tolstoy's angry attack upon it.

7

Bosanquet and Tolstoy

In this chapter, we look at two more figures who wrote on aesthetics during the 1890s, a period as fruitful as the final decade of the previous century – from Britain, Bernard Bosanquet, and from outside Britain, Leo Tolstoy. Bosanquet, though working within the framework of British Hegelianism, broadened Hegel's own conception of art in ways compatible with the breadth of spirit we found in Pater and Wilde. Tolstoy, however, in spite of the breadth of mind and spirit manifest in his great novels of earlier decades, above all *War and Peace* (1869) and *Anna Karenina* (1877), reacted against a narrow conception of aestheticism with an equally narrow conception of art as exclusively a vehicle for the communication of religious feelings. We might then see the narrowness of aesthetic theory in Britain in the first decades of the twentieth century, to be considered in Volume 3, as a defense of the narrow conception of aestheticism that Tolstoy had attacked in his 1898 tract *What is Art?*, which was in fact first published in Britain rather than Russia.

1. BOSANQUET

Bernard Bosanquet (1848–1923) was born in Northumberland, the son of an evangelical clergyman, and attended Harrow School and Balliol College, Oxford, where his teachers included the leading British Neo-Hegelian idealists Benjamin Jowett, Thomas Hill Green, and Edward Caird. Upon graduation, he was elected to a fellowship at University College, which he held from 1871 to 1881, when he received an inheritance from his father, moved to London, and devoted himself to philosophy, social work, and adult education. He was active in the Charity Organization Society from 1881 until his death; in the Home, Arts, and

Industries Association; in the Ethical Society, where he gave many of the courses of lectures that would later become books; and he chaired the School of Sociology and Social Economics from 1903 until its incorporation into the London School of Economics in 1912. Also in 1903, he returned to academic life as Professor of Moral Philosophy at St. Andrews University in Scotland, but served in that position only five years. Most of his many works were written during his years as an independent scholar and activist in London. Among his early contributions were his translations of the introduction to Hegel's *Philosophy of Fine Arts* (1886) and Lotze's *System of Philosophy* (1888). During the 1880s he also laid down the general outlines of his philosophy in *Knowledge and Reality*, a critique of F.H. Bradley (1885), and *Logic, or the Morphology of Knowledge* (1888). In his work on logic, which continued as late as his 1920 *Implication and Linear Inference*, and which he understood in the broad sense comprising metaphysics and epistemology that was characteristic of the use of this term by the British idealists, Bosanquet argued for a coherence view of truth, on which individual claims to knowledge are true because of their consistency with a larger body of knowledge, for the absence of rigid boundaries between individuals and larger wholes as well as between body and mind, neither of which can be understood without the other, and for the infinitude of reality and thus the incompleteness and provisional character of knowledge at any particular time. In his political philosophy, epitomized in his *Philosophical Theory of the State* (1899), Bosanquet argued that individuals can develop only through cooperation in the larger whole of society although society should not be thought of as having a value independent of the individuals who constitute it. Bosanquet summarized his metaphysical views and their moral and political implications in his two volumes of Gifford lectures, *The Principle of Individuality and Value* (1912) and *The Value and Destiny of the Individual* (1913).

Bosanquet was unique among the British idealists of his and the previous generation (thus Caird, Jowett, Green, and Bradley) in writing on aesthetics throughout his career, and unique among all Anglophone aestheticians in making his major statement in aesthetics in the form of *A History of Æsthetic* (1892, revised 1904),[1] although as we will see, Bosanquet's suggestion of his views in this work needs to be supplemented by his *Three Lectures on Aesthetic*, published in 1915.[2] Indeed, the

---

[1] Bernard Bosanquet, *A History of Æsthetic* (London: Swan Sonnenschein, 1892), second edition (London: George Allen and Unwin, 1904).
[2] Bernard Bosanquet, *Three Lectures on Aesthetic* (London: Macmillan, 1915).

History needs to be supplemented by the *Lectures* precisely because it is in the latter work that Bosanquet most fully recognizes the importance of the element of play in aesthetic experience and attempts to synthesize it with the synthesis of formalist and expressivist theories of art that dominates the *History*. Thus Bosanquet ultimately endorses a threefold synthesis of approaches to aesthetics, but only over the course of a pair of works bridging the divide between the nineteenth and twentieth centuries.

Bosanquet's aesthetics as well as his philosophy as a whole is very loosely Hegelian,[3] and his Hegelianism is expressed in the fact that he first presents his aesthetic theory in the form of a history, indeed a history in which what he calls "aesthetic consciousness" or the actual aesthetic experience of historical periods evolves simultaneously with more self-conscious philosophical theory about aesthetic experience, a form of experience that existed, of course, long before the eighteenth-century invention of the term "aesthetic."[4] Bosanquet's *History* thus purports to be a history of the development of artistic style at the most general level as well as a history of theorizing about art. The argument of the work is that ancient art and ancient art theory were focused on the pleasures of form, that modern art and modern art theory have focused on the expression of feeling, but that the ultimate aim of art and the most satisfying kind of beauty must be the expression of both concrete content and our feelings about it through peculiarly appropriate form – what Bosanquet calls "the characteristic," as had Goethe before him. As he puts it, "Among the ancients the fundamental theory of the beautiful was connected with the notions of rhythm, symmetry, harmony of parts: in short, with the general formula of unity in variety," while "Among the moderns we find that more emphasis is laid on the idea of significance, expressiveness, the utterance of all that life contains; in general, that is to say, on the conception of the characteristic," and that the two elements of form and expression must be synthesized in artistic practice and recognized to be conjoined in aesthetic theory, leading to a definition of beauty in a broad rather than narrow sense that identifies it exclusively with pleasing form:

> If these two elements are reduced to a common denominator, there suggests itself as a comprehensive definition of the beautiful, "That which has

---

[3] In a rare recent treatment of Bosanquet's aesthetics, Marie-Luise Raters describes it as part of "Second Oxford Hegelianism"; see *Kunst, Wahrheit und Gefuuhl*, pp. 325–35, 346–98.
[4] Bosanquet, *History*, p. 1.

characteristic or individual expressiveness for sense-perception or imagination, subject to the conditions of general or abstract expressiveness in the same medium."[5]

By "general" or "abstract" expressiveness in a medium Bosanquet refers to beauty of form in the narrow sense, by "characteristic or individual expressiveness" to the particular content and the feeling about it that a successful work of art must communicate; and by distinguishing "sense-perception" from "imagination" Bosanquet leaves room for the idea that the pleasure of aesthetic experience comes not just from the cognition of content and feeling through form but also from creative free play with these elements. But that idea is not much developed until his *Lectures*, published twenty years after the first edition of the *History*.

Bosanquet stresses that the movement from purely formal beauty to the expressive "characteristic" in aesthetic consciousness and artistic practice as well as in aesthetic theory does not take place in a single stage, but in a series of moves including the recognition of the sublime in the eighteenth century (by both Burke and Kant)[6] and the artistic representation of ugliness (as by Rosenkranz)[7] in the nineteenth. He writes:

> But when with the birth of the modern world the romantic sense of beauty was awakened, accompanied by the craving for free and passionate expression, it became impossible that impartial theory should continue to consider that the beautiful was adequately explained as the regular and harmonious, or as the simple expression of unity in variety. The theory of the sublime now makes its appearance, at first indeed outside the theory of the beautiful; but it is followed by the analysis of the ugly, which develops into a recognized branch of aesthetic inquiry, with the result of finally establishing both the ugly and the sublime within the general frontier of beauty. The instrument by which this conciliation is effected is the conception of the characteristic or the significant; and the conflict between the harsher elements thus recognized and the common-sense requirement that all beauty should give pleasure, is mitigated, on the one hand by a *de facto* enlargement of average æsthetic appreciation, and on the other hand by the acceptance of such primary relations as harmony, regularity, or unity, in the light of essential elements organically determining all imaginable contents, and demanding, in their degree, characteristic expression for sense.[8]

What Bosanquet means by this is that aesthetic consciousness has come to accept and aesthetic theory has come to recognize that beauty lies not

---

[5] Bosanquet, *History*, pp. 4–5.
[6] Bosanquet, *History*, pp. 203–6 and 275–9.
[7] Bosanquet devotes a section of his *History* to Rosenkranz (pp. 400–9).
[8] Bosanquet, *History*, pp. 5–6.

just in pleasing formal properties and relations that are independent of all content, nor just in the formally pleasing representation of formally pleasing objects, but in the formally apt, indeed uniquely or "organically" suitable expression of reality in all its complexity, including the sublime and the ugly, and of the human feelings associated with all of these aspects of life. The recognition that even the ugly in the narrow, everyday sense can be the content of art that is beautiful in the wide sense of being aptly and organically expressive is for Bosanquet the final step in modern aesthetic consciousness and theory. And he stresses that from this enlightened point of view, the only kind of art that can be truly ugly is art in which, whether from confusion or from insincerity, reality is badly expressed and our feelings about it falsified:

> We must look for insuperable ugliness in its highest degree in the falsely beautiful produced by the confusion of aims and feelings in conscious representation, *i.e.* in art. We shall find it in the sentimental presented as touching, the effeminate as tender, in the feeble taken to be delicate, the tawdry taken to be brilliant, and the monstrous taken to be strong. Its lower degrees we shall find in the utilitarian works of man, not always as ugly in themselves, except when they present a simulated show of ornament devoid of interest or vitality, or as in discords of sound and colour introduce an artificial definiteness that has no æsthetic relations, but creating by their simple abstract shapes and ungraded colours an element of interference with the subtle and variously graduated content of external nature. In external nature itself it is hard by this standard to pronounce anything insuperably ugly except perhaps those disfigurements of individuality which indicate an alien life asserting itself victoriously within a higher form of existence.[9]

What is ugly is not reality as such, but conflict, in part conflict within nature, such as between a creature and a parasite or infection destroying it from within, but, more relevant to aesthetics, conflict between form and content and form and feeling, produced by confusion but even more so by deception and pretense. Here aesthetic and moral theory come close to one another: ugliness is as much a moral as a purely aesthetic phenomenon, disharmony and falsehood produced by negligence or malevolence. Bosanquet's statement of the thesis that ugliness lies in failed expressions anticipates Bendetto Croce's now better-remembered version of it from a decade later, although with the difference, as we will see in the next volume, that while Croce thought it necessary to rigorously separate the aesthetic and the moral, Bosanquet did not, and

---

[9] Bosanquet, *History*, pp. 435–6.

held instead that failed and especially insincere expression is common to both aesthetic and moral dysfunction.

Bosanquet's *History* covers the ancients, the medievals, and many modern figures from the Renaissance to his own time, but the central characters in its story are Kant, Schiller, Schelling, and Hegel on the side of the philosophers, the developers of aesthetic theory, and Winckelmann, Goethe, and Ruskin on the side of the artists and critics who are closer to aesthetic consciousness itself. Winckelmann is a central figure for Bosanquet, but not because he introduces the notion of the idealization of nature, which for Bosanquet would be the falsification of nature and therefore ugliness, but rather because he finds in the "tranquil soul" something *in* nature that can jointly satisfy the demands of beautiful form and beautiful expression. Winckelmann begins with conceptions of beauty and expression that are "a direct antithesis" or "opposing qualities" because "Beauty is in the first instance the beauty of pure form, which appears to mean the beauty of shape as exhibiting unity in variety," while "Expression in art, on the other hand, is the imitation of the acting and suffering condition of our soul and body of passions as well as of actions." "But in spite of this abrupt antagonism between the two," Bosanquet continues, when we turn to Winckelmann's "analysis of actual artistic portrayal, and to the history proper," we see that he has glimpsed the possibility of a reconciliation of formal beauty with expressiveness in at least one case, namely the case of the tranquil soul:

> The style which is called the "beautiful" *par excellence* is compatible with more expression than the earlier or grand style, and ... the grand style itself has not the beauty of a mere vase-outline or geometrical pattern, but is beautiful as the expression of a tranquil soul. And thus, though according to the strict theory of formal beauty it would seem to be like pure water, best when most flavourless, and so to be an easy and simple matter, needing in the artist who is to represent it no knowledge of man nor experience of passion, yet really "beauty without expression would be characterless, expression without beauty unpleasant"[10] ... He does not find that beauty is in inverse ratio to expression; and he shows conclusively that in the concrete the two are never divorced, and that beauty breaks up into kinds and types in accordance with the mental content from which it issues. Though he fails to reduce the two elements to a common denominator, and they remain antagonistic in theory, he has done all that is necessary, in the realm of plastic art, to exhibit that correspondence between phases of the beautiful and

---

[10] Bosanquet quotes these words from Winckelmann's *History of the Art of Antiquity*, Book V, 3.4.

the development of its content which holds a chief place among the data of modern æsthetic.[11]

Winckelmann does not cross the Jordan into the promised land of modern aesthetic theory, because he sees the compatibility of formal beauty and the beauty of apt expression only in the case of one kind of feeling and in one medium of art. But his treatment of at least this one case is prophetic for Bosanquet. He mentions both Goethe and Hegel as successors who saw the importance of what Winckelmann had glimpsed and were able to generalize it.

Kant is the next key figure in Bosanquet's history, because, although in Bosanquet's view somewhat grudgingly, he creates philosophical space for the combination of beauty of form with the expression of content, and at the more concrete level moves past Winckelmann's recognition of the reconciliation of these two terms in the case of the "tranquil soul" to a more general account of human beauty as a synthesis of form and content. Bosanquet stresses the systematic role of judgment as the bridge between the sensible world of theoretical cognition and the supersensible domain of freedom for Kant:

> To be the meeting point of these two worlds, the representative of reason in the world of sense, and of sense in the world of reason, is the high position which Kant is here preparing to assign to the content of the æsthetic and teleological judgment. This content coincides ... with the sublime and the beautiful in reality and in art, and the products of organic nature. The preeminent importance thus assigned to real objects in which an idea seems indissolubly embodied, was the germ from which concrete idealism was to spring.[12]

For Bosanquet, Kant's central contribution was the thought that a form that pleases our senses could also be recognized to embody an intellectual idea in a way that neither "sensationalist" nor "intellectualist" philosophy could recognize,[13] the former inevitably eliminating all content from the strictly sensory and the latter allowing the sensory only as a confused consciousness of the intellectual. Kant does this, on Bosanquet's account, by affirming rather than rejecting the paradoxes represented by his four "moments" of the judgment of taste: a pleasure in an object that is not an interest in its existence, an "object of a pleasure which is *universal* and *necessary*, but without the intervention of a reflective idea,"

---

[11] Bosanquet, *History*, pp. 248–51.
[12] Bosanquet, *History*, p. 261.
[13] Bosanquet, *History*, p. 266.

and a form of purposiveness that lies "in a harmonious relation to our faculties of imagination and understanding" rather than in a determinate relation to an end.[14] Summing up Kant's account of these four moments of aesthetic judgment, Bosanquet writes:

> The æsthetic consciousness is now recognised in its positive essence as the meeting-point of sense and reason. All that we have thus far learnt about it has pointed to this conclusion, but Kant, with his usual calm audacity, was the first to lay down the principles which felicitously describe our everyday experience of the beautiful, while in the light of abstract metaphysic they appear to the flattest self-contradictions. A feeling of pleasure which has no relation to practical interest, which depends on the purposiveness of a perceived content, and lays claim to universality and necessity, though remaining at all time a pure feeling, wholly free from explicit conceptions of purpose or class or antecedent and consequent, – such a feeling is a sheer impossibility alike to a sensationalist and to an intellectualist philosophy. It is not a clarified form of sense-gratification; it is not a confused idea of perfection; these are merely efforts to explain it upon wholly inadequate bases. It is *bonâ fide* feeling, and *bonâ fide* reasonable. Such is the paradox which Kant propounds.[15]

Because Kant recognized that even the simplest case of aesthetic judgment breaks down the presumed boundaries between the sensory and the intellectual, the contingent and the necessary, and so on, Bosanquet reasons, Kant was also prepared to recognize in abstract terms that the boundary between form and content is not rigid either, even though he was still sufficiently under the sway of the "sensationalist and empiricist prejudices" of a British model of the "judgment of taste" to insist that when taste is in "close association with objective and abstract ideas" it must be "set down" as "impure."[16] But this inability of Kant to appreciate what he had done, as well as his insistence that the sublime is an alternative to beauty rather than a variety of it,[17] does not change the fact that he had created theoretical room for the conception of the beautiful as the formally pleasing but also apt expression of significant content.

On Bosanquet's account, moreover, Kant exploited the room for such a conception of beauty that he had created in his account of the ideal

---

[14] Bosanquet, *History*, pp. 263–4. Kant's four moments are reduced to three in this statement because Bosanquet correctly recognizes that Kant's second moment (universality) and fourth moment (necessity) really make the same point; see Guyer, *Kant and the Claims of Taste*, second edition, pp. 142–7.
[15] Bosanquet, *History*, pp. 265–6.
[16] Bosanquet, *History*, pp. 266, 268.
[17] Bosanquet, *History*, pp. 275–8.

of beauty, although again with some ambivalence because of his initial commitment to the "pure," sensationalist conception of the judgment of taste. As Bosanquet correctly saw, for Kant the ideal of beauty cannot be reduced to correctness or regularity in an individual's instantiation of the features of its species, but rather "consists in the revelation of moral import through bodily manifestation in the human form," something that can be seen in outward form only by "great powers of imagination" on the part of an artist and perhaps on the part of an audience as well.[18] For Kant, the ideal of beauty is an instance of "dependent" or "adherent" rather than "free" beauty because the appreciation of it does depend upon a determinate concept of what a thing, namely a human being, ought to be, but Bosanquet objects that

> That beauty which is the largest and deepest revelation of spiritual power is not the most dependent but the freest beauty, because it implies no purpose whatever excepting that which constitutes its own inmost nature, the expression of reason in sensuous form. It is plain that Kant felt this and practically recognized the true rank of such beauty, but was baffled in attempting to include it in his formal datum, the judgment of taste.[19]

Winckelmann had failed to cross the Jordan into modern aesthetics because he saw the possibility of recognizing the beauty of form and the expression of content in only one case, the case of the tranquil soul, and did know how to generalize from this case. Kant, obviously, thinks at a less concrete and more general level than Winckelmann, and offers a more general possibility of the expression of content in a form that is not merely harmonious in itself but also uniquely apt for what it is to express – that is the import of the fact that the ideal of beauty is more than merely "correct" or average – but because of his initial commitment to a simplistic conception of the judgment of taste he cannot quite recognize what he has done.

As Bosanquet argues in his discussion of the concluding thesis of Kant's treatment of aesthetic judgment, namely his thesis that the beautiful is the symbol of the morally good, Kant's revolution in aesthetic theory is also limited by the fact that he sees beauty as an expression only of moral ideas, and still does not have the conception of beauty as the apt expression of any aspect of reality and our feeling about it: "Only in Kant a trace of moralism remains in as far as the permanent value of

---

[18] Bosanquet, *History*, p. 272.
[19] Bosanquet, *History*, pp. 272–3.

the beautiful is referred by him exclusively to its representation of moral ideas and the moral order, in consequence of the subjectivism which hinders him from plainly asserting the existence of any more general system which might express itself not only through morality in the world of conduct, but otherwise in other spheres." Or rather, Bosanquet is willing to recruit Kant for his own cause by some gentle reinterpretation, we might say pushing Kant back toward Shaftesbury: "In pointing however to a supra-sensuous unity common to the world of nature and of freedom, he really transcends this false subordination; and we might say that beauty is for him a symbol of morality only because and in as far as he understands morality to symbolize the order of the universe."[20] This statement must be qualified, of course: for Kant it could be morally dangerous to think that morality ever already *is* the order of the universe, as opposed to the order that we *ought* to strive to impose upon the universe and that we may rationally believe that we *can* so impose. But though Bosanquet may be too generous in his account of Kant's contribution to his own conception of aesthetics, it does seem fair enough for him to conclude that in Kant "The formal principle of unity and variety, which stood in the way of a concrete analysis of beauty, is being transformed into the principle of expressiveness, characterisation, significance."[21]

On Bosanquet's account, the next steps from the ancient to the modern theory of beauty were taken by Schiller, Goethe, Schelling, and Hegel. Bosanquet regards Schiller as a key figure in the history of aesthetics because he stresses that aesthetic experience is not just passive response to beautiful form, but involves activity as well: he sees that "in the enjoyment of beauty or of æsthetic unity there takes place an actual union and interpenetration of matter with form and of receptivity with activity."[22] (Of course, since for Kant sensibility is defined by receptivity and understanding by activity, it could be argued that Schiller is just making explicit what was implicit in Kant's conception of aesthetic experience as the imagination's free play between sensibility and understanding.) That aesthetic experience involves both matter and form also means that it is the experience of an embodied being, an experience that involves the senses as the link between embodied human beings and the world in which they are embodied: in Schiller's own words, quoted by Bosanquet and endorsed in his own philosophy, "man is not obliged

---

[20] Bosanquet, *History*, p. 283.
[21] Bosanquet, *History*, p. 283.
[22] Bosanquet, *History*, p. 290.

to escape from matter in order to assert himself as spirit."[23] In particular, he credits Schiller with clearly recognizing that what activity in aesthetic experience must add to the traditional notion of formal beauty passively apprehended is expression:

> He is quite sure that the pseudo-classical idea of beauty cannot be stretched so as to cover romantic art ... Therefore he thinks a new term must be chosen, which merely indicates the need of expression and of a matter to be expressed, and he sees that this characteristic matter will be found among the Greeks as in modern art. Now that the valuable quality of art, whether we call it "beauty" or by some other name, is understood to be a necessary and objective expression of human life and the unit of nature, there is no reason for trying to narrow the scope of its manifestations. And therefore the thinker who was the first to proclaim its concrete objectivity was also the first who in set terms discarded all formal and traditional limitations to the compass of its unity.[24]

Bosanquet does not make it clear exactly what in Schiller gives rise to this appreciation of his contribution, but he evidently believes that Schiller has taken a major step beyond Winckelmann and Kant in recognizing that beauty in the broadest sense consists in the apt expression of an unlimited range of human conditions and human emotions, not just the particular "tranquil soul" of Winckelmann or the broader but still limited concept of morality as in Kant's ideal of beauty. However, at this stage of his own thought, Bosanquet is critical of Schiller's use in the *Letters on Aesthetic Education* of the concept of play, more precisely the "play-impulse," to characterize the distinctive activity involved in making and experiencing beauty, the creation and recognition of forms of expression. He claims that Schiller is "under stress" from the "metaphor which he adopts":

> The two real links between beauty and the play-impulse are their common freedom from practical ends, and their common tendency to simulation or, in the very largest sense, the ideal treatment of reality. In other respects "play" suggests to us amusement and the relaxation of our faculties, and seems not to do justice to the serious need of self-utterance, nor to the element of expressiveness involved in all work in which the craftsman has any degree of freedom. The play impulse is in short only æsthetic where its primarily negative freedom is charged with a content which demands imaginative expression; and any impulse which takes such a form is æsthetic, whether or not it chances to remind us of "play."[25]

[23] Bosanquet, *History*, p. 291, quoting from a letter to Goethe.
[24] Bosanquet, *History*, p. 303.
[25] Bosanquet, *History*, pp. 295–6.

The basis for Bosanquet's rejection of Schiller's conception of play would appear to be that it does not capture the value of expression as a form of cognition of the outer and inner realities of human life, and that any pleasure that play as a characteristic of artistic or spectatorial activity might generate apart from the cognitive significance of expression would be trivial in comparison with the latter. As we will see later in this volume and in the next, Bosanquet's reservation that interpreting aesthetic creation and experience as a form of play does not do justice to its seriousness was not an uncommon criticism.

Bosanquet credits Goethe with the first unequivocal recognition of the "characteristic" as the essence of beauty in the wide sense. The core of his discussion is a long quotation from Goethe's famous essay "On German Architecture," his plaidoyer for Gothic architecture originally published in 1773 in the collection *On German Style and Art* together with Herder's essay on Shakespeare.[26] In his meditation on the cathedral at Strassburg, Goethe praises the way in which in this building individually "capricious" forms nevertheless "agree together; for a single feeling has created them into a characteristic whole." Here Bosanquet thinks that Goethe has put his finger on the essence of beauty in the wide sense: the apt expression of a distinctive sort of human feeling by means that considered apart from their expressive function might not satisfy formal standards of harmony but that are in utter harmony with what they are to express. He quotes Goethe further: "Now this characteristic art is the only true art. When it acts on what lies round it from inward, single, individual, independent feeling, careless and even ignorant of all that is alien to it, then whether born of rude savagery or of cultivated sensibility, it is whole and living."[27] He also stresses that unlike Winckelmann, who started with a formalist conception of beauty but who recognized the value of expression in at least the one case where what is expressed is not in tension with that formalist beauty, Goethe "approached" the beauty of form and expression "*in the reverse order*": "His point of departure was the idea of the characteristic as the excellent in art, that is to say, as the beautiful in the wider sense of the word which we have determined to adhere to," only "supplemented … by the limiting postulate of formal beauty, beauty in the narrower sense, chiefly as a safeguard against

---

[26] In a review of Bosanquet's *History* published in 1893, John Dewey perceptively noted the complete absence of Herder from Bosanquet's story; given the anti-formalist impetus of Herder's work throughout his career, there is indeed no good reason for this absence. See *Philosophical Review* 2 (1893): 63–9, at p. 67.

[27] Bosanquet, *History*, p. 310.

misunderstandings and eccentricities."[28] (One might also think here of Kant's claim that taste may sometimes have to clip the wings of genius.)[29] In Bosanquet's view, subsequent progress in the history of philosophical aesthetics is only a matter of giving abstract expression to this concrete insight of the artist Goethe.

Schelling and Hegel then made indispensable steps toward giving philosophical expression to Goethe's advance in aesthetic consciousness. "With Schelling we are fairly launched on nineteenth century æsthetic," he writes, because in Schelling "The objectivity and necessary historical continuity of the sense of beauty – Schelling will have it to be *the* supreme expression – of the absolute or divine reality as uttering itself through man, has become an axiom of philosophy."[30] However, Schelling tends to conceive of the absolute or infinite as being constrained by the necessity of appearing in sensuous and finite form, of "the infinite (ideal) [as] narrowed down to the finite (sensuous), and ... the finite (sensuous) [as] racked and stretched and brought to an expressiveness more like that of feeling and thought, to admit the import of the ideal," and, according to Bosanquet, "It is indeed painful to us, and we hold it false, when we are told that modern art is essentially allegory, which is the conclusion that Schelling draws from the entire subordination of symbol to import in the modern imagination."[31] In other words, Schelling does not recognize that beauty lies in a true harmony between matter, form, and content, but thinks that intellectual content must always exceed the grasp of sensuous matter and form. In Schelling's view, "In the modern or Christian world ... the intellectual or spiritual import is dominant, and refuses to be measured by the carrying capacity of any object or person presented to fancy or perception."[32] This leads Schelling to regard mythology as the paradigm of art, and Bosanquet will not accept this conclusion or the "supra-sensuous and theosophic world of beauty, into which pseudo-Platonic abstractions Schelling fell in later years."[33]

Bosanquet thinks that Hegel developed a more balanced view of expression, recognizing the necessity that the absolute or what Hegel calls the "Idea" show itself to sense, but he also holds that this recognition remains abstract for Hegel, and that he fails to give full weight to

---

[28] Bosanquet, *History*, p. 305; emphasis in the original.
[29] Kant, *CPJ*, §50, 5:319.
[30] Bosanquet, *History*, p. 333.
[31] Bosanquet, *History*, p. 324.
[32] Bosanquet, *History*, pp. 323–4.
[33] Bosanquet, *History*, p. 321.

the beauty of nature as something that is itself perfused with human thought and feeling. Bosanquet approves of Hegel's formulations that "Beauty is the Idea as it shows itself to sense"[34] or "the Idea so translated into the terms or tendencies of the imagination as to be capable of direct or indirect presentation to sense."[35] He likewise approves of Hegel's view that "However concrete and particular may be the forms of art, they must be different for having passed through the mind, which is the faculty of universals," which implies a genuine synthesis of sensuous media and intellectual and emotional content, and of Hegel's application of this insight at least in principle to the case of nature as well: "If the artist imitates nature, it is not because she has done this or that, but because she has done it *right*," obviously a judgment that can only be made from the human point of view – natural beauty is also human, nature as humans think it ought to look. But he thinks that Hegel nevertheless did not "fully feel" the beauty of nature, which is to say he did not appreciate how extensively human beings may use the forms of nature, whether directly or in artistic representation, for the expression of their own thoughts and emotions, how fully human beings may infuse nature with humanity.

> The beauty of nature, as distinguished from man, which Hegel begins by considering, was something that he did not fully feel. He understood that inanimate nature may be in apparent sympathy with human moods, but he had no detailed justification to offer for their coincidence, nor any sense of character and import in mountain form or cloud formation or water movement. His gaze is concentrated on the individual organism and its progressive manifestation of life, in which for the first time the idea seems to him to attain a partially adequate self-revelation, and he devotes more attention to the plant than to the rocks, more to the animal than to the plant, and subsequently more to the human being than to the animal.

But, speaking for himself, Bosanquet continues,

> We do not feel, I believe, this exact progression of æsthetic value in the ratio of organic development. The landscape, and plant life as the vesture of the earth, seem to us more yielding and sympathetic to our moods than the concentrated life of the individual animal.[36]

This is a way of saying that Hegel did not fully appreciate the power of human imagination and its centrality to aesthetic expression. He favored

---

[34] Bosanquet, *History*, p. 336.
[35] Bosanquet, *History*, p. 340.
[36] Bosanquet, *History*, p. 337.

the beauty of animals over that of landscape and plants because he thought that animals themselves approximate more of the powers of the human being as in turn the vehicle for the manifestation of the spirit; in other words, he evaluated natural beauty from a strictly cognitive point of view – how much can it reveal to us of the essence of Spirit? – and did not regard the creation of expression as valuable in its own right. Bosanquet, on the contrary, values the beauty of landscape and flora, whether in nature or in artistic representation, precisely because the human imagination can use that as a vehicle for the expression of human feelings more freely than it can use the beauty of animals for that purpose.

Bosanquet sums up this part of his discussion of Hegel with the comment that "Hegel's treatment of the Ideal is the greatest single step that has ever been made in æsthetic," but "Subject to the reservation which has been indicated, and which is practically represented by the life-work of Ruskin."[37] His *History* concludes with a chapter on Ruskin and William Morris, in which he argues that "at least within the theory of formative art a new vitality of connection is supplied by the work of our great writers, which precisely justifies, by an undesigned coincidence, the conception of the early concrete Idealists of Germany, and supplements what is defective in the arid formalism of their successors," by whom he means especially "exact" aestheticians such as Gustav Fechner (to be briefly discussed later in this volume), who merely reproduced "the theory of antiquity armed with the methods of modern science,"[38] and writers such as Robert Zimmerman[39] and Max Schasler,[40] who primarily rang permutations on Schelling's and Hegel's systems for classifying the arts, although in Bosanquet's view those were the least valuable part of their work. Bosanquet calls Ruskin's affinity with the "early concrete Idealists" "undesigned" because he believes that "True English æsthetic has not sprung from philosophy or philosophers, except through the negative contact of Mr. Ruskin with Alison and Burke," and that any transmission of "pregnant" German ideas to Ruskin through Coleridge and Carlyle remains unproven.[41] Bosanquet's assessment of Ruskin's philosophical sources and lack thereof is consistent with the judgment reached in the present work, where Ruskin was presented as having arrived at an aesthetics of truth and truthfulness similar in spirit to the aesthetics of German

[37] Bosanquet, *History*, p. 342.
[38] Bosanquet, *History*, p. 387.
[39] Bosanquet, *History*, pp. 373–81.
[40] Bosanquet, *History*, pp. 414–24.
[41] Bosanquet, *History*, pp. 441–2.

Idealism but independent of any actual influence from that quarter. But what Bosanquet stresses is that Ruskin recognized, at least for the visual arts of painting, sculpture, and architecture, that all of nature is a candidate for the apt or truthful expression of its essential forms and character, and also that all of nature is a potential vehicle for the expression or reflection of human feelings. The first point Bosanquet makes by saying that Ruskin's *Modern Painters* – the first volume of which he takes some glee in pointing out was published the same year as John Stuart Mill's *System of Logic* (1843) –

> brought nature nearer to man, and showed him his own intelligence both mirrored in its causation and rooted in its evolution; and secondly, it revealed in all phenomena, inorganic, organic, and belonging to humanity, the definite distinctive characteristics which on the one hand had stamped them for what they individually were, and on the other displayed them in their microcosmic relations as meeting-points of the complex influences that permeate the universe.[42]

That is, natural beauty reveals the continuity between humankind and the rest of nature, and consists in the first instance in the expression of the individual essence of the beautiful natural object, whether seen directly or as captured by the likes of Turner, and in the second instance in the expression of the relation between the microcosmic and the macrocosmic, the relation between the individual character of the object at hand and the rest of nature. The second point is that Ruskin recognized that beauty is not only the expression of the essence of the natural object perceived or depicted but also the expression of human feeling about that:

> The characteristic thus apprehended, including in its expression signs of the feeling with which the sympathetic or idealised self enters into the world-life thus symbolised, is fully in the sense of Hegel, but possesses a wealth and vigour which in the beauty of landscape scenery his eye was never trained to appreciate. And here, in its simplest form, if we bear in mind the nature of the curves and graduated surfaces demanded according to the above exposition, is the vital bond between content and expression.[43]

For Bosanquet in his *History of Æsthetic*, then, the history of both aesthetic consciousness and aesthetic theory culminates with Ruskin's recognition that beauty lies in the truthful expression of the essential character of nature without us and of our own feelings in the presence of nature,

---

[42] Bosanquet, *History*, p. 444.
[43] Bosanquet, *History*, p. 451.

which of course are also part of nature. Beauty is a form of cognition, but cognition of the essential characteristics of nature and of that special part of nature that consists of human feelings about the rest of nature.

The Bosanquet of the *History* thus remains within the cognitivist framework of most nineteenth-century aesthetics, but clearly adds human feelings and emotions to the subject matter of aesthetic cognition. And as we saw in his comments on Schiller, he shared with most of his contemporaries the rejection of play as an essential component of aesthetic experience. In the *Three Lectures on Aesthetic* published more than two decades after the first edition of the *History*, however, Bosanquet gives much more scope to the role of imagination in aesthetic experience, and therefore to the idea of play. In the *Lectures*, Bosanquet also drops the use of the term "characteristic" and the suggestion that beauty lies in the apt expression of essential characteristics of *objects*, and instead explains beauty primarily as the expression or, as he more often says, embodiment of *feeling*. The *Lectures* thus point toward a threefold synthesis of the cognitivist approach to aesthetics with the emotional impact of aesthetic experience and a more generous attitude toward the conception of aesthetic experience as a form of play.

Bosanquet begins the first lecture, on "The General Nature of the Aesthetic Attitude – Contemplation and Creation,"[44] by enumerating the criteria of aesthetic experience: it is (i) "a *stable* feeling," which does not "pass into satiety, like the pleasures of eating and drinking"; (ii) "a *relevant* feeling," that is, "it is attached, annexed, to the quality of some object – to all its detail – ... a special feeling, or a concrete feeling"; and (iii) "a *common* feeling," that is, "You can share it; and its value is not diminished by being shared."[45] But the object that can satisfy these criteria in Bosanquet's view is nothing other than feeling itself: we get a feeling that is stable, relevant, and common in response to the organization or "incarnation" of feeling itself. It is "feeling which has found its incarnation or taken plastic shape" that "cannot remain the passing reaction of a single 'body-and-mind,'" but instead produces a stable, shareable, and object-directed feeling of pleasure.[46] The remainder of the first lecture is then devoted to the description of the transformation of feeling itself into an object by means of imagination: "the aesthetic attitude is

---

[44] Bosanquet, *Lectures*, p. 1.
[45] Bosanquet, *Lectures*, pp. 4–5.
[46] Bosanquet, *Lectures*, p. 7.

that of feeling embodied in 'form.'"[47] And now, unlike in the *History*, Bosanquet gives an account of form. First, "Form means outline, shape, general rule, *e.g.* for putting together a sentence, or an argument; or it means the metre in poetry, or the type of poem, sonnet, or what not" – in other words, an organization that is imposed upon some material from without, "something superficial, general, diagrammatic." But second, "when you push home your insight into the order and connection of parts, not leaving out the way in which this affects the parts themselves; then you find that the form becomes (as a lawyer would say) 'very material'; not merely outlines and shapes, but all the sets of gradations and variations and connections that make everything what it is – the life, soul, and movement of the object."[48] This might make it seem as if form in the second sense is something that is inherent in the object rather than externally imposed upon it, and that the activity of both artistic creation and aesthetic appreciation is simply a matter of letting the real character of the object come forth without distortion by anything superficial imposed upon it (as Schopenhauer's earlier account of beauty or Heidegger's later account of truth would suggest). But this is not what Bosanquet wants to say. Rather, he claims that form in this deep rather than superficial sense is created only by the interaction of the object and the subject, and in the case of feeling as the aesthetic object in the interaction of the feeling as we first encounter it with our efforts to give it shape, to find a vehicle for expressing it.

> You always, in contemplating objects, ... experience bodily tensions and impulses relative to the forms which you apprehend, the rising and sinking, rushing, colliding, reciprocal checking, etc. of shapes. And these are connected with your own activities in apprehending them; the form, indeed, or law of connection in any object, is ... just what depends, for being apprehended, upon activity of body-and-mind on your part. And the feelings and associations of such activity are what you automatically use, with all their associated significances, to compose the feeling which is for you the feeling of the object or the object as an embodied feeling.

The object of the aesthetic attitude is embodied feeling; in the interval between his two works in aesthetics, Bosanquet was clearly influenced by the "empathy" theorists whom we will discuss shortly. Indeed, feeling must be embodied, that is, though of course it emanates from our bodies, it does not come with a distinctive form for its expression, but one

---

[47] Bosanquet, *Lectures*, p. 13.
[48] Bosanquet, *Lectures*, pp. 15–16.

must be created for it, through the activity of our body directly, as in song or dance, or through the creation of further bodies by the use of our own bodies, as in painting or sculpture.

In addition to stressing that it is feeling itself which is embodied in aesthetic creation and appreciation, Bosanquet also now emphasizes that these activities are imaginative, free from the constraints of antecedent theory and free to create new and appropriate form:

> The aesthetic attitude must be imaginative. That is to say, it must be the attitude of a mind which freely tracks and pursues the detail of experience for the sake of a particular kind of satisfaction – not the satisfaction of complete and self-consistent theory, but the automatic satisfaction, so to speak, of a complete embodiment of feeling. The important point seems to me to be that "contemplation" should not mean "inertness," but should include from the beginning a creative element.

This is what Bosanquet now calls "expression."[49] Bosanquet stresses the creativity of expression by arguing that "We must not suppose that we first have a disembodied feeling, and then set out to find an embodiment adequate to it." Rather, "imaginative expression creates the feeling in creating its embodiment, and the feeling so created not merely cannot be otherwise expressed, but cannot otherwise exist, than in and through the embodiment which imagination has found for it."[50]

Bosanquet does not explicitly say so, because he does not explicitly discuss aesthetic pleasure at all, but it seems obvious that even though part of the pleasure of aesthetic experience must arise from the satisfaction in the fact of having found a suitable form for the expression of some feeling, part of it must also arise from the satisfaction in the act of *creating* such a form – that there is pleasure in aesthetic creation and appreciation because it is not just a matter of recognizing the true form of a feeling, but of actively creating a form for the expression of the feeling without the guidance and domination of some rule for doing this. This also seems implicit in one of the central points of the second lecture. In a passage reminiscent of Adam Smith's argument that the pleasure in imitation comes not from the antecedent similarity of the medium of a representation to the thing represented but rather from the feat of overcoming the dissimilarity of the medium of representation to its object, Bosanquet says about "the Homeric description of the metal-working deity's craftsmanship in the shield of Achilles":

---

[49] Bosanquet, *Lectures*, p. 33.
[50] Bosanquet, *Lectures*, p. 34.

> Surely the miracle lies in what Homer accents when he says, "Though it was made of gold." It lies here; that without the heavy matter and the whole natural process of the reality, man's mind possesses a magic by which it can extract the soul of the actual thing or event, and confer it on any medium which is convenient to him, the wall of a cave, or a plate of gold, or a scrap of paper. And when these great poets insist on the likeness of the imitation, I take it that the real underlying interest is in the conquest of the difference of the medium. So that really, in the naïve praise of successful imitation, we have, if we read it rightly, the germ of the fundamental doctrine of aesthetic semblance. That is to say, what matters is not the thing, but the appearance which you can carry off, and deal with apart from it, and recreate.[51]

Aesthetic semblance is a central concept for Bosanquet in the *Lectures*, but what is crucial to his conception of semblance is precisely that it is an invention, a product of imagination, rather than something given, a product of passive perception. The aesthetic "semblance of external things" is "that which imaginative perception freely apprehends, and remodels in the interest of feeling."[52] "Imagination finds in experience the instrument of that immense embodiment of feeling which it constructs,"[53] and it seems clear that the stable, shareable pleasure of imagination comes as much from the act of construction – itself first performed by the artist but re-performed by the audience – as well as from the product of the construction, the embodiment. For, as Bosanquet concludes the third lecture, "Beauty is above all a creation, a new individual expression in which a new feeling comes to exist.... If we understand it otherwise, as a rule previously prescribed, then it is something which must be hostile to free and complete expression for expression's sake."[54]

In making the transition from his own aesthetics of the nineteenth century to his aesthetics of the twentieth century, Bosanquet stressed the imaginative, creative element of embodying feeling as well as the cognitive significance of the embodiment of feeling, and suggested that the pleasure of aesthetic experience has as much to do with the former as it owes with the latter. Bosanquet thus resurrected the idea of play and gave it a novel interpretation that straddles the boundary between the physical and mental. Had Bosanquet explicitly combined this new theory of play with his previous theory of the "characteristic" as the combination of form and feeling, where indeed the latter element is both the cognition and the experience of feeling, he would have counted

---

[51] Bosanquet, *Lectures*, pp. 50–1.
[52] Bosanquet, *Lectures*, p. 54.
[53] Bosanquet, *Lectures*, p. 55.
[54] Bosanquet, *Lectures*, p. 109.

among the great synthesizers of the history of modern aesthetics. He did not quite make this synthesis explicit – he did not write a third book in aesthetics to combine his first two. But his approach was certainly far more comprehensive than that of many of his contemporaries. In the remainder of this chapter, we will see how Leo Tolstoy produced a much narrower response to his narrow interpretation of nineteenth-century aestheticism. When we return to the further development of aesthetics in early twentieth-century Britain in Volume 3, we will see how a philosophical defense of a narrow aestheticism emerged, as if in reaction to Tolstoy's attack upon it, while the more comprehensive approaches of Pater, Bosanquet, and even Wilde were ignored.

2. TOLSTOY

The Russian novelist Leo Tolstoy's *What is Art?* first published not in his native language but in an English translation in 1898,[55] and thus at least in part a British as well as a Russian document, is an attack upon both the art and the aesthetic theory of the nineteenth century that had culminated in the aestheticist movement in the arts and the theory of art for art's sake, as Tolstoy understood that movement. British aesthetics after the turn of the twentieth century can then be considered a response to Tolstoy, but was at first a defense of aestheticism conceived as narrowly as Tolstoy had conceived it in his attack. Only gradually did anything like a defense of the more comprehensive aestheticism of Pater and Wilde emerge in twentieth-century Britain – although, as we will see, a more comprehensive aesthetic theory was advanced earlier in the United States, by George Santayana, even before the nineteenth century was over. But all that will be considered later. For now, we will complete our survey of nineteenth-century aestheticism with Tolstoy's attack upon it, and then return to Germany to survey the later nineteenth-century developments in aesthetics there, before we fully plunge into the twentieth century in Volume 3.

Count Leo (Lev Nikolayevich) Tolstoy (1828–1910) was born to a family of ancient Russian nobility on their estate of Yasnaya Polyana in the Tula province of central Russia, which he would inherit after the death of several brothers. After failing to complete studies in Oriental

---

[55] Leo Tolstoy, *What is Art?* trans. Alymer Maude (London: Oxford University Press, 1930); trans. Richard Pevear and Larissa Volokhonsky (London: Penguin Books, 1995). The latter translation will be cited here.

languages and law at the university at Kazan and a period of gambling and womanizing in Moscow, he published a translation of Laurence Sterne's *Sentimental Journey* (1851) and then served in the Russian army during the Crimean war, during which period he published *Childhood* (1852) and, while the siege of Sevastopol was still going on, the three historical fictions *Sevastopol Sketches* (1855). After a further period of traveling among European literati, he settled down on his estates, where he turned to the education of his peasants and married in 1862. The following years saw his greatest literary accomplishments, *War and Peace* (serial publication completed in 1869) and *Anna Karenina* (1877). While writing *Anna Karenina* he turned toward Christianity, first toward the Orthodox church but after 1880 toward his own brand of Christian communitarianism. Many of his writings after that time, even his remaining fictions, were polemical, and *What is Art?* is part of that polemical work, arguing as it does that the mere enjoyment of beauty cannot justify the great social and financial costs of the production of art, but that only art's communication of sound religious feeling can.

What is Art? begins with a scathing but hilarious indictment of the costs of putting on a full-dress production of a nineteenth-century grand opera to be enjoyed by a wealthy elite that could only have been written by a member of that elite who had detailed familiarity with such productions. It then continues with a well-informed survey of (continental) aesthetic theories from Baumgarten to his own time (he evinces no familiarity with any of the British work we have just been considering). Tolstoy implausibly ascribes to Baumgarten the view that "The aim of beauty itself is to be pleasing and to arouse desire,"[56] and then argues that although many after Baumgarten opposed such a conception of the value of beauty with an "objective and mystical one, which merges this concept with the highest perfection, with God," such a definition is "fantastic ... not based on anything."[57] In his view, the only informative definition to have come out of the tradition of aesthetic theory is the subjective one that beauty is simply "that which affords us a certain kind of pleasure,"[58] supposedly "without awakening lust,"[59] but a pleasure that cannot in fact be clearly separated from the pleasure of for example eating as understood "by people who stand at the lowest level of moral development (savages, for instance)." Tolstoy thinks that it is possible for

[56] Tolstoy, *What is Art?* ch. III, p. 17.
[57] Tolstoy, *What is Art?* ch. IV, p. 31.
[58] Tolstoy, *What is Art?* ch. IV, p. 32.
[59] Tolstoy, *What is Art?* ch. IV, p. 33.

people to ascribe a higher meaning than mere pleasure to eating if they have a higher understanding of the meaning of life, but "Just as people who think that the aim and purpose of food is pleasure cannot perceive the true meaning of eating, so people who think that the aim of art is pleasure cannot know its meaning and purpose, because they ascribe to an activity which has meaning in connection with the other phenomena of life the false and exclusive aim of pleasure."[60] Mere pleasure cannot justify the sacrifice of "the labours of millions of people, the very lives of people,"[61] which art costs. Instead, "In order to define art precisely, one must first of all cease looking at it as a means of pleasure and consider it as one of the conditions of human life. Considering art in this way, we cannot fail to see that art is a means of communion among people."[62] This leads to Tolstoy's definition of art as the communication of feeling from one person (the artist) to others (the audience) through external means (artistic media), a process that Tolstoy describes, remarkably, as "infection": feeling is communicated from artist to audience in the way that a cold is, thus without any special activity, especially any free play of the imagination, at least on the part of the latter. Of course, such a definition can also be a justification of art only if the feelings that are so communicated are valuable ones. This requirement is reflected in the two stages of Tolstoy's exposition of his alternative to the merely pleasure-seeking conception of art. First he emphasizes with his own italics the communication of feeling:

> *To call up in oneself a feeling once experienced and, having called it up, to convey it by means of movements, lines, colours, sounds, images expressed in words, so that others experience the same feeling* – in this consists the activity of art. Art is that human activity which consists in one man's consciously conveying to others, by certain external signs, the feelings he has experienced, and in others being infected by those feelings and also experiencing them.[63]

But then Tolstoy adds the requirement that the communication of feeling will justify the cost of art only when the feelings communicated are "necessary for life and for the movement towards the good of the individual man and of mankind," in other words, what he considers to be religious feelings once religion has been stripped of all that is unessential or even contradictory to its true message:

---

[60] Tolstoy, *What is Art?* ch. IV, p. 35.
[61] Tolstoy, *What is Art?* ch. IV, p. 36.
[62] Tolstoy, *What is Art?* ch. V, p. 37.
[63] Tolstoy, *What is Art?* ch. V, pp. 39–40.

> This special significance has always been given to all people to the part of this activity which conveys feelings coming from their religious consciousness, and it is this small part of the whole of art that has been called art in the full sense of the word.[64]
>
> Always, in all times and in all human societies, there has existed this religious consciousness, common to all people of the society, of what is good and what is bad, and it is this religious consciousness that determines the worth of the feelings conveyed by art.[65]

All art that aims at beauty for its own sake, that is, merely for the sake of the pleasure that it affords, is degenerate, even though that may indict most Western art since the Middle Ages: "The concept of beauty not only does not coincide with the good, but is rather the opposite of it, because the good for the most part coincides with a triumph over our predilections, while beauty is at the basis of all our predilections."[66] What is genuine and valuable is not the beauty sought by the elite who have lost their faith, beauty that has inevitably become "fanciful and unclear," "artificial and cerebral,"[67] but art that "must then be accessible to all people,"[68] for example heartfelt stories about peasants that can be understood and appreciated by peasants.

Tolstoy's "infection" model of artistic creation and communication might seem to impute a remarkable degree of passivity to artist as well as audience, to leave no room for the activity of imagination on the part of either – after all, when one person passes a cold on to another, it is not usually as a result of some intentional, voluntary action on the part of the former (although perhaps there might have been some voluntary actions that the former could have taken to reduce the likelihood of infecting others if he had sufficiently understood his own condition or cared about the health of others). And indeed, Tolstoy never suggests that the audience needs any preparation or activity on their own part to understand the message of genuinely accessible art; for the audience, apparently, the unchanging "properties of human nature" will suffice.[69] However, Tolstoy's description of art as an "activity" by which the artist uses a medium to "consciously convey" his own experience to others seems to impute intentional, voluntary action to the artist, action

---

[64] Tolstoy, *What is Art?* ch. V, p. 41.
[65] Tolstoy, *What is Art?* ch. VI, p. 43.
[66] Tolstoy, *What is Art?* ch. VII, p. 52.
[67] Tolstoy, *What is Art?* ch. IX, p. 59.
[68] Tolstoy, *What is Art?* ch. VIII, p. 57.
[69] Tolstoy, *What is Art?* ch. XVI, p. 125.

that presumably draws upon both trained technique and thought or indeed imagination in the artist. So it might seems as if "infection" could describe the passive reception of art but not the active creation of art. However, Tolstoy's emphasis upon *sincerity* as the fundamental quality of the artist minimizes the importance of activity and imagination in artistic creation. What Tolstoy requires is that the artist have experienced religious feeling deeply and then let his expression of it flow naturally from his experience rather than obscuring it with complicated technique and clever invention. The artist should avoid "borrowing," "imitation," "effectfulness" (or "being Striking" as Alymer Maude translated), and "diversion,"[70] as well as professionalization, advanced training, and refined art criticism;[71] instead, the essential task for the artist is negative, that of avoiding the disruption of the communication of his genuine feeling "by the superfluity of details."[72] The work of art is more a matter of stripping away barriers to the transmission of feeling than of the invention of elaborate means for that communication. All the artist really needs is sincerity, "the chief and most precious property of art";[73] all that is necessary for art will be found when and "only when a man gives himself to his feeling.... And therefore schools can teach what is required for creating something resembling art, but never art itself."[74]

The reduction of artistic creation to sincerity might seem too simple; even Tolstoy himself seems to suggest that there are several conditions for successful communication in art, not just this one. Thus he writes:

> Art becomes more or less infectious owing to three conditions: (1) the greater or lesser particularity of the feeling conveyed; (2) the greater or lesser clarity with which the feeling is conveyed; and (3) the artist's sincerity, that is, the greater or lesser force with which the artist himself experiences the feeling he conveys.[75]

It might seem as if finding out how to make a feeling particular and clear requires both training and imagination, and it might also seem as if by listing these requirements first Tolstoy means to suggest that they are at least as important if not more important than sincerity. However, he quickly makes it clear that he thinks that the first two conditions for successful art follow directly from the third:

---

[70] Tolstoy, *What is Art?* ch. XI, p. 84; in the Oxford translation, p. 181.
[71] Tolstoy, *What is Art?* ch. XII, p. 93.
[72] Tolstoy, *What is Art?* ch. XI, p. 88.
[73] Tolstoy, *What is Art?* ch. XII, p. 93.
[74] Tolstoy, *What is Art?* ch. XII, p. 100.
[75] Tolstoy, *What is Art?* ch. XV, p. 121.

I am speaking of three conditions of infectiousness and worth in art, but in fact only the last is a condition, that the artist must experience an inner need to express the feeling he conveys. This condition includes the first, because if the artist is sincere, he will express his feeling as he has perceived it. And since each man is unlike all others, this feeling will be particular for all others, and will be the more particular the more deeply the artist penetrates, the more heartfelt and sincere he is. And this sincerity will force the artist to find a clear expression of the feeling he wishes to convey.

And therefore this third condition – sincerity – is the most important of the three.[76]

Sincerity presumably may take effort – surely it will take effort for the artist growing up in an artificial, elite culture with a professional education virtually forced upon him – but once sincerity has been achieved, it seems as if everything else necessary for art will flow automatically from it; the sincere artist will not be able to avoid successfully communicating his feeling, and to that extent "infection" seems to be an apt characterization for Tolstoy's conception of artistic creations as well as of the reception of art.

One point that needs to be made here is that Tolstoy's notion of particularity cannot be confused with any idea of idiosyncrasy, that is, any idea that individuality is as such an intrinsic value in art. That cannot be his idea, for his position is that art is valuable just insofar as it communicates from one person to others feelings on which a genuine community can be based, feelings that bring people together rather than separate them. His view can only be that people differ within a common framework, and that the function of the artistic transmission of feelings must be to create empathy, that is, an identification with the feelings of others that allows all to recognize that they share more than they differ, that they can be members of a single community in spite of their superficial differences.

Tolstoy's conception of art is not that art is a vehicle for the communication of metaphysical truth, but it is oriented toward truth nevertheless: the artist must be truthful to his own feelings, and by being so he will communicate to others feelings that will be the true basis for genuine human community. Such a theory is of course profoundly moralistic, and thus the furthest thing from the original idea of art for art's sake, in which the value of beauty was strictly separated from the values of truth and goodness. Tolstoy certainly emphasized the emotional impact of art, but so restricted the emotions that art should communicate and so minimized the role of either knowledge or imagination on the part

---

[76] Tolstoy, *What is Art?* ch. XV, p. 122.

of either artist or audience that he hardly contributed to a broadening of aesthetic theory – instead, he offered as narrow an aesthetic theory as we have seen throughout our survey of the eighteenth and nineteenth centuries. And we will see that, at least in Britain, it took some time in the twentieth century for this narrowness to be overcome, although what initially prevailed was a narrow version of aestheticism as if in defiance of Tolstoy's narrow attack upon it. But before we can begin our survey of twentieth-century aesthetics, we must first return to Germany and see how aesthetic theory developed there following the post-Hegelian period with which we ended our earlier survey.

PART THREE

GERMAN AESTHETICS IN THE SECOND HALF OF THE NINETEENTH CENTURY

8

In the Shadow of Schopenhauer

In Part One of this volume, we saw how Schelling cast a large shadow over much thought about art both within and beyond Germany in the first decades of the nineteenth century, and that Hegel then cast an equally large shadow, especially on aesthetics in the German academy, in the three decades following his death. In the later years of that period, especially in the time between 1848 and his own death in 1860, Schopenhauer's star began to rise. Following our discussion of British aesthetics from Ruskin to Bosanquet, we now return to the German scene to consider the influence of Schopenhauer on a new generation of aestheticians. Friedrich Nietzsche will be our primary subject, but we will also touch upon the aesthetic theory of Eduard von Hartmann. In the subsequent two chapters of this volume, we will examine the reviving influence of Kant, first among philosophers who considered themselves to be Neo-Kantians – although the most self-avowedly Neo-Kantian among them did not in fact revive Kant's concept of free play – and then among a group of philosophers, all German-influenced although not all German, who did not think of themselves as Neo-Kantians but some of whom did revive Kant's concept of play. Among this group, some, such as Herbert Spencer, revived the concept of play; others, such as Theodor Lipps, opposed the concept of empathy to it; and some, such as Karl Groos, tried to find room for both notions. But among all the philosophers to be considered in this part, it was probably Wilhelm Dilthey, an unorthodox Neo-Kantian who was also deeply influenced by Friedrich Schleiermacher, who developed the most comprehensive view of aesthetic experience, synthesizing, as Schleiermacher had before him, the aesthetics of truth, the aesthetics of feeling, and the aesthetics of play.

1. NIETZSCHE: INTRODUCTION

In 1872, the twenty-seven-year-old professor of classical philosophy at Basel, Friedrich Nietzsche, published not the scholarly monograph that had been expected from him following his early appointment, but *The Birth of Tragedy Out of the Spirit of Music*, a speculative interpretation of the sources of Greek tragedy leading to an *apologia* for the music of Richard Wagner that would do as much to damage his academic career as did the poor health that required him to resign his position seven years later. Fourteen years later, he issued a new edition of this first work, now entitled *The Birth of Tragedy: Or Hellenism and Pessimism*, not with a new preface but with "An Attempt at Self-Criticism" of this "questionable book."[1] The older Nietzsche complained that his youthful work is "impossible," "badly written, clumsy, embarrassing, with a rage for imagery and confused in its imagery, emotional ... lacking the will to logical cleanliness, very convinced and therefore too arrogant to prove its assertions, mistrustful even of the *propriety* of proving things, a book for the initiated, 'music' for those who were baptized in the name of music," and more[2] – yet in spite of these faults, he was willing to reissue it, and it has remained one of his most popular books ever since. But what really seems to have bothered the older Nietzsche was, in personal terms, that his youthful work had "the bad manners of a Wagnerite," and that, philosophically, it had sought to justify its "provocative sentence ... that the existence of the world is *justified* only as an aesthetic phenomenon" by appeal to the "true *metaphysical* activity of man."[3] The older Nietzsche, in addition to having come to see the intoxicating music of Wagner as inimical rather than advantageous to the development of human freedom, had also come to

---

[1] Friedrich Nietzsche, *The Birth of Tragedy and Other Writings*, ed. Raymond Geuss and Ronald Speirs, trans. Ronald Speirs (Cambridge: Cambridge University Press, 1999). Henceforth "*BT*." Other works of Nietzsche cited in this section will include *Human, All Too Human: A Book for Free Spirits*, tr. R.J. Hollingdale (Cambridge: Cambridge University Press, 1986) ("*HAH*"); *The Gay Science*, ed. Bernard Williams, trans. Josefine Nauckhoff (Cambridge: Cambridge University Press, 2001) ("*GS*"); *Beyond Good and Evil*, ed. Rolf-Peter Horstmann and Judith Norman, trans. Judith Norman (Cambridge: Cambridge University Press, 2002) ("*BGE*"); *On the Genealogy of Morality*, ed. Keith Ansell-Pierson, trans. Carol Diethe, revised edition (Cambridge: Cambridge University Press, 2007); *The Anti-Christ, Ecce Homo, Twilight of the Idols, and Other Writings*, ed. Aaron Ridley and Judith Norman, trans. Judith Norman (Cambridge: Cambridge University Press, 2005) ("*AC*"); and *Writings from the Early Notebooks*, ed. Raymond Geuss and Alexander Nehamas, trans. Ladislaus Löb (Cambridge: Cambridge University Press, 2009) ("*EN*").
[2] *BT*, pp. 6–7.
[3] *BT*, p. 8.

doubt that art could reveal a metaphysical justification of human existence. In *The Birth of Tragedy*, the young Nietzsche, adapting the philosophy of Arthur Schopenhauer, his enthusiasm for which he then shared with Wagner, had argued that art – first in the form of the Greek tragedy of Aeschylus and Sophocles and now at last again in the form of the operas of Richard Wagner – can reveal the metaphysical truth that makes human life bearable, the joyous truth that beneath the level of appearance that is full of suffering and destruction humans are really at one with each other and with the world in a "primordial ground" that is "indestructible and eternal."[4] The older Nietzsche rejected the domineering music of Wagner and the dualistic metaphysics of Schopenhauer – which he had in fact already mistrusted before coming under Wagner's spell[5] – and in some moments seems to have mistrusted art altogether. In some moments he continued to see the possibility of art as a sign of the possibility of human freedom, however, although a playful freedom by means of which we can make our lives bearable or even joyous *in* the real world of our natural existence rather than a freedom *from* the natural world, the flight into a metaphysical fantasy of primordial being that Schopenhauer had imagined. Nietzsche rejected the eighteenth-century ideal of disinterestedness, whether in aesthetics or in morality itself, and never considered art outside of his primary project of "transvaluing" conventional morality into a new model of the potential for human flourishing for "free spirits." Thus he never accepted the idea of aesthetic experience as a free play of our cognitive powers that has nothing to do with the rest of our lives. But in his later work he at least suggested that art's false promise of solace through metaphysical truth might be replaced with a genuine possibility of free play throughout our lives.

Nietzsche was born in Saxony in 1844 to a Lutheran pastor and his wife, herself the daughter of a pastor.[6] His father died when he was five, and the following year he moved with his mother and younger sister Elizabeth to live with his paternal grandmother and great-aunts in Naumburg.

---

[4] *BT*, §17, p. 81.
[5] See *EN*, "October 1867 – April 1868: On Schopenhauer," *EN*, pp. 1–8. In these notes, Nietzsche balks at Schopenhauer's attempt to identify Kant's supposedly unknowable "thing in itself" with something that is after all known, namely the will, as well as asking how Schopenhauer could suppose that the mind evolves in time if time is supposed to be the product of the mind, as it is for Kant. Even in his enthusiasm in *The Birth of Tragedy* for Schopenhauer's idea of something nonrational at the basis of reality, Nietzsche does not make the mistake of also insisting that this must be unknowable.
[6] For a magisterial biography of Nietzsche, see Julian Young, *Friedrich Nietzsche: A Philosophical Biography* (Cambridge: Cambridge University Press, 2010).

After attending local schools, from 1858 to 1864 he was a scholarship student at the selective school founded in 1543 by the Elector of Saxony at Pforta, an hour's walk away. The curriculum at Pforta emphasized classical languages and literature above all else, and it had produced some of Germany's most famous writers and intellectuals (eighty years earlier, Johann Gottlieb Fichte had also been a student there). Nietzsche started university at Bonn in 1864 as a theology student, but after one year followed the classical philologist Friedrich Ritschl to the university in Leipzig, where his philosophical interests were inflamed by reading Schopenhauer's *World as Will and Representation* and Friedrich Lange's Neo-Kantian *History of Materialism*,[7] and where he was first introduced to Richard Wagner. Nietzsche was an intimate of Wagner and his family for the next several years, and his turn toward philosophy was considerably influenced by Wagner, himself also an enthusiast for Schopenhauer. Nietzsche's student work in the classics was brilliant, and in 1869 his teacher Ritschl successfully recommended him for the professorship at Basel before he had even completed his Ph.D. (hastily granted by Leipzig on the basis of philological articles already published). With minimal financial resources of his own, Nietzsche could hardly turn down this surprisingly early opportunity for a secure position.[8] However, Nietzsche was not really committed to a career as a scholarly classicist – he tried without luck to get himself moved to the chair in philosophy after just two years in the classics chair[9] – and the imaginative and speculative *Birth of Tragedy* was met with harsh criticism by professional classicists upon its appearance in 1872, notably from the equally youthful Ulrich von Wilamowitz-Möllendorf, who had been a classmate at Pforta. This response cost Nietzsche most of his students,[10] but did not dissuade him from his new philosophical path.

Between 1873 and 1876 Nietzsche published four *Untimely Meditations*, the second of which still adulated Schopenhauer but the fourth of which, "Richard Wagner in Bayreuth," already showed signs of distance from the cult that Wagner was establishing around himself with the establishment of his personal opera house in Bayreuth – Nietzsche would flee from the

---

[7] R.J. Hollingdale provides an incisive analysis of the tensions between the philosophies that Nietzsche imbibed from Schopenhauer and Lange, which he only gradually and perhaps never entirely resolved; see *Nietzsche: The Man and His Philosophy*, revised edition (Cambridge: Cambridge University Press, 1999), pp. 36–7.
[8] See Hollingdale, *Nietzsche*, pp. 41–3.
[9] Hollingdale, *Nietzsche*, pp. 50–1.
[10] Hollingdale, *Nietzsche*, p. 82.

debut of the complete *Ring* cycle there in 1876. In 1878, Nietzsche published *Human, All Too Human: A Book for Free Spirits*, dedicated to Voltaire rather than to Schopenhauer and Wagner, which rejected the metaphysical claims for the importance of art made by the former and accepted by the latter as well as by Nietzsche himself six years earlier. After resigning his position in 1879 (receiving a pension for six years, supplemented by a small inheritance), Nietzsche led a nomadic life in Switzerland and Italy, devoting himself to bursts of writing between terrible migraines and other ailments. He published *Daybreak* in 1881 and *The Gay Science* in 1882, a year in which his life was thrown into further turmoil by a falling out with his best friend Paul Reé over the affections of a young Russian woman who had turned up in their lives, Lou Salomé, and by a break with his family over this incident. From 1883 to 1885 he published what he regarded as his central work, *Thus Spoke Zarathustra*, in four parts, and then published what are now considered along with *The Birth of Tragedy* his most important works, *Beyond Good and Evil* in 1886 and *The Genealogy of Morality* in 1887. In 1888, in a spurt of writing, he produced several short books, including *The Anti-Christ, Ecce Homo, Twilight of the Idols*, and *Nietzsche Contra Wagner*, as well as the essay "The Case of Wagner," all of which would be published under the supervision of others after the complete mental breakdown that Nietzsche suffered in Turin in January 1889. Nietzsche's mental collapse is generally attributed to syphilis, with which he is assumed to have been infected by a prostitute during his university years. After being retrieved from Turin by his loyal friend Franz Overbeck, Nietzsche spent the remainder of his life under the care first of his mother and then his sister. Elizabeth, who had been close to Nietzsche when they were younger, had by this time been married to a notorious anti-Semite, Bernhard Förster, who had then killed himself over the failure of an attempted colony in Paraguay.[11] Nietzsche had nothing but contempt for Förster and his anti-Semitism, but after his death Elizabeth would misrepresent her brother's intellectual legacy and ultimately foster his misappropriation by the Nazis, whose rise to power she would witness before her death in 1935.

After the early, mostly negative publicity that had greeted *The Birth of Tragedy*, Nietzsche had largely been ignored during the remainder of his creative years – at the end, he had to pay to have his works printed. But he was becoming noticed again just at the time of his breakdown, and then remained popular with European intellectuals

---

[11] On Förster and Elizabeth Nietzsche, see Hollingdale, *Nietzsche*, pp. 176–8.

of many political persuasions throughout the twentieth century. In the United States and Britain, the highly selective use of Nietzsche by the Nazis – Nietzsche held that the "slave morality" of Christianity originated with the Jews,[12] but at the same time utterly rejected the German nationalism and anti-Semitism of the 1870s and 1880s[13] – had a chilling effect on his reception during the decades around World War II, but interest in his work waxed again after the publication of works by Walter Kaufman in 1950[14] and Arthur Danto in 1965,[15] and has been unabated since in the United States, Britain, Germany, and France (where he was a major influence on Michel Foucault),[16] and many other places.[17]

2. NIETZSCHE: "THE DIONYSIAC WORLD VIEW"

Nietzsche first stated the central idea of *The Birth of Tragedy*, but with only hints at the Schopenhauerian metaphysics of the subsequent work and without its promotion of Wagner, in a lecture on the "Dionysiac World View" that he gave in 1870. In this early piece, it looks as if Nietzsche is on the verge of a wholehearted revival of the aesthetics of play after its long rejection by German idealism. Nietzsche begins by stating that

---

[12] E.g., *GM*, Part I, §7, pp. 17–18.
[13] For a few examples, see *HAH*, §475, pp. 174–5; *BGE*, §251, pp. 141–3; *GM*, Part I, §16, p. 32; Part II, §3, pp. 38–9; Part III, §26, p. 117. For further discussion, see Hollingdale, *Nietzsche*, p. 176.
[14] Walter Kaufman, *Nietzsche: Philosopher, Psychologist, Antichrist* (Princeton: Princeton University Press, 1950).
[15] Arthur C. Danto, *Nietzsche as Philosopher* (New York: Macmillan, 1965).
[16] See Eric Matthews, *Twentieth-Century French Philosophy* (Oxford: Oxford University Press, 1996), pp. 147–56; Foucault's best known works, *The Order of Things* (New York: Vintage, 1970), and *The Archaeology of Knowledge*, translated by A.M. Sheridan Smith (New York: Pantheon, 1972), employ a Nietzschean "genealogical" method.
[17] The literature on Nietzsche is extensive. In addition to the works already mentioned, valuable surveys of Nietzsche's philosophy as a whole include Richard Schacht, *Nietzsche* (London: Routledge, 1983); Bernard Reginster, *The Affirmation of Life: Nietzsche on Overcoming Nihilism* (Cambridge, Mass.: Harvard University Press, 2006); and Christopher Janaway, *Beyond Selflessness: Reading Nietzsche's Genealogy* (Oxford: Oxford University Press, 2007). Valuable work on Nietzsche's aesthetics includes M.S. Silk and J.P. Stern, *Nietzsche on Tragedy* (Cambridge: Cambridge University Press, 1981); Alexander Nehamas, *Nietzsche: Life as Literature* (Cambridge, Mass.: Harvard University Press, 1985); Julian Young, *Nietzsche's Philosophy of Art* (Cambridge: Cambridge University Press, 1992); Philip Pothe, *Nietzsche and the Fate of Art* (Aldershot: Ashgate, 2002); Aaron Ridley, *Nietzsche on Art* (London: Routledge, 2007); and the collection edited by Salim Kemal, Ivan Gaskell, and Daniel W. Conway, *Nietzsche, Philosophy, and the Arts* (Cambridge: Cambridge University Press, 1998).

"there are two states in which human beings attain to the feeling of delight in existence, namely in *dreams* and in *intoxication*." He maintains that each of these sources of pleasure leads to a style in art, that of "*playing with dream*" in making images, on the one hand, and, on the other, "play with intoxication," which involves the "two principal forces which bring naive, natural man to the self-oblivion of intoxication, namely the drive of spring," or drive to sex, "and narcotic drink," which leads to song and dance. Nieztsche associates the pleasure of playing or dreaming with Apollo, the god of light and form, and the pleasure of intoxication with the "Asian" (Thracian) deity Dionysos. He claims that "In the realm of art these names represent stylistic opposites which exist side by side and in almost perpetual conflict ... and which only once, at the moment when the Hellenic 'Will' blossomed, appeared fused together in the work of art that is Attic tragedy."[18] What he means by this is that tragedy arose from the fusion of the intoxicating exuberance of Dionysiac (or Bacchic) celebrations, basically fertility rites, with the calm image-making of epic poetry. By means of this unique combination, Nietzsche argues, "the *principium individuationis* is disrupted, subjectivity disappears entirely before the erupting force of the general element in human life, indeed of the general element in nature. Not only do the festivals of Dionysos" – to which the Apollonian images of the drama have now been added, but which nevertheless retain their original force – "forge a bond between human beings, they also reconcile human beings and nature.... All the caste-like divisions which necessity and arbitrary power have established between men disappear; the slave is a free man, the aristocrat and the man of lowly birth unite in the same Bacchic choruses. In ever-swelling bands the gospel of 'universal harmony' rolls on from place to place; as they sing and dance, human beings express their membership in a higher, more ideal community."[19] Although Nietzsche uses some Schopenhauerian language here, which would entail that we could sense primordial unity only by transcending the individuated level of appearance, he nevertheless seems to conceive of the possibility of harmonious life held out by the unification of the Dionysian and Apollonian elements of tragedy as something that can be found in nature as we ordinarily understand it, not in some realm of primordial being beyond mere appearance. And he also seems to think that the metaphor of play is the best way to characterize the aesthetic

---

[18] Nietzsche, "The Dionysiac World View," *BT*, pp. 119–20.
[19] Nietzsche, "The Dionysiac World View," *BT*, p. 120.

experience of tragedy, which is no part of Schopenhauer's account of tragedy:

> If intoxication is nature playing with human beings, the Dionysiac artist's creation is a playing with intoxication. If one has not experienced it for oneself this state can only be understood by analogy; it is rather like dreaming and at the same time being aware that the dream is a dream. Thus the attendant of Dionysos must be in a state of intoxication and at the same time he must lie in ambush, observing himself from behind. Dionysiac art manifests itself, not in the alternation of clear-mindedness and intoxication, but in their co-existence.[20]

In spite of his invocation of the Greek deities and his use of the image of intoxication, neither of which were any part of the eighteenth-century discussion of aesthetic experience, Nietzsche here seems ready to embark on an interesting expansion of earlier analyses of the experience of fiction, using the idea of play to characterize the bifurcated way in which we both give ourselves over to a fiction and yet at the same time retain our distance from it, our knowledge of its fictionality; and this in turn would suggest how we must balance an awareness of our own particularity and yet also our commonality with other human beings in order to achieve a harmonious form of life. This opening toward the idea of play is not immediately taken up in Nietzsche's next work, however.

3. NIETZSCHE: *THE BIRTH OF TRAGEDY*

There is no mention of Wagner in "The Dionysiac World View." But *The Birth of Tragedy*, which Nietzsche wrote about a year later than this lecture, has a more complicated agenda: it aims to give not only an historical but also a more metaphysical analysis of the origin and significance of Greek tragedy, to criticize the "rationalism" of both Euripides and Socrates, whom Nietzsche saw as jointly ending the magic moment of Hellenic tragedy, now confined to Aeschylus and Sophocles, and to herald the work of Richard Wagner as the first rebirth of the spirit of Greek tragedy since the time of those giants. In *Ecce Homo*, what turned out to be the valedictory work of 1888 in which Nietzsche summed up his previous books, Nietzsche gives *The Birth of Tragedy* work credit for the rising fame of Wagner[21] (when in fact it may have been the urging of Wagner that pushed Nietzsche to make his original account of the Dionysian

---

[20] Nietzsche, "The Dionysiac World View," *BT*, p. 121.
[21] Nietzsche, *AC*, p. 107.

and Apollonian both more Schopenhauerian and more Wagnerian),[22] but also gives a perceptive account of his interpretation of tragedy and his critique of Socratism. Nietzsche exaggerates in saying that the book "smells offensively Hegelian and only a few formulas are tainted with the cadaverous fragrance of Schopenhauer": "the opposition between Dionysian and Apollonian – translated into metaphysics" which is the core of his understanding of tragedy is his version of Schopenhauer's distinction between the phenomenal world of appearance and the noumenal reality of the will in itself. (It might seem as if Nietzsche violates the conventions of transcendental idealism by treating the Dionysian as well as the Apollonian as something we can actually experience, but neither does Schopenhauer himself keep the will entirely on the other side of the fence around what can be experienced.) Nevertheless, Nietzsche accurately sums up the gist of his interpretation of tragedy as the life-affirming emergence of the Dionysian primordial unity of being into the Apollonian world of illusory individuality, and of the radical difference between his own understanding of tragedy and the classical one:

> "Saying yes to life, even in its strangest and harshest problems; the will to life rejoicing in its own inexhaustibility through the *sacrifice* of its highest types – *that* is what I called Dionysian, *that* is what I understood as the bridge to the psychology of the *tragic* poet. *Not* in order to escape fear and pity, not in order to cleanse yourself of a dangerous affect by violent discharge – as Aristotle mistakenly thought –: but instead, over and above all fear and pity, in order for *you yourself to be* the eternal joy in becoming, – the joy that includes even the eternal *joy in negating* ..." In this sense, I have the right to understand myself as the first *tragic philosopher* – which is to say the most diametrically opposed antipode of a pessimistic philosopher.[23]

By saying that he was the "diametrically opposed antipode of a pessimistic philosopher," the late Nietzsche means to say that he had rejected the fundamental attitude of Schopenhauer. *The Birth of Tragedy* did indeed express a more optimistic philosophy than Schopenhauer's, but within a metaphysical framework that was more Schopenhauerian than that employed in "The Dionysiac World View." To appreciate the development of Nietzsche's view of the value of art from this early lecture to *The Birth of Tragedy* and then beyond, we must first see how he valued art while he was most committed to Schopenhauer's framework and then see how he thought about art once he had left Schopenhauer behind.

---

[22] See Hollingdale, *Nietzsche*, pp. 78–9.
[23] Nietzsche, *AC*, pp. 109–10.

Schopenhauer, as we saw earlier,[24] began from Kant's distinction between the phenomenal world of spatio-temporal appearance and the noumenal reality that lies behind it, although while Kant thought that we could describe the noumenal only from the standpoint of morality as a pure will governed by the moral law, Schopenhauer thought that our own experiencing of willing requires us to describe the noumenal ground of phenomenal appearance as a willing of ceaseless activity with no rationally explanatory beginning and no morally rational end – Schopenhauer's use of our own experiencing of willing to characterize reality as it is in itself is precisely what makes the boundary between the phenomenal and the noumenal more permeable for him than it was for Kant, and prepares the way for Nietzsche to treat both the Apollonian and Dionysian as possible objects of aesthetic experience. The young Nietzsche accepted Schopenhauer's transformation of Kant's dualism, and indeed would argue throughout his career that Kant's moral ideal of a universally valid moral law – the "categorical imperative" – was neither a true description of any reality nor a norm that is valid for all human beings; here too he can be thought of as following Schopenhauer's attack upon the validity of Kant's categorical imperative.[25]

In aesthetics, Schopenhauer began by transposing Kant's doctrine of "aesthetic ideas" as the "spirit" of the fine arts out of its decidedly moral key. He claimed that all the arts from architecture through literature represent essential, "Platonic" forms of the "objectification of the will," that is, the paradigmatic forms in which the will manifests itself in appearance, while music copies not the objectifications of the will but the will itself – in Platonic terms, it is not at two removes from truth but only one. In his transposition of Kant's idea of disinterestedness, Schopenhauer located the value of art in the fact that it can induce a state of pure will-less, subject-less, painless knowing. It is initially hard to see how anything that represents the ever-striving, unsatisfied, and unsatisfiable character of the will as it really is could be painless, but as we saw Schopenhauer's idea was that precisely because art deals with universally valid forms, whether of the will itself in the case of music or of the objectifications of the will in the case of all the other arts, it distracts one from the frustration of one's *own* will, the source of all pain – paradoxically,

---

[24] See also the illuminating sketch of Schopenhauer's philosophy and aesthetics in Hollingdale, *Nietzsche*, pp. 67–72.
[25] See Schopenhauer, *On the Basis of Morality*, trans. E.F.J. Payne, introduction by David E. Cartwright (Indianapolis and Cambridge: Hackett Publishing, 1995), Part II, §7, pp. 88–94.

the contemplation of the will and its inevitable frustration is pleasurable rather than painful as long as what is contemplated is universal rather than particular. (As we also saw, Friedrich Theodor Vischer used a similar strategy to reconcile the emotional impact of aesthetic experience with its disinterestedness.) But Schopenhauer also held that the contemplation of the Platonic ideas of the objectifications of the will in the nonmusical arts or of the will itself in the case of music offers only momentary respite from the painful frustration of the individual will; real relief from phenomenal willing is offered only by ascetic renunciation of one's own desires and compassion with all others, whom one recognizes to be identical with oneself at the ultimate level of reality.

In *The Birth of Tragedy*, Nietzsche transforms the deities Apollo and Dionysos, whom he had already identified in the 1870 lecture as the "god of all image-making energies," of image-makers such as sculptors, and in general "the magnificent divine image of the *principium indivuationis*,[26] on the one hand, and the god of intoxication, orgy, and music,[27] on the other, into images for the distinct realms of rationally organized appearance and arational underlying reality from Schopenhauerian metaphysics, which he had not done in the earlier piece, and then finds art to promise us harmony not within nature but beyond it.[28] As in the earlier work, he sees tragedy as arising from the imposition of the limpid imagery of epic poetry onto the Dionysian or Bacchic rites through the vehicle of the tragic chorus. "Both the sculptor and his relative, the epic poet, are lost in the pure contemplation of images. The Dionysiac musician, with no image at all, is nothing but primal pain and the primal echo of it."[29] They are unified in the tragedy: "At this point our gaze falls on the sublime and exalted art of *Attic tragedy* and the dramatic dithyramb as the common goal of both drives whose mysterious marriage, after a long preceding struggle, was crowned with such a child – who is both Antigone and Cassandra in one"[30] – those two being, of course, paradigmatic figures in Sophoclean and Aeschylean tragedy respectively. In the first instance, it is not the audience for tragedy but the artist who maximally benefits from its creation:

---

[26] Nietzsche, *BT*, §1, pp. 14, 16, and 17.
[27] Nietzsche, *BT*, §1, pp. 14, 17; §2, pp. 19–21.
[28] Although there are still traces of the earlier, more naturalistic assessment of the benefits of art in the opening section of *The Birth of Tragedy*, §1, p. 18. Nietzsche will return to the more naturalistic stance in later works.
[29] Nietzsche, *BT*, §5, p. 30.
[30] Nietzsche, *BT*, §4, p. 28.

> The entire opposition between the subjective and objective (which Schopenhauer ... still uses to divide up the arts, as if it were some criterion of value) is absolutely inappropriate in aesthetics since the subject, the willing individual in pursuit of his own, egotistical goals, can only be considered the opponent of art and not its origin. But where the subject is an artist, it is already released and redeemed from the individual will and has become, as it were a medium, the channel through which the one truly existing subject celebrates its release and redemption in semblance. For what must be clear to us above all ... is that the whole comedy of art is certainly not performed for us, neither for our edification nor our education, just as we are far from truly being the creators of that world of art; however, we may very well assume we are already images and artistic projections for the true creator of art, and that our highest dignity lies in our significance as works of art – for only as an *aesthetic phenomenon* is existence and the world eternally *justified* – although, of course, our awareness of our significance in this respect hardly differs from the awareness which painted soldiers have of the battle depicted on the same canvas. Thus our whole knowledge of art is at bottom entirely illusory, because, as knowing creatures, we are not one and identical with the essential being which gives itself eternal pleasure as the creator and spectator of that comedy of art. Only insofar as the genius, during the act of artistic procreation, merges fully with that original artist of the world does he know anything of the eternal essence of art; for in this condition he resembles, miraculously, that uncanny image of fairy-tale which can turn its eyes around and look at itself; now he is at one and the same time subject and object, simultaneously poet, actor, and spectator.[31]

This passage is remarkably complex. Its latter part characterizes "the act of artistic procreation" as one in which the subject is both fully absorbed in its object and yet still conscious of itself, but without suggesting that this is the essence of aesthetic play, as Nietzsche's earlier lecture had. Its first part rejects Schopenhauer's division of the arts into more subjective and more objective ones, although this might have seemed to be one way of parsing the distinction between Dionysian (more subjective) and Apollonian (more objective) arts; but it does this precisely because it is Nietzsche's view that the true synthesis of the Apollonian and the Dionysian in tragedy overcomes the distinction between subjective and objective by revealing the ultimate identity of the individual with the primordial ground of being – the ultimate aim of Schopenhauerian metaphysics and ethics, after all. But it reserves this experience for the artist, not for the audience, although Schopenhauer had stressed that the artistic genius is one who obtains the metaphysical insight and ethical benefit of art before his audience can but who can also communicate these to

---

[31] Nietzsche, *BT*, §5, pp. 32–3.

his audience. Finally, Nietzsche hints at the idea that in order to flourish, the individual must turn his own life into a work of art, an idea that will be emphasized more in later works.[32]

Without resolving all of the tensions lurking in this passage, Nietzsche subsequently extends the benefit of the experience of tragedy from the artist to his audience, first of all the Greek audience, but then, since this passage actually comes in the transition to his paean for his contemporary palladin, Wagner, to his potential audience, that is, all of us. Here there is no contrast between artist and audience, but all are subsumed in a single "we":

> Dionysiac art ... wants to convince us of the eternal pleasure of existence; but we are to seek this pleasure not in appearances but behind them. We are to recognize that everything that comes into being must be prepared for painful destruction; we are forced to gaze into the terrors of individual existence – and yet we are not to freeze in horror: its metaphysical solace tears us momentarily out of the turmoil of its changing figures. For brief moments we are truly the primordial being itself and we feel its unbounded greed for existence and pleasure in existence; the struggle, the agony, the destruction of appearances, all this now seems to us to be necessary, given the uncountable excess of forms of existence thrusting and pushing themselves into life, given the exuberant fertility of the world-Will; we are pierced by the furious sting of these pains at the very moment when, as it were, we become one with the immeasurable, primordial pleasure in existence and receive an intimation, in Dionysiac ecstasy, that this pleasure is indestructible and eternal. Despite fear and pity, we are happily alive, not as individuals, but as the *one* living being, with whose procreative pleasure we have become one.[33]

Nietzsche's central thought here, indeed his central contribution to the century-old debate about the paradox of tragedy, is that while the depiction of tragic events, all of which he interprets as symbols for the rending of the body of Dionysos by the Titans,[34] might seem painful, it is actually profoundly pleasurable because it intimates our underlying unity with the fertile unity of being that underlies all merely apparent individuality. Or, as he puts it later in this section, "In the old tragedy" – pre-Euripidean, pre-Socratic, that is – "the spectator experienced metaphysical solace, without which it is quite impossible to explain our pleasure in tragedy; the sounds of reconciliation from another world can perhaps be heard at their purest in *Oedipus at Colonus*."[35] This is the basic metaphysical

---

[32] On this see Nehamas, *Nietzsche: Life as Literature*, especially ch. 6.
[33] Nietzsche, *BT*, §17, pp. 80–1.
[34] See Nietzsche, *BT*, §10, p. 52.
[35] Nietzsche, *BT*, §17, p. 84.

claim of Schopenhauer, read back into a specific moment in the history of art.

Even while accepting this core of Schopenhauer's metaphysics, however, Nietzsche makes two key modifications to his master's view. First, for Nietzsche the medium of art that reveals the underlying nature of reality or the Dionysian is not music, as Schopenhauer thought it was, but tragedy, which is born "out of the spirit of music" in the sense that it historically arises from a Greek form of music – the satyr chorus dedicated to the god Dionysos – but also in the sense that it philosophically replaces music within Schopenhauerian aesthetics. But second, for Nietzsche art does not offer a solace from the frustration of the will that needs to be and can be superseded by the genuinely ethical solace of ascetic resignation and compassion; rather, it offers the only but sufficient "metaphysical solace" without any taint of either asceticism or compassion, both of which Nietzsche violently rejected as healthy values throughout his work.[36] This is to say that even at his most Schopenhauerian, Nietzsche replaces Schopenhauer's view that the truly enduring relief of pain can only come through asceticism and compassion, with an even grander claim for joy based solely on metaphysical cognition through art. One might even say that this departure from Schopenhauer happens within the passage before us: at the start of this passage, Nietzsche suggests, like Schopenhauer, that the solace offered by Dionysiac art is only momentary, but by the end of it he suggests that its intimation of our own identity with all existence, which taken as a whole is certainly indestructible though any given piece of it is equally certainly destructible, offers us a pleasure that is "indestructible and eternal." But whether or not Nietzsche holds that the pleasure offered by art is permanent, it is clear that in *The Birth of Tragedy* he does not think that our pleasure in art is only an anticipation of a more permanent pleasure offered by an ethical attitude toward underlying reality; our understanding of our metaphysical identity with reality through Dionysian art is our only source of metaphysical solace.

In Nietzsche's historiography of tragedy, "the tendency of Euripides … was to expel the original and all-powerful Dionysiac element from tragedy and to rebuild tragedy in a new and pure form on the foundations of a non-Dionysiac art, morality, and view of the world,"[37] "putting

---

[36] For Nietzsche's polemic against compassion and asceticism, see *GM*, Part III.
[37] Nietzsche, *BT*, §12, p. 59.

drama on to purely Apolline foundations." The art of Euripides was in turn the exemplification of "*aesthetic Socratism*, whose supreme law runs roughly like this: 'In order to be beautiful, everything must be reasonable' – a sentence formed in parallel to Socrates' dictum that 'Only he who knows is virtuous.' With this canon in his hand, Euripides measured every single element – language, characters, dramatic construction, choral music – and rectified it in accordance with this principle."[38] The scorn dripping from Nietzsche's unusual latinate word "rectified" – *rectificirte* – is palpable. "Socrates is the archetype of the theoretical optimist whose belief that the nature of things can be discovered leads him to attribute to knowledge and understanding the power of a panacea"[39] instead of recognizing that redemption lies only in Dionysian absorption into the one primordial ground of being. Nietzsche then introduces Wagner into his argument by claiming that Wagner "has put his own stamp" on Schopenhauer's "insight, the most important in all aesthetics," that music – but now transformed into true tragedy – "represents *the metaphysical in relation to all that is physical in the world*." Wagner did this by writing, in his essay on Beethoven, "that music is to be assessed by quite different aesthetic criteria from those which apply to all image-making arts, and not at all by the category of beauty," and by inventing, in his *Gesamtkunstwerk*, a wholly new, or renewed, relation of music "to image and concept."[40]

This leads Nietzsche to a remarkable historiography of opera: "Nothing can define the innermost substance of ... Socratic culture more sharply than the *culture of the opera*"[41] as it has been practiced before Wagner, because the essence of pre-Wagnerian ("Alexandrian") opera has been to purchase clarity of word and concept at the cost of the music. "Are we not driven to assume that its idyllic seductions, its Alexandrian arts of flattery, will cause the supreme and truly serious task of art to degenerate into an empty, amusing distraction...? What will become of the eternal truths of the Dionysiac and the Apolline ... where the music is regarded as the servant and the libretto as the master...? – where music is deprived of its true dignity, which consists in being a Dionysiac mirror of the world, so that all that remains to music, as the slave of the world of appearances, is to imitate the forms of the world of appearances and

---

[38] Nietzsche, *BT*, §12, p. 62.
[39] Nietzsche, *BT*, §15, p. 74.
[40] Nietzsche, *BT*, §16, p. 77.
[41] Nietzsche, *BT*, §19, p. 89.

to excite external pleasure in the play of line and proportion."[42] With that last remark, Nietzsche condemns not only opera from "the amusement-hungry luxury of certain circles in Florence"[43] to contemporary Italy and France but also an entire line of aesthetic thought in modern times, from Hutcheson and Hogarth to Gerard and Kant: the aesthetics of play with beautiful form. Through the example of *Tristan and Isolde*, however, Nietzsche argues that in the music of Wagner the Dionysian element in art is finally restored to its rightful place. Nietzsche describes this opera as a struggle between the Apollonian and the Dionysian, in which the Apollonian aspect of the work first "tears us away from Dionysiac generality and causes us to take delight in individuals" and in "compassion" with them, but in which "In the total effect of tragedy the Dionysiac gains the upper hand once more," the opera "closing with a sound which could never issue from the realm of Apolline art. Thereby Apolline deception is revealed for what it is: a persistent veiling, for the duration of the tragedy, of the true Dionysiac effect, an effect so powerful, however, that it finally drives the Apolline drama itself into a sphere where it begins to speak with Dionysian wisdom and where it negates itself and its Apolline visibility."[44] It does this both with its music – no "true musician" could "fail to be shattered" by its third act, "having once put their ear to the heart of the universal Will, so to speak, and felt the raging desire for existence pour forth into all the arteries of the world"[45] – and in its words, ending with the verses "In the surging swell/ Where joys abound/ ... /To drown thus – sink down thus/ – all thought gone – delight alone!"[46] – but with words and music together, not through the former at the expense of the latter. Thus, Nietzsche claims, for the first time since Aeschylus and Sophocles Wagner has produced an art "whose enormous Dionysiac drive ... consumes this entire world of appearances, thereby allowing us to sense, behind that world and through its destruction, a supreme, artistic, primal joy in the womb of the Primordial Unity."[47] Thereby Wagner brings Schopenhauer to the stage, tragedy having originated from the spirit of music and music now being recreated in the spirit of tragedy.

---

[42] Nietzsche, *BT*, §19, p. 93.
[43] Nietzsche, *BT*, §19, p. 89.
[44] Nietzsche, *BT*, §21, pp. 102–4.
[45] Nietzsche, *BT*, §21, p. 100.
[46] Nietzsche quoting Wagner at *BT*, §22, p. 205.
[47] Nietzsche, *BT*, §22, p. 205.

4. NIETZSCHE AFTER *THE BIRTH OF TRAGEDY*

Although art would never again be as central to Nietzsche's thought as it was in *The Birth of Tragedy* – all of Christian morality and Schopenhauer's beloved Vedic asceticism awaited their transvaluation, after all – much of what he did subsequently have to say about art consisted in the repudiation of both the music of Wagner and the metaphysics of Schopenhauer. Nietzsche repudiated Wagner in "The Case of Wagner," written in Turin in 1888 – five years after the death of Wagner, with whom Nietzsche had ultimately broken after seeing the spectacle of Wagner's self-deification at Bayreuth in 1876, but *against* whom he perhaps could never have so openly turned while his one-time patron was still alive. Always an enthusiast, however, Nietzsche turned against Wagner and *Tristan* by replacing him with new idols, Bizet and *Carmen*, which he first saw in Genoa in 1881[48] and which he claimed to have seen twenty times by 1888.[49] Nietzsche writes of *Carmen*: "This music seems perfect to me. It approaches lightly, supplely, politely. It is amiable, it does not *sweat*. 'All good things are light, everything divine runs along on delicate feet': first principle of my aesthetics.... Has anyone noticed that music" – *this* music, that is – "makes the spirit *free*? gives wings to thought? that you become more of a philosopher, the more of a musician you become? – The grey sky of abstraction illuminated as if by lightning; the light strong enough for the whole filigree of things."[50] The "orchestral timbre" of Wagner, on the other hand, is "brutal, artificial, ... harmful."[51] "*Does Wagner liberate the spirit?*" Quite the contrary, "he wages war on *us*, us free spirits! How his magic-maiden tones pander to every type of cowardice in the modern soul! – There was never such a *deadly hatred* of knowledge! – You need to be a cynic to stop being seduced here, you need to be able to bite in order to stop worshipping here."[52] This comes after some sarcastic parodies of Wagner's characters and plots, reminiscent of Tolstoy's attack upon opera a few years later, but makes a point that at least some feel in listening to Wagner: beautiful as the music may be, it is also manipulative, the *Gesamtkunstwerk* designed to employ all of the arts of stage and pit not in order to free the imagination of the audience but to ensure that they respond precisely and only as the composer intends, seducing

---

[48] Hollingdale, *Nietzsche*, p. 130.
[49] Nietzsche, *AC*, p. 234.
[50] Nietzsche, "The Case of Wagner," *AC*, pp. 234–5.
[51] Nietzsche, "The Case of Wagner," *AC*, pp. 234–5.
[52] Nietzsche, "The Case of Wagner," *AC*, p. 257.

them rather than liberating them. Nietzsche's critique may have had its origin in his revulsion against his earlier domination by Richard Wagner the man, but raises an objection against his music that resonates with at least some listeners.

Of course, this sea change in Nietzsche's view of Wagner goes with a sea change in his view of art: the point of art is not to absorb all its audience into one primordial being, to offer them, so to speak, the negative freedom of liberation from self, but rather to free those who are capable of being so to be themselves. The repudiation of the music of Wagner thus goes with a repudiation of the metaphysics of Schopenhauer. Nietzsche repudiated the metaphysical interpretation of art in *Human, All Too Human* in 1878, long before he was ready to formalize his break with Wagner. In the section of the work entitled "From the Souls of Artists and Writers," he recognizes the overwhelming attraction of attributing metaphysical meaning to art, but says that the test of "intellectual probity" for the "free spirit" – though it is not clear whether this refers to artist, audience, philosopher, or all of these – is the ability to withstand this temptation:

> *Art makes the thinker's heart heavy.* – How strong the metaphysical need is, and how hard nature makes it to bid it a final farewell, can be seen from the fact that even when the free spirit has divested himself of everything metaphysical the highest effects of art can easily set the metaphysical strings ... vibrating in sympathy; so it can happen, for example, that a passage in Beethoven's Ninth Symphony will make him feel he is hovering above the earth in a dome of stars with the dream of *immortality* in his heart ... – If he becomes aware of being in this condition he feels a profound stab in the heart and sighs for the man who will lead him back to his lost love, whether she be called religion or metaphysics. It is in such moments that his intellectual probity is put to the test.[53]

The interpretation of the greatest art as revealing Dionysian truth beneath Apollonian imagery had not promised personal immortality, to be sure, but had offered a substitute for it in the absorption of the individual in the greater unity of primordial being, and now Nietzsche rejects that.

Of course, that raises the question of what the value of art might be instead, and Nietzsche answers that by maintaining that art shows how individuals may affirm life and find joy within it without demoting the natural, spatio-temporal world to mere appearance and seeking solace in identification with a supposed reality beyond it:

[53] Nietzsche, *HAH*, Vol. I, Part 4, §153, p. 82.

What is left of art. – It is true, certain metaphysical presuppositions bestow much greater value on art, for example, when it is believed that the character is unalterable and that all characters and actions are a continual expression of the nature of the world: then the work of the artist becomes an image of the *everlastingly steadfast* ... The same would be so in the case of another metaphysical presupposition: supposing our visible world would come to stand quite close to the real world, for there would then be only too much similarity between the world of appearance and the illusory world of the artist; and the difference remaining would even elevate the significance of art above the significance of nature ... – These presuppositions are, however, false: after this knowledge what place still remains for art? Above all, it has taught us for thousands of years to look upon life in any of its forms with interest and pleasure, and to educate our sensibilities so that at last we cry: "life, however it may be, is good!"[54] –

a line that comes from Goethe's poem *"Der Bräutigam"* ("The Bridegroom"), *"Wie es auch sei, das Leben, es ist Gut"* ("However life is, it is good"), but that also perhaps looks forward to Nietzsche's later use of the idea of "eternal recurrence" as a test of how you live your life: have you lived your life to the fullest, so that you would be able to will its eternal recurrence even with all of its pains, knowing that those are the necessary price for the joys you have created for yourself?[55] However, Nietzsche does not expand upon how art may teach us to find interest and pleasure in all forms of life in *Human, All Too Human*. Indeed, in the second volume that he added in 1886 he suggests that it might be embarrassing for poets to pretend to be "teachers of adults" in the modern age,[56] and then adds that in order to "reach out" for the art of such wise artists as "Homer, Sophocles, Theocritus, Calderón, Racine, Goethe" we – the audience – "must already have grown wiser and more harmonious."[57] In other words, instead of accepting Schiller's theory of aesthetic education, that aesthetic experience is the only route to a harmonious life, he seems to consider the reverse, that only a life that is independently harmonious allows for the appreciation of great art.

However, a few key passages in *The Gay Science*, four years after the first volume of *Human, All Too Human*, suggest that although Nietzsche would become critical of the traditional German ideal of aesthetic education,

---

[54] Nietzsche, *HAH*, Vol. I, Part 4, §222, p. 105.
[55] For this approach to the eternal recurrence, see Nehamas, *Nietzsche: Life as Literature*, ch. 5, "This Life – Your Eternal Life," pp. 142–69. For a more traditional approach that sees eternal recurrence as a fact about temporal reality rather than a purely normative idea, see Hollingdale, *Nietzsche*, pp. 164–7.
[56] Nietzsche, *HAH*, Vol. II, Part I, "Assorted Opinions and Maxims," §172, p. 254.
[57] Nietzsche, *HAH*, Vol. II, Part 1, §173, p. 254.

he was willing to consider that the idea of free play might be a way to bring out the continuity between aesthetic experience and what he had come to recognize as the greatest aim of life and of his transvaluation of all values, the development of individual freedom and creativity. One passage in this 1882 work, halfway between Nietzsche's early adulation of Wagner and his later repudiation of him, calls for us to "remain faithful to Wagner in what is *true* and original in him." "It doesn't matter that as a thinker he is so often wrong," Nietzsche continues:

> Enough that his life is justified before itself and remains justified – this life which shouts at every one of us: "Be a man and do not follow me – but yourself! Yourself!" Our life, too, shall be justified before ourselves! We too shall freely and fearlessly, in innocent selfishness, grow and blossom from ourselves![58]

Nietzsche then concludes this Book of *The Gay Science* with an expression of "*Our ultimate gratitude to art*" in which he argues that art's imagination of better possibilities for human life is a necessary complement to the scientific investigation of the failures of human will – this is how he is now characterizing an essential part of his own work – and then suggests that these better possibilities are to be understood precisely as forms of play. He writes:

> *Honesty* would lead to nausea and suicide. But now our honesty has a counterforce that helps us avoid such consequences: art, as the *good* will to appearance. We do not always keep our eyes from rounding off, from finishing off the poem ... As an aesthetic phenomenon existence is still *bearable* to us, and art furnishes us with the eye and hand and above all the good conscience to be *able* to make such a phenomenon of ourselves. At times we need to have a rest from ourselves by looking at and down at ourselves and, from an artistic distance, laughing *at* ourselves or crying *at* ourselves ... And precisely because we are at bottom grave and serious human beings and more weights than human beings, nothing does us as much good as the *fool's cap*: we need it against ourselves – we need all exuberant, floating, dancing, mocking, childish, and blissful art lest we lose that *freedom over things* that our idea demands of us. It would be a *relapse* for us, with our irritable honesty, to get completely caught up in morality and, for the sake of the overly severe demands that we there make on ourselves, to become virtuous monsters and scarecrows. We also have to *be able* to stand *above* morality and not just to stand with the anxious stiffness of someone who is afraid of slipping and falling at any moment, but also to float and play above it! How then could we possibly do without art, without the fool?[59]

---

[58] Nietzsche, *GS*, Book Two, §100, p. 97.
[59] Nietzsche, *GS*, Book Two, §107, pp. 104–5 (translation modified).

Here Nietzsche clearly lowers some of his earlier hopes for art by suggesting that the "aesthetic phenomenon" will make life *bearable* for us rather than *justifying* it. He also suggests one addition to such earlier ideas as Du Bos's "artificial emotion," Mendelssohn's idea of distance, and Kames's "ideal presence": we do not just need a degree of distance from the *objects* of drama or other depiction in order to be able to enjoy rather than be pained by emotional response to them; rather, we need a certain degree of distance *on ourselves* in order not to take ourselves too seriously, more specifically in order not to take the constraints of conventional morality to which it is so easy for us all to subscribe, and thereby have the freedom to create, presumably not merely new works of art (that would make the means into the end), but new, more fulfilling ways of life. This can also be seen as a subtle response to Schopenhauer: the point of aesthetic experience is not simply to free ourselves from our individuality, but rather to free ourselves from the constraints that we ourselves accept that block our creativity. Nietzsche also distances himself from Kant's aesthetics in his next and last major work, *The Genealogy of Morality*, when he accuses Kant's aesthetics of being an aesthetics entirely for spectators "instead of viewing the aesthetic through the experiences of the artist (the creator)," that is, of treating aesthetic experience as a contemplative, passive experience rather than a creative one – and he there charges Schopenhauer as still being, in spite of standing "much closer to the arts than Kant," unable to "break free of the spell of Kant's definition."[60]

In spite of this hint at a renewed interest in the idea of play as the key to aesthetic experience and its larger significance in our lives, as an indication of the possibility of creating our own lives as artists would create their works of art, Nietzsche does not further develop the concept of play. Instead, in the *Genealogy of Morality*, he uses the opportunity to take another swipe at the metaphysical pretensions of artists in general and of Wagner in particular:

> Let us put aside artists for the time being: their position in the world and *against* the world is far from sufficiently independent for their changing evaluations *as such* to merit our attention! Down the ages, they have been the valets of a morality or philosophy or religion: quite apart from the fact that they were, unfortunately, often the all-too-glib courtiers of their hangers-on and patrons and sycophants ... At the very least, they always need a defender, a supporter, an already established authority ... So, for example, Richard Wagner took the philosopher Schopenhauer as his front man, his defender.[61]

[60] Nietzsche, *GM* III, §6, p. 74.
[61] Nietzsche, *GM* III, §5, p. 72.

Having backed off from his original metaphysical interpretation of art in *Human, All Too Human* and having suggested the possibility in *The Gay Science* that creative play in art might be a model for human creativity in general, in his final works Nietzsche remained torn between the idea that art can be a genuine form of free play, as he suggests in his appreciation of *Carmen* in "The Case of Wagner," and that art cannot escape the domination of metaphysics, as he holds in *The Genealogy of Morals*.

For the most part, then, Nietzsche continued the cognitivist approach to aesthetic experience that dominated the nineteenth century, although after his earliest work he rejected the value of the metaphysical cognition to which, in his view, art pretends. A renewed and fuller analysis of aesthetic experience as a form of play, as well as a renewed and developed appreciation of the value of such a form of experience, would largely have to wait for others. In the following chapters, we will see that there were some among Nietzsche's contemporaries who did do more with the idea of play, for example Wilhelm Dilthey among the Neo-Kantians and Herbert Spencer and Karl Groos among more naturalistic philosophers. Before we turn to these philosophers and their contexts, however, we will take a brief look at another heir to Schopenhauer and a close contemporary of Nietzsche, Eduard von Hartmann.

5. VON HARTMANN

Von Hartmann (1842–1906) came from a Prussian military family, but his own career in the officer corps was cut short at the age of twenty-three by injury. He then turned to philosophy, earning a Ph.D. at Rostock at twenty-five, and at age twenty-seven he published *The Philosophy of the Unconscious*, which quickly became a best seller.[62] This work was deeply influenced by Schopenhauer but also by Schelling, and postulated an unconscious will as the underlying, absolute reality beneath appearances; von Hartmann differed from Schopenhauer, however, in arguing that the collective exercise of human reason rather than individual asceticism was the only path toward salvation – not that human reason could mediate the suffering brought on by the will, but that it could reveal the ultimate insignificance of it and thus release the human species from its so to speak second-order concern over its suffering. The details of

---

[62] Eduard von Hartmann, *Philosophie des Unbewußten: Versuch einer Weltanschauung* (Berlin, C. Duncker, 1869); *Philosophy of the Unconscious*, trans. William Chatterton Coupland, 3 vols. (New York: Macmillan, 1884).

this now largely forgotten book, however, need not detain us, as von Hartmann wrote numerous other works, some of which are still of considerable interest independently of his cosmic pessimism. These include a *Phenomenology of Moral Consciousness: Prolegomena to Any Future Ethics* (1879), in which von Hartmann argues that morality must be based on feeling, not reason (that Kant is a target of the work is of course indicated by the echo of Kant's own *Prolegomena to Any Future Metaphysics* in von Hartmann's subtitle), yet not, as in Schopenhauer, on the single feeling of compassion, but on a range of feelings and drives including feelings for piety, truthfulness, love, and duty as well as for sympathy,[63] and a two-part work in aesthetics, a history of *German Aesthetics since Kant* and a systematic *Philosophy of the Beautiful*, both originally published in 1887.[64] Von Hartmann's aesthetic theory hovers between the metaphysical aesthetics of German idealism and the reemerging aesthetics of feeling of the late nineteenth century, but in both moods remains well within the tradition of the aesthetics of truth rather than the aesthetics of play.

Von Hartmann begins his theory of beauty in a Kantian mood, starting from Kant's initial analysis of our pleasure in beauty as an immediate pleasure in the representation of objects rather than pleasure in the use of actual objects or, for that matter, pleasure in actual empirical cognition of the external world obtained through the representation of objects. "The aesthetic attitude [*Verhalten*] toward subjective appearance is distinguished primarily and specifically from the theoretical and practical attitudes towards the same thing by the fact that it entirely abstracts from the transsubjective reality that causally grounds the subjective appearance, and satisfies itself with the appearance as such, as long as it is beautiful."[65] Going beyond Kant, however, von Hartmann adds that aesthetic *Schein* or appearances produces *Scheingefühle*, or apparent feelings and emotions, which must be merely apparent or "aesthetically-ideal" in order to satisfy Kant's premise that "all enjoyment of the beautiful must be really disinterested satisfaction."[66] Von Hartmann does not seem troubled by the question of why we should take pleasure in merely apparent feelings, for he does not consider these apparent feelings to be causes of

---

[63] Selected chapters of this work have been reprinted as Eduard von Hartmann, *Die Gefühlsmoral*, ed. Jean-Claude Wolf (Hamburg: Felix Meiner Verlag, 2006).
[64] Eduard von Hartmann, *Die deutsche Aesthetik seit Kant: Erster historisch-kritischer Theil der Aesthetik* (Leipzig: Wilhelm Friedrich, n.d.), and *Die Philosophie des Schönen: Zweiter systematischer Theil der Aesthetik*, *Ausgewählte Werke*, second edition, vol. IV (Leipzig: Hermann Haacke, n.d.).
[65] Von Hartmann, *Philosophie des Schönen*, p. 12.
[66] Von Hartmann, *Philosophie des Schönen*, p. 41.

aesthetic pleasure; rather, their chief effect is to concentrate our attention on the properties of the appearance or *Schein* of the aesthetic object itself, and it is the latter that is the source of our pleasure in beauty. "The aesthetic appearance that has been enriched and fulfilled with the reflection of the aesthetic apparent feelings is thus the seat or the carrier of beauty; it is that which is enjoyed as beautiful by the aesthetic subject who is apprehending it." The feeling of pleasure in the beautiful object thus enriched is itself real, von Hartmann emphasizes, not apparent: "This aesthetic enjoyment is evidently a real feeling of pleasure, no ideal apparent feeling like those that are called forth by the aesthetic appearance as it is first given through perception of the product of fantasy."[67] It seems to be just an empirical fact that we are pleased by the contemplation of the appearances of objects enriched by the appearances of the feelings that such objects would induce in us if they were real. Von Hartmann makes no mention of the play of our cognitive or imaginative powers with such appearances, so it seems as if our pleasure in them is cognitive: we are just pleased to know how things look and feel. This, as we will see in the next chapter, was to become a widespread view among the aestheticians of the late nineteenth and early twentieth centuries, many of whom attempted to subsume the aesthetics of feeling into the aesthetics of truth while ignoring the aesthetics of play altogether.

However, von Hartmann does not leave matters there; he subsequently says that this first level of his account of our pleasure in the beautiful is "merely empirical," and has not yet "concerned itself with the causal explanation" of beauty.[68] Here, in a section of his chapter on "The Place of the Beautiful in the World-Whole" entitled "The significance and the value of the beautiful for the conscious spirit" is where, as his titles suggests, he turns back toward the metaphysical aesthetics of German idealism. He first claims, using language adopted from Schopenhauer, that if we confine ourselves to truths about "the real world of individuation," then there will seem to be no connection between beauty and truth at all, indeed, beauty will seem to be just "an *hors d'oeuvre*" before the main course of truth, a mere "calculation of the playing fantasy"[69] – here is a rare place where he speaks of play, but he speaks of it in what is evidently a derogatory way. Rather, he next argues, the real ground of our pleasure in beauty is that beauty reveals to us in the microcosm of a single

---

[67] Von Hartmann, *Philosophie des Schönen*, pp. 64–5.
[68] Von Hartmann, *Philosophie des Schönen*, p. 486.
[69] Von Hartmann, *Philosophie des Schönen*, p. 436.

appearance the truth of our connection to the macrocosm, even if only evanescently:

> As an objective-real individual of appearance the subject is really separated from the absolute spirit, and it feels itself as an individual self-consciousness existentially divorced from that, although it remains immanent to it as the unconscious ground of being. But in its surrender to the beautiful the subject feels the annulment of this divorce, and feels itself phenomenally restored to unity with the absolute spirit through the aesthetic appearance of the idea, even if this *restitutio in integrum* is merely a psychological illusion, which will disappear again with the end of the aesthetic act.
>
> All objective real appearances present themselves to the subject as something alien, first and foremost as something hostile ... Only the pure appearance of the beautiful is an object with which, when the transcendental relation to a transcendental reality falls away, all alienness, potential enmity, and real opposition against the subject is also removed, and it is thereby made possible for the subject to forget its opposition to the object and by means of the aesthetic apparent feelings and the real aesthetic pleasure to be drawn entirely to and into it.[70]

Here von Hartmann draws on Schelling in conceiving of aesthetic experience as a moment in which the subject pleasurably realizes its identity rather than difference with the object rather than on Schopenhauer, who held that in aesthetic experience the subject simply forgets its own identity and is thus freed from the pain of the ever immanent frustration of its will, although he had earlier, at the merely empirical stage of his account, agreed with Schopenhauer that one loses one's sense of one's own identity in aesthetic experience.[71] But he also agrees with Schopenhauer here that the pleasure in the metaphysical recognition of the identity of self and object in aesthetic experience is evanescent, lasting only as long as the aesthetic experience itself lasts, and in this he differs from the Nietzsche of *The Birth of Tragedy*, who had not suggested that the aesthetic justification afforded by our insight into the Dionysian beneath the Apollonian is necessarily fleeting. Neither for von Hartmann nor for Schopenhauer is aesthetic experience a permanent solution to the problem of human existence.

Von Hartmann's metaphysical aesthetics thus looks back to the idealism of a half-century before, and was not the aspect of his work that was to be developed or at least echoed in the four following decades. His language in the last paragraphs cited anticipates the existential aesthetics

---

[70] Von Hartmann, *Philosophie des Schönen*, pp. 487–8.
[71] Von Hartmann, *Philosophie des Schönen*, pp. 33–5.

propounded by Martin Heidegger a half-century later, however. So, as we turn to the aesthetics of feeling developed by both Neo-Kantians and others from the time of von Hartmann until the 1920s, we should keep in mind that the aesthetics of truth still present in his work by no means died out with it, but would return with a vengeance.

9

Neo-Kantian Aesthetics

Neo-Kantianism "officially" began with the command, or plea, "Back to Kant!" issued by the twenty-five-year-old Otto Liebmann, subsequently professor of philosophy at Strassburg and Jena, in 1865. But what this call meant is far from simple.[1] The import of the plea must be understood in its historical context, where the authority of Kant was to be used to criticize both the speculative, "absolute" idealism of Fichte, Schelling, and Hegel that had immediately followed Kant as well as the attempt to ground philosophy on empirical psychology by Gustav Theodor Fechner, Hermann von Helmholtz, and others that had been a previous response to post-Kantian idealism.[2] However, while it might have been expected that a Neo-Kantian movement in aesthetics would develop Kant's synthesis of the aesthetics of truth and the aesthetics of

---

[1] There is little literature on Neo-Kantianism, and what there is has even less to say about aesthetics in Neo-Kantianism. For a work on the development of Neo-Kantianism but only up to 1881, see Klaus Christian Köhnke, *Entstehung und Aufsteig des Neukantianismus: Die deutsche Universitätsphilosophie zwischen Idealismus und Positivismus* (Frankfurt am Main: Suhrkamp, 1986) (the English translation, *The Rise of Neo-Kantianism: German Academic Philosophy between Idealism and Positivism*, by R.J. Hollingdale [Cambridge: Cambridge University Press, 1991], cannot be recommended because, remarkably, it omitted all the endnotes of the original); Thomas E. Willey, *Back to Kant: The Revival of Kantianism in German Social and Historical Thought, 1860–1914* (Detroit: Wayne State University Press, 1978), covers a longer period, but is restricted to the topics indicated by its subtitle; Christopher Adair-Toteff, "Neo-Kantianism: The German Idealism Movement," in Thomas Baldwin, editor, *The Cambridge History of Philosophy 1870–1945* (Cambridge: Cambridge University Press, 2003), pp. 27–42, provides a brief orientation; and Rudolf A. Makkreel and Sebastian Luft, "Dilthey and the Neo-Kantians: The Dispute over the Status of the Human and Cultural Sciences," in Dean Moyar, editor, *The Routledge Companion to Nineteenth Century Philosophy* (London: Routledge, 2010), pp. 554–97, focuses on the differences between Dilthey and the other Neo-Kantians.

[2] See Andrea Poma, *The Critical Philosophy of Hermann Cohen*, trans. John Denton (Albany: State University of New York Press, 1997), pp. 1–4.

play and perhaps find a way to add recognition of the emotional impact of art and nature on to Kant's own theory of aesthetic ideas, that is not what initially happened in Neo-Kantianism. Instead, certainly the first great Neo-Kantian, Hermann Cohen, the leader of the Marburg school, retained the outlines of Kant's analysis of judgments of taste but dropped his explanation of the pleasure that underlies such judgments as the product of the free play of imagination and understanding; he then recognized the importance of emotions in aesthetic experience, but framed that recognition within an essentially cognitivist approach to aesthetic experience, finding the essence of aesthetic experience to be cognition of the nature of human feelings through art. He thus rejected the speculative metaphysics of Hegelian aesthetics, but retained a cognitivist approach by making human emotions themselves the object of aesthetic cognition. Jonas Cohn, a figure not from the first but from the second generation of the other main school of Neo-Kantianism, the Heidelberg or Southwest school founded by Wilhelm Windelband, made the communication of emotion central to his in this regard deeply un-Kantian aesthetic theory, and in this way came closer to recognizing the experience rather than merely the cognition of emotions as an essential part of aesthetic experience. Following our discussion of Cohn, we will consider another figure associated with the Southwest school of Neo-Kantianism, Hugo Münsterberg, who developed his own aesthetics on the basis of a Kantian idea not used by the others, namely the idea of apperception. However, among Neo-Kantians it was only the more independent and eclectic Berlin philosopher Wilhelm Dilthey, influenced as much by Schleiermacher as by Kant, who would find room for the idea of free play in his version of a Neo-Kantian aesthetics.

In the tradition of Karl Philipp Moritz, the founder of the journal for "experiential psychology," Dilthey would wrap his aesthetics – or more precisely, his poetics, since he focused his attention on literary art – in the mantle of "experience" (*Erlebnis*), but he was at pains to distinguish his approach from that of the experimental psychologists of the time who applied their methods to the case of aesthetic preferences, namely Fechner and Helmholtz. So we will begin this chapter with a glance at an example of this approach, namely the aesthetics of Fechner. In the following chapter, we examine the broader movement toward psychological aesthetics that took place outside of the framework of Neo-Kantianism. There we will see how Friedrich Theodor Vischer's idea of empathy interacted with a revival of the concept of play.

1. FECHNER

Thus we begin with a glance at the transitional figure of Gustav Theodor Fechner (1801–87), who would become a target for Wilhelm Dilthey. Fechner was appointed professor of physics at Leipzig at the age of thirty-three, although ironically had to give up that position five years later because of eye problems; after a period of recuperation, he resumed a life of lecturing and writing. He is best remembered for his research into "psychophysics," or the physics of perception, summed up in his *Elements of Psychophysics* (1860). From early in his career, he also wrote speculative works about the mind and its place in nature, including *The Little Book on Life after Death* (1836), *Nanna, or the Soul of Plants* (1848), and *Zend-Avesta, or on the Things in Heaven and Beyond* (1851). In aesthetics, he took over the title used earlier by Jean Paul and published a *Preschool for Aesthetics* (*Vorschule der Ästhetik*) in 1876. In this work, he criticized the aesthetics "from above" of the German idealists, which subsumes the "domain of experience" under "ideal frames" characterized by conceptions of the "absolute" and "divine creativity," and insisted that aesthetics must begin "from below," with an empirical investigation of the "laws" of pleasure and displeasure and through that of the "objective essence of beauty," although, in line with his speculative as well as empirical bent, he did not reject speculative aesthetics out of hand but rather expressed the expectation that ultimately – not in his "preschool" – they can be brought together, aesthetics "from above" describing the goals that can be fulfilled by aesthetics "from below."[3] But he also criticized the work of the eighteenth-century British aestheticians – he mentions especially Hutcheson, Hogarth, and Burke – whom one might have thought he would have claimed as forerunners, as too "particular" and "unorganized" to carry much weight.[4]

However, although Fechner made genuine advances in psychological technique, developing methods for testing preferences by having subjects compare samples rather than just asking them about their response, there is nothing in the content of his empirical aesthetics that was not already known to the eighteenth century. He promulgated two introductory principles – one that our perception of potentially beautiful properties must rise to a certain "threshold" before we will take pleasure in them and the other that different aesthetic properties may "help" or

---

[3] Gustav Theodor Fechner, *Vorschule der Aesthetik*, second edition, 2 vols. (Leipzig: Breitkopf & Härtel, 1925; reprinted Hildesheim: Georg Olms, 1978), vol. I, pp. v, 1–2.
[4] Fechner, *Vorschule*, vol. I, pp. 2–3.

"intensify" each other, or that the sum of an aesthetic effect of a whole is greater than the sum of the effects its parts would have if experienced separately.[5] He promoted three "primary" principles – that beautiful objects please in virtue of the "unity of the manifold" of our perception of them, the "truth" or freedom from contradiction of our perception, and the "clarity" of our perception.[6] And he held one final principle, the "principle of association," according to which a large part of the pleasurable effect of an aesthetic object depends on its associations, the recollections it causes, and the like.[7] He uses the example of a table for one illustration of the effect of associations: we do not just perceive a table as a rectangular surface a few feet above the floor, rather we cannot but perceive it as a gathering place, a place where we have enjoyed meals or work, or not, as the case may be: "we see it not just with a sensible but with a spiritual [*geistigen*] eye."[8] Our associations with the object do not present themselves to us discretely, though, but coalesce together with the more formal properties of the object picked out by the previous three principles to form a single, conscious impression of the object, pleasing or not as the case may be. Fechner goes on to enumerate a variety of types of association that may contribute to the aesthetic effect of the perception of an object: associations of color, of space and/or time, of situation, and more,[9] but, he argues, it is "the human being as the center of associations" that is the largest factor in our pleasure or displeasure in an object: whatever is the "natural expression of human mood, passion, intellectual and moral quality" is foremost among our associations with an object. For example, the overturning of a tree by wind or racing clouds are interpreted in human terms, and "many natural sounds owe their impression entirely to such associations."[10] Poetry works primarily with associations,[11] and "fantasy" – Fechner does not use the term "imagination" – works with associations but does not create new ones: "the circle of associative moments is the room for play [*Spielraum*] within which only it can move."[12] Fechner's conception of room for play here is passive rather than active, confining rather than liberating; he nowhere uses

---

[5] Fechner, *Vorschule*, vol. I, pp. 46, 49, 51.
[6] Fechner, *Vorschule*, vol. I, pp. 53, 80, 82.
[7] Fechner, *Vorschule*, vol. I, p. 86.
[8] Fechner, *Vorschule*, vol. I, p. 93.
[9] Fechner, *Vorschule*, vol. I, pp. 96–100.
[10] Fechner, *Vorschule*, vol. I, p. 108.
[11] Fechner, *Vorschule*, vol. I, p. 109.
[12] Fechner, *Vorschule*, vol. I, p. 112.

the term "play" as part of a positive account of the source of our pleasure in aesthetic experience. But Fechner's conception of association does recognize the emotional dimension of aesthetic experience.

Fechner claims that his principles have been confirmed by his empirical investigations with human subjects, but there is nothing original about them. No one in the eighteenth century formulated his preliminary principles of "threshhold" and "intensification," but neither would any eighteenth-century aesthetician have objected to them. The principles of unity, truth, and clarity were well known to both British and German aestheticians in the eighteenth century, although grounded in tradition and introspection rather than in any formal method of interrogating subjects in a laboratory setting. Fechner claimed no special originality for his principle of association, acknowledging that it had been anticipated by Kames and Lotze[13] but surprisingly not mentioning Archibald Alison, who clearly had already argued precisely that our emotional responses to human qualities are the primary source of our associations with aesthetic objects in general – Alison, who did not know the German philosophy of his own century, seems to have been repaid by being ignored in Germany in the next century. Fechner blames Kant's preference for "free" over "adherent" beauty for discrediting emotional associations in aesthetic experience in German thought, and claims that Schelling and Hegel were completely ignorant of it. This is only partially fair to all three. Kant did not say that the experience of free beauty is more important than that of adherent beauty, only that it is "purer," and in particular in his explicit theory of fine art, which Fechner does not consider, he made moral associations central to the experience of artistic beauty, indeed to the experience of all beauty, through his theory of "aesthetic ideas." To be sure, he did reject "charm" and "emotion" as core elements of the experience of beauty in the "Analytic of the Beautiful,"[14] and thus suppressed the undeniable fact that the moral ideas that are conveyed through "aesthetic ideas" are obviously associated with powerful emotions. And it would seem fairer to say that Schelling and Hegel give little weight to the ordinary emotional associations of things in their own accounts of the experience of beauty than to assert that they denied it altogether; at least Schelling's image of aesthetic experience is fraught with the emotional associations we are supposed to have toward the metaphysical character of human existence.

---

[13] Fechner, *Vorschule*, vol. I, p. 86.
[14] Kant, *CPJ*, §13.

Fechner's claim to originality is thus belied by the previous history of aesthetics, and his empirical methods seem only to confirm what had been described by many authors a century before. Fechner's principle of association could have opened the door to a greater recognition of the importance of emotions as part of aesthetic experience than had been allowed by Kant or German Idealism, but that was not the immediate response to his work. While Fechner stressed the pleasure or displeasure that we take in an object because of its emotional associations, he did not argue that aesthetic experience is at its core nothing less than the cognition of emotions themselves. But Neo-Kantian aesthetics would continue to be dominated by the aesthetics of truth, although the aesthetics of truth turned inward: by most authors, aesthetic experience and art would not be seen as vehicles for metaphysical insight, but as vehicles for insight into the nature of human emotions. Fechner put human emotions back onto the table of aesthetic experience, but he did not anticipate the particular role they would play in the aesthetic schools that would follow his own "preschool."

2. COHEN

The approach to aesthetic experience as a medium for the cognition of human emotions begins with the Neo-Kantian movement in Germany. In the spirit of Kant, the Neo-Kantians attempted to develop accounts of the fundamental, *a priori* principles of the main forms of human thought that did not assert that these principles give us insight into some transhuman reality and yet did not reduce them to empirically discoverable principles of human cognitive and conative psychology. But the Neo-Kantians did not feel compelled to stick closely to the letter of the philosophy of the historical Kant (although it was due to the impetus of the Neo-Kantian movement that the foundations of modern Kant scholarship were laid, including the commencement of the critical edition of Kant, the *Akademie* edition,[15] under the leadership of some of the Neo-Kantians, such as Wilhelm Dilthey and Wilhelm Windelband, whose own uses of Kant certainly departed considerably from the letter of Kant's philosophy), and they often developed approaches and arguments that differed considerably from Kant's own.

[15] *Kant's gesammlte Schriften*, edited by the Royal Prussian (later German, now Berlin-Brandenburg) Academy of Sciences (Berlin: Georg Reimer, later Walter de Gruyter & Co., 1900 –), 29 volumes (volume 26 currently incomplete, and others currently under revision).

This was certainly the case in aesthetics. Perhaps surprisingly, given the interest of all of the main schools of Neo-Kantianism in developing a general philosophy of human culture, few of the leading figures in the movement devoted much of their efforts to aesthetics, although aesthetics was a central field in German philosophy throughout the nineteenth century. But the leader of the "Marburg" school of Neo-Kantianism, Hermann Cohen (1842–1918) did, devoting one of his three books on Kant's philosophy to *Kants Begründung der Aesthetik*[16] ("Kant's founding of aesthetics") and one of the three multi-volumed books of his own philosophical system to an *Ästhetik des reinen Gefühls*[17] ("aesthetics of pure feeling"). And while neither of the leaders of the "Baden," "Heidelberg," or "Southwestern" school of Neo-Kantianism, Wilhelm Windelband and Heinrich Rickert, devoted either an historical or a systematic book to aesthetics, one of the significant figures of the second generation of Southwestern Neo-Kantianism, Jonas Cohn (1869–1947), published an *Allgemeine Ästhetik* ("general aesthetics") in 1901 that purported to approach the subject on Kantian lines and that may be regarded as the main treatise on aesthetics from this school,[18] while Hugo Münsterberg (1863–1916), as much a psychologist as a philosopher, also published works on aesthetics both before and after his permanent move to the United States in 1897. Cohen, Cohn, and Münsterberg all made independent use of certain key, but different, elements of Kant's aesthetics at crucial points in their own work. But they arrived at views that are very different from Kant's own, although similar in their most basic ideas not only to each other but also to other leading approaches to aesthetics in the late nineteenth and early twentieth centuries that were developed independently of Kantian premises. The common approach to aesthetics developed by Cohen, Cohn, and Münsterberg in spite of differences between their schools of Neo-Kantianism and their particular starting points in Kant can certainly be considered as an alternative to the speculative, metaphysical aesthetics of Schelling and Hegel on the one hand[19] and to the psychological aesthetics of Fechner and Helmholtz on the other, but their approach reflects the general tendency of aesthetics in their own times as much as Kant's own intentions. This is by no means to

---

[16] Hermann Cohen, *Kants Begründung der Aesthetik* (Berlin: Ferd. Dümmlers Verlagsbuchhandlung, 1889).
[17] Hermann Cohen, *Ästhetik des reinen Gefühls*, 2 vols. (Berlin: Bruno Cassirer, 1912).
[18] Jonas Cohn, *Allgemeine Ästhetik* (Leipzig: Wilhelm Engelmann, 1901).
[19] On the speculative or metaphysical turn of aesthetics after Kant, see Schaeffer, *Art of the Modern Age*, chs. 2–3.

deny the interest or importance of their approach; on the contrary, their work, along with the related and now better-known work of such slightly later figures as Edward Bullough and R.G. Collingwood, may constitute an enduring contribution to the field of aesthetics. But that approach should definitely be considered a supplement to the enduringly important ideas of Kant, not an interpretation of them.

We begin our discussion of Neo-Kantian aesthetics with Hermann Cohen, in particular with his commentary on *Kants Begründung der Aesthetik* rather than on his subsequent, more systematic *Ästhetik des reinen Gefühls*, as the earlier work lays down the central themes of the latter while also revealing how Cohen managed to transform Kant's original theory to his own purposes.[20]

Hermann Cohen (1842–1918) was the most significant Jewish philosopher in Germany since Moses Mendelssohn, and the first to hold a prominent university professorship. He studied at the gymnasium in Dessau, Mendelssohn's home town, at the Jewish Theological Seminary in Breslau, and at the German universities of Breslau, Berlin, and Halle. In 1873 he became a *Privatdozent* at Marburg, the Hessian university that had welcomed Christian Wolff after his banishment from Halle a century and a half earlier, but that had been in philosophical decline since Wolff's triumphant return to Halle in 1740; Cohen became professor in 1875, and initiated Marburg's second golden age in philosophy, with Paul Natorp and then Ernst Cassirer among his foremost students. In addition to his Kant commentaries and his own systematic works, Cohen wrote on Jewish philosophy throughout his career; his culminating work in this area, completed during his retirement in Berlin and posthumously published in 1919, was *Religion der Venunft aus der Quellen des Judentums* ("Religion of reason from the sources of Judaism"),[21] a lengthy riposte to Kant's argument in his *Religion within the Boundaries of Mere Reason*,

---

[20] The only extended discussion of Cohen's aesthetics I have been able to find is in Poma, *Critical Philosophy*, pp. 131–47. Poma's discussion is useful, but it does not emphasize how fundamentally different both Cohen's method and his substantive results in aesthetics are from Kant's, as I will do in what follows. Poma also devotes two essays to particular topics in aesthetics in his collection *Yearning for Form and Other Essays on Hermann Cohen's Thought* (Dordrecht: Springer, 2006), "Cohen and Mozart: Considerations on Drama, the Beautiful and Humaneness in Cohen's Aesthetics," pp. 87–110, and "The Portrait in Hermann Cohen's Aesthetics," pp. 145–68.

[21] A recent edition is Hermann Cohen, *Religion der Vernunft aus der Quellen des Judentums: Eine jüdische Religionsphilosophie*, with an introduction by Ulrich Oelschläger (Wiesbaden: Marx Verlag, 2008); an English translation is Cohen, *Religion of Reason: Out of the Sources of Judaism*, trans. Simon Kaplan, introduction by Leo Strauss (New York: Frederick Ungar, 1972).

itself directed at least in part to Mendelssohn, that Christianity is a better expression of the religion of pure reason than Judaism. The connections to both Mendelssohn and Kant are acknowledged in Cohen's final work, though as the title suggests he is far more interested in demonstrating the presence of a religion of reason in traditional Jewish sources such as the Talmud than in his eighteenth-century predecessors.

Kants Begründung der Aesthetik was published in 1889, eighteen years after Cohen's initial statement of his approach to Kant's transcendental epistemology and philosophy of science in *Kants Theorie der Erfahrung* (1871) and seventeen years after his interpretation of Kant's practical philosophy in *Kants Begründung der Ethik* (1872) (work on his detailed commentary of the *Critique of Pure Reason* and on the theory of infinitesimals intervened). It is an ambitious work. It begins with a review of the history of aesthetics, in which Cohen, revealing the nationalism of the German *Gründerzeit*, argues that the discipline of aesthetics could have originated only in Germany, with its recognition of the depths of the human spirit, and that, although important contributions to the discipline were made by Mendelssohn and Winckelmann, who emphasized the centrality of the activity of the idealization of nature in art, aesthetics as a part of philosophy was established only by Kant, because he was the first to include aesthetics in a systematic philosophy – something else only a German could have done. Next, Cohen reviews the central themes of Kant's philosophy of nature and morality, and makes some general claims about the relations of aesthetics to nature and morality, preparing the way for his claim that although "the beautiful originates as a special interest of the soul, as a special activation of the powers of the soul" – that is what Winckelmann discovered with his conception of the "ideal of the beautiful" – at the same time "science and morality are the matter for art, which this to be sure has to cultivate independently and transform into new creations."[22] After this "Systematic Introduction" Cohen expounds his aesthetics and derives it from Kant's in three lengthy chapters on "The Lawfulness of Aesthetic Consciousness," "The Content of Aesthetic Consciousness," and "The Arts as the Modes of the Generation of Aesthetic Content." He concludes with a chapter on "The Friends and Opponents of the Critical Aesthetics," in which he reviews the history of aesthetics, again exclusively German aesthetics, since Kant, and argues that his approach is the only right one.

---

[22] Cohen, *Begründung*, pp. 92–3.

Two points about Cohen's systematic assumptions will be important for what follows. First, following Kant's claim that "Our cognitive faculty as a whole has two domains, that of the concept of nature and that of the concept of freedom,"[23] and that the fundamental principle of judgment, although it is distinct from the *principles* of nature and freedom, will still have to apply to the *objects* of nature and freedom, that is, natural and human products, Cohen also argues that there are only two primary domains of objects, the objects of natural science and of morality, and that the objects of aesthetics, namely works of art – he already departs from Kant, and in fact follows the Hegelian tradition, in deemphasizing the importance of natural beauty – will somehow have to supervene on the objects of science and morality. Science and morality, in turn, he argues, here inspired by Kant (and many years before G.E.M. Anscombe introduced this idea into Anglo-American philosophy),[24] differ in their "direction of consciousness." On the one hand, although our experience of nature is a conceptualized product "generated" by our own activity, it nevertheless begins with sensations that we are given, and so the direction of our consciousness in the case of nature is toward a "reality that is independent from the conditions of consciousness":[25] in other words, we try to fit our representation of nature to data that are given to us rather than trying to fit the data to a preconceived notion of nature. The "direction of consciousness" in the "generation of the moral," however, is the opposite: "here there is not a thoroughly subsisting reality which is merely to be copied; the generation is not intended reconstructively, but is aimed at the future of a reality."[26] In other words, in morality the point is not to form our concepts to fit nature, but to transform nature to realize our moral goals. But these two opposed directions of fit seem at least *prima facie* exhaustive, and it is not immediately obvious what third direction of consciousness could be the goal of aesthetic experience and of the production of art. Explaining that is one task for Cohen's aesthetics.

The second general point about Cohen's approach to philosophy in general is that it is ultimately based on the model of Kant's "analytical" style of argument in the *Prolegomena to any future Metaphysics* and the "fact of reason" argument in the *Critique of Practical Reason* rather than on what we might consider to be the synthetic proof-strategies of the first

[23] Kant, *CPJ*, Introduction, section II, 5:174.
[24] G.E.M. Anscombe, *Intention* (Oxford: Blackwell, 1957), p. 56.
[25] Cohen, *Begründung*, p. 97.
[26] Cohen, *Begründung*, p. 98.

Critique, the third section of the *Groundwork for the Metaphysics of Morals*, or the deduction of aesthetic judgments in the third *Critique*. That is, Cohen does not regard it as the task of philosophy to prove the very possibility of natural science, morality, or art; rather, starting from the "fact" of natural science, morality, or of the existence of art, philosophy's task is to elucidate the *a priori* principles or "lawfulness" of the relevant domain. In *Kants Theorie der Erfahrung*, Cohen argues that Kant begins from the validity of Newtonian physics and infers the *a priori* forms of space and time and the *a priori* categories of the understanding as the conditions of the possibility of that science, and in *Kants Begründung der Ethik* he advocates the second *Critique*'s strategy of inferring freedom from the fact of our consciousness of our obligation under the moral law; indeed, in his later *Ethik des reinen Willens* he argues that ethics begins from actual systems of laws and elucidates their underlying *a priori* principle. He then claims that he will follow this methodology in aesthetics as well, and that it is "The productions of the arts that are the *Factum* to which, in analogy with the fact of the sciences and the 'fact as it were' of the moral law the foundation of the beautiful has to conform itself."[27] We might think that since Kant clearly organized the "Analytic of the Beautiful" and the "Deduction of judgments of taste" around the task of proving synthetically that such judgments are possible at all, and for the third *Critique* wrote no *Prolegomena* in which he clearly used the analytic rather than the synthetic method, Cohen's use of his own method in the case of aesthetics is a clear departure from Kant's method in aesthetics. Substantively, Cohen's use of his preferred method in aesthetics, namely an appeal to "fact," opens up the possibility that his results will be influenced as much if not more by his own experience or contemporary views about the arts than by any identifiably Kantian premises, and this could well explain why his views end up seeming more like other contemporary aesthetic theories than like Kant's own theory.

Let us now turn from these general premises to the central ideas of Cohen's aesthetics. The first and foremost of his theses is that the aim of art is the expression of the feelings associated with our representations of nature and our own volitions and actions – that is, science and morality – that are not captured by the concepts of those two domains, and that the pleasure of beauty is the pleasure of enjoying those feelings. He gives an argument of his own for this view and then claims that Kant was conveying the very same view with his conception of the free play of

[27] Cohen, *Begründung*, p. 305.

our cognitive powers. He begins his own argument by reiterating that if knowledge of reality on the one hand and the determination of the will to change reality on the other exhaust the directions of consciousness, if "all psychological elements" are exhausted by "concepts on the one side and representations of the will on the other," then it is not clear that "art could be" or have "a special content" of its own.[28] But it does: "The new mode of consciousness is called feeling." By calling feeling "new," Cohen means not just that it is being newly introduced into his analysis at this point, but also that the recognition of feeling as the subject matter of art was a theoretical innovation, one that he places just before Kant, observing that Johann Georg Sulzer did not yet devote an article to it in his otherwise exhaustive *Allgemeine Theorie der schönen Künste* of 1771–74 although Moses Mendelssohn had made it central to his aesthetics beginning in the 1750s and Johann Nicolaus Tetens had also emphasized it in his *Philosophische Versuchen* of 1776.[29] Kant had been influenced by both of these authors, and had begun his own "Analytic of the Beautiful" with the statement that "the feeling of pleasure or displeasure" is the one aspect of our consciousness of objects that cannot be included in cognition of them.[30] Cohen does not immediately appeal to this Kantian premise, however, because his thesis is that we have a multitude of feelings associated with the representation of objects or with the determination of the will that are not captured by our cognitive or practical concepts, that these are the subject matter of art, and that these are not identical with or reducible to some singular feelings of pleasure and displeasure but rather that pleasure or displeasure supervenes on the experience of these multiform feelings.

Thus he begins his argument by saying that "If one is to determine feeling, its significance for the connections of consciousness-processes, as well as the kind and degree of consciousness which it may exhibit, then one must abstract from the *quale* of being-conscious [*Bewusstheit*] that is designated as pleasure and displeasure."[31] Rather, Cohen argues, we must begin from the idea that we have an initial level of consciousness that we are conscious, being-conscious that we are conscious ("*Dass Bewusstsein überhaupt von Statten geht ... das ist Bewusstheit*"),[32] and that "feeling" is, in the first place, this consciousness of being conscious, and,

---

[28] Cohen, *Begründung*, p. 151.
[29] Cohen, *Begründung*, pp. 151–2.
[30] Kant, *CPJ*, §1, 5:204.
[31] Cohen, *Begründung*, p. 153.
[32] Cohen, *Begründung*, pp. 153–4.

second, everything about this consciousness that will not be captured by our subsequent conceptualization of our consciousness, whether that take the form of a conceptualized representation of an object or of a determination of the will. Thus he writes:

> Now if one properly abstracts from pleasure and displeasure, then feeling in general remains as the universal and fundamental kind of consciousness, as the expression of the fact that we have consciousness, without the specification, however, of to what content this consciousness determines itself. This meaning of feeling [*Gefühls*] I call *to feel* [*Fühlen*] in order to indicate that this first manifestation of consciousness consists in a kind of becoming conscious [*Bewusstwerdens*] that is preserved in the more developed levels of feeling.[33]

By the last comment Cohen suggests the two-leveled view I have imputed to him, that is, that we have a layer of feeling associated with all consciousness of objects that precedes and is not exhausted by our conceptualization of that consciousness, and that our aesthetic pleasure or displeasure supervenes on that level of consciousness (as contrasted to prudential or moral pleasure in a state of affairs, which supervenes only on a conceptualization of an object and/or a determination of the will). More precisely, Cohen continues, consciousness of objects consists of "sensations" (*Empfindungen*) that are organized by concepts, but the primordial level of consciousness or "feeling" precedes both, so there are feelings associated with sensations and feelings associated with concepts that are preserved in, yet not exhausted by, both of the latter. So "the feeling of sensation is the primordial process of becoming conscious that preserves itself" in subsequent consciousness, and likewise there are feelings associated with conceptualized "representations" that "form the substratum of abstract and intellectual processes of consciousness" but are not included in the conceptualized representations that result from those processes. He then maintains that the "unique direction" of "aesthetic consciousness" is precisely its direction at these primordial feelings of becoming-conscious that precede determinate sensation and conceptualization of objects and determinations of the will and are not taken up into them. This solves the problem of the "direction of consciousness" for aesthetic experience and the content of art: we could not introduce an entirely new domain of actual objects or intended states of affairs to play this role, because the distinction of objects into real objects of knowledge and intended objects of the will was exhaustive; but there is

[33] Cohen, *Begründung*, pp. 154–5.

a whole range of primordial feelings associated with our consciousness of those two kinds of objects, and that range of feelings, itself never fully exhausted by our two exhaustive forms of conceptualization, is the subject matter of art and aesthetic experience. Or, as Cohen puts it much later in the work:

> No single object, even were it the highest, counts as the content that is to be determined [in aesthetic experience and art], but consciousness itself grasped in the totality of its directions, and this totality organized as proportion; this interweaving of all objects in a mere relationship is the aesthetic content. And this interweaving of objects itself forms the new object: feeling as feeling, and not as an annex of sensation or representation.[34]

From this general model of the contents of aesthetic experience, one of Cohen's more particular theses follows pretty directly: since art deals with the feelings that underlie our other, more specific forms of consciousness, and the latter are exhausted by the scientific knowledge of nature on the one hand and the moral representation of a better world on the other, the subject matter of art must be either science or morality, or more precisely the objects of science and of morality, nature on the one hand and human actions and intentions on the other.

Thus far, however, nothing positive has been said about the pleasure (or displeasure) of aesthetic experience. Cohen charges that it was a mistake on Kant's part to reduce all the feelings that are the content of the aesthetic to a single feeling of pleasure (or displeasure), but he certainly concedes that aesthetics must explain the pleasure of its domain of experience. His initial suggestion seems to be that pleasure and displeasure are *one* of the dimensions of primordial consciousness, and that art has a special charge somehow to capture this dimension of consciousness in its productions, so that the pleasure and displeasure captured by art are then communicated to us as the audience for art. He says, "In fact aesthetic consciousness comes down to this: that the specific moments of pleasure and displeasure press themselves upon us and yet do not become dissolved, but rather intensify and heighten themselves. Joy and pain should move the human heart when it becomes aware of the art-feeling. And through the qualia of anxiety and empathy blessed peace should spread itself over the mind."[35] But this does not explain why art should focus on only those dimensions of primordial consciousness, and it presupposes a theory of empathy that is not worked out or defended. In any

---

[34] Cohen, *Begründung*, pp. 399–400.
[35] Cohen, *Begründung*, pp. 161–2.

case, Cohen's more considered view seems to be that pleasure in particular (not displeasure) supervenes on the expression of the whole range of primordial feelings in art because aesthetic experience is not directed at the objective content of experience but at the "motility [*Regsamkeit*] of consciousness itself"; aesthetic feeling is "the feeling of animation and of the disposition of consciousness to activity in general."[36]

Here is where Cohen attaches his analysis to his interpretation of Kant: he presents his own theory as an interpretation of Kant's theory that the pleasure of aesthetic experience arises from the free play of our cognitive powers. He interprets Kant's claim that the free play takes place between the "powers of representation" rather than among "representations" themselves[37] to be based on Kant's recognition that aesthetic experience concerns "domains of consciousness [*Bewusstseinsgebiete*] rather than individual images of consciousness [*Bewusstseinsgebilde*],"[38] that is, the primordial level of consciousness rather than the conceptualized representations of actual or possible objects of consciousness that constitute the subject matter of science and morality. However, he also says that Kant's image of the play of the mental powers is a "seductively imagistic [*bildlicher*] expression,"[39] and its seductiveness seems to consist in its abstractness leading Kant to focus on pleasure as the unique product of the free play of the faculties and to suppress what he should have recognized, namely Cohen's own view that what animates the mind to its free play is its awareness of the whole range of preconceptual and never fully conceptualized feelings that constitute the primordial level of consciousness.

Now Cohen is certainly right to turn to Kant for the idea that the free play of the mind with any content whatsoever is potentially pleasurable, just because it is an exercise of one of our most distinctive capabilities and as a crucial part of what it is for a human to be alive can lead to a heightened feeling of life. And he is right to associate this with the Leibnizian tradition in German philosophy,[40] for the thought can already be found in Sulzer, although it is unfortunate that in his German nationalism Cohen overlooks the presence of this thought in Scottish aesthetics in the mid-eighteenth century, especially in Alexander Gerard, who seems to have been more influential for Kant than Sulzer. But in any

---

[36] Cohen, *Begründung*, pp. 175–6.
[37] Cohen, *Begründung*, p. 170.
[38] Cohen, *Begründung*, p. 172.
[39] Cohen, *Begründung*, p. 173.
[40] Cohen, *Begründung*, p. 172.

case, Cohen seems to have no justification at all for his interpretation of Kant's conception of free play as expressing a contrast between a play of representational powers and a play of particular representations, and for using this interpretation to ground his own view that the content of aesthetic experience is all that aspect of primordial consciousness that is not otherwise captured by the determinate concepts of science and morality. As Kant makes clear in the very first section of the "Analytic of the Beautiful," already cited, he himself does not recognize any ineluctably subjective content of consciousness other than the feeling of pleasure and displeasure itself. Kant simply did not recognize the existence of other aspects of primordial consciousness that cannot be captured by our theoretical and practical concepts but that might somehow be captured in art. Indeed, Kant thought that the paradigmatic content of art is *ideas* of pure reason, paradigmatically moral ideas, which need to be intimated by the wealth of imagery in a successful work of art because they *outrun* or can never be fully captured by ordinary experience, but not because they in any way *precede* ordinary experience. Kant has his reason for preferring to call the central thoughts of morality "ideas" rather than "concepts," but certainly with respect to Cohen's own distinction between "primordial being-conscious" and worked-up, conceptualized "representation," they fall on the latter rather than the former side. So Kant's own theory of art is very different from Cohen's. Cohen can successfully appeal to Kant for his theory of aesthetic *pleasure* as resulting from the "lawful" but nevertheless "free" play of our cognitive powers, but he cannot appeal to Kant for his theory of aesthetic *contents*. That seems to be his own invention, reflecting his own experience and perhaps artistic tendencies of his own time, or at least post-Kantian times. Again, that is not to say his theory is a mistake: it can be considered as part of the same emphasis on feelings or the subjective dimension of experience in general as the special subject of art that we will find in such representative writers of the next half-century as Bullough and Collingwood, to be discussed in the next volume. That tendency can be considered to be an enduring contribution to aesthetics. But it is not Kant's contribution.

A few further points will confirm that Cohen's approach leads to results rather different from Kant's. First, as mentioned earlier, Cohen's conception of the direction of philosophical argument is the opposite of Kant's preference for the synthetic over the analytic method of argument in all cases except the "fact of reason" argument for freedom in the second *Critique*: while Kant's general conception of philosophy is that it needs to provide a transcendental deduction of the fundamental principles that license the practices of natural science, aesthetic judgment, and, at least in the *Groundwork*, moral judgment as well, Cohen's method is to start from the undisputed actuality of a domain of facts and then merely to elucidate rather than prove the principles of their possibility. I have already suggested that Cohen's specification of the content of aesthetic experience and the arts is certainly not deduced from Kant's theory, but may better represent his own experience of the arts. In this context, it is interesting to remember a passage cited earlier, in which Cohen states that the productions of the arts are "the fact" for aesthetics that is analogous to "the fact of the sciences and the 'as it were fact' of the moral law," and in which he also says that "The arts are the factual lever of the beautiful, so that the transcendental foundation of aesthetics has not overstepped its boundaries in seeking what is characteristic in the arts."[41] Here Cohen makes clear that an analysis of what the arts as we actually find them are concerned with is the starting point for aesthetic theory, but that this in his view does not compromise the claim of aesthetics to be called transcendental, any more than the fact that his philosophy of science begins from the actual accomplishments of science compromises its claim to be called transcendental.

Cohen's methodology is also evident in his appeal to the "fact of genius." Cohen certainly accepts from Kant the claim that judgments of taste claim universal validity, although they do this without the "pretense to laws" and *a priori* "grounds of proof."[42] He also recognizes that Kant attempted to derive the justification of the universal validity of judgments of taste from the commonality of human cognitive powers, but he dismisses this deduction as psychological rather than transcendental. Instead, for him the basis for the assertion of the "lawfulness of aesthetic consciousness" is the existence of genius, the sheer fact that there are artists who are able to capture the emotional dimensions of human experience in a way that all find valid. He states plainly:

> The transcendental method stands on the status of its conditions as cultural facts to be examined, on the "fact of experience," the "as it were fact," the "analogue of a fact" of the moral law, and so also on the works of the art of genius: in order to communicate in its objective effect the conditions of the feeling corresponding to the cognitive faculty and practical reason.[43]

---

[41] Cohen, *Begründung*, p. 305.
[42] Cohen, *Begründung*, pp. 186, 188.
[43] Cohen, *Begründung*, p. 190.

In other words, the problem of the possibility of intersubjectively valid judgments of taste is solved by the actuality of universally recognized works of artistic genius, which express the universally valid emotional concomitants of the conceptualized representations of nature and of morality. Again, this seems to be very different from Kant's approach to the problem of universal validity, because Kant introduces his conception of genius as an ability to create universally accessible works of art only after he has, at least to his own satisfaction, deduced the possibility of universally valid judgments of taste from the commonality of human cognitive powers, and thus, since part of what characterizes genius is that its products are exemplary but not determined by a rule, proven the very possibility of genius.

A further point at which Cohen seems to draw more on the actual experience of the arts than on any transcendental argument is his claim that the arts concern not merely the feelings associated with our conceptions of nature *or* of morality – we saw how his argument for that went, and how it might be considered *a priori* although not Kantian – but the feelings associated with the unification of art *and* nature. Cohen argues that art always idealizes – this is the insight that he traces back to Winckelmann – but that in particular it idealizes nature by representing it as more moral than it normally seems to be and it idealizes morality by representing it as more natural, or more fully realized in nature, than it normally seems to be. The "higher task" of art is to be the vehicle for the "idealization" of nature into an "image of morality. Only insofar as art presents the natural object as an image of morality is it capable of transforming both nature and morality into "art-feeling." He continues:

> And the opposite holds as well: Only insofar as art is capable of presenting the object of morality as an object of nature can it first transform the object of morality into an object of art. Art demands both, holding both together, combining both. A natural object that is not displaced into the relations of morality so that the sympathy of minds that breathe as a final end does not become effective, such a natural object can never become an object of art, no matter how precise the drawing nor how lively the colors. Nature must pass through morality if it is to be able to become art.[44]

This might be taken to be inspired by Kant's claim that we have an intellectual interest in the beauty of nature insofar as it gives us a hint that our moral purposes can be realized in nature,[45] but it goes beyond this

---

[44] Cohen, *Begründung*, pp. 230–1.
[45] Kant, *CPJ*, §42.

claim that we can see a *parallel* between natural beauty and moral success as well as beyond Kant's claim that all art must ultimately concern ideas of reason, maintaining instead that all art ultimately *directly* concerns the realization of morality in nature, or the possibility of a higher degree of that realization than we ordinarily experience. Kant did not maintain that all art concerns the possibility of the realization of aesthetic ideas *in* nature. Here again Cohen seems to be drawing on a supposed fact about the arts rather than any *a priori* argument to make his claim (although we might observe that Kant's own claim that all art concerns aesthetic ideas is also not obviously grounded on any *a priori* argument). Here we may further note that while there might initially seem to be a tension between Cohen's claim that all philosophy begins from facts but that art idealizes rather than presenting nature or human efforts to be moral to us as they actually are, there is not: it is just a fact about art as a third form of culture besides natural science and morality that it does this.

Of course, it could also be objected that Cohen owes us an explanation of the connection between the idealizing function of art and its function of expressing our primordial feelings underlying our representations of both nature and morality, and it is not immediately obvious what this explanation is. Perhaps his idea is that among our primordial feelings is a never fully expressed yearning that nature and morality fully coincide, and that we express this feeling through art. This would at least be consistent with another feature of Cohen's aesthetics (and of his philosophy as a whole), namely his remarkable reinterpretation of Kant's idea of the thing in itself, or in the case of aesthetics of the "supersensible substratum" of both humanity and nature. The role of the "supersensible substratum" in Kant's resolution of the "antinomy of taste" is problematic, because Kant seems to have solved the problem of reconciling the non-rule-governedness of judgments of taste with their claim to universal validity through the essentially epistemological concept of the free play of shared cognitive powers, and it is not at all clear why he should suddenly resort to the metaphysical conception of a supersensible substratum or common noumenal character of all mankind to explain the possibility of agreement in taste, or to a common supersensible substratum of both mankind and nature to explain the natural existence of things we find beautiful.[46] Cohen characteristically avoids this problem

---

[46] I have argued that this move is problematic in *Kant and the Claims of Taste* (Cambridge, Mass.: Harvard University Press; expanded edition, Cambridge: Cambridge University Press, 1997), ch. 10. Kant's introduction of the supersensible into the resolution of the antinomy of judgments of taste has been defended by Henry E. Allison, *Kant's Theory of*

by insisting that Kant's conception of the thing in itself and in the case of aesthetics of the supersensible substratum is not a metaphysical conception at all, but something more like a practical conception of an infinite task the realization of which we can approach only asymptotically: the idea of the thing in itself in epistemology is the ideal of a complete knowledge of nature that we can never fully attain,[47] the idea of the thing in itself in morality is the ideal of a moral world or realm of ends that we can never fully realize, and the idea of the supersensible substratum in aesthetics is perhaps the ideal of a realization of our primordial desire for a unification of the natural and the moral that can never be fully realized in reality nor fully expressed in art. Cohen writes:

> And since every idea manages a particular purposiveness, so every kind of purposiveness is a particular kind of thing in itself. The thing in itself, however, always signifies a task, through which reason bounds the understanding, which without reason would regard itself as limited in its task. Aesthetic purposiveness also presents such a task as the aesthetic idea, as a "supersensible ground," as a thing in itself of consciousness. And hereby we come to the genuine and highest fulfillment of the problem of the end which aesthetic lawfulness sets and solves.[48]

That Cohen refers to a "thing in itself of consciousness" shows how far his view has departed from Kant's, for this idea would seem to be self-contradictory for Kant. Cohen is here obviously also completely reinterpreting Kant's notion of an "aesthetic idea," or using Kant's term for a very different purpose. His idea that art gives expression to our conception of an infinite task of reconciling nature and morality seems to be based entirely on his own interpretation of our primordial feelings and of the task of art.

Cohen's interpretation of the task of art may be determined not just by his general reinterpretation of Kant's concept of the thing in itself but

---

Taste: A Reading of the Critique of Aesthetic Judgment (Cambridge: Cambridge University Press, 2001), ch. 11, and Jennifer K. Dobe, "Kant's Common Sense and the Strategy for a Deduction," *Journal of Aesthetics and Art Criticism* 68 (2008): 47–60.

[47] Cohen's conception of the thing in itself is thus analogous to his contemporary Charles Sanders Peirce's (1839–1914) conception of the "real" as the object represented in "The opinion which is fated to be ultimately agreed to by all who investigate," in his famous paper "How to Make Our Ideas Clear" (1877), in *The Essential Peirce*, edited by Nathan Houser and Christian Kloesel, 2 vols. (Bloomington: Indiana University Press, 1992), vol. 1, pp. 124–41, at p. 139, with the difference that Peirce seems to conceive of the real as something that could actually be known in the fullness of time, while for Cohen our knowledge could only approach it asymptotically.

[48] Cohen, *Begründung*, p. 208.

also by his experience of a kind of art that Kant did not live to experience. At least this suggestion gives me an excuse to quote the concluding peroration of Cohen's book, which is too indicative of the character of the man and his times to omit:

> Bach and Beethoven are German artists. The one stems from Luther, who understood how to touch the aesthetic consciousness of his people in word and song. Like Schiller, Bach fulfills German internalization ... Beethoven, however, follows the path of Goethe. Everything Faustian is only the outline of life. What should be brought to expression is not the drama, not the epic, not the opera and not the oratorium, in general nothing that is stuck onto the thoughts of men, their clever knowledge and the superstitious belief. Their passion alone and in this passion their joys, that is the divine spark[49] by which Beethoven becomes Prometheus. He makes feeling as such the object of his creativity. And thus he invents feelings that in such determinacy and with such power had tempted no composer before him. He articulates the mind that lives in the current of feelings with a firmness and gives this human mind full of variation an endurance of feelings that no previous musical artwork was able to accomplish in such intensity.... Is it an accident that the Germans completed the foundation of aesthetics?[50]

Cohen's view of the infinite task of art in expressing human emotions and the possibility of the complete interpenetration of nature and morality is obviously based on an experience of art that Kant never had, and at least in the case of late Beethoven could not have had, more than on a reconstruction of Kant's own theory of art. Again, this is hardly to criticize Cohen's theory of art, only his pretense to be interpreting Kant's theory of art.

As we have now seen, for all his allegiance to Kant, Cohen's aesthetics departs from Kant's in radical ways. It employs an analytical rather than synthetic method. It constructs a far more definite connection between art and morality than Kant was willing to accept. But for our purposes, what is most important is that while emphasizing that feelings are the content of art in a way that Kant certainly did not, Cohen transforms Kant's theory of free play with our cognitive powers into a theory of cognition of the most subjective aspects of experience, and thus transforms what might have been a recognition that the experience of emotions is central to aesthetic experience into a theory of the cognition of emotions through art that essentially rejects the theory of free play. Let us

---

[49] *Götterfunke*, a word Cohen is lifting from the text of Schiller's "Ode to Joy" that Kant used in the fourth movement of the Ninth Symphony.
[50] Cohen, *Begründung*, pp. 432–3.

now turn the purple prose with which Cohen completed his characteristic work of the late nineteenth century to a work from the first year of the twentieth century that differs completely in its philosophical style and method but reaches conclusions that are in some ways similar to Cohen's but in some ways different. This is the *Allgemeine Ästhetik* of Jonas Cohn. The crucial difference between Cohn and Cohen (apart from an "e") is that the former comes closer than the latter to straightforwardly acknowledging the actual experience of the emotional impact of art, and does not reduce the emotions to the subject matter of art as a form of cognition.

3. COHN

Jonas Cohn (1869–1947) was a follower of the Southwest school of Neo-Kantianism led by Wilhelm Windelband and Heinrich Rickert rather than a leader of his own school, but since neither Windelband nor Rickert wrote extensively on aesthetics, we must turn to Cohn's *Allgemeine Ästhetik* of 1901 for an example of the Southwest school's approach to aesthetics. This book grew out of Cohn's work for his habilitation under Windelband, after earlier studies that included philosophy and experimental psychology but culminated in a doctorate in botany. In the same year in which he published the work, Cohn was appointed as associate professor in philosophy and pedagogy in Freiburg im Breisgau, where he became full professor in the Institute of Psychology in 1919. He held that position until he was forcibly "retired" after the advent of the Nazis in 1933, but he managed to emigrate to Britain in 1939 and to complete his career at the University of Birmingham. His relocation to Britain seems fitting, because after the overheated rhetoric of Cohen's book, Cohn's work reads like a work of more recent analytical philosophy – although naturally Schiller and Goethe loom larger in Cohn's stock of examples than they would in any British or American work in analytical aesthetics.

Rather than beginning from the alleged "facts" of natural science, social mores and law, and art, as did the Marburg Neo-Kantians, the Southwest Neo-Kantians began with conceptions of the "domains of value" and their formal criteria, and then turned to experience to determine what phenomena satisfy the criteria of the various domains of value. This approach is evident in Cohn's aesthetics. He begins by defining the domain of aesthetics as that of the beautiful broadly rather than narrowly understood, so that the beautiful in the everyday sense is only one species of the beautiful in the philosophical sense and the sublime, the tragic, and the comic are other species. He then turns to Kant for guidance in determining the formal criteria of the domain of aesthetic value rather than for the substance of his aesthetic theory; indeed, he explicitly rejects Kant's conception of the free play of the cognitive powers as a positive characterization of our experience of the beautiful and self-consciously arrives at a different substantive aesthetic theory using Kant's formal criteria for aesthetic value. He believes that Kant was correct to begin from an analysis of aesthetic judgment, and so himself starts with an analysis of judgments of the beautiful in the broad sense as a form of value judgments. According to Cohn, every value judgment has three aspects or "determinations," namely something valued, the value that is attributed to that subject, and a particular kind of validity that is claimed for that value.[51] He then argues that in the case of aesthetic judgment what is valued is the "intuition" or "immediate experience" afforded by an object rather than the class to which it belongs or the motivation or outcome it may have (in the case in which the object is an action);[52] the aesthetic judgment, in other words, is not a cognitive or a practical judgment. Second, the value that is attributed to an intuition in aesthetic judgment is "purely intensive" (*rein intensiv*);[53] this is Cohn's way of saying that it is intrinsic or non-instrumental, or in Kant's terminology disinterested. Cohn immediately considers the objection that the values of the true and the good are also intrinsic rather than instrumental, but responds that while that is to a certain extent true, those values are "transgredient" rather than "immanent":[54] a truth in science or ordinary cognitive discourse always both points to some fact outside of itself (to which it corresponds, or which makes it true) and is also linked in all kinds of ways to innumerable other truths, so that it can only be evaluated as part of a larger theory; and the morally good will always seeks a goal beyond itself, even though of course it is still good if it does not actually achieve that goal; but a beautiful object, specifically a beautiful work of art, though it is of course the product of a goal-directed activity, is nevertheless complete in itself and can be valued for what it is by itself. In Cohn's words, "In the completed work of art what counts is no longer what is willed [*das Wollen*] but what has been achieved [*das Erreichte*]."[55]

---

[51] Cohn, *Ästhetik*, p. 17.
[52] Cohn, *Ästhetik*, p. 18.
[53] Cohn, *Ästhetik*, p. 23.
[54] Cohn, *Ästhetik*, p. 27.
[55] Cohn, *Ästhetik*, p. 30.

Cohn sums up his reconstruction of Kant's conception of disinterestedness by observing that Kant's connection of it with the free play of the faculties is instructive in a negative sense, for the immanence of aesthetic value requires that it be appreciated free from constraint by other values, but cannot provide a positive characterization of aesthetic value: "From the consideration of all possible [kinds of] play the characteristic peculiarities of the aesthetic will never be derived."[56] So, unlike Cohen, Cohn does not attempt to re-interpret Kant's concept of the free play of the faculties for his own powers, but simply accepts Kant's formal analysis of aesthetic judgment while rejecting Kant's substantive theory of aesthetic experience and thus of the grounds of that judgment. Finally, in his interpretation of Kant's conception of the universal subjective validity and exemplary necessity of aesthetic judgments, Cohn argues that the kind of validity characteristic of aesthetic judgments is the "character of a demand" (*Forderungscharakter*), or an imperatival character:[57] "The beautiful, the great work of art presents itself to me with the demand to be appreciated,"[58] and likewise of course an object that has properly presented itself to me in this way will similarly present itself to anyone else.

Cohn recognizes that Kant did and that others may expect a justification of the *Forderungscharakter* of the aesthetic judgment, but he rejects Kant's deduction of the aesthetic judgment's claim to universal subjective validity by grounding it on a free play of the same powers that are involved in ordinary cognition precisely because this leads to a restriction of "pure beauty to the formal, ornamental domain," which is a product more of "the effort to derive the demand-character of aesthetic value from that of logical value, the effort to conduct a gap-free proof of its demand-character"[59] than of anything intrinsic to aesthetic judgment itself. In other words, Cohn claims that Kant's conception of the free play of the faculties as the core of aesthetic experience and the ground for aesthetic judgment is a product of his effort to force his analysis of the aesthetic onto the Procrustean bed of transcendental deduction rather than of an open-minded encounter with aesthetic experience itself. In Cohn's own view, for a justification of the demand-character of aesthetic judgments we must merely turn to the history of art as the "battleground of aesthetic values" from which "great works of art" emerge

---

[56] Cohn, *Ästhetik*, p. 31.
[57] Cohn, *Ästhetik*, p. 37.
[58] Cohn, *Ästhetik*, p. 38.
[59] Cohn, *Ästhetik*, p. 43.

victorious, that is, self-evidently justify their demand to be appreciated.[60] In other words, the justification of the demand-character of aesthetic judgment lies not in a transcendental deduction but in the test of time that is passed by great works of art. Here Cohn's method coincides with Cohen's, although Cohn does not use the Marburg expression of "facts" nor appeal explicitly to the "fact" of genius in addition to that of the existence of great works of art. (We might also say that Cohn ultimately prefers Hume's empiricist solution to the problem of taste to Kant's more *a priori* solution.)

Cohn's substantive account of the object of aesthetic value also coincides with Cohen's, although his methodology is clearer than Cohen's argument about the primordial layer of consciousness. Cohn argues simply that once we have defined the formal criteria of aesthetic value, then we should turn to experience to find out what best satisfies them, specifically to discover what kind of intuition immediately presents itself to us as intrinsically valuable and demanding our appreciation. The answer to this question, which "cannot be won through a logical deduction" but "must first be given hypothetically and then justified" by experience, is that "intuition can maintain the value of a demand insofar as it is grasped as the expression of an inner life." He writes:

> What this means, and how much intuition itself is thereby altered for us, can readily be seen when one compares ... the swing of the pendulum in a clock and the wave of a human hand. It is also readily comprehensible that an intuition has a higher, indeed a fundamentally different value for us, when it is regarded as "expression." For us human beings the inner life of another is in general accessible only insofar as we grasp intuited movements or other sensibly perceivable processes as expression and with their assistance sympathetically experience [*miterleben*] what is expressed. The only possibility for us to escape from the narrowness of our own individuality, or expanding our personality beyond its limits, lies in this sympathetic life [*Mitleben*].[61]

Cohn argues that the feeling of identification with another, in which "his suffering becomes our suffering, his pleasure our pleasure, his want our want," is the most intense kind of feeling that we can have, and thus that the experience of "complete inhabitation of the life [*Hineinleben*]" of another satisfies the criterion that aesthetic value be "purely intensive."[62] Here a subtle but important difference between Cohn and Cohen

---

[60] Cohn, *Ästhetik*, pp. 44–5.
[61] Cohn, *Ästhetik*, pp. 48–9.
[62] Cohen, *Ästhetik*, pp. 65–6.

emerges: by adapting the terminology of the empathy theorists whom we will discuss in the next chapter, Cohn signals that the actual experience of emotions and not just cognition of them is an essential aspect of aesthetic experience.

Building on his recognition that emotions are communicated and thus shared through art, Cohn has not only replaced Kant's free play of the faculties with our appreciation of the expression of the inner life of other living beings as the basis of aesthetic value, but also assumed a very different relation between the aesthetic and the moral than Kant did. For Kant, as we saw in Volume 1, the experience of the beautiful and the sublime may *prepare* us for morality in certain ways, the beautiful may be a *symbol* of the morally good, and we may take an "empirical interest" in the fact that our pleasure in beautiful objects is shared, that is, take an additional enjoyment from the fact that we enjoy the same things as others.[63] But for Kant all of these are *consequences* of our basic enjoyment of the beautiful because of the free play of our cognitive powers that it stimulates, whereas for Cohn our essentially moral desire to empathize with others is the *basis* for our appreciation of the beautiful, and our enjoyment of occasions for successful communication of feelings with or at least from others is constitutive of the pleasure of the beautiful. Kant himself used the fact that all art expresses aesthetic ideas to find the axes for his classification of the arts, but he did not use the premise that art expresses and communicates the inner life of others to ground his underlying explanation of our pleasure in art. For Kant, this would have made emotion, namely *Rührung*, being touched, an essential aspect of aesthetic experience, which he wanted to avoid. But Cohn makes no effort to avoid this conclusion.

To be sure, given his initial acceptance of the traditional as well as Kantian tripartion of the domains of values into the true, the good, and the beautiful, Cohn does not want simply to collapse the beautiful into the moral, so he identifies what is unique to the aesthetic by arguing that in the case of the beautiful we experience the expression of an inner life "in a determinate form [*Gestaltung*] corresponding to our capacity for apprehension," and thus that "in the aesthetically complete form and expression constitute [*bilden*] a necessary unity."[64] Here again Cohn does not appeal to Kant's own division of expression into content and form

---

[63] See Kant, *CPJ*, §41, and my article "Pleasure and Society in Kant's Theory of Taste," in Ted Cohen and Paul Guyer, editors, *Essays in Kant's Aesthetics* (Chicago: University of Chicago Press, 1982), pp. 21–54.
[64] Cohn, *Ästhetik*, p. 48.

under the rubrics of articulation, gesticulation, and modulation, but defines form or *Gestaltung* in his own, abstract way. He does not identify it with any particular aspect of perception or of the objects of perception, as Kant did when he separated gesticulation and modulation from articulation or when he identified the aesthetically significant form of a painting with its drawing rather than its color.[65] Rather, Cohn identifies form with whatever allows "what is essential in the expression" of the inner life of another "to come forth clearly" out of the background of the noise of various kinds against which our experience always takes place.[66] Much of the content of Cohn's work is then concerned with the description of the ways in which the different media of the arts allow the expression of inner life to become clear as well as with the differences in the kinds of inner life or feelings that the different varieties of beauty – the beautiful narrowly understood, the sublime, the tragic, and the comic – express through the different media of the arts.

After his analysis of the different arts and the different forms of beauty, which of course takes up a good part of his book, Cohn returns to the question of the "significance of the aesthetic domain of values."[67] Here he maintains that "the great domains of value all belong to the collaboration of human beings in a cultural life."[68] The need to be heard and understood by each other is the most fundamental of human needs, and aesthetic value has its foundation in this. Kant had recognized this in a very general way, but had not allowed the communication of emotion to be an essential function of aesthetic experience. Cohn can allow this, because for him what distinguishes the aesthetic from the other domains of values is not the absence of feelings but rather the purity and intensity of the communication of feelings that it allows through its unification of expression and form,[69] the way in which it allows us to transcend the boundaries of our individuality and to communicate with others more fully than we can do anywhere else. Departing from Cohen on this point, Cohn argues even more generally that while we can never completely realize our goals in science and ethics, in aesthetic experience we can and do attain the completion that we long for elsewhere. "The aesthetic is completed in present intuition [*als Anschauung vorhanden*], it attains fulfillment, it is not longing but possession. Thereby it elevates

---

[65] Kant, *CPJ*, §14, 5:225.
[66] Cohn, *Ästhetik*, p. 75.
[67] Cohn, *Ästhetik*, p. 224.
[68] Cohn, *Ästhetik*, p. 228.
[69] Cohn, *Ästhetik*, p. 231.

the human being above the narrowness of his own life."[70] To be sure, Cohn carefully argues that the special intensity of aesthetic experience cannot be confused with an actual cognition of the essence of things or with a guarantee that "the kind of life and harmony that is represented in the beautiful also dominates in the extra-aesthetic world";[71] he rejects any claim that the aesthetic gives us actual knowledge of the Idea or a genuine guarantee of the possibility of the complete realization of the demands and goals of morality. In this way, he maintains his allegiance to Neo-Kantianism and his rejection of absolute idealism, still an issue even at the turn of the twentieth century.

Nevertheless, Cohn, like Cohen, has departed considerably from Kant. He has accepted the formal framework of Kantian aesthetics, its analysis of the logic of aesthetic judgment, but has largely dismissed Kant's theory of free play and replaced it with a theory, grounded in experience and therefore inevitably in his own experience of the arts and the experience of the arts in and of his time, in which the aesthetic is more closely linked to the experience of emotions and through that to the moral than Kant was ever prepared to concede. For Cohn, aesthetic experience is essentially a medium not for insight into the external world in general but for experience of the feelings of others, and the value of the aesthetic is ultimately founded in the importance of such experience of the inner life of others for the achievement of a cultural community, thus for the achievement of the essential goal of morality. The rejection of Kant's theory of aesthetic experience as a form of free play leads both of our proponents of Neo-Kantianism to greater claims for the cognitive and moral significance of the aesthetic than Kant ever countenanced. Once again, we might well think that the Neo-Kantians' departure from the letter of Kant's aesthetics and their emphasis on human feelings as the essential subject matter to be clarified and communicated by art is hardly anything to be criticized but is rather an enduring contribution to aesthetics. But we might also think that the modesty of Kant's claims for the cognitive and moral significance of the aesthetic, which is based on his view that aesthetic experience is in the end a form of play rather than a genuine form of scientific or moral knowledge, remains salubrious, a strong cup of coffee that needs to be drunk after indulging in some of the more intoxicating claims not only of his most immediate critics in the heyday of absolute

[70] Cohn, *Ästhetik*, p. 285.
[71] Cohn, *Ästhetik*, p. 252.

idealism but even of those who claimed, in his name, to be returning to a more sober approach to aesthetics.

4. MÜNSTERBERG

Before turning to the less orthodox Neo-Kantian Wilhelm Dilthey, we may consider another figure at least initially associated with the Heidelberg school of Neo-Kantianism, who developed an aesthetic theory with a focus on the Kantian conception of disinterestedness on the foundation of Kant's theoretical philosophy, specifically its central concept of the unity of apperception or self-consciousness. This is Hugo Münsterberg (1863–1916), a prolific author whose works ranged from industrial psychology to the earliest book on cinema that is still read, but one of whose central works was a philosophy of values very much in the Southwestern Neo-Kantian tradition, which contains an extended treatment of the value of aesthetic experience. Münsterberg, born in Danzig, received a Ph.D. in psychology in 1885 at Leipzig under Wilhelm Wundt and then completed an M.D. at Heidelberg in 1887. During this time, Kuno Fischer and Wilhelm Windelband, the latter of whom is generally regarded as the founder of the Heidelberg or Southwestern school of Neo-Kantianism, were teaching philosophy at Heidelberg; this school's emphasis on the concept of value would mark Münsterberg's eventual philosophy. At the outset of his career, however, Münsterberg's emphasis was primarily on psychology, and it was in this field that he became a *Privatdozent* and then an assistant professor in Freiburg in Breisgau, which was to become the second center of Southwestern Neo-Kantianism (and later, through Edmund Husserl and then Martin Heidegger, the home of the competing movement of phenomenology as well). It was as a psychologist that Münsterberg met William James at an international conference in 1891, after which James invited him to run the laboratory in experimental psychology that he had established at Harvard. Münsterberg did this from 1892 until 1895, at which point, in spite of James's entreaties, he returned to Germany. After two more years, however, he submitted to James's pleas, and returned to Harvard as a professor in the not yet divided department of philosophy and psychology. He then began publishing extensively in English as well as German and in philosophy as well as psychology, where his books included pathbreaking work in industrial psychology and other areas of applied psychology. He also wrote extensively on American-German relations and on his experience of America as a German immigrant, and when World War I broke out he campaigned actively although in vain to keep the United States from entering on the Allied side. Although he had previously been a highly popular teacher at Harvard, this activity made him deeply unpopular, even bringing accusations that he was a German spy, and he died in December 1916, from a cerebral hemorrhage brought on, at least in the opinion of his family, by the public pressure on him. But he had remained intellectually active until this bitter end, having published most of his important books within the preceding decade and his book on cinema just earlier that year.

Münsterberg's central philosophical work was *The Eternal Values*[72] of 1909, the English counterpart to his German *Philosophie der Werte: Grundzüge einer Weltanschauung* of the previous year.[73] This book discusses aesthetic values as one of the four basic kinds of values, the others being logical values, ethical values, and "metaphysical" values, including the religious value of holiness as well as the value of "absoluteness." Münsterberg frames the problem of values by distinguishing, in Neo-Kantian fashion, between nature understood purely physically, including the "causal psychology" of human beings, which allows for description and explanation but not valuation,[74] and the realm of values, which is founded on will, something that does not enter into the description or explanation of nature.[75] However, values cannot be reduced simply to personal preferences – "There exists no bridge from the individual pleasure and displeasure to the absolute value"[76] – because those have no intersubjective validity – they give rise to "modern relativism in all its forms"[77] – and are also subject entirely to causal explanation. But neither will Münsterberg allow that objective values exist, like Platonic forms, independent of human experience altogether. Instead, absolute values must be connected with the conditions of the possibility of experience of a world that is coherent both theoretically and practically. First Münsterberg describes the connection between absolute value and a theoretically coherent world:

> [T]he idea of super-reality has been definitely removed from critical philosophy by Kant. The world of experience is the only world to which our

---

[72] Hugo Münsterberg, *The Eternal Values* (Boston: Houghton Mifflin, 1909).
[73] Hugo Münsterberg, *Philosophie der Werte: Grundzüge einer Weltanschauung* (Leipzig: Barth, 1908).
[74] E.g., Münsterberg, *Eternal Values*, p. 17.
[75] Münsterberg, *Eternal Values*, p. 27.
[76] Münsterberg, *Eternal Values*, p. 28.
[77] Münsterberg, *Eternal Values*, p. 34.

knowledge can have reference, and the reality which we want to grasp in our truth is therefore completely bound up with the conditions of our mental experience. The true world is independent of the single individual as such, and therefore absolute with reference to the individual; but it is a world of which we can have knowledge at all only if its forms are determined by the conditions of consciousness.

Likewise,

> The absolute values must therefore completely lie in a world whose totality stands under the condition of being a possible object of experience. Even where the conviction transcends the world of experience and seeks an over-experience, such a last reality must still remain dependent upon the conditions of consciousness.
>
> The absolute world with its eternal values, if it exists, is thus certainly not something which hangs in its own atmosphere, eternally separated from our consciousness.... On the contrary, everything which can be acknowledged as unconditional must be conceived beforehand as belonging to the sphere of possible material of consciousness ... The absolute values have unexceptional validity because they are valid for every possible subject who shares the world with us, and who relates his thinking and striving to our world.... The values stand above the individual. But they would become meaningless if they were conceived as independent of the conditions of consciousness.[78]

Specifically, values are connected with the conditions of the possibility of consciousness of a coherent and organized world. But, as Münsterberg's juxtaposition of "thinking and striving" might already suggest, he does not conceive of the idea of experiencing a coherent world as without effect on our affects; on the contrary, he conceives of the experience of a coherent world as the most fundamental goal of the will as well as the intellect, although not the contingent will of the "individual personality" but rather "a pure will which is not touched by personal pleasure and displeasure."[79] We all seek to experience a coherent world, independent of whatever preferences may have been formed by the peculiarities of our particular nature and nurture, and achievement of such coherence in experience brings us a kind of satisfaction that is distinct from the gratification of merely personal preferences.

Thus, Münsterberg's conception of objective, absolute, or "eternal" values has a cognitive dimension on the one side – connection or coherence is the fundamental form of all cognition – but a conative and

---

[78] Münsterberg, *Eternal Values*, pp. 48–9.
[79] Münsterberg, *Eternal Values*, p. 64.

affective dimension on the other – such coherence is the most fundamental object of the will, and its realization the most fundamental source of satisfaction:

> We seek the identity of experience. That is the one fundamental fact which secures for us a world. It is the one act which we cannot give up, and yet which has nothing whatever to do with personal pleasure and pain. We demand that there be a world; that means that our experience be more than just the passing experience, that it assert itself in its identity in new experiences. Here is the one original deed which gives eternal meaning to our reality, and without which our life would be an empty dream, a chaos, a nothing. We will that our experience is a world.... the experienced content itself becomes such a world for us by that one fundamental deed of seeking identities.[80]

Münsterbeg combines the fundamental ideas of Kant's theoretical and practical philosophies, the idea of the necessary unity of apperception on the one hand and the idea of the pure will on the other, to form his basic idea of eternal values. Logical, aesthetic, ethical, and metaphysical values will all be specific ways of satisfying the will in its search for a world. But even though the idea of freedom from personal interest has been a parameter for Münsterberg's conception of absolute value from the outset and his account of aesthetic value will give particular emphasis to its disinterestedness, what is almost entirely omitted from his synthesis of Kantian theoretical and practical ideas is Kant's own explanation for distinctively aesthetic value, namely the free play of the imagination. Imagination and its play has no central role in Münsterberg's account of natural or artistic beauty, although he touches upon the idea of play in passing.

Münsterberg erects a complex classification of values on the basic idea of experience of a world as the fundamental object of our common will rather than idiosyncratic wills. There are four main classes of value because there are four main forms of unity that we may find in our experience.

> If experiences are to assert themselves as a self-dependent world, and are to realize themselves in new and ever new experiences, we must demand a fourfold relation. First, every part must remain identical with itself in the changing events; secondly, the various parts must show in a certain sense identity among themselves, and thus show that they agree with one another and that no one part of the world is entirely isolated; thirdly, that which changes itself in the experience must still present an identity in its change

---

[80] Münsterberg, *Eternal Values*, pp. 75–6.

by showing that the change belongs to its own meaning and is only its own realization.... But if the world is completely to assert itself, that is, to hold its own identity, these three values must ultimately be identical with one another, one must realize itself in the other. Then only the pure will gains its absolute satisfaction; and then we gain the fourth value of completion.[81]

Specifically, the logical values or values of science concern the connections among objects of experience over time and space; the aesthetic values concern the internal coherence of the experience of individual objects; ethical values concern the realization of a coherent self and coherent relations with others in a world; and metaphysical values, whether in religious form (the value of "holiness") or philosophical form (the value of "absoluteness") concern the recognition of the underlying unity of these various forms of unity.

But our concern is Münsterberg's conception of aesthetic value. Münsterberg presents the experience of beauty, which he recognizes may be provided by works of nature or works of art, as the experience of unity or coherence within an object, but specifically, once again effacing the boundary between the theoretical and the practical, as experience of the unity or coherence of the *will* within an object, the presentation of a coherent volition within the object that satisfies our own volition for coherence. The "beautiful comes to us in the real experience with the whole richness of its own striving and feeling and willing."[82] There must be natural as well as artistic beauty because we can experience beauty in "naïve life" as well as in "the conscious work of civilization ... the functions of art,"[83] and our experience of the unity of the object's volition must be metaphorical in the case of natural beauty, the beauty of flowers and landscapes to which we do not ordinarily ascribe any volition at all, while it can at best be indirect in the case of works of art, where we may ascribe volition literally to artists but not to their works, although it is our experience of their works that is crucial for aesthetic value. Nevertheless, Münsterberg insists that "If we really start from experience, we must acknowledge that the beautiful is never given to us as a naturalistic object, but as a free expression of attitudes and will which we as willing personalities can understand by feeling with them."[84] Münsterberg illustrates his claim with examples from both nature and art. First, although

---

[81] Münsterberg, *Eternal Values*, p. 78.
[82] Münsterberg, *Eternal Values*, p. 171.
[83] Münsterberg, *Eternal Values*, p. 165.
[84] Münsterberg, *Eternal Values*, p. 171.

here most authors would have described the experience he adduces as sublime rather than beautiful,

> In the real experience the beautiful unity exists for us in nature itself or in the work of art, and it is our part to understand and to feel, and not to create it. The lightning flashes, the thunder rolls, the black clouds threaten, the rugged rocks stretch upward in defiant power, the surging sea rages and demands its victim. If we feel with that sympathizing, we do not seek the unity of the excited nature in ourselves, but in this raving of the elements. They are not only filled with the will which we share, but their volitions belong together, support one another, reënforce one another, and point to one another. The rocks and the clouds and the waves all really want the same thing, and we feel excited with their common emotion.

Münsterberg then goes on to the case of art:

> It is not different when the unity of the work of art speaks to us. The charming little rococo picture gossips of light shepherds' play. The position of the figures betrays the gallant tone; the features, the eyes, the lips, frivolously say the same; the laughing landscape in the background agrees with the flowers in the meadow, and the slender willow with the fleecy little clouds and the glancing brooklet. Every ribbon in the light gown flutters in tender play. In the soft colors and the mildly curved lines all wills are the same, all wills the one, and their real unity must be felt if we want to understand the picture. The unity of the beautiful is the agreement of its real volitions, which we share only in our feelings.[85]

We may note in the second passage that a work of art that represents nature can of course display the kind of unity that we find in nature itself as well as that which might be peculiar to art. We may also note that in this passage Münsterberg does mention the play of both people (shepherds) and things (the ribbons of the gown), but as part of the coherent content of the work, what it represents, not as a central part of our experience of the work. On the contrary, our experience in both cases is an experience of the unity of volition, whether in actual nature, represented nature, or the artistic representation of nature – but there is no mention of the volition of the artist. It should also be noted that Münsterberg treats our own satisfying sense of coherence as an empathetic response to or "sharing" of "the agreement of [the] real volitions" of the beautiful work of nature or art, and does not treat the unified volition of the object as a projection of our own feeling onto the object. In this regard his theory is diametrically opposed to the theory of empathy of the two Vischers and Theodor Lipps, which interprets empathy as a

---

[85] Münsterberg, *Eternal Values*, p. 173.

form of projection rather than reception,[86] and which we will consider in the next chapter. Münsterberg insists that "We know now that æsthetic values can be given in the world of things only when the things have their own will.... An æsthetic value is given to us only when a manifoldness of volitions approaches us, and when those volitions point to one another and agree with one another ... only a nature which wills can come under the æsthetic point of view."[87]

At this point it becomes clear that both Schopenhauer as well as Kant have influenced Münsterberg. His ascription of will to nature of course smacks of Schopenhauer rather than Kant, and when his discussion turns to disinterestedness it also reveals the same ambivalence that Schopenhauer's did. On the one hand, Münsterberg argues that we must approach beautiful objects in a disinterested frame of mind, free from our personal and practical concerns, if we are to experience their beauty:

> It always remains essential that we can understand this phase of the outer world when our practical desire which serves our personal interests is little concerned. The purple sunset may transmit its own excitement to our soul, but when the sun troubles us with its burning rays at noon-time, we try to protect ourselves from them, and this effort inhibits every sympathizing feeling with the own will of the sun which expresses itself in its fiery glow.[88]

On the other hand, particularly in the case of art, Münsterberg suggests that the experience of beauty turns us away from our usual concern with our personal practical needs rather than presupposing that we have already turned away from that concern. Thus art leads to a "suppression of all felt relations," and in that "lies the true unreality of the life which art offers to us": "The unreal is that which offers itself completely in its presentation; it is that which is a whole, which does not point to anything outside of itself"[89] and thereby turns our attention away from anything outside of itself, such as our ordinary practical concerns. Münsterberg sounds just like Schopenhauer, whose theory of sympathy as the basis of ethics he has earlier explicitly acknowledged,[90] when he writes that "That which offers itself as unreal excludes every expectation of practical effects. Hence the effect on ourselves and our own surroundings

---

[86] See Theodor Lipps, *Ästhetik: Psychologie des Schönen und der Kunst*, 2 vols. (Hamburg and Leipzig: Voss, 1903–1906).
[87] Münsterberg, *Eternal Values*, p. 177.
[88] Münsterberg, *Eternal Values*, p. 175.
[89] Münsterberg, *Eternal Values*, p. 210.
[90] Münsterberg, *Eternal Values*, p. 190.

is excluded, and that annihilates by principle our interest in entering with an own action and in taking attitudes. There is no point of contact between the work of art and our practical personality."[91] Of course, there is no actual contradiction in the idea that we may need to approach art (or natural beauty) with a certain degree of disinterestedness but that the experience of beauty thereby made possible can then intensify our absorption in the object and our disinterestedness or lack of concern with reality.

Münsterberg divides aesthetic values into the values of harmony, love, and happiness, and correlates these categories with a distinction among the "outer world" of objects, the "fellow-world" of other people, and the "inner world" of one's own feelings. He then correlates the main branches of art with these three domains and therefore with these three values:

> The self-agreement of the world in our life-experience gave us the value of harmony for the outer world, of love for the fellow-world, of happiness for the inner world. If art is called systematically to bring the self-agreement of the world to its expression in the history of civilization, fine art [that is, visual art] is fulfilling this task for the outer world, literature for the fellow-world, and music for the inner world.[92]

Münsterberg's theory of music as forming "our own inner world to a unified tissue of volitions," in which "the tones lead us back to ourselves" and "Everything remains related to the striving and counter-striving of the feeling and willing of the self and returns to it in the unity of the I"[93] is also clearly influenced by Schopenhauer's analysis of music as the representation of the will itself rather than of any of the externalizations of the will in the characteristic or Platonic forms of objects. But instead of following the further details of Münsterberg's classification of the arts, we can conclude this discussion of his work with a look at his pioneering book on film, *The Silent Photoplay in 1916*, or as it was later renamed, *The Film: A Psychological Study*.[94]

After a brief history tracing the origin of cinema in various devices for creating the illusion of motion from series of drawn pictures in the earlier part of the nineteenth century through Eadweard Muybridge's

---

[91] Münsterberg, *Eternal Values*, p. 213.
[92] Münsterberg, *Eternal Values*, p. 204.
[93] Münsterberg, *Eternal Values*, p. 253.
[94] Hugo Münsterberg, *The Silent Photoplay in 1916* (New York: Appleton, 1916); retitled *The Film: A Psychological Study*, with a new foreword by Richard Griffith (New York: Dover Publications, 1970).

stop-motion photography later in the century and then the rapid growth of the popularity of silent films in the two decades following the introduction of Edison's "kinetoscope" in 1895, Münsterberg gives a detailed description of the roles of depth and movement, attention, memory and imagination, and emotions in our experience of the images of the film. Central to Münsterberg's analysis is our own projection of movement onto a sequence of images, each of which is itself static. Here, in contrast to his account of aesthetic experience in *The Eternal Values* a half-dozen years earlier, Münsterberg emphasizes the role of the imagination in the transformation of experience; for example, "*The objective world is molded by the interests of the mind. Events which are far distant from one another so that we could not be physically present at all of them at the same time are fusing in our field of vision, just as they are brought together in our own consciousness.*"[95] But, consistently with his earlier work, Münsterberg stresses our sense of the unreality of the images before us, so that our experience of film is described as a complex experience involving a sense of both reality and unreality, and an oscillation between them: "Even in the most objective factor of the mind, the perception, we find this peculiar oscillation. We perceive the movement; and yet we perceive it as something which has not its independent character as an outer world process, because our mind has built it up from single pictures rapidly following one another. We perceive things in their plastic depth; and yet again the depth is not that of the outer world. We are aware of its unreality and of the pictorial flatness of the impressions."[96] Because of the importance of a sense of unreality as part of our experience of cinema, Münsterberg rejects any interpretation of it as a mere imitation of ordinary life and, further, as an imitation of traditional theater: "moving pictures ... *are not and ought never to be imitations of the theater.*"[97] This is the basis for an argument that live theater and film are two very different arts, which is important for later film studies; but what is important for our purposes is that it is also the basis for Münsterberg's argument that, in spite of its basis in photography, which we often take to be a transparent reproduction of the actual world, film, like other arts, achieves "unreality" in the specific sense of detachment from our ordinary practical concern with reality, and that our pleasure in it arises from its self-contained completeness rather than from its reference to

---

[95] Münsterberg, *The Film*, p. 46. The italics in this and following quotations are Münsterberg's, the emphasis setting them off as among the author's central theses.
[96] Münsterberg, *The Film*, p. 58.
[97] Münsterberg, *The Film*, p. 60.

anything beyond itself. Film *"becomes art just insofar as it overcomes reality, stops imitating itself and leaves the imitated reality behind it."*[98] Thus film, like other arts, *"shows us the things and events perfectly complete in themselves, freed from all connections which lead beyond their own limits, that is, in perfect isolation."*[99] Münsterberg then draws the same conclusion he had drawn in *The Eternal Values*, namely that the value in the art of cinema "lies just in the deviation from reality in the service of human desires and ideals ... the desire and ideal of the artist in every possible art is to give us things which are freed from the connection of the world and which stand before us complete in themselves,"[100] and which thereby give us a sympathetic sense of our own self-completeness. The remarkable thing about film in Münsterberg's analysis is that it does this in spite of the fact that it might initially seem to be a mere copy of reality rather than a projection of "unreality" in his sense; but all of his analysis of the perception of motion in the experience of cinema was aimed at showing precisely that we do not respond to it as a mere imitation of real motion. Of course, since his claim that "every possible art" aims to free us from the connection to the world and give us things that are complete in themselves, other arts must have their ways of doing this too, even if they do not involve the particular oscillation between a sense of reality and a sense of unreality that is characteristic of film.

A child of his own moment in history, Münsterberg was convinced that the use of either color or sound in film would interfere with the creation of the sense of unreality in film; it can be debated whether he was right about that. But we will not pursue that debate here; instead, we will now turn to a Neo-Kantian who worked independently of the two main schools of Marburg and Southwestern Neo-Kantianism, and who, unlike any of the figures we have been considering, did make room for the Kantian concept of play in his aesthetic theory, while also emphasizing the place of cognition and emotion in aesthetic experience. This is the Berlin philosopher Wilhelm Dilthey, who was thus the only figure in Neo-Kantianism, indeed in late nineteenth-century Germany altogether, to continue the development of a threefold approach to aesthetics that had been started by a few in the eighteenth century, such as Kames, and only by Schleiermacher, the subject of one of Dilthey's main works, among the German Idealists.

---

[98] Münsterberg, *The Film*, p. 62.
[99] Münsterberg, *The Film*, p. 64.
[100] Münsterberg, *The Film*, p. 65.

5. DILTHEY

Turning from the orthodox Neo-Kantians of the provincial Marburg and Heidelberg schools to the more cosmopolitan philosophers of Berlin, we find in Wilhelm Dilthey (1833–1911) a similar emphasis that the proper subject matter of art is human feeling, but a comprehensive approach to this thesis that uses what Dilthey finds best in Kant and his predecessors, in his idealist successors, and in the more recent psychological aesthetics of Fechner and others that neither accepts anything from these earlier approaches without independent validation from experience nor rejects any of them completely. Dilthey presented his major statement in aesthetics in the form of a "poetics" or a theory of literature rather than of the arts in general, in this formal regard thus returning to the tradition of Baumgarten, but his position was clearly meant to apply to the arts in general.[101]

In the central essay on "The Imagination of the Poet," first published in 1887, Dilthey claims that the content of poetry, and by implication of the other arts, is "lived experience" or *Erlebnis*, the entire range of human feelings, and not "ideas," that is, metaphysical truths of the sort imputed to art by the absolute idealists. Thus he writes that

> This to and fro of life at its fullest, of perception enlivened and saturated by feeling, and of the feeling of life shining forth in the clarity of the image: that is the essential characteristic of the content of all poetry. Such lived experience is fully possessed only when it is brought into an inner relation with other lived experiences and its meaning is grasped thereby. Lived experience can never be reduced to thoughts or ideas.[102]

---

[101] The chief work on Dilthey remains Rudolf A. Makkreel, *Dilthey: Philosopher of the Human Studies* (Princeton: Princeton University Press, 1975). The substantial Part Two of this work (pp. 77–202) is devoted to "The Concept of the Imagination" and Dilthey's aesthetics. See also Frithjof Rodi, *Morphologie und Hermeneutik: Zur Methode von Diltheys Ästhetik* (Stuttgart: Kohlhammer, 1969). See also Matthias Jung, *Dilthey zur Einführung* (Hamburg: Junius Verlag, 1996), which discusses "Dilthey's middle phase: aesthetics, pragmatism, and descriptive psychology" at pp. 87–138. Several other general works on Dilthey are Michael Ermarth, *Wilhelm Dilthey: The Critique of Historical Reason* (Chicago: University of Chicago Press, 1978), and Hans Peter Rickman, *Wilhelm Dilthey: Pioneer of the Human Studies* (London: Elek, 1979). Hans-Georg Gadamer discusses Dilthey in *Truth and Method*, trans. Joel Weinsheimer and Donald G. Marshall, second, revised edition (London: Continuum, 2004), especially pp. 213–51.

[102] Wilhelm Dilthey, "The Imagination of the Poet," trans. Louis Agosta and Rudolf A. Makkreel, in Wilhelm Dilthey, *Selected Works, Volume V: Poetry and Experience*, ed. Rudolf A. Makkreel and Frithjof Rodi (Princeton: Princeton University Press, 1985), p. 59. All quotations from Dilthey will be from this volume.

And then again,

> Every living work of major scope takes its subject matter from something factual that has been experienced. In the last analysis, it expresses only lived experience, transformed and generalized by the feelings. For this reason, no idea may be sought in literature[103] –

a claim that Dilthey makes explicit is addressed against the Hegelian tradition of speculative, metaphysical aesthetics: "Thus the interpretation of literary works as presently dominated by *Hegelian aesthetics* must be opposed." Any attempt to give a metaphysical interpretation of *Hamlet*, for example, can offer only "a paltry description of the incommensurable facts [to] which Shakespeare has given a universally valid meaning in his drama ... the lived experience of the poet and its unnerving symbols constitute a dramatic core that cannot be expressed in any proposition."[104] But these few quotations suggest how complex Dilthey's aesthetics actually is. While he rejects the metaphysical interpretations of art in idealist aesthetics as wringing the life out of art in behalf of some abstract propositions (precisely the kind that are better dealt with by philosophy itself), he accepts the idealist thesis that works of art are embedded in the cultures that produced them and cannot be understood entirely apart from such cultures. Yet at the same time, while he rejects the Kantian reduction of the feelings relevant to art to the single feeling of pleasure in favor of his view that the arts concern the entire range of human feelings, from the most painful to the most pleasurable, in all their multiplicity, he also accepts the Kantian demand that aesthetic experience be universally valid, and seeks to explain how human feelings embedded in the context of one culture are nevertheless universal and accessible to other cultures. And while he certainly assigns art the task of bringing us to *understanding* our feelings, or cognizing them – thus he continues the first passage just quoted by saying that the "lived experience" constituted by the "to and fro of life at its fullest" is

> fully possessed only when it is brought into an inner relation with other lived experience and its meaning is grasped thereby. Lived experience can never be reduced to thought or ideas. However, it can be related to the totality of human existence through reflection, especially through generalization and the establishment of relationships, and thus it can be understood in its essence, that is, its meaning. All poetry – its elements and their

---

[103] Dilthey, "Imagination of the Poet," p. 137.
[104] Dilthey, "Imagination of the Poet," pp. 138–9.

forms of connection – is composed of lived experience understood in this sense[105] –

he also emphasizes that there is a strong element of enjoyment of the sheer play of forms and contents in the experience of art, of the enjoyment of the feeling of life for its own sake rather than for the sake of generalizable knowledge. (This is also part of what he means by choosing as his term for "experience" *Erlebnis* rather than the more traditional *Erfahrung*, which for those brought up on Kant could only mean experience as it is subsumed under concepts rather than as it is grasped more immediately.)[106]

Thus, unlike the Neo-Kantians previously considered, Dilthey by no means rejects Kant's theory of aesthetic experience as the free play of our mental powers, but argues that, along with comprehending and communicating our emotions, enjoying the play of the full range of our mental powers, including our emotional as well as cognitive capacities, is central to our experience of art. Although his rejection of the view that art concerns abstract ideas can be taken as a criticism of Kant's theory of "aesthetic ideas" as well as of the post-Kantian idealist aesthetics that to some extent took its inspiration from that Kantian conception, Dilthey would nevertheless reconnect the idea of the free play of the imagination with an idea of truthfulness to significant content, although this content becomes the concrete reality of human emotions rather than the abstract ideas of morality. And as Dilthey stresses, our experience of the emotional content of art is *lived* experience; thus through art we do not just cognize emotions, but feel their impact. Dilthey's poetics thus represents one of those points in the history of modern aesthetics where the aesthetics of truth and the aesthetics of play, both understood in the broadest possible sense, were joined to the aesthetics of emotional impact to create a comprehensive account of aesthetic experience – although confining himself to the case of poetry as he does, Dilthey does not generalize his position to all the arts, let alone to the aesthetic experience of nature.

Like so many other German philosophers of his day, Dilthey was originally sent to university to study for the ministry, but studied classical philology and philosophy along with theology and in spite of familial resistance pursued an academic career in philosophy. Yet although his

---

[105] Dilthey, "Imagination of the Poet," p. 59.
[106] On the contrast between *Erlebnis* and *Erfahrung*, see Makkreel, *Dilthey*, pp. 8–9 and 387–8.

own work became fully secular, with religion being treated only as one form of the cultural self-expression of mankind among others, his early study of theology produced lasting effects: one of Dilthey's lifelong projects was *The Life of Schleiermacher*, one volume of which was published during his lifetime (1870) and the other of which, as was true of much of his work, only posthumously; Dilthey also published a work specifically on Schleiermacher's hermeneutics in 1860.[107] Another of Dilthey's biographical works was *The History of the Young Hegel* (1905), focusing on Hegel's most theological period. Dilthey's work on Schleiermacher and Hegel was facilitated by his appointment at their University of Berlin in 1883, following appointments at Basel, Kiel, and Breslau. He was already fifty years old when appointed at Berlin, but taught and wrote copiously for twenty-five years before retiring from that position. In addition to his biographical works and many works on the history of philosophy and of ideas in Germany, especially since the Renaissance, Dilthey wrote a series of systematic works on the foundations of the *Geisteswissenschaften*, the "human sciences" or better, as Rudolf Makkreel translates the term, the "human studies," including what we now distinguish as humanities and social sciences. He is sometimes described as attempting to add a fourth critique to Kant's three, namely a "critique of historical reason," although that focus misrepresents Dilthey's view that all of the "human sciences," and not just art, are concerned with the expression of the full range of human experience, not just abstract thought. Chief among these works are the *Introduction to the Human Sciences* of 1883, published the year Dilthey started teaching in Berlin; the *Ideas for a Descriptive and an Analytical Psychology* (1894); the *Origins of Hermeneutics* (1900); and the *Construction of the Historical World in the Human Sciences* published in 1910, one year before Dilthey's death.[108]

But we are concerned with Dilthey's approach to aesthetics, or his "poetics." This was presented not only in the 1887 essay on "The Imagination of the Poet: Elements for a Poetics," originally published in a *Festschrift* for the great historian of classical philosophy Eduard Zeller (although its only concession to Zeller's interests is an opening discussion in which

---

[107] See Dilthey, *Selected Works*, ed. Rudolf A. Makkreel and Frithjof Rodi, vol. IV (Princeton: Princeton University Press, 1996), pp. 33–227.
[108] See Dilthey, *Selected Works*, ed. Rudolf A. Makkreel and Frithjof Rodi (Princeton: Princeton University Press, 1985–2010): Vol. I, *Introduction to the Human Sciences* (1989); Vol. II, *Understanding the Human World* (2010); Vol. III, *The Formation of the Historical World in the Human Sciences* (2002); and Vol. IV, *Hermeneutics and the Study of History* (1996).

it praises Aristotle's *Poetics* as deriving sound principles for a dramaturgy of the imitation of human action but criticizes Aristotle for failing to recognize that art should really concern the inner life of human beings),[109] but also in a series of essays on Goethe, Hölderlin, Lessing, and Novalis that he began early in his career and which, when finally published in a volume edited by his students in 1906, proved to be his most popular work.[110] Here we will focus on "The Imagination of the Poet." Following in the tradition of Baumgarten with his characterization of the *felix aestheticus* and the aesthetics of genius in Kant and others, Dilthey organizes this work around the characteristic and techniques of the poet: its two main sections concern the "Description of the Poet's Constitution" with "An Attempt to Explain Poetic Creativity Psychologically" (Section Two) and "A Theory of Poetic Technique to be Derived from these Psychological Foundations" (Section Four). But Dilthey argues throughout that the aim of the poet is to make it possible for the audience to experience what the poet experiences, the full range of human feelings in all their play and in all their significance, so he draws no hard line between the aesthetics of creation and the aesthetics of reception, and his analysis of the conditions for poetic creation is also explicitly intended as an analysis of aesthetic experience. Thus, Dilthey begins his description of poetic creativity with the claim that the difference between what it takes to create art and what it takes to experience art is only a matter of degree, not of kind, and that successful art brings the experience of the audience close to the intensity of the experience of the artist:

> The nexus of events provided by our experiences of life need only undergo a transformation in order to become an aesthetic plot. There is no special morality of the theater, there are no resolutions which satisfy us in a novel but not in life itself. That is precisely what is powerfully gripping about a work of literature – that it originates in a psyche similar to ours, only greater and more vigorous. It expands our heart beyond its actual confines without displacing us into the thin, rarefied atmosphere of a world unfamiliar to us. The activities of the [artist's] imagination ... should foster and strengthen whatever is best in the reader or listener, teach him to understand better his own emotions, to look for hidden life in the monotonous stretches of his own path, to tend his modest garden, as it were, and then also to be equal to whatever extraordinary things occur there.[111]

---

[109] Dilthey, "Imagination of the Poet," pp. 37–9.
[110] Makkreel and Rodi's *Selected Works, Volume V* includes the essays on Goethe (pp. 235–302) and Hölderlin (pp. 303–83).
[111] Dilthey, "The Imagination of the Poet," p. 57.

Art has its origins in the human drives to experience, to understand experience, and to express and communicate experience: "it emerges in the life of the human mind, which expresses its content in gestures and sound, transposes the power of its impulses to a beloved form or to nature, and enjoys the intensification of its experience in images of the conditions that produced it." The urge to experience and the urge to communicate are inseparable, so the artist's experience would be incomplete without its communication to an audience, and the audience's reception of the communication is also a recreation of the experience that is communicated to them: "One and the same human nature generates both artistic creation and taste that re-experiences feelings." To be sure, Dilthey continues, "this process works more powerfully in the creator than in the spectator," and it is more active and voluntary in the creator, who is "guided by the will," that is, whose intentions determine the nature of the work more than the audience's intentions do (although of course the audience must voluntarily decide to go to the theater or read the book), "but its constituents are predominantly the same."[112] Thus the analysis of the elements of poetic creativity will also be the analysis of the elements of aesthetic experience, and in practice Dilthey constantly switches back and forth between a poetics of artistic creation and an aesthetics of artistic experience. But what is most important here is that for Dilthey the urge to understand human emotions cannot be separated from the urge to feel and communicate them; thus he links the aesthetics of truth and the aesthetics of emotional impact.

The two main parts of Dilthey's work are the analysis of the elements of poetic creativity and of the general rules of poetic technique. He makes it clear in both parts that he is attempting to do justice to the eighteenth-century and especially Kantian concern for the possibility of universal validity in judgments of taste. Thus he writes that "The task of a poetics which derives from [the] living relationship to the artistic pursuit itself is to determine whether it can attain universally valid laws that are useful as rules of creativity and as norms for criticism,"[113] and that "The central question of all poetics – that concerning the *universal validity* or historical variability of the judgment of taste, of the concept of beauty, of technique and its rules – must be answered if poetics is to be of use to the creative poet, to guide the public's judgment, or to furnish a firm foundation for aesthetic criticism and philology."[114] These remarks make

---

[112] Dilthey, "Imagination of the Poet," p. 121.
[113] Dilthey, "Imagination of the Poet," p. 34.
[114] Dilthey, "Imagination of the Poet," p. 54.

clear Dilthey's conviction that the theories of aesthetic creation and of aesthetic experience are at bottom one and the same. Their larger context also makes clear his complex view of the relationship of the universal validity of aesthetic creations and experiences to history on the one hand and psychology on the other. Thus, following the latter remark, he continues that universal laws of taste cannot be found by a purely historical method, for "every empirical, comparative method can only derive a rule from the historical past, whose validity is thus historically restricted. It cannot make any binding claims or judgments about what is new and belongs to the future. Such a rule applies only retrospectively, and contains no law for the future." Instead, "the law of beauty and the rules of poetry can be derived only from human nature ... poetics must seek this firm basis in the life of the psyche."[115] By the last, he means that aesthetics must be founded in a descriptive psychology, a characterization of the most general cognitive, conative, and emotional tendencies of human nature. But at the same time, he argues at length that the experimental psychological aesthetics popularized especially, as we saw, by Fechner, can only capture particular, subordinate elements of aesthetic experiences – preferences for one sort of shape over another – and that while such results are valid in the laboratory, where the subject responds to isolated forms or features, real aesthetic experiences are not aggregates of such preferences but unified responses to complex works, and the complexity of such works and the unity of our responses to them cannot be captured by experimental psychology but only by his own, more complex descriptive psychology. (As we also saw, this simplifies Fechner's actual analysis of aesthetic experience.)

But Dilthey also argues – and this is his solution to the question "How is the technique of a particular period and particular nature related to ... universal rules? How do we overcome the difficulty, which all the human sciences must face, of deriving universally valid principles from inner experiences, which are personally limited, composite, and yet incapable of analysis?"[116] – that the fundamental commonality of the human psyche must manifest itself differently in different historical and cultural epochs, yet at the same time that commonality of the human psyche must also make it possible for humans from one historical and cultural epoch to understand those of another, at least if adequate information about their whole culture and way of life is available. This is so because

---

[115] Dilthey, "Imagination of the Poet," p. 54.
[116] Dilthey, "Imagination of the Poet," p. 34.

of course it is part of his theory that a work of art does not capture and express a universally valid human feeling in isolation, but only in a complex cultural nexus, so naturally that experience can be recaptured in some other time and place only if adequate information about that entire nexus is available. (Here Dilthey shows the influence of Herder as well as Schleiermacher.) From all of this, Dilthey concludes that it is possible to infer general principles of aesthetic creation and reception, general guidelines for poetic techinque and critical evaluation, but not formulae that can be mechanically or algorithmically followed:

> Thus, the works of the poet also possess *universal validity* and *necessity*. But here these features do not signify what they do in the propositions of science. "Universal validity" signifies that every heart with feelings can re-create and appreciate the work in question. That which is selected from our life and taken together as being necessary for the nexus of life as such, we call "essential." "Necessity" signifies that the nexus existing in a work of literature is as compelling for the spectator as for the creative artist. When these requirements are satisfied, then the real manifests the essential.[117]

This interpretation of the universal validity and necessity of aesthetic experience is of course completely consistent with Kant's thesis that judgments of taste speak with a "universal voice" and achieve "exemplary" necessity but that they are "not determinable by grounds of proof at all" and thus can never be "forced" on anyone.[118] The "rules" that Dilthey offers are, to use several of his own terms, "norms" or "guidelines" that can inspire artistic creation and reception, not algorithms that can mechanically determine such production and response. In this regard, Dilthey's aesthetics is genuinely Kantian (and for that matter, Humean as well).

The non-determinate character of Dilthey's "rules" is also implied by the fact that, unlike those of the Marburg and Heidelberg Neo-Kantians, Dilthey's account of aesthetic experience makes room for play with the inner life as well as experience and cognition of it, and ultimately insists upon an intimate and inseparable connection between play and these other two dimensions of aesthetic experience. This becomes clear in his analysis of artistic creativity as well as in his exposition of the general principles of artistic technique. The first main part of Dilthey's poetics consists of the "Description of the Poet's Constitution."[119] Here,

---

[117] Dilthey, "Imagination of the Poet," p. 116.
[118] Kant, *CPJ*, §8, 5:216; §18, 5:237; §33, 5:284.
[119] Dilthey, "Imagination of the Poet," section 4, ch. 1, pp. 56–68.

drawing on the tradition of the analysis of the *felix aestheticus* and genius, he enumerates the special qualities of the creative poet: "intensity and precision of his *perceptual images*," "the clarity of delineation, strength of sensation, and energy of projection peculiar to his memory images and their formations," "the power with which he <expresses or> recreates psychic states, both states experienced in himself and those observed in others," "a capacity to truly *enliven images*, and the attendant satisfaction from perception ... *saturated by images*," and, finally, "the poet stands apart in that his images and their connections unfold freely *beyond the bounds of reality*."[120] This list intertwines heightened powers of perception and cognition with powers of imagination and invention, powers for the experience and apprehension of the real character of human perceptions and the feelings associated with them and powers for the creation of complexes of perceptions and feelings going beyond anything actually experienced. This duality in Dilthey's conception of poetic power is manifested throughout his work with an emphasis on the truthfulness of the poet's perception and expression of feeling on the one hand and on the freedom of the poet's inventions from the constraints of ordinary reality on the other – truth and play in the realm of feelings – but ultimately resolved with the suggestion that none of these – truth, feeling, and play – can exist without the other.

Dilthey's next chapter, "An Attempt to Explain Poetic Creativity Psychologically,"[121] attempts to give a "scientific" foundation to the previous analysis. Here Dilthey situates "The Place of Artistic Creativity in the Nexus of Psychic Life" in general.[122] The first point that he emphasizes here is the element of play in poetic creation and therefore experience: when the poetic "will controls [the] elementary and formative processes" of ordinary perception, cognition, and feeling "with intense energy and with a consciousness of its goal, a fundamental distinction arises which differentiates the play of our representations from logical thought,"[123] and the "formative processes of the artistic imagination are produced by the play of feelings."[124] This emphasis on play with both feelings and "logical thoughts" characterizes the first four stages of Dilthey's analysis of a series of "spheres of feeling,"[125] culminating in a sphere of feelings

---

[120] Dilthey, "Imagination of the Poet," pp. 61–6.
[121] Dilthey, "Imagination of the Poet," pp. 68–107.
[122] Dilthey, "Imagination of the Poet," p. 73.
[123] Dilthey, "Imagination of the Poet," p. 74.
[124] Dilthey, "Imagination of the Poet," p. 77.
[125] Dilthey, "Imagination of the Poet," p. 79.

comprising "the great variety of feelings that spring from the cognitive *connection* of our *representations* and which are aroused by the mere forms of our representational and thought processes, without regard to the relationship of their content to our being."[126] Here Dilthey's description is Kantian, emphasizing the freedom of the imagination to play with the materials of cognition without the constraints of the ordinary rules and purposes of cognition: "In summary, we find an artwork pleasing because the forms of the representational and thinking processes which occasion its apprehension by the recipient" – note how he has glided from analyzing the character of aesthetic production to analyzing that of aesthetic experience – "are accompanied by pleasure, still quite apart from the relation of the content to our concrete impulses."[127] Although Dilthey immediately follows this claim about aesthetic experience with the remark that it was anticipated by "Leibniz's idea that plurality must emerge *from unity* and reemerge in unity" and claims that "this principle was made the basis for art and poetry especially" at the end of the seventeenth and the beginning of the eighteenth centuries, it also recapitulates Kant's claim that the detachment of our experience and judgment from the ordinary interests of cognition and practice leaves room for the free play of the imagination within the most general conditions of cognition. But then Dilthey goes on to describe a fifth sphere of feeling that "results from the particular *material impulses* which pervade the whole of life and whose entire content is possessed in a reflexive awareness obtained through feelings." The feelings he has in mind here are those associated with "the drives for nourishment, for self-preservation or the will-to-live, for procreation, and love of offspring," as well as "a second group of feelings in which we experience the pain and pleasure of others as our own," in which we "appropriate another's life in our own ego, as it were, through sympathy, pity, or love." He then maintains that "the elementary material of poetry" is to be found in this final, twofold sphere of feelings, and thus that the "more firmly motif and plot are rooted in life, the more powerfully do they move our senses. The great elemental drives of human existence, the passions that derive from them and the fate of these passions in the world, these constitute the authentic basis of all poetic ability" (here Dilthey has switched from the analysis of aesthetic experience back to that of aesthetic creation)._[128] This sphere of

---

[126] Dilthey, "Imagination of the Poet," p. 81.
[127] Dilthey, "Imagination of the Poet," p. 82.
[128] Dilthey, "Imagination of the Poet," p. 83.

feelings leads Dilthey to formulate a *"principle of truthfulness* in the sense of the powerful reality of a person and of the elementary drives in him" that holds for all of the arts. This principle of truthfulness holds even or especially for the arts that are not overtly representational, "For where no external truth, in the sense of a depiction of reality, is aimed at, as in architecture and music, there the forms are rooted in the inner power of a substantial human being, rather than in the mere imitation of the life of others or even the forms created by them."[129]

In this analysis of the spheres of feelings as the proper subject matter of art and aesthetic experience, Dilthey has clearly rejected the metaphysical aesthetics of absolute idealism in favor of a conception of art focused on the expression of human emotions. He has gone beyond Cohen in recognizing that we must feel as well as cognize such emotions, beyond Cohn in reviving Kant's notion of play, and beyond Münsterberg in that regard as well. But, although he has clearly recognized the importance of a free play with such emotions and the perceptions and thoughts that arouse them as an essential component of aesthetic experience, it may still look as if he has subordinated the importance of this free play to his principle of truthfulness, the principle that art accurately capture and express the kinds of emotions that we really do have in life. As Dilthey continues, however, the opposite seems to be the case: the principle of truthfulness becomes subordinated to the principle of play, or at least to a version of what Cohen had recognized as the principle of idealization in art: the most intense emotions and the most intense "feeling of life" itself can only be evoked by works of poetic imagination that start with the situations of real life and the emotions associated with them but then free themselves from the bonds of the ordinary. Thus under the rubric of "Laws governing the free transformation of representations beyond the bounds of reality under the influence of the life of the feelings," he writes that "the powerful effect of art and literature does not depend solely on our enjoyment of those constituents of consciousness that already possess an aesthetic effect in the course of our life; it also depends on *images that are formed to evoke a still purer kind of aesthetic pleasure.*"[130] Several pages later he writes:

> The poet is aware of the nexus of reality and he distinguishes his images from it. He differentiates reality from the realm of beauty and illusion. However much these images approximate the character of reality, they

---

[129] Dilthey, "Imagination of the Poet," p. 84.
[130] Dilthey, "Imagination of the Poet," p. 93.

nevertheless remain separated from it by a fine line. During his creative work, the poet lives in a dream world where these images receive the mark of reality. But they do not receive this through the obscure natural power of hallucinations, but rather through the freedom of a creative capacity in possession of itself.... The typical and the ideal in poetry transcend experience so that it can be felt and understood more profoundly than in the most faithful copies of reality.[131]

But what is really happening here is that the aesthetic of truth, the aesthetics of emotional impact, and the aesthetics of play are all being joined, because it is only through the free play of the imagination unconstrained by the confines of ordinary life that the emotions of real life can be evoked in their purest form and thus be most fully understood.

At bottom, this is Dilthey's conclusion, although he still sometimes emphasizes one element more than the other even though in successful art none can exist without the others. Thus he follows the paragraph just quoted, which comes in the conclusion of his analysis of poetic creativity (and thus aesthetic experience), with the remark that "This kind of belief in images of things that are unreal, and the illusion that results, can best be compared with what takes place in *children at play*. Literature is akin to play, as Schiller has demonstrated. In play, the energy of the child's psychic life becomes active and free," and in "later stages of life the distinguishing trait of play is that its activities stand in no causal relation to the purposive nexus of this life." But at the outset of his analysis of poetic "technique," the second main part of his poetics,[132] he again suggests that the free play of the imagination is the necessary condition for the expression of the most intense forms of imagination on the part of the artist and the communication of that to the audience rather than the aim of art on its own. Thus he makes a series of statements which we may regard as revealing the core of his position. First he states that "poetic creativity ... initially has its standard and distinguishing characteristic in the fact that the nexus of images produced satisfies the creator himself. At the same time, however, the satisfaction of the reader or listener becomes the goal of the poet and the standard of his achievement." This leads Dilthey to one of his highlighted "principles," which certainly does not have the form of a rule that can be mechanically followed but instead states a goal of art in the most general terms:

---

[131] Dilthey, "Imagination of the Poet," p. 101.
[132] Dilthey, "Imagination of the Poet," section 4, chapter 2, pp. 127–60.

The poet's technique is a transformation of the content of lived experience into an illusory whole existing merely in the reader's or listener's representations. The sensuous energy of this structure of images has a powerful feeling-content, is significant for thought, and produces a lasting satisfaction with the aid of other lesser means.

This is followed by the remark that "It is constitutive of the *artist's character* that his work does not intrude into the purposive system of real life and is not limited by it." Disinterestedness and the freedom of the imagination that it permits become the enabling condition for the artist's and the audience's experience and enjoyment of human feelings and emotions in their purest form:

> Disinterestedness, together with the deep reflection stemming from it, for which everything becomes lived experience, and which hovers over its objects with a calm and contemplative eye, forms a more ideal reality that evokes belief and simultaneously satisfies both the heart and the head: these are the characteristics of the poet.[133]

On the next page, Dilthey reiterates that "Art is play," that "The entire effect which it would like to produce consists of a present and lasting satisfaction" rather than any satisfaction of "direct interests," but then again suggests that free play is the necessary condition of the experience of emotion in all of its intensity:

> Such a satisfaction, however, is bound to the illusion which makes imitation a lived experience of reality. The basis of all genuine art is the agreement of the product of the imagination with the laws and value-determinations of reality contained in the acquired nexus of psychic life, the probability and plausibility stemming from them, and the sensory impact of the work. Modern technique, which consistently and capably strives to establish this foundation, is completely justified in its opposition to so-called poetry of ideas or illustrations of thoughts. Without this foundation, how would we be moved to experience the destinies of others as our own and what is invented as real? Today's poets forget all too often that their object must really move the heart and that its theoretical relations must be meaningful.[134]

Dilthey follows these claims with an appeal to Schiller and Goethe for corroboration; the invocation of these heroes of German culture indicates that we have reached the bedrock of his thought, just as it did even in such a sober analyst as Jonas Cohn.

While very much a piece of its own time, for example in its invocation of the authority of experimental psychology (while rejecting Fechner's

---

[133] Dilthey, "Imagination of the Poet," p. 129.
[134] Dilthey, "Imagination of the Poet," p. 130.

specific version of it), Dilthey's aesthetics is also a work of synthesis that is as comprehensive as only a few of the most important aesthetic theories of the preceding two centuries. Like the more orthodox Neo-Kantians, Dilthey rejected the metaphysical aesthetics of German Idealism, according to which art expresses the progress of the "spirit," in favor of the view that art expresses our own thoroughly human emotions. But unlike the other Neo-Kantians, he emphasized the relation between art and its historical context, characteristic of an idealist like Hegel although also of a more naturalistic philosopher like Herder. Also unlike orthodox Neo-Kantians such as Cohen and Cohn, although in this regard similar to the younger Münsterberg, Dilthey was hospitable to the psychological aesthetics of the third quarter of the nineteenth century, although he integrated the piecemeal results of the experimental aesthetics of Fechner and others into his own unifying "descriptive" psychology of aesthetic creation and reception. Like Cohn, he accepted Kant's analysis of the universal but "exemplary" rather than "logical" validity of aesthetic experience and judgments of taste, but, in this unlike any of the other Neo-Kantians, he recognized the importance of the free play of the imagination as a source of aesthetic pleasure in its own right but also as the necessary condition for the intensified experience of emotions and of the "feeling of life" itself. Both the free play of the imagination and the "feeling of life" are unmistakably Kantian ideas, but Dilthey linked the two ideas in a new way by arguing that the free play of the imagination produces a heightened feeling of life through producing a heightened experience of particular human emotions, which Kant had attempted to keep out of the proper subject matter and experience of art, in favor of the more intellectual "aesthetic ideas" that prepared the way for the metaphysical excesses of the aesthetics of German idealism. And in his revision of Kantian aesthetics, Dilthey also recaptured one of the deepest ideas of pre-Kantian aesthetics, notably Mendelssohn's idea, in turn developed from Du Bos, that it is precisely our recognition of the artificiality of what is presented on stage or in another artistic form that frees us to experience the emotions that it arouses most intensely, that artificiality is not an obstacle to emotionally intense aesthetic experience but an enabling condition for it. Both drawing on key moments in eighteenth-century aesthetics and adding ideas of his own, Dilthey re-established connections among the aesthetics of truth, the aesthetics of feeling, and the aesthetics of play that a few of the greatest aestheticians of the previous century had established but that many of the aestheticians of his own century had rejected. We will shortly see that only a few aestheticians of the twentieth century also attempted to connect all three approaches to aesthetics. But first we will conclude the present volume by reviewing some of the German and German-inspired aesthetic theories of the late nineteenth century that were also inspired by contemporary psychology but remained outside the framework of Neo-Kantianism. We will see that in these theories too it proved difficult to sustain a synthesis between the aesthetics of play and other approaches to aesthetics.

10

Psychological Aesthetics

Play and Empathy

As we saw previously, one thing that unified authors as diverse as Schelling, Hegel, Schopenhauer, and many of their followers was the rejection of the concept of aesthetic experience as a form of play that had been central to the aesthetics of Gerard, Kant, and Schiller in the eighteenth century, and that had then been revived by only a few writers in the nineteenth century, such as Schleiermacher, Dilthey, and perhaps Nietzsche, although only toward the end of his career. As we will see, an attack upon the notion of aesthetic experience as play would again become prominent in many quarters at the beginning of the twentieth century, notably in the aesthetics of Benedetto Croce, himself influenced by Kant in some regards but by Hegel in this regard, and by many influenced by him, especially in Great Britain. Were those philosophers just flogging a horse that had been killed a century earlier? By no means, because there was a revival of enthusiasm for the concept of play as the central concept of aesthetics among several writers in the second half of the nineteenth century. However, as we will see in due course, the character of the renewed attack on the theory of play that would follow its revival would be similar to the original attack of German Idealism against the theory of play in Kant and Schiller: the idea that aesthetic experience involves the pleasurable play of our powers, including our cognitive powers, but not for the sake of cognition or any other determinate goal, would once again be rejected in favor of the theory that aesthetic experience is itself an important form of cognition.

But the response to the revived aesthetics of play in the later nineteenth century is more complicated than that suggests, for this time the attack came not only from the side of those who endorsed a primarily cognitivist approach to aesthetics, but also from some who endorsed the aesthetics of emotional impact, specifically some who developed the concept of "empathy" that had been introduced by Friedrich Theodor Vischer in his attempt to make some room for the emotional impact of both nature and art in an otherwise Hegelian approach to aesthetics. The leaders in the aesthetics of empathy were Vischer's son Robert and Theodor Lipps, and we shall see that even though the idea of the enjoyment of our own mental activity was central to Lipps's conception of aesthetic experience, he nevertheless tried to distance his recognition of this aspect of aesthetic pleasure from the traditional conception of play. But then others, notably Karl Groos, tried to synthesize the aesthetics of empathy with the aesthetics of play.

But even this still simplifies the somewhat complicated narrative to be presented in this chapter. Thus far, only German characters have been mentioned. And given the title of the present part of this volume, that is what would be expected. However, in this chapter national boundaries are going to have to be breached, because the revival of the theory of aesthetic experience as a form of play that triggered the responses of Lipps and then Groos was in fact the work of an Englishman, namely Herbert Spencer, and then because several of the most interesting writers to be influenced by the empathy theorists were also Anglophone, the American Ethel Puffer, herself a student of Hugo Münsterberg, and the expatriate Englishwoman Vernon Lee. However, what ties these figures together is the influence of psychology in their work. Herbert Spencer's aesthetic theory was part of his psychology, Lipps and Groos were psychologists as much as philosophers, and Ethel Puffer studied psychology rather than philosophy with Hugo Münsterberg and taught psychology as well. Vernon Lee was neither a philosopher nor a psychologist, indeed she did not have formal academic training at all, but since her works on aesthetics were so heavily influenced by Lipps she clearly belongs with the other figures to be discussed in this chapter rather than among the British aestheticians to be discussed in the next volume.

This chapter is thus called "Psychological Aesthetics: Play and Empathy," rather than, say, "German-influencing, German, and German-influenced non-Neo-Kantian Aesthetics in the Late Nineteenth and Early Twentieth Centuries." I trust there will be no objection to the simpler title. The point of the chapter is to describe the new version of the aesthetics of play that would be so strongly rejected by many early twentieth-century philosophers, but also to show how some philosophers of the group to be considered here combined the idea of play with the idea of empathy to provide a more comprehensive account of aesthetic experience than either approach could provide by itself – although not as comprehensive an approach to aesthetics as Dilthey was developing at the same time.

1. SPENCER'S REVIVAL OF THE CONCEPT OF PLAY

The revival of the theory of play was led by the British sociologist and philosopher Herbert Spencer (1820–1903).[1] Spencer, the son of a dissenting schoolteacher in Derby, England, did not enjoy a traditional university education like his close contemporary John Ruskin; instead, after receiving an early education by his father and his uncle, a vicar, he worked as a civil engineer during Britain's early railway boom. But he started writing as a journalist as well, and in 1848 he was taken on as a sub-editor by *The Economist*, where he would work for five years. During this period he published his first book, *Social Statics*,[2] in which he argued for the "law of equal freedom," that "every person has freedom to do all that he wills, provided he infringes not the equal freedom of any other man,"[3] and for a minimalist or "nightwatchman" state the function of which should only be to protect the equal spheres of freedom that each person should enjoy.[4] This classical statement of nineteenth-century liberalism brought Spencer renown, and his publisher, John Chapman, introduced him to his salon, where Spencer met luminaries such as the couples John Stuart Mill and Harriet Martineau as well as Mary Ann Evans (George Eliot) and George Henry Lewes, and into which circle Spencer himself introduced Thomas Henry Huxley, later "Darwin's bulldog." But before the publication of *The Origin of Species* in 1859, Spencer began to work out an evolutionary approach to all questions of philosophy, influenced by the sociology of August Comte, to which he was introduced by Mill's *System of Logic*, and the pre-Darwinian thinking of Charles Darwin's grandfather Erasmus Darwin and the French naturalist Jean Baptiste Lamarck. Under their influence, as well as that of Schelling, transmitted by Coleridge, Spencer developed a view

---

[1] Monographs on Spencer focusing on his sociology and political philosophy: John David Yeadon Peel, *Herbert Spencer: The Evolution of a Sociologist* (London: Heinemann, 1971); Michael W. Taylor, *Man versus the State: Herbert Spencer and Late Victorian Individualism* (Oxford: Clarendon Press, 1992); and Tim S. Gray, *Herbert Spencer's Political Philosophy: Individualism and Organicism* (Hampshire: Avebury, 1996).

[2] Herbert Spencer, *Social Statics: or the Conditions Essential to Human Happiness and the First of them Developed* (London: Chapman, 1851).

[3] Spencer, *Social Statics*, p. 103.

[4] See Tim S. Gray, "Spencer, Herbert," in *Routledge Encyclopedia of Philosophy*, ed. Edward Craig (London: Routledge, 1998), vol. 9, pp. 87–9, at p. 87.

of evolution as development toward ever-increasing complexity in which characteristics developed in one generation could be passed on to the next. In spite of the publication of Darwin's work a few years after his own next book, *The Principles of Psychology* of 1855, Spencer never gave up his own more teleological conception of evolution, and it remained the basis of the "System of Synthetic Philosophy" that he conceived in 1861 and expounded in a vast corpus of subsequent books. This system would incorporate *The Principles of Psychology* and include *First Principles* (1862), *Principles of Biology* (1864), *Principles of Sociology* in eight parts (1876–96), and *Principles of Ethics* in six parts (1879–93).[5] It took six years to sell out the initial edition of the *Principles of Psychology*, but during the 1860s Spencer's increasing fame made a second edition possible. When this appeared, now in two volumes, in 1870 and 1872, it contained a new final part of "Corollaries," and Spencer concluded this with a section on "Æsthetic Sentiments."[6] Here is where Spencer revived the theory of play as the basis of aesthetic experience, and his brief treatment, only twenty pages out of the more than twelve hundred of the whole work, would trigger an extensive discussion among aestheticians.

The general argument of Spencer's psychology is that life is "The continuous adjustment of internal relations to external relations,"[7] and that "mind" or consciousness evolves in increasingly complex organisms as a representation of internal relations that allows organisms to manage their increasingly complex external relations with their environment. Spencer rejects any rigid separation or "impassable chasm" between body and mind,[8] or, in his terminology, between physiology and psychology, but does allow that as creatures become increasingly complex they add to their capacities for sensation, perception, reflex, and instinct, which are the foundation for their interaction with their environment, the further capacities of memory, reason, feeling, and will.[9] These higher faculties together constitute "intelligence." The basis for Spencer's aesthetics is then the assumption that in the highest and most complex creatures, namely humans, these faculties need to be exercised and maintained even when their exercise is not immediately necessary for the survival of the creature, and that the function of play in all its forms – although

[5] See Gray, "Spencer, Herbert," p. 88.
[6] Herbert Spencer, *The Principles of Psychology* (New York: Appleton, 1895), vol. II, pp. 627–48.
[7] Spencer, *Principles of Psychology*, vol. I, p. 293.
[8] Spencer, *Principles of Psychology*, vol. I, p. 396.
[9] Spencer, *Principles of Psychology*, vol. I, pp. 444–504.

not the conscious intention of those who play when they play – is the exercise of these faculties for the sake of their maintenance. The forms of play that ground aesthetic production and experience, the activities of artists and audiences, particularly exercise our capacities for perception and for feeling.

Spencer introduces his discussion of the aesthetic sentiments with the remark that

> Many years ago I met with a quotation from a German author to the effect that the æsthetic sentiments originate from the play-impulse. I do not remember the name of the author; and if any reasons were given for this statement, or any inferences drawn from it, I cannot recall them. But the statement itself has remained with me, as being one which, if not literally true, is yet the adumbration of a truth.[10]

Spencer's history as an autodidact and his pose as a systematic philosopher may have led him to suppress his source, but those who subsequently responded to him had no doubt that he was referring to Schiller's *Letters on Aesthetic Education*.[11] Yet Spencer could just as easily have had Kant in mind; in any case, what he goes on to maintain could certainly be taken as an interpretation of the idea that aesthetic experience is essentially disinterested, and for that reason can only be understood as a form of play. Spencer asserts that "The activities we call play are united with the æsthetic activities, by the trait that neither subserve, in any direct way, the processes conducive to life." He argues that "the bodily powers, the intellectual faculties, the instincts, appetites, passions and even [the] highest feelings," everything ranging from the "vital actions" of the "viscera" to the "egoistic" and "altruistic" sentiments which "prompt care of property and liberty" or "regulate conduct toward others" "have maintenance of the organic equilibrium of the individual, or else maintenance of the species, as their immediate or remote ends," but yet that these same faculties may function in cases in which they do not aim at any proximate ends, although their exercise "may bring the ulterior benefits of increased power in the faculties exercised; and that thus the life as a whole may be afterwards furthered." Spencer further explains that

> From the primary action of a faculty there results the immediate normal gratification, *plus* the maintained or increased ability due to exercise, *plus* the objective end achieved or requirement fulfilled. But from

---

[10] Spencer, *Principles of Psychology*, §533, vol. II, p. 627.
[11] See Karl Groos, *The Play of Animals*, trans. Elizabeth L. Baldwin, with preface by J. Mark Baldwin (New York: Appleton, 1898), p. 3.

this secondary action of a faculty exhibited in play or in an æsthetic pursuit, there results only the immediate gratification *plus* the maintained or increased ability[12] –

but *not* the gratification connected with the achievement of any particular end, the satisfaction of any particular need. Aesthetic experience and aesthetic activity are play without any immediate end, although no doubt as such play – or artistic activity – becomes more complicated, it generates various internal goals within its ultimately goal-less – although ultimately beneficial – activity.

What makes play both possible and necessary for higher or more complex creatures is that their "time and strength are not wholly absorbed in providing for immediate needs,"[13] or that they have, so to speak, excess capacity, and that their capacities, when dormant or not required for immediate needs, have an "unusual readiness" to discharge themselves anyway, or to produce "a simulation" of their normal activities when circumstances offer the possibility of that "in place of the real activities." Thus "Play is ... an artificial exercise of powers which, in default of their natural exercise, become so ready to discharge that they relieve themselves by simulated actions in place of real actions."[14] Spencer illustrates this with the tendency of rats to gnaw anything they can get hold of even when they are not eating (which is not actually an "artificial exercise" of powers, because rats need to do this to keep the constant growth of their teeth in check) and of cats to scratch at chairs even when they are not scratching at prey, but also with the tendency of little girls to simulate adult activities such as tea parties and "The sports of boys, chasing one another, wrestling, making prisoners," which "obviously gratify in a partial way the predatory instincts"[15] that they naturally have and will exercise for specific ends as adults. In such exercises of their capacities, "activity of the intellectual faculties in which they are not used for purposes of guidance in the business of life," the players will experience a twofold pleasure, "the pleasure of the activity itself" and "the accompanying satisfaction of certain egoistic feelings which find for the moment no other sphere."[16] The additional feelings gratified by an experience of play need not, however, be only egoistic.

---

[12] Spencer, *Principles of Psychology*, §533, vol. II, pp. 527–8.
[13] Spencer, *Principles of Psychology*, §534, vol. II, p. 628.
[14] Spencer, *Principles of Psychology*, §534, vol. II, p. 630.
[15] Spencer, *Principles of Psychology*, §534, vol. II, p. 631.
[16] Spencer, *Principles of Psychology*, §534, vol. II, p. 631.

This theory of the discharge of excess capacity combined with the two-fold pleasures of the exercise of the faculties themselves plus the gratification of various feelings, such as the egoistic satisfaction in winning a game (which can generate an internal goal in an externally goal-less activity), provides the foundations for Spencer's theory of specifically aesthetic play. Spencer holds that the play of any of our capacities of consciousness may be pleasurable, but particularly stresses the capacities for sensation and perception on the one hand and the capacity for feeling or emotion on the other. Thus, he argues that ordinary survival does not require very fine visual or auditory discriminations – the color-blind feel "comparatively small inconvenience," he blithely observes – so "though the faculty which appreciates colour has a life-serving function, the relation between its activity and its use is not close," and "the gratification derivable from this activity, carried on for its own sake," for example making fine discriminations of colors, "becomes conspicuous," and likewise in the case of sounds. Spencer adds that "the sensations brought by non-useful exercise" do not "*necessarily* have the æsthetic character," only that "separableness from life-serving function is one of the *conditions* to the acquirement" of this character.[17] So he will have to spell out some additional condition besides the non-necessary exercise of mental capacities to make their exercise aesthetically pleasurable. But before he does that, he comments on the "other extreme" of the capacities involved in aesthetic experience, the capacity for feeling or sentiment rather than sensation or perception. Here Spencer notes first that self-referential or "egoistic" feelings may be gratified by activities that do not directly contribute to biological survival, for example one might take pride in one's own capacity for fine sensory discriminations even when that is not directly useful. But more important perhaps is "the conspicuous fact that many æsthetic feelings arise from the contemplation of the attributes and deeds of other persons, real or ideal." He continues that

> In these cases, the consciousness is remote from life-serving function, not simply as is the consciousness accompanying play or the enjoyment of a beautiful colour or tone, but also in the further way that the thing contemplated as a source of pleasure, is not a direct action or affection of the self at all, but is a secondary affection produced by contemplation of acts and feelings known as objective, and present to the self only by representation. Here the separateness from life-serving function is extreme; since neither a

---

[17] Spencer, *Principles of Psychology*, §535, vol. II, p. 633.

beneficial end, nor an act conducive to that end, nor a sentiment prompting such act, forms an element in the æsthetic feeling.[18]

Here Spencer seems to be combining two separable ideas: first, that the arousal of sentiment is not functional but a form of play when it is aroused by a representation, even by the representation of another real person instead of a mere image of one, rather than by one's own condition, and, second, that the arousal of sentiment is aesthetic rather than functional when it does not lead to a specific action. These conditions need to be separated more carefully than Spencer suggests, since there are no doubt many cases in which feeling what another person does or would feel in a certain circumstance is a direct prompt to action (this is the assumption of, for example, Adam Smith's account of human motivation in *A Theory of Moral Sentiments*),[19] and even some in which arousal of feeling by an image is a direct spur to action (this is the condition of the efficacy of rhetoric). But be this as it may, Spencer's point is that in the exercise of a variety of our capacities for consciousness ranging from sensation to sentiment without an immediate objective, there is still the possibility for two elements of pleasure, namely the immediate pleasure in the sheer exercise of our faculties and and pleasurable feelings triggered by representations of the exercise of these faculties, whether in ourselves or in others and whether real or fictional. Insofar as pleasures of the second sort depend upon representations of states of affairs, whether veridical or not, this aspect of Spencer's theory may be considered to contain a cognitive element.

Spencer will shortly add a third source of pleasure to aesthetic experience, but before he does that he offers a solution to the problem raised a moment ago, namely that the mere discharge of excess capacity is a necessary but not a sufficient condition for the satisfaction of aesthetic expectation. What distinguishes the mere discharge of excess cognitive capacity from its aesthetic exercise is the organization of complexity in the successful case. Spencer writes:

> In the more complex combinations, including many forms presented together, it is relatively difficult to trace out the principle; but I see sundry reasons for suspecting that beautiful arrangements of forms, are those which effectually exercise the largest numbers of the structural elements

---

[18] Spencer, *Principles of Psychology*, §535, vol. II, p. 634.
[19] See Adam Smith, *A Theory of Moral Sentiments* (1759), edited by D.D. Raphael and A.L. Macfie (Oxford: Oxford University Press, 1976), or by Knud Haakonssen (Cambridge: Cambridge University Press, 2002).

concerned in perception, while over-taxing the fewest of them. Similarly with the complex visual wholes presented by actual objects, or by pictorial representations of objects, with all their lights and shades and colours. The requirements for harmony, subordination, and for proportion – the demand for a variety sufficient to prevent monotony, but not a variety which too much distracts the attention, may be regarded as all implied by the principle that many elements of perceptive faculty must be called into play, while none are over-exerted.[20]

In keeping with his practice, Spencer does not mention any predecessors for his views, but it is impossible to read this without thinking of Kant's conception of the free play of the cognitive powers: Spencer's claim is that aesthetic experience is not simply the experience of the exercise of the powers of consciousness, but the experience of the harmonious play of multiple cognitive capacities, a harmonious play made possible by formal properties – such as "subordination" and "proportion."[21] Turning from sight to sound, Spencer illustrates his point by saying that "greater heterogeneity implies greater variety of excitements in the percipient, and avoidance of that over-excitement of some perceptive agency which uniformity implies,"[22] while the pleasurability of the experience also requires the harmony that appropriate relations of subordination and proportion facilitate.

Having almost in passing introduced this central theme of traditional aesthetics into his contemporary psychological account, Spencer now adds a third source of aesthetic pleasure, which is also deeply reminiscent of eighteenth-century theories. As Spencer says, "something must be added in elucidation of the third kind of æsthetic pleasure accompanying perceptive activity – that more special kind which results from the special associations formed in experience."[23] By such associations Spencer means the "feelings from time to time received along with perceptions" of objects that may in turn be represented or otherwise invoked in aesthetic activity or appreciation, for example, feelings of happiness associated with the graceful movements of dancers at a ball, which can in turn be invoked by an image of such an event, or with "architectural, plastic, pictorial" "art-products" that have themselves been associated with "occasions of happiness, social or otherwise." Spencer observes that

---

[20] Spencer, *Principles of Psychology*, §537, vol. II, pp. 639–40.
[21] Spencer's idea in this passage also points forward to the most Kantian among more recent aestheticians, namely Monroe Beardsley; see Volume III, 3.
[22] Spencer, *Principles of Psychology*, §537, vol. II, p. 640.
[23] Spencer, *Principles of Psychology*, §537, vol. II, p. 640.

the dimension of pleasurable association greatly increases the potential for aesthetic pleasure beyond what is offered by the first two dimensions of pleasure, that in the sheer exercise of our capacities and that in the feelings, such as pride, most directly connected with such exercise. Putting the point in a way that reveals that nineteenth-century liberalism is a long way from later conceptions of egalitarianism, Spencer says that association "is a reason why the æsthetic pleasure derived from form, though not great in the uncultured, becomes relatively voluminous in the cultured."[24] But perhaps more important, Spencer suggests that it is at this third level of aesthetic pleasure, the pleasure of associations, that the involvement of our emotional capacities in aesthetic experience becomes most pronounced. "When the emotion suggested" by a musical cadence, for example, "is a joyous one, opportunity is given for pleasurable sympathy; and when a painful emotion is suggested, there comes an opportunity for the pleasurable pain of pity."[25] Here we could say that Spencer departs from the Kantian model of play by including within his own conception of play the exercise of our own emotional capacities when, not needed for immediate practical purposes, they would otherwise lie dormant; and he swiftly addresses the traditional paradox of tragedy by suggesting that the exercise of our emotional capacities is just as enjoyable as the exercise of our cognitive capacities, even when the feelings directly aroused by the content of an artistic representation (through our cognitive capacities, of course) are not immediately pleasant. Situating Spencer's view even more deeply in the history of aesthetics than he would ever do, we could also contrast his views to Aristotle's by saying that he does not think that we suffer from an excess of feelings of pity and fear that needs to be purged, but rather that we have an excess capacity for feelings of pity and fear that needs to be exercised.

Spencer sums up his account by stating that "the most perfect form of æsthetic excitement is reached when these three orders of sensational, perceptional, and emotional gratification are given, by the fullest actions of the respective faculties, with the least deduction caused by painful excess of action."[26] Thus the most pleasing works of art would be ones that combine "the pleasures derivable from simple sensation, as of sweet odours, beautiful colours, fine tones," with "those pleasurable feelings that go along with perceptions more or less complex, of forms, of

---

[24] Spencer, *Principles of Psychology*, §537, vol. II, p. 641.
[25] Spencer, *Principles of Psychology*, §537, vol. II, p. 642.
[26] Spencer, *Principles of Psychology*, §539, vol. II, p. 645.

combined lights and shades, of successive cadences and chords; rising to a greater height where these are joined into elaborate combinations of forms, and ... structures," with the even greater opportunities for complexity and especially associations provided when "the presentative elements are incidental and the representative elements essential," in other words, what can be offered by the content rather than by the matter and form of works of art.[27] But he also recognizes that it is very rare for any work of art or body of works to exploit all these potential sources of pleasure to an equal degree: even "many admired works of modern art,... good in *technique*, are low in the emotions they express and arouse, such as the battle-scenes of Vernet and the pieces of Gerôme."[28] But success in exploiting all three dimensions of pleasure in that high form of play which is art is a true measure of artistic success.

Spencer sums up his theory of the aesthetic sentiments by reminding us that

> The æsthetic feelings and sentiments are not, as our words and phrases lead us to suppose, feelings and sentiments that essentially differ in origin and nature from the rest. They are nothing else than particular modes of excitement of the faculties, sensational, perceptional, and emotional – faculties which, otherwise excited, produce those other modes of consciousness constituting our ordinary impressions, ideas, and feelings. The same agencies are in action; and the only difference is in the attitude of consciousness towards its resulting state[29] –

the difference, that is, between gratification at the accomplishment or satisfaction of some concrete objective, and pleasure in the mere exercise of our capacities along with that in the feelings and associations that may accompany such exercise. Spencer ends by reminding us of the point with which he began, namely that only highly evolved creatures will be capable of aesthetic experience: "only when there is reached an organization so superior, that the energies have not to be wholly expended in the fulfilment of material requirements from hour to hour" is aesthetic experience possible.[30] But since Spencer's version of evolutionary theory is not just teleological but also profoundly optimistic, he sees no reason to think that aesthetic capacity and correspondingly artistic development has reached a maximum in his own or any past time. On the contrary, his concluding claim is that "the æsthetic activities in general may be

---

[27] Spencer, *Principles of Psychology*, §539, vol. II, pp. 644–5.
[28] Spencer, *Principles of Psychology*, §539, vol. II, p. 646.
[29] Spencer, *Principles of Psychology*, §540, vol. II, p. 646.
[30] Spencer, *Principles of Psychology*, §540, vol. II, p. 647.

expected to play an increasing part in human life as evolution advances," and that particular forms of art will themselves also evolve, thus "they will in a greater degree than now appeal to the higher emotions."[31] Thus Spencer's revival of the theory of aesthetic experience as play does not just reject German idealism's rejection of this conception; it specifically rejects Hegel's famous claim that art for us is a thing of the past. On the contrary, the continuing evolution of humankind that Spencer expects promises the increasing importance of art and aesthetic experience in human life.

Spencer's conception of play as exercise of both our cognitive and our emotional capacities might have been recognized as a way of synthesizing the separate approaches of the aesthetics of truth, the aesthetics of feeling, and the aesthetics of play into a comprehensive theory of aesthetic experience. But many of those who responded to him did not look past his biological account of play as developing abilities needed for survival and then releasing excess capacity in these capacities once developed. This, Spencer's readers clearly felt, was beneath the dignity expected of a philosophical theory of aesthetic experience. So Spencer's theory of play would be rejected and its potential for a nonreductive aesthetic theory largely ignored.

2. THE AESTHETICS OF EMPATHY: ROBERT VISCHER, LIPPS, AND VOLKELT

Spencer appealed to psychology to revive the notion of play in his account of the "aesthetic sentiments." The main school of psychological aesthetics in Germany was not initially concerned to revive the notion of play, but instead developed the recognition of the emotional impact of art in the form of empathy that Friedrich Theodor Vischer had first introduced to break out of the cognitivist confines of Hegelian aesthetics. Without the antipathy toward psychology sometimes characteristic of Neo-Kantianism, especially Marburg Neo-Kantianism, philosophers within this approach had no reason not to recognize the arousal or "experience" (that is, *Erlebnis*, not *Erfahrung*) of emotion as an essential aim of aesthetic experience in general and of our experience of the arts in particular. The term "empathy" (*Einfühlung*), the idea that we immediately experience aesthetic objects, whether human or not, in terms of emotions that we ourselves have in fact projected onto them, is most

---

[31] Spencer, *Principles of Psychology*, §540, vol. II, p. 647.

closely associated with the name Theodor Lipps (1851–1914). But it was previously promoted by Robert Vischer (1847–1933), in his 1873 doctoral thesis *On the Optical Sense of Form*, and after Lipps the position that empathy is indispensable to aesthetic response although not its only aspect was defended against attacks from supposedly more "objectivist" accounts of aesthetic qualities by Johannes Volkelt (1848–1930). We will discuss these three figures in this section, and in the following section will consider a figure who tried to combine the results of the play theorists and the empathy theorists, Karl Groos (1861–1940).[32]

Vischer

Robert Vischer studied in Zürich, Heidelberg, Bonn, and Munich before taking his degree at his father's university of Tübingen. He completed his habilitation in Munich and then taught art history at Breslau and Aachen, where he became professor of art history and aesthetics. From 1893 until his retirement in 1911 he taught at Göttingen. In addition to editing his father's works, he published on different periods of art history, including works on Luca Signorelli (1879) and Peter Paul Rubens (1904).[33] Vischer developed his account of empathy in his 1873 doctoral dissertation *Über das optische Formgefühl* ("On the Optical Feeling of Form").[34] But he attributed the idea of empathy to his father, who, in a later "critique" of his earlier system of aesthetics, had maintained "against the Herbartian school" that there can "be no form without content" and then suggested that "forms devoid of emotional content ... are supplied with emotional content that we – the observers – unwittingly transfer to them."[35] Actually, according to the son, the father had already

---

[32] There is a discussion of the "Theory of Einfühlung" in the Earl of Listowel, *A Critical History of Modern Aesthetics* (London: George Allen & Unwin, 1933), pp. 51–82. Robert Vischer, Lipps, and Volkelt receive some discussion in two works by Christian G. Allesch, *Geschichte der psychologischen Ästhetik* (Göttingen: Hogrefe, 1987), and *Einführung in die psychologische Ästhetik* (Vienna: Facultas Verlags- und Buchhandels, 2006). The latter contains an extensive bibliography of work in psychological aesthetics from the period considered here to the present. Lipps is also discussed in Louis Agosta, *Empathy in the Context of Philosophy* (Basingstoke: Palgrave Macmillan, 2010).

[33] Vischer's work was discussed by Hermann Glockner, "Robert Vischer und die Krisis der Geisteswissenschaften im letzten Drittel des 19. Jahrhunderts: Ein Beitrag zur Geschichte des Irrationalitätsproblem," *Logos* 14 (1925): 297–343, and 15 (1926): 47–102.

[34] Robert Vischer, *Über das optische Formgefühl* (Leipzig: Hermann Credner, 1873); reprinted in Robert Vischer, *Drei Schriften zum ästhetischen Formproblem* (Halle: Max Niemeyer Verlag, 1927).

[35] Robert Vischer, *On the Optical Sense of Form: A Contribution to Aesthetics* (Leipzig: Hermann Credner, 1873), translated in Henry Francis Mallgrave and Eleftherides Ikonomou, eds.,

hinted at the new idea in two places in his original multi-volumed treatise on aesthetics, in a section on architecture and a section on natural beauty, where he had argued that "the aesthetic effect of all inorganic phenomena, even the lower organic world of plants and the whole realm of landscape, appears with an intuitive investment on our part, that is, we involuntarily read our emotions into them."[36] The son would develop this idea on the premise that humans have a "pantheistic urge for union with the world, which can by no means be limited to our more easily understood kinship with the human species but must, consciously or unconsciously, be directed toward the universe."[37] In other words, the foundation of empathy is our desire for fellowship with our own kind, which depends upon the possibility of understanding our fellows, but we project this on to the whole world as we experience it, and thus experience the nonhuman world in terms of the same emotions by means of which we understand each other. Theodor Lipps, who adopted the stance of a more sober psychologist than the art historian Vischer, would drop the idea of a "pantheistic urge," and treat the empathetic projection of our own emotions into other human beings as an essential part of aesthetic experience and not just a basis for it. But before we turn to Lipps, let us continue with Vischer's development of his father's idea of the projection of our own emotions into the nonhuman as an essential part of aesthetic experience.

Vischer's idea of empathy is based on two premises. First, he holds that it is possible to distinguish between "ideal associations and a direct merger of the representation with objective form,"[38] that is, between the classical association of ideas in which we remain aware of the distinction between a stimulus and an idea to which it leads us, on the one hand, and an experience that seems unitary, with no awareness of distinction between what might be the external stimulus and what might be added by the mind. Vischer argues that much although not all aesthetic experience takes the latter form, an idea that he in turn credits to an 1861 book on *The Life of Dreams* by Karl Albert Scherner.[39] Vischer's

---

Empathy, Form, and Space: A Problem in German Aesthetics 1873–1893 (Santa Monica: Getty Foundation, 1994), pp. 89–123, at p. 89, citing Friedrich Theodor Vischer, *Kritische Gänge*, vol. 5 (Stuttgart: Cotta, 1866).

[36] Robert Vischer, *Optical Sense of Form*, p. 90.
[37] Vischer, *Optical Sense of Form*, p. 109.
[38] Vischer, *Optical Sense of Form*, p. 92. Mallgrave and Ikonomou rendered Vischer's word *Vorstellung* as "imagination"; I have used the more customary "representation."
[39] Karl Albert Scherner, *Das Leben des Traums* (Berlin: Heinrich Schindler, 1861).

second point is that this second form of experience, the union of subjective response with the perception of "objective form" that he calls *Einfühlung* or empathy, is based on the projection of our own bodily form or attitude into the perceived form of objects, a projection that, because of the union of our own body and soul, carries with it the projection of our own emotional as well as physical characteristics into the perception of the object. "The body, in responding to certain stimuli" – in dreams, as Scherner had argued, but in aesthetic experience in general, as Vischer is now arguing – "objectifies itself in spatial forms. Thus it unconsciously projects its own bodily form – and with this also the soul – into the form of the object. From this I derived the notion that I call empathy [*Einfühlung*]."[40] This projection, Vischer argues, is based on a feeling of harmony between a perceived object and our own body, "a harmony between the object and the subject, which arises because the object has a harmonious form and a formal effect corresponding to subjective harmony."[41] This harmony is in the first instance a harmony between the object and the organ that perceives it: for example, "the horizontal line is pleasing because our eyes are positioned horizontally."[42] But this feeling of harmony quickly extends itself to the "structure of the whole body,"[43] and then along with feeling the harmony or resemblance between an object and our own body, or more precisely with a particular condition or posture of our body, we also feel and project into the object the emotional state that goes along with that bodily condition. Thus,

> When I observe a stationary object, I can without difficulty place myself within its inner structure, at its center of gravity. I can think my way into it, mediate its size with my own, stretch and expand, bend and confine myself to it. With a small object, partially or totally confined and constructed, I very precisely concentrate my feeling. My feeling will be compressed and modest ... When, on the contrary, I see a large or partially overproportioned form, I experience a feeling of mental grandeur and breadth, a freedom of the will ... the compressed or upward striving, the bent or broken impression of an object fills us with a corresponding mental feeling of oppression, depression, or aspiration, a submissive or shattered stated of mind[44] –

---

[40] Vischer, *Optical Sense of Form*, p. 92.
[41] Vischer, *Optical Sense of Form*, p. 95.
[42] Vischer, *Optical Sense of Form*, p. 97.
[43] Vischer, *Optical Sense of Form*, p. 97.
[44] Vischer, *Optical Sense of Form*, pp. 104–5.

and such feelings are projected on to the object in such a way that we do not distinguish between them and the more objective perception of the object, that is, they become part of the unitary experience of the object.

With further examples, and perhaps with greater plausibility, Vischer argues that we have this response not just to static forms of objects but also to the perception of motion or the possibility of motion in objects – we feel harmony between the actual or possible motions of objects and those of our own bodies and then project into our experience of the objects the emotions that accompany such motions in our own bodies. Thus "the responsive sensation considers ... the outline of the form ([e.g.] mountain silhouette) or follows ... the path of movement ([e.g.] flight of a bird apart from [the form of] the bird itself." The perception of motion in the object is then accompanied by the emotion that would accompany such motion in our own body: "The apparent movement of form is thus unconsciously accompanied by a concrete emotional element of feeling."

> When I, for instance, look at the undulations and curves in a road, my thoughts also trace them – sometimes with dreamy hesitation, sometimes at a bounding speed. I seek and find, ascend triumphantly and fall to destruction, and so on. The direction and tempo of this motion are related to the perceived form and thus emulate human impulses and passions. Thus the responsive sensation intensifies into a **responsive feeling** [*Nachfühling*],[45]

one of the forms of *Einfühlung*.

Vischer further argues that even though the "association of ideas," which "evokes an *other* – absent images, thoughts, and vital feelings that have nothing to do with the symbolism of form" immediately before us, where "symbolism of form" is what has been explained by empathy, is "of only minor importance," nevertheless once the unification of perceived form with emotional response by means of the harmony between object and body has taken place, even the association of ideas is swept up into the sense of unity thereby created. Thus

> We must bear in mind and never forget that *in every image the symbolization of form discussed here always work together, first with each other and second with the association of ideas. They become entwined into an inextricable whole, and only by virtue of this absolute interlacing and togetherness does a true aesthetic appreciation of form arise.*[46]

---

[45] Vischer, *Optical Sense of Form*, pp. 106–7.
[46] Vischer, *Optical Sense of Form*, pp. 108–9.

In other words, a feeling of complete unity in our experience of what would otherwise be considered physical properties of an object and of our emotional response to it is not just a feature of empathy but is a defining feature of aesthetic experience as such and what makes empathy paradigmatic for aesthetic experience.

Although Vischer has not explicitly asserted that aesthetic appreciation is pleasurable, presumably he assumes that it is, and the explanation of its pleasure would be that our pleasure in our own emotions is incorporated into our unitary experience of the object, so that the object itself is indistinguishable from our emotional response to it and our pleasure in the latter becomes part of our pleasure in the former. Thus Vischer's theory of empathy can be considered a forerunner of the theory developed by George Santayana two decades later that beauty is pleasure "objectified," although Santayana makes no mention of Vischer or the other empathy theorists.[47] Unlike Santayana's later theory, however, Vischer's theory is based on the assumption that our primary psychological drive is for union with other human beings – the "natural love for my species is the only thing that makes it possible for me to project myself mentally ... A pure and complete union between the subjective and objective imagination ... can take place only when the latter involves another human being"[48] – but accompanied with the further assumption that this urge for union with other humans, which in turn depends upon the ability to project our own feelings into others, leads to a less discriminating urge to project our feelings onto nonhuman objects of experience as well. This second assumption is important for Vischer, for he hardly means to argue that aesthetic experience is restricted to our experience of other human beings or images of them, or that our projection of emotion onto nonhuman objects depends upon imagining in some way that they are representations of humans. The feeling of harmony between external objects and our own bodies on which the projection of emotion depends does not involve a stage in which we imagine that the external objects are human.

Vischer's theory of the empathetic projection of emotion as the dominant part if not the whole of aesthetic response also leads to the premise for a theory of artistic production. The basic idea here is that we do not simply feel a harmony between an object and possible motions of our

[47] George Santayana, *The Sense of Beauty* (New York: Charles Scribner's Sons, 1896; New York: Dover Publications, 1955), §11, p. 31.
[48] Vischer, *Optical Sense of Form*, p. 103.

own, as in the case of the flight of a bird or the undulating road, and then project the appropriate emotions onto such objects; we also have a tendency actually to move our own bodies in response to our imagination of their possible motions, and then to make some sort of physical record of those motions. "To suggest something unfurled or magnificent, for instance, we open our arms wide; to indicate greatness and majesty, we raise them high; to show something contemplated, doubtful, or untrue, we shake our heads and hands." Thus, our internal emotional states, which are responses to our perceptions of objects and projected into them, also "express themselves externally in analogous movements of our muscles and limbs," and then "Nothing is more natural, then, than that this hand that traces designs in the air should also seek to set down its images in a more permanent presentation with a solid material."[49] Some people, of course, have a greater drive and a greater gift for the later stages of this process, that is, for expressing their feelings in their bodily movements and finding ways to set those movements down into more permanent presentations. Those are the people who may become artists. But they speak or express for the rest of us, because the emotional responses and projections that they express and record are universal. Thus art "delivers a universally valid product and knows how to translate the indefinability and instability of mental life, as well as the chaotic disorder of nature, into a magnificent objectivity, into a clear reflection of a free humanity." Vischer concludes that "every work of art reveals itself to us as a person harmoniously feeling himself into a kindred object, or as humanity objectifying itself in harmonious forms."[50] But every work of art potentially reveals itself to every one of us as humanity objectifying itself in harmonious forms, because our underlying perceptual and emotional processes are fundamentally similar.

Vischer's theory of art is thus based on the assumption that we have a natural tendency not only to project our emotions onto objects external to ourselves but also to express our emotions in our own bodies, and then to record such expression in yet other physical media, thus giving rise to the variety of the arts – and even those of us who are not very good at doing the latter, presumably many if not most of us, appreciate the products of others who are gifted at that. This theory of Vischer's is at least in part a response to the Hegelian idealism of the previous generation of German aestheticians, and should be kept in mind when we come

---

[49] Vischer, *Optical Sense of Form*, p. 115.
[50] Vischer, *Optical Sense of Form*, pp. 116–17.

to a revival of Hegelian idealism in a subsequent generation, namely the aesthetic idealism of Benedetto Croce, which once again deemphasizes the importance of the bodily and further physical expression of artistic ideas.[51] For Vischer, at least, there is a natural continuum between aesthetic experience as a mental response to bodies, the expression of that response in one's own bodily movement, and recording that response in physical media, and there is no point to introducing any rigid boundaries within this continuum. Vischer's theory that (visual) art is a record of our feelings and movements in response to the perception of objects rather than of the appearance of the object itself could also be seen as a fundamental attack upon the traditional notion of imitation and as a theoretical basis for the development of modern art, especially abstract expressionism; we will later find an echo of Vischer's approach, although again probably unwitting, in R.G. Collingwood's pages on Cézanne.[52]

Lipps

Theodor Lipps was the best-known theorist of empathy. Lipps received his doctorate in Bonn and then followed in the career path of Robert Vischer, teaching first in Breslau and then in Munich, although he arrived there the year after Vischer had left for Göttingen and was the successor to Carl Stumpf in a chair for philosophy, not the successor in Vischer's chair in art history and aesthetics. Lipps was a prolific author known for work in psychology as well as philosophy. His career began with a dissertation on Herbart's ontology,[53] but among his other early works were *The Fundamental Facts of Psychical Life*[54] (1883) and *Psychological Studies*[55] (1885); his first work exclusively in aesthetics was *The Debate about Tragedy*[56] (1891). In the last decade of the nineteenth century and the first of the twentieth, he published massive treatises on logic,[57] psychology,[58] and aesthetics,[59] the last of which is organized around the notion of empathy.

[51] See Volume 3, Part Two.
[52] See R.G. Collingwood, *The Principles of Art* (Oxford: Clarendon Press, 1938), pp. 144–5.
[53] Theodor Lipps, *Zur Herbart'schen Ontologie* (Bonn: n.p., 1874).
[54] Theodor Lipps, *Grundtatsachen des Seelenlebens* (Bonn: Cohen, 1883).
[55] Theodor Lipps, *Psychologische Studien* (Heidelberg: Weiss, 1885).
[56] Theodor Lipps, *Der Streit über die Tragödie* (Hamburg: Voss, 1891); modern printing (Teddington, Middlesex: Echo Library, 2006) will be cited here.
[57] Theodor Lipps, *Grundzüge der Logik* (Hamburg: Voss, 1893).
[58] Theodor Lipps, *Leitfaden der Psychologie* (Leipzig: Engelmann, 1903).
[59] Theodor Lipps, *Ästhetik*, 2 vols.: Vol. I, *Grundlegung der Ästhetik* (Hamburg: Voss, 1903), and Vol. II, *Die ästhetische Betrachtung und die bildende Kunst* (Hamburg: Voss, 1906).

He remained active until his death in 1914, at only age sixty-three, publishing yet another treatise on empathy as late as 1913.[60] Lipps also translated Hume's *Treatise of Human Nature* into German (1904–1906),[61] a fact that confirms the eighteenth-century sources of much of his thought about aesthetics in spite of his composition of his main work in aesthetics in a contemporary idiom entirely without historical references. Here we shall focus on the idea of empathy as expounded in his main work on aesthetics, though the idea was introduced in earlier works, but shall also turn to his little book on tragedy for a more concrete illustration of his conception of empathy at work.

Lipps does not indulge in metaphysical language such as Vischer's "pantheistic urge," preferring instead the language of descriptive psychology. "Aesthetics is a psychological discipline," he says, a "*descriptive* and *explanatory* science," although he also insists that there is no conflict between such a descriptive enterprise and a "normative" one, since from an adequate description of aesthetic phenomena "I can also say without further ado what conditions must be fulfilled and what is to be avoided if the feeling of beauty in question is to be called into being."[62] As this remark makes clear, Lipps regards the discipline of aesthetics as the psychology of beauty, although his conception of the beautiful is quite broad, including under it such categories as the comic and the tragic, which were often distinguished from it; and he regards art as "the intentional production of the beautiful."[63] Beauty itself is defined as "the capacity of an object to produce a particular *effect* in me,"[64] an effect which is none other than pleasure: aesthetic value, Lipps writes, is, like all value, a form of pleasure: "it is, like everything valuable, *pleasurable.*"[65] Of course, not everything that is pleasurable is beautiful or aesthetically valuable; there are different kinds of pleasures, and the beautiful is what reveals itself to be pleasurable in "aesthetic contemplation": "aesthetic value is the value that reveals itself to us in aesthetic contemplation" (*ästhetische Betrachtung*).[66] Lipps does not define what he means by "aesthetic contemplation" until his second volume, but when he does, he

---

[60] Theodor Lipps, *Zur Einfühlung* (Leipzig: Engelmann, 1913).
[61] David Hume, *Traktat über die menschliche Natur*, reprint of edition of 1904–1906 with introduction by Reinhard Brandt (Hamburg: Felix Meiner Verlag, 1973).
[62] Lipps, *Ästhetik*, vol. I, pp. 1–2.
[63] Lipps, *Ästhetik*, vol. I, p. 3.
[64] Lipps, *Ästhetik*, vol. I, p. 1.
[65] "Er ist, vie alles Wertvolle, *lustvoll*"; Lipps, *Ästhetik*, vol. I, p. 6.
[66] Lipps, *Ästhetik*, vol. I, p. 8.

explains it as a form of consideration in which we simply do not raise any question about the reality or nonreality of the objects that we experience and the properties in them that we experience with pleasure. An aesthetic experience, for example the experience of aesthetic empathy, is one that simply does not ask about the reality (*Wirklichkeit*) of its object:[67] "Aesthetic contemplation, in short, is that which remains absolutely *on this side* of the *question about reality*."[68]

Thus far, Lipps remains firmly within the conceptual framework of eighteenth-century aesthetics in spite of the trappings of nineteenth-century psychology: beauty is the most general aesthetic property, and the beautiful is what causes us a disinterested pleasure where such a pleasure is defined precisely in Kant's terms as pleasure in the "mere contemplation" of the appearance of an object rather than in any judgment about its existence.[69] Lipps also reveals the eighteenth-century and indeed Kantian background of his approach by arguing that we experience beauty in both nature and art, art differing from nature, as has already been stated, only in that it is the intentional production of beauty. Lipps likewise demonstrates the influence of Kant (and Herbart, the subject of his doctoral dissertation) on his thought by beginning his treatise with an account of our pleasure in the aesthetic contemplation of form, an account that is deeply Kantian in spite of his pointed refusal to use the term "play" in his description of the aesthetic experience of form. His account clearly departs from the Kantian approach only when he introduces the idea of empathy into it, for which he borrows not only Vischer's term *Einfühlung* and Vischer's equation of empathy with "symbolization" but also Vischer's basic conception of empathy as the projection of human emotions into external objects in virtue of harmonies or resemblances between those objects, whether nonhuman or other humans, and ourselves – a process that Lipps calls "personification" or "humanization" (*Vermenschlichung*). Lipps thus shares with Neo-Kantians like Cohen the strategy of retaining Kant's analysis of judgments of taste

---

[67] Lipps, *Ästhetik*, vol. II, p. 35.
[68] Lipps, *Ästhetik*, vol. II, p. 36. Lipps's idea of leaving questions about reality "to one side" cannot fail to remind one of Edmund Husserl's conception of "bracketing" or "transcendental *epoché*" as the foundation of the discipline of phenomenology, although Husserl did not emphasize this notion until his *Cartesian Meditations* of 1909, thus three years after the remark of Lipps just quoted. Further, since Husserl used this notion as the characteristic of the "phenomenological reduction" in general, he could not use it as a criterion of aesthetic experience in particular, and did not develop an aesthetics, although numerous of his followers did.
[69] Kant, *CPJ*, §2, 5:204.

while dropping Kant's explanation of aesthetic response as the free play of imagination and understanding, but will substitute the empathetic feeling of emotion rather than the Neo-Kantian idea of the cognition of emotion as his own explanation of aesthetic response.

But before we turn to Lipps's account of empathy, let us take a brief look at his account of our aesthetic response to formal features of objects, insofar as that does not yet involve empathy – for in fact the two aspects of his account are deeply connected. Lipps's most basic idea is that all pleasure arises from "the activations [*Betätigungen*] of the soul that ... find in the soul conditions conducive to their completion,"[70] or find in the impressions given to the mind conditions that facilitate its activities. His "general proposition" is that "A ground for pleasure is given to the degree that psychic processes – or complexes thereof – thus sensations, perceptions, representations, thoughts, and connections among them, are 'natural' for the soul."[71] This might have seemed a natural place for Lipps to have appealed to the Kantian idea of free play, but Lipps introduces a different Kantian idea here, saying that what pleases us is what can readily be taken up into our "apperception," or representation of the unity of our own impressions and thoughts, and thus that what pleases us aesthetically is what can readily be taken up into our apperception in aesthetic contemplation. Apperception consists in taking up a particular experience into the unity of our experience:

> It consists in grasping, comprehending, attending to sensation, perception, representation, in noticing it or its object, in directing attention to it. This noticing, comprehending, attending, this inner grasping, and the specific allowing a process or experience [*Erlebnisses*] to become effective in the connection of psychical life [*psychischen Lebenszusammenhang*] is what I call "apperception".... Accordingly we must make the previously stated rule more precise: Pleasure arises to the degree that a psychical process finds favorable conditions for its *apperception* in the soul, or to the degree that it is *harmonious* with the psychically given conditions of *apperception*.[72]

The first aspects of beauty are thus those that facilitate the apperception of the object that presents them, or facilitates taking our perception of such features of appearance into the unity of our apperception. Lipps then describes such traditional criteria of beauty as proportion, unity amidst variety, equilibrium, and what he names "monarchical subordination,"[73]

[70] Lipps, *Ästhetik*, vol. I, p. 9.
[71] Lipps, *Ästhetik*, vol. I, p. 10.
[72] Lipps, *Ästhetik*, vol. I, p. 11.
[73] Lipps, *Ästhetik*, vol. I, pp. 74–90.

the presence in our experience of an object as a central feature that seems to organize and dominate without eliminating or suppressing the others, as features of objects that facilitate our integration of our experience of them into the unity of our apperception. For example, "Regularity is a harmony among parts, elements, features of a whole," and "such harmony facilitates the apprehension of the whole" and by means of that facilitates the unity of the soul itself. "On this depends the pleasure."[74]

However, Lipps also describes our enjoyment of realizing the unity of apperception in our experience of an object as an enjoyment of our own mental activity in experiencing the object. Thus he writes that

> The fundamental condition of pleasure in the objective [*im Gegenständlichen*] for us was unity. This was first determined as inner harmony... Corresponding to this is also the unitariness of acting [*Einstimmigkeit des Tuns*] in itself, and the harmonization [*Zusammenfassung*] of inner activity in points of unity, the contradiction-free subordination of all acting under determinate, unified goals.

He then goes on to describe this mental state in terms of a feeling of the freedom of inner action:

> Or, to bring together what has here been said: All feeling of self-value is pleasure in the power, the wealth or breadth, and the inner freedom of my acting. Here inner freedom means nothing other than that unitariness and unity of my acting in itself.
>
> The acting, of which I here speak, is of many kinds. It may be my intellectual acting.... Another kind of my acting is my acting directed at practical goals.... Finally my acting is perhaps also merely the acting that consists in the grasping and holding of an object, the in itself harmonious, thus internally free turning to something perceived or represented and the free turning away from it, the active going hither and yon, taking together and taking apart, penetrating, the internal appropriation and domination.

A beautiful object is one that allows me this unhindered and free mental activity; an object pleases me in aesthetic contemplation when it allows such "free grasping and holding"; "it is also something beautiful on account of the capacity for enjoyment that consists in such power and freedom of grasping and giving" myself to the object.[75]

In all of this, it certainly sounds as if Lipps is offering his own interpretation of Kant's central notion of the free play of the imagination and understanding. However, Lipps refuses to call the mental state of

---

[74] Lipps, *Ästhetik*, vol. I, pp. 18–19.
[75] Lipps, *Ästhetik*, vol. I, pp. 98–9.

response to a beautiful object "a free play of fantasy" because "it occurs ... with psychological necessity,"[76] that is, it does not seem like an optional and additional response to the perception of a beautiful object, but rather like part and parcel of our original experience of the object. Whether that aspect of the experience of beauty, previously emphasized by Vischer, is an adequate ground for refusing to call the psychological state that Lipps has described a state of free play might well be contested. After all, Kant too had noticed that we tend to think of beauty as if it were really a property of the object rather than a separable feature of our response to it, although his explanation of why we do this lay in our assumption of the intersubjective validity of our judgments of beauty rather than in descriptive psychology.[77]

Be that as it may, the basis of Lipps's conception of empathy lies in his view that we enjoy our own mental activity, now coupled with the view that we project an idea of mental activity onto whatever stimulates our own mental activity in aesthetic contemplation and then project as well onto such an object the emotional accompaniment of our own mental activity. The key move here is that the possibility of unhindered mental activity that we enjoy in our experience of a beautiful object is projected into the object as "liveliness and the possibility of life" (*Lebendigkeit und Lebensmöglichkeit*), so that the subjective character of our experience of the object is fused into our conception of the object itself – for the purposes of aesthetic contemplation, of course. Thus Lipps now states that "All enjoyment of beauty is an impression of the liveliness and possibility of life lying in the object; and all ugliness is in its ultimate essence the negation of life, lack of life, restriction, crippling, destruction, etc."[78] Of course, the most obvious object for such an experience is nothing other than our fellow humans, whom we can experience as themselves enjoying and promoting a free and harmonious mental life or as negating such a life, and this might seem to stand in the way of a generalization of empathy to all forms of beauty, including the beauty of inanimate nature, animate but nonhuman nature, and even human artifacts. But Lipps points out that even our experience of human beauty is not an immediate response to the human body as such – "The external appearance of the human being offers nothing that considered in itself could appear beautiful and indeed as the most beautiful"[79] – and infers from

---

[76] Lipps, *Ästhetik*, vol. I, p. 165.
[77] See Kant, *CPJ*, §6, 5:211.
[78] Lipps, *Ästhetik*, vol. I, p. 102.
[79] Lipps, *Ästhetik*, vol. I, p. 103.

this that our experience of the beauty of other humans must be empathetic, a projection onto their bodies of the feelings and emotions that we would associate with the postures and motions we observe in them if we were undergoing or undertaking those ourselves. We associate bodily symmetry, for example, with the possibility of successful physical activity or "life-activity" (*Lebensbetätigung*),[80] and that in turn with our own experience of mental harmony and its pleasure, which we then project onto the body. Lipps argues that "We experience [*erleben*] that this value is not attached to something sensuous, but to something human, to a life that lies behind [the sensuous] and expresses itself therein. I said about the form of the female body: When we have an impression of its beauty, we so to speak see through the form to a life; and we know that we do this."[81] But my understanding of the inner life has to come from my own case – "This inner is always me" – and has to be projected by me onto the other. Thus, "The consciousness of aesthetic value is always consciousness of a depth, in the object and in me, which I experience as a value, i.e., enjoy in myself,"[82] and this has to be projected into my experience of the other. My experience of the other – that is, my *Erlebnis* – is, phenomenologically, a unity, so I experience the depth of life in the other as being as much of a property of her as her bodily form, but it is nevertheless projected from my experience of my own mental life.

And once we have realized that even in the case of the beauty of another human being we have projected our own feeling of life into our experience of her, then of course the way is open for the thought that we perform this kind of projection in our experience of nonhuman and artistic beauty as well. This is exactly what Lipps argues next. Using a favorite term of Friedrich Theodor Vischer, he begins with the case of other animals, and argues that our aesthetic experience of them involves the projection of human emotions on to them:

> We consider animals as ensouled. Nobody can doubt that we know of a life of the soul in animals only because we ground the expressions of life in animals on a psychic life similar to our own, an I. This is in its origin my own. Insofar as I do not merely add this psychic life to the external appearance of the animal or think it in addition thereto, but internally experience it, the external appearance of the animal becomes aesthetically comprehensible to me and thereby wins aesthetic significance.[83]

---

[80] Lipps, *Ästhetik*, vol. I, p. 105.
[81] Lipps, *Ästhetik*, vol. I, p. 157.
[82] Lipps, *Ästhetik*, vol. I, p. 159.
[83] Lipps, *Ästhetik*, vol. I, p. 160.

Immediately preceding this argument Lipps had equated the empathetic injection of feeling into what we experience as beautiful as symbolism – "Everything beautiful is the 'symbol' of such a personal life and self-expression [*Sichauslebens*]"[84] – so this account of our aesthetic experience of animals is also an account of how they become symbols of human feelings for us. Immediately following his argument about animals, Lipps applies the same analysis to the case of non-animate nature: here too we experience appearances in nature as if they were bodily states or actions of human beings and then project onto them the feelings that we associate therewith. He begins his lengthy description of this sort of empathy with the case of sounds (again revealing his indebtedness to the older Vischer):

> In nature we encounter sounds everywhere. We hear the trees moan and groan, the storm howl, the leaves whisper, the stream murmur.... These sounds are not identical to our sounds of affect, but are comparable.... And to the degree that this is the case, they also seem to originate from a drive to make themselves audible, and to carry in themselves a corresponding affective moment.... And this is: making audible something internal, something human, something personal in general. Thus the sounds that we encounter in nature animate nature, humanize it, make of it an analogue of our own personality.[85]

Here Lipps equates empathy with the personification or humanization (*Vermenschlichung*) of the objects of aesthetic experience.

But although Lipps has displayed the eighteenth-century roots of his thought as well as his debts to Friedrich Theodor as well as Robert Vischer with the attention that he gives to the aesthetics of nature, he is sufficiently a child of the nineteenth-century to devote the bulk of his theory – the whole of the second volume of his *Aesthetics* – to the experience of art. Now of course it is no surprise that we should experience works of art as expressions of human emotion, since they are products of human activity and thus (often) expressions of the actual emotions of actual artists – even if we have to project our own emotions onto those artists in order to understand theirs, since after all we do not experience the emotions of each other directly. But the point that Lipps wants to make is that we experience expressed emotions as if they were part of works of art themselves, not merely part of the causal chain that has produced works of art. We do this in spite of our recognition that the work

---

[84] Lipps, *Ästhetik*, vol. I, p. 159.
[85] Lipps, *Ästhetik*, vol. I, pp. 161–2.

of art before us is just a block of inanimate stone, in the case of a sculpture, or even in the case of a performance art, such as theater, human actors who are not identical with the characters they are portraying – thus the work of art, or the characters portrayed in it, is always "ideal" rather than actual, and yet we experience it as if it were human, as if it had an emotional life of its own. So we experience the work of art not just as a human product but as if it were itself human; in a poem or a play or a sculpture we encounter a human personality that can only be a product of our own personification or humanization of what is actually before us. The experience of art is "in the final analysis always the experience of a *human being*. But this is the experience of myself. Thus I feel myself as a human being in the form that presents itself to me."[86] Using a term that Edward Bullough would make famous a decade later,[87] Lipps says that we are always aware of "distance" between ourselves and the work of art, or its "objecthood" (*Gegenständlichkeit*),[88] but that we at the same time experience it as having an emotional life that is grounded in our own. "We demand that in every case a *human being* comes before us in the work of art," one whose experience we can "co-experience" (*Miterleben*),[89] which of course we can do because its experience is in fact our own, projected into it by means of empathy.

Lipps spends most of the second large volume of his *Aesthetics* working out this idea in detail, and even then discusses only the "spatial" arts, the visual arts of painting, sculpture, architecture, and ornament. There is no space here to follow him through these details. We will conclude our discussion of Lipps with the following point only. Recall that at the outset of his theory Lipps had grounded aesthetic experience in the pleasure that we take in the unhindered activity of our own minds stimulated by an object, the activity that sounded so much like the Kantian free play of our cognitive powers but from which Lipps withheld that designation. This means that the mental life that we project onto other objects by means of empathy must ultimately be a positive form of life, something pleasurable rather than not. It is certainly easier for Lipps to maintain this position throughout a discussion of visual art rather than

---

[86] Lipps, *Ästhetik*, vol. II, p. 49.
[87] See Edward Bullough, "'Psychical Distance' as a Factor in Art and an Æsthetic Principle," *British Journal of Psychology* V (1912): 87–118, reprinted in Bullough, *Æsthetics: Lectures and Essays*, trans. Elizabeth M. Wilkinson (Stanford: Stanford University Press, 1957), pp. 91–130.
[88] Lipps, *Ästhetik*, vol. II, p. 51.
[89] Lipps, *Ästhetik*, vol. II, pp. 53–4.

other art forms, for example tragic drama, where the inner life that is represented on stage and to which we respond with the empathetic projection of our own emotions seems anything but pleasurable or affirmative – this is of course the traditional paradox of tragedy. In spite of not explicitly addressing the case of tragedy in his systematic work on aesthetics, as we noted one of Lipps's earlier publications was a small book on *The Debate about Tragedy*. Although Lipps does not yet explicitly deploy the concept of empathy in this work and thus does not directly address the question of how our empathetic response to art is supposed to be consonant with the underlying assumption that aesthetic response is supposed to be pleasurable, his main point in this work nevertheless shows how he could resolve this question. For what he argues is that tragedy pleases us not because it offers us an image of "poetic justice"[90] or "moral world-order"[91] in which characters receive the fate they deserve – from an array of ancient and modern examples, he argues that the main characters in the most effective tragedies usually receive a fate far worse than they deserve – but because it offers us the experience of compassion (*Mitleid*) with the powers and efforts of the characters to resist the inexorable forces of fate. Thus what we respond to in *Antigone* is not the unfairness of Creon's refusal to let Antigone give her brother a proper burial but "the force and powerful measure of moral passion in Antigone," and even in the case of Shakespeare's Richard III what we respond to is not his spite but rather the "extraordinary force of human willing" that is therein expressed.[92] More generally, Lipps states that

> *No* suffering, whatever it may be called, can please through its mere existence. The ground of enjoyment can by no means consist in something merely negative, it also cannot consist in inner negation. Rather what constitutes here as everywhere else the enjoyment in suffering is that in the suffering something positively valuable in the personality comes to light. This positively valuable is here the voice of conscience and truth.[93]

Such a generalization about tragedy is no doubt debatable: one could argue that it is Oedipus's drive for truth that brings about his own destruction, and that this drive is therefore something to which we should respond negatively, although it might also be argued that it is his belated drive for truth in spite of his earlier casualness about it (when

---

[90] Lipps, *Der Streit über die Tragödie*, pp. 11–16, 23–5.
[91] Lipps, *Der Streit über die Tragödie*, pp. 17–22.
[92] Lipps, *Der Streit über die Tragödie*, p. 30.
[93] Lipps, *Der Streit über die Tragödie*, p. 38.

he killed the old man on the road without worrying much about who he might really be) that ultimately draws our admiration. But however that debate might ultimately be decided, Lipps's own commitment to ensuring that empathy is always a positive experience should be evident in this approach to tragedy.

Lipps's account of empathy was widely received, but also criticized. Before we proceed to one of the most important of these criticisms, let us take a look at the defense of empathy theory offered by Johannes Volkelt.

Volkelt

Johannes Volkelt received his doctorate in Jena in 1876, became a professor there in 1879, and then taught in Basel and Würzburg before becoming professor in Leipzig, where he taught until 1921. He published numerous works in epistemology as well as aesthetics, and also published individual works on Kant, Schopenhauer, Jean Paul, and even on *Franz Grillparzer as Poet of the Tragic*. One of his mid-career works was, as in the case of Lipps, a theory of tragedy.[94] His main work in aesthetics was a three-volume *System of Aesthetics*, first published from 1905 to 1912 and then substantially revised for a second edition published from 1925 to 1927.[95] In the first edition of this work, Volkelt explicitly presented himself as a synthesizer in the history of aesthetics, methodologically and substantively: he said that his aesthetics "proceeds in the manner of experiential psychology" but "at the same time acknowledges significant and illuminating truth in the older German aesthetics";[96] that the aesthetic is "closely connected with the sensory side of the human being, even with the so-called lower sensations," but at the same time he remains firm that "the aesthetic, with all of its connections with the sensory ground of our nature, in every case nevertheless first comes to be within the highest, most spiritual [*vergeistigtesten*] circles of activity of the life of our soul";[97] and finally that on his understanding "aesthetics has to make clear the connection of the beautiful and of art with the other

---

[94] Johannes Volkelt, *Ästhetik des Tragischen* (Munich: Oskar Beck, 1897).
[95] Johannes Volkelt, *System der Ästhetik*: Vol. I, *Grundlegung der Ästhetik*, second, "strongly altered" edition (Munich: C.H. Beck, 1927); Vol. II, *Die Ästhetische Grundgestalten*, and Vol. III, *Kunstphilosophie und Metaphysik der Ästhetik*, second edition (Munich: C.H. Beck, 1925).
[96] Volkelt, *System*, vol. I, pp. v–vi.
[97] Volkelt, *System*, vol. I, p. vi.

great goods of humankind, with the other activities of culture," and that "one makes idol worship out of art if one rips it out of its connection with the goods, the values of culture in general and will not accept that the standards of other cultural values must be acknowledged by art."[98] In the second edition, however, twenty years later, Volkelt was more concerned to separate the psychological description of aesthetic experience from "value-theoretic considerations."[99]

In spite of these large claims, for Volkelt the "Psychological Foundation of Aesthetics" was and remained the "Psychology of Empathy,"[100] and our concern here will only be his attempt to defend this concept from contemporary objections. Volkelt devoted himself to this task in a work of 1920, thus shortly before his revision of his *System*, titled *The Aesthetic Consciousness*.[101] Volkelt saw the aesthetics of empathy attacked as a "subjectivist" approach by "objectivist" approaches of two kinds, on the one hand, what we might call purely philosophical approaches, namely the phenomenological approach of Edmund Husserl and his followers and the "transcendental method" of the Neo-Kantians, and, on the other, the substantive approach of aesthetic formalists such as Konrad Fiedler (1841–95) and his followers,[102] like that of Herbart before them.[103] The latter, according to Volkelt, tried to reduce the objects of aesthetic experience to pure "spatial form, relations of colors, connections of tones, forms of words,"[104] and so on, but were such "enemies of feeling" that they "paid no attention to what an emptying and flattening of aesthetic experiences [*Erlebnisse*] they would introduce through the exclusion of feelings" literally "melted into" (*eingeschmolzenen*) the objects of our actual aesthetic experience:[105] to insist that we actually experience pure spatial or temporal forms or even colors or tones without any emotional value (or other meaning) is simply to deny the nature of our actual experience. That objects present themselves to us as sublime, magnificent,

---

[98] Volkelt, *System*, vol. I, p. vii.
[99] Volkelt, *System*, vol. I, p. x.
[100] Volkelt, *System*, vol. I, p. xi.
[101] Johannes Volkelt, *Das ästhetische Bewusstsein: Prinzipienfragen der Ästhetik* (Munich: C.H. Beck, 1920).
[102] See Konrad Fiedler, *Schriften über Kunst*, ed. Hermann Konnerth (Munich: R. Piper, 1913). For literature, see Podro, *The Manifold in Perception*, Chapter VIII, and Stefan Majetschak, editor, *Auge und Hand: Konrad Fiedlers Kunsttheorie im Kontext* (Munich: Wilhelm Fink Verlag, 1997).
[103] Volkelt, *Ästhetische Bewusstsein*, p. 18.
[104] Volkelt, *Ästhetische Bewusstsein*, p. 9.
[105] Volkelt, *Ästhetische Bewusstsein*, p. 11.

worthy, or pathetic is just as much as part of our experience as that they present themselves to us as shaped and colored, and thus "The aesthetics of empathy," in Volkelt's view, "is at the same time an aesthetics of objectivity."[106] Volkelt was equally unimpressed with the philosophical objections to the aesthetics of empathy as "subjectivist." In his view, Husserl's method of "essence-intuiting, eidetic, intuitive grasping"[107] is subject matter-neutral, and can be used to describe our experience of objects as emotionally meaningful as much as it can be used to describe any other form of perception or conceptualization of objects; Husserl's method tells us how to describe our experience of an object but not what kinds of properties we can actually experience objects to have. As for the transcendental method of a Neo-Kantian such as Cohen or for that matter of Kant himself, Volkelt the epistemologist agrees that it can describe the "immanent lawfulness of the thought" of objects as such,[108] but again maintains that this only determines the logical form of our experience of objects, not the substance of such experience. It remains to experience to tell us what the contents rather than the form of our experience of objects is, and in Volkelt's view what experience tells us, as Lipps before him had shown, is that we experience objects as laden with emotions. Thus he defends Lipps's aesthetics of empathy as well as his own in his *System of Aesthetics* as the substantive result of descriptive psychology, incompatible with the formalist aesthetics of the Herbartian tradition although compatible with either Husserlian phenomenology or Kantian transcendental principles of experience. He remains confident of his treatment of "empathy as a process widespread in human mental life, which is found by no means only in aesthetic contexts," all the more so because "his own method of work in aesthetics, for all its close connection to psychology, is predominantly determined by art" itself, "ruled by the effort to order and determine the impressions and experiences that have been imparted to me in uninterrupted traffic with art."[109]

Not in his account of the foundations of aesthetics in Volume I of his *System*, nor in his catalogue of particular forms of empathy in Volume II, nor in his account of artistic creativity or of the relations between aesthetic and other values in Volume III does the idea of aesthetic experience as either a form of cognition or a form of play appear, so from our

---

[106] Volkelt, *Ästhetische Bewusstsein*, p. 15.
[107] Volkelt, *Ästhetische Bewusstsein*, p. 17.
[108] Volkelt, *Ästhetische Bewusstsein*, p. 34.
[109] Volkelt, *Ästhetische Bewusstsein*, p. 43.

point of view Volkelt's aesthetics reduces aesthetic experience to the element of emotional in spite of the generous comments of its preface. One German aesthetician who attempted to revive the concept of play while acknowledging the importance of empathy, however, was Karl Groos.

3. GROOS: THE PLAY OF ANIMAL AND MAN

A critique of the particulars of Herbert Spencer's version of the aesthetics of play that nevertheless accepted the importance of play while also trying to find room for empathy within aesthetic experience was offered by Karl Groos (1861–1946), professor of philosophy at Giessen in Hesse, later at Basel, and finally at Tübingen, the university of Friedrich Theodor and Robert Vischer. Groos studied at Heidelberg, one of the seats of Southwest Neo-Kantianism, and his earliest publication was a work on the philosophy of Schelling.[110] That was quickly followed by an introduction to aesthetics,[111] and then for a decade Groos focused on the concept of play and its pedagogical importance. This work culminated in a book on *The Mental Life of Children*[112] that achieved great popularity in Germany, going through at least six editions. In his later career, Groos published numerous works on more standard topics in academic philosophy. But his wider reputation was based on his work on play, particularly a pair of books that were quickly translated into English, and indeed in the United States published by Spencer's publisher, namely *The Play of Animals* (1896) and *The Play of Man* (1899).[113] In these works Groos adopted Spencer's psychological approach to play and his foundation of aesthetics upon this concept, but objected to the idea that either play or developed aesthetic activity is simply the discharge of excess capacity with no direct advantage for the individual or species who plays. Born two years after the publication of *The Origin of Species* and convinced that every important characteristic of a creature must have an evolutionary advantage, Groos argued that higher animals and especially humans have a fundamental impulse or instinct to play and that this has the direct advantage of preparing them to use their capacities in ways that are certainly functional. At the same time, Groos, far more learned

---

[110] Karl Groos, *Die reine Vernunftwissenschaft* (Heidelberg: Georg Weiß, 1889).
[111] Karl Groos, *Einleitung in die Ästhetik* (Giessen: Ricker, 1892).
[112] Karl Groos, *Das Seelenleben des Kindes* (Berlin: Reuter und Richard, 1904).
[113] Karl Groos, *The Play of Animals*, trans. Elizabeth L. Baldwin, with Preface by J. Mark Baldwin (New York: Appleton, 1898), and *The Play of Man*, trans. Elizabeth L. Baldwin, with Preface by J. Mark Baldwin (New York: Appleton, 1901).

in the history of philosophy than Spencer, accepted the idea of the disinterestedness of aesthetic experience, and following Schiller and Kant as well celebrated aesthetic experience as an experience of freedom. How he reconciled the functionality of play with the aesthetics of freedom will be a central question in what follows.

The fundamental idea of Groos's approach to the concept of play is clearly asserted in the preface to *The Play of Animals*: "The play of youth depends on the fact that certain instincts, especially useful in preserving the species, appear before the animal seriously needs them. They are, in contrast with later serious *exercise* (*Ausübung*), a *preparation* (*Vorübung*) and *practice* (*Einübung*) for the special instincts.... The animal does not play because he is young, he has a period of youth because he must play."[114] That is, Groos supposes, higher animals will need for their survival physical and intellectual capacities of a kind that cannot be fully developed at birth but are only latent then, but their species must have evolved an instinct to develop these capacities by appropriate play as well as the parenting instincts that will allow and nurture such play in the developing young. In the first chapter of the book, Groos makes it clear immediately that his theory is directed against the "surplus energy principle" of Spencer, and defends the honor of Schiller while so doing: he emphasizes "Schiller's priority" in the theory of play but also insists that for Schiller the surplus energy principle "holds but a subordinate place" rather than being the whole explanation of the importance of play.[115] Instead of interpreting the play of the young, in both higher animals and humans, as mere discharge of surplus energy that may accidentally take the form of the imitation of adult activities, such as tea parties and war, Groos holds that

> The "experimenting" of little children and young animals, their movement, hunting, and fighting games, which are the most important elementary forms of play, are not imitative repetitions, but rather preparatory efforts. They come before any serious activity, and evidently aim at preparing the young creature for it and making him familiar with it.[116]

Fledglings flapping their wings while still in the nest, infants crowing and babbling, and boys romping – "all these do not imitate serious action, whose organ has been dormant for an interval 'longer than ordinary,' but rather, impelled by irresistible impulse, they make their first

---

[114] Groos, *Play of Animals*, p. xx.
[115] Groos, *Play of Animals*, p. 1.
[116] Groos, *Play of Animals*, p. 7.

preparations for such activities in this way."[117] Along with rejecting the idea that play is primarily an expenditure of surplus energy that just happens to take the form of imitation of adult activities, Groos also rejects the idea that play is primarily recreational or restorative. He does not deny that children or even adults can seek "recreation 'in a little game' after the burden and the heat of the day,'" but he denies that "the necessity for recreation originates play."[118] What originates play is the need for the young creature to develop the complex abilities that it will need in its later life. Of course, both those latent capacities and the instinct to play in order to develop them must be inherited: "The activity of all living beings is in the highest degree influenced by hereditary instincts."[119]

After devoting many pages to describing the varieties of play among animals, Groos turns to "The Psychology of Animal Play," but under this rubric in fact turns to the psychology of human play. Here he makes a reference to his Basel predecessor Nietzsche, noting that his conception of a "struggle for power" is a better description of the psychology of much play than Darwin's "struggle for survival," which as he notes is usually "no struggle at all" at the level of individuals; by this means he introduces the point that young creatures, including children, first struggle to attain mastery over their own bodies "by means of experimental and movement plays," which then lead to "playful chase and mock combats," and to further forms of play, involving "building, nursing, and curiosity," in which "the impulses of ownership and subjugation manifest themselves in various ways."[120] Through these forms of play, children develop the physical and social skills they will need in adult life. In this context Groos returns to the attack upon Spencer, criticizing the characterization of play as "aimless activity" and emphasizing that setting and trying to achieve goals is essential to the functional character of much play.[121]

But given the high degree of functionality that Groos has ascribed to the play of human children as well as to animals, how can he build upon the concept of play a conception of art that accepts the disinterestedness of aesthetic experience from the tradition of Kant and Schiller that he has taken as the origin of the theory of play? The answer to this question is that

---

[117] Groos, *Play of Animals*, p. 8.
[118] Groos, *Play of Animals*, p. 17.
[119] Groos, *Play of Animals*, p. 13.
[120] Groos, *Play of Animals*, pp. 290–1.
[121] Groos, *Play of Animals*, p. 291. Here Groos cites the French philosopher and aesthetician Paul Souriau.

> Here we must suppose a progressive development from mere satisfaction of instinctive impulse (where the act is performed neither for its own sake nor for the sake of an external aim, but simply in obedience to hereditary propensity) through what is subjectively considered akin to work, up to make-believe activity with an external aim as its second stage. Finally, as the outward aim gives way before the pleasure-giving quality of the act itself, the transition to art takes place. At this point the outward aim has but a very slight significance, though never vanishing entirely; for it can not be denied that in artistic execution it regains very considerable importance in an altered form.[122]

The suggestion is that play that is at first entirely instinctive can next be undertaken with a conscious recognition of its ulterior benefit, in which case it has some of the characteristics of work, but can finally be undertaken for sheer pleasure regardless of the benefits it may also be recognized to have. At this point Groos must be accepting from Spencer the idea that there is pleasure in the sheer exercise of our capacities, which do have excess capacity, and that we can find ways in which to exercise them that will please us long after their role as preparation for the serious business of adult life has been discharged. "So we find in this pleasure in the possession of power the psychological foundation for all play which has higher intellectual accompaniments"[123] and the foundations for the activities of producing and experiencing art in particular – although, as Groos suggested in the previous quotation, the production of art will ordinarily involve elements of acquired skill and effort that seem more like work than like play, and, we might add, sometimes even the appreciation of art can also involve work, such as learning classical languages, as Kant had long before pointed out.

In the concluding pages of *The Play of Animals*, Groos develops this premise into the foundations for a theory of art by identifying the form of play that leads to art as pretending, or "conscious self-illusion," and the pleasure characteristic of art and its experience as "pleasure in making believe." He writes that

> The origin of artistic fantasy or playful illusion is thus anchored in the firm ground of organic evolution. Play is needed for the higher development of intelligence; at first merely objective, it becomes, by means of this development, subjective as well, for the fact that the animal, though recognising that his action is only a pretence, repeats it, raises it to the sphere of conscious self-illusion, pleasure in making believe – that is, to the threshold of artistic production.

[122] Groos, *Play of Animals*, pp. 292–3.
[123] Groos, *Play of Animals*, pp. 295–6.

Groos continues that this brings us "only to the threshold of art," however, for to the production of true art there also "belongs the aim of affecting others by the pretence, and pure play has none of this aim. Only love play shows something of it, and in this respect it is nearest to art."[124] Here Groos says that the production of art also requires the desire to share the pleasure of making believe, and identifies the desire to share pleasure as the essence of love. So art emerges only when the individual and the species see past a purely egoistical pleasure in play and are ready to share that pleasure. Of course, since sharing is necessary to the individual survival of human beings as well as the propagation of more of the kind, Groos could easily argue, although he does not do so here, that this condition of the emergence of art is also a hereditary instinct, thus that the emergence of art is due to the conjunction of two instincts – the play-instinct and the instinct for love. This does not exactly replicate Schiller's view that the drive for play and art emerges out of the drive for matter and the drive for form, but has something of the same structure.

In any case, Groos explicitly associates his theory of artistic play as "self-conscious illusion" or "making believe" with Schiller's idea of "æsthetic appearance (*Schein*) which we distinguish from reality," which we like "because it is show, and not because we mistake it for anything else."[125] Groos then identifies two key facts about "conscious self-illusion" as the key to aesthetic experience. First, developing a view that he had already suggested in his 1892 introduction to aesthetics but that he also finds in his contemporaries the aesthetician Max Dessoir (1867–1947), who published a work called *The Double Self* in 1890,[126] and the art-historian Konrad Lange (1855–1921), professor of art history at Tübingen, and thus later Groos's colleague, as well as director of the Württemberg state art museum in Stuttgart, who introduced the idea into his book *Conscious Self-Deception as the Kernel of Aesthetic Enjoyment* in 1895,[127] Groos argues that in aesthetic experience – presumably here meaning either the experience of production or reception – the subject is always conscious of both the fantasy and reality and the difference between them. "Even the

---

[124] Groos, *Play of Animals*, pp. 302–3.
[125] Groos, *Play of Animals*, p. 303, citing Schiller's *Letters on the Aesthetic Education of Mankind*, Letter XXVI.
[126] Max Dessoir, *Das Doppel-Ich* (Leipzig: Günther, 1890). Dessoir's main work was *Ästhetik und allgemeine Kunstwissenschaft* (1906), translated as *Aesthetics and Theory of Art* by Stephen A. Emery (Detroit: Wayne State University Press, 1970).
[127] Konrad Lange, *Das bewusste Selbsttäuschung als Kern des ästhetischen Genusses* (Leipzig: Veit & Co., 1895). Lange would later develop the theory of illusion into a full-blown theory

child [who] is wholly absorbed in his play ... has the knowledge that it is only a pretence, after all," he states,[128] and all the more so the adult, whose grip on the difference between reality and illusion is at least as strong as that of the child if not stronger, has the difference in mind while nevertheless being absorbed in the creation or enjoyment of a work of art. Indeed, Groos follows Lange in locating the source of our pleasure in aesthetic experience precisely in playing in the gap between illusion and reality while being aware of the distinction between them. Lange, he says, "speaks of the 'oscillation between appearance and reality,' and regards it as the very essence of æsthetic enjoyment." Lange goes still further, Groos quotes:

> Artistic enjoyment thus appears as a variable floating condition, a free and conscious movement between appearance and reality, between the serious and the playful ... The subject knows quite well, on the one hand, that the ideas and feeling occupying him are only make-believe, yet, on the other hand, he continues to act as if they were serious and real. It is this continued play of emotion, this alternation of appearance and reality, or reason and emotion, if you like, that constitutes the essence of aesthetic enjoyment.[129]

It may be noted that here Groos and Lange introduce the experience of emotion into the theory of play, not, as Spencer did, by holding simply that our capacity for emotion is one of the capacities that is discharged in play, but by suggesting that we experience a complex play of emotions as we swing back and forth between the emotions appropriate to the contents of our illusion or make-believe and the emotions appropriate to our real circumstances. Thus this version of the theory of play finds a central role for the experience of emotions in response to art, which Kant had gone to such efforts to exclude from his own theory of play.

Groos does not expand upon this suggestion, although presumably the point could be developed into the assertion that our experience of make-believe allows us to experience emotions missing from our real life, at least in present circumstances, while our continuing awareness of the difference between reality and illusion tempers those emotions. Instead of further developing this point, Groos makes a second main point about aesthetic experience as self-conscious illusion, namely that

---

of the arts in *Das Wesen der Kunst*, 2 vols. (Berlin: G. Grote, 1901), second edition in one volume (Berlin: G. Grote, 1907).

[128] Groos, *Play of Animals*, p. 304. Here Groos also cites Eduard van Hartmann, *Ästhetik*, vol. II, p. 59.

[129] Groos, *Play of Animals*, p. 310, quoting Lange, *Die bewusste Selbsttäuschung*, p. 22.

it is a "feeling of freedom," a feeling of freedom from the constraints of ordinary life.[130] This point too Groos traces back to Schiller, indeed to as early an essay as "The Stage Considered as a Moral Institution" of 1784, written well before Schiller felt the influence of Kant. "Schiller is perfectly right," Groos says, "in designating the feeling of freedom as the highest and most important factor in the satisfaction derived from play."[131] "It may safely be said that we never feel so free as when we are playing," Groos continues, although he would prefer not to ground this point on "transcendental considerations" but on the fact that "free activity, regarded from a psychological standpoint, depends on our ability to do just what we wish to do."[132] The key idea is then that in our adult life creating and experiencing art is pretty much the only place we can do just what we wish to do. "Where can the feeling of freedom be purer or more intense than in conscious self-illusion in the realm of play? In real life we are always in servitude to objects and under the double weight of past and future."[133] But at the same time, we must preserve consciousness of the illusory character of make-believe if we are not to be swept away by it, and lose our freedom of thought and feeling in that way, different from but just as much a form of unfreedom as the constraints of everyday life.

This is the conclusion of *The Play of Animals*. We might expect to find much more about art and aesthetic experience in *The Play of Man*, since the creation and the enjoyment of art seems to be a specifically human possibility. In fact, while *The Play of Man* offers detailed descriptions of "Playful Experimentation" and "The Playful Exercise of Impulses of the Second or Socionomic Order," picking up on the suggestion that in play we develop mastery of both our own bodies and our social feelings that we noted earlier, it offers only a brief further discussion of the "æsthetic standpoint." What this adds to the conclusion of *The Play of Animals* is chiefly a criticism of the theory of "empathy" of Theodor Lipps from the point of view of the theory of play. Groos does not deny the importance of empathy in aesthetic experience. He is clearly sympathetic to the "conviction … among German students of æsthetics," by whom he has in mind in addition to Lipps also Volkelt, "that one of the weightiest problems of their science is offered by that familiar process by which we put ourselves into the object observed, and thus attain a sort of inward

---

[130] Groos, *Play of Animals*, p. 319.
[131] Groos, *Play of Animals*, p. 320.
[132] Groos, *Play of Animals*, p. 321.
[133] Groos, *Play of Animals*, p. 322.

sympathy with it."[134] Groos gives a precise description of "this very complicated process":

> 1*a*. The mind conceives of the experience of the other individual as if it were its own. 1*b*. We live through the psychic states which a lifeless object would experience if it possessed a mental life like our own. 2*a*. We inwardly participate in the movements of an external object. 2*b*. We also conceive of the motions which a body at rest might make if the powers which we attribute to it were actual ... 3. We transfer the temper, which is the result of our own inward sympathy, to the object and speak of the solemnity of the sublime, the gaiety of beauty, etc.[135]

Groos's objection is only to the supposition that empathy so described includes "the whole field" of aesthetic experience; what the theory of empathy fails to see, in his view, is that empathy is only one element in the play that we may enjoy with an aesthetic object. He illustrates his point by taking as an example "the latest utterance of Lipps on the impression produced by a Doric column." This example comes not from Lipps's systematic *Aesthetics*, which had not yet been published, but from his 1897 book *Spatial Aesthetics and geometrical-optical Illusions*.[136] Groos quotes Lipps as saying that "I sympathize with the column's manner of holding itself and attribute to it qualities of life because I recognize in it proportions and other relations agreeable to me. Thus all enjoyment of form, and indeed all æsthetic enjoyment whatsoever, resolves itself into an agreeable feeling of sympathy."[137] Groos does not object to Lipps's hasty generalization that all aesthetic experience involves the kind of empathy we are supposed to find in our experience of the column, although he might well have done so; rather, he objects that Lipps's description of empathy is incomplete, because it does not explain how our sympathetic projection of feeling onto the column is "part of a general psychological fact," how it fits into our apperception as a whole while still being "differentiated as a particular satisfaction from general apperception." He himself asserts that this can be done only by means of the idea of play, arguing that empathy becomes aesthetic "only when the hearer enjoys the emotional effect of the phenomenon as such, rendered possible by the process of fusion; when he has an independent, self-centered pleasure in this result – that is to say, when he plays."[138] "It

---

[134] Groos, *The Play of Man*, p. 322.
[135] Groos, *The Play of Man*, p. 323.
[136] Theodor Lipps, *Raumästhetik und geometrische-optische Täuschungen* (Leipzig: Barth, 1897).
[137] Groos, *The Play of Man*, p. 324, quoting Lipps, *Raumästhetik*, p. 5.
[138] Groos, *The Play of Man*, pp. 325–6.

is self-evident," he continues, "that we can not think of [the column's] upward spring without calling in our earlier experiences, but it seems to me to be just as apparent that in æsthetic perception the impression is intentionally lingered over only for the sake of its pleasure-giving qualities, i.e., playfully."[139] Thus Groos makes room for the emotional impact of art by allowing that empathy can be part of play, but also argues that aesthetic empathy can be understood only as part of play as he has analyzed it.

Whether it will be "self-evident" that empathy can be incorporated into yet differentiated within the unity of apperception of human mental life in general only as part of play will depend upon whether the reader has by this point accepted Groos's theory of play. But even if Groos's entire theory has not been accepted, his criticism might be taken to make the point (in anticipation) that in spite of the emphasis that he gives to the concept of apperception, Lipps does not in fact fully explain how his theory of empathy fits into this larger aspect of human mental life. Lipps does of course try to explain what differentiates aesthetic empathy from other sorts of empathy through his concept of aesthetic contemplation, but then it could be argued that this too needs a more explicit integration into Lipps's theory of apperception than he actually gives it.

Groos thus attempted to unify the approaches to aesthetics that emphasized the importance of play with aesthetic form and the emotional impact of art, although he had nothing to say about aesthetic experience as a form of knowledge. He thus developed a more comprehensive approach to aesthetic experience than Lipps or Volkelt did, but not as comprehensive an approach as Dilthey had suggested in his poetics, which seems to have been ignored by all these authors. In spite of their limitations, however, both the more restrictive empathy theory of Lipps and the more inclusive theory of Groos had considerable influence. We will now consider several examples of their influence outside of Germany. Although both of the authors now to be considered published their relevant works after the turn of the twentieth century, they were so influenced by the late-nineteenth-century theories we have just been discussing that we will consider them here before concluding the present volume and turning to the aesthetics of the twentieth century proper.

---

[139] Groos, *The Play of Man*, p. 326.

4. PSYCHOLOGICAL AESTHETICS IN THE UNITED STATES: PUFFER

A significant author of psychological aesthetics in the United States was the now little remembered Ethel Dench Puffer, later Ethel Puffer Howes (1872–1950), whose promising career as a psychologist was cut off by prejudice against women in academia in the early twentieth century, but who enjoyed a second career as a leading feminist writer and researcher. Puffer was one of four sisters from Framingham, Massachusetts, all of whom graduated from Smith College – Ethel at the age of 19, in 1891. In 1895 she traveled to Berlin to pursue advanced studies in psychology, but as a woman met with considerable resistance. She was treated better in Freiburg, where she spent 1896–97 working under Hugo Münsterberg. When he was called to Harvard, she came back with him, and completed work for a doctorate in 1898. But Harvard refused, again on account of her gender, to grant her a degree, which after a three-year delay was granted instead by Radcliffe College, not yet part of Harvard, in 1901. In that year Puffer published the first chapter of her dissertation, "Criticism and Æsthetics," in the *Atlantic Monthly*,[140] and the whole work was published in 1905 as *The Psychology of Beauty*.[141] Puffer taught at Wellesley College until she married Benjamin Howes, a civil engineer, in 1908, which ended her appointment at Wellesley and blocked her from other appointments, such as at Barnard, the women's college of Columbia University. In spite of this, she stayed abreast of the field of aesthetics, publishing detailed reviews of new works by leading German, British, French, American, and Italian aestheticians in 1913 and 1914.[142] She had two children in 1915 and 1917, well into her forties, and at that time became Executive Secretary of the National College Equal Suffrage League. In the 1920s, she published prominent articles, again in the *Atlantic*, on the difficulties put in the way of professional women. From 1925 to 1931, she headed an Institute for the Coordination of Women's Interest back at Smith with support from the Rockefeller Foundation, but when that grant ended Smith did not continue support. She subsequently moved to Washington with her husband, who became chief of the U.S. Housing Authority and Public Housing Administration, and devoted herself to civic activities but did not publish further.

---

[140] Ethel D. Puffer, "Criticism and Æsthetics," *Atlantic Monthly* 87 (June, 1901): 839–48.
[141] Ethel D. Puffer, *The Psychology of Beauty* (Boston: Houghton Mifflin, 1905).
[142] Ethel Puffer Howes, "Æsthetics," *Psychological Bulletin* 10 (1913): 196–201 and 11 (1914): 256–62.

In *The Psychology of Beauty*, Puffer argued that it is the role of philosophy to define beauty or "lay down what Beauty has to do," but of psychology to determine how beauty is actually experienced or to "deal with the various means through which this end is to be reached."[143] More fully,

> The aim of æsthetics being ... the determination of the Nature of Beauty and the explanation of our feelings about it, it is evident at this point that the Nature of Beauty must be determined by philosophy; but the general definition having been fixed, the meaning of the work of art having been made clear, the only possible explanation of our feelings about it – the æsthetic experience, in other words – must be gained from psychology.... How the beautiful object brings about the æsthetic experience, the boundaries of which are already known, is clearly a matter for psychology.

Puffer's work accordingly comprises both an analytical stratum, in which the definition of beauty is presented, and an empirical level, in which the experience of beauty is described. (Her conception of the relation between philosophical analysis and psychological description thus anticipates that suggested by Volkelt's response to phenomenology and transcendental philosophy.) She does not consider any other aesthetic category than beauty, although since her book concludes with her explanation of tragic emotions, it is clear that she meant the concept and experience of beauty to be understood broadly.

In view of this structure, one would expect Puffer to begin by defining beauty and then turning to her psychological account of the experience of it. In fact, she proceeds in the opposite order, first giving her basic description of the experience of beauty and only then showing how it fits into and completes traditional philosophical conceptions, before illustrating her results with discussions of the beauty of fine art, music, literature, and drama. Her account of the experience of beauty is not basically dissimilar to those we have found in Robert Vischer and Lipps, of the latter of whom at least she was well aware, emphasizing the effect of the perception of the work of art on our own emotions, but she does not follow them in arguing that we project our own emotion back onto the object, in other words she does not adopt their conception of empathy. She is also aware of the work of Groos, but does not include an element of play in her own account of aesthetic experience.

Puffer begins her chapter on "Criticism and Æsthetics" with a critique of the evolutionary theory of art of Ferdinand Brunetière (1849–1906),

---

[143] Puffer, *Psychology of Beauty*, pp. 37–8.

professor of French language and literature at the École Normale Supérieure and editor of the *Revue des deux mondes*, whose *L'Evolution de genres dans l'histoire de la littérature*[144] offered a pseudo-Darwinian account of the evolution of artistic genres and styles. Puffer argued that an evolutionary approach could explain the development of various stylistic characteristics of art but could never explain what makes them beautiful. Thus, it could explain the emergence of the "Greek temple [as] a product of Greek religion applied to geographical conditions" or various features of early Italian art as due to its ecclesiastical origins, but can never explain "how and why just those proportions" of Greek architecture "were chosen which make the joy and despair of all beholders" or "all that makes a Giotto greater than a Pictor Ignotus."[145] What actually makes an object beautiful, Puffer holds, can only be explained in psychological terms. The explanation lies in the effect of a work on one's own bodily condition and through that on one's emotional state and general sense of well-being. Thus,

> When I feel the rhythm of poetry, or of perfect prose,... every sensation of sound sends through me a diffusive wave of nervous energy. I *am* the rhythm because I imitate it in myself. I march to noble music in all my veins, even though I may be sitting decorously by my own hearthstone; and when I sweep with my eyes the outlines of a great picture, the curve of a Greek vase, the arches of cathedral, every line is lived over again in my own frame. And when rhythm and melody and forms and colors give me pleasure, it is because the imitating impulses and movements that have arisen in me are such as suit, help, heighten my physical organization in general and particular.... The basis, in short, of any æsthetic experience – [of] poetry, music, painting, and the rest is beautiful through its harmony with the conditions offered by our senses, primarily of sight and hearing, and through the harmony of the suggestions and impulses it arouses with the whole organism.[146]

Puffer emphasizes, as Vischer had thirty years earlier, that harmony between aspects of objects and the conditions of our perception of them diffuses a feeling of well-being throughout our bodies and psyches, but does not argue, as both Vischer and Lipps had, that we then in turn project our own emotional state back on to the object. Instead, she takes up another question, namely "What of the special emotions – the gayety or

---

[144] Ferdinand Brunetière, *L'Evolution de genres dans l'histoire de la littérature* (Paris: Hatchette, 1892).
[145] Puffer, *Psychology of Art*, p. 10. "Pictor Ignotus" is a poem by Robert Browning, describing an imaginary monastic painter.
[146] Puffer, *Psychology of Art*, pp. 12–13.

triumph, the sadness or peace or agitation – that hang about the work of art, and make, for many, the greater part of their delight in it?"[147] Explaining how objects stimulate specific emotions rather than the general emotion of pleasure or a feeling of well-being would be a necessary condition for explaining how we project specific emotional content back on to them, but Puffer is not interested in taking that further step. Instead, with a tacit appeal to the theory of emotion of William James – she uses his famous example of "fear at the sight of a bear" without mentioning his name[148] – she argues that specific emotions consist in specific "bodily changes," for example physical feelings of "preparation for flight" or, on the perception of a glass of wine, or image of one, "organic states which are felt emotionally as cheerfulness." Her thesis is that different bodily states have different "emotional tones," "And so if the music of a Strauss waltz makes us gay, and Händel's Largo serious, it is not because we are reminded of the ballroom or of the cathedral, but because the physical response to the stimulus of the music is itself the basis of the emotion." Or, "What makes the sense of peace in the atmosphere of the Low Countries?" or paintings of those landscapes? "Only the tendency, on following those level lines of landscape, to assume ourselves the horizontal, and the restfulness which belongs to that posture."[149] Here Puffer rejects the associationism of a century earlier as well as Eduard Hanslick's criticism that music cannot have specific emotional meaning because it can only make us feel its own properties, such as a fast or slow beat;[150] her position is that all sorts of physical properties of objects (such as landscapes or musical performances) or their representations (landscape paintings) have specific physical effects on us that are in turn characteristic of specific emotions, which we then experience without attributing to the objects. This is a physical and emotional process, not an intellectual one – Puffer rejects a cognitivist approach to art:

> If the crimson of a picture by Böcklin, or the golden glow of a Giorgione, or the fantastic gleam of a Rembrandt speaks to me like a human voice, it is not because it expresses to me an idea, but because it impresses that sensibility which is deeper than ideas, – the region of emotional response to

---

[147] Puffer, *Psychology of Art*, p. 14.
[148] See William James, *The Principles of Psychology* (1890), introduction by George A. Miller (Cambridge, Mass.: Harvard University Press, 1983), Chapter XXV, pp. 1058–97, at p. 1065.
[149] Puffer, *Psychology of Art*, pp. 14–15.
[150] See Eduard Hanslick, *The Beautiful in Music*, trans. Gustav Cohen (Indianapolis: Bobbs-Merrill Company, 1957), pp. 24–5.

color and to light.... It is the way in which the form in its exquisite fitness to our senses, and the emotion belonging to that particular form as organic reverberation therefrom, in its exquisite fitness to thought, create in us a delight quite unaccounted for by the ideas which they express. This is the essence of beauty, – the possession of a quality which excites the human organism to functioning harmoniously with its own nature.[151]

Here Puffer focuses on the emotional dimension of aesthetic experience, but leaves room for a larger sense of harmony as well.

Puffer returns to the general emotional tone of aesthetic experience rather than to specific emotions in relating her psychological explanation of aesthetic experience to the philosophical definition of beauty, the project of her second chapter, on "The Nature of Beauty." She begins with the premise that "Beauty is an excellence, a standard, a value ... because it fulfills an end, because it is good for something in the world."[152] It thus appears that she must be about to reject the traditional definition of aesthetic experience as disinterested and of the beautiful as completely different from the good as well as from the true. But in fact she endorses Hegel's statement that "It was Kant ... who spoke the first rational word concerning Beauty."[153] She can do this because she holds that the "two important factors ... of Kant's æsthetics are its reconciliation of sense and reason in beauty, and its reference of the 'purposiveness' of beauty to the cognitive faculty,"[154] though not for the purpose of determinate cognition. She argues that Schiller and Schelling basically have the same idea as Kant, namely that the experience of beauty is "the objective possibility for the bridge between sense and reason, ... the vindication of the possible unity of the real and the ideal, or nature and self,"[155] all of which point to her own idea that aesthetic experience constitutes a "reconciliation" "because I am for the moment complete, at the highest point of energy and unity." "The subject should not be a mirror of perfection but a state of perfection," she adds.[156] All of the idealist theories, except for Hegel's, which is too intellectualist for Puffer's taste, point to the idea of the experience of beauty as an experience of "unity and self-completeness" in the one who has the experience rather than the object. We saw indeed that this remained an aspect of aesthetic theory in Germany as late as Robert Vischer, and it could even be argued

---

[151] Puffer, *Psychology of Art*, p. 15.
[152] Puffer, *Psychology of Art*, p. 36.
[153] Puffer, *Psychology of Art*, p. 39.
[154] Puffer, *Psychology of Art*, p. 41.
[155] Puffer, *Psychology of Art*, p. 43.
[156] Puffer, *Psychology of Art*, p. 47.

that it is what lies behind Lipps's theory of apperception. Once again, Puffer could have argued that the subject goes on to project that experience of unity on to the object and that this is what is called its beauty, but she does not take that further step of the empathy theorists. Nor, although the experience she describes must clearly involve a sense of harmony among the different mental powers of the subject, does she describe it as any form of free play.

For Puffer, this is as far as philosophy can take the explanation of beauty. She states:

> Our philosophical definition of Beauty has thus taken final shape. The beautiful object possesses those qualities which bring the personality into a state of unity and self-completeness.... Beauty is to bring unity and self-completeness into the personality. By what means? What causes can bring about this effect? When we enter the realm of causes and effects, however, we have already left the ground of philosophy, and it is fitting that the concepts which we have to use should be adopted to the empirical point of view. The personality, as dealt with in psychology, is but the psychophysical organism; and we need to know only how to translate unity and self-completeness into psychological terms.[157]

And that Puffer has already done, by explaining how the experience of the physical features of works of art or natural beauties – shape, rhythm, and so on – produce complementary states in our own bodies that in turn induce a general feeling of well-being.

Eighteenth-century empiricists would not have drawn the rigid distinction between philosophical analysis and psychological explanation that Puffer does, although Kant already pointed in that direction.[158] Puffer does not contrast her view to that of the earlier empiricists, however, but concludes her chapter on "The Nature of Beauty" with some brief comparisons between her view and that of her contemporaries. According to her, "Lipps defines the æsthetic experience as a 'thrill of sympathetic feeling,'" which is too narrow an account of the range of emotions beauty can produce, and Groos defines it as "sympathetic imitation," which she thinks leaves out the element of "repose" that is crucial to her own account of the experience of beauty as an experience of

---

[157] Puffer, *Psychology of Art*, p. 49.
[158] This distinction has been a cornerstone of my own interpretation of Kant's aesthetics; see *Kant and the Claims of Taste*, second edition, pp. 106–18. I made my distinction there between the analysis of the logic of aesthetic judgments and the explanation of aesthetic response that allows it to satisfy before I discovered Puffer's work.

"unity and self-completeness" and thereby relates it to the idealist tradition.[159] Santayana's account of "Beauty as objectified pleasure" (which will be discussed in the next volume) she finds "neither a determination of objective beauty nor a sufficient description of the psychological state,"[160] that is, specific enough as a description neither of the properties of objects that cause aesthetic experience nor of the response to those properties. The contemporary who holds a view closest to her own is Jean-Marie Guyau (1854–88), author of *Problèmes de l'Esthétique Contemporaine*[161] as well as many other works during his short life, who wrote that "The beautiful is a perception of an action which stimulates life within us under its three forms simultaneously (i.e., sensibility, intelligence, and will), and produces pleasure by the swift consciousness of this general stimulation."[162] This passage comes closer to any of Puffer's own remarks to recognizing the involvement of all our mental capacities in aesthetic experience, though it too does not describe their relation as one of play.

The remainder of Puffer's book applies her theory to the fine or visual arts, music, literature, and drama. In her account of literature she expands upon her idea of the experience of beauty as one that gives us a sense of "unity and self-completeness":

> The perfect moment across the dialect of life, the moment of perfect life, must be in truth that in which we touch the confines of our being, look upon our world, all in all, as revealed in some great moment, and see that it is good – that we grasp it, possess it, that it is akin to us, that it is identical with our deepest wills. The work that grasps the conditions of our being gives ourselves back to us completed.... The development, the rise, complication, expectation, gratification, the suspense, climax, and drop of the great novel, corresponds to the natural functioning of our mental processes.[163]

The remark that the work "gives ourselves back" might sound like a tacit adoption of the idea of empathy, but for the fact that Puffer is discussing the art of the novel, an art form that explicitly describes human conduct and feelings and so of course can describe states that mirror those of the reader – it was not the novel that called forth the theory of empathy, but

---

[159] Puffer, *Psychology of Art*, p. 53.
[160] Puffer, *Psychology of Art*, p. 54.
[161] Jean-Marie Guyau, *Problèmes de l'Esthétique Contemporaine* (Paris: F. Alcan, 1884).
[162] Puffer, *Psychology of Beauty*, p. 54, quoting from p. 77 of a 1902 edition of Guyau's work.
[163] Puffer, *Psychology of Art*, p. 223.

rather the puzzle of describing works of non-descriptive art in terms of human emotions that did so.

Puffer writes that "In the end it might be said that literature gives us a moment of perfection, and is thus possessed of beauty, when it reveals ourselves to ourselves in a better world of experience."[164] But she then says that "because it is most often in the tragedies that the conditions of our being are laid bare, and the strings which reverberate to the emotions most easily played upon, it is likely that the greatest books of all will be the tragedies themselves."[165] Yet tragedies notoriously do not present to us a "better world of experience," and, perhaps with the exception of *Oedipus at Colonus*, they do not represent characters experiencing unity and self-completeness. So how does she fit the case of tragedy into her theory? She argues against the famous interpretation of Aristotle's conception of *katharsis* as the medicinal "purgation" of emotion offered by Jakob Bernays,[166] and develops her own view in two steps. First, she points out that "A necessary step to the explanation of our pleasure in supposedly painful emotions is to make clear how we can feel any emotion at all in watching what we know to be unreal,"[167] and resolves this problem by appeal to the Jamesian theory of emotions as an essentially physiological response to perception that does not fully, or at least immediately, involve the cognitive faculties and thus our discrimination between fact and fiction.[168] Having by this means established that drama can arouse emotions at all, she then turns to the paradox of our pleasure in supposedly painful emotions. Here what she argues is that tragedy is always a depiction of conflict or antagonism, and that it is only through the experience of conflict that the experience of resolution can in turn be enjoyed. The "tragic … is in the collision itself; it is the profound and, to our vision, the irreconcilable antagonism of different elements in life," she writes, and that would seem to leave us in tension; but she goes on that "In life we accept it because we must; we transcend it because, as moral beings, we may."[169] In other words, it is not the characters within the tragedy that experience the resolution of their conflicts; it is we, the audience, who realize the possibility of resolution. This solution to the

---

[164] Puffer, *Psychology of Beauty*, p. 224.
[165] Puffer, *Psychology of Beauty*, p. 225.
[166] Puffer, *Psychology of Beauty*, pp. 231–9; see Jakob Bernays, *Zwei Abhandlungen über die Aristotelischen Theorie des Dramas* (Berlin: Hertz, 1880), originally 1857.
[167] Puffer, *Psychology of Beauty*, p. 239.
[168] Puffer, *Psychology of Beauty*, p. 240.
[169] Puffer, *Psychology of Beauty*, p. 256.

paradox of tragedy is impressive. But it might also seem to go beyond the physiological foundation of Puffer's psychology of beauty; to experience the resolution of tragedy in this way seems to call upon our knowledge of our own moral potential and what morality requires. Perhaps here the limits of an approach to the emotional response to art without admission of the intellectual dimension of aesthetic experience are revealed.

5. PSYCHOLOGICAL AESTHETICS IN BRITAIN: LEE

The chief proponent of psychological aesthetics in Britain was Vernon Lee, the pseudonym of Violet Paget (1856–1935), who interpreted beauty on the basis of a theory of empathy developed on the basis of the work of Lipps, Groos, and her own lover Clementina Anstruther-Thomson, but who also argued that beauty was only one objective among many aims of art, even if it is the *sine qua non* of art. Lee can therefore be regarded as developing within the framework of *fin-de-siècle* psychological aesthetics a complex account of aesthetic experience that recognizes its cognitive and emotional dimensions while emphasizing beauty of form. But she interpreted the explanation of the beauty of form in terms of empathy as an alternative to its explanation by the concept of play, thus in contrast to the explanation of empathy offered by Karl Groos, whom she nevertheless admired and regarded as a good friend.

Lee was born to expatriate British parents in France, and spent much of her life in Italy; a childhood friend among expatriate circles was John Singer Sargent, who would later paint her portrait, now in the Tate Gallery. Later in life, she would number both Walter Pater and Oscar Wilde as friends and influences. She received little formal education, but was a precocious child and voracious reader who would go on to publish more than forty books, including stories and novels of the supernatural, historical novels, works of history and art history, books on music, travel, and gardening, and in mid-life the two volumes that establish her place in the history of aesthetics, *Beauty and Ugliness and Other Studies in Psychological Æsthetics* in 1912,[170] a volume of essays organized around the central essay on "Beauty and Ugliness" originally published

---

[170] Vernon Lee and Clementina Anstruther-Thomson, *Beauty and Ugliness and Other Studies in Psychological Æsthetics* (London: The Bodley Head, 1912). Anstruther-Thomson contributed the introspective reports on aesthetic experience in the original essay "Beauty and Ugliness."

with Anstruther-Thomson in 1897, and *The Beautiful: An Introduction to Psychological Aesthetics* in 1913.[171]

In both works, Lee distinguishes between aesthetics and the philosophy of art, arguing that aesthetics properly concerns only the nature of beauty and our response to it, or even more precisely that the "central problem of æsthetics" is that of explaining "the *intrinsic satisfactoriness* of visible form as such, and the pleasure (or displeasure) which its contemplation can awaken,"[172] while art can have multiple aims although beauty is always one of them and its achievement of beauty is always a necessary condition for our satisfaction with its other accomplishments. Lee makes this point in both books. She begins the first essay in *Beauty and Ugliness*, on "Anthropomorphic Æsthetics," by arguing that the word "aesthetics" should be understood as "the adjective referring to beauty" rather than to art in order to avoid "self-contradictions" (a linguistic recommendation recently accepted by many outside of professional philosophy, no doubt without knowledge of its source), for art aims at many things besides beauty and these other aims can at least potentially conflict with the achievement of beauty:

> No one, for instance, can deny that the drama, the novel, poetry in general, are of the nature of art. But no one can deny that in all of them, besides appeals to our desire for beauty, there are appeals to quite different demands of the human soul, such as the demand for logical activity, for moral satisfaction, and for all manner of emotional stimulation, from the grossest to the most exalted; let alone the demand for self-expression, for construction, and for skilful handicraft. All these demands, involved in every form of art, are of course demands for pleasure, but some of them are consistent with the production and perception not of beauty but of ugliness.[173]

While insisting upon the plurality of aims of art and thus of aspects of our response to it, however, Lee does not draw the inference that art may actually ignore the demand for beauty, let alone aim at ugliness rather than beauty; her view is rather that we are under an "imperative" for beauty and that all the other aims of beauty must be subordinated to the demand for beauty. Thus her position is not the same as that of Arthur Danto a century later, who argued that a specific work or style of art might aim for beauty, but that aiming for beauty is not necessary to art

---

[171] Vernon Lee, *The Beautiful: An Introduction to Psychological Aesthetics* (Cambridge: Cambridge University Press, 1913).
[172] Lee and Anstruther-Thomson, *Beauty and Ugliness*, p. 81.
[173] Lee and Anstruther-Thomson, *Beauty and Ugliness*, pp. 3–4.

in general.[174] Lee rather holds that "the definition of the word 'æsthetic' provides a clue to the whole question, 'What is art, and what has the beautiful to do with art?,'"

> For we shall find that it is the demand for beauty which qualifies all the other demands which may seek satisfaction through art, and thereby unites together, by a common factor of variation, all the heterogeneous instincts and activities which go to make up the various branches of art.[175]

Unlike Bosanquet two decades earlier, or Croce a decade earlier (to whom she does not refer in spite of her lifelong residence in Italy), Lee does not argue that beauty *is* successful expression, or success in any of the other aims of art, e.g., moral satisfaction or emotional stimulation, but rather that it is an independent goal but one that constrains the ways in which the other goals of art may be achieved. Thus she concludes,

> Art, therefore, is the manifestation of any group of faculties, the expression of any instincts, the answer to any needs, which is to any extent qualified, that is to say, restrained, added to, altered, or deflected, in obedience to a desire totally separate from any of these, possessing its own reasons, its own standards and its own imperative, which desire is the æsthetic desire. And the quality answering to this æsthetic desire is what we call Beauty; the quality which it avoids or diminishes is Ugliness.[176]

Whatever else it does, and it may do much else, art must achieve beauty and avoid ugliness.

Of course this leaves open the question of what beauty and our response to it are, and that is the "central problem" of aesthetics to which Lee devotes most of her work. She argues that beauty lies in shape, understood broadly to include audible as well as visible shape, and that our response to it, "shape preference," is based on empathy, understood in terms drawn from Lipps and Groos. But before we turn to her account of empathy with shape, we may observe that she repeats her argument that art has multiple aims that are however subordinated to the aesthetic aim or imperative in her introductory work on *The Beautiful*. Here she posits it as "historically probable that the habit of avoiding ugliness and seeking beauty of shape may have been originally established by utilitarian attention to the non-imitative ... shapes of weaving, pottery, and implement-making" and then "transferred from these crafts to the shapes intended

---

[174] Arthur C. Danto, *The Abuse of Beauty: Aesthetics and the Concept of Art*, Paul Carus Lectures 21 (LaSalle: Open Court Publishing Co., 2003), e.g., pp. 101–2.
[175] Lee and Anstruther-Thomson, *Beauty and Ugliness*, p. 5.
[176] Lee and Anstruther-Thomson, *Beauty and Ugliness*, p. 9.

to represent or imitate natural objects." Yet, she continues, "the distinction between *Beautiful* and *Ugly* does not belong either solely or necessarily to what we call *Art*," thus "the satisfaction of the shape-perceptive or æsthetic preferences must not be confused with any of the many and various other aims and activities to which art is due and by which it is carried on."[177] Thus art does not originate in the desire to experience beauty; art may originate in the attempt to fulfill practical needs for implements or in other needs such as the need for self-expression or moral instruction. But once the possibility of beauty has been discovered, it seems, in at least some circumstances these other aims will be subordinated to the aim at beauty, thus although "art has invariably started from some desire other than that of affording satisfactory shape-contemplation," it nevertheless submits itself to the "*æsthetic imperative*":

> All art, therefore, except that of children, savages, ignoramuses and extreme innovators, invariably avoids ugly shapes and seeks for beautiful ones; *but art does this while pursuing all manner of different aims.* These non-æsthetic aims of art may be roughly divided into (A) the making of useful objects ranging from clothes to weapons and from a pitcher to a temple; (B) the registering or transmitting of facts and their visualising, as in portraits, historical pictures or literature, and book illustration; and (C) the awakening, intensifying or maintaining of definite emotional states, as especially by music and literature, but also by painting and architecture when employed as "aids to devotion." And these large classes may again be divided and connected ... into utilitarian, social, ritual, sentimental, scientific and other aims, some of them not countenanced or not avowed by contemporary morality.[178]

The last remark implies that for Lee art is subject to the "aesthetic imperative" regardless of its other aims but not to the categorical imperative or at least to any particular current understanding of the demands of morality. Thus, though Lee does not think that art aims at beauty alone, but that it might in addition have a wide range of utilitarian, cognitive, and emotional goals, she does think that it may be free of the constraints of at least current, conventional morality. At this point Lee's approach to art might thus be thought to converge with the conception of the autonomy of art or "art for art's sake" associated with such of her contemporaries and indeed acquaintances as Oscar Wilde.

The phrase "satisfactory shape-contemplation" in the last series of quotations may suggest a Kantian conception of beauty, and indeed Lee does claim in the first chapter of *The Beautiful* that the "*kind of satisfaction*

---

[177] Lee, *The Beautiful*, pp. 98–9.
[178] Lee, *The Beautiful*, pp. 99–100.

connected with the word Beautiful is always of the Contemplative order" and illustrates this claim in the second chapter with a parable distinguishing a wayfarer who simply enjoys "contemplative satisfaction" of the view of a city such as Rome or Edinburgh from a hilltop from a practically minded one who immediately begins to think of the profit that might be derived from a tram or funicular to make the view more accessible and a "man of science" who immediately starts to think about the geological processes that produced the vista; indeed, Lee here goes so far as to distinguish the purely contemplative satisfaction in the vista from any desire to paint it or describe it in a work of literature.[179] However, Lee does not follow Kant in explaining our pleasure in contemplation of beauty as pleasure in the free play of our perceptive and cognitive faculties. Instead, she explicitly rejects this theory, which she associates primarily with Friedrich Schiller and Herbert Spencer rather than with Kant, as confusing a necessary condition for both the production and reception of art, namely the kind of leisure that allows us to play, with the aim of aesthetic experience. In *The Beautiful* she states that "although leisure and freedom from cares are necessary for both play and for æsthetic appreciation, the latter differs essentially from the former by its contemplative nature."[180] She argues this point at greater length in "Anthropomorphic Æsthetics." Here she presents the theory "according to which art is differentiated from other employments of human activity by being a kind of play," "first broached by Schiller ... and revived by Mr. Herbert Spencer," as an alternative to her theory that "the demand for beauty qualifies all the other demands which may seek satisfaction through art" rather than as an explanation of it.[181] She allows that the play theory correctly connects the arts "by the common characteristic of disinterested contemplation," although she implies, as her own theory of the multiple aims of art requires her to, that the play theory is mistaken to assume that the arts always "serve no practical aim and constitute a kind of holiday in life." But more importantly, she objects that the play theory, whether in the form of Spencer's theory that art simply vents stored up and otherwise unused energy or in that of Groos's "play-instinct," which "has merely returned to Schiller's

---

[179] Lee, *The Beautiful*, pp. 8–13. Because of her separation of the concepts of the aesthetic or beautiful and the concept of art, however, Lee does not infer from this, as Croce and later Collingwood would do, that the act of aesthetic contemplation exhausts the production of a work of art and thus that physical production such as painting is not actually part of the work of art. See Volume 3, Part Two.

[180] Lee, *The Beautiful*, p. 7.

[181] Lee and Anstruther-Thomson, *Beauty and Ugliness*, p. 5.

theory that the pleasurableness of art is due to the characteristic of all other kinds of play, namely, the sense of freedom or of holiday," "is surely an inversion of the true order of facts," namely that "We do not take pleasure in playing because playing makes us feel free; but, on the contrary, we get greater and more unmixed pleasure while playing, because we are free to leave off and alter – in fact, to do what we cannot do while working, accommodate our activity to our pleasure."[182] Lee's view is that the freedom, not in the abstract but in the specific sense of freedom from constraint by the demands of work, is simply a necessary condition for aesthetic experience and artistic experience, not their aim and the explanation of our pleasure in them. As she says,

> if a freedom from practical considerations is undoubtedly implied in ... making ... necessary things beautiful, that freedom is not the aim of this artistic process, but its necessary condition, since we do not act freely in order to take pleasure in freedom, but please ourselves because we happen to be free to do so.[183]

The connection between play and beauty is only that the same kind of freedom, that is to say, leisure, that is a necessary condition for our being free to play is also a necessary condition for our being free to create art and to enjoy it. Of course, given Lee's view of the multiple aims of art, which can include many practical aims, this freedom or leisure cannot be understood as the complete absence of all practical concerns or all concerns other than the concern with beauty itself. The freedom that is a necessary condition for artistic production and aesthetic experience must instead consist in the fact that the practical or other aims of art do not exhaust our relation to the work of art and preclude contemplative satisfaction with it.

But now the question of what does explain contemplative satisfaction becomes all the more pressing, so we must turn to Lee's positive account of beauty. Here is where she invokes the theory of empathy as developed by Lipps and refined by Groos, although she states that her original 1897 article on "Beauty and Ugliness," coauthored with Anstruther-Thomson, was written before she had discovered their work. Lee understands empathy as the projection of our own feeling of life on to objects, "the interpretation of form according to the facts of our own inner experience, the attribution to form of modes of being, moving, and feeling similar to our own." It might seem as if such projection could be either

---

[182] Lee and Anstruther-Thomson, *Beauty and Ugliness*, pp. 6–7.
[183] Lee and Anstruther-Thomson, *Beauty and Ugliness*, p. 8.

pleasant or unpleasant, depending on what feelings we project on to objects, and thus as if objects might be made either beautiful or ugly depending on the feelings that we project on to them. Thus, "this projection of our own life into what we see is pleasant or unpleasant because it facilitates or hampers our own vitality,"[184] and, Lee infers, it is only "when this attribution of our modes of life to visible shapes" and the "revival of past experience" that is also projected on to objects "is such as to be favourable to our existence and in so far pleasurable" that "we welcome the form thus animated by ourselves as 'beautiful.'"[185] However, Lee's deeper view appears to be that all activity is fundamentally pleasurable, and thus that all projection of our own feelings of activity – life in the broadest sense – onto objects is pleasurable and makes objects beautiful. Thus she endorses a passage from Rudolph Lotze's *Microcosmos*, which she, apparently unfamiliar with the Vischers, regards as the "first statement" of the theory of empathy, in which Lotze writes that

> Our fancy meets with no visible shape so refractory that the former cannot transport us into it and make us share its life. Nor is this possibility of entering into vital modes of what is foreign to us limited to creatures whose kind and ways approximate to ours; to the bird, for instance, who sings joyously in his flight.... We project ourselves not merely into the forms of the tree, identifying our life with that of the slender shoots which swell and stretch forth ... We extend equally to lifeless things those feelings which lend them meaning.[186]

She likewise cites Theodor Lipps's example of our empathetic experience of the Doric column (which had also been cited by Groos), summing up his description of our experience of such a nonhuman object (although a human-made artifact) by saying that we attribute to its "lines and surfaces, to the spatial forms, those dynamic experiences which we should have were we to put our bodies into similar conditions." She then makes it clear that we attribute to such an object a wide range of emotions connected to a wide range of human activities, and implies that we enjoy all of them as part of human life and thus find objects beautiful insofar as we project on to them all of these emotions:

> Moreover, just as sympathy with the grief of our neighbors implies in ourselves knowledge of the conflicting states – hope, resignation, pain, and

---

[184] Lee and Anstruther-Thomson, *Beauty and Ugliness*, p. 17.
[185] Lee and Anstruther-Thomson, *Beauty and Ugliness*, p. 21.
[186] Lee and Anstruther-Thomson, *Beauty and Ugliness*, pp. 17–18, quoting from Lotze, *Mikrokosmos*, Book V, Chapter 2, no edition given.

the efforts against pain – which constitute similar grief in our own experience; so this æsthetic attribution of our own dynamic modes to visible forms implies the realisation in our consciousness of the various conflicting strains and pressures, of the resistance and yielding which constitute any given dynamic volition experiences of our own. When we attribute to the Doric column a condition akin to our own in keeping erect and defying the force of gravitation, there is the revival in our mind of a little drama we have experienced many millions of times, and which has become registered in our memory, even like that less common drama of hope, disappointment, and anguish which has been revived in the case of our neighbor's grief and attributed to him.[187]

What is crucial is not that the individual feelings that we project on to objects (or even on to other people) be kinds of feeling that taken in isolation would be pleasurable rather than painful, but rather that objects stimulate in us a drama or "dynamic" of feelings that we then project back onto them, a drama that is enjoyable, as a mirror of life itself, even if every moment of it is not. Indeed, it could be argued that a drama necessarily includes some unpleasant moments, just as life necessarily includes obstacles that must be overcome, just as even in standing erect we must overcome the resistance of gravity. What we enjoy in the experience of objects is the experience of life itself in all its complexity and activity, and it is the projection of that back onto objects, not the projection onto them of individually pleasant feelings, that leads us to call them beautiful. In fact, in spite of her rejection of the account of aesthetic experience as play in the forms it had taken on in Spencer and before him Schiller, Lee comes close to connecting empathy and play: "we feel activity and life, because our own activity, our own life, have been brought into play."[188] It might be objected that this is just a verbal similarity between Lee's description of empathy and the theory of play, but the idea that play is enjoyable because it is activity and that activity is the essence of life itself goes back to the roots of the theory of aesthetic experience as play in Gerard and Kant.

In her account of empathy, Lee has built upon Lipps, but she takes from Groos, even though he is a play theorist rather than an empathy theorist, the point that the perception of objects produces in us bodily or "motor" responses, not just purely mental responses, and that we project those too onto the objects that stimulate them. Thus she writes that "our motor activities rehearse the tensions, pressures, thrusts, resistances,

---

[187] Lee and Anstruther-Thomson, *Beauty and Ugliness*, pp. 20–1.
[188] Lee and Anstruther-Thomson, *Beauty and Ugliness*, p. 22.

efforts, the volition, in fact, the life, with its accompanying emotions, which we project into the form and attribute to it."[189] This leads to a spirited but friendly polemic – Lee had by this time become personally acquainted with both Lipps and Groos – in which she charges that in order to avoid recognition of the bodily aspect of empathy Lipps had moved toward a "metaphysical" conception of the ego that experiences and projects. "One might almost believe that it is the dislike of admitting the participation of the body in the phenomenon of æsthetic Empathy which has impelled Lipps to make æsthetics more and more abstract, *a priori*, and metaphysical."[190] Lee deplores this tendency in Lipps, and thereby re-introduces into aesthetic theory an emphasis on the bodily dimension of aesthetic experience the likes of which had not been seen since Mendelssohn, except to the extent that Lee's own approach was anticipated by Groos. One might suggest that it is only with this emphasis that the century-long grip of idealism on aesthetic theory began to be loosened, although as we shall subsequently see the dominant influence of Croce on British aesthetics in the early decades of the twentieth century meant that this battle would continue to be fought for decades to come, and it is perhaps only in the psychoanalytically inflected work of Richard Wollheim three-quarters of a century later that the approach of Lee finally triumphs.

Although Lee's introductory book on *The Beautiful* begins with the Kantian emphasis on contemplation that has already been mentioned, it quickly introduces the theory of "Empathetic Interpretation" as its explanation of the experience of beauty,[191] and sums up the previous analysis of empathy "*as the merging of the activities of the subject in the object.*"[192] Empathy is the projection of imagined and physically felt activity into the forms of objects, although that is still contemplative because it is not identical to nor immediately leads to practical activities such as constructing funiculars: "I have already given the Reader an example of such Empathy when I described the landscape seen by the man on the hill as consisting of a skyline '*dropping down merely to rush up again in rapid concave curves*'; to which I might have added" – in a way that goes all the way back to Robert Vischer's 1873 dissertation – "that there was also a plain which *extended*, a valley which *wound along*, paths which *climbed*

---

[189] Lee and Anstruther-Thomson, *Beauty and Ugliness*, pp. 28–9.
[190] Lee and Anstruther-Thomson, *Beauty and Ugliness*, p. 60.
[191] Lee, *The Beautiful*, p. 55.
[192] Lee, *The Beautiful*, p. 58; emphasis in the original.

and roads which *followed* the *undulations* of the land"[193] – in all of this we are projecting our own activities and the emotions connected with them onto something that is actually inert, in this case a landscape that is partially natural and partially man-made. We do the same with works of art, which are completely man-made though not themselves human beings with their own emotions. But while in *The Beautiful* Lee expands on how "lines" and "shapes" stimulate our empathy, she also adds a second dimension to her account of aesthetic experience, arguing that "life has little leisure for contemplation; it demands *recognition*, inference and readiness for active adaptation," and thus "forces us to deal with shapes mainly inasmuch as they indicate the actual or possible experience of other groups of qualities which may help or hurt us," thus "Life hurries us into recognizing *Things*."[194] She then characterizes aesthetic experience, using the example of the experience of "Art of the visual-representative group," as "the interplay of the desire to be told (or tell) *facts about things* with the desire to *contemplate shapes*, and to contemplate them (otherwise we should *not* contemplate!) with sensuous, intellectual and empathic satisfaction."[195] Here Lee complicates her previous already complex analysis of aesthetic experience: while she had previously held that the shapes of visible objects, or the analogues of shapes in other art forms, may stimulate a variety of responses, including cognitive and moral as well as emotional responses, although the empathetic response to beauty must always be among them and indeed *prima inter pares*, she now argues that our response to a work of art or other aesthetic object is always a mixture of our already complex responses to its shape or other kind of form as well as our cognitive and practical responses to its actual existence and the implications of the latter, the advantages and threats that the object may really present to us. In other words, contemplative, aesthetic experience does not occur independently of our cognitive and practical response to objects – as Kant might have been thought to argue, at least in his initial exposition of aesthetic judgment – but as part of our overall response to objects. Indeed, she argues that "interference of the *Thought about Things* with the *Contemplation of Shapes* is essential to the rythm [*sic*] of our mental life, and therefore a chief factor in all artistic production and appreciation."[196] However, she also insists that "art is conditioned by the desire for beauty while pursuing entirely different

[193] Lee, *The Beautiful*, pp. 59–60.
[194] Lee, *The Beautiful*, p. 84.
[195] Lee, *The Beautiful*, pp. 100–1.
[196] Lee, *The Beautiful*, p. 105.

aims, and executing any one of a variety of wholly independent non-aesthetic tasks";[197] in other words, no matter how complex our experience of an aesthetic object is, no matter what a mixture of empathetic, intellectual, and moral responses, satisfaction of our desire for beauty is always a necessary condition for art.

Lee thus concludes the psychological movement in late nineteenth- and early-twentieth century aesthetics by complicating it. The movement began with Spencer introducing a simple physiological conception of play into his principles of psychology. Though that theory was refined by Groos, it was largely replaced by the theory of empathy developed by Vischer and Lipps and defended by Volkelt in Germany, then brought to the United States, although without the idea of projection, by Ethel Puffer. Lee combined the approaches of Lipps and Groos to develop her own account of empathy as projection of the full range of human emotions on to the shapes or other forms of objects, but also recognized cognitive and practical dimensions both within the aesthetic aspects of experience as well as the vital interplay between aesthetic and non-aesthetic dimensions of experience in the experience of aesthetic objects. She thus provided a model of the complexity of aesthetic experience that avoided the reductionism that had dominated the nineteenth century, whether in the cognitivist form of idealist aesthetics or the formalist approach of the early members of the "art for art's sake movement," although not perhaps the subtler theories of her own models Pater and Wilde.

But as our study of twentieth-century aesthetics shall now show, the struggle between reductionist approaches to aesthetics and more complex approaches like Lee's was by no means over. Particularly in Germany, where we shall now continue, the reductionist cognitivism of German Idealism was about to enjoy a new lease on life, and just as there had been a left and right wing in the original response to Hegel, so cognitivist aesthetics in twentieth-century Germany can also be divided into left- and right-wing forms. In Britain, to which we will subsequently turn, both the native aesthetics of the Bloomsbury school and the imported theory of Benedetto Croce can be seen as reductive theories, one lending academic dress to the original inspiration of the "art for art's sake movement" and the other developing a kind of cognitivism from a strange mixture of Hegel and Kant. There would be an immediate and forceful rejection of the immaterialism of Croce's aesthetics, but not until much

---

[197] Lee, *The Beautiful*, p. 110.

later in the twentieth century would the phenomena of play and of emotional impact be given their full due in British aesthetics. If, next, we regard twentieth-century American aesthetics – really American aesthetics altogether – as beginning with Santayana's *Sense of Beauty* of 1896, we shall see that here aesthetics begins with a comprehensive rather than reductive approach, and that many American aestheticians in the first half of the century did a better job than their counterparts elsewhere in keeping that synthetic spirit alive. But then, as we shall see, a new form of reductionism entered into both British and American aesthetics with the impact of Wittgenstein in the 1950s, and there was again a struggle to restore a sense of the complexity of aesthetic experience. Volume 3 will be completed with a description of some of the most recent phases of that struggle.

Bibliography

Primary Sources

Aristotle. *The Complete Works of Aristotle*, edited by Jonathan Barnes, 2 vols. Princeton: Princeton University Press, 1984.

Arnold, Matthew. *Poetry and Prose*, edited by John Bryson. Cambridge, Mass.: Harvard University Press, 1970.

Culture and Anarchy and other writings, edited by Stefan Collini. Cambridge: Cambridge University Press, 1993.

"The Study of Poetry." http://www.poetryfoundation.org/learning/essay/237186.

Bartram, William. *Travels through North and South Carolina, Georgia, East and West Florida*, etc. (Philadelphia, 1791), reprinted in *Travels and Other Writings*, edited by Thomas Slaughter. New York: Library of America, 1996.

Baudelaire, Charles. *Art in Paris 1845–1862: Salons and Other Exhibitions Reviewed by Charles Baudelaire*, edited by Jonathan Mayne. London: Phaidon, 1964.

The Painter of Modern Life and Other Essays, translated and edited by Jonathan Mayne. London: Phaidon, 1965.

Bentham, Jeremy. *The Rationale of Reward*. London: Robert Heward, 1830.

Bernays, Jakob. *Zwei Abhandlungen über die Aristotelischen Theorie des Dramas*. Berlin: Hertz, 1880.

Bosanquet, Bernard. *A History of Æsthetic*. London: Swan Sonnenschein, 1892, second edition, London: George Allen and Unwin, 1904.

Three Lectures on Aesthetic. London: Macmillan, 1915.

Brunetière, Ferdinand. *L'Evolution de genres dans l'histoire de la littérature*. Paris: Hatchette, 1892.

Bullough, Edward. "'Psychical Distance' as a Factor in Art and an Æsthetic Principle." *British Journal of Psychology* V (1912): 87–118; reprinted in Bullough, *Æsthetics: Lectures and Essays*, translated by Elizabeth M. Wilkinson. Stanford: Stanford University Press, 1957. Pp. 91–130.

Burke, Edmund. *A Philosophical Enquiry into the Origin of our Ideas of the Sublime and Beautiful*, edited by J.T. Boulton. London: Routledge and Kegan Paul, 1958.

Cohen, Hermann. *Ästhetik des reinen Gefühls*, 2 vols. Berlin: Bruno Cassirer, 1912.

Cohen, Hermann. *Kants Begründung der Aesthetik.* Berlin: Ferd. Dümmlers Verlagsbuchhandlung, 1889.
  Religion der Vernunft aus den Quellen des Judentums: Eine judische Religionsphilosophie. With an introduction by Ulrich Oelschläger. Wiesbaden: Marix Verlag, 2008
Cohn, Jonas. *Allgemeine Ästhetik.* Leipzig: Wilhelm Engelmann, 1901.
Coleridge, Samuel Taylor. *Biographia Literaria, with his Aesthetical Essays,* edited by J. Shawcross, 2 vols. Oxford: Oxford University Press, 1907.
  The Collected Works of Samuel Taylor Coleridge, Bollingen Series 75, general editor Kathleen Coburn, thus far 16 vols. Princeton: Princeton University Press, 1969–2002.
  Faustus: from the German of Goethe, translated by Samuel Taylor Coleridge, edited by Frederick Burwick and James C. McKusick. Oxford: Clarendon Press, 2007.
Collingwood, Robin George. *The Principles of Art.* Oxford: Clarendon Press, 1938.
Cousin, Victor. *Lectures on the True, the Beautiful, and the Good,* translated by O.W. Wight. New York: Appleton, 1873.
Dessoir, Max. *Aesthetics and Theory of Art,* translated by Stephen A. Emery. Detroit: Wayne State University Press, 1970.
  Das Doppel-Ich. Leipzig: Günther, 1890.
Dewey, John. Review of Bernard Bosanquet, *A History of Æsthetic. Philosophical Review* 2 (1893): 63–9.
Dilthey, Wilhelm. *Leben Schleiermachers.* Berlin: Georg Reimer, 1870.
  Selected Works, edited by Rudolf A. Makkreel and Frithjof Rodi, 5 vols. Princeton: Princeton University Press, 1985–2010.
Emerson, Ralph Waldo. *The Collected Works of Ralph Waldo Emerson,* Vol. I, edited by Alfred R. Ferguson, introductions and notes by Robert E. Spiller. Cambridge, Mass.: Harvard University Press, 1971.
  The Collected Works of Ralph Waldo Emerson, Vol. II, introduction and notes by Joseph Slater, text edited by Alfred R. Ferguson and Jean Ferguson Carr. Cambridge, Mass.: Harvard University Press, 1979.
  The Complete Works of Ralph Waldo Emerson, Vol. III, edited by Edward Waldo Emerson. Boston: Houghton Mifflin, 1904.
  The Collected Works of Ralph Waldo Emerson, Vol. VI, introduction by Barbara L. Packer, notes by Joseph Slater, text edited by Douglas Emory Wilson. Cambridge, Mass.: Harvard University Press, 2003.
Fechner, Gustav Theodor. *Vorschule der Aesthetik,* second edition, 2 vols. Leipzig: Breitkopf & Härtel, 1925; reprinted Hildesheim: Georg Olms, 1978.
Fiedler, Konrad. *Schriften über Kunst,* edited by Hermann Konnerth. Munich: R. Piper, 1913.
Gautier, Théophile. *Mademoiselle du Maupin,* translated by Helen Constantine. London: Penguin Books, 2005.
Gerard, Alexander. *An Essay on Genius.* London and Edinburgh: Strahan, Cadell, and Creech, 1774.
Goodman, Nelson. *Languages of Art: An Approach to a Theory of Symbols.* Indianapolis: Bobbs-Merrill, 1968.

Groos, Karl. *Einleitung in die Ästhetik*. Giessen: Ricker, 1892.
The Play of Animals, translated by Elizabeth L. Baldwin, with Preface by J. Mark Baldwin. New York: Appleton, 1898.
Die reine Vernunftwissenschaft. Heidelberg: Georg Weiß, 1889.
The Play of Man, translated by Elizabeth L. Baldwin, with Preface by J. Mark Baldwin. New York: Appleton, 1901.
Das Seelenleben des Kindes. Berlin: Reuter und Richard, 1904.
Guyau, Jean-Marie. *Problèmes de l'Esthétique Contemporaine*. Paris: F. Alcan, 1884.
Hanslick, Eduard. *The Beautiful in Music*, translated by Gustav Cohen. Indianapolis: Bobbs-Merrill Company, 1957.
Harrison, Charles, Paul Wood, and Jason Gaiger, *Art in Theory: 1815–1900*. Oxford: Blackwell, 1998.
Hartmann, Eduard von. *Die deutsche Aesthetik seit Kant: Erster historisch-kritischer Theil der Aesthetik*. Leipzig: Wilhelm Friedrich, n.d.
Die Philosophie des Schönen: Zweiter systematischer Theil der Aesthetik, Ausgewählte Werke, second edition, vol. IV. Leipzig: Hermann Haacke, n.d.
Philosophie des Unbewußten: Versuch einer Weltanschauung. Berlin, C. Duncker, 1869; *Philosophy of the Unconscious*, translated by William Chatterton Coupland, 3 vols. New York: Macmillan, 1884.
Die Gefühlsmoral, edited by Jean-Claude Wolf. Hamburg: Felix Meiner Verlag, 2006.
Hegel, Georg Wilhelm Friedrich. *Aesthetics: Lectures on Fine Art*, translated by T.M. Knox, two volumes. Oxford: Clarendon Press, 1975.
Vorlesungen über die Philosophie der Religion, Teil I, in *Vorlesungen*, edited by Walter Jaeschke. Hamburg: Felix Meiner, 1983.
Enzyklopädie der philosophischen Wissenschaften im Grundrisse (1830), edited by Wolfgang Bonsiepen and Hans-Christian Lucer, in Hegel, *Gesammelte Werke*, vol. 20. Hamburg: Felix Meiner Verlag, 1992.
Vorlesung über Ästhetik (1821), edited by Helmut Schneider. Berlin and New York: Peter Lang, Main, 1995.
Vorlesungen über die Philosophie der Kunst (1823), edited by Annemarie Gethmann-Seifert. Darmstadt: Wissenschaftliche Buchgesellschaft, 2003.
Philosophie der Kunst oder Ästhetik. Nach Hegel. Im Sommer 1826, Mitschrift Friedrich Carl Hermann Victor von Kehler, edited by Annemarie Gethmann-Seifert and Bernadette Collenberg-Plotnikov. Munich: Wilhelm Fink Verlag, 2004.
Hölderlin, Friedrich. *Werke – Dokumente – Briefe*, edited by Pierre Bertaux. Munich: Winkler Verlag, 1963.
Essays and Letters on Theory, translated and edited by Thomas Pfau. Albany: State University of New York Press, 1988.
James, William. *The Principles of Psychology*, introduction by George A. Miller. Cambridge, Mass.: Harvard University Press, 1983.
Kant, Immanuel. *Kant's gesammlte Schriften*, edited by the Royal Prussian, later German, then Berlin-Brandenburg Academy of Sciences, 29 vols. Berlin: Georg Reimer, later Walter de Gruyter & Co., 1900 –.
Practical Philosophy, edited and translated by Mary J. Gregor. Cambridge: Cambridge University Press, 1996.

Critique of the Power of Judgment, edited by Paul Guyer, translated by Paul Guyer and Eric Matthews. Cambridge: Cambridge University Press, 2000.
Anthropology, History, and Education, edited by Günter Zöller and Robert B. Louden. Cambridge: Cambridge University Press, 2007.
Lange, Konrad. *Das bewusste Selbsttäuschung als Kern des ästhetischen Genusses.* Leipzig: Veit & Co., 1895.
Das Wesen der Kunst, 2 vols. Berlin: G. Grote, 1901; second edition in one volume. Berlin: G. Grote, 1907.
Lee, Vernon. *The Beautiful: An Introduction to Psychological Aesthetics.* Cambridge: Cambridge University Press, 1913.
Lee, Vernon and Clementina Anstruther-Thomson. *Beauty and Ugliness and Other Studies in Psychological Æsthetics.* London: The Bodley Head, 1912.
Leibniz, Gottfried Wilhelm. *Philosophical Papers and Letters.* Edited by Leroy E. Loemker. Second editon. Dordrecht: D. Reidel, 1969.
Lipps, Theodor *Zur Herbart'schen Ontologie.* Bonn: n.p., 1874.
Grundtatsachen des Seelenlebens. Bonn: Cohen, 1883.
Psychologische Studien. Heidelberg: Weiss, 1885.
Der Streit über die Tragödie. Hamburg: Voss, 1891; modern reprint Teddington, Middlesex: Echo Library, 2006.
Grundzüge der Logik. Hamburg: Voss, 1893.
Raumästhetik und geometrische-optische Täuschungen. Leipzig: Barth, 1897.
Leitfaden der Psychologie. Leipzig: Engelmann, 1903.
Ästhetik: Psychologie des Schönen und der Kunst, 2 vols. Hamburg and Leipzig: Voss, 1903–1906.
Zur Einfühlung. Leipzig: Engelmann, 1913.
Loos, Adolf. *Ornament and Crime and Other Essays*, translated by Michael Mitchell. Riverside, Calif.: Ariadne Press, 1998.
Lotze, Hermann Rudolf. *Geschichte der Ästhetik in Deutschland.* Munich: Cotta, 1868.
Microcosmus: An Essay concerning Man and his relation to the World, translated by Elizabeth Hamilton and E.E. Constance Jones, 2 vols. Edinburgh: T. Clark, 1885.
Kleinere Schriften, vols. 1–2. Leipzig: S. Hirzel, 1885–86.
Logic, in Three Books, of Thought, of Investigation, and of Knowledge, translated by Bernard Bosanquet, second edition. Oxford: Clarendon Press, 1888.
Grundzüge der Ästhetik: Diktate aus den Vorlesungen. Berlin: Alexander Verlag, 1990.
Mill, John Stuart. *Autobiography and Literary Essays, The Collected Works of John Stuart Mill*, volume 1, edited by John M. Robson and Jack Stillinger. Toronto: University of Toronto Press, 1981.
Essays on Ethics, Religion, and Society, The Collected Works of John Stuart Mill, volume 10, edited by J.M. Robson, F.E.L. Priestly, and D.P. Dryer. Toronto: University of Toronto Press, 1969.
Essays on Politics and Society, Collected Works of John Stuart Mill, volume 18, edited by J.M. Robson and Alexander Brady. Toronto: University of Toronto Press, 1977.

Morris, William. *The Collected Works of William Morris*, edited by May Morris. London: Longmann, Green and Co., 1910–15.
  News from Nowhere and Other Writings. London: Penguin, 1993.
Münsterberg, Hugo. *Philosophie der Werte: Grundzüge einer Weltanschauung*. Leipzig: Barth, 1908.
  The Eternal Values. Boston: Houghton Mifflin, 1909.
  The Silent Photoplay in 1916. New York: Appleton, 1916; retitled *The Film: A Psychological Study*, with a new forward by Richard Griffith. New York: Dover Publications, 1970.
Nietzsche, Friedrich. *Human, All Too Human: A Book for Free Spirits*, translated by R.J. Hollingdale. Cambridge: Cambridge University Press, 1986.
  The Birth of Tragedy and Other Writings, edited by Raymond Geuss and Ronald Speirs, translated by Ronald Speirs. Cambridge: Cambridge University Press, 1999.
  The Gay Science, edited by Bernard Williams, translated by Josefine Nauckhoff. Cambridge: Cambridge University Press, 2001.
  Beyond Good and Evil, edited by Rolf-Peter Horstmann and Judith Norman, translated by Judith Norman. Cambridge: Cambridge University Press, 2002.
  The Anti-Christ, Ecce Homo, Twilight of the Idols, and Other Writings, edited by Aaron Ridley and Judith Norman, translated by Judith Norman. Cambridge: Cambridge University Press, 2005.
  On the Genealogy of Morality, edited by Keith Ansell-Pierson, translated by Carol Diethe, revised edition. Cambridge: Cambridge University Press, 2007.
  Writings from the Early Notebooks, edited by Raymond Geuss and Alexander Nehamas, translated by Ladislaus Löb. Cambridge: Cambridge University Press, 2009.
Pater, Walter. *Marius the Epicurean*, edited by Michael Levey. London: Penguin, 1985.
  The Renaissance: Studies in Art and Poetry, edited by Adam Philips. Oxford: Oxford University Press, 1986.
  Plato and Platonism: A Series of Lectures. London: Macmillan, 1893; reprinted New York: Macmillan, 1903.
  Imaginary Portraits, with The Child in the House and Gaston de Latour, with introduction by Bill Beckley. New York: Allworth Press, 1997.
Peirce, Charles Sanders. *The Essential Peirce*, edited by Nathan Houser and Christian Kloesel, 2 vols. Bloomington: Indiana University Press, 1992.
Poe, Edgar Allan. *Essays and Reviews*, edited by G.R. Thompson. New York: Library of America, 1984.
Puffer, Ethel D. "Criticism and Æsthetics." *Atlantic Monthly* 87 (June, 1901): 839–48.
  The Psychology of Beauty. Boston: Houghton Mifflin, 1905.
Puffer Howes, Ethel. "Æsthetics." *Psychological Bulletin* 10 (1913): 196–201 and 11 (1914): 256–62.
Reid, Thomas. *Thomas Reid's Lectures on the Fine Arts*, edited by Peter Kivy. The Hague: Martinus Nijhoff, 1973.

Essays on the Intellectual Powers of Man, edited by Derek R. Brookes. University Park: Pennsylvania State University Press, 2002.

(Richter), Jean Paul. *Flower, fruit, and thorn pieces; or, The wedded life, death, and marriage of Firmian Stanislaus Siebenkæs, parish advocate in the burgh of Kuhschnappel (A genuine thorn piece)*, translated by Alexander Ewing. London: G. Bell, 1897.

Horn of Oberon: Jean Paul's School for Aesthetics, translated by Margaret R. Hale. Detroit: Wayne State University Press, 1973.

Sämtliche Werke, edited by Norbert Müller, fourth edition. Munich: Hanser, 1987.

Rosenkranz, Karl. *Ästhetik des Häßlichen*. Königsberg: Gerüder Borntränger, 1853; edited by Dieter Kliche. Leipzig: Reclam Verlag, 1996.

Ruskin, John. *The Library Edition of the Works of John Ruskin*, edited by E.T. Cook and Alexander Wedderburn. 39 vols. London: George Allen, 1903–12.

The Seven Lamps of Architecture, introduction by Sir Arnold Lunn. London: Dent, 1956.

Modern Painters, 5 vols. Boston: Estes and Lauriat, n.d.

Selected Writings, edited by Philip Davis. London: J.M. Dent, 1995.

Selected Writings, edited by Dinah Birch. Oxford: Oxford University Press, 2004.

Santayana, George. *The Sense of Beauty*. New York: Charles Scribner's Sons, 1896; New York: Dover Publications, 1955.

Schelling, Friedrich Wilhelm Joseph. *Sämtliche Werke*, edited by K.F.A. Schelling, 14 vols. Stuttgart: Cotta, 1856–61.

System des transzendentalen Idealismus, edited by Walter Schulz. Hamburg: Felix Meiner Verlag, 1957.

System of Transcendental Idealism (1800), translated by Peter Heath, introduction by Michael Vater. Charlottesville: University Press of Virginia, 1978.

Ausgewählte Schriften, edited by Manfred Frank, 6 vols. Frankfurt am Main: Suhrkamp Verlag, 1985.

Ideas for a Philosophy of Nature, translated by Errol E. Harris and Peter Heath. Cambridge: Cambridge University Press, 1988.

The Philosophy of Art, edited and translated by Douglas W. Stott. Minneapolis: University of Minnesota Press, 1989.

First Outline of a System of the Philosophy of Nature, translated by Keith R. Peterson. Albany: State University Press of New York, 2004.

Philosophical Investigations into the Essence of Human Freedom, translated by Jeff Love and Johannes Schmidt. Albany: State University of New York Press, 2006.

Historical-critical Introduction to the Philosophy of Mythology, translated by Mason Richey and Markus Zisselsberger with a foreword by Jason M. Wirth. Albany: State University Press of New York, 2007.

Scherner, Karl Albert. *Das Leben des Traums*. Berlin: Heinrich Schindler, 1861.

Schiller, Friedrich. *On the Aesthetic Education of Man: In a Series of Letters*, edited and translated by Elizabeth M. Wilkinson and L.A. Willoughby. Oxford: Clarendon Press, 1967.

Schlegel, Friedrich. *The Aesthetic and Miscellaneous Works of Frederick von Schlegel*, translated by E.J. Millington. London: Bohn, 1849.

Lucinde: Ein Roman, edited by Karl Konrad Polheim, revised edition. Stuttgart: Philipp Reclam jun., 1999; *Friedrich Schlegel's Lucinde and the Fragments*, translated with an introduction by Peter Firchow. Minneapolis: University of Minnesota Press, 1971.

"Athenäums"-Fragmente und andere Schriften, edited by Andreas Huyssen. Stuttgart: Philipp Reclam jun.: 1978.

Philosophical Fragments, translated by Peter Firchow. Minneapolis: University of Minnesota Press, 1991.

On the Study of Greek Poetry, translated by Stuart Bennett. Albany: State University of New York Press, 2001.

Schleiermacher, Friedrich Daniel Ernst. *Friedrich Schleiermachers Ästhetik*, edited by Rudolf Odebrecht, Veröffentlichungen der Literatur-Archiv-Gesellschaft in Berlin, Volume 4. Berlin: Walter de Gruyter, 1931.

Ästhetik (1819/25)/Über den Begriff der Kunst (1831/32), edited by Thomas Lehnerer. Hamburg: Felix Meiner Verlag, 1984.

On Religion: Speeches to its Cultured Despisers, translated by Richard Crouter. Cambridge: Cambridge University Press, 1988.

Hermeneutics and Criticism and Other Writings, edited by Andrew Bowie. Cambridge: Cambridge University Press, 1998.

Schopenhauer, Arthur. *The World as Will and Representation*, translated by E.F.J. Payne, two vols. Indian Hills, Colo.: Falcon's Wing Press, 1958.

Parerga and Paralipomena, translated by E.F.J. Payne, 2 vols. Oxford: Clarendon Press, 1974.

On the Basis of Morality, translated by E.F.J. Payne, introduction by David E. Cartwright. Indianapolis and Cambridge: Hackett Publishing Co., 1995.

Shelley, Percy Bysshe. *The Major Works*, edited by Zachary Leader and Michael O'Neill. Oxford: Oxford University Press, 2003.

Solger, Karl Wilhelm Ferdinand. *Vorlesungen über Ästhetik*, edited by K.W.L. Heyse. Berlin, 1829; facsimile edition, Karben: Verlag Petra Wald, 1996.

Spencer, Herbert. *Social Statics: or the Conditions Essential to Human Happiness and the First of them Developed*. London: Chapman, 1851.

The Principles of Psychology, 2 vols. New York: Appleton, 1895.

Tolstoy, Leo. *What is Art?* translated by Alymer Maude. London: Oxford University Press, 1930.

What is Art? translated by Richard Pevear and Larissa Volokhonsky. London: Penguin Books, 1995.

Vischer, Friederich Theodor. *Aesthetik oder Wissenschaft des Schönen*, eight volumes. Reutlingen and Leipzig: Karl Mäcken's Verlag, 1846–57; second edition edited by Robert Vischer, 6 vol. Munich: Meyer and Jessen Verlag, 1922–23.

Das Schöne und die Kunst: Zur Einführung in die Ästhetik. Edited by Robert Vischer. Stuttgart: Cotta, 1898.

Kritische Gänge, edited by Robert Vischer, second edition. Munich: Meyer & Jessen Verlag, 1922.

Mode und Cynismus, edited by Michael Neumann. Berlin: Kulturverlag Kadmos, 2006.

Kritische Skizzen, edited by Hermann Bausinger. Tübingen: Klöpfer & Meyer, 2009.

Vischer, Robert. *Drei Schriften zum ästhetischen Formproblem*. Halle: Max Niemeyer Verlag, 1927.
On the Optical Sense of Form: A Contribution to Aesthetics, translated in Henry Francis Mallgrave and Eleftherides Ikonomou, editors, *Empathy, Form, and Space: A Problem in German Aesthetics 1873–1893*. Santa Monica: Getty Foundation, 1994. Pp. 89–123.
Volkelt, Johannes. *Ästhetik des Tragischen*. Munich: Oskar Beck, 1897.
System der Ästhetik, Vol. II, *Die Ästhetische Grundgestalten*, second edition. Munich: C.H. Beck, 1925.
System der Ästhetik, Vol. III, *Kunstphilosophie und Metaphysik der Ästhetik*, second edition. Munich: C.H. Beck, 1925.
System der Ästhetik: Vol. I, *Grundlegung der Ästhetik*, second edition. Munich: C.H. Beck, 1927.
Wilde, Oscar. *The Artist as Critic: Critical Writings of Oscar Wilde*, edited by Richard Ellmann. New York: Random House, 1969; reprinted Chicago: University of Chicago Press, 1982.
Intentions. London: Osgood, McIlvaine, 1891. Cited from www.wilde-online. info/the-artist-as-critic.html.
Wordsworth, William. *The Major Works*, edited by Stephen Gill. Oxford: Oxford University Press, 1984.
Zimmermann, Robert, Edler von. *Aesthetik*. Vienna: W. Braumüller, 1858–65.
Studien und Kritiken zur Philosophie und Aesthetik. Vienna: W. Braumüller, 1870.

Secondary Sources

Abrams, M.H. *The Mirror and the Lamp: Romantic Theory and the Critical Tradition*. Oxford: Oxford University Press, 1953.
Natural Supernaturalism: Tradition and Revolution in Romantic Literature. New York: W.W. Norton, 1971.
Adair-Toteff, Christopher. "Neo-Kantianism: The German Idealism Movement." In Thomas Baldwin, editor, *The Cambridge History of Philosophy 1870–1945*. Cambridge: Cambridge University Press, 2003. Pp. 27–42.
Agosta, Louis. *Empathy in the Context of Philosophy*. Basingstoke: Palgrave Macmillan, 2010.
Allen, Gay Wilson. *Waldo Emerson: A Biography*. New York: Viking, 1981.
Allesch, Christian G. *Geschichte der psychologischen Ästhetik*. Göttingen: Hogrefe, 1987.
Einführung in die psychologische Ästhetik. Vienna: Facultas Verlags- und Buchhandels, 2006.
Allison, Henry E. *Kant's Theory of Taste: A Reading of the* Critique of Aesthetic Judgment. Cambridge: Cambridge University Press, 2001.
Anscombe, G.E.M. *Intention*. Oxford: Blackwell, 1957.
Bann, Stephen. "Pater, Walter." In *Encyclopedia of Aesthetics*, edited by Michael Kelly, 4 vols. New York: Oxford University Press, 1998. Vol. 3, pp. 445–7.
Bate, Walter Jackson. *Coleridge*. London: Macmillan, 1968.
Baum, Günter and Dieter Birnbacher, editors. *Schopenhauer und die Künste*. Göttingen: Wallstein Verlag, 2005.
Behler, Ernst. *Frühromantik*. Berlin: Walter de Gruyter, 1992.

Beiser, Frederick C. *The Romantic Imperative: The Concept of Early German Romanticism.* Cambridge, Mass.: Harvard University Press, 2003.
  Hegel. London: Routledge, 2005.
Benjamin, Walter. *Der Begriff der Kunstkritik in der deutschen Romantik.* Bern: Francke, 1920; Frankfurt am Main: Suhrkamp Verlag, 1973.
Berner, Christian. *La Philosophie de Schleiermacher: Herméneutique, Dialectique, Ethique.* Paris: Editions du Cerf, 1995.
Böhme, Gernot. *Aisthetik: Vorlesungen über Ästhetik als allgemeine Wahrnehmungslehre.* Munich: Wilhelm Fink Verlag: 2001.
Bowie, Andrew. *Schelling and Modern European Philosophy.* London: Routledge, 1993.
  From Romanticism to Critical Theory: The Philosophy of German Literary Theory. London: Routledge, 1997.
  Aesthetics and Subjectivity: From Kant to Nietzsche, second edition. Manchester: University of Manchester Press, 2003.
Bruyn, Günter de. *Das Leben des Jean Paul Friedrich Richter.* Halle: Mitteldeutscher Verlag, 1975.
Buell, Lawrence. *Emerson.* Cambridge, Mass.: Harvard University Press, 2003.
Bungay, Stephen. *Beauty and Truth: A Study of Hegel's Aesthetics.* Oxford: Clarendon Press, 1987.
Capaldi, Nicholas. *John Stuart Mill: A Biography.* Cambridge: Cambridge University Press, 2004.
Cartwright, David E. *Schopenhauer: A Biography.* Cambridge: Cambridge University Press. 2010.
Cavell, Stanley. *In Quest of the Ordinary: Lines of Skepticism and Romanticism.* Chicago: University of Chicago Press, 1988.
  Emerson's Transcendental Etudes, edited by David Justin Hodge. Stanford: Stanford University Press, 2003.
  Cities of Words: Pedagogical Letters on a Register of the Moral Life. Cambridge, Mass.: Harvard University Press, 2004.
Clements, Elicia and Leslie J. Higgins. *Victorian Aesthetic Conditions: Pater Across the Arts.* Basingstoke: Palgrave Macmillan, 2010.
Collingwood, William Gershom. *The Life of John Ruskin.* London: Methuen & Co., 1893.
Daley, Kenneth. *The Rescue of Romanticism: Walter Pater and John Ruskin.* Athens: Ohio University Press, 2001.
Danto, Arthur C. *Nietzsche as Philosopher.* New York: Macmillan, 1965.
  After the End of Art: Contemporary Art and the Pale of History, Bollingen Series XXXV:44. Princeton: Princeton University Press, 1997.
  The Abuse of Beauty. Chicago and LaSalle: Open Court, 2003.
Desmond, William. *Art and the Absolute: A Study of Hegel's Aesthetics*, Albany: State University Press of New York, 1986.
Dobe, Jennifer K. "Kant's Common Sense and the Strategy for a Deduction." *Journal of Aesthetics and Art Criticism* **68** (2008): 47–60.
Donner, Wendy. "Morality, Virtue, and Aesthetics in Mill's Art of Life." In Ben Eggleston, Dale E. Miller, and David Weinstein, editors, *John Stuart Mill and the Art of Life.* New York: Oxford University Press, 2011. Pp. 146–65.
Eldridge, Richard. *The Persistence of Romanticism: Essays in Philosophy and Literature.* Cambridge: Cambridge University Press, 2001.

Engell, James. *The Creative Imagination: Enlightenment to Romanticism.* Cambridge, Mass.: Harvard University Press, 1981.
"*Biographia Literaria.*" In *The Cambridge Companion to Coleridge*, edited by Lucy Newlyn. Cambridge: Cambridge University Press, 2002. Pp. 59–74.
Ermarth, Michael. *Wilhelm Dilthey: The Critique of Historical Reason.* Chicago: University of Chicago Press, 1978.
Feger, Hans. *Poetische Vernunft: Ästhetik und Moral im Deutschen Idealismus.* Stuttgart: J.B. Metzler, 2007.
Fischer, Kuno. *Geschichte der neueren Philosophie*, vol. VII, third edition. Heidelberg: C. Winter, 1902.
Förster, Eckart. *The Twenty-Five Years of Philosophy*, translated by Brady Bowman. Cambridge, Mass.: Harvard University Press, 2012.
Forster, Michael N. *After Herder: Philosophy of Language in the German Tradition.* Oxford: Oxford University Press, 2010.
Foster, Cheryl. "Ideas and Imagination: Schopenhauer on the Proper Foundation of Art." In *The Cambridge Companion to Schopenhauer*, edited by Christopher Janaway. Cambridge: Cambridge University Press, 1999. Pp. 213–51.
Foucault, Michel. *The Order of Things.* New York: Vintage, 1970.
The Archaeology of Knowledge, translated by A.M. Sheridan Smith. New York: Pantheon, 1972.
Frank, Manfred. *Das Individualle-Allgemeine: Textstruktuierung und -interpretation nach Schleiermacher.* Frankfurt am Main: Suhrkamp Verlag, 1977.
Eine Einführung in Schellings Philosophie. Frankfurt am Main: Suhrkamp Verlag, 1985.
Einführung in die frühromantische Ästhetik. Frankfurt am Main: Suhrkamp Verlag, 1989.
Unendliche Annäherung: Die Anfänge der philosophischen Frühromantik. Frankfurt am Main: Suhrkamp Verlag, 1997; *The Philosophical Foundations of Early German Romanticism*, translated by Elizabeth Millán-Zaibert. Albany: State University of New York Press, 2004.
Franke, Ursula and Annemarie Gethmann-Seifert, editors. *Kulturpolitik und Kunstgeschichte: Perspektiven der Hegelschen Ästhetik*, Sonderheft des Jahrgangs 2005 der *Zeitschrift für Ästhetik und allgemeine Kunstwissenschaft.* Hamburg: Felix Meiner Verlag, 2005.
Fricke, Hermann. *K. W. F. Solger: Ein Brandenburgisch-Berlinisches Gelehrtenleben an der Wende vom 18. zum 19. Jahrhundert.* Berlin: Hauder & Spener, 1972.
Funk, Holger. *Ästhetik des Häßlichen: Beiträge zum Verständnis negativer Ausdrucksformen im 19. Jahrhundert.* Berlin: Agora Verlag, 1983.
Gadamer, Hans-Georg. *Truth and Method*, translated by Joel Weinsheimer and Donald G. Marshall, second revised edition. London: Continuum, 2004.
Gardiner, Patrick. *Schopenhauer.* Harmondsworth: Penguin Books, 1963.
"Kant and Hegel on Aesthetics," in Stephen Priest, editor, *Hegel's Critique of Kant.* Oxford: Clarendon Press, 1987. Pp. 161–72.
Gethmann-Siefert, Annemarie. *Einführung in die Ästhetik.* Munich: Wilhelm Fink Verlag, 1995.
Einführung in Hegels Ästhetik. Munich: Wilhelm Fink Verlag, 2005.

Gilbert, Katharine Everett and Helmut Kuhn. *A History of Esthetics*, second edition. Bloomington: Indiana University Press, 1953.
Gjesdal, Kristin. *Gadamer and the Legacy of German Idealism*. Cambridge: Cambridge University Press, 2009.
Glockner, Hermann. "Robert Vischer und die Krisis der Geisteswissenschaften im letzten Drittel des 19. Jahrhunderts: Ein Beitrag zur Geschichte des Irrationalitätsproblem." *Logos* **14** (1925): 297–343, and 15 (1926): 47–102.
Gombrich, E.H. *Art and Illusion: A Study in the Psychology of Pictorial Representation*. Bollingen Series XXXV:5. Princeton: Princeton University Press, 1960.
Goodman, Russell B. *American Philosophy and the Romantic Tradition*. Cambridge: Cambridge University Press, 1990.
Gray, Tim S. *Herbert Spencer's Political Philosophy: Individualism and Organicism*. Hampshire: Avebury, 1996.
"Spencer, Herbert." In *Routledge Encyclopedia of Philosophy*, edited by Edward Craig, 10 vols. London: Routledge, 1998. Vol. 9, pp. 87–9.
Guyer, Paul. "Pleasure and Society in Kant's Theory of Taste." In Ted Cohen and Paul Guyer, editors, *Essays in Kant's Aesthetics*. Chicago: University of Chicago Press, 1982. Pp. 21–54.
Kant and the Experience of Freedom: Essays on Aesthetics and Morality. Cambridge: Cambridge University Press, 1993.
Kant and the Claims of Taste. Cambridge, Mass.: Harvard University Press; expanded edition, Cambridge: Cambridge University Press, 1997.
"Hegel on Kant's Aesthetics: Necessity and Contingency in Beauty and Art." In *Kant and the Experience of Freedom*, pp. 161–83.
"Nature, Art, and Autonomy." In *Kant and the Experience of Freedom*, pp. 229–74.
"Absolute Idealism and the Rejection of Kantian Dualism." In *The Cambridge Companion to German Idealism*, edited by Karl Ameriks. Cambridge: Cambridge University Press, 2000. Pp. 37–66.
"Free and Adherent Beauty: A Modest Proposal." *British Journal for Aesthetics* 42 (October, 2002) 357–66.
Values of Beauty: Historical Essays in Aesthetics. Cambridge: Cambridge University Press, 2005.
Hamilton, Paul. "The Philosopher." In *The Cambridge Companion to Coleridge*, edited by Lucy Newlyn. Cambridge: Cambridge University Press, 2002. Pp. 170–86.
Hamlyn, D.W. *Schopenhauer*. London: Routledge & Kegan Paul, 1980.
Harris, H.S. *Hegel's Development: Toward the Sunlight, 1770–1801*. Oxford: Clarendon Press, 1972.
Hegel's Development: Night Thoughts, Jena 1801–1806. Oxford: Clarendon Press, 1983.
Haskins, Charles Homer. *The Renaissance of the Twelfth Century*. Cambridge, Mass.: Harvard University Press, 1927.
Haym, Rudolf. *Die Romantische Schule: Ein Beitrag zur Geschichte des deutschen Geistes*. Berlin: R. Gaertner, 1870.

Helsinger, Elizaebth K. *Ruskin and the Art of the Beholder.* Cambridge, Mass.: Harvard University Press, 1982.
Henckmann, Wolfhart. "Die geistige Gestalt K.W.F. Solgers." *Philosophisches Jahrbuch* 81 (1974): 172–86.
"Symbolische und Allegorische Kunst bei K.W.F. Solger." In Jaeschke and Holzhey, editors, *Frühe Idealismus und Frühromantik*, 1990. Pp. 214–240.
Henrich, Dieter. *Selbstverhältnisse.* Stuttgart: Philipp Reclam jun., 1982.
The Course of Remembrance and Other Essays on Hölderlin, edited by Eckart Förster. Stanford: Stanford University Press, 1993.
Between Kant and Hegel: Lectures on German Idealism, edited by David S. Pacini. Cambridge, Mass.: Harvard University Press, 2003.
Fixpunkte. Frankfurt am Main: Suhrkamp Verlag, 2003.
Heydt, Colin. *Rethinking Mill's Ethics: Character and Aesthetic Education.* London: Continuum, 2006.
Hilton, Tim. *John Ruskin: The Early Years.* New Haven and London: Yale University Press, 1985.
John Ruskin: The Later Years. New Haven and London: Yale University Press, 2000.
Hollingdale, R.J. *Nietzsche: The Man and His Philosophy*, revised edition. Cambridge: Cambridge University Press, 1999.
Holub, Robert C. *Reception Theory: A Critical Introduction.* London: Routledge, 1984.
Honour, Hugh. *Neo-Classicism.* Harmondsworth: Penguin Books, 1968.
Hopkins, Vivian C. *Spires of Form: A Study of Emerson's Aesthetic Theory.* Cambridge, Mass.: Harvard University Press, 1951.
Horstmann, Rolf-Peter. "Zur Hegel-Kritik des späten Schelling." In Horstmann, *Die Grenzen der Vernunft: Eine Untersuchung zu Zielen und Motiven des Deutschen Idealismus.* Frankfurt am Main: Anton Hain, 1991. Pp. 245–68.
Houlgate, Stephen, editor. *Hegel and the Arts.* Evanston, Ill.: Northwestern University Press, 2007.
Huch, Ricarda. *Die Romantik: Ausbreitung, Blüte, und Verfall.* Leipzig: H. Haessel, 1908.
Iannelli, Francesca. *Das Siegel der Moderne: Hegels Bestimmung des Hässlichen in den Vorlesungen zur Ästhetik und die Rezeption bei den Hegelianern.* Munich: Wilhelm Fink Verlag, 2007.
Inwood, Michael. "Hegel." In Berys Gaut and Dominic McIver Lopes, *The Routledge Companion to Aesthetics*, second edition. London: Routledge, 2005. Pp. 71–82.
Iser, Wolfgang. *The Act of Reading: A Theory of Aesthetic Response.* Baltimore: Johns Hopkins University Press, 1978.
Jacquette, Dale. "Idealism: Schopenhauer, Schiller and Schelling." In Berys Gaut and Dominic McIver Lopes, *The Routledge Companion to Aesthetics*, second edition. London: Routledge, 2005. Pp. 83–96.
The Philosophy of Schopenhauer. Montreal and Kingston: McGill-Queen's University Press, 2005.
Jacquette, Dale, editor. *Schopenhauer, Philosophy, and the Arts.* Cambridge: Cambridge University Press, 1996.

Jaeschke, Walter and Helmut Holzhey, editors. *Früher Idealismus und Frühromantik: Der Streit um die Grundlagen der Ästhetik (1795–1805)*, 2 vols. Hamburg: Felix Meiner Verlag, 1990.
Jähnig, Dieter. *Schelling: Die Kunst in der Philosophie*, 2 vols. Pfüllingen: Neske, 1966–69.
Janaway, Christopher. *Schopenhauer*. Oxford: Oxford University Press, 1994.
Beyond Selflessness: Reading Nietzsche's Genealogy. Oxford: Oxford University Press, 2007.
Janaway, Christopher, editor. *The Cambridge Companion to Schopenhauer*. Cambridge: Cambridge University Press, 1999.
Jauss, Robert. *Aesthetic Experience and Literary Hermeneutics*, translated by Michael Shaw. Minneapolis: University of Minnesota Press, 1982.
Toward an Aesthetic of Reception, translated by Timothy Bahti. Minneapolis: University of Minnesota Press, 1982.
Jung, Matthias. *Dilthey zur Einführung*. Hamburg: Junius Verlag, 1996.
Jung, Werner. *Schöner Schein der Häßlichkeit oder Häßlichkeit des schönen Scheins*. Frankfurt am Main: Athenäum, 1987.
Kaminsky, Jack. *Hegel on Art: An Interpretation of Hegel's Aesthetics*. Albany: State University Press of New York, 1962.
Kaufman, Walter. *Nietzsche: Philosopher, Psychologist, Antichrist*. Princeton: Princeton University Press, 1950.
Kelley, Theresa M. *Wordsworth's Revisionary Aesthetics*. Cambridge: Cambridge University Press, 1988.
Kemal, Salim, Ivan Gaskell, and Daniel W. Conway. *Nietzsche, Philosophy, and the Arts*. Cambridge: Cambridge University Press, 1998.
Köhnke, Klaus Christian. *Entstehung und Aufsteig des Neukantianismus: Die deutsche Universitätsphilosophie zwischen Idealismus und Positivismus*. Frankfurt am Main: Suhrkamp Verlag, 1986.
The Rise of Neo-Kantianism: German Academic Philosophy between Idealism and Positivism, translated by R.J. Hollingdale. Cambridge: Cambridge University Press, 1991.
Kruft, Hanno Walter. *A History of Architectural Theory from Vitruvius to the Present*, translated by Ronald Taylor, Elsie Callander, and Antony Wood. New York: Princeton Architectural Press, 1994.
Krukowski, Lucien. *Aesthetic Legacies*. Philadelphia: Temple University Press, 1992.
Kuhn, Helmut. "Die Vollendung der klassischen deutschen Ästhetik durch Hegel." In Kuhn, *Schriften zur Ästhetik*, edited by Wolfhart Henckmann. Munich: Kosel, 1966.
Landow, George P. *The Aesthetical and Critical Theories of John Ruskin*. Princeton: Princeton University Press, 1971.
Ruskin. Oxford: Oxford University Press, 1985.
Lear, Jonathan. "Katharsis." In Amélie Oksenberg Rorty, editor, *Essays on Aristotle's Poetics*. Princeton: Princeton University Press, 1992. Pp. 315–40.
Levey, Michael. *The Case of Walter Pater*. London: Thames and Hudson, 1978.
Listowel, Earl of. *A Critical History of Modern Aesthetics*. London: George Allen & Unwin, 1933.

Magee, Bryan. *The Philosophy of Schopenhauer*. Oxford: Clarendon Press, 1983.
Magee, Judith. *The Art and Science of William Bartram*. University Park: Pennsylvania State University Press, 2007.
Majetschak, Stefan, editor. *Auge und Hand: Konrad Fiedlers Kunsttheorie im Kontext*. Munich: Wilhelm Fink Verlag, 1997.
Maker, William, editor. *Hegel and Aesthetics*. Albany: State University Press of New York, 2000.
Makkreel, Rudolf A. *Dilthey: Philosopher of the Human Studies*. Princeton: Princeton University Press, 1975.
Makkreel, Rudolf A. and Sebastian Luft. "Dilthey and the Neo-Kantians: The Dispute over the Status of the Human and Cultural Sciences." In Dean Moyar, editor, *The Routledge Companion to Nineteenth Century Philosophy*. London: Routledge, 2010. Pp. 554–97.
Mariña, Jacqueline, editor. *The Cambridge Companion to Friedrich Schleiermacher*. Cambridge: Cambridge University Press, 2005.
Marx, Werner. *The Philosophy of F.W.J. Schelling: History, System, and Freedom*, translated by Thomas Nenon. Bloomington: Indiana University Press, 1984.
Matthews, Eric. *Twentieth-Century French Philosophy*. Oxford: Oxford University Press, 1996.
Millán-Zaibert, Elizabeth. *Friedrich Schlegel and the Emergence of Romantic Philosophy*. Albany: State University Press of New York, 2007.
Moran, Michael. "Emerson, Ralph Waldo." In *Encyclopedia of Philosophy*, second edition, edited by Donald M. Borchert, 10 vols. Farmington Hills, Mich.: Thomson-Gale, 2006. Vol. 3, pp. 194–7.
Muirhead, John H. *Coleridge as Philosopher*. London: George Allen & Unwin, 1930.
Müller, Götz. "Jean Pauls Ästhetik im Kontext der Frühromantik und des deutschen Idealismus." In Jaeschke and Holzhey, *Früher Idealismus und Frühromantik*, pp. 159–73.
Nehamas, Alexander. *Nietzsche: Life as Literature*. Cambridge, Mass.: Harvard University Press, 1985.
  "Pity and Fear in the *Rhetoric* and the *Poetics*." In Amélie Oksenberg Rorty, editor, *Essays on Aristotle's Poetics*. Princeton: Princeton University Press, 1992. Pp. 291–314.
  Only a Promise of Happiness: The Place of Beauty in a World of Art. Princeton: Princeton University Press, 2007.
Neill, Alex and Christopher Janaway, editors. *Better Consciousness: Schopenhauer's Philosophy of Value*. Chichester: Wiley-Blackwell, 2009.
Nussbaum, Martha C. "Nietzsche, Schopenhauer, and Dionyus." In *The Cambridge Companion to Schopenhauer*, edited by Christopher Janaway. Cambridge: Cambridge University Press, 1999. Pp. 344–74.
Oelmüller, Willi. *Friedrich Theodor Vischer und das Problem einer nachhegelschen Ästhetik*. Stuttgart: Kohlhammer, 1959.
Orsini, G.N.G. *Coleridge and German Idealism: A Study in the History of Philosophy with Unpublished Materials from Coleridge's Manuscripts*. Carbondale: Southern Illinois University Press, 1969.

Bibliography 453

Peel, John David Yeadon. *Herbert Spencer: The Evolution of a Sociologist.* London: Heinemann, 1971.
Pester, Reinhard. *Hermann Lotze–Wege seines Denkens und Forschens: Ein Kapitel deutscher Philosophie- und Wissenschaftsgeschichte im 19 Jahrhundert.* Würzburg: Könighausen & Neumann, 1997.
Pinkard, Terry. *Hegel: A Biography.* Cambridge: Cambridge University Press, 2000.
Pippin, Robert. "What Was Abstract Art? (From the Point of View of Hegel)." In Stephen Houlgate, editor, *Hegel and the Arts.* Evanston: Northwestern University Press, 2007. Pp. 244–70.
"The Absence of Aesthetics in Hegel's Aesthetics." In *The Cambridge Companion to Hegel and Nineteenth-Century Philosophy,* edited by Frederick C. Beiser. Cambridge: Cambridge University Press, 2008. Pp. 394–418.
Pochat, Götz. *Geschichte der Ästhetik und Kunsttheorie: Von der Antike bis zum 19. Jahrhundert.* Cologne: DuMont, 1986.
Podro, Michael. *The Manifold in Perception: Theories of Art from Kant to Hildebrand.* Oxford: Clarendon Press, 1972.
The Critical Historians of Art. New Haven: Yale University Press, 1983.
Poma, Andrea. *The Critical Philosophy of Hermann Cohen,* translated by John Denton. Albany: State University Press of New York, 1997.
Yearning for Form and Other Essays on Hermann Cohen's Thought. Dordrecht: Springer, 2006.
Pothast, Ulrich. *Die eigentliche metaphysische Tätigkeit: Über Schopenhauers Ästhetik und ihre Anwendung durch Samuel Beckett.* Frankfurt am Main: Suhrkamp Verlag, 1982.
Pothe, Philip. *Nietzsche and the Fate of Art.* Aldershot: Ashgate, 2002.
Proust, Marcel. *On Reading Ruskin: Prefaces to* La Bible d'Amiens *and* Sésame et les Lys, translated and edited by Jean Autret, William Burford, and Phillip J. Wolfe. New Haven and London: Yale University Press, 1987.
Raters, Marie-Luise. *Kunst, Wahrheit und Gefühl: Schelling, Hegel und die Ästhetik des angelsächsischen Idealismus.* Freiburg: Verlag Karl Alber, 2005.
Reginster, Bernard. *The Affirmation of Life: Nietzsche on Overcoming Nihilism.* Cambridge, Mass.: Harvard University Press, 2006.
Richards, Ivor Armstrong. *Coleridge on Imagination.* London: Routledge & Kegan Paul, 1934.
Richardson, Robert D., Jr. *Emerson: The Mind on Fire.* Berkeley and Los Angeles: University of California Press, 1995.
Rickman, Peter. *Wilhelm Dilthey: Pioneer of the Human Studies.* London: Elek, 1979.
Ridley, Aaron. *The Routledge Guidebook to Nietzsche on Art.* London: Routledge, 2007.
Ritter, Joachim. *Vorlesungen zur Philosophischen Ästhetik,* Marbacher Schriften, Neue Folge 6, edited by Ulrich von Bülow and Mark Schweda. Göttingen: Wallstein Verlag, 2010.
Rodi, Frithjof. *Morphologie und Hermeneutik: Zur Methode von Diltheys Ästhetik.* Stuttgart: Kohlhammer, 1969.

Rosenberg, John D. *The Darkening Glass: A Portrait of Ruskin's Genius.* New York: Columbia University Press, 1961.
Rutter, Benjamin. *Hegel on the Modern Arts.* Cambridge: Cambridge University Press, 2010.
Ryan, Alan. *J.S. Mill.* London: Routledge & Kegan Paul, 1974.
Safranski, Rüdiger. *Schopenhauer and the Wild Years of Philosophy,* translated by Ewald Osers. Cambridge, Mass.: Harvard University Press, 1989.
  Romantik: Eine deutsche Affäre. Munich: Carl Hanser Verlag, 2007.
Santayana, George. *Lotze's System of Philosophy,* edited by Paul Grimley Kuntz. Bloomington: Indiana University Press, 1971.
Sartwell, Crispin. "Art for Art's Sake." In *Encyclopedia of Aesthetics,* edited by Michael Kelly, 4 vols. New York: Oxford University Press, 1998. Vol. I, pp. 118–21.
Schacht, Richard. *Nietzsche.* London: Routledge, 1983.
Schaeffer, Jean-Marie. *Art of the Modern Age: Philosophy of Art from Kant to Heidegger,* translated by Steven Rendall. Princeton: Princeton University Press, 2000.
Scheer, Brigitte. *Einführung in die philosophische Ästhetik.* Darmstadt: Wissenschaftliche Buchgesellschaft, 1997.
Schmidt, Jochen. *Die Geschichte des Genie-Gedankens in der deutschen Literature, Philosophie und Politik 1750–1945,* 2 vols. Darmstadt: Wissenschaftliche Buchgesellschaft, 1985.
Scholz, Günter. *Die Philosophie Schleiermachers.* Darmstadt: Wissenschaftliche Buchgesellschaft, 1984.
Sharpless, F. Parvin. *The Literary Criticism of John Stuart Mill.* The Hague: Mouton, 1967.
Silk, M.S. and J.P. Stern. *Nietzsche on Tragedy.* Cambridge: Cambridge University Press, 1981.
Simmel, Georg. *Schopenhauer and Nietzsche* (1907), translated by Helmut Loiskandl, Deena Weinstein, and Michael Weinstein. Amherst: University of Massachusetts Press, 1986.
Skorupski, John. *John Stuart Mill.* London: Routledge, 1989.
Snow, Dale E. *Schelling and the End of Idealism.* Albany: State University Press of New York, 1996.
Sonderegger, Ruth. *Für eine Ästhetik des Spiels: Hermeneutik, Dekonstruktion und der Eigensinn der Kunst.* Frankfurt am Main: Suhrkamp Verlag, 2000.
Stansky, Peter. *Redesigning the World: William Morris, the 1880s, and the Arts and Crafts.* Princeton: Princeton University Press, 1985.
Strauss, David Friedrich. *Das Leben Jesu kritisch bearbeitet.* Tübingen: Osiander, 1835–36; translated by Marian (Mary Anne) Evans (George Eliot), *The Life of Jesus, Critically Examined,* 3 vols. London: Chapman Brothers,1846.
Taylor, Charles. *Hegel.* Cambridge: Cambridge University Press, 1975.
Taylor, Michael W. *Man versus the State: Herbert Spencer and Late Victorian Individualism.* Oxford: Clarendon Press, 1992.
Teukolsky, Rachel. *The Literate Eye: Victorian Art Writing and Modernist Aesthetics.* Oxford: Oxford University Press, 2009.
Thompson, E.P. *William Morris: Romantic to Revolutionary,* revised edition. New York: Pantheon, 1977.

Thompson, Paul. *The Work of William Morris*. London: Heinemann, 1967.
Tilliette, Xavier. *Schelling: Une Philosophie en Devenir*, 2 vols. Paris: Vrin, 1970.
Volhard, Ewald. *Zwischen Hegel und Nietzsche: Der Ästhetiker Friederich Theodor Vischer*. Frankfurt am Main: Kohlhammer, 1932.
Wellek, René. *Immanuel Kant in England 1793–1838*. Princeton: Princeton University Press, 1931.
Wheeler, Kathleen M. *Sources, Processes, and Methods in Coleridge's* Biographia Literaria. Cambridge: Cambridge University Press, 1980.
White, Alan. *Schelling: An Introduction to the System of Freedom*. New Haven: Yale University Press, 1983.
Wicks, Robert. "Hegel's Aesthetics: An Overview." In *The Cambridge Companion to Hegel*, edited by Frederick C. Beiser. Cambridge: Cambridge University Press, 1993. Pp. 348–77.
Wilcox, John. "The Beginnings of L'art pour L'art." *Journal of Aesthetics and Art Criticism* 11 (1953): 360–77.
Will, Frederic. *Flumen historicum: Victor Cousin's Aesthetic and its Sources*. Chapel Hill: University of North Carolina Press, 1965.
Willey, Thomas E. *Back to Kant: The Revival of Kantianism in German Social and Historical Thought, 1860–1914*. Detroit: Wayne State University Press, 1978.
Williams, Carolyn. *Transfigured World: Walter Pater's Aesthetic Historicism*. Ithaca: Cornell University Press, 1989.
Witte, Egbert. *Logik ohne Dornen: Die Rezeption von A.G. Baumgartens Ästhetik im Spannungsfeld von logischem Begriff und ästhetischer Anschauung*. Hildesheim: Georg Olms Verlag, 2000.
Wyss, Beat. *Hegel's Art History and the Critique of Modernity*, translated by Caroline Dobson Salzwedel. Cambridge: Cambridge University Press, 1999.
Young, Julian. *Nietzsche's Philosophy of Art*. Cambridge: Cambridge University Press, 1992.
  Schopenhauer. London: Routledge, 2005.
  Friedrich Nietzsche: A Philosophical Biography. Cambridge: Cambridge University Press, 2010.

Index

absolute
  in Jean Paul's account of genius, 60
  in Schelling's *The Philosophy of Art*, 50–1
absolute (objective) idealism, 21–2. *See also* Schelling, Friedrich Wilhelm Josef von
absolute Idea, Friedrich Vischer's account of, 161–4
absolute spirit, Hegel's account of
  classical art, 133–6
  continuing significance of, 143
  genius, 141–2
  history of art, 128–31
  overview, 126–8
  rejection of natural beauty, 140
  romantic art, 135–8
  sublime, 141
  symbolic art, 131–3
absolute values, Münsterberg's account of, 354–60
abstraction, in Pater's account, 254
The Aesthetic Consciousness (Volkelt), 407–9
aesthetic contemplation, Lipps's account of, 397–8
aesthetic idea
  Kant's account of, 14–15
  Schleiermacher's version of, 148–9
æsthetic imperative, Lee's account of, 429

aesthetic Socratism, Nietzsche's account of, 313
aesthetic values, Münsterberg's account of, 357–60
aestheticism. *See* "art for art's sake" movement; Pater, Walter; Wilde, Oscar
Aesthetics (Lipps), 397–404
Aesthetics: Lectures on Fine Art (Hegel), 123–4
Aesthetics of the Ugly (Rosenkranz), 173–8
Aesthetik oder Wissenschaft des Schönen (*Aesthetics or the Science of the Beautiful*), Friedrich Vischer
  absolute Idea, 161–4
  beauty, 165–6
  emotional impact of aesthetic experience, 166–7
  overview, 160–1
  rehabilitation of Kant in, 164–5
agreeable, Lotze's account of, 182
Alison, Archibald, 329
Allgemeine Ästhetik (Cohn), 345–6
American aesthetics. *See also specific philosophers by name*
  in nineteenth century, 3–4
  psychological aesthetics, 418–26
  twentieth-century, 437
analytic method, in Cohen's account, 334–5
animals, projection of emotions on, 402–3

anthropomorphism, in Hegel's history of art, 133–6
Apollonian art, Nietzsche's account of, 305, 309–11, 312–14
apperception, in Lipps's account, 399–400
architecture
  Hegel's account of symbolic art, 131–2
  Ruskin's account of relation, 213–15
  Ruskin's account of truthfulness in, 218–24
  Schopenhauer's account of, 116
Aristotle, in Wilde's "The Critic as Artist," 262–3
Arnold, Matthew, 225–8
art. *See also* "art for art's sake" movement; greatness in art, Ruskin's sources of; history of art, Hegel's account of; *specific arts by name*
  in Bosanquet's *History of Æsthetic*, 272–5
  Cohen's account of feelings in, 335–9
  Cohen's account of higher task of, 342–5
  Coleridge's account of, 66, 69–71
  Dilthey's account of, 367–8, 370–7
  Emerson's account of, 96–9
  Friedrich Vischer's account of, 165–72
  Groos's account of, 411–15
  Hegel's cognitivist view of, 119–22, 127–8
  Jean Paul's account of, 58–62
  Kant's account of, 13–17
  Lee's account of, 427–9, 430–1
  Lipps's account of projection of emotions on, 403–4
  Lotze's account of, 184–5
  Mill's account of poetry, 84–91
  in Münsterberg's account, 357, 358–9, 360, 362
  Nietzsche's account of, 300–1, 309–14, 316–20
  Pater's account of free play, 251–4
  Pater's account of integrative character of, 246–51
  Pater's account of morality, 255–6
  Puffer's account of, 424–6
  Robert Vischer's account of, 394–6
  Rosenkranz's account of ugliness in, 174–8
  Ruskin's account of truthfulness in, 216–18
  Schelling's *The Philosophy of Art*, 50–4
  Schelling's system of transcendental idealism, 41–50
  Schlegel's account of truth as aim of, 28–34
  Schlegel's "Letters on Christian Art," 37–8
  Schlegel's "On the Study of Greek Poetry," 28–34
  Schleiermacher's account of, 144, 146–52
  Schopenhauer's account of, 112–19, 308–9
  Solger's account of, 153, 154–8
  Spencer's account of, 387–9
  Tolstoy's *What is Art?*, 291–6
  Wilde's basic account of, 258–9
  in Wilde's "The Critic as Artist," 261–8
  in Wilde's "The Decay of Lying," 258–9
  in Wilde's *The Picture of Dorian Gray*, 268–9
"Art" (Emerson), 97–9
"art for art's sake" movement (aestheticism), 7. *See also* Pater, Walter; Wilde, Oscar
  Baudelaire, 241–4
  Cousin, 230–4
  Gautier, 234–6
  Lee's approach as similar to, 429
  overview, 227–8, 229–30
  Poe, 236–42
  Tolstoy's attack upon, 290–6
artificiality, in Dilthey's account, 376
artistic beauty
  Emerson's account of, 96–7
  Hegel's account of, 140

in Münsterberg's account,
    357, 358–9
  Schelling's account of natural
    beauty versus, 49
associations
  Fechner's principle of, 328–30
  in Robert Vischer's account,
    391, 393–4
  Ruskin's account of, 212–15
  in Spencer's account, 386–7
associative imagination, Ruskin's
  account of, 209–10
Athäneum fragments (Schlegel), 33–7
audience
  in Dilthey's account, 367–8
  in Kant's account, 16
  in Mill's account, 87–8
  in Nietzsche's account, 311–12
  in Schleiermacher's account, 146–7
  in Schopenhauer's account, 114–15
  Tolstoy's account of art as
    communication of feeling, 292–6
  in Wordsworth's account of
    poetry, 76–8
autonomy of aesthetic experience.
  See "art for art's sake" movement

"Baden" school of Neo-Kantianism.
  See Neo-Kantianism; *specific
    philosophers by name*
Baudelaire, Charles, 241–4
Baumgarten, Alexander Gottlieb
  in Solger's account, 155
  in Tolstoy's account, 291
*The Beautiful: An Introduction to
  Psychological Aesthetics* (Lee),
  428–30, 434–6
"The Beautiful and Art" (*Das Schöne
  und die Kunst*), Friedrich Vischer,
  167–72
beauty
  Baudelaire's account of, 242–4
  Bosanquet's basic account
    of, 272–5
  Bosanquet's discussion of
    Goethe, 281–2
  Bosanquet's discussion of
    Hegel, 282–4

Bosanquet's discussion of
  Kant, 276–9
Bosanquet's discussion of
  Ruskin, 285–6
Bosanquet's discussion of
  Schelling, 282
Bosanquet's discussion of
  Schiller, 280
Bosanquet's discussion of
  Winckelmann, 275–6
Cohen's account of pleasure
  of, 335–9
Cohn's account of, 350–1
Coleridge's account of, 65–6
Cousin's account of, 231–4
Emerson's account of, 95–7, 101–2
Friedrich Vischer's account of,
  162–4, 165–6, 167, 170–2
Gautier's account of, 236
Hegel's rejection of natural, 139–40
Kant's account of, 14–15, 16–17
Lee's account of, 427–33
Lipps's account of, 397–8, 399–400
Lotze's account of, 181–4
Mill's account of, 88–9
Münsterberg's account of, 357–60
Pater's argument against general
  rules for, 248–9
Poe's account of, 238, 240–1
Puffer's account of, 419–26
Ruskin's account of, 192, 203–12,
  216–17
Schelling's account of, 47–9, 51–2
Schlegel's account of limits of, 25–8
Schlegel's account of objectivity
  of, 28–34
in Schlegel's account of romantic
  poetry, 37
Schopenhauer's account of, 115–16
Solger's account of, 156–7
in Tolstoy's account, 291, 293
von Hartmann's account of, 321–3
in Wilde's "The Critic as
  Artist," 261–8
in Wilde's "The Decay of Lying,"
  259–60
in Wilde's *The Picture of Dorian
  Gray*, 268–9

Beauty and Ugliness and Other Studies in Psychological Æsthetics (Lee), 427–8, 430–4
Beethoven, Ludwig van, 345
being, Hölderlin's account of, 20–1
Beiser, Frederick, 125
Bell, Clive, 4
Biographia Literaria (Coleridge)
   art, 69–71
   central idea of, 65–9
   discussion of Wordsworth in, 72–4
   genius, 69–71
   overview, 64
The Birth of Tragedy (Nietzsche), 300–1, 306–14
Bizet, Georges, 315
Bloomsbury aesthetics, 4, 7
bodily dimension of aesthetic experience
   Lee's account of, 433–4
   Puffer's account of, 421
   Robert Vischer's account of, 394–6
Bosanquet, Bernard, 3–4, 8, 269
   on Goethe, 281–2
   on Hegel, 282–4
   on Kant, 276–9
   overview, 270–5, 289–90
   on Ruskin, 284–6
   on Schelling, 282
   on Schiller, 279–81
   Three Lectures on Aesthetic, 286–9
   on Winckelmann, 275–6
British aesthetics. *See also specific philosophers by name*
   in eighteenth century, 1
   in nineteenth century, 2–4, 187–9
   psychological aesthetics, 426–36
   twentieth-century, 436–7
British Romantics. *See also* Coleridge, Samuel Taylor
   Mill, 84–91
   Shelley, 79–83
   Wordsworth, 75–8

capacities, discharge of excess
   Groos's disagreement with, 410–11
   Spencer's account of, 383–4, 385–6
Carmen (Bizet), 315

"The Case of Wagner" (Nietzsche), 315–16
categorical imperative, in Nietzsche's account, 308
celebration, in Schleiermacher's account of art, 151–2
characteristic
   Bosanquet's account of, 272–3
   Bosanquet's discussion of Goethe's concept, 281–2
Christian religiosity
   in Hegel's account of romantic art, 136–7
   in Schlegel's aesthetics, 37–8
cinema, Münsterberg's account of, 360–2
classical art, Hegel's account of, 130, 133–6. *See also* Greek art
cognition, in Kant's account of free play, 11–13
cognitivist approach to aesthetic experience
   Arnold's account, 226–8
   Bosanquet's account, 286, 289–90
   Cohen's account, 345–6
   Cohn's account, 352
   Coleridge's account, 66
   Cousin's account, 231
   Dilthey's account, 364–5, 368, 370–7
   Emerson's account, 96, 97–101, 102, 103–4
   in German Idealism, 106
   Hegel's account, 119–22, 127–8, 140
   Hölderlin's account, 23
   Jean Paul's account, 60
   in Kant's account, 16–17
   Lee's account, 435–6
   Lotze's account, 181–2
   metaphysical version of, 13, 15–16, 23
   Münsterberg's account, 355–6
   Neo-Kantianism, 330
   in nineteenth century, 4–8
   Puffer's rejection of, 421–2
   by Romantic writers, 57

Rosenkranz's account,
172–3, 175–6
Ruskin's account, 191–3, 225
Schelling's account, 43, 47, 49–50,
51–2, 53–4
Schleiermacher's account, 144,
147–9, 150, 152
Schopenhauer's account, 106–7,
112–15, 118–19
Shelley's account, 79, 80–2
Solger's account, 155, 157
Spencer's account, 385, 389
von Hartmann's account, 322–4
Wordsworth's account, 75, 78
cognizing functions, in
Schleiermacher's account, 147–9
Cohen, Hermann, 326, 331
background of, 332–3
feelings in art, 335–9
free play theory, 339–40
genius, 341–2
higher task of art, 342–5
versus other Neo-Kantians, 331–2
overview, 333–5, 345–6
philosophy, 334–5, 340–1
coherence, in Münsterberg's account,
354–6, 357–9
Cohn, Jonas, 326, 331–2, 346–53
Coleridge, Samuel Taylor
art, 69–71
background of, 63–4
central idea in aesthetics of, 65–9
discussion of Wordsworth by, 72–4
genius, 71–2
influence on Mill, 84
comedy
Hegel's account of, 137
Rosenkranz's account of, 173–4
communication
of cognition by geniuses,
Schopenhauer's account of,
114–15
in Dilthey's account, 368
of feeling, Tolstoy's account of art
as, 292–6
in Schleiermacher's account, 148–9
complexity, organization of in
Spencer's account, 385–6

concept, in Hegel's account, 126–7
concreteness, in Pater's account,
247–8, 254
The Conduct of Life (Emerson), 101–2
conscious, in Coleridge's account of
genius, 72
conscious intelligence, Coleridge's
account of, 66–8
conscious self-illusion, in Groos's
account of art, 412–15
conscious thought, in Schelling's
account, 41–50
consciousness, Cohen's account of,
334, 335–9
contemplation, Lipps's account of
aesthetic, 397–8
contemplative imagination, Ruskin's
account of, 211–12
content
in Hegel's history of art, 129–31
Pater's account of effacement of
distinction between form and,
249–50
contingency, in Friedrich Vischer's
absolute Idea, 162
Cousin, Victor, 230–4
creation, in Bosanquet's
account, 288–9
creativity
Dilthey's account of, 367–8, 370–3
Emerson's account of, 97
"The Critic as Artist" (Wilde), 261–8
criticism
Gautier's attack on, 236
in Pater's account, 247–9
Croce, Benedetto, 4
Culture and Anarchy (Arnold), 225–6

Danto, Arthur C., 143
Das Schöne und die Kunst ("The
Beautiful and Art"), Friedrich
Vischer, 167–72
The Debate about Tragedy
(Lipps), 405–6
"The Decay of Lying" (Wilde), 258,
259–61
deceitfulness, in Ruskin's account of
architecture, 220–2

decoration, in Ruskin's account of architecture, 222–4
deduction of judgments of taste, 12
"Defence of Poetry" (Shelley), 79–83
demand-character of aesthetic judgments, Cohn's account of, 348–9
detachment, in Emerson's account of art, 98
"Dialectic of the Aesthetic Power of Judgment" (Kant), 12–13
Dilthey, Wilhelm, 7–8, 299, 326
  background of, 365–6
  overview, 362–5, 366–8
  synthesis of aesthetic theories by, 370–7
  universal validity of judgment of taste, 368–70
"Dionysiac World View" (Nietzsche), 304–6
Dionysian art, Nietzsche's account of, 304, 309–14
direction of consciousness, in Cohen's account, 334, 337–8
discharge of excess capacity
  Groos's disagreement with, 410–11
  Spencer's account of, 383–4, 385–6
disinterestedness
  Cohn's account of, 347–8
  in Dilthey's account, 375
  in Emerson's account of art, 98
  in Friedrich Vischer's account, 169–70, 171–2
  in Kant's account of taste, 11
  in Münsterberg's account, 359–60
  in Schopenhauer's account, 308–9
displeasure, Cohen's account of, 335–9
dissolution of art, Hegel's account of, 135–6
distance, in Nietzsche's account, 319
divine. *See also* God
  in Hegel's account of classical art, 133–6
  in Jean Paul's account, 58–9, 60
  in Solger's account, 154–5, 156–8

drama
  Friedrich Vischer's account of, 166–7
  Hegel's account of, 138
Du vrai, du beau, et du bien (*The True, the Beautiful, and the Good*), Cousin, 230–4

early German Romanticism. *See also* Schlegel, Friedrich
  Hölderlin, 19–23
  overview, 18–19, 24–5
Ecce Homo (Nietzsche), 306–7
education, Hegel's views on art in, 121–2
Egyptian art, Hegel's account of, 132
eloquence, versus poetry, Mill's account of, 87–8
embodied feeling, object of aesthetic attitude as, 286–8
Emerson, Ralph Waldo
  art, 96–9
  background of, 91–3
  beauty, 95–7, 101–2
  imagination, 102–5
  poetry, 99–101
  Transcendentalism, 92, 93–5
emotion, Spencer's account of capacity for, 384–5, 388
emotional impact of aesthetic experience
  Bosanquet's account, 286, 289–90
  Cohn's account, 349–50, 351–2
  Dilthey's account, 364–5, 368, 370–7
  in Emerson's account, 103
  empathy school, 389–90
  Fechner's account, 329–30
  Friedrich Vischer's account, 160, 166–72
  Groos's combination of play and empathy, 409–17
  Hegel's rejection of, 120–2
  Lee's account, 431–5
  Lipps's account, 396–406
  Mill's account, 85–91
  Münsterberg's account, 355–6

in nineteenth century, 4–8
Puffer's account, 420–6
and revival of free play theory,
378–80
Robert Vischer's account, 390–6
Romantic writers, 57
Schleiermacher's account, 144,
146–50, 152
Schopenhauer's account, 107
Shelley's account, 79, 81–3
Spencer's account, 387–8, 389
Tolstoy's account, 295–6
Volkelt's account, 406–9
in Wilde's "The Critic as Artist,"
261, 263–7
Wordsworth's account, 75–8
empathy
in Cohn's account, 349–50
Friedrich Vischer's account
of, 170–1
Groos's combination of play and,
409–17
Lee's account of, 431–5
Lipps's account of, 396–406
in Münsterberg's account of
beauty, 358–9
overview, 3, 6, 389–90
and revival of free play theory,
378–80
Robert Vischer's account
of, 390–6
Volkelt's account of, 406–9
Encyclopedia of the Philosophical Sciences
(Hegel), 120
end
of art, Hegel's account of, 135–6
Friedrich Vischer's account of
Kant's concept of, 164
endless striving, in Schopenhauer's
account of will, 111
ensoulment, Friedrich Vischer's
account of, 170–1
esemplastic imagination, Coleridge's
account of, 65–6, 68, 69, 73–4
Essays: First Series (Emerson), 94, 97–9
Essays: Second Series (Emerson),
99–101

The Eternal Values (Münsterberg),
354–60
ethics, affinity with nature as
expressed in, 95
Euripides, Nietzsche's account of,
312–13
evolution
Puffer's criticism of theories of
beauty based on, 419–20
Spencer's conception of,
380–1, 388–9
excellence, in Emerson's account of
beauty, 101
excess capacity, discharge of
Groos's disagreement with,
410–11
Spencer's account of, 383–4, 385–6
experience
in Dilthey's account, 363–5, 368
in Ruskin's account of truth,
198–203
expression
in Bosanquet's account, 275–6, 288
in Cohn's account, 350–1

fancy. *See also* imagination
Coleridge's account of, 68–9
Emerson's account of, 104–5
Fechner, Gustav Theodor, 327–30
feeling. *See also* emotional impact of
aesthetic experience
in art, Cohen's account of,
335–9
Dilthey's account of spheres
of, 371–3
embodied, Bosanquet's idea of
object of aesthetic attitude
as, 286–8
of life, in Dilthey's account, 376
Spencer's account of capacity for,
384–5, 388
Tolstoy's account of art as
communication of, 292–6
in von Hartmann's account of
beauty, 321–2
festival, in Schleiermacher's account
of art, 151–2

The Film: A Psychological Study (Münsterberg), 360–2
fine art, Kant's account of, 13–17
finite, in Jean Paul's account of modern art, 61–2
form
　in Bosanquet's account, 286–8
　in Cohn's account, 350–1
　in Friedrich Vischer's account, 168–9
　in Hegel's history of art, 129–31
　human, in Emerson's account of beauty, 101
　Pater's account of effacement of distinction between content and, 249–50
formative arts, Schelling's account of, 52
formlessness, in Rosenkranz's account of ugliness in art, 176
fragmentary conception of aesthetic cognition, 25–6, 33–7
free play theory
　Arnold's account, 226
　Bosanquet's account, 273, 286, 289–90
　Cohen's account, 339–40
　Cohn's account, 347–8
　Coleridge's dismissal of, 65–6
　Dilthey's account, 364–5, 370–7
　Emerson's account, 100–1, 105
　Fechner's account, 328–9
　Friedrich Vischer's account, 161, 164–5
　Groos's combination of empathy and, 409–17
　Hegel's rejection of, 120
　in Kant's account of taste, 11–13
　Kant's theory of genius, 14, 15, 16–17
　Lee's objections to, 430–1, 433
　Lipps's avoidance of, 400–1
　Lotze's account, 179, 181–4, 185
　Münsterberg's account, 356
　Nietzsche's account, 301, 304–6, 317–19
　in nineteenth century, 4–8
　Pater's account, 246, 251–4

revival of in late nineteenth century, 378–80
in Schlegel's account of beauty, 26–8
Schleiermacher's account, 144, 149–51, 152
Schopenhauer's account, 107, 114–15
in Solger's account, 155
Spencer's revival of, 380–9
free will, Schelling's account of, 54–6
freedom
　in Cohen's account, 334
　in Groos's account, 414–15
　Mill's account of, 90
　in Rosenkranz's account, 172–3, 174–5, 177–8
　in Ruskin's account, 224–5
　in Schelling's account of will, 54–6
　in Schleiermacher's account of art, 150–1
French aesthetics, 3
frustration, in Schopenhauer's account of will, 111
"The Function of Criticism at the Present Time" (Arnold), 226

Gautier, Théophile, 234–6
The Gay Science (Nietzsche), 317–19
The Genealogy of Morality (Nietzsche), 319–20
generic vital beauty, Ruskin's account of, 209
genius
　Cohen's account of, 341–2
　Coleridge's account of, 71–2, 73–4
　in Emerson's account of art, 100
　Hegel's account of, 141–2
　Jean Paul's account of, 59–60
　Kant's account of, 13–17
　in Schelling's account, 45–6
　Schleiermacher's account of, 151
　Schopenhauer's account of, 113–15
German aesthetics. *See also specific philosophers by name*
　empathy school, 389–90
　in nineteenth century, 187–8, 299

periodization, challenge of, 1–3
twentieth-century, 436
German Idealism, 2, 106. *See also* Neo-Kantianism; *specific philosophers by name*
German Romanticism.
  See also Schlegel, Friedrich
  early, 18–19, 24–5
  Hölderlin, 19–23
  Jean Paul, 58–62
  overview, 6
God
  in Cousin's account, 231, 233–4
  in Ruskin's account of beauty, 205–6, 208
  in Schelling's account of will, 54–5
  in Schelling's *The Philosophy of Art*, 50–1
  in Solger's account, 154–5, 156–8
gods, anthropomorphic representation of, 133–6
Goethe, Johann Wolfgang von, 281–2
good, in Lotze's account, 183–4
Gothic architecture, Ruskin's account of, 223–4
grace, in Emerson's account of beauty, 102
great art, Ruskin's account of truthfulness in, 216–18
greatness in art, Ruskin's sources of
  beauty, 203–12
  imitation, 196–8
  overview, 195
  power, 195–6
  relation, 212–15
  truth, 198–203
Greek art
  Hegel's account of, 134
  Jean Paul's account of, 61–2
  Nietzsche's account of tragedy, 306–14
  Schlegel's "On the Study of Greek Poetry," 28–34
  in Wilde's "The Critic as Artist," 262–3
Groos, Karl, 409–17
Guyau, Jean-Marie, 424

hand-work, in Ruskin's account of architecture, 222–4
harmony
  Hölderlin's account of poetry, 22–3
  in Lipps's account, 399–400
  in Poe's account, 241
  purposive, in Lotze's account, 181–2
  in Robert Vischer's account, 392–3
  in Schlegel's account of Greek poetry, 29–34
Hegel (Beiser), 125
Hegel, Georg Wilhelm Friedrich
  background of, 122–4
  Bosanquet's discussion of, 282–4
  classical art, 133–6
  cognitivist approach to aesthetic experience, 5–6, 119–22
  Friedrich Vischer's independence from, 160–3
  genius, 141–2
  history of art by, 128–31, 139
  influence of Kant's ideas on, 17
  influence of on German aesthetics, 153
  influence of on others, 6–7
  natural beauty, rejection of, 139–40
  opinion of Solger, 154–5
  overview, 106, 142–3
  philosophical system of, 125–8
  romantic art, 135–8
  sublime, 140–1
  symbolic art, 131–3
Hegelian aesthetics.
  See also Bosanquet, Bernard; Vischer, Friedrich Theodor
  Lotze, 179–85
  overview, 153, 158
  Rosenkranz, 172–8
"Heidelberg" school of Neo-Kantianism. *See* Neo-Kantianism; *specific philosophers by name*
high art, Ruskin's account of truthfulness in, 216–18
higher task of art, Cohen's account of, 342–5

historical truth, Ruskin's account of, 212–15
A History of Æsthetic (Bosanquet)
  Goethe, 281–2
  Hegel, 282–4
  Kant, 276–9
  overview, 272–5
  Ruskin, 284–6
  Schelling, 282
  Schiller, 279–81
  Winckelmann, 275–6
history of art, Hegel's account of
  classical art, 130, 133–6
  overview, 128–31, 139
  romantic art, 130–1, 135–8
  symbolic art, 130, 131–3, 141
Hölderlin, Friedrich, 19–23
holy style in art, Schleiermacher's account of, 151–2
Hotho, Heinrich Gustav, 123–4
Howes, Ethel Puffer (Ethel Dench Puffer), 418–26
Human, All Too Human: A Book for Free Spirits (Nietzsche), 303, 316–17
human form
  in Emerson's account of beauty, 101
  in Hegel's account of classical art, 133–6
human vital beauty, Ruskin's account of, 209
humanization, Lipps's account of, 402–4
humor, Jean Paul's account of, 62
Husserl, Edmund, 398

Idea, absolute, Friedrich Vischer's account of, 161–4
ideal
  Hegel's contrast between idea and, 129–31
  in Schelling's account of art, 52–3
ideal beauty
  Bosanquet's discussion of Kant's concept of, 277–8
  Cousin's account of, 233–4
idealism. *See also* Neo-Kantianism; *specific philosophers by name*
  absolute, 21–2
  German, 2
  of Hegel, 125–6
  overview, 106
  Schelling's system of transcendental, 41–50
idealization in art
  in Cohen's account, 342–5
  in Dilthey's account, 373–4
ideas
  in Hegel's account, 126–7
  Hegel's contrast between ideal and, 129–31
  Platonic, Schopenhauer's account of, 112–18
"Ideas" (Schlegel), 36–7
identity of thought, in Schelling's system of transcendental idealism, 45–6
identity philosophy, Schelling's, 42, 50–1
imagination
  in Bosanquet's account, 288–9
  Coleridge's account of, 65–6, 68–9, 73–4
  Cousin's account of, 232
  Emerson's account of, 102–5
  in Jean Paul's account of genius, 60
  in Kant's account of free play, 11–13
  in Pater's account, 254–5
  in Ruskin's account of beauty, 209–12
  Shelley's account of, 79–80, 82
  in Tolstoy's account, 293–4
  Wilde's account of, 260–1
"The Imagination of the Poet: Elements for a Poetics" (Dilthey)
  overview, 363–5, 366–8
  synthesis of aesthetic theories in, 370–7
  universal validity of judgment of taste, 368–70
imaginative reason, in Pater's account, 254–5

Index

imitation
  of Greek art, Schlegel's account of, 32–3
  of nature, Coleridge's account of, 70–1
  Ruskin's account of, 196–8, 199–200
  in Wilde's "The Decay of Lying," 259–60
impression, Ruskin's truth of, 198–203
incorrectness, in Rosenkranz's account of ugliness in art, 176–7
independence of aesthetic experience. See "art for art's sake" movement
individuality
  Jean Paul's account of genius, 59–60
  Mill's account of, 90
  in Pater's account, 247–8
  in Tolstoy's account, 295
  in Wilde's "The Critic as Artist," 265–6
infection model of art, Tolstoy's, 292–6
infinite, in Jean Paul's account of modern art, 61–2
infinite task of art, Cohen's account of, 342–5
infinity
  in Jean Paul's account of genius, 60
  in Ruskin's account of beauty, 207
  in Schelling's system of transcendental idealism, 47–8
insight, genius as capacity for metaphysical, 71–2
integrative character of aesthetic experience, Pater's account of, 246–51
intellect
  in Emerson's account of beauty, 96
  in Poe's account of poetry, 239–40
  in Ruskin's account of beauty, 203–4
intellectual beauty, Cousin's account of, 233–4
intellectual interest, in Lotze's account, 179, 183
intellectual intuition, Hölderlin's account of, 20–2
intelligence, Coleridge's account of, 66–8
intensification principle, Fechner's, 327–8
intention, in Schelling's system of transcendental idealism, 44–6
intoxication, in Nietzsche's account, 304–6
intuition
  in Cohn's account, 349
  in Hegel's account, 126–7
  intellectual, Hölderlin's account of, 20–2
iron, in Ruskin's account of architecture, 221
irony of art, Solger's account of, 157–8
Italian aesthetics, 4

Jean Paul (Johann Paul Friedrich Richter), 58–62
judgment
  Cohn's account of aesthetic, 347–9
  Hölderlin's account of, 20–1
"Judgment and Being" (Hölderlin), 20–1
judgments of taste
  Bosanquet's discussion of Kant, 276–7
  Cohen's account of, 341–2
  Dilthey's account of, 368–70
  Kant's account of, 11–13

Kant, Immanuel, 50
  Bosanquet's discussion of, 276–9
  central themes of aesthetics of, 11–17
  Cohen's departure from methods of, 334–5, 340–1
  Cohen's interpretation of free play theory of, 339–40
  Cohen's reinterpretation of supersensible substratum, 343–4
  Cohn's reconstruction of ideas of, 347–8, 350–1

Kant, Immanuel (*cont.*)
  emotional impact of aesthetic experience, 329
  Friedrich Vischer's rehabilitation of, 161, 164–5, 168–9
  Hegel's transformation of account of, 126–7
  Hölderlin's anti-Kantian viewpoint, 21
  influence of on Lipps, 398–9
  Lotze's discussion of, 182–4
  natural beauty, 139
  Neo-Kantianism, 325–6, 352–3
  reviving influence of in nineteenth century, 299
  Schlegel, influence of on, 25–8
  Schopenhauer's transformation of account of, 107, 110–11, 114–15, 118–19
  in Solger's account, 155
  sublime, 140–1
  synthesis of aesthetic theories by, 4–5, 16–17
Kants Begründung der Aesthetik ("Kant's founding of aesthetics"), Cohen, 332
  feelings in art, 335–9
  free play theory, 339–40
  genius, 341–2
  higher task of art, 342–5
  overview, 333–5, 345–6
  philosophy, 334–5, 340–1
knowledge
  Coleridge's account of, 66–8
  of self, in Schopenhauer's account, 109–10

lamps of architecture, Ruskin's account of, 218–23
landscape painting, Lotze's account of, 184–5
Lange, Konrad, 413–14
Lee, Vernon (Violet Paget), 426–36
"Letter to B—" (Poe), 237
Letters and Social Aims (Emerson), 102–5

"Letters on Christian Art" (Schlegel), 37–8
liberation, in Emerson's account of art, 100–1. *See also* freedom
life, feeling of in Dilthey's account, 376
"The Limits of the Beautiful" (Schlegel), 25–8
Lipps, Theodor, 396–406, 416–17, 433–4
literature
  Friedrich Vischer's account of, 166–7
  Puffer's account of, 424–6
lived experience, in Dilthey's account, 363–5, 368
Loos, Adolf, 222–3
Lotze, Hermann Rudolf, 179–85
love
  of beauty, Ruskin's account of, 216–17
  Poe's account of, 240–1
lying in art, Wilde's account of, 259–61
lyric poetry, Friedrich Vischer's account of, 166
Lyrical Ballads, Preface to (Wordsworth), 75–8

Mademoiselle du Maupin (Gautier), 234–6
making believe, in Groos's account of art, 412–15
man, Ruskin's account of vital beauty in, 209
"Marburg" school of Neo-Kantianism. *See* Cohen, Hermann; Neo-Kantianism
matter, in Hegel's account, 125–6
mental activity, in Lipps's account of empathy, 400–2
metals, in Ruskin's account of architecture, 221
metaphysical (moral) truth
  in Nietzsche's account, 300–1
  in Ruskin's account of beauty, 203–12

metaphysical insight, genius as
    capacity for, 71-2
metaphysical version of cognitivist
    aesthetics
  Hölderlin's account of, 23
  Kant's theory of genius, 15-16
  overview, 13
metaphysics
  Dilthey's rejection of aesthetics
    based on, 364
  of Hegel, 125-8
  in Nietzsche's account, 306-14,
    316-17, 319-20
  in von Hartmann's account,
    322-3
metempsychosis, 72
Mill, John Stuart, 84-91
Millán-Zaibert, Elizabeth, 33
mind, in Emerson's
    Transcendentalism, 94-5
moderation, in Ruskin's account of
    beauty, 207-8
modern art, Jean Paul's account
    of, 61-2
Modern Painters (Ruskin), 191-3
  beauty, 203-12
  imagination, 209-12
  imitation, 196-8
  power, 195-6
  relation, 212-13
  sources of greatness in art, 195
  truth, 198-203
  truthfulness, 215-18
monadology, in Schlegel's account of
    romantic poetry, 35-6
moral (metaphysical) truth
  in Nietzsche's account, 300-1
  in Ruskin's account of beauty,
    203-12
moral beauty, Cousin's account
    of, 233-4
moral sense, in Poe's account of
    poetry, 239-40
morality
  in Bosanquet's account,
    274-5, 278-9
  in Cohen's account, 334, 342-5

  in Cohn's account, 350
  in Emerson's account of
    beauty, 101-2
  in Friedrich Vischer's
    account, 163-4
  Kant's theory of genius, 15-16
  in Lotze's account, 183-4
  in Pater's account, 255-6
  in Ruskin's account of
    beauty, 204-9
  in Shelley's account, 81-2
  in Tolstoy's account, 292-3
  in Wilde's works, 264, 267-9
morally good, beauty as symbol of, 17
Morris, William, 224
motion, in Robert Vischer's account,
    393, 394-6
Münsterberg, Hugo, 331-2
  background of, 353-4
  The Eternal Values, 354-60
  The Silent Photoplay in 1916, 360-2
music
  Hegel's account of, 137-8
  in Münsterberg's account, 360
  Nietzsche's account of, 313-14,
    315-16
  Pater's account of, 249-50
  Schopenhauer's account of, 117-18

natural beauty
  Emerson's account of, 95-6
  Hegel's rejection of, 139-40
  Schelling's account of, 49
nature
  Bosanquet's discussion of
    Hegel, 282-4
  Bosanquet's discussion of
    Ruskin, 285-6
  in Cohen's account, 334, 342-5
  Coleridge's account of, 66-8, 69-71
  in Emerson's account, 93-9, 103
  Jean Paul's account of, 58-9
  Lipps's account of projection of
    emotions on, 403
  in Münsterberg's account, 357-9
  Rosenkranz's account of ugliness
    in, 174

nature (*cont.*)
  in Ruskin's account of truth, 199–200, 202
  Schelling's philosophy of, 41–2
  in Schelling's *The Philosophy of Art*, 50–1
  Schelling's system of transcendental idealism, 43–5
  truthfulness to organic whole of, 29–34
  in Wilde's "The Decay of Lying," 259–61
Nature (Emerson), 93–4, 95–7
necessity
  of aesthetic experience, Dilthey's account of, 370
  in Friedrich Vischer's account of absolute Idea, 162
negative pleasure
  in Ruskin's account of imitation, 197–8
  in Schelling's account, 46
  in Schopenhauer's account, 111–13
Neo-Classicism, Hegel's rejection of, 142
Neo-Kantianism. *See also specific philosophers by name*
  departures from Kant within, 352–3
  overview, 3, 6–7, 299, 325–6
  plurality of approaches in, 330–2
Neo-Platonism, Schlegel's, 25–7
Nietzsche, Elizabeth, 303
Nietzsche, Friedrich, 7
  after *The Birth of Tragedy*, 315–20
  The Birth of Tragedy, 306–14
  "Dionysiac World View," 304–6
  influence of Emerson on, 92–3
  overview, 300–4
nineteenth century aesthetics.
  See also specific aesthetic theories or movements; specific philosophers by name
  major themes covered in, 4–8
  overview, 436–7
  periodization, challenge of, 1–4
  revival of free play theory in, 378–80

non-human world, projection of emotions on, 391–3, 402–4
non-rational will
  Schelling's account of, 54–6
  Schopenhauer's account of, 109–11
noumenal, in Schopenhauer's account, 308
noumenal basis for taste, 12–13

obedience, Ruskin's lamp of, 219
object, Coleridge's account of, 66–8
objectification of non-rational will, Schopenhauer's account of, 112–18
objective (absolute) idealism, 21–2. *See also* Schelling, Friedrich Wilhelm Josef von
objective form, in Robert Vischer's account, 391–4
objective values, Münsterberg's account of, 354–60
objectivity
  of beauty, Schlegel's account of, 28–34
  Nietzsche's account of, 310–11
  in Schelling's system of transcendental idealism, 42–3
"On German Architecture" (Goethe), 281–2
On Liberty (Mill), 90
"On Poesy or Art" (Coleridge), 69–71
"On the Conditions of Beauty in Art" (Lotze), 181–2
"On the Study of Greek Poetry" (Schlegel), 28–34
opera, Nietzsche's historiography of, 313–14
oratory versus poetry, Mill's account of, 87–8
organic whole of nature, truthfulness to, 29–34
organization of complexity, in Spencer's account, 385–6
organizing functions, in Schleiermacher's account, 147–9
ornament, in Ruskin's account of architecture, 222–4
"The Over-Soul" (Emerson), 94

Paget, Violet (Vernon Lee), 426–36
painting
   Hegel's account of, 137
   Lotze's account of, 184–5
   Ruskin's account of truth in, 198–203
paradox of tragedy
   Lipps's account of, 404–6
   Nietzsche's account of, 311–12
   Puffer's account of, 425–6
   Schopenhauer's account of, 116–18
   Shelley's account of, 82–3
particulars, focus on in art, 31–2
passion, Poe's account of, 238
Pater, Walter, 229–30
   free play theory, 251–4
   integrative character of aesthetic experience, 246–51
   morality, 255–6
   overview, 244–6, 256–7
Peirce, Charles Sanders, 344
penetrative imagination, Ruskin's account of, 210–11
perception
   in Schopenhauer's account, 111–12
   in Spencer's account, 384, 385–6
periodization, challenge of, 1–4
personality, in Friedrich Vischer's absolute Idea, 163
personification, Lipps's account of, 402–4
phenomenal, in Schopenhauer's account, 308
phenomenological truth, in Ruskin's account, 198–203
Phenomenology of Moral Consciousness: Prolegomena to Any Future Ethics (von Hartmann), 321
Philosophical Investigations into the Essence of Human Freedom (Schelling), 54–6
philosophical system of Hegel, 125–8
philosophy
   Cohen's account of, 334–5, 340–1
   Coleridge's account of, 70
   Hegel's account of, 127–8, 129, 143
   of nature, Schelling's, 41–2
   Schelling's transcendental, 42–3
   Schlegel's assimilation of poetry to, 36–7
   of Solger, 154–5
The Philosophy of Art (Schelling), 40, 50–4
"The Philosophy of Composition" (Poe), 237–8
Philosophy of the Beautiful (von Hartmann), 321–3
The Philosophy of the Unconscious (von Hartmann), 320–1
physical beauty, Cousin's account of, 233–4
physical process, Puffer's account of aesthetics as, 421
The Picture of Dorian Gray (Wilde), 268–9
plastic quality of Greek poetry, Jean Paul's account of, 61
Plato and Platonism (Pater), 246
Platonic ideas, Schopenhauer's account of, 112–18
play. *See also* free play theory
   in Bosanquet's discussion of Schiller, 280–1
   interpretation of Schlegel centered on, 28
The Play of Animals (Groos), 409–15
The Play of Man (Groos), 409–10, 415–17
pleasure
   in Bosanquet's account, 288–9
   Cohen's account of, 335–9
   in Emerson's account of imagination, 104
   in Groos's account, 412–13, 414
   in Lipps's account, 397–8, 399–401, 404–6
   in Nietzsche's account of tragedy, 311, 312
   in Poe's account of poetry, 237–8
   in Robert Vischer's account, 394

pleasure (*cont.*)
    in Ruskin's account of
        imitation, 197–8
    Schelling's account of negative, 46
    in Schlegel's account of beauty, 27
    Schopenhauer's account of
        negative, 111–13
    Schopenhauer's account of positive,
        115–16
    in Shelley's account, 82–3
    in Spencer's account, 383–8
    in Tolstoy's account, 291–2
    in von Hartmann's account of
        beauty, 321–3
    in Wordsworth's account of
        poetry, 77–8
Poe, Edgar Allan, 236–42
poesy (verbal arts), Hegel's account
    of, 138
"The Poet" (Emerson), 99–101
"The Poetic Principle" (Poe), 238–41
Poetics (Aristotle), 262–3
poetics, of Dilthey
    overview, 363–5, 366–8
    synthesis of aesthetic theories
        in, 370–7
    universal validity of judgment of
        taste, 368–70
poetry
    Arnold's account of, 227
    Baudelaire's account of, 242
    Emerson's account of,
        99–101, 102–5
    Hölderlin's account of, 22–3
    Jean Paul's account of Greek, 61–2
    Mill's account of, 84–91
    in Pater's account, 256
    Poe's account of, 237–41
    Schlegel's account of
        romantic, 33–7
    Schlegel's "On the Study of Greek
        Poetry," 28–34
    Schopenhauer's account of,
        116–17
    Shelley's account of, 79–83
    Wordsworth's account of emotional
        impact of, 75–8

"Poetry and Imagination"
    (Emerson), 102–5
Poma, Andrea, 332
positive pleasure, in Schopenhauer's
    account, 115–16
post-Hegelian generation.
    See also Vischer, Friedrich
        Theodor
    Lotze, 179–85
    overview, 153, 158
    Rosenkranz, 172–8
power, Ruskin's account of, 195–6
practical responses, in Lee's
    account, 435–6
Preface to *Lyrical Ballads*
    (Wordsworth), 75–8
Preface to *The Renaissance*
    (Pater), 247–8
preparatory efforts, Groos's idea of
    play as, 410–11
Preparatory School for Aesthetics
    (*Vorschule der Ästhetik*), Jean
    Paul, 58–62
Preschool for Aesthetics (*Vorschule der
    Ästhetik*), Fechner, 327–30
pretending, in Groos's account of art,
    412–15
primary imagination, Coleridge's
    account of, 65–6, 68, 69, 73–4
primordial feelings in art, Cohen's
    account of, 335–9
primordial unity of being, Hölderlin's
    account of, 20–3
The Principles of Psychology
    (Spencer), 381–9
"The Procedure of the Poetic Spirit"
    (Hölderlin), 22–3
production, artistic, Solger's account
    of, 157
production aesthetics,
    Schleiermacher's account of,
    146–7, 148–9
projection of emotions
    Lee's account of, 431–5
    Lipps's account of, 401–5
    Robert Vischer's account of,
        391–3, 394–5

Proust, Marcel, 193
psychological aesthetics
 Dilthey, 369–70, 371–3
 Fechner, 327–30
 Groos, 409–17
 Lee, 426–36
 Lipps, 396–406
 overview, 378–80, 436–7
 Puffer, 418–26
 Robert Vischer, 390–6
 Spencer, 380–9
 Volkelt, 406–9
The Psychology of Beauty (Puffer), 419–26
Puffer, Ethel Dench (Ethel Puffer Howes), 418–26
purity, in Ruskin's account of beauty, 207
purposive harmony, in Lotze's account, 181–2
purposiveness, in Schelling's system of transcendental idealism, 44–6

"The Rationale of Verse" (Poe), 238
rationality, in Schopenhauer's account, 109–11
real, in Schelling's account of art, 52–3
reality
 in Dilthey's account, 373–4
 fragmentary character of, 25–6, 33–7
 in Groos's account of art, 413–14
 in Lipps's account, 397–8
 in Münsterberg's account, 359–60, 361–2
reason, in Cousin's account of beauty, 231–2
reception aesthetics, Schleiermacher's account of, 146–7, 148–9
reconstitution of original unity, Hölderlin's account of, 20–3
reductionism, 436–7
relation, Ruskin's account of, 212–15
relative vital beauty, Ruskin's account of, 209
relief, in Schopenhauer's account, 111–13

religion
 in Hegel's account, 127–8, 129, 136–7
 in Schlegel's aesthetics, 37–8
 in Schleiermacher's account of art, 151–2
 in Solger's account, 154–5, 156–8
 in Tolstoy's account, 292–3
Religion der Venunft aus der Quellen des Judentums ("Religion of reason from the sources of Judaism"), Cohen, 332–3
Rembrandt van Rijn, 217–18
The Renaissance (Pater)
 free play theory, 251–4
 integrative character of aesthetic experience, 245–6, 247–51
 morality, 255–6
repose, in Ruskin's account of beauty, 207
representation
 in Dilthey's account, 371–3
 in Hegel's account, 126–7
 in Spencer's account, 384–5
Richter, Johann Paul Friedrich (Jean Paul), 58–62
romantic art, Hegel's account of, 130–1, 135–8
romantic poetry, Schlegel's account of, 33–7
Romanticism. *See also* Coleridge, Samuel Taylor; Emerson, Ralph Waldo; Schlegel, Friedrich
 after Schelling, 57
 early, 18–19, 24–5
 Hegel's rejection of, 142
 Hölderlin, 19–23
 Jean Paul, 58–62
 Mill, 84–91
 overview, 6
 periodization, challenge of, 2
 Shelley, 79–83
 Wordsworth, 75–8
Rosenkranz, Karl, 172–8
rules for beauty, Pater's argument against, 248–9

Ruskin, John, 3, 188
  architecture, truthfulness in, 218–24
  background of, 193–5
  beauty, 203–12
  Bosanquet's discussion of, 284–6
  great or high art, truthfulness in, 216–18
  imagination, 209–12
  imitation, 196–8
  overview, 191–3, 225
  power, 195–6
  relation, 212–15
  sources of greatness in art, 195
  truth, 198–203
  truthfulness, overview of, 215–16

Santayana, George, 3–4, 189
Schelling, Friedrich Wilhelm Josef von, 6, 115, 329
  background of, 38–41
  Bosanquet's discussion of, 282
  cognitivist approach to aesthetic experience, 5
  Hegel's account versus that of, 125
  influence of Kant's ideas on, 17
  influence on Coleridge, 64, 66–7
  The Philosophy of Art, 50–4
  in Solger's account, 155
  System of Transcendental Idealism, 41–50
  will, 54–6
Schiller, Friedrich, 279–81
Schlegel, August Wilhelm, 24
Schlegel, Friedrich, 6
  Athänuem fragments, 33–7
  background of, 24–5
  fragmentary conception of aesthetic cognition, 33–7
  influence of Kant on, 25–8
  "Letters on Christian Art," 37–8
  "The Limits of the Beautiful," 25–8
  "On the Study of Greek Poetry," 28–34
  religious tone of aesthetics of, 37–8
  truth as aim of art, 28–34

Schleiermacher, Friedrich Daniel Ernst, 6, 144–52
"The School of Giorgione" (Pater), 248–50, 252–3
Schopenhauer, Arthur, 54, 105
  background of, 106–8
  classification of arts by, 116–18
  cognitivist approach to aesthetic experience, 5
  genius, 113–15
  Hegel's views on art versus, 121
  influence of Kant's ideas on, 17
  influence of on others, 7, 299
  influence on Nietzsche, 307–12
  negative pleasure, 111–13
  Nietzsche's repudiation of, 316–17
  non-rational will, 109–11
  overview, 106
  positive pleasure, 115–16
science, in Cohen's account, 334
sculpture, Hegel's account of classical, 133–6
secondary Imagination, Coleridge's account of, 68, 69
self-completeness, in Puffer's account, 422–3
self-consciousness
  Coleridge's account of, 67–8
  in Schelling's account, 43
self-directed pleasure, in Ruskin's account of imitation, 197–8
sensation, in Spencer's account, 384
senses, in Pater's account of free play, 252
sensible particulars, in Friedrich Vischer's absolute Idea, 162–3
sensual response to beauty, in Ruskin's account, 203–4
sentiment, Spencer's account of capacity for, 384–5, 388. *See also* emotional impact of aesthetic experience
The Seven Lamps of Architecture (Ruskin), 213–15, 218–23
shared feelings, in Wordsworth's account of poetry, 78
sharing, in Groos's account of art, 413

Shelley, Percey Bysshe, 79–83
signs, in Ruskin's account,
    199–200, 208
The Silent Photoplay in 1916
    (Münsterberg), 360–2
sincerity (truthfulness), Ruskin's
    account of, 192–3
  architecture, 218–24
  great or high art, 216–18
  overview, 215–16
sincerity, in Tolstoy's account,
    294–5
Social Statics (Spencer), 380
social style in art, Schleiermacher's
    account of, 151–2
Socratism, aesthetic, Nietzsche's
    account of, 313
Solger, Karl Wilhelm
    Ferdinand, 153–8
Sonderegger, Ruth, 28
Sophocles, Schlegel's characterization
    of, 30–1
sounds, Lipps's account of projection
    of emotions on, 403
"Southwestern" school of Neo-
    Kantianism, 346. *See also* Neo-
    Kantianism; *specific philosophers
    by name*
speculative version of cognitivist
    aesthetics. *See* metaphysical
    version of cognitivist
    aesthetics
Spencer, Herbert, 380–9
spheres of feeling, Dilthey's account
    of, 371–3
spirit. *See also* absolute spirit, Hegel's
    account of
  in Kant's theory of genius, 14
  in Lotze's account, 183–4
  of poetry, Hölderlin's account
    of, 22–3
  in Rosenkranz's account of
    ugliness, 174–5
spiritual beauty, Cousin's account
    of, 233–4
The Stones of Venice (Ruskin),
    193, 223–4

stories versus poems, Shelley's
    account of, 80–1
strangeness, in Baudelaire's
    account, 243–4
striving, endless, in Schopenhauer's
    account, 111
structural honesty, in Ruskin's
    account of architecture, 221–2
struggle for power, Groos's idea of
    play as, 411
"The Study of Poetry" (Arnold), 227
subject, Coleridge's account of, 66–8
subjective part of aesthetic pleasure,
    Schopenhauer's account of,
    115–16
subjectivism, Friedrich Vischer's
    account of Kant's, 164
subjectivity
  in art, 31–2
  in Coleridge's account of art, 69–70
  in Hegel's account of romantic
    art, 137–8
  Nietzsche's account of, 310–11
  in Pater's account, 247
sublime
  in Bosanquet's account, 273–4
  Hegel's account of, 140–1
  Jean Paul's account of, 58–9
  Schelling's account of, 48–9
  Schopenhauer's account of,
    115–16
supernal beauty, Poe's account
    of, 240–1
supersensible substratum, Cohen's
    account of, 343–4
support modes, in Ruskin's account of
    architecture, 221–2
surplus energy principle
  Groos's disagreement with, 410–11
  Spencer's account of,
    383–4, 385–6
symbolic art, Hegel's account of, 130,
    131–3, 141
symbols, in Ruskin's account of truth,
    199–200
symmetry, in Ruskin's account of
    beauty, 207

synthesis of aesthetic theories
  by Bosanquet, 286, 289–90
  by Dilthey, 7–8, 364–5, 370–7
  by Groos, 409–17
  by Kant, 4–5, 16–17
  by Lotze, 181–2, 185
  in nineteenth century, 4–8
  by Schleiermacher, 144, 147–50, 152
  by Spencer, 389
  by Wordsworth, 78
System of Aesthetics (Volkelt), 406–7
System of Transcendental Idealism (Schelling), 40, 41–50

taste
  Bosanquet's discussion of Kant, 276–7
  Cohen's account of, 341–2
  Cohn's account of, 348–9
  Dilthey's account of, 368–70
  Emerson's account of, 98–100
  Kant's account of, 11–13
  Poe's account of, 239–40, 241
teleological view of nature, Schelling's, 44–5
theoretic faculty, in Ruskin's account of beauty, 204–9
thought
  in Coleridge's account of art, 70–1
  in Emerson's account of beauty, 96
  in Hegel's account, 126–7
  in Schelling's *The Philosophy of Art*, 50–1
  in Schelling's system of transcendental idealism, 41–50
Three Lectures on Aesthetic (Bosanquet), 286–9
threshold principle, Fechner's, 327–8
Tolstoy, Leo, 8, 269, 270, 290–6
tragedy
  Friedrich Vischer's account of, 166–7
  Lipps's account of, 404–6
  in Nietzsche's account, 305–14
  Puffer's account of, 425–6
  romantic, Hegel's account of, 138

  Schopenhauer's account of, 116–18
  Shelley's account of, 82–3
  in Wilde's "The Critic as Artist," 262
tranquil soul, in Bosanquet's discussion of Winckelmann, 275–6
transcendental foundation of aesthetics, in Cohen's account, 340–1
transcendental idealism, Schelling's system of, 41–50
transcendental philosophy, Schelling's, 42–3
transcendental poetry, Schlegel's account of, 36
Transcendentalism, of Emerson, 92, 93–5
Tristan and Isolde (Wagner), 314
The True, the Beautiful, and the Good (*Du vrai, du beau, et du bien*), Cousin, 230–4
truth. *See also* cognitivist approach to aesthetic experience
  as aim of art, Schlegel's account of, 28–34
  in Arnold's account, 227
  Coleridge's account of, 67
  Cousin's account of, 231
  historical, Ruskin's account of, 212–15
  metaphysical, in Ruskin's account of beauty, 203–12
  phenomenological, Ruskin's account of, 198–203
  in Poe's account of poetry, 237, 241
  in Ruskin's account of architecture, 219–22
  Ruskin's basic account of, 191–3, 195
  in Shelley's account, 80–2
  in Tolstoy's account, 295
  in von Hartmann's account, 322–3
  in Wilde's "The Critic as Artist," 261–8
truthfulness (sincerity), Ruskin's account of, 192–3

architecture, 218–24
    great or high art, 216–18
    overview, 215–16
truthfulness, Dilthey's principle
    of, 372–4
Turner, Joseph Mallord William,
    191–2, 200–1, 202–3
twentieth-century aesthetics, 436–7
types, in Ruskin's account of
    beauty, 208
typical beauty, Ruskin's account
    of, 206–8

ugliness
    in Bosanquet's account, 273–5
    Rosenkranz's account of, 173–8
unconscious, in Coleridge's account
    of genius, 72
unconscious nature, Coleridge's
    account of, 66–8
unconscious thought, in Schelling's
    account, 41–50
understanding, in Kant's account of
    free play, 11–13
unfreedom, in Rosenkranz's account
    of ugliness, 177–8
unification, in Friedrich Vischer's
    account, 168
unitary experience of objects, in
    Robert Vischer's account, 391–4
unity
    of being, Hölderlin's account
        of, 20–3
    in Coleridge's account of art, 69–71
    in Emerson's
        Transcendentalism, 93–5
    in Lipps's account, 399–400
    in Münsterberg's account of
        beauty, 357–9
    organic, in Schlegel's account of
        Greek poetry, 29–34
    in Puffer's account, 422–3
    in Ruskin's account of beauty, 207
    in Schlegel's account of beauty, 26
    in Solger's account of art, 156–8
universal intelligibility of art,
    Emerson's account of, 98–100

universal poetry, Schlegel's account
    of, 33–7
universal validity of judgment of
    taste
    Cohen's account of, 341–2
    Cohn's account of, 348–9
    Dilthey's account of, 368–70
    Kant's account of, 11–13
universe, Lotze's account of purposive
    harmony of, 181–2
unreality, in Münsterberg's account,
    359–60, 361–2
Untimely Meditations
    (Nietzsche), 302–3
utilitarianism, 83–91
    Gautier's attack on, 235–6
    Ruskin's critique of, 204–6
utility
    in Ruskin's account of
        beauty, 204–6
    in Shelley's account, 83

value-judgments, Cohn's account
    of, 347–8
values, Münsterberg's account of,
    354–60
variety
    in Baudelaire's account, 243–4
    in Mill's account of individuality, 90
verbal art, Schelling's account of, 52
verbal arts (poesy), Hegel's account
    of, 138
virtue
    in Emerson's account of beauty, 96
    in Ruskin's account of vital
        beauty, 209
Vischer, Friedrich Theodor, 6
    absolute Idea, 161–4
    background of, 159–61
    beauty, 165–6
    emotional impact of art, 166–72
    independence from Hegel, 160–3
    rehabilitation of Kant by, 161,
        164–5, 168–9
Vischer, Robert, 6, 390–6
vital beauty, Ruskin's account of,
    207, 208–9

volition, in Schelling's system of
    transcendental idealism, 44–6.
    See also will
Volkelt, Johannes, 406–9
voluntarism, 55
von Hartmann, Eduard, 320–4
Vorschule der Ästhetik (*Preparatory
    School for Aesthetics*), Jean Paul,
    58–62
Vorschule der Ästhetik (*Preschool for
    Aesthetics*), Fechner, 327–30

Wagner, Richard, 300–1, 302,
    313–14, 315–16
What is Art? (Tolstoy), 290, 291–6
Wilde, Oscar, 229–30
    "The Critic as Artist," 261–8
    "The Decay of Lying," 259–61
    overview, 256–9, 269
    The Picture of Dorian Gray, 268–9

will
    in Münsterberg's account,
        355–6, 357–9
    non-rational, Schopenhauer's
        account of, 109–11
    Schelling's concept of, 54–6
    in Schopenhauer's account,
        112–18, 308–9
Winckelmann, Johann Joachim,
    253–4, 275–6
Wordsworth, William, 72–3
    Coleridge's discussion of, 72–4
    general discussion, 75–8
The World as Will and Representation
    (Schopenhauer)
    classification of arts, 116–18
    genius, 113–15
    negative pleasure, 111–13
    non-rational will, 109–11
    positive pleasure, 115–16

Lightning Source UK Ltd.
Milton Keynes UK
UKHW040611211022
410822UK00001B/5